Children's
Literature
Review

Guide to Gale Literary Criticism Series

When you need to review criticism of literary works, these are the Gale series to use:

If the author's death date is:

You should turn to:

After Dec. 31, 1959
(or author is still living)

CONTEMPORARY LITERARY CRITICISM

for example: Jorge Luis Borges, Anthony Burgess,
William Faulkner, Mary Gordon,
Ernest Hemingway, Iris Murdoch

1900 through 1959

TWENTIETH-CENTURY LITERARY CRITICISM

for example: Willa Cather, F. Scott Fitzgerald,
Henry James, Mark Twain, Virginia Woolf

1800 through 1899

NINETEENTH-CENTURY LITERATURE CRITICISM

for example: Fedor Dostoevski, George Sand,
Gerard Manley Hopkins, Emily Dickinson

1400 through 1799

LITERATURE CRITICISM FROM 1400 TO 1800
(excluding Shakespeare)

for example: Anne Bradstreet, Pierre Corneille,
Daniel Defoe, Alexander Pope,
Jonathan Swift, Phillis Wheatley

SHAKESPEAREAN CRITICISM

Shakespeare's plays and poetry

Antiquity through 1399

CLASSICAL AND MEDIEVAL LITERATURE CRITICISM

for example: Dante, Plato, Homer, Sophocles, Vergil,
the Beowulf poet

(Volume 1 forthcoming)

Gale also publishes related criticism series:

CHILDREN'S LITERATURE REVIEW

This ongoing series covers authors of all eras. Presents criticism on authors and author/illustrators who write for the preschool through high school audience.

CONTEMPORARY ISSUES CRITICISM

This two volume set presents criticism on contemporary authors writing on current issues. Topics covered include the social sciences, philosophy, economics, natural science, law, and related areas.

ISSN 0362-4145

volume 11

Children's Literature Review

Excerpts from Reviews,
Criticism, and Commentary
on Books for Children
and Young People

Guest Essay, "New Faces, New Directions
in Britain,"
by Marcus Crouch

Gerard J. Senick
Editor

Melissa Reiff Hug
Associate Editor

Gale Research Company
Book Tower
Detroit, Michigan 48226

STAFF

Gerard J. Senick, *Editor*

Melissa Reiff Hug, *Associate Editor*

Susan Miller Harig, *Senior Assistant Editor*

Motoko Fujishiro Huthwaite, *Assistant Editor*

Sharon R. Gunton, *Contributing Editor*

Lizbeth A. Purdy, *Production Supervisor*
Denise Michlewicz Broderick, *Production Coordinator*
Eric Berger, *Assistant Production Coordinator*
Kathleen M. Cook, Maureen Duffy, Sheila J. Nasea, *Editorial Assistants*

Victoria B. Cariappa, *Research Coordinator*
Maureen R. Richards, *Assistant Research Coordinator*
Daniel Kurt Gilbert, Keith E. Schooley, Filomena Sgambati,
Vincenza G. Tranchida, Mary D. Wise, *Research Assistants*

Linda M. Pugliese, *Manuscript Coordinator*
Donna Craft, *Assistant Manuscript Coordinator*
Maureen A. Puhl, Rosetta Irene Simms, *Manuscript Assistants*

Jeanne A. Gough, *Permissions Supervisor*
Janice M. Mach, *Permissions Coordinator, Text*
Patricia A. Seefelt, *Permissions Coordinator, Illustrations*
Susan D. Battista, *Assistant Permissions Coordinator*
Margaret A. Chamberlain, Sandra C. Davis, Kathy Grell,
Josephine Keene, Mary M. Matuz, *Senior Permissions Assistants*
H. Diane Cooper, Colleen M. Crane, Mabel Gurney, *Permissions Assistants*
Margaret Carson, Helen Hernandez, Anita Williams, *Permissions Clerks*

Arthur Chartow, *Art Director*

Frederick G. Ruffner, *Publisher*
Dedria Bryfonski, *Editorial Director*
Christine Nasso, *Director, Literature Division*
Laurie Lanzen Harris, *Senior Editor, Literary Criticism Series*
Dennis Poupard, *Managing Editor, Literary Criticism Series*

Library of Congress Catalog Card Number 75-34953
ISBN 0-8103-0343-4
ISSN 0362-4145

Computerized photocomposition by
Typographics, Incorporated
Kansas City, Missouri

Printed in the United States

CONTENTS

PREFACE

As children's literature has evolved into both a respected branch of creative writing and a successful industry, literary criticism has documented and influenced each stage of its growth. Critics have recorded the literary development of individual authors as well as the trends and controversies that resulted from changes in values and attitudes, especially as they concerned children. While defining a philosophy of children's literature, critics developed a scholarship that balances an appreciation of children and an awareness of their needs with standards for literary quality much like those required by critics of adult literature. *Children's Literature Review* (*CLR*) is designed to provide a permanent, accessible record of this ongoing scholarship. Those responsible for bringing children and books together can now make informed choices when selecting reading materials for the young.

Scope of the Series

Each biannual volume contains excerpts from published criticism on the literary works of authors and author/illustrators who create books for children from preschool through high school. The author list for each volume is international in scope and represents the variety of genres covered by children's literature—picture books, fiction, folklore, nonfiction, poetry, and drama. The works of approximately fifteen to forty authors of all eras are represented in each volume. Although earlier volumes of *CLR* emphasized critical material published after 1960, successive volumes have expanded their coverage to encompass criticism written before 1960. Since many of the authors included in *CLR* are living and continue to write, it is necessary to update their entries periodically. Thus, future volumes will supplement the entries of selected authors covered in earlier volumes as well as present criticism on the works of authors new to the series.

Organization of the Book

An author section consists of the following elements: author heading, author portrait, author introduction, excerpts of criticism (each followed by a bibliographical citation), and illustrations, when available.

- The **author heading** consists of the author's full name followed by birth and death dates. The portion of the name outside the parentheses denotes the form under which the author is most frequently published. If the majority of the author's works for children were written under a pseudonym, the pseudonym will be listed in the author heading and the real name given on the first line of the author introduction. Also located at the beginning of the introduction are any other pseudonyms used by the author in writing for children and any name variations, including transliterated forms for authors whose languages use nonroman alphabets. Uncertainty as to a birth or death date is indicated by question marks.

- An **author portrait** is included when available.

- The **author introduction** contains information designed to introduce an author to *CLR* users by presenting an overview of the author's themes and styles, occasional biographical facts that relate to his or her literary career, a summary of critical response to the author's works, and information about major awards and prizes the author has received. Where applicable, introductions conclude with references to additional entries in biographical and critical reference series published by Gale Research Company. These sources include past volumes of *CLR* as well as *Contemporary Authors, Something about the Author, Yesterday's Authors of Books for Children, Contemporary Literary Criticism, Twentieth-Century Literary Criticism, Nineteenth-Century Literature Criticism, Dictionary of Literary Biography,* and *Authors in the News.*

- **Criticism** is located in three sections: **author's commentary** and **general commentary** (when available) and within individual **title entries,** which are preceded by **title entry headings.** Criticism is arranged chronologically within each section. Titles by authors being profiled are highlighted in boldface type within the text for easier access by readers.

The **author's commentary** presents background material written by the author or by an interviewer. This commentary may cover a specific work or several works. Author's commentary on more than one work appears after the author introduction, while commentary on an individual book follows the title entry heading.

The **general commentary** consists of critical excerpts that consider more than one work by the author being profiled. General commentary is preceded by the critic's name in boldface type or, in the case of unsigned criticism, by the title of the journal.

Title entry headings precede the criticism on a title and cite publication information on the work being reviewed. Title headings list the work's title as it appeared in its country of origin; titles in languages using nonroman alphabets are transliterated. If the original title is in a language other than English, the title of the first English-language translation follows in brackets. The work's first publication date is listed in parentheses following the title. Differing U.S. and British titles of works originally published in English follow the publication date within the parentheses.

Title entries consist of critical excerpts on the author's individual works, arranged chronologically by publication date. The entries generally contain two to six reviews per title, depending on the stature of the book and the amount of criticism it has generated. The editors select titles that reflect the entire scope of the author's literary contribution, covering each genre and subject. An effort is made to reprint criticism that represents the full range of each title's reception —from the year of its initial publication to current assessments. Thus, the reader is provided with a record of the author's critical history.

● Selected excerpts are preceded by **explanatory notes,** which provide information on the critic or work of criticism to enhance the reader's understanding of the excerpt.

● A complete **bibliographical citation** designed to facilitate the location of the original book or article follows each piece of criticism. An asterisk (*) at the end of a citation indicates that the essay or book is on more than one author.

● Numerous **illustrations** are featured in *CLR.* For entries on author/illustrators, an effort has been made to include illustrations that reflect the author's styles as represented in the criticism. Entries on major authors who do not illustrate their own works may also include photographs and other illustrative material pertinent to the authors' careers.

Other Features

● A list of **authors to appear in future volumes** follows the preface.

● A **guest essay** appears before the first author entry. These essays are written specifically for *CLR* by prominent critics on subjects of their choice. Past volumes have included essays by John Rowe Townsend, Zena Sutherland, Sheila A. Egoff, and Rudine Sims. Volume 11 contains Marcus Crouch's "New Faces, New Directions in Britain." The editors are honored to feature Mr. Crouch in this volume.

● An **appendix** lists the sources from which material has been reprinted in the volume. It does not, however, list every book or periodical consulted for the volume.

● *CLR* volumes contain **cumulative indexes** to authors, nationalities, and titles.

The **cumulative index to authors** lists authors who have appeared in *CLR* and includes cross-references to *Contemporary Authors, Something about the Author, Yesterday's Authors of Books for Children, Contemporary Literary Criticism, Twentieth-Century Literary Criticism, Nineteenth-Century Literature Criticism, Dictionary of Literary Biography,* and *Authors in the News.*

The **cumulative nationality index** lists authors alphabetically under their respective nationalities. Author names are followed by the volume number(s) in which they appear. Authors who have changed citizenship or whose current citizenship is not reflected in biographical sources appear under both their original nationality and that of their current residence.

The **cumulative title index** lists titles covered in *CLR* followed by the volume and page number where criticism begins.

Acknowledgments

No work of this scope can be accomplished without the cooperation of many people. The editors especially wish to thank the copyright holders of the criticism included in this volume, the permissions managers of many book and magazine publishing companies for assisting us in securing reprint rights, and the staffs of the Kresge Library at Wayne State University, the University of Michigan Library, the Detroit Public Library, and the Wayne Oakland Library Federation (WOLF) for making their resources available to us. We are also grateful to Carole McCollough, Coordinator of Children's and Young Adults' Services for WOLF, and to Anthony J. Bogucki for his assistance with copyright research.

Suggestions Are Welcome

In response to various suggestions, several features have been added to *CLR* since the series began:

- Since Volume 3—**Author's commentary,** when available, which presents the viewpoint of the author being profiled.

  —An **appendix** listing the sources of criticism in each volume.

- Since Volume 4—**Author portraits** as well as **illustrations** from works by author/illustrators, when available.

  —**Title entries** arranged chronologically according to the work's first publication; previous volumes listed titles alphabetically.

- Since Volume 5—A **guest essay,** when available, written specifically for *CLR* by a prominent critic on a subject of his or her choice.

- Since Volume 6—**Explanatory notes** that provide information on the critic or work of criticism to enhance the usefulness of the excerpt.

  —A **cumulative nationality index** for easy access to authors by nationality.

- Since Volume 8—Author entries on retellers of traditional literature as well as those who have been the first to record oral tales and other folklore.

  —More extensive illustrative material, such as holographs of manuscript pages and photographs of people and places pertinent to the authors' careers.

- Since Volume 10—Entries devoted to criticism on a major work by a single author.

Readers are cordially invited to write the editor with comments and suggestions for further enhancing the usefulness of the *CLR* series.

AUTHORS TO APPEAR IN FUTURE VOLUMES

Aardema, Verna (Norberg) 1911-
Adams, Adrienne 1906-
Adams, Harriet S(tratemeyer)
  1893?-1982
Adams, Richard 1920-
Adler, Irving 1913-
Aesop 620?BC-564?BC
Anderson, C(larence) W(illiam)
  1891-1971
Arnosky, Jim 1946-
Arundel, Honor (Morfydd) 1919-1973
Asbjörnsen, Peter Christen 1812-1885
  and Jörgen Moe 1813?-1882
Asch, Frank 1946-
Asimov, Isaac 1920-
Avery, Gillian 1926-
Avi 1937-
Aymé, Marcel 1902-1967
Bailey, Carolyn Sherwin 1875-1961
Ballantyne, R(obert) M(ichael)
  1825-1894
Banner, Angela 1923-
Bannerman, Helen 1863-1946
Barrett, Judi(th) 1941-
Barrie, J(ames) M(atthew) 1860-1937
Baum, L(yman) Frank 1856-1919
Baumann, Hans 1914-1985
BB 1905-
Beatty, Patricia 1922- and John
  1922-1975
Behn, Harry 1898-1973
Belloc, Hilaire 1870-1953
Benary-Isbert, Margot 1889-1979
Benchley, Nathaniel 1915-1981
Berenstain, Stan(ley) 1923- and
  Jan(ice) 1923-
Berger, Melvin 1927-
Berna, Paul 1910-
Beskow, Elsa 1874-1953
Bianco, Margery Williams 1881-1944
Bishop, Claire Huchet
Blades, Ann 1947-
Blake, Quentin 1932-
Blos, Joan W(insor) 1928-
Blumberg, Rhoda 1917-
Blyton, Enid 1897-1968
Bodecker, N(iels) M(ogens) 1922-
Bødker, Cecil 1927-
Bonham, Frank 1914-
Brancato, Robin F(idler) 1936-
Branley, Franklyn M(ansfield) 1915-
Branscum, Robbie 1937-
Brazil, Angela 1869-1947
Breinburg, Petronella 1927-
Bridgers, Sue Ellen 1942-
Bright, Robert 1902-
Brink, Carol Ryrie 1895-1981
Brooke, L(eonard) Leslie 1862-1940

Brown, Marc 1946-
Brown, Marcia 1918-
Browne, Anthony (Edward Tudor)
  1946-
Bryan, Ashley F. 1923-
Buff, Mary 1890-1970 and Conrad
  1886-1975
Bulla, Clyde Robert 1914-
Burch, Robert 1925-
Burchard, Peter 1921-
Burgess, Gelett 1866-1951
Burgess, Thornton W(aldo) 1874-1965
Burnett, Frances Hodgson 1849-1924
Butterworth, Oliver 1915-
Caines, Jeannette
Carlson, Natalie Savage 1906-
Carrick, Carol 1935-
Chambers, Aidan 1934-
Childress, Alice 1920-
Chönz, Selina
Christopher, Matt(hew) 1917-
Ciardi, John 1916-1986
Clapp, Patricia 1912-
Clark, Ann Nolan 1896-
Clarke, Pauline 1921-
Cleaver, Elizabeth (Mrazik) 1939-1985
Cohen, Barbara 1932-
Colby, C(arroll) B(urleigh) 1904-1977
Colman, Hila
Colum Padraic 1881-1972
Cone, Molly 1918-
Coolidge, Olivia 1908-
Coolidge, Susan 1835-1905
Cooney, Barbara 1917-
Cormier, Robert (Edmund) 1925-
Courlander, Harold 1908-
Cox, Palmer 1840-1924
Cresswell, Helen 1934-
Crompton, Richmal 1890-1969
Cunningham, Julia 1916-
Curry, Jane L(ouise) 1932-
Dalgliesh, Alice 1893-1979
Daly, Maureen 1921-
Daugherty, James 1889-1974
d'Aulaire, Ingri 1904-1980 and Edgar
  Parin 1898-
de la Mare, Walter 1873-1956
de Regniers, Beatrice Schenk 1914-
Dickinson, Peter 1927-
Dillon, Eilís 1920-
Dodge, Mary Mapes 1831-1905
Domanska, Janina
Drescher, Henrik
Duncan, Lois S(teinmetz) 1934-
Duvoisin, Roger 1904-1980
Eager, Edward 1911-1964
Edgeworth, Maria 1767-1849
Edmonds, Walter D(umaux) 1903-

Ende, Michael 1930(?)-
Epstein, Sam(uel) 1909- and Beryl 1910-
Ets, Marie Hall 1893-
Ewing, Juliana Horatia 1841-1885
Farber, Norma 1909-1984
Farjeon, Eleanor 1881-1965
Field, Eugene 1850-1895
Field, Rachel 1894-1942
Fisher, Dorothy Canfield 1879-1958
Fisher, Leonard Everett 1924-
Flack, Marjorie 1897-1958
Forbes, Esther 1891-1967
Forest, Antonia
Freeman, Don 1908-1978
Fujikawa, Gyo 1908-
Fyleman, Rose 1877-1957
Galdone, Paul 1914-
Gardam, Jane 1928-
Garfield, Leon 1921-
Garis, Howard R(oger) 1873-1962
Garner, Alan 1935-
Gates, Doris 1901-
Gerrard, Roy 1935-
Giblin, James Cross 1933-
Giff, Patricia Reilly 1935-
Ginsburg, Mirra 1919-
Goble, Paul 1933-
Godden, Rumer 1907-
Goodrich, Samuel G(riswold) 1793-1860
Gorey, Edward 1925-
Goudge, Elizabeth (de Beauchamp)
  1900-1984
Gramatky, Hardie 1907-1979
Greene, Constance C(larke) 1924-
Grimm, Jacob 1785-1863 and Wilhelm
  1786-1859
Gruelle, Johnny 1880-1938
Guillot, René 1900-1969
Guy, Rosa (Cuthbert) 1928-
Hader, Elmer 1889-1973 and Berta
  1891?-1976
Hale, Lucretia Peabody 1820-1900
Haley, Gail E(inhart) 1939-
Harnett, Cynthia 1893-1981
Harris, Christie 1907-
Harris, Joel Chandler 1848-1908
Harris, Rosemary (Jeanne) 1923-
Haywood, Carolyn 1898-
Heide, Florence Parry 1919-
Highwater, Jamake 1942-
Hill, Eric
Hoban, Tana
Hoberman, Mary Ann 1930-
Hoff, Syd(ney) 1912-
Hoffman, Heinrich 1809-1894
Holland, Isabelle 1920-
Holling, Holling C(lancy) 1900-1973
Hughes, Langston 1902-1967

9

Hughes, Shirley 1929-
Hunter, Mollie 1922-
Ipcar, Dahlov 1917-
Iwasaki, Chihiro 1918-1974
Jackson, Jesse 1908-1983
Jacobs, Joseph 1854-1916
Janosch 1931-
Jeschke, Susan 1942-
Johnson, Crockett 1906-1975
Johnson, James Weldon 1871-1938
Jonas, Ann
Jones, Diana Wynne 1934-
Judson, Clara Ingram 1879-1960
Juster, Norton 1929-
Keith, Harold 1903-
Kelly, Eric P(hilbrook) 1884-1960
Kennedy, Richard 1932-
Kent, Jack 1920-1985
Kerr, Judith 1923-
Kerr, M. E. 1927-
Kettelkamp, Larry 1933-
King, Clive 1924-
Kipling, Rudyard 1865-1936
Kjelgaard, Jim 1910-1959
Kraus, Robert 1925-
Krauss, Ruth 1911-
Krumgold, Joseph 1908-1980
La Farge, Oliver 1901-1963
La Fontaine, Jean de 1621-1695
Lang, Andrew 1844-1912
Langton, Jane 1922-
Latham, Jean Lee 1902-
Lauber, Patricia 1924-
Lavine, Sigmund A(rnold) 1908-
Leaf, Munro 1905-1976
Lenski, Lois 1893-1974
Levy, Elizabeth 1942-
Lewis, Elizabeth Foreman 1892-1958
Lightner, A(lice) M. 1904-
Linklater, Eric 1899-1974
Lofting, Hugh 1866-1947
Lunn, Janet 1928-
MacDonald, George 1824-1905
MacGregor, Ellen 1906-1954
MacLachlan, Patricia
Mann, Peggy
Marshall, James 1942-
Martin, Patricia Miles 1899-
Masefield, John 1878-1967
Mayer, Marianna 1945-
Mayne, William 1928-
Mazer, Harry 1925-
Mazer, Norma Fox 1931-
McCaffrey, Anne (Inez) 1926-
McGovern, Ann
McKillip, Patricia A(nne) 1948-
McNeer, May 1902-

Meader, Stephen W(arren) 1892-1977
Means, Florence Crannell 1891-1980
Meigs, Cornelia 1884-1973
Meltzer, Milton 1915-
Merriam, Eve 1916-
Merrill, Jean 1923-
Miles, Betty 1928-
Milne, Lorus 1912- and Margery 1915-
Minarik, Else Holmelund 1920-
Mizumura, Kazue
Molesworth, Mary Louisa 1842-1921
Moore, Lilian
Morey, Walt(er) 1907-
Naylor, Phyllis Reynolds 1933-
Neufeld, John (Arthur) 1938-
Neville, Emily Cheney 1919-
Nic Leodhas, Sorche 1898-1969
Nichols, Ruth 1948-
North, Sterling 1906-1974
Nöstlinger, Christine 1936-
Ofek, Uriel 1926-
Olney, Ross R(obert) 1929-
Oneal, Zibby 1934-
Ormondroyd, Edward 1925-
Ottley, Reginald
Oxenbury, Helen 1938-
Parish, Peggy 1927-
Peck, Richard (Wayne) 1934-
Peck, Robert Newton 1928-
Peet, Bill 1915-
Perl, Lila
Perrault, Charles 1628-1703
Petersham, Maud 1890-1971 and Miska 1888-1960
Petry, Ann (Lane) 1908-
Picard, Barbara Leonie 1917-
Platt, Kin 1911-
Politi, Leo 1908-
Prelutsky, Jack
Price, Christine 1928-1980
Pyle, Howard 1853-1911
Reeves, James 1909-1978
Richards, Laura E(lizabeth) 1850-1943
Richler, Mordecai 1931-
Robertson, Keith 1914-
Rockwell, Anne 1934- and Harlow
Rodgers, Mary 1931-
Rollins, Charlemae Hill 1897-1979
Ross, Tony 1938-
Rounds, Glen 1906-
Rylant, Cynthia 1954-
Sánchez-Silva, José María 1911-
Sandburg, Carl 1878-1967
Sandoz, Mari 1896-1966
Sawyer, Ruth 1880-1970
Scarry, Huck 1953-
Scott, Jack Denton 1915-

Sebestyen, Ouida 1924-
Seton, Ernest Thompson 1860-1946
Sharmat, Marjorie Weinman 1928-
Sharp, Margery 1905-
Shotwell, Louisa R(ossiter) 1902-
Sidney, Margaret 1844-1924
Silverstein, Alvin 1933- and Virginia 1937-
Sinclair, Catherine 1880-1864
Skurzynski, Gloria 1930-
Sleator, William 1945-
Slobodkin, Louis 1903-1975
Smith, Doris Buchanan 1934-
Snyder, Zilpha Keatley 1927-
Spence, Eleanor 1928-
Sperry, Armstrong W. 1897-1976
Spykman, E(lizabeth) C. 1896-1965
Spyri, Johanna 1827-1901
Steele, William O(wen) 1917-1979
Stevenson, James 1929-
Stolz, Mary 1920-
Stratemeyer, Edward L. 1862-1930
Streatfeild, Noel 1897-
Taylor, Sydney 1904?-1978
Taylor, Theodore 1924-
Ter Haar, Jaap 1922-
Titus, Eve 1922-
Tolkien, J(ohn) R(onald) R(euel) 1892-1973
Treadgold, Mary 1910-
Trease, Geoffrey 1909-
Tresselt, Alvin 1916-
Treviño, Elizabeth Borton de 1904-
Tudor, Tasha 1915-
Turkle, Brinton 1915-
Twain, Mark 1835-1910
Udry, Janice May 1928-
Unnerstad, Edith 1900-
Uttley, Alison 1884-1976
Ventura, Piero 1937-
Vincent, Gabrielle
Vining, Elizabeth Gray 1902-
Voigt, Cynthia 1942-
Waber, Bernard 1924-
Wahl, Jan 1933-
Walter, Mildred Pitts
Ward, Lynd 1905-1985
Wells, Rosemary 1943-
Westall, Robert (Atkinson) 1929-
Wiese, Kurt 1887-1974
Wilkinson, Brenda 1946-
Williams, Barbara 1925-
Yates, Elizabeth 1905-
Yonge, Charlotte M(ary) 1823-1901
Zemach, Harve 1933-1974 and Margot 1931-
Zion, Gene 1913-1975

Readers are cordially invited to suggest additional authors to the editors.

GUEST ESSAY

New Faces, New Directions in Britain
by Marcus Crouch

In the early 1970s I was asked to write a survey of the children's novel in postwar Britain which was subsequently published as *The Nesbit Tradition: The Children's Novel in England, 1945-70* (London: Benn, 1972). At the time I was not thinking of 1970 as a very significant watershed date, merely a convenient resting place. Looking back now after more than fifteen years, I am inclined to believe that it was, if no dramatic turning point, at least in some degree a point of change.

I am no great believer in "movements," at least so far as children's literature is concerned. Good books come about because there are good writers to make them. During the Second World War a new generation was growing up; the previous one was preoccupied with immediate problems and had little time for creativity. With the end of war and, after a few years, the easing of many restrictions (notably a chronic shortage of paper), there was a burst of literary activity in every field, not least that of the children's book. New writers of outstanding promise appeared: Rosemary Sutcliff in 1950, William Mayne in 1953, Philippa Pearce in 1955, and a little later John Rowe Townsend and Helen Cresswell, Leon Garfield and Alan Garner. The list could readily be extended.

All of these writers have continued to be active beyond 1970. Most of them had set the pattern of their work by that date—even William Mayne! Mayne, who began as the *enfant terrible* of his generation, no longer shocks with the audacity of his ideas, and his stylistic virtuosity, still a constant source of delight, has lost some of its ability to surprise. For most of the others, fine craftsmanship and integrity ensure that each new book will have its own power to give pleasure and extend horizons, but we know more or less what to expect. The foundations were laid, the creative battles won, in earlier decades.

I was tempted to call this paper "New Faces" and concentrate on writers who have emerged since 1970. To do this would cut out some established writers whose work has undergone significant changes in direction in recent years. One cannot call Kathleen Peyton a "new face"; her first books were published, under her maiden name of Herald, while she was at school in the 1940s. Throughout her writing life Mrs. Peyton has been restlessly searching for her kind of book. She seemed to have found it in the first of the "Flambards" stories, *Flambards* (1967), and again in the "Pennington" books—*Pennington's Seventeenth Summer* (1970), *The Beethoven Medal* (1971), and *Pennington's Heir* (1973)—with their offbeat anti-hero who perhaps reflected in part her own independent view of society. The search continues. It has taken her into the fairly recent past in *A Pattern of Roses* (1972), an original exploration of a "time-shift" theme which contains some of her most sensitive writing. Mrs. Peyton shares with some of her young readers a love of horses, and in some of her stories she has lifted the "pony" book on to an altogether higher level. *Dear Fred* (1981) is a horse story of a different order. Here is a picture of the world of professional horse racing, an oblique portrait of the greatest of British jockeys, Fred Archer, and, not for the first time but here with greater subtlety, a moving and deeply understanding study of first love. Since then Mrs. Peyton has written a genuine comedy in *Who, Sir? Me, Sir?* (1983), which relates how four lower-class, inexperienced students are entered into a tetrathlon against a team from a privileged school. In the past she has kept a rein on her undoubted sense of humour; here it breaks out unrestrained. Hoomey and his friends (and enemies) are recognisable denizens of a real world. In their struggles to meet the unreasonable demands laid on them by a thoughtless teacher, they grow in stature without losing any of their animal high-spirits. A Moral Tale this, and a very funny one. It may indicate the direction in which Mrs. Peyton is moving.

My good friend Barbara Willard will, I know, forgive me if I say that even less than Kathleen Peyton can she be called a new face. She began her career as an adult novelist in the year of *Swallows and Amazons* (1930). Her work was always marked by intelligence and high professionalism, but for many admirers it lacked focus. In 1970 she found her theme. For many years, she had lived in the Weald of Sussex on the edge of Ashdown Forest, absorbing its history and atmosphere. *The Lark and the Laurel* (1970) was the first fruit of this love affair with a landscape. She created a manor house in the forest and peopled it with vividly realized and individual inhabitants. In the following ten years she followed the fortunes of the house and the family through eight reigns and a century and a half in *The Spring of Bloom* (1971), *A Cold Wind Blowing* (1972), *The Iron Lily* (1973), *Harrow and Harvest* (1974), *The Miller's Boy* (1976), *The Eldest Son* (1977), and *The Keys of Mantlemass* (1981). Mantlemass became, if not an obsession, a preoccupation which at times threatened to obliterate the contemporary world. The "Mantlemass" novels, seven of them with a slighter story and a pendant of short stories filling in gaps in the chronicle, are a remarkable example of concentrated creativity, of a writer's personal "daemon" (in Rosemary Sutcliff's word) taking over and lifting a competent author into an altogether higher league. The effect has been lasting. Since the Mantlemass sequence was brought to and end —by the publisher's insistence, I fancy, rather than by loss of inspiration—Miss Willard has continued to produce novels which are much superior to those of the pre-Mantlemass days. *Ned Only* (1985), the story of a kitchen boy who lives on a Sussex estate during the post-Restoration period, is especially notable for being better written, sharper in observation, and having a keener sense of period than Miss Willard's earlier works.

Alan Garner, too, has not stayed still. When the rather tentative fantasies of his 'prentice days were followed by *The Owl Service* (1967) it seemed to some observers that he had found his metier and might be expected to follow this achievement with other interpretations of present dilemmas by reference to the mythical past. *Red Shift* (1973) disturbed such notions. Here was a brilliantly experimental, and extremely difficult, examination of time in parallel, closely based on an actual Cheshire landscape. For the full effect one needs to read it map in hand! Structurally forward-looking as *Red Shift* is, it in some ways marks the end of a phase for Garner, the "Owl Service" formula pushed to its ultimate limits. His next major project was of a very different order in theme and manner, although the scene remained the same. This was the so-called "Stone Book Quartet": *The Stone Book* (1976), *Granny Reardun* (1977), *Tom Fobble's Day* (1977), and *The Aimer Gate* (1978). In four short books he looks at life in a Cheshire village a generation or so on each side of 1900 and the impact on the scene, the community, and the family of the work of country craftmen. In celebrating these past artizans—stonemason, blacksmith and the like—Garner has been moved to match their skill with a craftmanship of his own, purifying and refining his style down to the bare bones. The resulting stories are small only as regards length; in wisdom as much as in strength and style, they are not only Garner's best work but writing more profound and more personal than anything he has done before or since.

For different reasons and by different paths both Alan Garner and Barbara Willard go back to the past for their material. In a chapter in *The Nesbit Tradition,* I suggested that this had been one of the most productive areas of children's literature in the postwar period. No longer. Relatively few of the new writers seem to find satisfaction in the conventional historical romance. There are exceptions. Both Peter Dickinson (who, although he had written before 1970, has so broadened and intensified his work that he may fairly be called a new writer) and Jill Paton Walsh turned to the story of the Byzantine Empire, Dickinson to the high noon of its power in *The Dancing Bear* (1972), Miss Paton Walsh to the death-throes of the Empire at the fall of Constantinople in the *The Emperor's Winding Sheet* (1974). The latter is perhaps this talented writer's finest essay in historical fiction with its bold sweep and grandeur of concept which do not obscure the intimacy of its detail. I have a personal preference for her *A Parcel of Patterns* (1983). This takes for its subject the pathetic story of Eyam, the Derbyshire village which, having involuntarily introduced the plague into the community, shut itself off from the outside world in order to contain the disease. The story is true, the characters—with the exception of narrator Mall Percival—have historical authority, and the writer meets the challenge of her subject with enormous integrity.

In her first novel Mary John goes back even further in time, to the Bronze Age and the building of Stonehenge. I admit to a personal affection for *Bluestones* (1982), for this was the prizewinner in a competition, sponsored by the Welsh Arts Council and Harlech Television, in which I was privileged to be a judge. Mary John's is a remarkable exercise in imaginative reconstruction. There is no documentary evidence, yet she brings the period vividly to life by the vitality of her portraiture. Her central characters are two young girls chosen to die as sacrificial victims on the blue stones of ancient ritual circle in the Preselli Hills. They are saved, and the lives of their tribe transformed, by the arrival of a representative of the new culture, come to bargain for the blue stones which are needed for the hub of Bronze Age life at Stonehenge. Archaeological facts support Mrs. John's thesis, but the reader is concerned more with the passions and the aspirations of these remote people. *Bluestones,* which comes from a Welsh publishing house set up initially to publish the competition prizewinners, has not won the wider appreciation which its real qualities deserve.

If not for historical fiction, the last decade or two has been a great time for reminiscence. Writers, and their characters, look back to their own childhoods. I would claim some of the most memorable books of the period for this category, most of them by women writers. Nina Bawden began writing adult novels and turned to children's books; Penelope Lively was a children's writer first, an adult writer later. Both of them, it seems to me—but others would disagree—

sometimes hold back a little of themselves in their children's books as if they have not quite reconciled themselves to this role. This is true of Nina Bawden's early books, but by the time she came to write *Carrie's War* (1973) she had shed most of these inhibitions. This is a story of the tragicomedy of the Second World War called evacuation, in which many children were sent into the country for safety. Carrie and her young brother go to live with a Welsh shopkeeper and his repressed sister, where they find a little cautious affection and learn much of the effects of a narrow mind on human relationships. There is, as in the earlier books, rather too much contrivance in the plot, but of Mrs. Bawden's power to penetrate her characters to the heart there can be no question. *The Peppermint Pig* (1975) is a slighter book but structurally more perfect. No contrivance here, just the kind of enrichment with which memory is apt to adorn reality; the perfect Grandmother tale, in fact. Way back in a world without aeroplanes and bombs, Poll shares a year of childhood with scarlet fever and the peppermint pig, Johnnie. The runt of the litter, Johnnie is adopted by the Greengrass family and grows up with them; clever and greedy, he brings much fun to counterbalance the family's many troubles. In the end, when the inevitable happens and Johnnie goes to the butcher, Poll grows up, abruptly and painfully. This is a wise, humane story, told with unaffected simplicity and great tenderness.

Penelope Lively established her reputation with a series of novels in which there was more than a hint of the supernatural. The best of these is *The Ghost of Thomas Kempe* (1973), a Carnegie Medal winner in which a seventeenth-century magician intrudes, mostly with comic effect, into the life of a modern child. She has not abandoned this vein, which has its most recent expression in *The Revenge of Samuel Stokes* (1981). Here a famous (fictional) landscape gardener of the Capability Brown/Repton school, which promoted both the artistic and practical in gardens, objects to what has been done to his masterpiece by modern developers, and reinstates it—lake, terraces, statuary and all—in the middle of a model housing estate. A very funny story, not without its pertinent social comment, is somewhat marred by the physical intrusion of Samuel Stokes himself. This touch, for me, destroys the credibility without adding to the excitement. Excellent as these books are, I find Penelope Lively most truly herself in *Going Back* (1975), a work set during the Second World War. This cannot be autobiographical—the writer was born in Egypt and, I believe, stayed there until after the war—but it bears all the marks of personal experience. During the war two children live in reasonable physical comfort in a lovely house for which they have deep affection, but they have no mother, and their father is a distant, indifferent, sometimes hostile force. The story, in which there are no contrived episodes, is set in a real Somerset landscape, hardly ever overtly described but conveyed clearly through the children's eyes. The details of wartime life are equally convincing. The story is remembered by Jane, now a grown woman with her own family, who returns with her husband and lets the happiness and the sadness of those distant days wash over her, a device which gives the story a sharp, bittersweet reality.

There is something of the same tender melancholy in Jill Paton Walsh's *Goldengrove* (1972) and *Unleaving* (1976), two novels linked by their titles (derived from a familiar poem of Gerard Manley Hopkins), their scene, and central character. The first has as its underlying theme two children on the brink of adolescence; in the second the girl, a child no longer, discovers the anguish of first love and the wonder and pain of growing up. Both books are full of the most subtle observations of child and adult behaviour, and are written with a delicacy and penetration which invite comparison—as does some of the subject matter—with Virginia Woolf. Here is the work of a major novelist writing not for children but in order to put down some personal and original ideas about the importance of living and the nature of relationships. Perhaps it is inappropriate to mention these books in a consideration of children's literature, but their honesty and candour, as well as their pervading humour, have surely something to say to readers of any age. Miss Paton Walsh knows how to pack simple sentences with meaning. Early in *Unleaving* the children take Gran, the owner and presiding genius of the house, Goldengrove, down to the beach for a picnic. She is dying, and the children, unknowing, play at burying in the sand. "Gran sits, eyes closed, looking out to sea."

Most of the books I have mentioned have, at least in large part, a country setting. This is not so much because old children's book traditions die hard, but because many writers find that what they have to say fits best into the compass of a small community. They write, moreover, most happily and effectively about what they know best. Witness Jane Gardam's *The Hollow Land* (1981), a joyous celebration of Cumbria. In a series of separate episodes, each involving the same maturing characters, she explores the changing colours and moods of the seasons and the fun of country folk following their own affairs. These people are as odd and idiosyncratic as the place where they live and as absorbingly fascinating. No writer of our time has captured more vividly, with little direct description, the wonder of a frost-bound land than Mrs. Gardam in the chapter "The Icicle Ride." There is sensitive handling of landscape, too, in Alison Morgan's *Leaving Home* (1979), in which a small boy is taken, for his own good, away from the mountain cottage where he has lived happily with his grandfather and goes to live on a suburban estate with kindly but conventional cousins. As Paul insists on bringing his goat with him, trouble inevitably follows, and in time he goes back home, making an epic journey alone to his native mountains. Paul's dilemma, and the nature of the home for which he yearns, are projected with a force which is the more effective for being always understated.

These are stories in which the countryside is identified with home. In *The Maps of Time* (1983), Peter Hunt brings a party of town folk into the country on holiday. This book underlines the changes which have overtaken the children's story in recent years. The basic situation is not unlike that of an Arthur Ransome book, although Ransome would have been astonished at the sexual maturity and freedom of the characters. The everyday events of a riverside holiday are presented with much animation and humour, and with an affectionate understanding of young people, but I find the main thesis of the book, which involves the manipulation of time by means of old maps bought in one of the celebrated bookhops of Hay-on-Wye, incompletely realized. The starting point of Brigid Chard's *Voices on the Wind* (1980) is more like E. Nesbit than Ransome. This fine and undervalued novel shows a family leaving London to escape the attentions of the press—their father is missing, believed dead, in dramatic circumstances—and going to live in a remote cottage on the Welsh border. It might almost be an updated *Railway Children*, but not for long. Again, some of the mechanics of the plot are unsatisfactory, but the delight of the children in exploring their new environment and their involvement in a rural community are conveyed with a most tender understanding.

Mention of *The Hollow Land* brings me to a book in which setting is subordinated to character and which is for me the central achievement of the past fifteen years. This is Jane Gardam's *Bilgewater* (1976), a novel which for no discernable reason other than the publisher's whim was included in the children's book list, but which in its vitality, its wisdom, and its pervading humour demands the delighted capitulation of readers of all ages. *Bilgewater* is a variant on the theme of the Ugly Duckling. The eponymous heroine grows up in the unnatural atmosphere of a boys' Public School—in England, remember, Public Schools are not public but the province of a privileged few—of which her unworldly father is a housemaster. With no mother, she is dependent on the school matron, Paula, a strong-minded woman with a contempt for human frailty—"Beware of Self Pity!" Paula is usually too much preoccupied with the boys' underwear and defects of the crumbling school buildings to be aware of Bilge's frequent dilemmas. Bilgewater's real name is Marigold, but the boys' nickname—a variation of "Bill's daughter"—sticks. She is plain, uncertain, and dislexic, and has acquired an undeserved reputation for stupidity. She also wears thick glasses and deplorable clothes and is convinced that she is physically undesirable. In a rare moment of emotion, Paula points to the heart of Bilge's problem: "She sees clear and pure and sometimes it's a bit more than she nor anybody can bear." As she grows up, surprising everyone with her academic brilliance, she falls in love with a sequence of schoolboys, starting with the Head Boy, handsome, talented, but with small eyes which betray the small mind within. Poor Bilgewater narrates the story herself, exposing in marvellously memorable phrases her many shortcomings as she blunders from one disaster to the next. This is high comedy, expressed with unfailing wit, but tears are never far behind the laughter.

Jane Gardam seems to me to be in the classic tradition of the English novel, in direct descent from Jane Austen. Like Jane Austen she is aware of the world outside her circle, but not to be deflected from her purpose by it. For many writers today, perhaps most, that world and its problems are the central theme. Poverty, drugs, race, violence, sex: all are the subjects of novels of greater or lesser significance. The relatively recent problem—in this country—of racial relations has produced some interesting stories, although none anywhere near as good as the best in the States, such as Virginia Hamilton's. Jan Needle — *My Mate Shofiq* (1978) and *Piggy in the Middle* (1982), Len Webster—*The Turban Wallah* (1984), and Susan Gregory, whose short stories entitled *Martini on the Rocks* (1984) take a more relaxed and humourous look at the subject, are the most satisfactory of English writers in this field. There is an attractive picture of friendship breaking down the barriers between races in an adventure story by Bernard Ashley, written originally for television. The main of *Running Scared* (1986) is gangsterism in London's East End, but the interest of the book springs most from its picture of two girls, one from each community, whose affection and respect for each other are the basis of the final resolution. Bernard Ashley is typical of a new generation of writers whose concern for and understanding of young people comes from personal experience; he is a headmaster in a London school. All of his books are concerned with the difficulties of children growing up in a hostile world. His motives are worthy, but Ashley's performances are sometimes not up to his motives. In *Dodgem* (1981), however, he moves freely within the context of the book. *Dodgem* concerns the growth of a truant boy who escapes from a juvenile center to a fairground; due to its convincing characterization and atmosphere, it is perhaps Ashley's most successful work to date.

Violence is a recurrent theme in Ashley. It is inevitably at the heart of a number of books set in Northern Ireland. Peter Carter's *Under Goliath* (1977) is set in Belfast at the outbreak of the present troubles, and shows how a promising friendship between Protestant and Catholic boys is eroded by traditional hatreds. No comfort here. Not much either in Lynne Reid Banks' *Maura's Angel* (1984), in which a little girl's guardian angel is projected by an explosion into a Catholic household. The experience does everyone some good, but Miss Reid Banks offers no easy solutions. There is violence in most of the remarkable and varied novels of Robert Westall, whose first book, *The Machine Gunners* (1975), disturbed some adult readers with its revelation of the latent aggression in quite normal Tyneside boys. Westall's work is endlessly intriguing and his manner is seen at its best and least controversial in *The Wind Eye* (1976), a contemporary time fantasy which describes how the lives of a family are transformed through their involvement with

14

a seventh-century saint. However, I am perhaps not alone in finding many of his stories disfigured by a gratuitous aggressiveness. Another contemporary problem, terrorism, is the subject of a clever and stressful novel by Gillian Cross, *On the Edge* (1984). It has its most brilliant exposition in Peter Dickinson's *The Seventh Raven* (1981). Here the frightening actuality of the terrorists is heightened by a brilliantly presented setting: the production of a new opera by child players, one of whom—one of the seven ravens who feed the Prophet Elijah—is the son of a diplomat and consequently a target for terrorist activity. The ordinary hazards of amateur dramatics generate some good fun, and the story—narrated by a precocious teenager—has additional edge because the terrorists have a case: they are fighting a corrupt dictatorship.

In children's book terms, sex has come a long way since Josephine Kamm, with conscious temerity, introduced an unmarried mother into *Young Mother* (1965). Now anything goes. We are offered a "wealth" of detail in adolescent romance, a fictional rape (a happy amnesia prevents me from naming this book), and the rapture and tragedy of a homosexual relationship which Aidan Chambers evokes in *Dance on My Grave* (1982). Such stories are mostly unmemorable. I found Gina Wilson's *Family Feeling* (1986) remarkably successful in dealing with a familiar situation: a second marriage bringing together two disparate readymade families, and showing how friendship between stepbrother and stepsister can turn to sexual experimentation. Perhaps the most convincing study of adolescent passion in recent fiction is by Liz Berry in *Easy Connections* (1983) and its sequel *Easy Freedom* (1985). In these clever novels, drama and near-tragedy come from the clash between boy and girl, career and career. A young girl, with a brilliant career in art before her, is seduced by the leader of a rock group and thereafter forced by the pressures of the ruthless young man and of conventional society into a marriage which threatens to destroy her career and her own personality. Although the novels are maddening because Cathy is not given the breaks she deserves and the plot comes periously close to that of the standard "romance," the treatment is penetrating and forceful. The descriptions of rock concerts are in themselves performances of startling virtuosity.

Cathy's problem, in *Easy Connections*, is one of identity; how can she remain true to herself in the face of sexual and social pressures? This is a common dilemma among fictional heroines, and some heroes. One finds it often in the admirable novels of Jan Mark, where cheerfulness is often breaking through to lighten the burden [see entry on Mark beginning on p. 134 of this volume]. In *The Ennead* (1978), Mrs. Mark's invented planet Erato has an authoritarian government committed to the elimination of individual identity. The efforts of malcontents like Isaac, Eleanor, and Moshe to follow, by very different means, their own courses lead to disaster. Their only satisfaction comes from holding fast to their own identities, but they die for it. *The Ennead* is a grim and powerful book. Something of the same idea is developed much more lightheartedly in *Handles* (1984), whose tough and vulnerable heroine finds her essential self among the motorbikes of the "smallest industrial estate in the world," where she earns her "handle," handles being special names which, as in folktales, have much potency in them.

Perhaps the strongest expression of this quest for identity comes in Mollie Hunter's *I'll Go My Own Way* (1984). This is the most personal as it is arguably the most powerful of Ms. Hunter's many books. It has social implications as a study of life among the Scottish "travellers," but its greatest interest lies in its portrait of a young girl growing into adulthood. Cat (Catriona) is no "thieving tink," as the police regard all her kind, but a strong woman in the making. Wise in poaching and other country crafts, bravely delivering her mother's new baby, she comes at the close of the story to face with confidence a harsh future with her man. Knowing herself and her husband, she has no doubt that she will overcome.

With so much notable writing about the real world, fantasy has lost some of its preeminence in recent years. Vivian Alcock's *The Stonewalkers* (1981) is an interesting exercise in the Nesbit manner. (Her earlier *The Haunting of Cassie Palmer* (1980) enters the all-too-real world of the fake spiritualist medium with greater penetration and high spirits.) Kenneth Lillington blends the natural and the supernatural in *What Beckoning Ghost?* (1983) and, more convincingly, in *Selkie* (1985). Diana Wynne Jones (*The Homeward Bounders*, 1981) is the current master of all matters magical. There is laughter in her works, but its function is mainly to relieve the fears generated by her vividly imagined stories. Geraldine Harris's "Seven Citadels" quartet—*The Children of the Wind* (1982), *The Dead Kingdom* (1983), *The Prince of the Godborn* (1983), and *The Seventh Gate* (1983)—is an imaginative *tour-de-force* which invites and almost deserves comparison with Ursula K. Le Guin's "Earthsea" trilogy: *A Wizard of Earthsea* (1968), *The Tombs of Atuan* (1971), and *The Farthest Shore* (1972).

In sheer power of imagination, sustained vitality, and bulk—it makes *Watership Down* (1972) look like a short story—Pat O'Shea's *The Hounds of the Morrigan* (1985) is the fantasy of the decade. Into her first book the author packs the experience of many lifetimes. It is a story of modern Ireland involving, as principal actors, two small children of the present day with their frankness and their freedom from inhibition. For complex reasons they become agents in the renewed war between the forces of good and evil. The combatants are creatures of the old Ireland of legend: the Morrigan, a deadly trinity of female goddesses, on the one hand, on the other heroes like Cuchulain, wearing until the end homely modern disguises. Despite the seriousness of the theme and the excitement of its many episodes, this is often a very funny book, the humour springing from the earthy toughness of the little girl Brigit and the equally earthy philosophy of some very memorable animals, earwigs, spiders, rats, and an endearing and amorous frog. *The Hounds of the Morrigan* must be among the longest children's books ever, but it is tightly constructed with no padding and no loose ends, and it is above all enormously readable, driving forward to a thrilling and satisfying conclusion.

Pat O'Shea can, I suppose, be described as an amateur writer, in the sense that Lewis Carroll and Kenneth Grahame were, in the context of their children's books, amateurs. Nevertheless, the keynote of children's books in Britain today is professionalism. Children's writers take themselves very seriously. Their concern for their craft is far removed from the unstudied outgoing writing of, say, Arthur Ransome. With this professionalism comes high standards. If there are no more books now than in previous generations that are likely to stand the test of time, there are far fewer poor, loosely written or incompletely thought-out books. Sometimes, I feel, in their concern for their craft writers may lose sight of their audience; they often mislay their sense of humour. Nevertheless, it is no bad time to be young, or to be a writer for the young. Children's books are in a healthy state. But I suspect that, in the next ten or fifteen years, we may be looking for new and creative ideas not so much to Britain or even to the States but to Australasia. To my mind the outstanding talent in this field today is the New Zealander Margaret Mahy. The qualities which make me place her so high are her versatility, wit and humor, originality, and intensity of imagination. Writing with equal effectiveness for picture-book readers, teenagers, and the groups in between, Miss Mahy has a genuinely comic view of life which she expresses without failing to achieve total seriousness when appropriate. Miss Mahy has a most fertile mind, producing ideas which are startlingly original; she also writes with powerful conviction, and carries the reader with her into many strange situations. There are indications that she is no isolated star but just the brightest of a new constellation.

Bibliography

Adams, Richard. *Watership Down*. London: Collings, 1972.

Alcock, Vivien. *The Haunting of Cassie Palmer*. London: Methuen, 1980.

Alcock, Vivien. *The Stonewalkers*. London: Methuen, 1981.

Ashley, Bernard. *Dodgem*. London: MacRae, 1981.

Ashley, Bernard. *Running Scared*. London: MacRae, 1986.

Banks, Lynne Reid. *Maura's Angel*. Illustrated by Robin Jacques. London: Dent, 1984.

Bawden, Nina. *Carrie's War*. Illustrated by Faith Jacques. London: Gollancz, 1973.

Bawden, Nina. *The Peppermint Pig*. Illustrated by Alexy Pendle. London: Gollancz, 1975.

Berry, Liz. *Easy Connections*. London: Gollancz, 1983.

Berry, Liz. *Easy Freedom*. London: Gollancz, 1985.

Carter, Peter. *Under Goliath*. London: Oxford University Press, 1977.

Chambers, Aidan. *Dance on My Grave: A Life and a Death in Four Parts, One Hundred and Seventeen Bits, Six Running Reports and Two Press Clippings, with a Few Jokes, a Puzzle or Three, Some Footnotes and a Fiasco Now and Then to Help the Story Along*. London: Bodley Head, 1982.

Chard, Brigid. *Voices on the Wind*. London: Collings, 1980.

Cross, Gillian. *On the Edge*. Oxford: Oxford University Press, 1984.

Crouch, Marcus. *The Nesbit Tradition: The Children's Novel in England, 1945-1970*. London: Benn, 1972.

Dickinson, Peter. *The Dancing Bear*. Illustrated by David Smee. London: Gollancz, 1972.

Dickinson, Peter. *The Seventh Raven*. London: Gollancz, 1981.

Gardam, Jane. *Bilgewater*. London: Hamilton, 1976.

Gardam, Jane. *The Hollow Land*. Illustrated by Janet Rawlins. London: MacRae, 1981.

Garner, Alan. *The Aimer Gate*. Illustrated by Michael Foreman. London: Collins, 1978.

Garner, Alan. *Granny Reardun*. Illustrated by Michael Foreman. London: Collins, 1977.

Garner, Alan. *The Owl Service*. London: Collins, 1967.

Garner, Alan. *Red Shift*. London: Collins, 1973.

Garner, Alan. *The Stone Book*. Illustrated by Michael Foreman. London: Collins, 1976.

Garner, Alan. *Tom Fobble's Day*. Illustrated by Michael Foreman. London: Collins, 1977.

Gregory, Susan. *Martini-on-the-Rocks*. London: Kestrel, 1984.

Harris, Geraldine. *The Children of the Wind*. London: Macmillan, 1982.

Harris, Geraldine. *The Dead Kingdom*. London: Macmillan, 1983.

Harris, Geraldine. *The Prince of the Godborn*. London: Unwin, 1983.

Harris, Geraldine. *The Seventh Gate*. London: Macmillan, 1983.

Hunt, Peter. *The Maps of Time*. London: MacRae, 1983.

Hunter, Mollie. *I'll Go My Own Way*. London: Hamilton, 1985.

John, Mary. *Bluestones*. Port Talbot, Wales: Barn Owl Press, 1982.

Jones, Diana Wynne. *The Homeward Bounders*. London: Macmillan, 1981.

Kamm, Josephine. *Young Mother*. Leicester, England: Brockhampton, 1965.

Le Guin, Ursula K. *The Farthest Shore*. Illustrated by Gail Garraty. New York: Atheneum, 1972.

Le Guin, Ursula K. *The Tombs of Atuan*. Illustrated by Gail Garraty. New York: Atheneum, 1971.

Le Guin, Ursula K. *A Wizard of Earthsea*. Illustrated by Ruth Robbins. Berkeley, Calif.: Parnassus Press, 1968.

Lillington, Kenneth. *Selkie*. London: Faber, 1985.

Lillington, Kenneth. *What Beckoning Ghost?*. London: Faber, 1983

Lively, Penelope. *The Ghost of Thomas Kempe*. Illustrated by Antony Maitland. London: Heinemann, 1973.

Lively, Penelope. *Going Back*. London: Heinemann, 1975.

Lively, Penelope. *The Revenge of Samuel Stokes*. London: Heinemann, 1981.

Mark, Jan. *The Ennead*. London: Kestrel, 1978.

Mark, Jan. *Handles*. Illustrated by David Parkins. London: Kestrel, 1983.

Morgan, Alison. *Leaving Home*. London: Chatto & Windus, 1979.

Needle, Jan. *My Mate Shofiq*. London: Deutsch, 1978.

Needle, Jan. *Piggy in the Middle*. London: Deutsch, 1982.

Nesbit, E. *The Railway Children*. Illustrated by C. E. Brock. London: Wells Gardner, 1906.

O'Shea, Pat. *The Hounds of the Morrigan*. Oxford: Oxford University Press, 1985.

Peyton, K. M. *The Beethoven Medal*. London: Oxford University Press, 1971.

Peyton, K. M. *Dear Fred*. London: Bodley Head, 1981.

Peyton, K. M. *Flambards*. Illustrated by Victor G. Ambrus. London: Oxford University Press, 1967.

Peyton, K. M. *A Pattern of Roses*. London: Oxford University Press, 1972.

Peyton, K. M. *Pennington's Heir*. Oxford: Oxford University Press, 1973.

Peyton, K. M. *Pennington's Seventeenth Summer*. London: Oxford University Press, 1970.

Peyton, K. M. *Who, Sir? Me, Sir?* Oxford: Oxford University Press, 1983.

Ransome, Arthur. *Swalllows and Amazons*. London: Cape, 1930.

Walsh, Jill Paton. *The Emperor's Winding Sheet*. London: Macmillan, 1974.

Walsh, Jill Paton. *Goldengrove*. London: Macmillan, 1972.

Walsh, Jill Paton. *A Parcel of Patterns*. London: Kestrel, 1983.

Walsh, Jill Paton. *Unleaving.* London: Macmillan, 1976.

Webster, Len. *The Turban-Wallah*. Oxford: Oxford University Press, 1984.

Westall, Robert. *The Machine-Gunners*. London: Macmillan, 1975.

Westall, Robert. *The Wind Eye.* London: Macmillan, 1976.

Willard, Barbara. *A Cold Wind Blowing.* London: Longman, 1972.

Willard, Barbara. *The Eldest Son.* London: Kestrel, 1977.

Willard, Barbara. *A Flight of Swans.* London: Kestrel, 1980.

Willard, Barbara. *Harrow and Harvest.* London: Kestrel, 1974.

Willard, Barbara. *The Iron Lily.* London: Longman, 1973.

Willard, Barbara. *The Keys of Mantlemass.* London: Kestrel, 1981.

Willard, Barbara. *The Lark and the Laurel.* Illustrated by Gareth Floyd. London: Longman, 1970.

Willard, Barbara. *The Miller's Boy.* Illustrated by Gareth Floyd. London: Kestrel, 1976.

Willard, Barbara. *Ned Only.* London: MacRae, 1985.

Willard, Barbara. *The Sprig of Broom.* Illustrated by Paul Shardlow. London: Longman, 1971.

Wilson, Gina. *Family Feeling.* London: Faber, 1986.

Marcus Crouch is an English author, critic, editor, and librarian. Author of *Treasure Seekers and Borrowers: Children's Books in Britain, 1900-1960* (1962) and *The Nesbit Tradition: The Children's Novel in England, 1945-1970* (1972), he is also the editor of *Chosen for Children: An Account of the Books Which Have Been Awarded the Library Association Carnegie Medal* (1957; second edition, 1967; third edition with Alec Ellis, 1977). Since 1948, Mr. Crouch has reviewed books for children in *Junior Bookshelf;* he was also a reviewer for the (London) *Times Literary Supplement* for twenty-five years and has contributed to a number of other publications. Mr. Crouch was Deputy County Librarian, Kent, from 1948 through 1977. Before his retirement, Mr. Crouch wrote twenty books of nonfiction, many on British history and typography. After retiring, he wrote several free versions of folktales in collaboration with the English illustrator William Stobbs, which include *The Home Countries* (1975), *Brer Rabbit* (1977), *Six against the World* (1978), and *The Ivory City* (1980). Past chairman of both the Youth Libraries Group of the (British) Library Association and the Kent Branch of the School Library Association, Mr. Crouch has also been honorary secretary of the Library Association.

Children's
Literature
Review

Nancy (Barbara) Bond
1945-

American author of fiction.

Bond is noted for creating perceptive novels which reflect her fascination with setting and her concern for adolescents coping with change. Her books deal with evocative places—Wales; Concord, Massachusetts; Hadrian's Wall; Cape Cod—and characteristically touch upon other times ranging from second-century England to New England in the future. Combining plots integral to the locale with themes of adaptation and reconciliation, Bond portrays families who adjust to death, remarriage, gradual fragmentation, and hostile environments. Her works stress respect for the individual, the recognition of personal differences, and the honest effort to resolve conflicts. Although Bond writes predominantly realistic stories, she is best known for her fantasy *A String in the Harp*, which revolves around a motherless American family in Wales and features Peter's adventures with a sixth-century magic harp key. In most of her later books, Bond keeps the action in the present but uses historical and supernatural allusions to add another dimension to her suspenseful tales.

Critics regard Bond as a writer of originality, skill, and depth, one who employs sharply focused settings, insightful human relationships, and unique, well-developed characters. Some observers object to the length of her books, the result of her leisurely writing style and liberal use of description. However, most reviewers esteem Bond as a novelist whose tightly interwoven plots, thought-provoking themes, and rich prose have added quality to young adult literature.

A String in the Harp was named a *Boston Globe-Horn Book* Honor Book in 1976 and a Newbery Honor Book in 1977. *The Voyage Begun* was a *Boston Globe-Horn Book* Honor Book in 1982.

(See also *Something about the Author*, Vol. 22; *Contemporary Authors New Revision Series*, Vol. 9; and *Contemporary Authors*, Vols. 65-68.)

Photograph by William Bond. Courtesy of Nancy Bond

AUTHOR'S COMMENTARY

[The following essay is based on a speech given by Bond on March 12, 1983 at a conference on "War as Metaphor in Children's Literature."]

Conflict, in its various forms, is one of a novel's essential ingredients. It provides the shape, the drama, the tension, the movement of a story. You introduce a group of characters, you put them in a setting, and then you make something happen. Conflict is the something that happens, and it progresses through the novel to a resolution—or at least a recognition—and you have a climax. I am very much aware of this myself in practical terms, because I recently met it head on in writing *A Place to Come Back To*. I reached what would have been the resolution of my story, only to discover to my infinite dismay that I had developed no real conflict to resolve. I felt as if I had no story, and I had to go back and find it.

To explore further the role of conflict in fiction, I have identified three general kinds of conflict which I propose to define

and then to discuss, chiefly in terms of my own books, because I can examine the process of constructing them and show how various aspects shifted and developed as I learned what I was writing about.

The first kind of conflict I call global. This is an external conflict; it involves a great number of people at the same time, fighting against each other or some other force—fire, flood, famine, or war in the military sense: the World Wars, the Korean, the Vietnam, the Civil War, the Revolution, or a kind of unofficial terrorist war. This kind of conflict has been the subject of many novels for children, among them *Johnny Tremain* (Houghton), *My Brother Sam Is Dead* (Four Winds), *The Dolphin Crossing* (St. Martin), *The Little Fishes* (Houghton), *Friedrich* (Holt), *The Seventh Raven* (Dutton), *After the First Death* (Pantheon).

The second kind of conflict I've termed personal. By this I mean the kind of conflict or hostility that arises between individuals—one person against another or one person against a familiar group of people: a child against a gang, as in *The Chocolate War* (Pantheon), or Patty struggling with her parents in *Summer of My German Soldier* (Dial) or Ivan Southall's Josh against all the kids in Ryan Creek or James against the ghost of Thomas Kempe.

The third kind of conflict is internal. It's the kind of conflict that occurs within a character. *A Wizard of Earthsea* (Parnas-

21

sus/Houghton) is a metaphorical exploration of this internal conflict. Ged's external struggle with the shadow he has thoughtlessly loosed is actually his struggle to recognize and to reconcile the two conflicting sides of his own nature, the dark and the light.

What I have said so far seems fairly simple and straightforward, but most novels do not actually deal with only one kind of conflict; they deal with a combination of two, or with all three.

I want first to look a little more closely at the idea of global conflict in children's novels. There is quite a large body of fiction dealing with war and its effects on children. Right now I'm speaking only of "real" war, not the wars of fantasy, which have rules of their own and almost always involve child characters in a very different way. Real—historical—war imposes two big limitations on a novelist. First, there is the simple fact that a child in any war has little—often no—chance of affecting what happens. Wars of this kind are fought by adults and involve children. Second, history has happened. Unless you are writing fantasy, no fictional character can alter the facts. I remember, years ago, reading Stephanie Plowman's novels about the Russian Revolution—*Three Lives for the Czar* and *My Kingdom for a Grave* (both Houghton). I vividly recall the heavy sense of doom I felt because I knew beforehand what had happened and I knew that her characters couldn't change it. I have the same feeling of predestination when I read a novel about World War II, for instance; the horrors that happened will happen again in the book—it is inevitable.

So you put a child character in a situation of war; he or she is witness or victim; in *Friedrich*, as an example, there is one of each. What are you as writer going to do with a character whose fate is, as it were, sealed? It seems to me that one of the greatest strengths—if not *the* greatest strength—of fiction is to turn statistics, which we all have coming out of our ears these days, back into human beings. This is certainly true of books about global conflict. Understanding something intellectually is very different from coming to terms with it emotionally. If we understood emotionally all the horrors that daily bombard us in newspapers and on television and radio, many of us would be incapable of functioning. How many people died in the camps in Lebanon or in the massacres of Bengali refugees in Assam? So many that they are not people to us; they are undifferentiated masses. We hear numbers, and we see terrible pictures, but we are removed from the tragedy because we don't identify individuals; we are not involved first-hand.

But out of that mass a writer takes on one person or a family; he or she tells a single story about a human being, and suddenly you begin to comprehend. The truth of war is awful, but without a perception of that truth our inclination is to remain uninvolved, passive, doing little to alleviate and nothing to prevent.

Here lies also the power of fiction. The writer uses imagination and human experience to create three-dimensional characters—characters with pasts, futures, parents, siblings, hopes, fears, sorrows, happiness. At the same time that the writer shows us individuals, he or she is showing us our common humanity, inviting identification and involvement.

From my own reading experience I will say that seldom—I can't really think of any instance—is the conflict in a novel global only, for all the reasons I have just mentioned, and for one other. Part of our common humanity is conflict—it is a fact of life.

To show you what I mean, I'll use my book *The Voyage Begun*. I had the idea for that book long before I actually wrote it. But when I sat down to work on it, I realized that the idea which had seemed so complete to me wasn't nearly ready to become a book. I have been a passionate conservationist for a long time. The original catalyst for *Voyage* came from a chance remark I heard a geologist make about the natural instability of Cape Cod: the fact that it is moving and changing and is unlikely to exist as a permanent geologic feature. The phrase that got me started was: "The dunes are marching." At that time there were a great many spectacular natural phenomena taking place around the world: earthquakes, droughts, fires, floods, mud slides, volcanic eruptions, unexpected weather patterns. My initial plan was to write a book in which the inanimate forces of nature actually seemed to rebel against the kind of treatment we have been giving the world: dumping wastes into air and water, clear-cutting jungles, spreading pesticides, building insufficiently safe nuclear plants—making drastic, fundamental, and widespread changes without any clear notion of future consequences. I saw myself using all of the natural disasters mentioned, indicating that this rebellion was going on all over the world, not just in one little corner. And that was my problem, right there, although it took me quite a while to recognize it.

The point of a novel, as I see it, is specificity. Two things I have learned about my own writing: It must be specific as to place and as to character. The global business was out; I couldn't begin to cope effectively with it, and I was right not to waste time trying but to turn instead to another, entirely different book. To give myself time to define the problem and to work out a solution.

The Voyage Begun is actually the story of two characters, each within a family, each family within the same small community, which is located in a small, isolated part of the northeast coast of the United States. There is no place in that book for volcanic eruptions in Hawaii or droughts in Africa, although those things may be happening offstage at the same time. I would consider my initial idea one of global conflict: war between humans and nature, which is on the periphery of the book. But that's a matter of statistics. In order to make the conflict immediate and understandable in human terms, I had to be specific. I needed to write about individuals responding to a particular situation, attempting to cope with it and with each other and to survive. Within the situation of global conflict I focused on personal and internal conflict. When I examine *Voyage* in this light, I see at once that it is full of conflict: Everyone in it is in conflict with someone or something. The most striking example is Mickey, the eleven-year-old girl, one of the two main characters; at the beginning she is in conflict with everyone.

Here I would like to look a little further at the nature of personal conflict. What are the qualities that put a character in conflict? Very often they are qualities we do not consider particularly admirable: anger, misunderstanding, jealousy, competition, greed, vanity, self-preservation, ambition, cowardice, insensitivity, fear, obsession, revenge, passion. These are strong human drives. If we are being completely honest with one another and with ourselves and baring our souls, we have to admit that we have all felt most, if not all, of these urges and emotions to some degree at one time or another. They are the dark side of our character, and by recognizing them in ourselves, we can begin to control them and to understand them in other people. By denying or ignoring them, we don't make them go away.

Conflict in itself is not necessarily bad. If we were perfect and lived in a perfect world, it would be, but we aren't and don't. In *The Once and Future King* (Putnam), T. H. White's King Arthur has his great idea for the Round Table. He says:

> Now what I have thought . . . is this, Why can't you harness Might so that it works for Right? I know it sounds nonsense, but, I mean, you can't just say there is no such thing. The Might is there, in the bad half of people, and you can't neglect it. You can't cut it out, but you might be able to direct it, if you see what I mean, so that it was useful instead of bad.

In *A Wizard of Earthsea* Ged stands and faces—no, turns and *pursues*—his dark self, forcing recognition of it. "Ged reached out his hands, dropping his staff, and took hold of his shadow, of the black self that reached out to him. Light and darkness met, and joined, and were one." And afterward, he says to his companion, "'I am whole, I am free.'"

It is hard to acknowledge this dark side of ourselves, however. We all like to think of ourselves as good. We want our children to be good. We want to give them our values, which we consider worthwhile, and we want them to lead good lives.

Let me say at this point that one of the hardest characters to construct believably is a *good*, a totally, thoroughly *good* character. I always hope, when I write a book, that a reader somewhere will identify with one, or even part of one, of my characters; when that happens, there is a real sharing, and I write to share. I myself read fiction in the hope of that same identification, a recognition of mutual humanness. I have a lot of trouble identifying with a completely virtuous character, but one who is in conflict, who is struggling with problems and faults—now there's someone who speaks to me.

The most difficult and important task I face when I begin to write a book is getting to know my characters. First I must find names, and then I must begin to define the people behind them. Interestingly enough, one of the best approaches for me is through their flaws and weaknesses. The rough parts offer much better handholds than the smooth ones. The rough parts are almost invariably more interesting as well. If a good character does something good—that's nice but only to be expected. If a weak or a flawed character does something good—or brave or unselfish—that's a story.

Now what I have just been talking about also has a great deal of bearing on the third kind of conflict I mentioned: the internal conflict. This is, or ought to be, going on simultaneously with either or both of the other kinds of conflict. As an example, let me take my second book *The Best of Enemies*. This isn't really about global conflict, but let me pretend for a minute that it is; the book is, after all, about a kind of war, a reenactment of the battle between the British and the colonists at the Old North Bridge in Concord. Two groups of people are fighting one another—on the one hand, a motley assortment of British soldiers and, on the other, an old man and a handful of kids.

Just for a moment imagine this conflict to be global. It is an external, collective conflict, even a very small war. But it is also a personal conflict; in fact, it's several personal conflicts, some more serious and intense than others. There is the conflict between Commodore Shattuck and his old friend and rival, Captain MacPherson; this is really a game, not hostile, but competition is involved, and pride and ambition. And the game-playing of the two adults involves the safety and well-being of other people—in the ultimate confrontation, for instance, where it seems entirely likely that someone will get hurt. There is also a personal conflict between two of the children—Charlotte and Oliver—which is not at all a game. It involves jealousy, anger, resentment, mistrust, fear—a lot of serious feelings.

The story is told completely from Charlotte's point of view; she is the character through whom the readers see everything that is going on. Hers are the primary reactions; every other character's are secondary—that is, filtered through her. So the main internal conflict is also hers. She is struggling with her own conflicting feelings, learning to recognize them and beginning to deal with them. She sees that Oliver is not a very sympathetic person, distinctly unfriendly, even hostile; but she also comes to see that he is unhappy, unsure, and lonely. She can recognize these feelings in him because she knows them from her own experience. It would be far easier in many ways for her to forget about him than for her to try to understand him. Which will she do? And there is her internal struggle over feelings toward her older brother Eliot. All her life he has been her best friend; now he suddenly announces that he is leaving home for graduate school in Montana. Charlotte feels betrayed and resentful, hurt and angry. Eliot is happy; he is going to do something he wants to do, and Charlotte feels left out. *The Best of Enemies* is partly about her struggle to reconcile her negative emotions with the love she also feels toward Eliot and that she knows he feels for her.

As I was working all this out, something else occurred to me about these sorts of conflict as they appear in fiction. There are two possible conclusions—resolution and recognition. External conflict—the first two kinds—seem to me more likely to be resolved; the battle at the Bridge is resolved; it is finished. Internal conflicts are more likely to be recognized. I feel strongly that it would be wrong to think Charlotte had, or could, resolve her inner struggles during a weekend—the space of the story. Among other things such a resolution would belittle their seriousness. And I think this is a very important point. It is a gross oversimplification to imply or to demonstrate through fiction that all conflicts can be resolved quickly, or sometimes even at all, just as it is oversimplifying people to show them as completely good or completely bad. People and life are extremely complex. Not to acknowledge this is to miss what it is to be human and alive and filled with contradictions and opposing feelings—rage and love, joy and despair, all at once. To try to show that complexity is an important part of my job as a writer of fiction, as I see it.

In the process of my self-exploration as a writer, I have discovered a curious thing about myself. It has to do with conflict; it has to do with character; it has to do with my villains. These are the characters used to create a good deal of the internal and external conflict in a story. They are obstacles or counterforces which provide some, much, or all of the drama, action, and tension in a novel. In my own opinion I have, so far, been unable to construct a person I feel is thoroughly, undeniably bad. Not that I haven't tried to have a villain or thought, when I started a book, that there wouldn't be one. Let me look at the evolution of two of my prospective villains and try to explain what happened to them on the way to the book.

The setting for *Country of Broken Stone* is modern-day Northumberland, Hadrian's Wall, where a group of students and archaeologists is conducting a dig on the site of a Roman fort. The most obvious conflict is between these people and a local family who used to be tenant farmers on the site but who were displaced by the former owner. Aha, I thought. Here are my villains, a whole family of them, the Robsons, who will try all kinds of nasty and dangerous tactics to dislodge these unwelcome outsiders. Here is a cunning, unpleasant, and reclusive old mother who holes up in an isolated farmhouse and sends her equally unpleasant sons out to revenge the accidental death of her husband on my main—and innocent—characters. As it turns out, those people are not like the Robsons who actually appear in the story.

The basic discrepancy between my initial idea and the finished book caused me to write a very different story from what I had at first envisioned. What went wrong? Why couldn't I get my material to do what I expected it to do? The answer lies in the characters. When I start writing, I have only the haziest notion who my characters are, and they ultimately become the most important part of my stories. As I work on a book, I become increasingly familiar with them; I find out more and more about them—their interests, their passions and fears, their strengths and their weaknesses—and I find out, because it's my job to, what makes them act the way they do. In the case of my villains, I think what happens is that I find out more than I had originally bargained for. I feel compelled to understand what has made them what they are. That doesn't mean I have to like them or condone their actions, but I cannot make them arbitrary villains, and that's precisely what happened to the Robsons.

In the course of our acquaintance, I discovered that Mrs. Robson had nothing to do with the nasty tactics I mentioned—she was actually an invalid, semi-paralyzed after a stroke, and not responsible for nor happy about her son Archie's sabotage. I found out, as my protagonist Penelope did, that the youngest son Ran not only was not a villain, but he was someone to value as a friend, a person from a very different background, who saw life in very different terms. The evolution of their unexpected friendship became one of the most important parts of the book; their acceptance of each other, not without friction and misunderstanding but with the growing determination that their relationship was worth working for.

So that left me with Archie as my only villain, and by the end of the story I saw him less as a bad man than as one overwhelmed by circumstances he had not the strength to resist, someone too weak to stand up against the dark side of himself. Even as Penelope and Ran are different people, so are the two brothers Archie and Ran; Ran has the strength Archie lacks.

In retrospect, which is invariably when I understand what it is I have been writing about, I could see that one of the major themes in *Country of Broken Stone* concerns the deceptiveness of first appearances; Penelope's and my first impressions of the Robsons are very different from our final knowledge of them. Because Penelope and Ran come from family situations that are dissimilar, each must learn to see the other in context in order to understand. Different lives demand different adaptations and impose different limitations.

This is true also in *The Voyage Begun*. The villains in this book, as I originally conceived them, are the members of the teenage gang, the Salvages, who loot and vandalize the abandoned houses around a Cape Cod town. One of the Salvages is Mickey's fifteen-year-old brother Shawn. These boys are violent, and they destroy for the sake of destruction, and I—like Paul—loathe destruction and violence. The Salvages, and Shawn in particular, provide a great deal of the conflict in the

book; they create the main problem by burning out an old boat builder and sending him into a nursing home. So far so good.

I got myself into trouble with Shawn, however, by asking *why* he was a member of the gang. The fact that he has an older brother Patrick, who is conscientious, responsible, and law-abiding, doesn't automatically mean that Shawn is bad; he's different. He has responded differently to the same set of conditions. He is trapped; he sees no future for himself in the town he can see no way of leaving. His motivations are anger, frustration, and boredom. When I realized this, I began—I must confess—to have a creeping sympathy for him. I also found him to be much more interesting than I had originally thought he was, and that's significant. He began to be a person, rather than a device. Along the way I discovered in Shawn a latent potential for constructive activity *if* he were presented with something that engaged his interest. He could go either way; he needed a purpose. In the beginning the Salvages provided that purpose, and it is a negative one; by the end my protagonists have provided him with an opposing purpose. Reluctantly, he becomes involved with them.

I have said that the power of fiction is to illuminate individuals in a world that is all too often intent on reducing people to anonymity and to remind us of our kinship with one another. I think this is vital. We need, at all ages, to be reminded that behind each faceless number is a human being with a life as complex as our own, and a right to that life.

But good fiction goes even further. It not only illuminates other people, but it illuminates oneself. If I find self-exploration in writing a book, I also find it in reading one. This is not a process of being taught so much as it is one of sharing. There is no point in telling people it is easy to be good—you are isolated in your struggle if you are convinced no one else is struggling. Each of us is a mixture of conflicting qualities and emotions, and unless we acknowledge this we can't begin to arm ourselves for the struggle. Only by learning what the dark side of ourselves consists of can we hope to gain control of it—to use Might for Right and not to believe that Might *is* Right. (pp. 297-306)

Nancy Bond, "Conflict in Children's Fiction," in The Horn Book Magazine, *Vol. LX, No. 3, June, 1984, pp. 297-306.*

[*The following essay is based on a speech given by Bond on April 24, 1984 at the Children's Literature Association convention.*]

This article has been haunting me for quite a long time. Freedom and peace are momentous, solemn, immense words, and every time I've sat myself down to confront them I've found myself wallowing in amorphous generalities and platitudes, thinking about things that are certainly worthy of serious thought, but things that given my limited area of professionalism here—that of writing novels for children—seem much too subjective and idiosyncratic to spout off to you. Not to mention ill-defined and difficult to explain. I do have lots of strong feelings about freedom and peace in the general sense, but so I'm sure have all of you.

Instead, what I propose to do is spend a little time discussing freedom, and what it means to me personally as a writer of children's novels. This will necessarily mean that I do give you a few of my grand and vague thoughts on the subject, but I hope I can tether them rather more satisfactorily to something practical and demonstrable.

Initially, to me as a writer of children's books in the United States in the 1980s, what freedom means is that I can write about virtually anything I want, and that if I have done it well enough, in a manner that appeals to an editor within some publishing company, who can make a case for publishing my book, it will be published. As those of you in publishing know, that's a tiny oversimplification, but let it stand for now. What I mean to say is, that I do not feel, if I am doing my best, that I must limit myself to a list of specific subjects, rule out many others, and treat my material in a manner dictated to me by someone else. I can sit down at my typewriter and write those books that I have within me to write. This is what I've always done, since I began writing novels for children, and what I will continue to do as long as I am able.

If this sounds particularly self-centered, in a very real way I suppose it is. But this freedom—to write what I want—is like any other kind of true freedom, a paradoxical one. Possessing it does not mean that I can throw out all of the rules and do anything I please. Being given this freedom means that I must take responsibility for using it properly, and take responsibility as well for myself within a society that allows such freedom. I must not take it for granted, but must be constantly aware of having it, or there is real danger that I may misuse, or even lose it.

How does this work in terms of my writing? To me it means that I must do the best job I can, and that I must be honest—with my material, with my characters first, and ultimately with my readers. Let me add that I ought to feel this way no matter what audience I write for, not just an audience of innocent and impressionable children.

I have said that at this time in this country I feel that I have the freedom to write about any subject at all. That's true in the sense that there are virtually no forbidden subjects anymore. Writers are only one segment of the society that has been knocking them down for quite a long time. Whether you *like* the idea of novels about child abuse, drugs, sex of various kinds, runaways, violence, and alcoholism among the young, they are being written and published and read. In cold, practical terms, I believe censorship is impossible. We live in the kind of society that makes it ineffective. The mass media are exactly that—paperbacks are cheap and ubiquitous, and they are only a small proportion of the total flood of material that uses such themes as its substance—whether with good intentions or prurient, thoughtful and responsible or exploitive and commercial. It's my own very strongly held view that we can only hope to combat the worthless, misleading, and obscene with acknowledgement and discussion. I don't see how it can be effectively suppressed, not now—not in this world.

For me, anyway, it isn't primarily subject matter that makes a book good or bad, it's the writer's *treatment* of the subject. An author writing a good book about a difficult subject, writes about his or her characters with honesty and perception, not obvious sensationalism; without glossing over problems or horrors, but without using them for shocks. I also feel he or she ought not to be working out personal emotional hang-ups, or making overt moral pronouncements, or lecturing. When I am reading I have little trouble picking out those books which are about problems that have characters, from those about characters who have problems. The latter are the ones I find satisfying.

But let me return to myself as a writer with the freedom to write about anything. I don't really have it, not if I'm going

to be honest and responsible. Within the unlimited range of possible stories, there is only a handful I can pull out of myself and go to work on, because I need a sense of commitment to and confidence in what I write. I must create a set of characters, put them in a place, and make things happen to them which will cause them to react to one another, and—with luck and good planning—to develop. Through them I explore my world, the people around me, and myself. Each novel is a voyage of discovery which I hope will attract some readers as it progresses.

Just as there's a paradox about freedom, there's a paradox about fiction. You have fiction, you have non-fiction; non-fiction means real, fiction means made-up, simple, elementary school library definitions. But made up out of what? Not out of nothing, surely. There's a hoary old writing maxim handed routinely to would-be-writers of fiction: *write about what you know*. Like so many things, it's a puzzling over-simplification, and I found it difficult to understand until I'd been writing for a while. At first I thought if I limited myself to the substance of my own life I might as well give up writing novels before I began—I have led a very quiet, sheltered, well-educated, well-adjusted, encouraged, middle-class life, surrounded by an affectionate family, and friends—satisfying in many ways, but not very dramatic. What I learned was that doesn't mean I can't make dramatic things happen to my characters in a novel, however. It's just that those *characters* have to come from me—from my understanding of people, of myself, of my emotions. I can only put into them what I have—they draw their life from me. There are many people I will never be able to write about because I will never know and understand them well enough. There are situations I cannot imagine, too far outside my experience. The older and more widely experienced I become, the wider I hope to expand my boundaries. Still, there will always be things I won't write about because I don't want to; lives I cannot approach because they are too alien; characters I can't be true to because I haven't the background. I feel it's part of my responsibility as a writer to recognize that, to admit my limitations.

Fiction doesn't come out of thin air. By choosing to write fiction I don't turn myself completely free to write anything at all, any way I fancy. Last year I performed a very useful exercise for myself. I found it necessary to look at the first book I wrote, *A String in the Harp*, which is a time-shift fantasy among other things, to remind myself of the process of constructing it. It's been about ten years since I wrote that book, and it's the only fantasy of that sort I have yet written. I think many would-be writers for children seize eagerly on the idea of writing fantasy at the beginning because they have gotten as far as understanding that fiction has limitations, rules—shoals lurking under the deceptively smooth surface of making-things-up—and they think that fantasy will be less restrictive because the rules of the real world needn't apply. Fantasy, at first glance, seems to truly be the land of make-believe.

I hate to disillusion anyone, but that's not so. Fantasy has just as many rules to follow as realistic fiction. They're different. They require a different approach, a great deal of planning, a lot of hard thought, patience and perseverance, because the writers of fantasy must *make up most of the rules*, then apply them consistently and logically. A fantasy world, to succeed, must have order and structure, just as the real world has. But in fantasy the writer must create the order and structure instead of simply building on something already well-established and accepted. I took myself step-by-step through the constructing of the fantasy in *A String in the Harp,* the logic behind the time shifts, the choice of the character who saw into the past and understood it, the reasons why others did not, the bits of "visible magic" I allowed people outside to see—why, when and how, the ways in which I let the past and present touch each other, even the basic reason I had chosen fantasy as a device for my story in the first place—did it do what I had put it there for? Was it the most effective means of doing that? And I found to my delight (and relief) that I did indeed have answers and reasons. Obviously these are subjective; but I have the reassurance of knowing that other readers have responded to *A String in the Harp* in ways that make me believe it works for them as I wanted it to. And the whole exercise reminded me forcibly that fantasy should not be arbitrary.

Fiction of all kinds ought not to be arbitrary. It's the writer's responsibility to see that it isn't.

For me as a reader the most satisfying fiction is that from which I get a feeling of communication, of sharing. I look forward to learning from a novel, but I would rather not feel I am being taught. As a writer, I want more than anything else to achieve with some reader somewhere that same sense of sharing; it is *not* my intention to teach through my books. The kind of fiction I write aims to be about people; about relationships, feelings, understandings, misunderstandings, mistakes, choices, fears, and triumphs—all kinds of human things. It takes me a long time to write a book—to get to know my characters, to learn enough about them so that I understand the way they fit together, how they see their lives. I write about people who engage my emotions, people I can care about.

I find, having written five books now, that I do not tie up my endings in gift packages, much as I would often like to. I do care about my characters, and I'd dearly love to have everything work out for them. One of the things I am waiting for someone to jump on me for is that three of my books—so far—end in parting, in separation. One important character must say goodby to another—for a while, forever. I don't make that happen because I'm perverse enough to take pleasure in it. I make it happen because that's what *does* happen, and I have to be honest about it.

I am at least an optimist; in my books I give my characters hope, because I have it myself. I do my best not to give them *false* hope, however. They have hope because of the way they deal with their situations, the way they confront themselves. I try very hard not to give them happily-ever-after endings because that's the stuff of fairy tales, seldom real life, and my characters go through their stories grappling with real problems that cannot be solved at a wave of a wand. To be honest with them, and by proxy with the reader, I must allow solutions to be equal to problems—if the problem is important, the solution must not be contrived for the sake of an artificially happy conclusion. It doesn't matter how old the characters in the story, or the potential readers. Of this I am convinced. The freedom to write carries with it the responsiblity to write honestly. (pp. 169-71)

Nancy Bond, "A Writer's Freedom," in Catholic Library World, *Vol. 56, No. 4, November, 1984, pp. 169-71.*

A STRING IN THE HARP   (1976)

At first the motherless American Morgans are miserable in Wales, where their withdrawn, newly widowed father has taken a teaching year at the University; fifteen-year-old Jen becomes even more worried about her uncharacteristically brooding brother Peter, twelve, when he tells her that he has found Taliesin's harp key and that through its powers he actually "sees" episodes in the life of the 6th-century bard. Soon, though, not only the boy but others in his presence begin to observe strange events and appearances that can only be explained by his story. How Peter evades a relentless museum director and finally "gives back" the key to Taliesin constitutes the major plot of this relatively mild adventure involving no high deeds or danger to the children; the family's gradual healing and emotional reunion is seen as the more important outcome. Surprisingly, Bond has squeezed a solid, readable story out of this nearly exhausted tradition. The bits of imagined past are incorporated without a break in the rhythm or shift of scene; the four family members and their various new friends are separately likable despite their familiarity as types; the harsh Welsh climate and countryside are newly realized; and the key's uncertain future maintains tension to the appropriate end. Further, this avoids the solemn airs and tremulous harpstrings that fantasies of this ilk and length pass off as serious import.

A review of "A String in the Harp," in Kirkus Reviews, *Vol. XLIV, No. 5, March 1, 1976, p. 255.*

[*A String in the Harp*] masterfully integrates a Welsh legend into the story of young Peter Morgan. . . . Natural dialogue flows smoothly; the characters are finely wrought. There is no villain in the usual sense—i.e., no evil force—yet an inexorable tension between those who sense a power beyond human comprehension and those who insist upon rational explanations pervades this tightly written book.

Susan Davie, in a review of "A String in the Harp," in School Library Journal, *Vol. 22, No. 8, April, 1976, p. 84.*

The line between hack work and literary art is sometimes very fine: The hack, though obviously in it for the money, occasionally gets carried away somehow, and, despite his plot cliches, stereotypic characters and cheap dogmatism (all hacks are dogmatic—it's the quickest and easiest way to write), the hack achieves something that feels curiously like real literature. On the other hand, with just a little carelessness, just a little too much faith in the power of authentic concern and inspiration, a relatively serious literary artist like Nancy Bond can achieve mere hack work. The hack goes for spectacular effects, and if they rarely turn out to be spectacular, the reason is mainly that they've been achieved before, usually by some serious artist. The serious artist, on the other hand, goes only for those dramatic effects which are consistent with telling—or artistically figuring out—the truth. The truth may be realistic or fabulous or both; but whatever it is, it's impossible to confuse with lying, that is, forcing the plots down unnatural channels, bullying one's characters into doing what they would not naturally do, or saying about the world what is simply not so.

A great deal in *A String in the Harp* is well outside the dreary domain of hack work, and if the book were to become a popular success—for a short while, since in the end its weak timbers will certainly bring it down—I would not be surprised or distressed. It is at times a beautiful and moving book, original and texturally rich as only true art ever is, so that whatever its faults it is already a better book than many one comes across.

The story concerns an American professor, David Morgan, and his three children, Jen, 15, Peter, 12, and Becky, 10, and their attempt to cope with, simultaneously, a new setting—a small, isolated Welsh village near Aberystwyth—and the death, a year ago, of the children's mother. As the novel opens, Jen is just arriving on what the family expects will be a short vacation before her return to high school in America; but Jen's plans are soon changed. The family, she finds, is falling apart. During all his free hours, her father shuts himself up in his study, burying himself in work, avoiding his children's unhappiness and his own; little Becky, though a naturally cheerful child, quick to adjust to a new setting and new friends, is frightened by what is happening to her brother; and Peter, even after Jen's arrival, becomes increasingly cold and angry, increasingly withdrawn, and perhaps, Jen thinks, a little crazy.

So far so good: a novel about adjustment, about a family's learning to deal with grief and learning, after a breakdown, to trust one another again, develop faith. Wales becomes the symbol of what has happened and of what is happening in the progress of the novel; and this, too, is mostly superb. Borth, the village where the Morgans have settled, is in wintertime a fair equivalent of the mother's death—a long, drab, wind-bitten string of houses, oppressed by dark mountains, leaden skies and unrelenting rain, dug in between treacherous Borth Bog and the iron gray water of Cardigan Bay. But like all of North Wales, Borth changes as spring moves in, just as the Morgan family changes as its collective heart begins to warm. Bond's descriptions of Wales in all weather are poetic and powerful, as they had better be, since Wales has been inspiring bards for a thousand—maybe thousands—of years.

I've described so far the novel's realistic side, that part of the story that qualifies *A String in the Harp* as art. The novel has another side. What's wrong with 12-year-old Peter is not only sorrow and anger. He has discovered the thousand-year-old harp-tuning key of the long-dead bard Taliesin—and the key, it turns out, has strange powers. . . . The power of the key is so great, in fact, that not only Peter but sometimes people around him see the past as if it were the present. At one point, for instance, Peter and a young Welshman named Gwilym, are riding toward a reservoir. The key is at work and the result is:

> The moon disappeared for a minute, the cloud across it was edged in silver, and when the moon passed out of it, the view ahead caused Gwilym to swerve the bike dangerously. He gave a sharp, startled exclamation.
>
> There was no reservoir.
>
> Where the moon should have been reflected on the long sheet of water, it shone instead on a deep, wooded valley that twisted between the hills.

The fracturing of paragraphs—a hack writer's way of getting emphasis (a typographical equivalent to screaming)—is symptomatic of something deeper: the vision has gone tragic. The key and its visions serve well enough symbolically: Peter's psychological disorientation becomes disorientation in time (he sometimes literally can't tell whether he's in the present or in the bardic age); and the beauty or at least fascination of the key's images of "songs" aptly dramatizes Peter's withdrawal to a magical, inner world. But Bond will not stop at that. There are no escape clauses; the novel's magic is real, and those who do not believe in it are not too subtly identified as bad guys. Peter, out of his great generosity, may feel "pity" for the scientific, hard-nosed Professor Owen of Cardiff (a polluted city and a bad-guy place) but any fool can see that the linguist

and folklorist, Professor Rhys (of lonely, much more rural Aberystwyth), who believes in magic is morally superior. Bond, in short, makes the silliest, most obvious of aesthetic mistakes: she insists, almost belligerently, that her metaphors are true.

Actually, we do believe and shudder at some of the weird events—for instance when Peter has his first vision, one of a disastrous ancient flood, or when, on a pleasant—ominously pleasant—day Peter and a group of friends find an ancient Welsh boat and fish trap where no such objects can have been for many years. The fact is, it's easy for us to believe the unexplainable, especially when we see not ghosts but only the frightening signs of their proximity. The trouble comes when the mysterious is trivially explained (all these years, it turns out, the dead but immortal Taliesin has been pining for his lost key) when, worse, the author insists that we believe the explanation. I do not believe it—neither will any child—and the result, at least for me, is, what ought to have been a beautiful and moving story of sorrow, struggle, and reaffirmation has been cheapened. That glorious power, the imagination, and that wonderful, dark country where true imagination has long been native, are both turned shoddy, almost contemptible. The reason is of course not that there is anything wrong with the imagination, much less with mysterious old Wales. The reason is that Bond's imagination fails here: trying to do justice to one half of reality, the spiritual and mythic, she has carelessly, inadvertently, chopped off the head of the other, the world of tea and biscuits, pleasant chit-chat, and absolute loss.

> *John Gardner, "Fantasy in a Minor Key," in* Book World—The Washington Post," *May 2, 1976, p. L1.*

In polished, descriptive writing the relentless rain, the sea, and the mountains are given a vitality of their own, a background for the mood and the action. The spaciousness of the story permits a range of Welsh characters, whose speech makes one aware of how accurately the author's ear was tuned to the cadence of the English spoken in Wales. The story of the modern family and the tale of Taliesin are skillfully meshed in the narrative which rises in suspense and intensity. A substantial achievement.

> *Virginia Haviland, in a review of "A String in the Harp," in* The Horn Book Magzine, *Vol. LII, No. 3, June, 1976, p. 287.*

In a most impressive first novel, Bond deftly blends fantasy and realism; realism predominates, but it is a successful setting for the fanciful element that affects the everyday life of twelve-year-old Peter and his family. . . . The interweaving of Welsh background, the intermittently-told story of Taliesin, and the problems of family adjustment is adroit. The characters are drawn with depth, changing and growing in their maturity and in their understanding of each other.

> *Zena Sutherland, in a review of "A String in the Harp," in* Bulletin of the Center for Children's Books, *Vol. 29, No. 11, July-August, 1976, p. 171.*

The story has an excellent sense of place. The relationship between Mr. Morgan and his children is well developed. The Evans and Davies families and Dr. and Mrs. Rhys are also very real. Because reality fades into fantasy without any warning the story is sometimes hard to follow. All the episodes involving the fantasy appear believable so long as the fantasy is being observed. But the episode in which Peter and Gwilym participate to return the key is less credible. (p. 211)

Marilyn Leathers Solt, "The Newbery Medal and Honor Books, 1922-1981: 'A String in the Harp,'" in Newbery and Caldecott Medal and Honor Books: An Annotated Bibliography *by Linda Kauffman Peterson and Marilyn Leathers Solt, G. K. Hall & Co., 1982, pp. 210-11.*

THE BEST OF ENEMIES   (1978)

Happy in the protective closeness of her family, Charlotte feels no need for other friends. Recently, however, things are changing and she doesn't like it: her mother has taken a job, brother Max has married, sister Deb is moody and bad tempered, and her special favorite Eliot seems always busy. As Concord's Patriots' Day approaches, Charlotte is looking forward to being with Eliot and the other Minutemen actors in the annual festivities. Then almost against her will she is drawn into a plan with Oliver, a morose classmate, and his great-uncle, the eccentric Commodore Shattuck, to save the celebration from a band of Englishmen who plan to sabotage the event. A snowstorm and numerous complications intensify Charlotte's own reluctance to become involved, but at the time of confrontation she is swept into the milieu and consequently finds new depths within herself. As in *A String in the Harp* . . . , Bond successfully interweaves a two-level plot, and although the realistic confrontation here somewhat lacks the urgency of the harpkey fantasy line, the contemporary scene is handled with humor and skill while Charlotte's adjustment is done as perceptively as was Peter's. Each character is finely etched and stands vividly against the wintry chill and historical pageantry of Concord.

Barbara Elleman, in a review of "The Best of Enemies," in Booklist, *Vol. 74, No. 14, March 15, 1978, p. 1185.*

A disappointing offering from the author of *String in the Harp*. . . . The plot lacks any real intrigue; the characters fit into categories; and the climax, in which snowballs successfully repel state troopers and all are reconciled, works not at all. Moreover, Charlotte's perpetual whining hardly makes for invigorating reading.

Cyrisse Jaffee, in a review of "The Best of Enemies," in School Library Journal, *Vol. 24, No. 8, April, 1978, p. 91.*

The author of *A String in the Harp* again shows her skill in delineating family relationships and in creating individual characters. Her sense of place, as in her first book, is keen and specific, and her portrayal of a reluctant New England spring is exact as well as evocative. A leisurely narrative, in which an ingenious plot is skillfully subordinated to the setting and the characterization. (p. 274)

Paul Heins, in a review of "The Best of Enemies," in The Horn Book Magazine, *Vol. LIV, No. 3, June, 1978, pp. 273-74.*

The evolution of Charlotte's relationship with her adored elder brother Eliot who is preparing to leave home is sensitively handled, as is Charlotte's resentment towards her mother who has decided to work as a design consultant. However, the novel suffers from long digressions and top-heavy descriptions. The author is a talented writer who as yet lacks the discipline essential to fine fiction.

Brigitte Weeks, in a review of "The Best of Enemies," in Book World—The Washington Post, *August 13, 1978, p. E4.*

This totally unexciting novel of a twelve-year-old girl's involvement in a Patriot's Day Celebration in Concord, Massachusetts, does not move well, drags with too much contrived dialogue, lacks a substantially interesting plot, and contains an assortment of characters who remain colorless and underdeveloped. Although the only redeeming quality offered in this novel is its theme—that of an adolescent "baby of the family" who must accept the fact that her older siblings are moving out of her life—the theme alone, without proper story development, makes for an unsatisfactory novel and a potential shelf-sitter.

Jeanette Cohn, in a review of "The Best of Enemies," in Children's Book Review Service, *Vol. 7, No. 1, September, 1978, p. 6.*

Original storylines are harder and harder to come by in juvenile literature. Almost every path has been trod countless times, and the action viewed from a kaleidoscope of views. So it is understandable that an author can produce the plot of *The Best of Enemies*. Even the previously established quality of the writer (as seen in *A String In the Harp* . . .) is no guarantee against weaving a tattered cloth of jumbled characterizations, stultifying action lines bogged down in repetitious description (how many times can one describe snow falling, cold penetrating or families exchanging glances over the heroine's head?), and mediocre attempts to stir interest in American history.

Hildegarde Gray, in a review of "The Best of Enemies," in Best Sellers, *Vol. 38, No. 9, December, 1978, p. 290.*

COUNTRY OF BROKEN STONE   (1980)

A dig for a second-Century Roman fort has brought 14-year-old Penelope, her archaeologist stepmother, and the rest of her recently expanded family to an old, isolated house in the north of England for a summer. The expedition has been beset with difficulties in the past, and this summer is no exception as mysterious problems plague the project. Penelope strikes up an acquaintance with Randall, younger brother of a hostile farmer who holds a grudge against the expedition. Ultimately, she finds herself deeply involved in circumstances that lead to violence and potential disaster. Although there are suggestions of fantasy here, as a sense of foreboding and vague superstitions pervade the mood, all action stays within the realm of reality. A nice balance is maintained between the brooding, mysterious atmosphere and the day-to-day life of the family. Penelope's difficulties in coping with new family members and some revealing glimpses into the essential problems of a second marriage keep the story down-to-earth. Setting and tone are important, and Bond's rich, evocative descriptions allow the bleakness of the environment to surround the story without smothering it. The pace is slow, but Bond's prose has that same fluid grace that distinguished her earlier book, *A String in the Harp*. . . .

Marilyn Kaye, in a review of "Country of Broken Stone," in School Library Journal, *Vol. 26, No. 8, April, 1980, p. 120.*

The strong sense of place, suspenseful events, and ever-accelerating pace provide a unified rhythm that allows the masterfully delineated characters varied strata for interaction. Bond's thoughtful and perceptive structuring brings a multitude of details into vivid focus while never obscuring the major theme—adjusting one's perspective to meet life's changing patterns. (p. 1121)

> *Barbara Elleman, in a review of "Country of Broken Stone," in* Booklist, *Vol. 76, No. 15, April 1, 1980, pp. 1120-21.*

Country of Broken Stone is both a contemporary family story of remarriage and adjustment and a story of an archaeological dig. These are interwoven with an unusual backdrop and a persistent, unsettling sense of history repeating itself....

Interfamily conflicts are played off against the historic and contemporary conflicts at the archaeological site. Historically, the Roman invaders attempted to subdue the native barbarians and eventually failed. In a contemporary version of this, archaeologists have reclaimed land from a resentful native farmer, and the bitter struggle is far from over. It is a struggle for territory. The archaeologists hope for coexistence.

Independence and coexistence are central themes for the Ibbetson-Prine family as well. They struggle to work out a balance with each child looking for his place in the new family and both parents still sorting through their new responsibilities and adjustments....

Country of Broken Stone is a many-layered story with complex, believable characters and strong personal relationships. It is enriched by lively dialogue, complete with true-to-life arguments and 12-year-olds' jokes, and by luxurious detail: descriptions of the countryside, its weather and its people, information about the history of the wall and the workings of the dig. It is a long book with room for local color, character development, and mounting suspense.

> *Christine McDonnell, "Many-Layered Family Drama," in* The Christian Science Monitor, *May 12, 1980, p. B11.*

A well-upholstered (271-page) novel with the characteristic British combination of new family, old house, and ancient mystery—the last of which, in this case, never develops. The new family is formed when mystery-writer Ted, father of 14-year-old Penelope and her older brother, marries archaeologist Valerie, who has three younger children.... Penelope has very little part in what happens (and very little happens). She is forever summing up the situation and trying to understand people, but her thoughts are rather ponderous. The family relationships, the locale, and the interface between them would make a substantial, atmospheric background for a conventional story, but the story never materializes. Penelope feels the house's bad vibrations; Ted goes sniffing into local history and present activity, indicating a new book afoot; Valerie digs away at the Roman bathhouse, sure of a find—but nothing comes of any of this. There are other, smaller let-downs: Off on a forbidden outing with Ran, Penelope returns home with foreboding as she has left her small stepsister alone; but all that has happened is that Ted yelled at the child for bringing a dog in the house. In the end, everyone just drifts away, and despite the raging fire, the story does too.

> *A review of "Country of Broken Stone," in* Kirkus Reviews, *Vol. XLVIII, No. 10, May 15, 1980, p. 649.*

A beautifully written novel, dealing in various ways with the theme of conflict and resolution.... Events are all seen through Penelope's eyes; she is a sensitive, thoughtful girl, and her increasing affection for both her stepsister and her stepmother as well as her perception of the family's growing unity is beautifully handled. Each incident and observation in the narrative is firmly and neatly placed—like the stones in the Roman Wall—in relation to the organic whole. Randall's dialect is a bit difficult to read, and the book is somewhat too long; but it is extraordinary for the verisimilitude of its background, the solidity of its characterizations, and for subtlety of feeling. (pp. 303-04)

> *Ann A. Flowers, in a review of "Country of Broken Stone," in* The Horn Book Magazine, *Vol. LVI, No. 3, June, 1980, pp. 303-04.*

The story has an interesting setting and solid structure, but it is the writing style, polished and fluent, that dominates the story; Bond's characters are drawn with depth, they are distinct and consistent, and she uses dialogue—and dialect within the dialogue—masterfully, both to develop characterization and to establish mood. (p. 208)

> *Zena Sutherland, in a review of "Country of Broken Stone," in* Bulletin of the Center for Children's Books, *Vol. 33, No. 11, July-August, 1980, pp. 207-08.*

THE VOYAGE BEGUN (1981)

The physical format of Nancy Bond's novels, weighty and bulky, will discourage some readers, which is a pity. Her leisurely storytelling is for those who have the patience to read a series of in-depth character studies and the wit to follow their juxtaposition, as complex as a fugue, from which the plot is created. The characters are: Maggie Rudd, fervent conservationist; her friend, Gabe, the wanderer; Mickey, a tough, uncompromising realist at age 11; the elderly boatmaker, Walter Jepson, who won't admit dependency or loneliness; and Paul Vickers, 16, searching for values and answers. All of the characters seek perspective in a world that has changed too rapidly. Also important in this book of relationships are Paul's mother, brittle, vain, shallow, and Paul's father, a government-funded researcher and a true "company man." These two typify, as does Mickey's whining, fault-finding mother, those who pine after the "good old days" when food and fuel were plentiful, when "need" and "want" were synonymous. Other characters see and comprehend the impact that the loss of the tourist industry has had on the small Cape Cod town. They know things can never be as they were, and yet, as they help Walter take up again his life's work after it has been nearly destroyed by vandals, they are hopeful, indomitable voyagers on an uncertain sea.

> *Holly Sanhuber, in a review of "The Voyage Begun," in* School Library Journal, *Vol. 28, No. 1, September, 1981, p. 132.*

Within the evocative framework of an energy-starving America, just barely removed from the present, the author ties a subtle plea for conservation into an involving story of two young people who come together to renew an old man's interest in life. Bond sharply delineates her two protagonists, contrasting both their personalities and backgrounds. Irascible, suspicious Mickey Cafferty stifles her feelings beneath a tough, unrelinquishing pose that protects her from a bleak future. Sixteen-year-old Paul Vickers is a loner, set apart as much by his complacency as by his privileged life-style. Adult characters, skillfully and naturally integrated into the plot, are vividly individualized also. Depth and pull come primarily from characterizations, intricate detailing, and graceful prose style, rather than elaborate plot complications, potentials for which exist but remain undeveloped. But everything is accomplished with skill, perception, and delicacy.

> *Stephanie Zvirin, in a review of "The Voyage Begun," in* Booklist, *Volume 78, No. 2, September 15, 1981, p. 98.*

[*The Voyage Begun*] is probably Bond's most gripping story (and the others have been very good indeed) and one that is most pertinent to our lives. The characters, drawn with depth and nuance, are oddly assorted. . . . The chapters are usually from either Paul's or Mickey's (the girl's) viewpoint and move together in a smooth fusing that is like the fusing of Mickey's interests and those of the old man, or of Mickey's friendship with Paul, a relationship that begins with suspicion and hostility. Hard to say which is the more impressive, the merging of characters and story line, or the convincingly bleak context for the events.

> *Zena Sutherland, in a review of "The Voyage Begun," in* Bulletin of the Center for Children's Books, *Vol. 35, No. 3, November, 1981, p. 42.*

With its well-developed characters and strongly defined, passionately felt theme, the book is a provocative novel which probes personalities and interweaves many threads into a carefully wrought fabric. But it should be noted that the leisurely descriptive writing, in addition to the overall length, may prove to be an obstacle for many readers.

> *Mary M. Burns, in a review of "The Voyage Begun," in* The Horn Book Magazine, *Vol. LVIII, No. 1, February, 1982, p. 50.*

The characters in Nancy Bond's new novel live in an uncertain and inhospitable world, made so by man's own profligacy. Almost all fossil fuel has been depleted; there are no longer fish off the New England coast. Cape Cod . . . has become mainly a series of ghost towns. The people who remain protect what they have and turn a blind eye on marauding bands of young people who trash and loot the once fine summer homes. Orderly civilization is treading on very thin ice.

Obviously, Bond believes this is the kind of world we are heading for, if we don't mend our ways. Yet she rarely preaches: She's too good a storyteller. An environment spoiled by man simply provides a backdrop for the rich collection of characters, all of them misfits of some sort. . . . Deftly, through her characters and what they say, Bond gets her message across.

> *Alice Digilio, in a review of "The Voyage Begun," in* Book World—The Washington Post, *February 14, 1982, p. 11.*

[Nancy Bond] has been frequently praised for her fine characterization, strong sense of place and ability to depict human relationships. Her latest novel lives up to her reputation in every respect. . . .

[The] novel is a testimony to human courage and resourcefulness. Bond imagines for us how people would react in a society facing increasing shortages of food and energy coupled with pollution and radiation leaks. This serious and timely theme motivates her memorable characterizations.

Using a skillfully interwoven double third person point of view, Bond introduces Paul Vickers . . . and Mickey (Michelle) Cafferty . . . , whose fifteen year old brother, Shawn, is a member of the feared Salvagers, a gang which loots and destroys deserted property. (p. 21)

When Shawn's gang burns down Jepson's house and half-built boat, Mickey's fierce determination to rescue the old man from the nursing home to which he has been sent gradually involves the rest in a daring quest to find a new ship for the old man. The sailboat and Jepson, like some 21st century Noah and his ark, become a symbol which suggests that those willing to help complete the boat will find passage into the future, while those blinded by selfishness and the desire to hold onto the past will dwindle like the resort towns. Bond's concluding paragraphs offer the positive images of the boat, the sun and an open gate and the assurance that Mickey and Paul will be "all right." Their voyage has begun. A really excellent book, and not only for its nominally young adult audience. (pp. 21-2)

> *M. P. Esmonde, in a review of "The Voyage Begun," in* Science Fiction & Fantasy Book Review, *No. 2, March, 1982, pp. 21-2.*

A PLACE TO COME BACK TO (1984)

Charlotte, who was twelve years old in *The Best of Enemies* . . . is now an adolescent. She doesn't quite understand why it is so unsatisfying that she is always paired with Andy, and Oliver with Andy's sister Kath; her developing awareness of her love for Oliver is one of the two plot lines of the book— the other is Oliver's painful adjustment to the death of the great-uncle with whom he happily has lived. Oliver inherits the house, and it (as well as the Concord setting) is his "place to come back to," a promise for the future after he goes away with his mother and her new husband, who feel he is too young to stay in Concord on his own. This is more cohesive than the first book, a perceptive story written in polished style.

> *Zena Sutherland, in a review of "A Place to Come Back To," in* Bulletin of the Center for Children's Books, *Vol. 37, No. 7, March, 1984, p. 122.*

In all of her books, sometimes more prominently than others, Bond has addressed the problem of change in young people's lives; here, she brings this theme to the very forefront, making it an integral part of her work. . . . Though this is somewhat short on plot, the characters are so finely etched, the background so well-realized, and the details of place and time so carefully attended to that the story flows out fully, leaving a richly encountered experience that echoes long after. (p. 1055)

> *Barbara Elleman, in a review of "A Place to Come Back To," in* Booklist, *Vol. 80, No. 14, March 15, 1984, pp. 1053, 1055.*

Like [*The Best of Enemies*], this is distinguished by fine characterization, an excellent sense of place and by the author's insight into the confusion of adolescence and the dynamics of a loving family. It is marred only by a very slow beginning. But those who stay with it will experience, along with Charlotte, the difficulties of change: painful decisions that must be faced and accepted in the course of life.

Anne Connor, in a review of "A Place to Come Back To," in School Library Journal, *Vol. 30, No. 8, April, 1984, p. 122.*

In her essay in this issue [see the first excerpt under Author's Commentary], the author states that conflict is an essential ingredient of fiction—a premise beautifully illustrated in her fifth, and perhaps finest, novel. . . . The story takes place in a little more than a week, its leisurely pace leaving room for the author to use her remarkable ability to animate both setting and characters through her selectivity of detail and imagistic writing. For with sensitivity and grace she probes personalities, young and old alike, and the ebb and flow of their often turbid interactions. Respecting the reader as she does her characters, she has written a quietly powerful novel of friendship, love, and responsibility. One finds neither pretense nor patronizing but, rather, an amplitude of thoughtfulness: Charlotte "had come to realize that friendship was a matter of accepting the whole person, difficult as that might be, not picking out the bits you liked and discarding the rest." (pp. 335-36)

Ethel L. Heins, in a review of "A Place to Come Back To," in The Horn Book Magazine, *Vol. LX, No. 3, June, 1984, pp. 335-36.*

This quietly moving story of two young adults caught up in the aftermath of the death of someone dear to them is one of the best young adult novels of the year. A companion book to **Best of Enemies,** it stands on its own merits.

Lucy Marx, in a review of "A Place to Come Back To," in Children's Book Review Service, *Vol. 13, No. 1, September, 1984, p. 7.*

While the supposedly close relationship of the four youths seemed rather bleak, the warmth of family is strong in this novel. Bond has written a fine novel touching on the feelings that surround the death of a loved one, the disbelief, the hurt, the anger, the emptiness, and the sorrow.

Lynn Popham, in a review of "A Place to Come Back To," in Voice of Youth Advocates, *Vol. 7, No. 5, December, 1984, p. 262.*

Virginia Lee Burton (Demetrios)

1909-1968

American author/illustrator of picture books, reteller, and illustrator.

A major figure in American children's literature, Burton is noted for creating lively, well-designed picture books which generally convey a dislike of technological progress and a yearning for the simple life. Characterized by flowing, intricate pictures, nostalgic themes, and rhythmic, suspenseful texts, these tales introduce such memorable, anthropomorphic characters as Mary Anne the steam shovel, Katy the crawler tractor, and Maybelle the cable car who are in danger of being replaced by more modern machinery. Burton's attraction to the pastoral life is dramatically expressed in her most acclaimed work, *The Little House,* **in which a dirty, fast-paced city eventually surrounds a rural house. Her eight books also include a retelling of Hans Christian Andersen's** *The Emperor's New Clothes* **as well as her only nonfiction title,** *Life Story,* **which ambitiously and accurately relates the history of the earth. Recognized for their expert fusion of texts and pictures, Burton's works display a variety of artistic styles ranging from the expansive black crayon drawings of** *Choo Choo* **to the finely patterned scratchboards of** *Calico, the Wonder Horse* **and the detailed watercolor paintings of** *Life Story.* **Inspired by the child's desire for knowledge, she often used borders and endpapers to present interesting background information, mechanical data, and historical facts as addenda to her stories.**

While commentators praise Burton for her original and absorbing plots, her art work generates the most critical esteem. Reviewers admire her skill in endowing inanimate objects with a spirited personality and applaud her proficiency in creating mood through an adept use of color. They especially appreciate Burton as a masterful designer whose works demonstrate a dynamic sense of composition and movement.

Burton received the Caldecott Medal in 1943 and the Lewis Carroll Shelf Award in 1959 for *The Little House.*

(See also *Something about the Author,* **Vol. 2;** *Contemporary Authors Permanent Series,* **Vol. 1;** *Contemporary Authors,* **Vols. 13-14, Vols. 25-28, rev. ed. [obituary]; and** *Dictionary of Literary Biography,* **Vol. 22:** *American Writers for Children, 1900-1960.*

Courtesy of Aris and Michael Demetrios

AUTHOR'S COMMENTARY

[The following excerpt is taken from Burton's Caldecott Medal acceptance speech of June 14, 1943.]

In the first speech I ever made I told the sad story of my first book, an effort upon which the blessing of printer's ink never fell. I wrote and drew that book with all the ardor of an aspiring novice. My friends and I thought that it was very good and very clever, but thirteen juvenile editors disagreed with us. When the manuscript finally came back to me for the last time I discovered the reason for its editorial unpopularity. For then I read it to my son Aris, who was about four years old, and he was so bored that he went to sleep before I could finish the reading. That was the best criticism I have ever received, and by its principle I have been guided ever since.

Children's books are for children. That, of course, is a truism, bald and obvious, but just because it is obvious it is too often ignored or forgotten. Children live in a world of their own, different in many ways from our adult world, and books for children must deal with the things of their world. What we may imagine interests them often leaves them perfectly cold, and, on the other hand, what we dismiss as being of no interest may be fascinating to them. Naturally, then, they are the best of all critics of the books they are to read. I am fortunate in having two boys, two alert little critics for whom and with whom I write and draw all my books. And my boys, like most children, are both frank and keen in their criticism, and they tell me exactly what is right and what is wrong in my illustrations and in my manuscripts. (pp. 228-29)

I have often been asked how I create my books. Actually I make them in collaboration with my children and their friends. I show them the pictures I have drawn, and I tell them the story that explains the pictures. I watch their fluctuations of interest, and I let them be my guides. When their interest lags, I know that I must delete whatever it is that bores them; when I hold their attention I know that I am on the right track; and when their interest is fixed but unsatisfied I know that I must elaborate my point, or make it more vivid.

In this creative collaboration with children I have learned several things. First, one must never "write down" to children. They sense adult condescension in an instant, and they turn away from it. Moreover, their perception is clear and sharp, perhaps more so than ours. Little things interest them. No detail escapes them. In the crowd scenes in *The Little House* there were so many people and cars and trucks it was difficult to keep track of heads and feet and wheels. Michael, my youngest son's job was to see that they were all on. Purposely, in the end papers, I put a flat tire on a car. He immediately spotted it. Indeed, every detail, no matter how small or unimportant, must possess intrinsic interest and significance and must, at the same time, fit into the big design of the book.

Second, the text and the pictures must be perfectly correlated, and it is vastly preferable to have them on the same page, or on facing pages of the book. Any one who has experienced the ordeal of reading aloud to a child a book with illustrations on a different page from the text will appreciate this point. A hundred times the continuity of the story is broken by the child's demand to see the picture on "the other page," and long before one reaches the end of the book its meaning and its pleasure have been lost in the fluttering pages. In all but one of my books, a case where circumstances dictated otherwise, I have not only placed text and illustrations on the same page, I have also worked the typography of the text into the pattern of the page. Many times I have sacrificed the length of the text or added to it to make it fit the design.

Third, children have an avid appetite for knowledge. They like to learn, provided that the subject matter is presented to them in an entertaining manner. The extent of this desire to learn was something of a revelation to me. In *Mike Mulligan,* for example, the diagram of the steam shovel, with each part carefully labeled, which I put on the end papers because I thought it too complicated and too detailed for the body of the book, aroused intense interest in the children. Or again, in *The Little House,* the border pattern, on the end papers, representing the history of transportation, proved to be one of the most appealing features of the book.

But if the children learn something from my books, I, too, learn in making these books, for they entail not a little research work, to say nothing of a variety of experiences. For instance, on one occasion I drove some three hundred miles over icy roads to attend a New England town meeting, which ultimately found no place in the book I was writing. Other experiences, such as examining steam shovels, snow plows, hydraulic bull dozers and a dozen other mechanical monsters of our time, were more fruitful. Especially memorable is the day that my son Aris and I rode in a grimy, greasy engine cab, with a battery of levers and gauges in front of us, and an "awful noise" of escaping steam all around us—an experience which, I confess, I enjoyed more than Aris did.

To return, however, to the essential qualities of children's picture books, one must strive to give children what they like and want, and I am convinced that they like and want the best qualities. Among these qualities are clarity, well-defined detail, imagination and fantasy in the pictures; rhythm, simplicity and significance in the text—and in both there must be humor, from subtle (for, contrary to much adult belief, children are fully capable of appreciating subtlety) to blatantly obvious. To cite only one instance from my own work, my children never look at the bowed legs of Stewy Slinker without smiling. In brief, children's books must contain the same human and aes- thetic elements that appeal to adults, but these elements must be selected from the children's world.

Perhaps I should say from the children's *worlds,* for there are different worlds for children of different ages. Thus one must pattern one's books for definite age groups. *Choo Choo,* my first published book, was written for my son Aris, who was then four years old. It was the story of a run-away locomotive, a rampant adventure of the sort which Aris often produced in miniature in his toy play. This was something which he could and did understand and which held his interest because it was to him a super-dramatization of one of his daily diversions. My second book, *Mike Mulligan and His Steam Shovel,* was for my second son, Mike, when he had reached the age of four; and again, it was a story of things with which he was familiar in his play, about which he wanted to know more, and which he liked to see dramatized. When I wrote my next book Aris was nine years old, and he had fallen prey to the dime comic books. Hoping to counteract the not too elevated taste induced by this variety of literature, I did *Calico, the Wonder Horse.* . . . *Calico* was a new thing in the way of children's books, an experiment, as it were. . . . (pp. 229-31)

In *The Little House,* next in the sequence of my publications, I dared to make another departure from the usual in books for children. This time I was writing for the age span of from four to eight. The heroine of my story was the little house, but unlike most central characters the little house is stationary until the end of the book while its surroundings change. And the changing surroundings represent the sweep of social history, or to make a very bad pun "her-story." My problem was to convey the idea of historical perspective, or the passage of time, in terms comprehensible to a child. At the outset, the rising and setting of the sun signify the passing of the hours of the day; the waxing and waning of the moon, the succession of the days of the month; and the rotations of the seasons, the evanescence of the year. Once this rhythm is established, the child grasps the idea of change and perspective, and conceives the century of a city's growth, with the development of transportation, of paved streets, of reinforced concrete buildings, and the general idea of urbanization. A nocturnal scene every four or five pages spaces the bright colors and accentuates the sense of the flow of time. Many people have said that *The Little House* has a message, that the further away we get from nature and the simple way of life the less happy we are. For my part, I am quite willing to let this be the message of *The Little House.* . . .

But apart from the significance of any one book, it seems to me that books for children are among the most powerful influences in shaping their lives and tastes. In this sense these books are important means of advancing to a better world, for the future lies to some extent in the hands of the children of today. Tomorrow their ideas and their tastes will be the ones that count. Books created primarily for entertainment can do much to form the norms of future thought and action. Educational books can perhaps do still more. The drawings in educational books now used in the schools are not often of the best quality, and yet they have had more influence on the aesthetic and intellectual standards of the country than most of us realize. In recent years these standards may have been raised somewhat, but there is still ample room for improvement. Few of our best illustrators have gone into educational work, and the consequence is that most schoolbooks are not as well illustrated as they might be. Remember that taste begins with first impressions. Remember, too, that children are taught reading by seeing, that is, by associating a picture with a word. If the picture is well drawn and finely designed they learn more than a literal definition. They acquire a sense of good design, they learn to appreciate beauty, and they take the first step in the development of good taste. Primitive man thought in pictures, not in words, and this visual conception of the outside world is much more natural and far more fundamental than its sophisticated translation into verbal modes of thought. The basic things are always the most important, and good art, certainly a basic thing, impressed on young minds through the medium of children's books is without doubt one of the best possible ways of giving a true conception of the world they live in. (pp. 231-32)

> *Virginia Lee Burton, "Making Picture Books," in* The Horn Book Magazine, *Vol. XIX, No. 4, July-August, 1943, pp. 228-32.*

My subject material, with a few exceptions such as **Calico,** I draw directly from life, and I literally draw my books first and write down the text after—sort of "cart before the horse." I pin the sketched pages in sequence on the walls of my studio so I can *see* the book as a whole. Then I make a rough dummy and then the final drawings, and at last when I can put it off no longer, I type out the text and paste it in the dummy. Whenever I can substitute picture for word I do. Each new book is a new experience, not only in subject material and research, but in learning a new medium and technique for the drawings.

> *Virginia Lee Burton, "Virginia Lee Burton," a promotional piece by Houghton Mifflin Company, 1968?*

GENERAL COMMENTARY

L. FELIX RANLETT

Gusto is the quality, of all others, that my boys and I most enjoy in a story read aloud to them. By gusto we mean speed, action, a leaning forward into the breeze. We mean savor and relish in the telling. We mean vigor of line and movement in the illustrations. Gusto is the twinkle in the storyteller's eye infused into his printed words. It is the carrying over into type of a tongue racing to keep pace with a swift story. It is the quick push of the artist's pencil; dashing strokes caught on paper. It is spontaneity and vim. (p. 412)

In our experience the authors who draw their own pictures, or the artists who write their own stories, have the most gusto. Leading the field are Virginia Lee Burton, Robert McCloskey, Ludwig Bemelmans, Dr. Seuss, Howard Pyle, Hardie Gramatky, and James Daugherty. (pp. 412-13)

[*Choo Choo*] is the perfect example of gusto. Happy was the day five years ago when a copy was given to us. It is the story of a little engine who ran away because she was tired of pulling heavy trains and who thought, anyhow, that she would show off better by herself. The cover sets the pace: the locomotive leaning forward with speed, like a racing photograph, and, instead of smoke, the words "Choo Choo" billowing out of the smokestack. The title page carries on: the engine followed by clouds of smoke and dust whizzing round a great curve of track, a horse leaping in fright, dogs scuttling, a woman tossing a basket of eggs into the air upside down, a policeman losing his hat, phone poles bending with the rush, birds holding back with their wings, and crowds running and pointing. And so it goes throughout the book which is a triumph of speed, even

CHOOO choo choo choo ch
ch   CHOOoo .... choo ...... choo
choooo ..... choo ...... ch ..... ch
ch ....ch ....ch ....ch
a a a a a   AH CHOO! And there she sat!

as Peter Newell's *Hole Book* was in its day. "Whee" is the one word that describes it.

In **Choo Choo** even the form of the text serves to give the book gusto. It is hand lettered, in leaning characters that emphasize the motion of the story. The boys find that this confuses the pictures a bit. I agree, but believe that they would not be quite so steamed up if the text was in type. In **Mike Mulligan and His Steam Shovel,** Mrs. Burton's second book, the text is in type and the book is wholly successful, as is **Choo Choo,** but one cannot quite say that this proves anything. The pictures in **Mike Mulligan** are colored and the text is black. This separates the two satisfactorily though they are together on the page. In **Choo Choo** pictures and text are both black, crayon work.

Mike Mulligan has the same gusto as **Choo Choo.** The lines of the steam shovel curve as her speed grows. Her eyes and mouth grin in content when she has finished digging the cellar in just one day. People in hundreds lean over the pit gesticulating. They leap and wave their arms in a big way. Horses' manes stream upward. There is never a picture of things standing still. Even houses move.

Both of these books contain, besides the many drawings alive with speed, several that give the broad view; fields, towns, cities, tunnels, bridges, rivers, railroads, the ocean, ships. One can look at them for hours, constantly finding something new. The end papers of *Choo Choo* are the best. They have definitely set the style of drawing in our family.

Alongside of speed, humor rollicks through every page of words and pictures in these books. . . . (pp. 413-14)

[*Calico the Wonder Horse*] never rang any bells with us in spite of our fondness for *Choo Choo* and *Mike Mulligan*. . . . Why? The pictures are not clear. The device of printing on colored paper does not do away with the obscurity of too much black. As for the humor, we suspect that somebody is being kidded. Could it be us? We like our funnies and our books kept separate and we don't know whether *Calico* is a book or a funny. (pp. 414-15)

　　　　　L. Felix Ranlett, "Books and Two Small Boys," in
　　　　　The Horn Book Magazine, *Vol. XVIII, No. 6, November-December, 1942, pp. 412-16.**

GRACE A. HOGARTH

[*In the early 1940s, Hogarth headed the children's book department at Houghton Mifflin, where she was Burton's editor.*]

There is a difference in children's picture books—between the book that has bright appeal for the moment, and the book that has behind its appeal the integrity of purpose and art work that make it worthy of lasting attention. Behind all of Virginia Lee Burton's picture books, with their absorbing interest for children, lie her very sound and well-practiced principles of artistic design. . . .

At various times she has taught dancing and swimming, and art at the Burroughs Newsboys Foundation and at a Y.M.C.A. camp. But her drawing became most important when she worked as a sketcher . . . on the music and drama section of *The Boston Transcript*, attending first nights and openings of revues and musical events, prize fights, wrestling matches, and college carnivals. As Miss Burton's sketching during this time depended largely on memory work, she began to develop one of the most distinguishing features of her drawing—her remarkable ability to define the human body in all sorts of action. This keen sense of action she has carried into all her work; her designs are all based on lines of movement, progression, and growth. *Choo Choo, Mike Mulligan and His Steam Shovel*—and *The Little House*—are all about inanimate objects, but there is nothing inanimate about her drawings of them; the engine is going somewhere, the steam shovel moves with a purpose, and the perpetual changes in the world of the little house are reflected in her appearance and expression. (p. 517)

[Miss Burton's] ideas for a book come slowly, sometimes over a period of a year. *Choo Choo* and *Mike Mulligan* both took days and weeks of mechanical research, as did *Katy and the Big Snow*. . . . about a crawler tractor who is a snowplow in winter. *The Little House* began to grow in her mind when she and her husband bought some land in Folly Cove and moved the small house from the roadside back into the apple orchard. She works out the text and pictures of her books together, and her theories on design, which she teaches to a small group in Folly Cove, are an integral part of all her work. (pp. 518-19)

Miss Burton feels strongly the effect a book has upon a child and the responsibility that rests with the author and illustrator because of this. She points out the contrast between the German and Italian recognition of books as a means of training young minds and the scarcity of well-designed and illustrated educational books in this country. . . . In each of her books there is the fundamental idea that every child comes to learn at some

time—what lies behind the runaway train, the willing steam shovel, or the wistful house—and it is not always a moral. In *Choo Choo,* the child learns that curiosity doesn't always pay, but he also gains the sense of responsibility which plays such a large part in his life. In *Mike Mulligan and His Steam Shovel,* he senses that the newest, most mechanized affairs are not always the best—that human qualities count for more—and with *The Little House,* despite all the changes of seasons and surroundings, he feels secure. In this upside-down world, children need this sense of security more than ever before. (p. 519)

　　　　　Grace A. Hogarth, "Virginia Lee Burton, 1942 Caldecott Winner," in Library Journal, *Vol. 68, No. 12, June 15, 1943, pp. 517-19.*

GRACE ALLEN HOGARTH

[My] first introduction to Virginia Lee Burton was through her first two published books, *Choo Choo* and *Mike Mulligan and His Steam Shovel.* Long before I met their creator, all steam shovels had become Mike Mulligans and all engines not choo-choos, but "Choo Choo" to my children.

And then, one day, I happened into [manager] Lovell Thompson's office when he was talking to a young girl. "Jinnee and I," he said, "are trying to compete with the comics. Have you any ideas on the subject?" (p. 221)

The result of the conference about comics plus the help of Virginia Lee Burton's two boys, Aris and Michael, and the neighborhood children, was *Calico the Wonder Horse or the Saga of Stewy Slinker.* Calico and the villain . . . were created at great cost in time and effort. I think I am right in saying that Virginia Lee Burton worked longer and harder on this book than any she has ever done. The rhythm of the many designs that carry Stewy along to the climax of his tale required hours of thought and planning and hard work. (p. 222)

The Little House is so completely Virginia Lee Burton's own that the business of turning it into a book was as routine and frictionless as any publishing adventure I have ever had. The idea had been in her mind for some time, and it seemed to me *right* from the moment when she first told me the story. As the work progressed, World War II also progressed and there was one moment when Jinnee began to have doubts about her work—stirrings of conscience over her war effort. I felt then, as I do now, that if *The Little House* does nothing more than reaffirm the realities, the peace and security of a little child's world, it is building for a future in which these realities may be unquestioned.

Most editors have learned the odd fact that when nature bestows creative gifts, she is apt to lavish them all at once. The painter is so often something of a musician. The illustrator, often under protest, discovers that he is also a writer. That Virginia Lee Burton is both, is at once evident. (p. 224)

　　　　　Grace Allen Hogarth, "Virginia Lee Burton, Creative Artist," in The Horn Book Magazine, *Vol. XIX, No. 4, July-August, 1943, pp. 221-27.*

ANNIS DUFF

[*Duff was an American librarian and bookseller who wrote* Bequest of Wings *and* Longer Flight, *which record her reactions and those of her children to various books they read as a family. In the following excerpt from* Bequest of Wings, *Duff refers to her son while discussing* Choo-Choo *and* The Little House.]

I had wondered for a while if investing a mechanical object with a human personality was not an altogether bad thing. I have come to the conclusion that it is not necessarily fatal, just very dangerous. [Wallace Wadsworth's] *Choo-Choo, the Little Switch-Engine* overdoes the "human hopes and fears" element, and falls rather flat; whereas, in Virginia Lee Burton's **Choo-Choo, the Story of a Little Engine Who Ran Away,** the device is used with a lighter touch, just enough to engage the sympathies of little boys who know what it is to want to run away. Miss Burton knows the value of economy in telling a story to a small child, and lets the pictures do most of the work. They are fine pictures with sweeping boldness, rhythm, speed and drollery, very much to the taste of our young man when he was three years old, and increasingly delightful to him now that he is four. (pp. 43-4)

The Little House has all sorts of mechanical things in it, automobiles and steam-shovels and trucks and an elevated train; and these were and still are, of great interest. But the loveliness of the countryside and the beauty of the changing seasons shine so radiantly from the pages that even a masculine four-year-old falls under the spell. There is something very touching in hearing a little boy reading to himself about the little house that was "curious about the city" until it grew up all around her, destroying her field full of daisies and shutting the moon and stars away from her. There is distress in his voice as he tells about the noise and dust and smoke, and the people hurrying past without even a glance at the poor shabby little house; and warm satisfaction when she is taken back again to the country and set upon a hilltop, to be lived in and loved once more. **The Little House** is a beautiful book, with a soundness of philosophy in both story and pictures that I think will leave a deep impression on the mind of the happy child who lives with it. (pp. 56-7)

Both drama and beauty are in the pictures [of **The Little House**] that show the rising up and the going down of the sun, the waxing and waning of the moon, and the changing colors of the countryside as the seasons turn. The text that describes them is simple and rather poetic; you feel that the author really values these things. And the boy who owns the book sees moon and stars, snowflakes and apple blossoms and flying autumn leaves with perception sharpened because they have been shown to him, with affection and beauty, in a book. (pp. 146-47)

> Annis Duff, " 'The Man of It' " and " 'Of Brooks, . . . Blossoms, Birds and Bowers'," in her "Bequest of Wings": A Family's Pleasures with Books, The Viking Press, 1944, pp. 39-57, 139-48.*

MAY HILL ARBUTHNOT

If artists have any facility with words, they should make good storytellers, because graphic representation means the ability to see clearly and to bring to life for others what is taking place. Virginia Burton . . . uses her brush and words in the happiest possible combination. Her books are all picture-stories, that is, stories in which the pictures are an integral part of the text, interpreting and even adding to the word story. Her subjects are machines, or inanimate objects in a world of machines. This preoccupation with machinery very likely came as a natural response to the interests of her sons when they were small. (p. 307)

Katy and the Big Snow, the story of a snow shovel, has [the] similar format and manner [of **Mike Mulligan and His Steam Shovel**] but is not so popular as Mike is. **Choo Choo** preceded **Mike** by two years and is a favorite also. A new large edition of **Choo Choo** gives room for the exciting action drawings the author-illustrator does so well. These machine stories have

Burton's sons Michael and Aris Demetrios. Courtesy of Aris and Michael Demetrios.

certain marked characteristics which help to explain their popularity. The plot always involves a staggering task or action and has considerable suspense. The illustrations heighten the feeling of action by swirling, circular lines that rush across the page and stem from or center on the cause of it all. You can almost see movement in the pictures of Mary Anne tearing around that hole with dirt flying in all directions and of the crowd of tiny figures with their gaze focused on the snorting steam shovel. In the pictures of **Choo Choo,** trees, bridges, and telegraph poles yield to the onrushing momentum of the reckless runaway. The eye follows Choo Choo past or into or out of the next set of obstacles. The action of the text, together with the rhythmic movement in the pictures, keeps young readers (or read-tos) fairly breathless.

Another appeal to the children is the personification of the machines. This personification is not overdone and consists only of a face, but what a face! For instance, Mary Anne droops, or takes heart, or snorts with determination, or gets red in the face with effort, or smirks complacently. These pictures merely illustrate what every automobile driver has always felt about his car. He knows perfectly well when it sulks, or feels affable, or strives mightily. Of course his car has a personality. Virginia Burton sees her machines through her boys' eyes and makes an engine or a steam shovel alive and responsive. If animals talk to their owners, why shouldn't machines also come heroically to life?

The Little House . . . is Virginia Burton's finest and most distinguished book so far. (pp. 307-08)

There is a significance to this book that should make it permanently valuable both as literature and art. The evolution of cities in all their complexity and the resultant loss of some of the sweetness of earth and sky are implied in text and picture but not underscored or rubbed in. The house has only a delicately suggested face—a legitimate one, too, since the placement of the windows and door makes it look like a face. In this book the personification is subordinate to the pattern of these illustrations, something for children and adults to study with growing astonishment and delight. The pattern of every picture is the same—rhythmical curving lines which, in the country, are gracious and gentle but, in the city, become more and more violent and confused. The children's activities on the farm in each of the four seasons, the new event in each picture of urban growth, and the hundreds of dashing, darting people in the city are a part of the rich panorama and minute details which make this a book to be looked at again and again. It is a profound interpretation of one of the riddles of modern life, told and illustrated with sensitive perception. (p. 308)

> *May Hill Arbuthnot, "New Magic," in her* Children and Books, *Scott, Foresman and Company, 1947, pp. 276-359.**

JAMES C. MacCAMPBELL

The record of Miss Burton's published work begins with *Choo Choo,* which appeared in 1937. . . . One can almost hear [her son] Aris chuckle as he hears the book read. It is, in every sense, a story the four-to-six-year-old will enjoy. But, and this, of course, is true with all the books of Miss Burton, this book cannot be wholly enjoyed without the pictures which are an integral part of the text.

All little children, in common with many older ones and their fathers, are fascinated by trains. And often they wish to give them personality and a life of their own. When they find a book which does just this they are delighted. (p. 4)

Best of all, from the point of view of the young child, Choo Choo makes fascinating noises. Anyone reading this book to little children, parents, teachers, or librarians, must be prepared to use the author's words effectively so that the noises of the engine are childlike and meaningful to these young listeners. There is also a very important person in Jim, Choo Choo's engineer, who took such good care of her. Less important characters to the story but characters whose names have good sounds for children are Oley, the fireman, and Archibald, the conductor. The story of Choo Choo is an exciting story for the young child. It includes the elements of plot and conflict and suspense which are necessary components of stories for readers of all ages. *Choo Choo* is uniquely designed in this respect to delight the young child.

In *Choo Choo,* as in Miss Burton's other stories, the illustrations are so much a part of the whole that the reader and the listener are affected by both at the same time. So as we read of the adventures of Choo Choo we can also see her as she races over the tracks after Jim and Oley and Archibald had left her alone. The incident of the runaway train is told vividly in story and in picture. One without the other is less than satisfactory to children. (pp. 4-5)

Mike Mulligan and His Steam Shovel has an advantage over *Choo Choo* in its attractiveness to children because there is much beautiful color included as part of the illustrations. Children are immediately drawn to this story by the lavish splashes of color and the effective way it is used to increase the sustained interest in the story plot. Again, as in *Choo Choo,* the inanimate object which is the central character is given personality and a name. (p. 5)

[On the first page], the story is delineated for the children who are reading it or for the younger ones who are hearing it. This is an essential requirement for interesting writing for young children. Where interest span and attention span are short at best, interest must be captured without delay. Then the story can unfold with close attention to the detail which is necessary to fulfill the story's requirements.

Again, as in *Choo Choo,* the story of Mike Mulligan and Mary Anne includes passages developing understanding of vocabulary which, while not the central purpose of the book, in any sense, do supply needed background for young children as they prepare and develop their ability to read for themselves. The illustrations are childlike and are arranged to serve the text well by appearing on the page where they are needed. This book, along with *Choo Choo,* augments the repertoire of read-aloud books which parents and teachers should develop for themselves.

With the appearance of *Calico, the Wonder Horse* in 1941, Miss Burton made an attempt to challenge the appeal of the comics. . . . The general format consists of two drawings on most pages with the text for each achieved by the use of various colored pages on which the black drawings and print show up vividly. Experienced teachers of young children know that the most consistently popular stories for the pre-adolescent are horse stories. In most of these the ingredients are a horse, a man who is young and usually a cowboy, and lots of adventure which can be as exaggerated as the author wishes. All these ingredients are found in *Calico, the Wonder Horse.* (pp. 5-6)

[Along] with Calico there is a cowboy named Hank. Calico and Hank made a contented pair of inseparable friends who lived in a contented, happy place. But the happiness was short-lived because Stewy Stinker, the villain, appeared and began to stir up trouble. He and his men were cattle rustlers and hold-up men and all that was despicable in the Old West. After much trouble with the bad men, Hank and Calico triumph in true Western style and everyone lives happily once again in Cactus County.

Boys and girls in the intermediate years like this story with its stereotyped plot and exaggerated action placed there purposely to entertain and intrigue its readers. It's a tall tale reminiscent of Paul Bunyan and has the same appeal. It is an excellent attempt to show how authors and publishers might work constructively on the problem of comics. (p. 6)

It is an outstanding effort and might well be emulated by other authors as they seek new means of interesting young readers in literature.

With *The Little House* Miss Burton reached a summit of her artistic work. . . . It is truly an outstanding artistic creation which is difficult adequately to describe in an article of this kind in which the actual pages cannot be displayed. Perhaps outstanding in the book is Miss Burton's use of color, particularly on the many full-page spreads which so beautifully illustrate the text material. There are the bold, gawdy colors of autumn to help the child see [Fall]. . . . (pp. 6-7)

And on the very next page by tremendous contrast, the child sees winter in delicate blues and whites with just enough red and brown to show the movement of the people. . . .

Here truly are pictures to keep the little child entranced for long periods as he investigates the possibilities of each new page. He sees the dark nights and knows how the little house feels as she sits alone and watches the stars twinkle and flash in the darkness. The child can see the city creeping in closer and closer and shutting the little house away from the things she loves most.

So often in outstanding picture books for children, the illustrations shut out the story so that the story is only a weak part of the total book. In *The Little House* the story and the pictures form an integrated whole and complement and supplement each other. There is a very real story involved in this book; it is one which is seen by those who have watched and been concerned with the encroachment of cities on rural areas. In *The Little House* the child can learn of permanence and happiness and the quiet of living. (p. 7)

[*The Little House*] is a story for young children which carries with it some of the basic realities of life: permanence in an atmosphere of change, peace and security which is the undergirding for well-adjusted, happy children who will become the people to whom the future must look for happiness and security.

In *Katy and the Big Snow,* Virginia Lee Burton returns to the ever-fascinating story of a big machine. In this case, Katy is a ''beautiful red crawler tractor,'' with both a bulldozer blade ''to push dirt around with'' and a snow plow ''to plow snow with.'' The story is the simple one of the way in which the snow plow gets the city back to work after it has been paralyzed by a big snow storm.

Again in this book the illustrations and the text go along side by side. The format is unusual and different from the other books by this author. This is the case with each new Burton book and is a quality which the reader has come to expect. In Katy there is an unusual map of the city with red, numbered flags flying from the important buildings. Since many adult maps are built in this way, children are particularly drawn to this page and pore over it as they find in the legend the buildings to which the numbers refer. In all geographical areas which occasionally are likely to receive big snow storms this book will have particular attraction for children who see their own community in the story. . . . (p. 8)

Another interesting and different aspect of this book are the wide decorative margins which surround each page. These are not all merely decorative, however; they illustrate and further develop the text material on many pages. Again, insightful parents and teachers can use this book to help children augment direct experiences which they have had.

In her most recent book, Virginia Lee Burton delves into an incident in interesting history as the subject matter of *Maybelle, the Cable Car.* This book is dedicated to the City of San Francisco and to the woman who was most responsible for saving the cable cars when they were threatened with removal. This book is briefly documented and the adult reader is informed in the foreword of the historical interest in the cable car.

Next to *The Little House, Maybelle* impresses this reviewer as the most beautiful of all Miss Burton's work. She has again

used light, unusual combinations of color which are particularly pleasing to illustrate the text material. In some ways, the illustrations in this book are better than the use of text to tell the story. On pages two and three the margin consists of clear diagrams of the cable car itself. These are important and interesting to the children who read the book. (p. 9)

The book tells the story of the campaign to save the cable cars and the celebration of Maybelle when success was assured. Here is an interesting story of a subject which is unknown to most children. It is told so well with words and pictures that all young children will be delighted with it.

It does not seem likely that Miss Burton had instruction in mind when she wrote and illustrated these charming books for young children. There are, however, many bases for developing concepts which pre-school children need to enhance their development in learning to read for themselves. The books are rich in the vocabulary of occupations, in the activities of people, and in the thoughts of children. Descriptions of things about which children are curious abound in all these stories. In *Choo Choo* is found the vocabulary of trains: tender, conductor, and drawbridge. In *Mike Mulligan* there are steam shovels and diesel engines and caterpillar trucks. In *The Little House* are seen such words as elevated railways, tenement houses, and the subway. In *Katy and the Big Snow* children learn of bulldozers and truck plows and, finally, in *Maybelle* they learn of cable cars and how they work.

In these words and in the many other such passages found in the books, the vocabulary employed is explained only to the degree that the child needs to know in order to enjoy the story fully. Broad meaning is not an objective but rather meaning which affects the story and the life of children at the particular time of their development which these stories serve.

In all the books written and illustrated by Virginia Lee Burton, the illustrations constitute a major function of the story-telling art. This is perhaps because the author-artist herself is more interested in the illustrations. (pp. 9-10)

These books by Virginia Lee Burton are books primarily for young children at both the pre-reading stage as read-along books and in the early years of reading when the child is so eager to read for himself. With these books and an eager audience of Mother or Dad, he will read stories of excitement and pleasure. In *Calico,* Miss Burton enters the interest area of the nine-to-eleven-year-olds where good stories of the right vocabulary and interest level are sometimes hard to find. A large new audience will await her work among the children of this age bracket if she chooses to work with stories in which they are interested.

In every book which has come from the pen and brush of this woman, uniqueness and originality are apparent. Her obvious love of young children and her interest in the things that interest them provide the field of literature for children with refreshing, useful material which will lead children toward a love for good reading which none of the other media of communication can so thoroughly satisfy. (p. 10)

James C. MacCampbell, ''Virginia Lee Burton: Artist-Storyteller,'' in Elementary English, *Vol. XXXIII, No. 1, January, 1956, pp. 3-10.*

LEE KINGMAN

[*Kingman succeeded Grace Allen Hogarth as Burton's editor at Houghton Mifflin. At Hogarth's suggestion, she studied life drawing for two weeks with artist George Demetrios, Burton's hus-*

band, "to train my eye enough to work intelligently with artists and illustrators." Kingman became a close friend of Burton, and later studied in her Folly Cove Design workshop.]

When Virginia Lee Burton created her final book, *Life Story,* published in 1962, she was in total command of her ability to combine design, illustration, and text in a manner distinctively her own. But the student of illustration, book production, or design can learn much by seeing how she developed her theories from the time her first book, *Choo Choo,* was published. . . .

The strong black-and-white patterns of the trains racing across the pages of *Choo Choo* are bursting with motion. Choo Choo never waits placidly at the station; the engine always looks ready to spring out along the track.

This sense of movement, whether derived from the action inherent in an illustration, or from the changes and contrasts in a design, is an essential quality in all Virginia Lee Burton's work. She studied art at the California School of Fine Arts in San Francisco, but she also studied ballet and even planned at one point to become a professional dancer. Her love for and appreciation of dancing was an important part of her whole life. (p. 449)

To one so kinesthetically motivated as Jinnee, drawing must have seemed an extension of dance, the capture of motion on paper. But another vital element in her work, the clarity of her drawing, certainly came from her study with her husband, George Demetrios, one of the few great teachers of Life Drawing. . . .

Given these two qualities, the exuberant sense of movement and the clear ability to depict it, Jinnee had to find a way to hold them down on a page. With her second book, *Mike Mulligan and His Steam Shovel* . . . , she began to use the double-spread pages as a unit and also began to place the lines of text in a specially shaped area. She felt that the illustrator should be allowed by the publisher to command all the elements on the page—the type and unit of text as well as the pictures. (p. 450)

There is a relaxed freedom in [*Mike Mulligan*], . . . even though the vitality of its many figures depends upon the organization of each page, an indication of things to come in her later work.

In 1941, Jinnee was distressed by the influence of comic strips and comic books on children. She deplored the bad drawing and meaningless themes, and took great delight in offering her boys a substitute—*Calico the Wonder Horse or the Saga of Stewy Stinker.* Whether she would have cared to admit it or not, the comic-strip format of squared-off sequences influenced the development of her design techniques in *Calico.* The book was originally published on very poor wartime paper. There was a controversy, too, as a most proper librarian of the period felt Stinker was not an appropriate name for children to utter. Jinnee, always a forthright woman and knowledgeable about small boys' utterances, did not care for the librarian's criticism. The book was reissued in 1950 on better paper, with the name Stewy Stinker triumphant.

My copy of *Calico,* a 1950 reprint, is quite battered, worn out by my children and their friends, but one of its delights is its end papers. Prebound or rebound library copies may have lost this feature, and the loss is unfortunate, for the end papers tell a lot about Virginia Lee Burton's methods of working. They show the complete design of the whole book in quick sketches of the action appearing in the black-and-white pattern of each

page. Of course, almost every artist works out a dummy before beginning any finished illustration. But Jinnee always lived in the middle of hers. Once the dummy was made, up went the sketches for each page, tacked in sequence around the studio, gradually replaced by "finished" illustrations still in sequence. One of her habits in criticizing her own work—illustration or linoleum block print—was constant visual criticism of that segment of work by itself and in relation to anything before it or after it. Suddenly looking up, she might see, in a page supposedly completed days ago, an area or a line she knew needed changing. To do one book, she filled wastebaskets full of what other artists might well have considered completely satisfactory work. (p. 451)

The illustrations for *Calico* were done in black and white on scratchboard, the perfect medium for an artist who keeps enriching and changing the black-and-white areas as the illustration emerges. A black line in a white area can be quickly eliminated by scraping it off the surface. A white line in a black area can be easily incised. Black dots are quickly penned for tone and texture, or white dots cut out of the black. Compared to the precise and exquisite work Virginia Lee Burton did for [Ann Malcolmson's] *Song of Robin Hood* six years later, *Calico* is an early stage in both her design and her use of the medium. But the quickness and dash of the illustration excitingly carries out the comic-strip feeling she obviously used and transcended. The double-spread on pages 6 and 7 of *Calico* carries a continuing flow of design, yet is a good example of how each illustration can stand alone. Even the distant cattle are contributing to the motion of the whole as they stand in swirling loops that grow in size. After the subject of her designs or illustrations—here the cowboys—the next important element in her design theory was called "sizes." The contrast in size of the subject—the cowboys and horses being larger on the left-hand page than they are seen in perspective on the right-hand page—helps to build a sense of motion. The third important element of her design was "tones"—the black, white, and gray areas being used, in this case, to emphasize each other. A far too simple definition of her theory, which became internationally known as Folly Cove Design, is that it is based on the interplay of the subject in contrasting sizes and tones.

Calico reflects these theories as Jinnee worked them out. She had already taught her version of design to a class which met in her barn during the years 1939-1941. Where "Watch those sizes!" might indicate to most people an admonition to diet or exercise earnestly, the phrase was actually a watchword for the designers group. It meant squinting hard, with an honest second look at the design being criticized, to see where a larger or a more varied contrast in the sizes of lines, or a contrast in tones, would make that design come alive. (pp. 452-54)

After Virginia Lee Burton's death in October, 1968, I asked her former editor and friend through the years, Grace Allen Hogarth, about her special memories of Jinnee, and she wrote:

> I started to work for Houghton Mifflin just after *Mike Mulligan* was published. There was a long pause then, when Jinnee said she hadn't any other ideas at all. I knew that as a new editor I should be getting something out of this very talented person, but I was at a loss. After quiet nagging, which I think she rather enjoyed, I had a telephone call and a hint that an idea had come. I instantly asked her to come into Town and lunch with me which she did. . . . She was very diffident, but bit by bit the idea for *The*

Hank and Calico saw them go and slid down the mountainside to look for them.

They found Stewy Stinker hanging up in a tree by his gun belt. Hank took the gun and unhooked him.

From Calico, the Wonder Horse; or, The Saga of Stewy Stinker, *written and illustrated by Virginia Lee Burton. Houghton Mifflin, 1950. Copyright 1941, 1950 by Virginia Lee Demetrios. Copyright © renewed 1969 by Virginia Lee Demetrios. All rights reserved. Reprinted by permission of Houghton Mifflin Company.*

Little House emerged. She needed, as she always did, immense encouragement and I had no hesitation whatever in giving it to her. After that day we became firm friends and I went often to Folly Cove to watch each step of the work as it progressed. We worked together also on the type-setting about which she was most particular. I don't think that I have ever enjoyed working with any author or illustrator as much as I did with Jinnee. We both had the feeling that we were necessary to each other and the book which emerged seemed to be the special property of both of us! I can hear myself calling it ''My'' book and this particular kind of pride pleased Jinnee because she was the most generous-hearted person about her work that I have ever known. This modesty and what, at first sight, appeared to be lack of self-confidence in her was most touching. Each book required a great deal of encouragement, each idea was a fledgling that had to learn to fly and all editors realize the excitement of these first flights. After I left I think I missed Jinnee more than any one else.

With *The Little House,* . . . Virginia Lee Burton's name was permanently established in children's literature, and this book is so known and loved around the world that it does not need to be described here. . . . In the book Jinnee made her Little House small and simple and gave her a traditional shape, to emphasize her survival through decades of change. But the country setting, as seen in the cycle of the seasons, is very close to the appearance of the Demetrioi yard itself.

Jinnee was strongly influenced by her physical surroundings and while there has been criticism of her using the same theme more than once—*Life Story* recapitulates some of *The Little House* in its last twenty pages—it was only natural for her to use what she saw and felt around her. A basic tenet she always upheld to the Folly Cove Designers was: *Draw what you see and what you know. Don't copy, but draw from nature itself.*

Since nature is omnipresent, yet ever-changing, she apparently felt no limiting sense of repetition in using the theme of small home and changing seasons more than once. Not long before she died, she was discussing a book with her editors at Houghton Mifflin, which would have been about the actual building of a little house, and she planned to accompany the text and large illustrations with diagrams to show the fine points of structure and carpentry. Since she found writing more difficult by far than drawing, she always needed a strong simple theme, and apparently did not feel at ease with a conventional story having a child or animal for a hero. At one point when she was searching for an idea, I suggested using Lefty, her very large, very present, part-Newfoundland dog, in a story. But while she loved Lefty, who always accompanied her to the cove where she swam and he chased sea gulls, she could not see him as the protagonist in a plot—possibly because she was not subjective, as a writer can be, but was naturally an observer, an objective illustrator.

If you want to see Virginia Lee Burton at home, as her environment looked in recent years, do enjoy pages 51 to 58 of *Life Story* in all its detail. She even introduces this section, Act V of the book, by changing the little figure on stage left from the professor-lecturer of the earlier pages to herself, and in the text she invites:

> Twenty-five summers have passed quickly since we bought the old orchard, meadow, and woodland and moved a little house and my barn studio into the middle of it. The old apple trees have been trimmed, the woods cleaned up, and in the meadow we have put sheep to keep the grass down. Evergreens and flowering plants have been planted. Ferns and mosses grow by the running brook. Here is where we raised our children until they grew old enough to begin living a life of their own.

And it is her own environment that she shows, beginning on page 56, in realistic detail. In Folly Cove there really is a driveway curving in and up hill to the house with its yellow blinds. . . . There really are forsythia bushes on the left and a sheep meadow behind the fence on the right. There is a small sheep shed, featured not only in her book, as on pages 66 and 68 of *Life Story,* but also on one of her family Christmas cards; and there is one of her procession of Siamese cats, usually named Zaidee, on the shed roof. (pp. 454-57)

There are other personal notes in *Life Story*. In the autumn illustration, there is the wood pile where George's impressive wood piles always stand; and the apple tree by the house is where the Swing Tree, as Jinnee called it, grew and still stands today, though without its swings. This tree was a delightful motif in both her books and her black prints. . . . (p. 459)

.   .   .   .   .   .

While I was an editor at Houghton Mifflin, [Burton] was working on *Katy and the Big Snow*. . . . Snowblowers were news then, and I remember her making a rush trip from Gloucester in a snowstorm to sketch from the office windows and then to follow a snowblower around the streets of Boston, even though the new machine never appeared in her book. She had merely convinced herself that Katy, with her shiny, shapely V-plow, made a much better heroine than a fussy, sputtering snowblower ever could. (p. 594)

With *The Emperor's New Clothes* . . . , Jinnee turned again to color. The story was one she had liked as a child when her father read it aloud, and the theme of parade, panoply, and elegance was fun to treat with design and embellishment. She retold the story in her own words, so she could control the length of the text and make the type area on each page an integral part of the whole design. (p. 601)

The study for *Life Story* and the painstaking painting of the full-color originals absorbed eight years of Virginia Lee Burton's life and was exhausting to her, physically and creatively. She talked later about other books she wanted to do, especially one with a Japanese background—after her trip to Japan in the spring of 1964. But she was not in the best of health during her last five years. This bothered her, since she was a great

believer in mind over matter and felt that any kind of illness was a sign of weakness. She had a strong New England conscience. What else could have driven her to the years of early rising and the extremely long days of work on her books? But like any disciplined artist, she accepted the necessity of boring routine and infinite detail to make what she did perfect, and she had little patience with anyone's work that she felt too quick, too unfinished, or imative. (pp. 601-02)

As she could not do another book, it is appropriate that *Life Story* was her final, all-encompassing creation. And knowing her deep appreciation for life and all living, growing things, I like to think of her taking a walk through the woods by her little house, and returning to paint her feelings and describe her observations, as she did in her last book:

> Yesterday was a day to remember—one of those beautiful warm spring days when one could almost see the plants growing. Lowly little lichens clinging to the rocks brightened, liverworts and velvety mosses carpeted the damp ground, ferns pushed up and unfurled their delicate fronds, new bright green needles tipped the evergreens, buds opened and tiny little leaves unfolded, and the apple trees burst into blossom. In the meadow the sheep grazed happily on the tender new shoots of grass. The miracle of spring was here.
>
> (p. 602)

Lee Kingman, "Virginia Lee Burton's Dynamic Sense of Design," in The Horn Book Magazine, Vol. XLVI, Nos. 5 and 6, October and December, 1970, pp. 449-60; 593-602.

JOHN ROWE TOWNSEND

[*The Little House*] is one of the most affectionate and likeable of picture-books. (But the Little House, though spelled with initial capitals and referred to as 'she', is somewhat lacking in personality, to say nothing of architectural distinction. And can the happy ending be permanent, or will the city catch up once more?) A similar loving approach, giving life to inanimate creatures, was successful in *Maybelle the Cable Car*. . . . (p. 201)

John Rowe Townsend, "Craftsmen in Two Media," in his Written for Children: An Outline of English-Language Children's Literature, revised edition, 1974. Reprint by The Horn Book Incorporated, 1981, pp. 194-205.*

MARGERY FISHER

Many vehicles in picture-books have more described personality than Katy has. The vehicle comes to life simply through the firm, cumulative, rhythmic prose statements of her exploits and by the equally firm composition of pictures in which her busyness is contrasted visually with the stillness of trucks, cars and people. The simplicity and directness of Katy's story has made the book a prime favourite with more than one generation of children. (p. 165)

A classic picture-book, . . . *The Little House* is a rare example of the successful personalization of a building; perhaps it is simple for an artist to represent a face on a house-front, but to suggest real personality, in words and in line and colour, is another matter altogether. (p. 178)

Margery Fisher, "Who's Who in Children's Books: Katy" and "Who's Who in Children's Books: Little House," in her Who's Who in Children's Books: A

From Maybelle, the Cable Car, *written and illustrated by Virginia Lee Burton. Houghton Mifflin, 1952.*
Copyright 1952 by Virginia Lee Demetrios. Copyright © renewed 1980 by Michael Demetrios. All rights
reserved. Reprinted by permission of Houghton Mifflin Company.

Treasury of the Familiar Characters of Childhood,
Holt, Rinehart and Winston, 1975, pp. 165, 178.

BARBARA BADER

Burton knew exactly what she wanted in a picturebook, hers
or another's, and she wanted a good deal—information and
significant detail as well as the accustomed clarity, humor and
imagination. The wonder is that she achieved what she wanted
without losing the spontaneity that Ranlett [see excerpt dated
1942], among many, praises in her work. One can open *Mike
Mulligan and His Steam Shovel* almost at random and find a
spread that fits the bill, but read it, look into it, and you are
carried off posthaste with the heroes.

Or rather with all deliberate speed:

Mike Mulligan had a steam shovel,
  a beautiful red steam shovel.
    Her name was Mary Anne.
      Mike Mulligan was very proud of Mary Anne.
        He always said she could dig as much in a day
          as a hundred men could dig in a week,
            but he had never been quite sure
              that this was true.

Sympathetic, succinct, provocative, it is the best of beginnings,
prompting reflection, promising action. In the accompanying
picture, Mike introduces Mary Anne; they are not still again
until the last page, and the words are never again so important.

When Mary Anne and Mike come rolling over the hills (Wanda
Gág-child-peasant hills), leaving dark downtown towers and
dark dormitory houses for the sunny world of Popperville, the
progression is a story in itself. In Popperville, meanwhile, so
much is going on that one could play the old child's game of
committing items to memory and still overlook, perhaps, the
two women gesticulating over the fence or that characteristic
Burton touch, the posts, hedges, tree-rows and fences that
border the backyards and enclose the scene. Elsewhere no detail
distracts and Mary Anne and Mike themselves succumb to the
smoke and steam and flying dirt. Swirls and sweeps of smoke
and steam and dirt, orchestrated with sound—''BING! BANG!
CRASH! SLAM! LOUDER AND LOUDER, FASTER AND FASTER''—
and timed by the spreading setting sun.

Furiously dug, the cellar of the new town hall is finished in a
day, but the final triumph is not all Mike Mulligan's and Mary
Anne's; they have in fact dug themselves into a hole. Says
mean, cantankerous Henry B. Swap: ''The job isn't finished
because Mary Anne isn't out of the cellar, so Mike Mulligan

won't get paid.'' But the little boy who cheered Mike and Mary Anne along has an out (which Burton, with an asterisk, credited to one Dickie Birkenbush): let Mary Anne be the furnace and Mike Mulligan be the janitor of the new town hall. Even Henry B. Swap smiles—just as, when last seen, Old Sneep is savoring an ice cream cone. Like *Lentil, Mike Mulligan and His Steam Shovel* is cracker-barrel Americana, tow-headed lad subduing local grouch.

The pastoral strain comes to the fore in *The Little House,* a record of urban decay and a brief for rural blessedness that, appearing in 1942, bridges Model T mistrust of cities and low octane flight from them. As Burton observes, she had a problem: the Little House remained in one place while change occurred around her. (pp. 199-201)

Never had riverboat melodrama a maiden more grievously abandoned, a more precipitate rescue, a more sanguine end. But easy as it is to mock *The Little House,* the book provides a magic-lantern look at modern city development before wholesale leveling blurred its lineaments. Thirty years later it is history become historical truth, what happened become the nub of what happened. For children it had and has the dimensions of legend, and every left-behind rundown frame structure on a city street is the Little House.

Between *Mike Mulligan* and the Caldecott-winning *Little House,* Burton did *Calico, the Wonder Horse.* . . . ''A symphony in comics'' Burton's family dubbed *Calico* as she carefully calculated the circles, spirals, right angles and diagonals to get just the feeling of movement or repose she wanted; the figures, silhouetted, are secondary to the evolving design. Originally printed in eight different colors, a deliberate rainbow that dominated the story, the book was redone in 1950 in black and white with a colored border—redone and redrawn, with more modeling and less dynamism. In either version, however, *Calico* is not a comic book but a take-off on comic books, and the illustrations have more in common with the strip silhouettes of Caran d'Ache, the nineteenth-century French comic illustrator, than with the crypto-naturalism of contemporary comics. (pp. 202-03)

> *Barbara Bader, ''The Storytellers,'' in her* American Picture Books from Noah's Ark to the Beast Within, *Macmillan Publishing Company, 1976, pp. 199-211.**

MYRA POLLACK SADKER AND DAVID MILLER SADKER

There are few portrayals of female vehicles and, indeed, feminists have commented that although our language refers to cars, boats, and trains as ''she,'' in children's literature they all turn into males. However, in the picture book *Katy and the Big Snow* . . . , we have the story of a competent, persevering female steam shovel who plows out an entire city by herself. (p. 248)

To many authors who are concerned with ecology, the city becomes an example of a disrupting and dysfunctional environmental influence. Focusing on the population density, pollution, and alienation of urban life, many authors exclude any mention of the redeeming qualities of the city, offering instead a simplified presentation of the city as an enemy of a pure and clean environment.

One example of a slanted presentation of the city is Virginia Lee Burton's *The Little House.* . . . This popular picture book relates the story of an attractive, pink house that leads a pleasant life in the country watching the seasons change along with the gentle daily activities of the people. The little house is curious about the lights of the city seen in the distance, but it is not until a road is built and the city begins to expand that the little house gets to experience city life firsthand. As stores and tenements are built, the little house becomes the victim of neglect. The illustrations turn muddy brown and the beautiful countryside is lost amidst rushing people, tall buildings, dust, smoke, bright lights, and the noise of the city. The little house becomes rundown and dilapidated and takes on the appearance of a victim of a mugging. The house is saved from this fate worse than death (i.e., living in a city) and is transported back to the country. Totally renovated, the house is now happy and seems to have learned an important lesson:

> Never again would she be curious about the city. . . . Never again would she want to live there. . . . The stars twinkled above her. . . . A new moon was coming up. . . . It was spring . . . and all was quiet and peaceful in the country.

Although this Caldecott winner is in many respects an excellent and charming picture book, it does, unfortunately, offer an overly negative and one-dimensional portrayal of city life. (p. 276)

[A] creative response to fast paced, and potentially inhumane, industrial change is Virginia Lee Burton's *Mike Mulligan and His Steam Shovel.* (p. 277)

Although *Mike Mulligan and His Steam Shovel* does not directly deal with the city, it does reflect the kind of creative and positive response to technological change that is too frequently omitted from children's books about city life. (p. 278)

> *Myra Pollack Sadker and David Miller Sadker, ''Breaking Out of the Pumpkin Shell: The Image of Women in Children's Literature'' and ''Spaceship Earth: Ecology in Children's Literature,'' in their* Now Upon a Time: A Contemporary View of Children's Literature, *Harper & Row, Publishers, 1977, pp. 231-66, 269-85.**

DONNA E. NORTON

Movement, rhythm, line, repetition, and contrast are all elements of design found in Virginia Lee Burton's illustrations. . . .

Both text and illustrations become part of Burton's design, and the page conveys a feeling of total unity between the visual and written elements. This design technique was used very effectively in *The Little House.* As an introduction to the little house on top of a green hill, the written text forms a pathway up the hill toward the house. Later, a repetition of trees is seen that causes the viewer's eyes to travel back toward the horizon. This movement is strengthened with brown dirt roads circling the hill and fields plowed on the hillsides; each field has a progressively smaller figure of a farmer plowing. This spring scene is followed by three illustrations depicting the changing seasons; rows of field crops add to the repetition in the summer picture; shocks of corn cover the fields in autumn; snow and children playing are seen in winter. This idealistic scene is jarringly shattered as a dirty line of highway equipment brings civilization, a blacktopped road, to the country. Now, rows of brown houses cover the hills with repetitive rhythm; the clouds are even black. Repetition in larger and larger buildings progresses until the little house is finally rescued and moved to a new hill in the country. (p. 120)

Children usually see nothing wrong with a house that thinks, a doll that feels, or a steam shovel that responds to emotions. Virginia Lee Burton, a favorite writer for small children, is a master of personification. In *Mike Mulligan and His Steam Shovel,* Burton creates a credible personality for a steam shovel because Mike names her and believes in her. The author creates drama as the two friends try to dig the basement of Popperville's town hall in only one day. The author provides suspense as mean old Henry B. Swap hopes that Mary Anne, the steam shovel, will fail; if she does, Mike will not be paid. The suspense builds as more and more people come to watch. . . . Sympathy for the steam shovel is enhanced as she works faster and faster when people cheer for her. . . .

Two other books by Burton have personified objects as main characters. Katy, an extraordinary red crawler tractor, is the heroine in *Katy and the Big Snow.* Credibility for the tractor is created as snow reaches the second floor windows in Geopolis and the chief of police calls for help. Katy says, "Sure," and then, "Follow me." She responds the same way to the postmaster, the telephone company, the water department, the hospital, the fire chief, and the airport. When such real city departments believe in her, it is easy for the reader to believe also. In *The Little House* Burton creates a heroine who is both strong and needs love. Burton's descriptions and illustrations of the changes around the house as she watches the city lights come closer and closer seem real. When the house feels sad and lonely, Burton shows her with cracked paint and broken windows. The house proceeds, like a real person, through a series of emotions until she is moved away from the city and happily settles down on her new foundation. . . . (p. 164)

> *Donna E. Norton, "Artists and Their Illustrations" and "Picture Books," in her* Through the Eyes of a Child: An Introduction to Children's Literature, *Charles E. Merrill Publishing Company, 1983, pp. 104-33, 134-93.**

CHOO CHOO: THE STORY OF A LITTLE ENGINE WHO RAN AWAY (1937)

[Virginia Lee Burton] proves herself an able story-teller in this picture book of a railroad engine's escapade.

Choo Choo, as smart and shiny a little engine as ever cocked a headlight in a pedestrian's eye, was not content, even under the ministrations of a devoted crew, to merely pull a train of cars. Her vanity was fired by the vision of a stellar performance, and in a burst of the rankest kind of individualism she gayly left duty behind and started off on a wild and glorious jaunt by herself.

The furor which a runaway engine caused among the startled populaces, among panicky cows and horses along the way, was more than Choo Choo had dreamed of. Nor did Choo Choo, careering madly down unfamiliar tracks, losing a tender, jumping a drawbridge here, causing a traffic jam there, have any time to savor her triumph. She was a chastened and repentant little engine, too exhausted to give more than one feeble toot when the anxious crew found her, lost and frightened on an abandoned siding, a tired little engine who was glad enough to go back to the well-regulated life of a railroad schedule.

Miss Burton tells the story in a tempo which emphasizes the speed of a runaway, and the mad-cap Choo Choo emerges as an ingratiating, if naughty, personality from the large and vital drawings, which are done in a crayon as soft and black as coal

soot, but considerably more decorative and appealing to 6 and 8 year olds and their younger brothers.

> *Ellen Lewis Buell, "A Runaway Engine," in* The New York Times Book Review, *August 15, 1937, p. 10.*

In this picture book of bold crayon drawings, so expressive of our age, Choo Choo creates the same kind of havoc and excitement on a large machine scale that John Gilpin did on a small horse scale with his famous ride in Caldecott's pen and ink and watercolor drawings.

> *A review of "Choo, Choo, the Story of a Little Engine Who Ran Away," in* The Horn Book Magazine, *Vol. XIII, No. 5, September-October, 1937, p. 283.*

The very brief text narrating Choo Choo's adventure is a mere commentary on the pictures. And what pictures they are!

Virginia Lee Burton established herself firmly in [England] with *Mike Mulligan and His Steam Shovel,* and readers will look forward to every new book by this artist with the keenest anticipation. *Choo Choo,* being a large sized book, offers scope for Miss Burton's style; for that bold, free handling of her pencil; those immense and sure curves; that fine sense of the possibilities offered by perspective. Her pictures have an air of intense movement, a strong, almost inexorable movement, and she uses light and shade with most expressive boldness.

It is usual to say that children should have colour in their pictures; I cannot feel that colour is necessary here. Miss Burton has conveyed her message with a completeness that will not fail to impress any child who has the good fortune to see this book.

> *A review of "Choo Choo," in* The Junior Bookshelf, *Vol. 8, No. 3, November, 1944, p. 93.*

[*Choo Choo*] is as expressive acoustically as it is visually. . . . The poor tired little steam-driven engine with the onomatopoetic name, her energy spent, has come to a sad end. Changing letter sizes, fragmented words, and dotted lines—CHOO choo ch. . . . . ch. . . . ch. . . aa, and so on, "printpaint" a vivid picture of exhaustion, almost a piece of acoustic concrete poetry.

Burton's *Choo Choo* is apparently the earliest important children's book where printed language is consistently used for both visual and acoustic purposes in a manner that pleasantly heightens the humor and the dynamic quality of the story. (pp. 80-1)

> *Joseph H. Schwarcz, "Visible Sound," in his* Ways of the Illustrator: Visual Communication in Children's Literature, *American Library Association, 1982, pp. 77-85.**

MIKE MULLIGAN AND HIS STEAM SHOVEL (1939)

[*Mike Mulligan and His Steam Shovel*] is good entertainment. The book has originality and is funny. How Mike and Mary Anne, as he called his faithful steam shovel, went to Popperville to dig the cellar for a new town hall and the good fortune that follows will interest children of many ages.

> *Florence Bethune Sloan, in a review of "Mike Mulligan and His Steam Shovel," in* The Christian Science Monitor, *November 13, 1939, p. 12B.*

From Mike Mulligan and His Steam Shovel, *written and illustrated by Virginia Lee Burton. Houghton Mifflin, 1939. Copyright 1939 by Virginia Lee Demetrios. Copyright © renewed 1967 by Virginia Lee Demetrios. All rights reserved. Reprinted by permission of Houghton Mifflin Company.*

This picture book should appeal to all small boys. It tells a dramatic story, and the pictures . . . are bright and full of humorous details. . . . Very good reading aloud and a child's interest in machinery will assure it of appreciation.

> *Irene Smith, in a review of "Mike Mulligan and His Steam Shovel," in* Library Journal, *Vol. 64, No. 22, December 15, 1939, p. 999.*

This is one of the jolliest books of the fall season. Every one who has stood and watched a steam shovel at work and fallen a victim to its fascination will enjoy it, but it belongs especially to the small boy who can most easily perceive the personality in Mary Anne. He will understand why Mike Mulligan was so proud of Mary Anne and took such good care of her, and he will sympathize when the new kinds of shovels came and took all the jobs away. And best of all he will rejoice when a little boy had a good idea that gave a new kind of work for Mary Anne and made all the people in Popperville happy. The pictures are as much fun as the text.

> *Alice M. Jordan, in a review of "Mike Mulligan and His Steam Shovel," in* The Horn Book Magazine, *Vol. XVI, No. 1, January-February, 1940, p. 42.*

This American creation is the best picture-story book this year has seen so far. . . . It is a very amusing conception both in text and pictures. The latter, brightly coloured lithographs, have a vitality and hearty spirit which are most invigorating. I have tried it out on a number of young readers with great success.

> *A review of "Mike Mulligan and His Steam Shovel," in* The Junior Bookshelf, *Vol. 6, No. 2, July, 1942, p. 61.*

A certain amount of personification and a definite story line have helped make Virginia Lee Burton's *Mike Mulligan and His Steam Shovel* a classic. The steam shovel named Mary Anne is given an expressive face; she's a willing coworker as

Mike digs the foundation for the town hall. Yet this author/artist knows the limits of the device. She knows that her subject's major appeal is a realistic one, and her illustrations show how a real steam shovel works. The impact seems to derive from realistic presentation, even though the thin layer of fantasy may add to enjoyment. (p. 261)

> *Sam Leaton Sebesta and William J. Iverson, "Realistic Fiction," in their* Literature for Thursday's Child, Science Research Associates, Inc., *1975, pp. 243-306.**

Mike Mulligan and his Steam Shovel has been a favorite for over three generations. . . . Like all great works, it is forever fresh and new. . . . As in all of Burton's books, progress is the villain and people and implements which live a simpler, more rural life are happiest. This nostalgic longing for a simpler life is a fairly common American theme—what makes *Mike Mulligan* so satisfying a book is the fact that Virginia Lee Burton has used language, color and time rhythms so successfully in conveying the theme. No child should miss the experience of reading this classic.

> *Jon C. Stott, in a review of "Mike Mulligan and His Steam Shovel," in* The World of Children's Books, *Vol. III, No. 1, Spring, 1978, p. 28.*

CALICO, THE WONDER HORSE; OR, THE SAGA OF STEWY SLINKER (1941)

AUTHOR'S COMMENTARY

I have found out by sad experience that the best way to write or draw a book for children is to work with them. What we think they would like is so often wrong.

Choo Choo, my first book, was for my son Aris, then aged four. *Mike Mulligan and His Steam Shovel* was written for Michael when he was about the same age. Now Aris is nine and it is his turn again. I started the new book (it was about cars), but found him unenthusiastic. The comics, the funnies, and the radio programs absorbed him completely; not only him but all the other boys his age. Here was something to look into. What was it that held them so enthralled? Comic books were like currency. They could be traded for toys. They were collected like treasures. There must be a reason for it.

I soon found out that these books and programs satisfied a natural craving for excitement . . . action . . . drama; gave the children a hero to worship and an escape to thrilling adventure that is wanted by any normal child. Further investigation showed that the wordy, muddled, full color pictures and over-crowded pages were passed by in favor of the simpler ones. The hero must be endowed with more than the average physical and mental powers, besides being all that was chivalrous and virtuous, and the villain the antithesis. Women were not necessary. There must be action, suspense, and tremendous but possible odds against the hero, but no one must get seriously hurt. Humor was welcome. Westerns were the most popular.

In the West they say, "When in doubt, trust to yo' hoss." That was my cue. I made the central character—the hero—or rather the heroine—Calico The Wonder Horse. "She wasn't very pretty, but she was very smart. . . ." All her senses were acutely developed—"she had a nose like a real blood-hound." Her master, Hank, was a cowboy and I made him young enough so that he could have been Aris. Instead of one villain I had five, with a chief villain whom I called Stewy Stinker (my publishers have now edited to *Slinker*, but I am still hopeful). "He was so mean he would hold up Santa Claus on Christmas Eve, if he had a chance. . . ." I made Stewy Stinker and his Bad Men—Butch Bones, Snake Eye Pyezon, Buzzard Bates, and little Skunk Skeeter—both villainous and comic, and got them into the most ridiculous positions the boys and I could contrive. We laid the scene in Cactus County with the Bad Lands over the river.

I told a story continued from night to night and built up the characters and action. I sketched the characters and plot, then went to my publishers. They suggested dividing the book into eight different colors to give a rainbow effect and 64 pages. I welcomed the idea. The change of color would help the serial effect and develop the plot. Moreover I could make the drawings in black and get the two color effect the children liked.

I had been working on design and now had a chance to use it. In design, movement is opposed to monotony. The circle or half-circle is at rest. Developed into a spiral, it moves. A right angle is stationary. A slight variation in degree and it immediately takes on life. My book began to be what my family called "a symphony in comics." Stewy Stinker, in his rare moments of repose, notably when he is thrown into a cactus bed, describes a right angle, but the minute he moves the angle becomes acute until, as the plot fully develops, he and his bad men are accented with a lightning chain of angles. Calico's and Hank's theme in action produces wave-like spirals that sweep through the book to end at last in a quiet half circle, complete repose, and peace.

The colors help. Soft pastels start off the story describing the quiet life in Cactus County, Calico, Hank, and the cattle round-ups. The scene shifts to Bad Men and Bad Lands and the color is lavender. Blacks are always heaviest for the Bad Men, giving a sinister effect. The capture of Stewy Stinker by Calico is in light brown, and his escape in pale green. Cerise and brilliant orange, spirals and zigzag angles bring the story to its climax. Blue with a violent storm starts the *dénouement*, and a soft

warm yellow brings the happy ending with Christmas, stolen presents recovered, Bad Men turned good, and the pattern quiet.

In creating this book, I have not, as you can see, been a complete reactionary. I couldn't be, with any hope of competing with the lurid tales on the market . . . so I offer *Calico the Wonder Horse, or The Saga of Stewy Stinker,* approved and made possible by Aris, Michael, Dick, David, Billy, Carl, etc. (pp. 307-11)

> *Virginia Lee Burton, "Symphony in Comics," in* The Horn Book Magazine, *Vol. XVII, No. 4, July-August, 1941, pp. 307-11.*

Fresh and original in treatment, [*Calico*] is the perfect answer to the Comics. Small boys, everywhere, will read this real "Western," in which a horse and a cowboy and a proper list of villains fill the stage with excitement and delight. At the same time, the composition and design of the pictures cannot fail to arrest the attention of older people interested in illustration. The progress of the story calls for backgrounds of different colors and we wait to see what effect these will have on a child's liking. Altogether, Virginia Lee Burton has made a noteworthy experiment.

> *Alice M. Jordan, in a review of "Calico the Wonder Horse or The Saga of Stewy Slinker," in* The Horn Book Magazine, *Vol. XVII, No. 5, September-October, 1941, p. 356.*

[How Stewy Slinker's band] were brought in and reformed makes a very humorous story. This story . . . is as tall a tale as any about Paul Bunyan, and Calico is every bit as unusual as Babe, the Blue Ox. Here is a book to give your comic-crazy customers. The follow-up with other books in our collections will be a challenge to each children's librarian. . . . This is an earnest attempt to displace the "funny books," and worth consideration as an experiment if nothing more.

> *Marguerite Nahigian, in a review of "Calico, the Wonder Horse," in* Library Journal, *Vol. 66, No. 19, November 1, 1941, p. 951.*

Here is a remarkable little book that strikes a fresh and original note in book making for children and bids fair to provide a solution to the problem of what to do about "the comics." . . .

While child readers are entranced by the speed, excitement and fun of Stewy Slinker's saga, their elders will find the design and composition of the drawings, and the backgrounds of different colors which help to develop the plot, extraordinarily interesting.

> *Anne T. Eaton, "A Wonder Horse," in* The New York Times Book Review, *November 2, 1941, p. 35.*

To what extent is [*Calico, the Wonder Horse, or the Saga of Stewy Slinker*] likely to appeal to English children, who will have seen nothing that corresponds to any extent to the American comic strip? I have tried it out on two English children (both girls, unfortunately), and although both of them thought it funny in parts, neither of them was moved to any great show of interest. That the pictures are strikingly original there is no doubt. The artist has achieved startling effects and the whole is amusing. (p. 97)

A review of "Calico the Wonder Horse, or The Saga of Stewy Slinker," in The Junior Bookshelf, *Vol. 6, No. 3, November, 1942, pp. 96-7.*

At first glance this seems to be a book of cowboy comic strips. It consists of a series of small pictures with a brief commentary. A closer look reveals that it is a highly sophisticated production. The drawings (scraper-boards) are elegant compositions, with many subtle touches. The whole thing is a good-humoured leg-pull. It will be liked most, I fancy, by boys approaching their teens, particularly those whose aesthetic appreciation is well-developed.

M. S. Crouch, in a review of "Calico the Wonder Horse," in The School Librarian and School Library Review, *Vol. 9, No. 4, March, 1959, p. 323.*

THE LITTLE HOUSE   (1942)

In the most fascinating picture book of the season, Virginia Lee Burton tells the story of a little house which wins its way into the very center of our heart. Stunning pictures in color show the changing scene of summer and winter, as the house watches the sun rise and set, and lights begin to twinkle in the nearby city, until she felt the city grow up around her, step by step. Both city and country children will study these pictures with absorption, for there is much exciting detail in them. Besides the seasonal sports and activities of children who played around the house, there is the panorama of the passers-by, in horse-drawn vehicles at first, and then in every kind of motor car you can think of. The pictures are full of life and movement, of work even more than play. And in the end we have the joy of seeing the little house, now shabby and forlorn, move back into the green and sunny country, where the stars shine over her at night. This is the best of Virginia Lee Burton's books, so far, and we predict for it a long and favored life.

From The Little House, *written and illustrated by Virginia Lee Burton. Houghton Mifflin, 1942. Copyright 1942 by Virginia Lee Demetrios. Copyright © renewed 1969 by George Demetrios. All rights reserved. Reprinted by permission of Houghton Mifflin Company.*

Alice M. Jordan, in a review of "The Little House," in The Horn Book Magazine, *Vol. XVIII, No. 6, November-December, 1942, p. 419.*

In **The Little House** Virginia Lee Burton, with lively imagination and genuine power, has made an original and charming picture book that tells in absorbing fashion what happens as cities grow larger and encroach more and more on the green of fields and orchards. . . .

In these days of rapid moving from one apartment house to another, children miss, without knowing it, a sense of permanence, and Miss Burton's book will help boys and girls to appreciate what it means to be able, in the same surroundings, to see the seasons come and go, or, unimpeded by tall buildings, to watch sunset and moonrise. There is something fortifying for them in the lasting qualities of The Little House and the steady round of the turning year. The text is rhythmical and lovely and the pictures are full of fascinating detail in the sports of the children, in the occupations of the different seasons, the vehicles of all kinds, the lively construction work. The artist has given The Little House real personality, and children catch and enjoy the charming humor of the varying expressions she assumes as her life story unfolds. There is indeed so much meaning in every line Miss Burton has drawn, and so much to see in every picture, that the interest of the book to children is practically inexhaustible. The colors are clear and beautiful and effectively suggest day and night in both country and city, and the aspects of the seasons. A picture-story book that will delight not only boys and girls from 5 to 10 but the older members of the family as well.

Anne T. Eaton, in a review of "The Little House," in The New York Times Book Review, *December 6, 1942, p. 9.*

We have been impatiently awaiting the publication of this book for some time. It is indeed a delight. Less exuberant than **Mike Mulligan,** and in a quieter vein, it, nevertheless, shows the movement and vitality, the excellent sense of composition, and the humour that we expect from Miss Burton. . . . This is undoubtedly the most charming picture book we have had for some time, but the text could with advantage have been translated from American into English.

A review of "The Little House," in The Junior Bookshelf, *Vol. 11, No. 1, March, 1947, p. 34.*

An extremely simple, but endearing, story of the life history of a little house overwhelmed by urbanization and industrialization, the story is clearly a parable about the development of American society. This little house which had weathered the seasons for an untold number of years sees the beginning of the destruction of its country idyll with the coming of the first horseless carriage "down the winding country road." Inexorably, the car is followed by steam shovels, highways, houses, tenements, trolleys, subways, skyscrapers, and abandonment. "No one wanted to live in her and take care of her any more," but she remained because she was so well-built. Furthermore, her wise original builder had said, "This Little House shall never be sold for gold or silver and she will live to see our great-great-grandchildren's great-great grandchildren living in her."

It is this stipulation which suggests that the house represents something more than just rural life. The house stands for a whole civilization and perhaps also for the American Constitution—the system of government which many conservatives felt was threatened by the New Deal as well as by increasing industrialization. The story preaches a nostalgia for the past and the rural innocence of snow and stars and apple trees and daisies. And when "the great-great-grand-daughter of the man who built the Little House so well" recognized "the shabby Little House" in the midst of the hurly-burly city, there was an obvious solution—move it to the country. (p. 169)

The flight to suburbia as a return to innocence and beauty is the message of *The Little House*. The world of the past was better, while the city and all of modern industrialization is evil and dirty. Nor is there any possible compromise or evolution, only escape. Even the class element is quite blatant, for it is only the well-to-do who can stop all the traffic to move a house out of the city. In this case it is also an "old" family, a fifth-generation family in 1942, which is thus representative of only a very small proportion of the population. (Interestingly enough, at approximately thirty years per generation, this also makes the house the same age as the constitution.) (p. 170)

> *Ruth B. Moynihan, "Ideologies in Children's Literature: Some Preliminary Notes," in* Children's Literature: Annual of the Modern Language Association Seminar on Children's Literature and The Children's Literature Association, *Vol. 2, 1973, pp. 166-72.*

F. O. Matthiessen's statement that "although literature reflects an age, it also illuminates it" is true not only of adult literature, but also of children's literature, for good children's books often strike into the social fabric of a culture, becoming more than mere entertainment. A case in point is Virginia Lee Burton's *The Little House*. . . . [It is a] profound representation of two main aspects of American social history; the fear of spreading urbanization and the yearning for a return to a simpler, rural way of life. The book thus is related to the pastoral tradition in America, although Burton's attitudes and artistry render it a departure from the main stream of this tradition.

The opening third of *The Little House* contains little plot development but emphasizes the harmony which has long existed among the house, its human occupants, and the environment. The story of the changed days, months, years, and generations takes place in an almost timeless, preindustrial, preurban realm. Details and activities may be altered, but the all-encompassing pattern of the life of the Little House remains the same. However, the fact that only two pages are required to describe and illustrate the destruction of a mood built up by the opening third of the book itself reflects the speed of the process by which the natural harmonies and rhythms of the Little House's earlier life are destroyed. With assembly line quickness and efficiency, a highway is built, slashing diagonally across and through the gentle curves of the rural landscape. The machine, to use Leo Marx' phrase, has entered into the garden, and with devastating rapidity.

Significantly, rescue comes for the Little House in Spring, when, everywhere but in the city, there is a bringing forth of new life and a rebirth of that which had appeared dead. The woman who carries out the rescue is a link to the rural past, for she remembers that her grandfather had lived in a house "way out in the country on a hill covered with daisies and apple trees growing around." The Little House makes a journey back in time from the skyscrapers of now, past tenements, small houses, and roadside gas stations of earlier times, off the black-topped highway onto a road curving past farm houses like those of the Little House's earlier years. It is the reverse of the temporal progress depicted earlier in the book. By trav-

elling through space, the house reaches a spot where the old-fashioned, rural way of life, with its close harmony with nature, still exists.

The power of *The Little House* arises in part because the central character assumes symbolic proportions. The house is deliberately personified, the windows and stoop representing eyes and mouth, the smoke issuing from the chimney, her vitality or spirit. She is consciously aware of and responsive to changes in her environment. She belongs to a tradition of dwellings in American literature in which houses are embodiments of personality: the House of Usher, the House of Seven Gables, and the House of Dies Drier, to name but three. That she is, at the outset, small, rural, and compatible with the landscape may well make her symbolic of the ordinary rural American of some generations ago—the type of person who provided the foundation of the Republic, one might say. And that the House is specified as feminine adds further dimensions to the symbolic portrait. For Burton, women—or the so-called "feminine" traits—are in opposition to the overbearing threat of technology, and they possess qualities for caring, nurturing, and extending kindness. It is significant that the woman who saves the House possesses these qualities as well as the ability to notice details (she is the only one who recognizes the Little House) and the energy to carry out a demanding and complicated act of compassion. Thus the house becomes, as well, symbolic of such values as compassion and friendliness, those also associated with this nineteenth century rural American. Accordingly, the adventures of the Little House are those of a representative, symbolic individual faced with a modern life which is purposeless and divorced from the rhythms of nature. The significance of this symbolic adventure must now be considered.

At first, *The Little House* might seem to belong within the pastoral tradition. Pastoralism is based on the tension between country and city life, between the purity and innocence and simplicity of the country, and the subtlety, complexity, and impersonality of the city. (pp. 33-4)

Virginia Lee Burton's works share the pastoralist's awareness of the tensions between the country and city ways of life. That she desires to escape the latter can be inferred by the strong strain of nostalgia in her books. Maybelle the Cable Car, Mary Anne the Steamshovel, and the Little House all dream of the old days when life was full and interesting, when people showed concern for one another. The structure of all three of the stories in which these characters appear is basically the same: an element of the older, more sensitive life is displaced by progress and technology and somehow this character finds its way back into the country—the place of innocence and purity. Unlike the pastoralists, Virginia Lee Burton allows the progressive element to be defeated and consistently idealizes the rural life to which her characters return.

This idealism and its resultant lack of the ironic vision characteristic of pastoralism is seen in the structure of *The Little House,* which is patterned not as a circular journey but as a linear one—the basic form of the romance, that type of literature in which the hero travels through a land filled with peril and arrives at an ideal land, a paradise, where lasting perfection and harmony are achieved. The romance form is predominantly one of wish fulfillment and is used in such works as Book One of *The Faerie Queene,* Hans Christian Andersen's "Thumbelina," and Doris Gates' *Blue Willow.* Virginia Lee Burton uses the artist's prerogative of choosing her version of reality to form patterns out of the stuff of our culture, and has resolved the tensions surrounding her symbolic character, a representative rural American crushed in an alien environment, through wish fulfillment, by sending the character, the Little House, on the linear journey of the romance form back to a time when the simple, rural, natural, harmonious, tension-free life existed.

But to the reader who is not convinced by the resolution of the conflicts in *The Little House,* there are some nagging questions. What is the significance of the fact that, in order to return to the quiet countryside she longs for, the house requires the aid of a giant truck, an agent of the progressive civilization which has nearly destroyed her? And if the ever present city has surrounded her once, who is to say that urban expansion will not continue, necessitating a future move? Will the rest of her life become a continual retreat from progress so that like those other searchers for a lost, simple past, Natty Bumpo and Daniel Boone, she will never find the rural past she desires? Virginia Lee Burton has presented both for herself and for many readers comforting solutions; but there are forces operating that she does not appear to have understood or, at least, wished to communicate. This may have been because, writing a children's book, she wished to present satisfying, unambiguous conclusions. More likely, she created in the Little House a character with whom she and other Americans could identify, and thus allowed herself to be deceived by a nostalgic vision which successfully shut out consciousness of forces she feared to acknowledge.

In essence, Burton's *The Little House* is escapism, although one of the great celebrations of an irrevocably past way of life that can be found in Children's Literature if not American Literature generally. It is a perfect expression of an author's vision. If there is a limitation in that vision, it is because she has created a character whose life reflects all too well the lives of many in modern American society and has given that character a way out impossible for, but deeply desired by, many people today. (pp. 35-6)

> *Jon C. Stott, "Pastoralism and Escapism in Virginia Lee Burton's 'The Little House'," in* North Dakota Quarterly, *Vol. 49, No. 1, Winter, 1981, pp. 33-6.*

Colorful, circular compositions, entwining and doubling back upon themselves, dominate the illustrations of *The Little House* in its country setting, until progress overtakes the country and turns it into a hustling, bustling city. The closer the city creeps toward the Little House, the more pronounced the vertical emphasis becomes; the soft, curving lines turn to a hard, vertical and horizontal environment for the Little House.

Virginia Burton not only utilizes her lines to convey the alienation the Little House begins to feel in this 1943 Medal Book, but she also transforms the light, clean blues, yellows, greens, and oranges of the country into darker grays and browns, reflecting the Little House's gloom as the city overtakes her. Spring, summer, winter, and fall all lose their color in this city—there seems to be no distinction between the seasons in the Little House's environment of subways, tenements, and masses of people.

But, finally, out of the hustle and bustle, the great-great-granddaughter of the building's original owner rescues the Little House and returns it to the country, where it can enjoy the quiet and serenity once again. The illustrations, too, return to the soft, curving compositions, full of the clear colors of the seasons.

It is clearly evident that Burton's illustrations reinforce and extend the text, and her skill in illustration enables her to mold the elements—color, line, composition—into a work that truly functions as a picture storybook. Burton's technique becomes evident as the illustrations change with the mood and visually reflect the impact of the city. Both the text and illustrations grow dependent upon each other so that to separate them would be to sever equally important facets of the book. It is works such as this that help define the concept of a picture storybook and build the reputation of the Caldecott Medal, rather than those books in which the text or illustrations dominate or overpower the other. (pp. 251-52)

> *Linda Kauffman Peterson, "The Caldecott Medal and Honor Books, 1938-1981: 'The Little House'," in* Newbery and Caldecott Medal and Honor Books *by Linda Kauffman Peterson and Marilyn Leathers Solt, G. K. Hall & Co., 1982, pp. 251-52.*

KATY AND THE BIG SNOW (1943)

Virginia Lee Burton has a way with such matters as tractors and steam rollers and locomotives which comes from a perfect understanding of what these mechanical contrivances mean to a child. . . .

Anyone who has ever watched a small boy's intense interest in one of these monsters of iron and steel that roll the roads or plow the fields will rejoice that this artist and author has made it possible for children to follow the fortunes of Katy, the beautiful red crawler tractor that belonged to the Highway Department of the City of Geoppolis. In the summer Katy worked on the roads. In the winter she had a snow plow to plow snow with, but she was so big and strong that there was not always enough snow for her to plow. However, a blizzard came, piling up snow to the second-story windows, and then the Highway Department sent Katy out. By the time she had plowed out the center of the city, made it possible for the Water Department to get at the broken water mains, for the firemen to go to a three-alarm fire and for the airplanes to land at the airport, the Highway Department was prouder of Katy than ever.

The pictures for this stirring saga have a fine quality of motion and Katy is presented with complete accuracy and an endearing humor. As always, Miss Burton's drawings have beauty and distinction, and the full and interesting detail furnishes lasting entertainment.

> *Anne T. Eaton, in a review of "Katy and the Big Snow," in* The New York Times Book Review, *December 19, 1943, p. 6.*

The characteristic charm of Miss Burton's *Little House* takes another shape, without losing its quality, in another of her successful personifications of objects that grown-ups call inanimate. Practically every building, large and small, appears in these wide pictures, with Katy stoutly cutting tracks. . . . Four-year-old boys in particular will hooray for Katy.

> *May Lamberton Becker, in a review of "Katy and the Big Snow," in* New York Herald Tribune Weekly Book Review, *January 2, 1944, p. 5.*

[*Katy and the Big Snow* is] delightfully filled with action, detail, and the cumulative element. . . . Although less successful artistically than the *Little House* . . . this book may have an even greater appeal for children—especially small boys.

From Katy and the Big Snow, *written and illustrated by Virginia Lee Burton. Houghton Mifflin, 1943.*
Copyright 1943 by Virginia Lee Demetrios. Copyright © renewed 1971 by George Demetrios. All rights
reserved. Reprinted by permission of Houghton Mifflin Company.

A review of "Katy and the Big Snow," in The Booklist, *Vol. 40, January 15, 1944, p. 184.*

[Katy is] a "character." She is named with the felicity that
the men of our Armed Services show when they name their
tanks. Few artists know as well as Mrs. Burton how to give
personality to inanimate objects. We can see Katy as a woman,
big and red-faced and jolly, sweeping all before her with her
energy and determination. . . .

She is strong and modern and efficient. In the marginal drawings we are shown her "horse-power"—a touch that small
boys will thoroughly appreciate. In a double-page spread, in
color, we are shown a map of the city, intricate and informing. . . .

Because of the delightful details that fill the pages, children
will want to own this book. It will take a long, long time to
follow Katy. And it will be lots and lots of fun.

Mary Gould Davis, "Katy Goes Home," in The Saturday Review of Literature, *Vol. XXVII, No. 5, January 29, 1944, p. 30.*

Continuing the excellent work we now know in *Mike Mulligan,*
and in *The Little House,* Miss Burton, in her latest book describes the accomplishments of a tractor. . . . The same hearty
humour that inspired *Mike Mulligan* and the same pages of
virile drawings though with less colour, are here, and will be
sure of the same grateful appreciation from all young readers.

A review of "Katy and the Big Snow," in The Junior
Bookshelf, *Vol. 11, No. 4, December, 1947, p. 163.*

THE EMPEROR'S NEW CLOTHES   (1949)

Hans Christian Andersen's story of *The Emperor's New Clothes*
has been made into a fresh and lovely picture book by Virginia
Lee Burton. The proud Emperor and the scheming weavers are

portrayed here for younger readers, with a wealth of tiny figures, all in soft colors so well reproduced it seems as if they
were the original designs and not the printed book.

There is an extraordinary feeling for rhythm and balance in
Miss Burton's work. This might well be the inspiration for
some school pageant. Costumes, actions and postures for the
dance are all vividly suggested. Turning the pages, one can
almost hear the tune of a minuet and see these figures move
in stately dance. This is indeed a delightful picture book.

Frances C. Darling, "Jolly Stories and Pictures for
You," in The Christian Science Monitor, *November*
15, 1949, p. 13.*

In these new pictures for a familiar old tale, Mrs. Burton
employs her familiar technique of scenes with many small
figures. A child would love to linger over the endpapers with
all the people waiting for the emperor to come along. Some
pages have still more of these little people on streets and in
palace rooms; others show the weavers busy at nothing, the
emperor, the courtiers. The colors are delightful, and the old
costumes and fantastic houses of old Denmark most decorative.

Louise S. Bechtel, in a review of "The Emperor's
New Clothes," in New York Herald Tribune Book
Review, *November 20, 1949, p. 10.*

Miss Burton has done no violence to the traditional tale by
expanding it here and there to admit of more pictures. Her gift
for imparting personality to strange houses and people in any
land is peculiarly her own and one to be cherished. As in all
her books, Miss Burton sees to it that the integrity of her design
has been fully preserved in the finished book.

Anne Carroll Moore, in a review of "The Emperor's
New Clothes," in The Horn Book Magazine, *Vol.*
XXV, No. 6, November-December, 1949, p. 523.

For this beloved and familiar story Virginia Burton has made the most entrancing and satisfying pictures it has ever had. Her sense of pageantry sets forth in beautiful colors the magnificence of the Emperor's domain and entourage; her sense of humor brings out rightly the ridiculous situation with all its implications. There will be those who feel that the version of the story is too much of a departure from the most exact and approved translations, but Virginia Burton has done no violence to the spirit and substance of Andersen's famous tale. Many more children will learn to love it in this new dress.

> *Alice M. Jordan, in a review of "The Emperor's New Clothes," in* The Horn Book Magazine, *Vol. XXV, No. 6, November-December, 1949, p. 524.*

MAYBELLE, THE CABLE CAR   (1952)

With the same wistful affection for days-gone-by expressed in **The Little House,** Miss Burton tells the story of a proud little cable car in San Francisco. For almost eighty years Maybelle and her sister cars have carried their passengers up and down the city's hilly streets. . . . Their peaceful nostalgic life is suddenly threatened, however, when the City Fathers announce their intention to abolish the cable cars in the interest of Progress and Economy.

Children will be caught up in the suspense of this story, for though Maybelle and her sisters are inanimate objects they become real and sympathetic characters in Miss Burton's book. The brightly colored line drawings are baroque in flavor, in keeping with the whimsey of the story, which is done in a loose-jointed blank verse, fine for reading aloud.

> *Mary Lee Krupka, "Car Troubled," in* The New York Times Book Review, *November 16, 1952, p. 39.*

[Some people] formed the Citizens' Committee to Save the Cable Cars and "got busy with posters, parades and publicity." All the excitement and suspense of those anxious times live within these pages. The artist, without drawing faces on Bill [the bus] and Maybelle, has nevertheless succeeded in giving even them exactly the right expression to suit the mood of the moment. And the Citizens are not just a group of people; each tiny figure has individuality. (p. 397)

> *Jennie D. Lindquist, in a review of "Maybelle the Cable Car," in* The Horn Book Magazine, *Vol. XXVIII, No. 6, December, 1952, pp. 396-97.*

People who voted "yes" in the San Francisco cable car question will love every page of this book and so will their children. With an affection for that city and cartoon ability that lends her pictures and her verse a definite cross country appeal Miss Burton sings of Maybelle and her mechanism—how the brakes, cables and front wheels work—of Maybelle through the years from the turn of the century. . . . *You'll* cheer too when the Citizen's Committee wins out.

> *A review of "Maybelle the Cable Car," in* Virginia Kirkus' Bookshop Service, *Vol. XX, No. 23, December 1, 1952, p. 739.*

[This story] is illustrated with fascinating drawings in soft, pastel colors, of the streets, the hills, the bridges, the waterfront, and the people of San Francisco. We especially admire the drawing of the citizens carrying the huge petition into the City Hall. Little boys and girls will spend many happy hours

following the story of Maybelle and the good people of San Francisco.

> *Mary Gould Davis, in a review of "Maybelle the Cable Car," in* The Saturday Review, *New York, Vol. XXXV, No. 50, December 13, 1952, p. 45.*

The story is written in rhythmic prose and illustrated in rather delicate, detailed pictures somewhat reminiscent of **The Little House.** Although this reviewer feels that a cable car that has seen so many years of service is deserving of a more robust treatment, the book has charm and will have a regional appeal to both children and adults.

> *A review of "Maybelle the Cable Car," in* The Booklist, *Vol. 49, No. 10, January 15, 1953, p. 177.*

The talents of the widely loved picture-book artist Virginia Lee Burton have turned to a rather specialized subject. In **Maybelle, the Cable Car** . . . , all her usual delightful detail and feeling for color and pattern occur again on many humorous pages, which, with a lively text, tell how the people of San Francisco voted to keep their cable cars. It is an attractive book, but we think it has slight general interest, compared to Gramatky's new book about "Sparky," an old trolley car which could have existed in so many places.

> *Louise S. Bechtel, in a review of "Maybelle, the Cable Car," in* New York Herald Tribune Book Review, *February 8, 1953, p. 10.*

LIFE STORY   (1962)

The story of the Earth's evolution from the time it swirled as a "red hot fiery ball of matter" to the planet we know today is depicted in terms of the various stages of development. "The world is truly a stage" here, for each full color painting is framed in a proscenium arch—a gimmick which in no way can redeem its ghastly flaws. Lifeless, dull and artificial, these illustrations are eons away from evoking the real drama of life on earth. In their conscious dramatic intent, they are pompous and uninspired. The text is somewhat better as it highlights each aspect of evolution—the formation of igneous and sedimentary rock, the earth's submarine epoch, the ages of ice, reptiles, volcanoes and the coming of man. In the end the story zeroes in on four scenes in the space of one day, focussing directly on the place of the individual on an everchanging planet.

> *A review of "Life Story," in* Virginia Kirkus' Service, *Vol. XXX, No. 7, April 1, 1962, p. 725.*

This is a magnificent book—imaginative in conception and masterful in execution. . . . [A] capsule summary can scarcely do it justice. The author's medium is highly visual—a few apt words set off a series of workmanlike multicolor paintings. It is these that make the book well worth the somewhat higher price than is usual for a physically slim volume for children. . . . It would appeal to any age.

> *Robert C. Cowen, in a review of "Life Story," in* The Christian Science Monitor, *May 10, 1962, p. 7B.*

Virginia Burton here presents, or makes a valiant attempt to present, life from its earliest beginnings to this morning. No one can really give the history of life in a picture book, but this is literally a dramatic effort. . . . The first stage setting

From Life Story, *written and illustrated by Virginia Lee Burton, Houghton Mifflin, 1962. Copyright ©*
1962 by Virginia Lee Demetrios. Reprinted by permission of Houghton Mifflin Company.

shows the astronomer with his telescope, introducing our galaxy. An effective picture, but, for the large age range given the book, one feels inadequacy in the brevity and the writing of the text. Matters improve as life begins and the story progresses—but always the text is too brief, even with accompanying diagrams. What does "Mammals were developing and experimenting in various forms" mean? The ages go racing by; then the pace slows, and we are on Virginia Burton's farm, where we stay a little long, but watch the passage of seasons through a period of years. Finally it is today and the young reader takes over: it is *his* life story.

Somewhat original in conception, this is an interesting book. The imaginative artist is pleasantly with us, for when *eohippus*, the ancestor of the horse, arrives he leaves the stage and steps forward to place his forefoot trustfully in the narrator's hand. What children *do* with the book will be the test; it may suggest many points of departure; it may lead on to other books. (p. 45)

> Alice Dalgliesh, "In and Out of This World," in
> Saturday Review, *Vol. XLV, No. 24, June 16, 1962,*
> *pp. 44-5.**

Miss Burton gives the reader a feeling for the sweep of life on earth. . . . This is more of an inspirational than a straight fact book, and to appreciate it the reader should already have a knowledge of the evolution of life. . . . Meticulous attention is given to both information and artistry, but the book is really over-ambitious and not quite successful. Miss Burton's talent seems to be more with the intimate and human than with the gusty sweeps of pre-history. In style and format the book is reminiscent of *The Little House.*

> Gertrude B. Herman, in a review of "Life Story,"
> in School Library Journal, *an appendix to* Library
> Journal, *Vol. 9, No. 1, September, 1962, p. 119.*

[The prose] is poetic, scientific and good for reading aloud. . . . Acts I and II present the Paleozoic and Mesozoic eras. And if words like these—and trilobite and cephalopod—are a bit difficult for parents, the latter need not be surprised to hear them roll easily off Junior's tongue, since nothing pleases a child like long words. . . .

After the terrors of primeval life [present-day America] may seem a little tame to children but the book as a whole is excellent because the author-artist has established a sense of continuity, making it easy for the reader to compare developments in different eras. The illustrations, as one would expect from the creator of *The Little House* are an outstanding feature, being both sensitive and scientific.

*Carolyn H. Lavender, in a review of "Life Story,"
in* The New York Times Book Review, *September
30, 1962, p. 28.*

The play analogy perfectly reflects Earth's on-going drama and
the temporal pattern of all things. Aside from the book's end
pages, no variety in presentation is given, but that is as it
should be—so much occurs on each page and the ever-changing
stage, so much life is acted out, that any other type of presentation would result in a confused "busyness." Two-page
spreads offer a poised counter-balance between information
and its illustration. On the left side a single paragraph of open-
spaced text is partially enclosed by simple black, white and
gray drawings that clarify or extend what is said: drawings
delineate the stages of Earth's formation, depict and name
extinct animals, chart the maturation of a tree. The opposite
page shows the literal stage on which the "play" unfolds: here,
boldly colored paintings illustrate the Earth's cooling surface,
a landscape inhabited by roaming dinosaurs, a shower-drenched
spring scene. The paintings are bright, semi-realistic portrayals
done in a slightly primitive style, further complementing the
book's ageless perspective.

The book's end pages alter this format, providing a sort of
historical or temporal frame to what they enclose. The opening
pages are pure black, followed by a two-page spread of a darkly
shaded paleontological, stratified chart. The closing pages are
bright yellow, preceded by another two-page spread done in
yellow and gray, representing a cut-away view of a natural
history museum filled with its residents and human visitors.
Obviously, a lot of information is being communicated through
Burton's near-perfect fusion of text, pictures, format and approach. Like a five-act play, the work conveys a sense of much
action, of countless characters living out the greatest theatrical
plot imaginable. . . . (p. 27)

*Joyce A. Thomas, "Non-Fiction Illustration: Some
Considerations," in* Children's Literature Association Quarterly, *Vol. 6, No. 4, Winter, 1981-82, pp.
25-8.**

Virginia (Esther) Hamilton

1936-

Black American author of fiction and nonfiction, reteller, and editor.

Considered among the most outstanding contemporary authors for young adults and preteens, Hamilton is distinguished by her originality, imagination, daring, and perceptiveness. Her works, which are characterized by their unique subjects, three-dimensional characters, and challenging writing style, are acclaimed for raising the quality of literature for young people as well as for stretching its boundaries. Hamilton generally writes realistic fiction, and also includes elements of fantasy, history, mystery, and folklore; in addition, she creates science fiction, biography, and short stories. Throughout her varied body of work, Hamilton focuses on consistent themes: self-discovery and self-acceptance, the importance of freedom and individuality, family unity and the bond between friends, and the influence of the past on the present. Weaving her themes around nontraditional characters and situations, she stresses the capabilities and endurance of her protagonists— young black people who find the inner strength to confront obstacles, survive them, and take responsibility for the results. Hamilton sets several of her books in rural Ohio, an area with which she has strong personal ties. By linking her own heritage with the heritage of a people, Hamilton provides a thread of continuity in her works which relates black history to the present and stresses the richness of black tradition. Songs, tales, chants, and other aspects of black folklore figure prominently in Hamilton's books as do the dreams, myths, and legends of her heritage. Her writing style, which includes such techniques as stream-of-consciousness narration, impressionism, flashbacks, and incomplete sentences, reflects Hamilton's fascination with the possibilities of language. Due to the complexity of her subjects and themes, literary sophistication, and frequent shifts in style, Hamilton is considered a difficult writer, but one whose intelligence and eloquence as a storyteller make her worth investigation.

Lauded for nearly every aspect of her literary style, Hamilton is especially praised for portraying believable, memorable characters and family relationships; critics also note her achievement in representing the black perspective while creating universal stories. Several of Hamilton's books, such as *Zeely*, *M. C. Higgins, the Great*, and *Justice and Her Brothers*, are recognized as juvenile classics. While some reviewers state that her works are too elusive and require an especially mature reader, most affirm that children who persist in reading Hamilton's works will be richly rewarded.

In 1975 Hamilton became the first author to receive both the Newbery Medal and the National Book Award for the same title, *M. C. Higgins, the Great*; this work was also selected for the *Boston Globe-Horn Book* Award in 1974 and the Lewis Carroll Shelf Award in 1976. Hamilton received the Edgar Allan Poe Award in 1969 for *The House of Dies Drear*. In 1972 *The Planet of Junior Brown* was chosen as a Newbery Honor Book and a National Book Award finalist; it also received the Lewis Carroll Shelf Award the same year. In 1983 Hamilton received the Coretta Scott King Award and the *Boston Globe-*

Photograph by Cox Studios. Courtesy of Virginia Hamilton

Horn Book Award for *Sweet Whispers, Brother Rush*, which was also named a Newbery Honor Book the same year.

(See also *CLR*, Vol. 1; *Contemporary Literary Criticism*, Vol. 26; *Something about the Author*, Vol. 4; *Contemporary Authors*, Vols. 25-28, rev. ed.; and *Dictionary of Literary Biography*, Vol. 33: *Afro-American Fiction Writers after 1955*.)

AUTHOR'S COMMENTARY

[The following excerpt is taken from a speech Hamilton delivered at the eleventh Loughborough International Seminar on Children's Literature on August 16, 1978.]

Some authors write particularly for young people because of the wonderfully clear and sweet memories they keep from their own childhoods, memories which they feel a strong need to share with others. But like all authors, we also write because creating fiction is what we care to do most of all. Each of us believes that he or she has a way of putting words down that is different from that of any other writer.

Recently I was on a panel of writers at a local college at home and was asked by a student, "If you had never been published, Miss Hamilton, would you have continued to write?" I answered promptly, "I never knew that I would *never* be published. But if I had somehow known, then no, I would not have continued writing.'' Most of the students were not pleased by this answer, believing that it smacked of mercenariness. What happened to the pleasures of self-expression, some wanted to know, and why wouldn't I have been willing to suffer through obscurity for my art? I said that probably I had always been too old for self-expression; that if I were to express myself in a book, they would toss it out of the window in less than five minutes; and that I've never been willing to suffer very long for anything. I don't believe in suffering, although I do believe that good work has its just rewards. But if it hadn't, I would have moved on to become a phys. ed. instructor, an occupation which at odd moments still appeals to me.

Somewhere in me is the Midwestern farmer, who after a long day, will listen to a good story and tell a few as well. I believe such stories might have begun as incidents or small occasions in the lives of busy, hard-working people and after years and years of talking, began to come together in lines of force that had beginnings, ends, and middles. I think where there were lapses in true memory, creativity came into play. An uncle or a cousin became known for telling tall tales; an aunt or a sister for keeping the perfect memory of Blind Martha, who could find her way two miles out of town and down the dusty road at the age of seventy-five to the exact place where the log cabin had stood in which she had been born and which had burned down fifty years before, leaving not a trace. It would take a gifted talker to tell a true story, like the one about Blind Martha, with the proper combination of drama and emotional wisdom, and it was Aunt So-and-So who could and did on occasions of solemnity.

In the succeeding generation—that is, my generation—stories and tall tales were less frequent but were told often enough so that the child I was learned to think and to manage feelings in terms of stories. When it came time for me to attempt my own telling, I found I was good at drawing on the lapses between true memories, which had grown large with the passage of time. I learned to create my stories and to solve the problems that storytelling makes for those who must write them down. If I express some of myself in the process or some flavor of my Midwestern past, then that's fine. But self-expression, the revealment of me, is not and has never been of any concern to me. This is difficult to explain to students of literature and writing, who are told repeatedly to express themselves. (pp. 609-10)

I work on a book in two ways, both of which have become important to me. One day there appears out of nowhere a small visual piece, a glimpse, say, of a small child struggling to put on rubber galoshes. At once the image disappears around a corner of my mind. So curious, so surprising it was, coming as it did from nowhere, that I have to chase after it to see where it's going. I may not discover another image like it for some time, but what of it? By then, I've been at the typewriter for hours. By the time I've explained why the child is putting on galoshes; that the hour is the middle of the night and she needs the galoshes to get through heavy snow to find her dad, whom she hears singing while he sleds down a nearby hill; that her hungry need for her father is greater than her large fear of the cold, dark outside—I'm into the book. I need no more glimpses; I may not yet know what the story has to do, but I've caught it, like a fever, or it's caught me. In another instance there is a whole story in the shape of the dreams and fears of one character, who appears in the mind completely realized. What becomes difficult is following this figure about

as he gathers to himself his neighbors, friends, and family and his surroundings and needs—all the way to the end. In either case, whether the story begins as a glimpse or as a whole idea, there is room within the novel for exploration in time, place, and mind and for change and growth.

Revision is the work that appeals to me most in writing. It is the creative process more than the initial creation, which is often like a frantic jotting down of glimpses and important signposts of the whole concept while it is still fresh. It is in the first and second revisions or drafts that the language of the first concept begins to take on signs of originality.

No Ohio visionary informed me that I was a novelist when I began writing novels. Nor did I discover the novel form hanging from some magical buckeye tree to be taken down and used for the rest of my days. In college I was a short-story writer out of necessity. Few novel-length books come out of the fast move and grind of co-op study. It was a classmate who convinced me, years after college, that one of those stories might make a children's book. But I recall having the presence to ask what is a children's book, which is like asking what is a book, both being the same question that hadn't crossed my mind until then. Now, a day doesn't pass without my looking closely within myself to see what a book is. Because the knowledge for making them is there in my being and must be a part of my nature.

The form of the novel can do about everything a novelist would have it do. It can fulfill the demands of character and plot to depths unknown in the short story. . . . The novel is capable of almost anything, but it would be best that it not remain what it once was, even if what it once was has communicated its meaning well. That is, it may stand complete, but it shouldn't stand still. The novel needs to grow and change and be in the process of becoming better than it has been.

A novelist can do about anything she wishes with the novel form, save stand still within it. She must grow and change and become better at revealing what is important. What's important is expressed by a kind of illumination at the core; better, at the mind's eye of the self. It is like a brief foresight of the all-important source: the experience of living and partly living, to use a T. S. Eliot phrase, that each novelist has and which is unique to each.

The novelist spends much of her life transforming the source, all that she is able to comprehend from the living experience, into a coherent form of the novel. Thus, writing over a period of time does indeed tend to stand for what she has lived and what living has meant to her. This may be the fundamental meaning of self-expression. The author must seek to discover new ways to express the source or the essence of living that belongs to her. I search to find the words and other words. As my writing changes and, I hope, grows, so must the language I use.

As a college student, I kept a card file on Africa—countries, governments, populations, climates, tribal mores, and languages. Crisscrossing the country on co-op jobs back then, the card file went with me. I believe I thought of it as a hobby, but I know now that it came to represent a kind of family, a comfort away from home. Studying it late at night, I often had strange visions. Past, present, and future formed a continuum, and I felt elemental yet indefinite in a series of written variations on the theme of racial continuity. The novel *Zeely* . . . eventually came out of my study and writings on Africa. And that book does speak of historical connections. Most readers find *Zeely* a nice story, simply written, which is what it was meant to be. And it was my interest in Africa and a certain longing for connections during that period of my life which made the book possible. But when I'm asked presently when I will write another *Zeely,* I am annoyed. Having covered a portion of ground, one needn't travel over it again. The moving writer having writ, as it were, has moved on beyond whatever it was she needed and was searching for in the writing.

But there is pleasure in going after something new down at the source, getting it right and telling it ture. There is no explaining knowing what is right and true, but the author seldom doubts the knowing. That in itself is the expression of her instinct or confidence, the certainty without which she would be lost. Yet there are times when the truth is so abstracted from the source, it's hard to demonstrate that the source is behind it, until one realizes that "living and partly living" is to say surviving, *in other words.* And I've been writing novels of survival for quite some time.

It's my hope never to be bored writing and never to bore children reading what I've written. This could be the reason that over the last decade I've become less preoccupied with my own roots. Only so much can be said about one's heritage, and five or so books on the subject seem quite enough. Not to say that at some time in the future I won't return to themes of the dark experience. But when I do, it may be from an entirely new vantage point and approached from the direction of humor and sorcery. There are huge sums of comedy hidden within the Black experience and unexplored in books for the young.

I am curious about survivors of all kinds. By definition survivors are fit for survival. Some people will survive the cataclysm, while most will perish. Is it chance or fate that the few survive, or do they survive because they are inherently different from the victims who go under? Who are survivors? Are they us or something within us? Are they our wit, our courage, our luck? Or are they our genes? Our genes certainly are within us. Perhaps they created us in body and mind just for themselves, with their preservation as the ultimate rationale for our existence, as some scientists now believe. What our genes may do for their own survival also benefits us, of course. And what a marvelous subject of speculation for the writer— that the fundamental unit of natural selection and, therefore, self-preservation or self-interest is neither the species nor the group nor the individual but the unit of heredity, the gene.

L. Larison Cudmore writes in *The Center of Life* (Quadrangle), "among the at least 800,000 unused genes we have, there may be [the power of] flight," which seems to be the ultimate end of evolution. "Birds and mammals came from the same reptilian ancestor.... Bats may have just renewed the flight capacity.... Flight is beloved and envied by almost every human being, [and is] an integral part of our myths, dreams, and religions.... The Icarus myth that fascinates us so may really be in our genes, not just in the imagination of an ancient storyteller." Might not the human survivors of a cataclysm have a built-in instinct to flee an area hours, even years, before the catastrophe? Was that most fabulous survivor of all time, old Noah, hearing messages from God or subconscious nudges from his distraught gene pool? Is it possible that telepathy, clairvoyance, the prophecy of the ancients, or genius might be a mutation of genes?

I imagine seemingly ordinary children, who have tapped new gene information, accessible after thirty million years of dormancy. They have powers which may be dangerous in the present world but are necessary, even vital, for a future one. So begins the novel concerning the young girl Justice in the *Justice* cycle.... These fantasies are fictions, which depend for effect on the weirdness of location or setting and on the increasing strangeness of the characters, as opposed to the realism I've written with its fidelity to real life and accurate presentations of the typical views and surroundings of the subjects. Writers of realism actually write a modified form, which is not so harsh as the real thing. I myself allow characters some amount of benevolent choice, although I know that in reality choices, benevolent or otherwise, are luxuries unavailable to them. Fantasy extends further than realism. It allows so many choices and so much power to weave the extraordinary into phantasmagoria. Unlike science fiction, fantasy permits every possibility. But one must sharply impose limits on the imagination, or the mind will commence to seem unfathomable, as a box within a box within a box.

There's no set or formal way books based on speculative scientific knowledge should be written. As in writing any fiction, one learns the way with each step and at every turn. Only with the last word am I aware of all the characters have to say as well as that which they can never put into words—how they feel secretly and what feelings they allow to come to the surface. As a book ends, one at last knows the fabric of it and the lives of characters, often over generations, even when the characters themselves have no interest in this history. A novelist will know much more about her subject than she ever puts into her fiction. Hardly any of the discussion here about genes and survival has found its way into the *Justice* cycle in any straight exposition. Yet it all will prove important to Justice and her brothers, who have unleashed the power to reach a future in which things are and are not as they seem.

All writing should appear smooth and fairly easy to comprehend once it is done. Most writing is hard to do, and I think writers should say this out loud; they should tell you that writing is hard. Many writers find one of the hardest problems is getting down to work, no matter what time the work begins. We use various devices to get us started. I know a writer who runs five miles before beginning his work. Naturally, there are days when he never quite begins, being already satisfied with his performance. They say Hemingway had to sharpen twenty pencils and that Willa Cather read passages from the Bible. I think William Faulkner must have sipped a large amount of sour mash bourbon with branch water. I like reading Faulkner way early in the morning just to remind myself that it's hard work to create the simplicity that begins a story. Or I might walk over to the high school track a half-mile away and run—in moderation, of course. I fancy the empty bleachers full of applauding fans as I come around, breaking the imaginary tape first. Always first. My husband, running with me, comes in first, also. Only through fantasy may two people come in first.

Novelists seem to work best over a stretch of four to six hours. That's steady thinking and writing—work that causes wear and tear on the mind. I get a sense that I'm a laborer, the way a sculptor or a painter is a laborer. A sculptor may get metal or marble dust all over himself, and a painter gets pigment deep in the pores. I think a novelist gets this noise, this irritation, at the tips of the fingers. I need to type, that is, to write with my hands. Words not only sound for me, they also seem. On paper they make designs as well as meanings. I have the distinct feeling that my hands are shaping. I am never remotely satisfied with my thinking about something until the story of it is in print. That's why I enjoy typing, creating my incantations in the first stages of print. But there is no feeling of completion for me until the final print. Writing is for me physical labor, and it must be published so that I know the labor is through.

My aim through this labor is to tell a really good story, to entertain. There are times when the texts will allow for my political and social beliefs in some specific way. Other times, I might write a small amount on racial and economic issues in the hope that my readers will take a position, will sympathize with the issues. Underpinning any number of my books are social issues, which I didn't create. I created stories and characters; but people, even imaginary ones, live within a social order.

In the *Justice* fantasies it's necessary to draw conclusions from the present concerning the future. We are aware now that some of the future may reflect our present dangerous failures. Biologist Cudmore informs us that there is no room for compassion when it comes to evolution. It matters little if one is beautiful and strong or feels important. There are simply too many organisms born, and many will have to die. From a biological point of view, what is significant is whether you leave life with more offspring carrying your genes than the next person leaves. Will it be your genes and the oak tree's and the dandelion's in the next generation? It is fantasy to assume that a catastrophic future awaits and that humanity will find ways to blunt the catastrophe. Yet these are the assumptions on which the *Justice* cycle is based.

Learning the new, having new knowledge stimulates the creative process through associative thinking. With the new the writer may combine something she has known for a long time, something with the quality of dream or superstition which is steadfastly believed in, the way one holds on to one's faith. The new knowledge connects with the old belief or memory and through the process of imagination brings about a unique concept. Thesis, antithesis, synthesis: A literature evolves through the careful and detailed settling down of words day after day.

When I decide to write a story, I don't say to myself, now I'm going to write a Black story. But it happens that I know Black people better than any other people because I am one of them and I grew up knowing what it is we are about. I am at ease with being Black. More than anything, I write about emotions, which are part of all people. But the constant is that the characters are Black, whether the story is fantasy or realism about a clairvoyant or a pole-sitter, because pole-sitters and clairvoyants might as well be of the Black race as any other, since race has nothing whatsoever to do with either talent. It might even be more interesting to have a Black pole-sitter or a Black clairvoyant, since race can give an added dimension to a story because of the clichés, prejudices, and assumptions readers will bring to stories with some amount of racial content. The writer uses the most comfortable milieu in which to tell a story, which is why my characters are Black. Often being Black is significant to the story; other times, it is not. The writer will always attempt to tell stories no one else can tell. She tries to realize the most natural way of telling. The way to know whether a story is told in the best manner is to try imagining it told some other way. If the writer can imagine a different telling, then she has not told it completely in the first place.

A day is wholly realized, nature's way of showing us a beginning, a fullness of light and shade, and an ending. A day is like no other day, yet still a day, unique to itself. In the same way, a story must reveal the finality of a completely imagined shape. Style has much to do with this shape, as opposed to plot. One may have a fine plot for a book, but not every plot is made clear through a decent style. My favorite author William Faulkner was a wonderful storyteller and a superb writer in spite of his incredibly complex style, which was not always successful with his readers. Nevertheless, his word-gift has an unearthly power and, for me, transcends the negative force of his style.

No one really knows what style is, but I think it must be a writer's personality, which means to me a public self that the writer feels comfortable having the reader recognize. This personality is not anywhere near the whole self, but it is a very human subterfuge of self, which the writer hopes the reader will go along with in order to appreciate the story. Style is rather like a signature which tells the reader that a writer is there and is interested in communicating through the story. (pp. 611-18)

A writer must have an audience, I believe—a reading audience. When you are sure of an audience, you know you're not writing for self-expression but for the effect that will interest readers. Since readers have the deepest feelings, what you write must never minimize their emotions, any emotions for that matter. Emotions are our humanity. It is the author's projection of emotional empathy with the reader's emotions that makes communication through literature the art it is capable of being. A most complex and highly literate process made simple through shared feelings. Always, we must feel for one another, which is the source and the art of living. (p. 619)

> *Virginia Hamilton, "Writing the Source: In Other Words," in* The Horn Book Magazine, *Vol. LIV, No. 6, December, 1978, pp. 609-19.*

[*The following excerpt is from a speech Hamilton delivered at the Children's Literature Association Conference in May, 1983.*]

I've often said that I write for children or young people, partly because of the fond memories I keep from my own childhood, memories which through an act of imagination I am able to transform into an entirely new "mind of a novel." Otherwise, I write because apparently I think or reason in terms of stories. I make up things in order to extrapolate from known sources what is right and wrong with the world.

My past childhood memories of stories told to me of my own experiences are quite vivid. The pictures I keep of my young self and others are the models, the forms I use when stumbling about in my mind to create characters. But also, stories come to me seemingly out of nowhere. They come from recent experiences, as well. One new story evolved from a vacation trip I had made by car from Ohio to Florida. (pp. 10-11)

Weeks later at home an idea grew, and the book that ensued is entitled *Sheema, Queen of the Road* [later published as *A Little Love*]. The seed of it was transformed and transposed from a fairly boring journey south. (p. 11)

It is interesting how the pine forests I saw on the trip to Florida are transposed into a character named Forrest. The Greyhound buses I saw become school buses. The nuclear power plants nearby translate into nightmarish fear of The Bomb.

Sheema, Queen of the Road is a proletarian novel. The people in the home town in which *Sheema* takes place live there not necessarily because the locale suits them, but because it is comfortably near the available whole-day labor. When the jobs die out, the lives of the people go into a decline. Or the entrenched work force finds the courage to move to other places that are convenient to other jobs. The book is not really about

Sheema's working-class background. And yet, the town and its people give the book a particular atmosphere or a kind of mind of its own. They give to the character, Sheema, a point of view, a way to dream and a reason to break loose. Knowing the socio-economic milieu of a book defines for me the way the characters speak, act, dress, think and feel. It provides me with knowledge of their wisdom, or lack of it.

Time, place and family are at the heart of a book like *Sheema, Queen of the Road.* Sheema, who lives with her grandparents, longs for a complete family, as did the character, Teresa, called Tree, in the novel, *Sweet Whispers, Brother Rush.* My commitment to family in my books has its foundation in my background and the intimate and shared places of the home town and the home town's parade of life.

Home town would seem to be the emotional landscape for my own spiritual growth, even when the home town folks pick themselves up and move to somewhere else. . . . [Time], place, the home town become almost mythical for me. I've suffered through every home town situation, or I have imagined how a situation might feel, just as my characters do, as historically, other people like myself have suffered through them. The real progress of a people across the hopescape of America has near the heart of it much restless comings and goings. Movement, change, is the soul of the home town folks' tireless dance across that continent.

I have always felt my rural Ohio landscape was eccentric, as is the history of my people prospering on it. Most of my books hold some element of fantasy, from little Jahdu who was born in an oven and the Night Traveller in *Zeely,* on to the dead James False Face speaking to the child, Arilla, in *Arilla Sun Down,* to the ghost in *Sweet Whispers, Brother Rush* and the divine power of the gods in *The Magical Adventures of Pretty Pearl.*

Sheema is the first realistic book I have done since *M. C. Higgins the Great,* in which the characters often express themselves in non-verbal ways. I am interested in people who do not have enough words. Some will call the language I use in books such as this and *Sweet Whispers, Brother Rush* Black English. Some will call it simply slang or colloquial speech. Truly I don't give it a name. Having recently published *The Magical Adventures of Pretty Pearl,* which takes place in the 1870s, I experimented with another kind of language. In *Pearl,* it was necessary to develop a language which resulted in a cross between some Afro-Caribbean dialects and what I surmised from my research might be the way the first free black generation after Surrender would speak. The language of the book was complicated, somewhat, by the fact that in it there are gods from Mt. Kenya in Africa who involve themselves with the black people in America. I decided the gods would speak as the black people spoke—since in a book of magic, the people would necessarily be made in their god's image. . . . (pp. 11-12)

Occasionally, people find black dialects difficult. Such speech is the sum total of local characteristics of speech, the spoken language peculiar to a region and no more difficult than a Milwaukee Polish dialect or Brooklynese. Black people speak in a wide variety of English, from so-called Standard English to regional and what I term "philosophical vernacular" English. This last is utilized by fairly educated blacks who need to travel through the many cultural and political situations of their country and thus create a more versatile language in order to ease their passage from one station to another.

It isn't possible to write and have characters speak without having them speak in a particular style. Such stylizations help make the world of the book more entertaining, I believe. Moreover, they can reveal character as clearly as narrative description can. Characters often define who they are through the manner in which they speak. Their language may reveal the limitations or freedoms they have. When the character, Tree, in *Sweet Whispers, Brother Rush,* says to Silversmith, her mother's manfriend, "Who you?" it is a kind of shorthand that has more the impact of an insult than if she had said indignantly, "Who do you think you are?" "Who you?" is unquestionably a clear put-down of Silversmith, phrased in the tough, no-nonsense of Tree's reality.

I have said often enough that I am descended from mid-western American farmers of African descent. Actually the progenitor was a fugitive from injustice and became a farmer because land was what he found before him, under him and all around him, and land was fairly easy to possess. I long ago became fascinated with the sons and daughters of Africa and how they survived on the American continent. My own ancestors delighted in story-telling, tall-tale telling and subtleties of verbal expression. But the one area that I have never heard them discuss was that dealing with their hard and secret venture north out of the South during the time of Slavery. It was as if, somehow, they knew that one of them would come along in some later generation to figure it out, to put it all together. And they knew that it would become a more profound experience the less that was known and told about it.

In *The Magical Adventures of Pretty Pearl,* a group of 150 blacks—orphaned children and stunned, misplaced adult former fugitive slaves—who call themselves inside folks, live hidden, sheltered in a vast Georgia forest. Out of their bereavement they form a society of sorts, a community and a family, in order to survive. Just as the character, Buddy Clark, forms a community as Tomorrow Billy in my novel *The Planet of Junior Brown.* The idea of gathering, of forming, an environment occurs again and again in my books. If something threatens the environment, the people escape, moving to somewhere else.

Pretty Pearl is my rendition of the dark secrets that surround the passage of the descendants of Africa from that continent onto the American one. It is in many ways a light-hearted book, full of gods, god-children, legend, myth and magic. But also in the book, descriptive narration is used to express the idea of uprooting, with which many readers can identify. (p. 12)

By listing the furniture of their lives . . . , that which the inside folks must take with them [in their journey out of the forest], as well as that which they must leave behind, the loads they thus are obliged to carry, become back breaking, symbolic of their life of suffering. The inside folks must move with all their own five hundred miles north and they must take their burdens with them. This is the way of community, of family, of black folk, the narration seems to mean.

What is transformed from myth, from history and family narrative in my books is derived from the certain progress of a people across the American hopescape. My writing can be lighthearted or moody, or dark and brooding, often in the same work. In the background of much of it is the dream of freedom which, even through this generation of the descendants of Africa, remains tantalizingly out of reach. Echoes of long past times often serve to feed my imagination. They may sound of African dreams; they may speculate about family truths and even the future. I find the past far easier to cope with than the present. But all of my literary concerns almost always derive out of my heritage experience, the collective unconscious, as it were, as I try to uncover new ways of expressing my creative triad of the known, remembered and imagined.

After seventeen books, . . . I am not yet bored with scribbling and hope never to bore young people reading what I've scribbled. I hope my sense of story will always interest readers. (pp. 12-13)

[Writers] such as myself often resist doing the familiar, resist writing entertainment for the sake of booksales. We struggle to balance our knowledge of young people and what they like or think they want with what we have to write and what we think they will comprehend and what they need to know. We struggle with complicated desires and literary considerations as well. I want my books to be read. I want an audience. I struggle daily with literary integrity, black cultural integrity, intellectual honesty, my desire for simplicity in the storytelling, and the wish for strong, original characterization, exceptional concepts for plots. (p. 13)

I am most happy creating fictions in which people interrelate, where we can go deep within them to where they test themselves, against nature, one another, or anti-nature, as with The Bomb in *Sheema.* It's my pleasure to transform ideas and vague images into coherent fictions. I discover the way to write a particular novel only by writing it. Word by word, sentence by sentence. That is the only way to do it. When I begin by thinking, now I'm going to really write a book, I cannot do it. But when I start with one word at a time, taking it slow, I can make words fit the pictures growing in my mind. Pictures come first to make the mind of the novel. Then the words come, to form the heart of the book. Mind and heart change, reshape and are multi-faceted.

The making of a fiction is foremost a self-view that becomes a force for communication and for life. It is greater than the sum of fact, memory and imagination that combine to create it. The art, the fiction, must stand independently from the self, more profound, more magical than anything the artist may have experienced. The artist strikes a tone. It is a call. The response is the key. Therein lies a medley of thought and feeling that we must learn to cherish.

Words that make *worlds* are magic for me. The miracle of words is that the language they convey can be made meaningful in terms of human desires. Language *is* magic, has always been magic, since the time sorcerers uttered their incantations and wrote their symbols, which steeped our human past in marvelous myth. Oh, I'm a believer in language and its magic monarchy! To bind its boundless spell to me is why I write. (p. 14)

Virginia Hamilton, ''The Mind of a Novel: The Heart of the Book,'' in Children's Literature Association Quarterly, *Vol. 8, No. 4, Winter, 1983, pp. 10-14.*

GENERAL COMMENTARY

JOHN ROWE TOWNSEND

I feel more hesitant in writing about Virginia Hamilton than about anyone else in the present book. This is not because she is particularly obscure or difficult; I do not think she is. Take her stories at their face value and they are usually quite simple, quite easy to follow. (*Arilla Sun Down,* it is true, moves back

and forth in time, but this ought not to cause any difficulty to an intelligent older child, or adult, with any experience of novel-reading or the cinema.) The problem is that the essence of her work is subtle and elusive, difficult to pin down on the page.

There are writers whose books are 'closed'; what appears in black and white is exactly what they have to say. Their goods are all in the shop window, ticketed and priced. There are others whose books are 'open': the reader is left to draw the inferences, make the connections, provide the interpretation. Virginia Hamilton's books are exceptionally open in this sense. Even at their simplest, her stories are capable of extension; they contain more than is expressed in their words. They cast shadows, and the shadows can vary according to the light the reader brings to them. One is reluctant therefore to offer a hard-and-fast interpretation or assessment. (p. 97)

According to a biographical note by Paul Heins, Virginia Hamilton 'often feels that she is a symbolist'. Without going into the historical intricacies of defining symbolism, one can certainly say that as the term is commonly used nowadays there is a great deal of it in her books. She remarked on this, humorously, in her Newbery Medal acceptance speech for *M. C. Higgins the Great* in 1975. . . . [The] pole, it seems, was not intended to be symbolic; yet surely it became so, willy-nilly, because of the way Miss Hamilton's imagination works. It seems safe to say that when M. C. Higgins is sitting atop the pole he is riding high, he is rising above his environment, he is holding a brilliant and confident though precarious balance. The pole indeed is obviously the throne of M. C. Higgins the Great. . . . I am reminded of Helen Cresswell's remark in *A Sense of Story:* 'Carefully worked-out symbolism is almost always cliché. You don't choose symbols—they choose you.'

With Virginia Hamilton, more than with many writers, it is helpful to have a personal context for the author. She is black. Her maternal grandfather, Levi Perry, was an escaped slave who settled in Ohio. She grew up among the 'large, extended and complex Perry clan' in the small town of Yellow Springs, where she lives today. The Perrys, from her account, are a lively, idiosyncratic family of storytellers; and Perrys appear, under that very name, in some of her books. Her grandmother was reputed to be part Cherokee Indian, and she herself is the mother of an interracial family; these two elements of her background are worth remembering in connection with *Arilla Sun Down.* She has a deep sense of roots: of rootedness in a family which itself is rooted in a place. And the place is in America. (pp. 98-100)

Clearly Virginia Hamilton is concerned as a writer with the black, or non-white, experience. To the best of my recollection, no fictional character in any of her work up to the time of writing is white. But there is no taint of racism in her books. . . . All through her work runs an awareness of black history, and particularly of black history in America. And there is a difference in the furniture of her writing mind from that of most of her white contemporaries: dream, myth, legend and ancient story can be sensed again and again in the background of naturalistically-described present-day events.

Her first book, *Zeely* . . . , exemplifies this and other Hamilton qualities. Elizabeth, who is calling herself Geeder by way of make-believe while on holiday in the country, sees the beautiful, regal, immensely-tall Zeely first as a night-traveller (a phrase which of course connotes escape from slavery) and then, obsessively, as a Watusi queen. At the end of the story, when for the first and only time she actually talks to Zeely, she faces the truth that Zeely is a very tall girl who looks after hogs. Zeely has accepted herself as what she is, and with the aid of a parable of seeking and finding she helps Geeder to do the same. She is not a queen; and perhaps there is an implication that for black Americans to look back towards supposed long-lost glories in Africa is unfruitful. Yet the story manages at the same time to hold within itself a different truth, almost a contradiction. There is a sense in which Geeder's illusions have not been illusions at all; in which the figure of Zeely does embody that of the night-traveller, who, according to Geeder's Uncle Ross, 'must be somebody who wants to walk tall . . . it is the free spirit in any of us breaking loose'; in which, as Geeder says at the end, Zeely truly is a queen as well as a hog-keeper. If there is a simple message here for younger children (and I do not think Virginia Hamilton would scorn to offer a simple message to young children) it can be summed up in those two words 'walk tall'; but it is a simplicity that has profound resonances.

The House of Dies Drear . . . , with its crowded action and melodramatic trappings, is in many ways at the opposite fictional pole from *Zeely*. Thomas is the eldest child of a black historian's family which moves into a great rambling old house, once a station on the Underground Railroad, supposedly-haunted home of a murdered abolitionist, and now guarded by 'that massive, black and bearded man some souls called Pluto'. Thomas and his father penetrate the labyrinthine complexities of the house, discovering at last the extraordinary treasure which is its ultimate secret; and they drive off those who have threatened it. Here is a tale of mystery and excitement; of all Miss Hamilton's novels it is the one with the most obvious attractions to the child reading for the story. Indeed, an adult reader may feel she has been rather too free with the Gothic embellishments.

The hidden buttons, sliding panels and secret passages can too easily suggest a commercially-inspired Haunted House from a superior fairground: at the same time gruesome and giggly. And the play-acting with which 'our' side frightens off superstitious intruders at the end is not really worthy of this author. One has initial doubts, too, about the marvellously-preserved treasure cave of Dies Drear, with its magnificent tapestries, carpets, glassware, Indian craft work and so on. Is it appropriate to the story that there should be a tangible, financially-valuable treasure, and anyway is it the right kind of thing for a dedicated abolitionist to have and to hide?

Here however one must recall Virginia Hamilton's comment on the tendency of the people and properties in her books to turn into emblems. It is a reasonable supposition that the treasure represents a cultural inheritance, of which Mr Pluto is the guardian or some kind of guardian spirit. The whole book has a strong, almost tangible sense of the presence of the past. It is a dramatic and at the same time a rather rambling piece of work, with something in it of the character of the house itself: much of it is below the surface, passages open out of the story in all directions, some are explored and some are only glanced into. It is highly interesting, highly readable, but it does not quite succeed in being both an exciting adventure story and a satisfying work of art.

The mysteries of *The Planet of Junior Brown* . . . are of a different order from those of *Dies Drear*: more akin to those of *Zeely* and of the later novels. *Junior Brown* is not fantasy, as the word is commonly understood: the laws of nature are never broken, and occasionally, as in the description of Junior's

mother's asthmatic attack, there is an insistent, almost cruel realism. Yet there is much in the book that requires a different kind of assent from that which we give to an account of everyday events. The ex-teacher janitor who has a large rotating model of the solar system erected in the hidden basement room to which his truant friends come; the 'planets' of homeless boys dotted around the big city, each with its 'Tomorrow Billy' as leader; the lowering of 262-pound Junior Brown into the basement of a deserted building by means of a specially-rigged hoist: these carry a conviction which has more to do with the character and atmosphere of the story, the hypnotic power of the author to compel belief, than with literal probability. (pp. 100-03)

A planet in this story is a person's refuge, and perhaps also his sphere of action. There is an analogy between the huge uncaring city and the vast indifference of space by which planets are surrounded. The school from which Junior Brown and Buddy are alienated, but in which they find a temporary home in the janitor's room, expresses the same analogy on a smaller scale. Buddy, coping and compassionate, instinctual and imaginative, 'swinging wild and cool through city streets', is a forerunner, a leader into the future, a kind of saint of the streets. Too good to be true? Too good to be literally true, I think; it is hard to suppose that a homeless street lad could be so noble, so uncorrupted by hardship and by the company of those already corrupted. But when Buddy affirms on the last page that 'the highest law is for us to live for one another', he surely speaks not as Buddy Clark but as Tomorrow Billy, a mythological figure, conceivably related to the High John de Conquer who was the hero and inspiration of slaves in the last century. (pp. 103-04)

[The protagonist of *M. C. Higgins, the Great*] is the early-teenage black boy who sits on that pole, which was his reward from his father for swimming the Ohio River. . . . The title 'the Great' is self-awarded, a joke, but by the time the book is read the reader is likely to feel it justified; for M. C. *is* great, he *does* ride high; though he is poor and presumably uneducated he has wisdom, competence, determination. . . . Unlike Buddy Clark, though, he is not a saint or an inspirational figure; he is human, makes mistakes, has his inadequacies.

On the surface, not a great deal happens in this novel. . . . But nothing is insignificant. Events in *M. C. Higgins the Great* either define the people and their situation or else, by apparently small redirections (like points on a rail track) change the courses of people's lives. The most important event happens inside M. C.: his acceptance of his own rootedness in Sarah's Mountain and his determination to stop that spoilheap.

Roots, more than anything else, are what this novel is about: roots in place and also the roots of ancestry. After telling M. C. how Great-grandmother Sarah came to the mountain, his father, Jones Higgins, sings some words from a song she used to sing. The words have been passed down through succeeding generations, but Jones doesn't know what they mean: I guess even Great-grandmother Sarah never knew. Just a piece of her language she remembered. Both Jones and M. C. occasionally have a sense of the presence of Sarah on the mountain. (pp. 104-05)

M. C. in fact has semi-mystical dreams and visions which link him with his past, and has a lingering half-belief in spirits. Jones is frankly superstitious, and this is harmful in his refusal to have anything to do with the 'witchy', six-fingered but perfectly harmless Killburns. M. C. does not go along with that; he is wiser, and Ben Killburn is his friend, though he has to assure himself that Ben's extra fingers aren't 'wildly waving and making magic'. It may be noted that M. C.'s wisdom is itself rooted in the earth and does not move away from it; he is hopelessly naïve about the visiting dude and about Mama's prospects of stardom. Two more small but significant events may be noted at the very end of the story: Jones accepts, albeit reluctantly, the presence of Ben Killburn on his property, helping M. C. to build the wall, and he gives the boys a gravestone to build into it.

> 'See it,' M. C. said. 'It's Great-grandmother Sarah's.' The markings were worn but the name was still readable.
>
> 'Why did your father bring it?' Ben wanted to know.
>
> 'Because,' M. C. said. He thought a long moment, smoothing his hand over the stone. Finally he smiled. 'To make the wall strong.'

It is the reinforcement, once more, of the present by the past.

The Adams family in *Arilla Sun Down* are interracial. Arilla's mother is a light-skinned black woman, beautiful, and a teacher of dancing. Her father is part-black, part American Indian; and her older brother Jack Sun Run, though neither more nor less Indian than Arilla, asserts himself to be 'a blood'. Arilla feels overshadowed; doesn't know who or what she is.

Jack Sun Run—handsome, flamboyant, a brilliant horseman—is the dominant figure in this novel; but he is a more subtly ambiguous creation than any in Virginia Hamilton's earlier books. There's a sense in which he is a phoney: 'playing the brave warrior', as his mother unkindly says. . . . Yet the phoney and the genuine are not entirely incompatible. There is something in Jack Sun Run's blood and background, and in his father's, that will come out and that will always be strange to Mother, who doesn't share it. And it is there in Arilla, too. In flashbacks to her earlier childhood, Arilla recalls half-forgotten experiences and encounters with the People: especially her friend, mentor, storyteller and source of wisdom, an old man called James False Face. Arilla receives—reluctantly, as a birthday present—a horse; she learns to ride well, and saves Jack Sun Run's life after an accident while out riding in fearful conditions. That is how she earns the name of Arilla Sun Down, becomes able to see Jack as human rather than as a being of sunlike power and brilliance, and also puts herself level with him, since he saved her life as a small child.

But in the end it is through her father that Arilla comes into a share of the Indian inheritance. Every year Dad, who is a supervisor in a college dining hall, disappears for a while, and Jack has to go and bring him back. Now, with Jack in hospital, the duty falls on Arilla. She finds Dad where he is known to be, up in the country of his people; and he has gone sledding—flying wild and free over the snow. Arilla sleds with him, as she did when a small child. Sledding, riding, even roller-skating: these are important, she needs the movement for the nomad that is in her. There is something of the experience, the transmitted wisdom of the People in her, too. All this is more real than the earlier posturings of Jack Sun Run.

Lastly there is the thing that is Arilla's own, the gift that is individually hers, that comes out in her urge to write. It goes with the name that old James has given her, along with his stories: her secret name. It is there in the book, at a key moment, a moment remembered by Arilla from years before. In

this memory James has just died; Arilla is feverish and she seems to hear him speaking to her of life and death, and concluding:

> 'Wordkeeper?'
> 'I hear you.'
> 'Remember who you are.'

In its movement back and forth in time, and its shifts of style, *Arilla Sun Down* may make one think occasionally of the Faulkner of *The Sound and the Fury*. But it is an original work, and a poetic one. Among many memorable lyric passages are Arilla's childhood recollection of sledding with Father, and, in her 'present-day' narrative, a parallel pages-long account of roller-skating, both capturing to an astonishing degree the poetry of motion. (pp. 105-07)

It is possible to do violence to a book by intrusive probing; by partial or misleading explanation. If I have given some impression of the power and strangeness of *Arilla Sun Down,* and left anyone feeling the need to read or reread it, I have probably done what is most useful. It is a book that takes risks. It is not for casual, easy reading, and among young people (or adults) it is likely to be appreciated only by a minority, and perhaps fully understood by none. The read book is always a collaboration between writer and reader, and this one requires that the reader should willingly contribute his or her own imaginative effort. It offers in return the high delight of sharing in an achieved work of art. (p. 108)

> *John Rowe Townsend, "Virginia Hamilton," in his* A Sounding of Storytellers: New and Revised Essays on Contemporary Writers for Children, *J. B. Lippincott, 1979, pp. 97-108.*

BETSY HEARNE

Virginia Hamilton has heightened the standards for children's literature as few other authors have. She does not address children or the state of children so much as she explores with them, sometimes ahead of them, the full possibilities of boundless imagination. Even her farthest-flung thoughts, however, are carefully leashed to the craft of writing. There is clearly a hard-worked development from the first two books, which were coated with some stiffness of language and incident, to three powerful novels weaving fantastic characters and situations with graceful, credible assurance.

Although comparatively awkward, the early *Zeely* and *The House of Dies Drear* leave indelible flashing impressions. . . . The second book is better built but still does not fully break surface formality to the power underneath. Then, in *The Time-Ago Tales of Jahdu,* Hamilton frees her words into strong, rhythmic patterns that can fit and follow her roving imagination.

The Planet of Junior Brown unites the graceful language of Jahdu with the sustained structure of imaginative fiction. The uncanny figure of Junior Brown—hugely fat, talented and unhappy—revolves in his own troubled universe while Buddy—strong, resourceful, streetwise—swirls around him, caring. . . .

Coming to Junior's rescue, Buddy develops his own philosophy of leadership in the underground "planets" established by older homeless boys to take care of younger ones. Early on he teaches, along with techniques of survival, "The highest law is to learn to live for yourself." By the end of the book, he has found a new trust. "We are together . . . because we have to learn to live for each other." Supporting such a resolution are two perfect portraits and a vivid setting.

As *The Planet* is a city book, quick in pace, **M. C. Higgins, The Great** is a country book, with slowgathering but inevitable power, natural images, and homemade music. (p. 22)

The pictures and the relationships and the sounds that fit together here deepen in perspective with each reading. There is a sure direction that never slips into preplanning, an opening and closure of another world that one wants to visit—a unique place where six-fingered, red-haired merino blacks have made a vegetable farming commune stretched over with a rope web where the children can climb and play. And they are as believeable as the strength M. C. finds in himself, his family, his friends, his mountain.

Arilla Sun Down is an adventurous book because it leaves the beaten paths of complete sentences and of Hamilton's previously successful award winners. That took a lot of nerve. In this first-person narrative are mixed chapters of present and past. . . .

The chapters of Arilla's memories are written in a stream-of-consciousness flow with impressionistic child language floating among half-buried images and snatches of adult conversation remembered piecemeal. Some, such as the scene of an old man's death, have a great impact, and on the whole they work effectively to undergird the adolescent's present-tense story of finding her name and place.

There are symbols in each of Hamilton's books that could be discussed at length, but the importance of her work is more than symbolism or sounding the black experience. The importance of it lies in taking artistic integrity as far as it will go, beyond thought of popular reading, but with much thought to communicating. This is a tradition which is accepted in adult literature and which must be accepted in children's literature if it is to be considered a true art form. With plenty of books that fit easily, there must be that occasional book that grows the mind one size larger. (p. 23)

Betsy Hearne, "Virginia Hamilton—An Eminent Writer for Children in the U.S.A.," in Bookbird, No. 4, (December 15, 1980), pp. 22-3.

SHEILA A. EGOFF

For the most part, the best American children's novels are more deeply rooted in social realism than are the British. They follow Stendahl's view of realistic fiction—a mirror traveling along a highway and giving an accurate though miniaturized picture of what is happening on it. This emphasis on specific reflections of social and political environments is most evident in the realistic fiction of American black authors or in stories of black American life. William Armstrong's *Sounder* (1969), Mildred Taylor's *Roll of Thunder, Hear My Cry* (1976), and Virginia Hamilton's **The Planet of Junior Brown** . . . are close to Steinbeck's *The Grapes of Wrath*, creating like it precise, deliberate social and historical images which convey the outrage of conscience and heart. (p. 50)

Perhaps the most timeless of the group will prove to be Virginia Hamilton's **The Planet of Junior Brown** because it is imbued with the fantastic. Everything seems larger and more surreal than life. . . . It is both a psychological and humanist drama, both an allegory and a social dissertation, but most of all it is a statement about friendship and freedom. (pp. 50-1)

Buddy Clark is a tender-tough street boy with a brilliant mathematical mind and wise heart who lives a mysterious life in deserted tenements, removed from the world of adults as a lone child-survivor. Junior Brown, suffocated and overprotected by his asthmatic, neurotic mother, finds solace from his deep unhappiness in his remarkable musical and artistic talents, in his fantasies, and in his friendship with Buddy. . . .

But Buddy has for many years lived yet another existence, in a role beyond his years as a "Tomorrow Billy," a guide for groups of homeless street children hiding from the controls of adult society. . . .

At the end of the novel, Junior has taken refuge in his new planet-underground home with Buddy and his new child family. (p. 51)

Hamilton portrays this communal sharing of love, friendship, and survival as socially unacceptable and heretical (almost early Christian) in the eyes of the conventional society of school, welfare, and home. It is fascinating that she has reversed the traditional archetypes, giving the children's underground "Tomorrow Billy" planets and their precursor, the janitor's cellar room, the value of heaven, of the planetary system of light, power, and conscious love rather than the dark realm of shades, despair, and the unconscious that the symbol of underground life has always evoked (Hades, Hell, and the underworld). (pp. 51-2)

The Planet of Junior Brown is also a "dangerous" survival story, but one with a positive, inspirational thread of salvation running through it. The world of eccentrics, misfits, and madness is given a sympathetic treatment; characters, both adults and children, are memorable and with both positive and negative attributes. They are whole, authentic human beings. There is also a visionary, or messianic note of the possibility of a new human race, self-fulfilled, a more humane and compassionate people than exists in the world today. Mr. Pool has always dreamed of a new human race for which life must be made ready and discovering the planets of the children has given him renewed faith in his dream. . . . (p. 52)

Hamilton writes with force. Her overall, imaginative theme and intricate plot line are joined to a natural and at times poetic prose with an appropriate use of black English that lends vitality to the dialogue. At the same time, her imagery is at times overpowering: there is that of music—the planetary music of the spheres and Junior's playing on the silenced keys of a piano; there is color—Junior's black vision of his spirit and sin, and the red of his paintings; there is the image of New York—Buddy's awareness of the darkness, danger, terror, even beauty of the city; there is the image of obesity—Junior's weight is seen as a metaphor for isolation and a Buddha-like abiding presence rather than as a physical problem.

Hamilton reverses her images in . . . [**M. C. Higgins the Great**], although in both she explores the tensions between individual freedom and responsibility and society's capacity for destroying those who are unusual, who are not easily molded. M. C. Higgins's achievement is to climb to the top of his majestic pole, viewing heaven and earth in brilliant, solitary isolation while Buddy's was to burrow into an underground world, creating a shared, cooperative venture for living in a group. **M. C. Higgins the Great** investigates light and love in a nuclear family, joy in song, and a struggle for the threatened countryside. . . . The earlier book investigates darkness, despair, madness, music of instruments, the love of a family of peers, and urban survival. The concepts in both are intriguingly similar to those in Alan Garner's *The Stone Book* (1976), in which Mary ascends to the top of the steeple and descends into the caves of the earth, experiencing the wisdom that lies within the heights and depths of both heaven and earth. What Hamilton and Garner are exploring is the archetype of opposites, the duality of existence, and the discovery of the ancient prophecy: "as above, so below." (pp. 52-3)

[A] persuasive melding of the intangible to the tangible, and the incredible to the credible [in science fiction] are the marks of such writers as K. M. Peyton in *A Pattern of Roses* (1972), Peter Dickinson in *The Gift* (1973), John Rowe Townsend in *The Xanadu Manuscript* (1977), and especially Virginia Hamilton in *Justice and Her Brothers*. . . . The change in actual human development due to the expansion of the human mind that has already been used in such adult science fiction as Arthur C. Clarke's *Childhood's End* and John Wyndham's *The Chrysalids* is encountered in these children's books as well. In them the children's newly developed powers also signal a change in society. Like Clarke and Wyndham, these writers for children keep their plots firmly rooted on present-day Earth and moreover portray the family life of their young protagonists realistically. (pp. 149-50)

[A] serious, even mystical, comprehension of transformation in human spirit and powers is seen in Virginia Hamilton's *Justice and Her Brothers*. While she concentrates on three children in one family, two of them identical twins, the effects of their psychic discoveries and manipulations are meant to show a fundamental change in the human race. Like most science fiction writers, Hamilton shies away from concrete, rational explanations. . . . However, she does offer an arresting, strongly physical treatment of Justice's initiation into her heretofore unsuspected powers by a next-door-neighbor, whose slatternly country persona is a disguise for secret pursuits as a medium. As does Don Juan to Carlos Castaneda, she escorts Justice along the mystical path of psychic knowledge.

While this exploration of the onset of newly developing human capabilities is almost earth-shaking in children's science fiction, it is the more human intimacy of family and sibling life that gives the novel its sense of naturalness and credibility. The family is composed of eleven-year-old Justice, her twin older brothers, Thomas and Levi, her skilled workman father and her loving mother, torn between studying at college and staying home to look after her family, all moving towards a crisis in summer days of almost unbearable heat. It erupts in the incredible mental power struggle among the children for dominance—that of Tom over Levi, and the final ascendance of the newly aroused Justice who will be "The Watcher." Justice knows that, "Our place isn't here. . . . Our time isn't now, but in the future." Having shown us both normal and supernatural children in strife and play, Hamilton reassures us with the abiding nature of childhood at the end:

> They were on their bikes, Thomas in the lead. Instantly, they raced in a flurry of shining, spinning wheels and glinting metal. . . . They had nothing more on their minds than beating the heat across town. Fresh cold drinks of water. Of getting home.
>
> Kids.

Yet the implication that children have the fate of the world in their hands is as strong in this children's story as it is in Doris Lessing's adult novel, *The Four-Gated City*, in which, after the collapse of western society, the exploration of ESP by two women leads to its discovery and development in a group of children.

While adult authors, from John Wyndham to Clarke to Lessing, have indicated through "childhood's end" a changing human consciousness, Virginia Hamilton is the first writer for children to see such transformation toward a new human race as a mystical necessity, a view that has its roots in her earlier novel, *The Planet of Junior Brown*. Hamilton's work underlines the fact that ESP and other psychological and psychic traits, increasingly to be found in fiction, really have little to do with either science fiction or fantasy in their classic forms. Since there does not seem to be any strong reason to expand the definitions of science fiction or fantasy, perhaps what Hamilton is offering is in fact a new genre. Is it too early to suggest that what we have here is the emergence of the parapsychological novel? (pp. 150-52)

> *Sheila A. Egoff, "Realistic Fiction" and "Science Fiction," in her* Thursday's Child: Trends and Patterns in Contemporary Children's Literature, *American Library Association, 1981, pp. 31-65, 130-58.**

LIZA G. BLISS

Justice and Her Brothers, Book One in *The Justice Cycle*, happens on the Quinella Trace, on our planet in our time. Eleven-year-old Justice and her older twin brothers come to recognize their interrelated supersensory powers. Justice has the Watcher in her, and with Thomas (the Magician) and Levi (who "suffered for them all") and their neighbor Dorian (the Healer), she forms the First Unit.

Book Two, *Dustland*, is set someplace, sometime else. The unit has traveled through the Crossover into a land of dust, inhabited by desperate Slakers and the golden, dog-like Miacis. Is it a nuked-out planet Earth? A zoo? A prison? When? Where? Why does the powerful Mal want the unit away from the dustwalkers?

In Book Three, *The Gathering*, Justice transfers the Watcher to Colossus machine. Now complete, Colossus will work through the thousand years of Reclaimen, extending domity (Dustland's green part).

Throughout the three books, the same themes are carried through numerous perspectives and seen against many backdrops: family relationships, the nature of being, the politics of power, the nature of communications, ecological balance, historical continuity. Together they form a complicated descriptive statement, gratifying to receive, about life. The cycle has everything going for it: imagination, variety, suspense, all executed with a brilliance of clarity and symmetry. The storytelling style is beautiful in its melody, its flow, and its ability to enchant. It's a sophisticated work: it calls for a reader who bothers both to concentrate and to believe. Re-reading reveals even more richness in the story and quality in the craft.

Since the cycle is demanding (Hamilton at her best is usually demanding) and puzzling (fantasy at its best is usually puzzling) and unexpected (though its style's charm is reminiscent of the soul of Hamilton's *Time-Ago Tales of Jahdu*, the *Justice Cycle*'s complicated structure makes a comparison silly), some readers have been miffed. Whether those qualities are nuisances or delights, of course, depends on the attitude of the reader. For those who let it, the *Justice Cycle* will show a striking new side of a trusted author.

> *Liza G. Bliss, in a review of "The Justice Cycle," in* Kliatt Young Adult Paperback Book Guide, *Vol. XVI, No. 1, Winter, 1982, p. 21.*

NINA MIKKELSEN

If any event in children's literature involving the black child after 1932 [when Arna Bontemps and Langston Hughes defined a more positive ethnic identity for the black child in *Popo and Fifina*] had revolutionary implications, it was the publication in the late '60's of three landmark books: Virginia Hamilton's *Zeely* . . . , John Steptoe's *Stevie* (Harper, 1969) . . . , and June Jordan's *Who Look At Me* (Crowell, 1969). . . . (p. 121)

The decade of the eighties should be the best of times for the black child in children's books, for some of the finest work in children's literature today is being produced by black authors and illustrators. The real story is being told now, but we need to know even more. The novels of Virginia Hamilton, for example, are just beginning to show us the rich complexities and possibilities of the black experience. Hamilton's theme, she says, is based on the fact that characters are black and share the black experience of being up "against the wall," the entrenched American way of life; and to Hamilton, this is the black experience—the black child surviving and enduring and going beyond, growing in spirit so that he sees no difficulties in living with pride. Thus her characters survive in terms they themselves define, having grown beyond all known means of survival.

We need more books like Hamilton's *M. C. Higgins the Great* . . . that depict the values and feelings of the many different groups of black people within the greater American culture. We need to know more about the mixture of native American and black heritage in families, as Hamilton has depicted in *Arilla Sun Down* . . . , and as Hamilton herself says, there is much more to be written about the "huge amounts of comedy," of "folk humor and magic," that have not yet been explored in books about the black child's experiences in America [see excerpt above in Author's Commentary dated 1978]. (pp. 121-22)

As a new canon of black children's fiction and poetry has emerged in the last decade, its dominant themes closely connected to the central subjects of black adult fiction—defining the cultural history of black people and determining how the black person lives in this country—the properties of such a genre, as they are separated from mainstream children's literature, will no doubt be noted by critics. On the other hand, in the future as the black child is simultaneously attaining his cultural identity and becoming more easily assimilated into the American cultural mainstream, critics might instead find themselves examining this literature, not so much for whether it is written by the black or white author, not for whether it addresses itself specifically to the issues of black experience in America, but instead for the integrity of the book itself in the larger perspective of American children's literature, the way Northrop Frye describes all literature as "the entire range of articulate human imagination," and the way many now regard the works of such a writer as Hamilton, for their total effect rather than for their specialized focus. Hamilton herself stated in 1978 that "over the last decade I've become less preoccupied with my own roots . . . and the themes of the dark experience. Now I find myself curious about survivors of all kinds" [see excerpt above in Author's Commentary dated 1978].

In either case, hopefully both black and white writers of the future will be producing more stories of the caliber of Hamilton. We need such books, not because they tell the real or the entire story of the black child (for no one writer could possibly achieve this), nor because they avoid the problems of censorship (for any book is always a potential target of someone's dissent),

but for the wisdom they engender, at a time when our survival as a culture is so dependent upon this knowledge. (pp. 123-24)

Nina Mikkelsen, "Censorship and the Black Child: Can the Real Story Ever Be Told?" in Proceedings of the Ninth Annual Conference of the Children's Literature Association: The Child and the Story, an Exploration of Narrative Forms, *1982, pp. 117-27.**

RUDINE SIMS

[*In* Shadow and Substance: Afro-American Experience in Contemporary Children's Fiction, *Sims conducts a survey and analysis of 150 examples of contemporary realistic fiction about Afro-Americans published from 1969-79. Sims contrasts social conscience literature addressed to non-blacks, books with a "melting pot" theme, and a third group where the characters, settings, and perspectives are Afro-American. In the following excerpt, she calls Hamilton "the most daring of the writers represented in the survey."*]

Virginia Hamilton is possessed of an imagination as fertile as the Ohio farmland on which her extended family, the Perrys, grew and flourished. (p. 86)

Hamilton is the most daring of the writers represented in the survey and among the most skilled writers of contemporary children's literature. Her books are often multilayered, multifaceted, full of symbols, and deep enough to be mined again and again for new insights or just savored for the quality of her imagination. Her willingness to take risks also results, in each of her books, in a touch of the unusual, the eccentric, perhaps even the bizarre—a 262-pound musical prodigy who plays a silent piano, a boy sitting and swaying on top of a forty-foot pole near the top of a mountain, a six and one-half foot tall pigkeeper who looks like a Watusi queen. From her father's stories about Paul Robeson, Hamilton absorbed the impression that "if one were to become anything, it would have to be not only the best, but wholly original, a new idea. I grew up yearning for the unusual, seeking something unique in myself. I longed, not only to write, but to newly write, and like no one else. Kenneth Hamilton wanted no less for his youngest child." Kenneth Hamilton would not be disappointed.

Virginia Hamilton's five realistic novels are all steeped in her own experiences and those of her family and her people, though she also stated, in her Newbery Award acceptance speech [for *M. C. Higgins, the Great*], that she has "never written demonstrable and classifiable truths". . . .

Her work is not autobiographical in any direct sense. Earlier, in an article called "High John Is Risen Again" . . . , she had said of her work:

What I am compelled to write can best be described as some essence of the dreams, lies, myths, and disasters befallen a clan of my blood relatives. . . . Some essence, then, of their language and feeling, which through space-time imagery I project as the unquenchable spirit of a whole people. . . .

(pp. 86-7)

In Hamilton's realistic fiction, the dreams, lies, and myths, as well as the truths of her heritage, are woven into the fabric of the stories—sometimes a major part of the design, sometimes background against which the design is etched. (p. 87)

Arilla Sun Down is not an easy book to read. Its language is impressionistic. It is full of flashbacks and symbols—most notably the never-ending circle, a symbol of continuity. In all, it is rather unconventional children's literature.

Written during the same time period as Hamilton's realistic fiction were the two Jahdu books, ***The Time-Ago Tales of Jahdu . . .*** and ***Time-Ago Lost: More Tales of Jahdu. . . .*** Both are set in Harlem and involve Mama Luka, who pulls Jahdu stories out of the air to tell to James Edward, whom she cares for while his parents are at work. The books are a mixture of fantasy and realism. They are fablelike, and through them James Edward acquires insights into himself and life in general. . . .

Whether fantasy, fiction, or biography, Hamilton writes about survivors. Her fantasy books move away from her personal heritage, but they continue the survival theme. Her realistic fiction, like some of the works of Clifton and Greenfield, stresses her heritage and, through it, the heritage and essence of a people. She, like Clifton and Greenfield, also stresses continuity—the circle in ***Arilla Sun Down,*** the legacy of ***Dies Drear,*** the circle that begins and ends with Sarah in ***M. C. Higgins, the Great.*** And while she plays with space-time imagery, she also stresses human emotions, human relationships, and human connections. (p. 89)

> Rudine Sims, "The Image-Makers," in her Shadow and Substance: Afro-American Experience in Contemporary Children's Fiction, *National Council of Teachers of English,* 1982, pp. 79-102.*

MARILYN APSELOFF

Yellow Springs, a small town in Ohio, was both the birthplace of Virginia Hamilton and the inspiration for the settings of most of her novels. Hamilton has transformed familiar settings into something new and sometimes startling; although ***Zeely, The House of Dies Drear, M. C. Higgins the Great, Arilla Sun Down,*** and the ***Justice Cycle*** trilogy all use Yellow Springs settings, no one reading those novels has any feeling of sameness from one to the other. Certainly characterization and plot are unique in each book, but creative geography also adds to their originality.

The seeds of Hamilton's versatility can be found in ***Zeely.*** . . . Here the Yellow Springs setting is principally farmland, the actual fields behind Virginia Hamilton's present home and the remembered farms of her uncles. Since her parents had raised hogs and chickens and had grown vegetables, she drew upon her background for the composite fictional farm of Geeder's uncle. . . . The fictional woods, based upon the glen of her childhood, will be more prominently featured in later novels. These realistic details, in giving a strong sense of place to ***Zeely,*** help to create the atmosphere that is necessary in this book about personal identity and maturation.

The next novel, ***The House of Dies Drear*** . . . , presents another view of Yellow Springs. This time the focus is on the limestone formations of the area, its hills and caves, a much more appropriate setting for a mystery. The house was based upon an actual place, Dies House, that Hamilton used to pass when she was a child (it no longer exists). Then it was "a narrow, abandoned Gothic mansion" that "gave her shivers of fear as she walked by—sometimes just for that purpose!" Another feature of Yellow Springs, Antioch College, is introduced in this novel, although it is not mentioned by name: Mr. Small, the protagonist's father, will be teaching history there, and his office and some of the buildings are described as he takes his family on a tour of the campus. Hamilton remembers eating in the college dining room with her family when she was a

child, and she incorporates that experience, refined in the telling, into her book.

The town is also described as Mr. Small shows his family the area; and the main street, Xenia Avenue, is actually named (in an interview, Hamilton told me, "People at home get a kick out of it."). Because this is a mystery, however, the brooding Dies House with its secret tunnels and the caves nearby is the principal setting, helping to intensify the mood and create tension. . . . (p. 17)

One of the characters, Mr. Pluto, actually lives in a cave whose secret room contains a rich treasure, a key to the past. Here the setting helps to connect past and present, as Thomas and his father piece together the mystery of Dies Drear. The Yellow Springs landscape and history provide ***The House of Dies Drear*** with the realism that is needed to frame the story's mystery.

Hamilton moved to New York City for a few years, and during that time the urban setting made a deep impression on her and influenced the settings of her two Jahdu books and ***The Planet of Junior Brown.*** Ohio was where her roots were, however, so she returned to Yellow Springs with her husband [poet/anthologist Arnold Adoff] and two children, bought some land from her mother, and built her present home. Her next novel, ***M. C. Higgins, the Great*** . . . , marked a return to Ohio settings. Again a feature of Yellow Springs is used, Glen Helen, which she explored as a child as did her brothers before her. (pp. 17-18)

Creative geography is at work here; Glen Helen has been transposed to an area along the Ohio River. Sarah's Mountain, with its top cut off because of strip mining and with its slag heap gradually descending upon the Higgins family, is also a part of Hamilton's imagination. But as she suggested to me, the glen itself and her love for it that shows through are real:

> I do know the glen very well, all the paths . . .
> I know how the land looks, the ravines and the
> ridges; that part of Ohio is nothing but a series
> of ridges. Of course you can't see them when
> you're walking, but I think that over ten to
> fifteen years you begin to surmise how they
> must look, how the weather affects it and so
> forth. That's what I was trying to write about.

Because the setting is vivid, believable through the richness of details given about it, the unusual characters are more acceptable. The Killburn clan, for example . . . do not seem nearly as exotic or unreal as they might if the setting did not help to anchor them to reality.

Setting is also used in this novel to reveal character. M. C. fears the slag heap, recognizing its deadly descent, and he tries to get his family to leave the mountain. His father, however, refuses to go, for his ancestors came to Sarah's Mountain:

> to think a solid piece of something big belongs
> to you. To your father, and his, too . . . And
> you to it, for a long kind of time. . . .

There his people are buried, and he feels that he cannot leave: his roots are too deep. . . .

Setting also reveals the effects of strip mining. The top of Sarah's Mountain, now flat and bald, was "where M. C. and his father once hunted wild game." . . .

In this novel setting is both cause and effect. It isolates the characters, and makes them suspicious but curious about strangers who come into their midst. Characters are tested by the setting: M. C. was rewarded with his pole when he swam the Ohio River, and the stranger, Lurhetta Outlaw, proves herself when she goes through the underwater tunnel with M. C. and then admits that she cannot swim. The other stranger, the dude, knows that Banina Higgins's voice is meant for the hills, not for the stage where her naturalness will be changed; he wants her voice left unspoiled, "like these hills were here unspoiled and beautiful in my father's time." . . . Lurhetta sees how isolation has drawn families closer together as she witnesses the loving relationships of the Higginses and the Killburns. In this, setting has a profound impact.

Hamilton used Glen Helen in her next novel, *Arilla Sun Down* . . . , but only as a part of the book's locale. This time the town of Yellow Springs (not named in the novel) and its environs are featured. Just as Jones Higgins was rooted to the mountain, Arilla's mother, Lillian Perry Adams, has her roots in the town. . . . Here there is no threatening slag heap, but a problem of identity . . . Flashbacks in truncated speech reveal [Arilla's] "rememories" of her early childhood in an Amerind setting, which serves as a contrast to the present where actual places are used: the Municipal Building, the park, streets and highways, the college, the glen, and the roller-skating rink.

The activities of a small town help to reveal the characters. The incident on the Fourth of July at Spangler Park (much larger in the novel than in reality) puts Jack in sharp focus; Arilla's birthday party at her mother's dance studio reveals much about the girl and her friends; and the escapade at the skating rink shows the reader still another side to the relationship between Arilla and Jack. The glen is the setting for the climactic ice storm, in which Jack is hit by a falling bird and his horse falls on him. (p. 18)

In the novel, Arilla comments about what writing is: "changing things around and disguising the for-real." . . . Hamilton has done just that. For example, the skating rink no longer exists; like Dies House, it was a part of the past, not the present. The glen is certainly a very different place from the way it was presented in *M. C. Higgins, the Great,* and is closer to actuality in *Arilla.* Again actual street names are used, and the technical college in the novel is based upon Antioch. The effect on the people in such a town is given: the "town kids" copy the "college kids" in the novel. . . . These realistic touches, combined with a strong sense of place, make the memorable characters more believable.

Virginia Hamilton's next project was a cycle of three tales, called the *Justice Cycle* after the protagonist. . . . Again the setting is Yellow Springs, although the town is not specifically named. Again there is a college, this time located twenty miles outside of town and called Marks College; Mrs. Douglass is a student there. Actual street names are used, including the location of Hamilton's present home, "the lane and her [Justice's] house were situated at the end of a narrow blacktop road called Union. At the entrance of the property was an enormous cottonwood tree". . . . Dayton Street, where Hamilton's mother lives, is also named. Other streets in Yellow Springs have been fictionalized: Grinell Road, for example, has become Quinella Road. Quinella Trace is based upon a stream that used to exist, but it was not the leech-infested water that it has become in *Justice.* The field behind the Douglass house where the children meet and where Thomas does his drumming is the field behind Hamilton's own home, complete with the towering osage hedgerow.

Where *Arilla Sun Down* dealt with the past and the present as Arilla searched for her identity, *Justice and Her Brothers* is concerned primarily with the future and with survival; the present is used to reveal the characters, to prepare the reader for the unit's trips into the future which will take place in the next two books. The *Arilla* setting was primarily in the town, but in *Justice* the concentration is on outlying areas such as the Trace and the road leading to it and the field behind the house. Also, a new element has been added, an unmitigating, unnatural heat wave with its consequent build-up of dust that covers everything and creates a different atmosphere from the previous novels. This new subject matter and very different tone leave the reader with no feeling of similarity between *Arilla* and *Justice,* despite the use of Yellow Springs for the setting of both.

Dustland . . . , the second book of the trilogy, is set primarily in the future. The reader later discovers that the novel began at the future site of Quinella Trace. . . . When the children return to the present at the end of the book, they are joined together there at Quinella Trace, where Dorian's mother, Mrs. Jefferson, has been anxiously awaiting their return. It is very late at night, and as Mrs. Jefferson and the children walk home, the streets of Yellow Springs provide a sharp contrast to the barren landscape of Dustland and its inhabitants, mutants and creatures who have evolved the ability to cope with an environment quite different from the southern Ohio town of the present. To evoke a stronger sense of place and create a welcoming atmosphere, Hamilton mentions specific streets and sights of the town as the group nears their homes.

The last book of the trilogy, *The Gathering* . . . , completes the cycle. The four children, the "unit of power," have joined hands while seated beneath the buckeye tree of the previous novels, ready to go into the future once more while Mrs. Jefferson watches over their bodies. (pp. 18-19)

The theme of the trilogy is survival: who will survive, and why? The setting establishes mood and creates situations that inhabitants must adapt to or perish. The characters in the future settings, then, are those people and creatures who have adapted or who are mutations that have developed. Special emphasis is placed upon how new characters have evolved, and the unit's return to the present after their Dustland and Sona experiences provides contrast and a framework for the theme. There is still the richness of the August fields and hedgerows and the love for the area that Justice feels and communicates to the reader, all the more vivid after the stay in Dustland and Sona.

Virginia Hamilton's latest novel, again has a southern Ohio setting, this time the Xenia-Wiberforce area. But it is another departure from what she has previously written. *Sweet Whispers, Brother Rush* . . . is a ghost story, but not a traditional one. Teresa, called Tree, fourteen, cares for her older but retarded brother Dabney (Dab) who is increasingly and mysteriously debilitated. Their mother is away for long periods on live-in jobs as a practical nurse. Because of her infrequent visits home to replenish the larder, she has not observed Dab's worsening condition. When the groceries are running low again, Tree first sees Brother Rush on the street as she heads home from school. Handsome and well-dressed, he takes her breath away; but when he later reappears in her room in the apartment with his body *through* a table, Tree realizes that he is a ghost. Through a mirror-like disc that he holds, Tree, and sometimes Dab, sees their family's past and Tree learns that Dab had been badly mistreated by their mother. Later she also learns that all of her mother's brothers died of porphyria, a little-known hereditary disease that now attacks Dab. Their father, whom Tree presumed was dead, deserted the family years ago.

Although specific streets and places are named, the richness of description found in the previous novels is missing, intentionally so, it seems, to create the necessary isolation of the children. Tree has no friends, for her life revolves around Dab and her mother's infrequent visits. She purposely avoids getting friendly with people in her apartment building so that her circumstances will not be revealed. She even has no past until Brother Rush begins to show it to her; since her mother's visits home are sporadic, when they are briefly together they concentrate on the present. The ghostly flashbacks sometimes give specifics of place, but the atmosphere evokes a season more than a specific locale. The apartment is central, especially the little room where Brother Rush appears; street names used en route to the hospital give verisimilitude but are perhaps used primarily to entertain readers in southern Ohio who would recognize them.

Relationships are of primary importance: the "sweet whispers" are the revelations about Tree's family years earlier, of their interaction and fates. Through this knowledge of the past comes a new understanding of her life. Time, then, is connected with characters and events rather than strongly with place. Virginia Hamilton's focus has always been on people; that focus is intensified in her latest novel. When Tree is with Brother Rush, she often feels herself to be part of her mother, as well as the child she is, bound inextricably to both. Virginia Hamilton has felt a similar kinship in her own family as one generation's story becomes a part of the next. For example, the sudden falling of the ivy from a house when Brother Rush is killed is from a tale told to Virginia by her mother. (p. 19)

Virginia Hamilton does not use geography for isolated references, dropping street names that stand out like raisins in raisin bread; instead, she uses realistic settings as stepping-stones to create landscapes, vividly real, that frame her fiction and establish mood. The rural summer setting in *Zeely* is languid, but the tempo picks up in *Dies Drear* with its Gothic overtones. The hills of the Higgins family sing a different song with an ominous note as the slag heap inches closer, and with the shift to the town setting in *Arilla,* there is an echo of drumbeats. More discordant music is felt throughout the *Justice Cycle* with its strained relationships and looks to the future, to survival. Finally, *Sweet Whispers, Brother Rush* combines harmony and dissonance as mood and situations change. (p. 20)

Marilyn Apseloff, *"Creative Geography in the Ohio Novels of Virginia Hamilton,"* in Children's Literature Association Quarterly, *Vol. 8, No. 1, Spring, 1983, pp. 17-20.*

DAVID REES

There is no doubt that Virginia Hamilton can write: as a painter of landscape or the creator of the apposite image and the memorably concise perception, only Paula Fox, Betsy Byars and Ursula Le Guin are her rivals among contemporary American writers of fiction for children. But the journey from *Zeely* to *Sweet Whispers, Brother Rush,* to borrow a phrase used twice in *Arilla Sun Down,* is "a long ride through a painted desert." Only two of her nine novels—*Zeely* and *M. C. Higgins, the Great*—are one hundred per cent successful, though *Sweet Whispers, Brother Rush* has some fine passages; in all the others there is some major flaw that spoils the finished product. In *The House of Dies Drear* and *The Planet of Junior Brown* it is credibility: the reader cannot believe in the reality of events

and people; these two books are fantasies, not reflections of deeply felt life. In *Arilla Sun Down* and *Justice and Her Brothers* there are too many words and not enough space between the words: narrative is slow to the point, at times, of tedium; page after page of descriptive prose with very little dialogue leaves the characters seen dimly, as if through a fog. The last two stories of the Justice trilogy, *Dustland* and *The Gathering,* suffer—as do some of Peter Dickinson's books—from too much concentration on technological paraphernalia; the characters do not develop, so their reactions and thought processes become predictable. The writing from *Arilla Sun Down* onwards is at times unnecessarily obscure or so fussy with detail that it acts as a barrier between the reader and the material; a child in particular may well give up the struggle:

> "Hur'm up, Strider!" Softly Run. Run making a squeaking with his mouth. Strider rushing into the wind. The town I see come quickly. Town spilling along crease of hills like scattering rocks. James-Face saying something as hooves pounding fast. We soon slow down and do not go into a town. Edge of crease, I see our house. Sun-up has not reached it. House always in shade. Is dark, as if we do not live there. Darkly hides among tall trees. Is James-Face a tall tree the first time I'm seeing him?

Individually the images in this quotation from *Arilla Sun Down,* which attempts to suggest a twelve-year-old remembering early childhood, work well, but there are too many of them, and the odd sentence structures which omit all sorts of key words sound pretentious. Few editors would allow the work of lesser writers to go to press in this way. In *The Gathering* difficulty comes from another kind of linguistic experimentation; there is a use here not of too many images but an excess of space jargon. . . . In the books from *Arilla Sun Down* to *The Gathering* language is often an endurance test, not a pleasure.

Yet the prose in *Zeely,* Virginia Hamilton's first novel, is uncluttered and luminous; sentences rise and fall with a poetry that leaves the reader admiring the clarity of thought and language, the vivid pictures—"The waning day she saw as clear as morning in the country; her father's words, bright as sunlight in the fields;" and "Long streets looked like spokes of a wheel connected to nothing and going nowhere."

> What they saw was no ordinary sight. They watched, spellbound, for nothing in the world could have prepared them for the sight of Miss Zeely Tayber.
>
> Zeely Tayber was more than six and a half feet tall, thin and deeply dark as a pole of Ceylon ebony. She wore a long smock that reached to her ankles. Her arms, hands and feet were bare, and her thin, oblong head didn't seem to fit quite right on her shoulders.
>
> She had very high cheekbones and her eyes seemed to turn inward on themselves . . .
>
> Zeely's long fingers looked exactly like bean pods left a long time in the sun.

This is as effective as anything Virginia Hamilton wrote in the books that followed: direct, simple description with the occasional image—the pole of Ceylon ebony, the fingers like bean pods—showing that the writer, even in this first novel, can use language with remarkable originality.

Zeely is a long short story for children; all Virginia Hamilton's subsequent work—with the exception of the two collections of Jahdu stories, *The Time-Ago Tales of Jahdu* and *Time-Ago Lost: More Tales of Jahdu*—has a teenage audience in mind. It is a pity she has not written more for younger readers, for *Zeely* has a straightforward, unpretentious narrative, clear-cut portraits of people, and in Geeder a sympathetic, highly imaginative central character. *Too* imaginative: that is the moral of the book. So "spellbound" is Geeder by Miss Tayber's looks and apparently odd behavior that she decides Zeely must be an African Queen, enslaved against her will by her brutal father to look after his hundreds of prize hogs; she goes around telling people this romantic nonsense, and eventually Zeely hears about it. There could, of course, be trouble at this point, but, in Geeder, Zeely recognizes herself when young, and while gently telling the girl that in everyday life she should stick to the facts, she also encourages her to cling to and develop the gifts of her imagination. "I stopped making up tales a long time ago," she says, "and now I am myself," but she adds, "You have a most fine way of dreaming. Hold onto that."

There is too much "dreaming" and not enough fact in *The House of Dies Drear,* which is a disappointment after *Zeely.* Its intentions are admirable, its background exciting. Virginia Hamilton's ancestors were slaves who fled from the South in the first half of the nineteenth century; "perhaps," she says (in an author's note in *The House of Dies Drear*), "with this book I have at last touched them the way they first touched me so long ago." The implausibility of much of the plot, however, stops the reader from being touched in the way she hoped. The Small family leave their home in North Carolina to live in Ohio (thus making the same journey as their black forefathers.) The house they rent had been used a hundred and fifty years previously as a staging post on one of the slaves' main escape routes; it belonged to Dies Drear, an abolitionist from a wealthy New England shipbuilding background. The house has many secret passages and false walls in which blacks on the run were hidden in times of trouble; the local community nowadays believes it is haunted. So far, so good: first-class material from which to fashion a story, though it is difficult to accept that Mrs. Small would agree to live in a haunted house. Unfortunately the author is not content with this. The neighbors, the Darrow family, try to frighten the Smalls into leaving the house because they think that hidden somewhere in it is a vast horde of treasure amassed by Dies Drear, and they want to get hold of it for themselves. The treasure does exist, in fact; it's hidden in an underground cave and has long ago been discovered by the caretaker of the house, Mr. Pluto, who himself lives in a cave. (The too obvious symbolic name Pluto, king of the underworld, is only one of many examples of clumsy thinking in this novel.) Mr. Pluto is old and ill, so his son, an actor, impersonates him, and together with the Small family he terrifies the Darrows into behaving themselves properly for the foreseeable future. This is all completely unbelievable: hidden treasure, greedy villains, ghosts and impersonations of ghosts belong to another genre than the one Virginia Hamilton probably wanted to explore; slave ancestry and color of skin are important and absorbing matters, but here they seem to be devalued into stage props, unlike, for example, similar material in Mildred Taylor's *Roll of Thunder, Hear My Cry.* The action is observed through the eyes of young Thomas Small, but he is not an interesting character out of whom events evolve; he is only a rather two-dimensional device for relaying the story to the reader. His parents are not much more than stereotypes, and the Plutos, father and son, are downright embarrassing. Yet the quality of the writing often impresses:

> The house of Dies Drear sat on an outcropping, much like a ledge, on the side of the hill. The face of the ledge was rock, from which gushed mineral springs. And these came together at the fertile land, making a narrow groove through it before emptying into the stream. Running down the face of the ledge, the springs coated the rock in their path with red and yellow rust.
>
> Thomas stared so long at the ledge and springs, his eyes began to play tricks on him. It seemed as if the rust moved along with the spring waters.
>
> "It's bleeding," he said softly.

The same problems exist in *The Planet of Junior Brown.* Here is a writer who certainly knows how to use words:

> A few trees struggled to grow in an atmosphere choked with automobile exhaust fumes. Junior found all of it beautiful—the stunted trees, the winter-brown plants and the old men and women. Out of the cheap retirement rooms of the side streets, the lonely old people rested awhile, like lost bundles on the cold, sunny benches.

All the characters are strange misfits. . . . Buddy Clark—intended as a sharp contrast to this bunch of grotesques—is the least convincing character of all. . . . There is not a trace of delinquency in him, not a hint of squalor in the basement where he camps out; he is every inch a saint. This might perhaps be credible if he were an adult with a wide and rich experience of life, but he's a boy of thirteen. As it is impossible to believe in the reality of the characters, it is difficult to be sympathetic to their problems or care very much about what happens to them; so ultimately, therefore, the reader may well become bored. The pace of the narrative is slower than in the previous books, though not as slow as in *Arilla Sun Down* or *Justice and Her Brothers,* and the astronomical symbolism, besides being simplistic and intrusive, shows little real connection between the "planet" of homeless children and Mr. Pool's solar system with its extra planet called Junior Brown.

In *M. C. Higgins, the Great* there is credible plot and convincing characterization, which, combined with the author's writing skills and talents, lead to her most satisfying book since *Zeely;* it is indeed a much finer achievement than *Zeely* as its range and depth are far greater. Landscape plays a more important role in this novel than any other of Virginia Hamilton's: we are in a remote mountainous part of Ohio; it is a landscape that has moulded the character of the few people who live there, including the protagonists of the book, M. C. and his parents, Jones and Banina Higgins. . . . It is impossible, when reading this book, not to be reminded of the tragedy that occurred in 1967 at Aberfan in Wales, when a heap of slurry crashed down a mountain-side and killed some eighty children who were in a school at the time: they were buried alive. Jones refuses to believe that the danger is real; even discussing the subject annoys him. But M. C. knows they will have to move. The idea of moving is effectively combined with M. C.'s knowledge that he is growing up—the idyllic mountain country becomes synonymous with childhood, and at thirteen he knows, regretfully, that he has to leave childhood behind. The other features of the story are simple and few. M. C. has a brief friendship with a girl he meets—his first experience of adolescence rather than childhood, and it is a transitory, bittersweet relationship, not at all like the certainties of his earlier life. . . . [By the end of the book he] has abandoned the idea of leaving, perhaps leaving the family; the last few pages show him for once contented and peaceful with his parents, brothers, sisters, and friends . . .—but it is no happy ending; the reader is left with the ominous sensation that tragedy will inevitably occur, just as it would be tragic not to move out of childhood. No wall, however massive and strong, can possibly hold back the force of thousands of tons of slurry. Or the arrival of adulthood. The wall's symbolic intention is similar to the use Jan Mark makes of the hole Matthew digs in *Under the Autumn Garden.*

All the characters in this book, even the mysterious interbred Killburns with their six fingers on each hand and reputations as witches, are complex, rounded, living people, and the different layers of love and caring, anger and irritation, in the Higgins family are totally convincing. Jones is a delightful portrait of a man who is at the age when he begins to regret the loss of his youthfulness; his eldest child, M. C., he regards with a mixture of affection and threat: M. C. is starting to compete with him on almost equal terms. This is neatly implied in the way Virginia Hamilton describes him:

> Jones was a powerfully built man. He wasn't tall, but he had a broad chest and lean but wide, muscular shoulders. He was narrow through the hips just as M. C. was, and his legs were long with muscles grown lengthwise. His toes were splayed with the bridge flattened wide, as were M. C.'s, the way a swimmer's feet will look. Jones was a swimmer. But somehow, his fine, physical equipment had never quite come together. As a man, he wasn't as good a swimmer as M. C. was right now.
>
> What will I be, at his age? M. C. wondered.
>
> *Be on this mountain,* his mind spoke for Jones.
>
> No, M. C. thought.

The relationship between M. C. and Jones is one of the most impressive father-son relationships in contemporary children's literature. We see a great deal, too, of the life M. C. shares with his mother, and also glimpses of his parents' marriage (a stable, loving, committed marriage), but if these are less striking, and Banina less frequently observed than Jones, that is because everything is viewed through M. C.'s eyes: he is at an age when his father is more important to him than his mother is. Again, it is part of the contrast between childhood and adolescence that is such a major theme in this novel—Banina represents for M. C. the certainties and happiness of childhood; Jones, he is aware, is not unlike what he will be himself because Jones is a man; his father, in this sense, represents the future as well as the past.

Landscape, as I said, is ever present, and so is the weather; Virginia Hamilton's prose brings this background vividly alive. . . . (pp. 168-76)

M. C. Higgins, the Great is a very fine achievement and thoroughly deserved the awards of the Newbery Medal and the National Book Award it received. . . .

Arilla Sun Down suffers from the old fault of some improbable characters, and a narrative pace that is far too slow. Events and people are smothered by the words: lengthy asides, interesting in themselves, distract the reader's attention, and descriptive passages lose their effect in language that is at times

unnecessarily complex. Almost all the characters in Virginia Hamilton's novels are black, but this is not a point worth discussing any more than it is worthwhile to speculate on why Alan Garner's characters are all white—except in **Arilla Sun Down,** where race *is* an issue. The Adams family are part black, part Indian; there is conflict between the women (Arilla and her mother) who think this is a matter of little importance, and the men (her father and her brother, Jack Sun Run) who are aware—or think they are aware—of the sad implications of their lost Indian heritage. This theme should, perhaps, have provided the book's main interest, but it gets lost under the weight of surface detail; it is only at the end that it seems more important than it has appeared to be, when Arilla chooses her Indian name—Sun Down. The plot moves from one lengthy static scene to another. The evening at the skating rink, Arilla's birthday party (odd—and oddly repetitive—that in most of Virginia Hamilton's novels the central character has a birthday party), the fourth of July celebrations when Jack Sun Run lassos two men he thinks have been rude to him, the snowstorm— all are big set-pieces, elaborate and leisurely like a carefully composed photograph: one is never aware of the excitement of a continuously developing narrative. The telling of the story is in two styles—Arilla's memories of early childhood, fragmentary, confusing, and written, as I said earlier, with most of the key words left out; and Arilla speaking quite normally as a twelve-year-old girl. The two styles do not harmonize well, for each shows up the other's inadequacies.

Jack Sun Run is quite unbelievable. At fifteen his skill with horses, his courage and judgment, are those of an experienced and mature man; as with Buddy Clark in **The Planet of Junior Brown** we are not really seeing a teenager at all, but an adult. (Even M. C. Higgins seems older than thirteen; his thinking processes and feelings are often those of a boy of at least fifteen.) The way Jack Sun Run is constantly presented as some kind of god is wearisome. . . . Maybe it is the first person narration that is the major fault. Though Arilla perceives her parents' placement of themselves in the town's social strata quite clearly, her eyes are, for the most part, too hazy to see character and event as having independent lives of their own.

Justice and Her Brothers, Dustland, and **The Gathering** form a trilogy called **The Justice Cycle.** These three books are works of science fiction, and the author seems as happy in this genre as she is in the realistic stories that had previously been her preoccupation. She says she feels less involved with her own heritage now and more interested in survivors. "Will the few who survive the cataclysm do so because they are genetically different?" she asks (in an author's note in **Dustland**). "Is it possible that telepathy, prophecy, and genius are genetic mutations? Could the striking talents of a few be the means of survival for many?" But the central character of the trilogy, the eleven-year-old girl, Justice, is involved to a great degree with her family, her roots, with the difficult and inharmonious relationship between her twin brothers, Thomas and Levi— there are several resonances here with other novels about twins, Katherine Paterson's *Jacob Have I Loved,* for example, and Penelope Farmer's *Year King*— and she uses the knowledge and power gained from the adventures she and her brothers have in the future to help heal the wounds of her family in the present.

The first hundred pages of **Justice and Her Brothers** give few hints to the reader that the story will ultimately be concerned with children who have extraordinary powers of extra-sensory perception, who have the ability to read minds and project themselves into the future. This first part of the book has an almost snail's pace narrative; place, weather, family, friends are portrayed in great detail, and the story seems to be revolving around only one event, the Great Snake Race that Thomas has organized for the kids of the neighborhood. It comes as quite a surprise when the novel departs from the realistic tale we have assumed it is going to be, but the clues are there; the science fiction genre to which it belongs isn't an afterthought, tacked on, as it were, because the author felt her realistic story was not going to function properly. *Justice and Her Brothers* is concerned with the development of the children's amazing abilities, not with the use to which those abilities are put— that is the function of *Dustland* and *The Gathering*. It is also concerned with the pattern of relationships in the Douglass family and the delineation of character. This, I think, is in some ways a mistake from a structural point of view; it leaves no room in the second and third books for development of character, for change. We know that whatever happens, Thomas is always the odd one out; the one who for entirely selfish reasons puts the other two and their friend, Dorian Jefferson, into some kind of danger; who, whatever happens, dislikes Justice because she has more power than he has. Levi is always the one who suffers most from Thomas's neurotic behavior; Dorian—whose character is never fully explored—invariably manages to heal him. (pp. 176-80)

Dustland and *The Gathering* are different from *Justice and Her Brothers,* less reflective, less analytical, more concerned with the creation of imaginary worlds. In *Dustland,* Virginia Hamilton's vision of the future on planet Earth, civilization destroyed apart from a few extraordinary creatures who have managed to survive the holocaust, the surface of the world totally barren, a desert of dust so thick that even the air chokes the sunlight, is a powerful and bleak picture of what just possibly could happen. Her gift for language, however, for the first time falters occasionally; the vague adverb or adjective is used when more precise descriptive words are needed: "They had passed through Dustland's unbelievable dawn an hour ago." No comment other than the dawn being "unbelievable" is unsatisfactory. It is a small fault, but it is also present in *The Gathering;* and in this final part of the trilogy language is sometimes used in a solemn, quasi-biblical way—"What was there they saw, yet did not see"—as if an attempt is being made to suggest a significance that the author has not otherwise justified. . . . There is quite a large collection of the usual bug-eyed monsters and intergalactic hardware one finds in a great deal of space fiction; Virginia Hamilton's creatures and machines are no more and no less convincing than those of several other writers. (One is reminded a little of the domed cities and strange beings in John Christopher's *City of Gold and Lead.*) Too much emphasis is given in *The Gathering* to these imaginings of future life: the result is that this novel has not enough narration, too much explanation. *Dustland,* therefore, is, of the three books, the most enjoyable to read.

Sweet Whispers, Brother Rush, though the first few chapters are slow, has a narrative that, for the most part, sets enough pace to hold the reader's attention, and the writing does not suffer from the obscurity that mars some of its predecessors; the result is Virginia Hamilton's best novel since *M. C. Higgins, the Great.* It is the story of fifteen-year-old Tree, left at home to look after her retarded elder brother, Dabney, while her mother is away in another town, working. Absence of mothers is a recurring theme in Virginia Hamilton's work— Justice's mother attends classes at college, Arilla's mother teaches long hours at a dance studio. In *Sweet Whispers, Brother*

Rush, the father is also missing—Ken deserted his wife and kids long ago. Tree is a very deprived child; when her mother's boy friend, Silversmith, takes her to a cafeteria, "She'd never seen such good-looking Jello, green and yellow and red and orange." When Silversmith says they'll take her out dancing, she says, "'Me?' Tree was astonished. 'Dancin? Me?'" Parental deprivation, however, is much worse for her than the absence of the ordinary pleasures of life. Her complex relationship with her mother, Vy, is the center of the book—a relationship that is at times warm and loving, but Tree is also angry and embittered by her mother's selfishness and the cold way she treats Dabney. Tree's love for her brother is a crucial element in the story. Elder brothers being important to younger sisters is another recurring theme of Virginia Hamilton's—it has a large place in the *Justice* trilogy and in *Arilla Sun Down:* but in *Sweet Whispers, Brother Rush* it is different in that it is without antagonism. Most of all, Tree is deprived of history— she knows nothing of her mother's background, her father, her uncles. It has been hidden from her, as it is from the reader for half of the book, and it is a tragic history—the uncles died young from porphyria, and the youngest (called Brother) let himself be killed in a car crash because he knew that he, too, was dying from the same disease. Dabney also dies of porphyria. It is a depressing, sad story; its message is, in the words of Silversmith,

> . . . you can't run away from what you've lost
> or what you love, either. I carried the love for
> my dad with me. I couldn't get away from it.
> I couldn't lose the loss of my mother.

But it ends hopefully—Silversmith is a good man, a substitute father for Tree; it seems probable that he will marry Vy, and his son Don begins to date Tree.

Tree discovers the family history through the appearance of the ghost of her Uncle Brother, which is an unsatisfactory device—in such a realistic novel as this, the use of the supernatural seems like a cheap short cut to give Tree knowledge: the author should have found a more convincing way of imparting information, particularly as the information, once given, leaves the ghost without any proper function in the story. Nevertheless, the need children have for a sense of the past, especially the past of their own families, is made convincing as Tree is so believable. . . . The prose style, though not easy, and on a few occasions pretentious—"It entered her mind, where her thoughts were shaken up and rearranged in preparation for that which was beyond her knowledge"—is on the whole excellent, uncluttered and musical, full of sharp, original observations. . . . It would seem that in *Sweet Whispers, Brother Rush,* Virginia Hamilton has, despite saying in *Dustland* that she is now more interested in survivors, returned to the idea of roots and heritage; in doing so she has produced a much more readable novel than any of those in the *Justice* trilogy.

The judgments in this essay may sound harsh, but Virginia Hamilton is too gifted an author to be assessed other than by the most exacting standards. Her achievement is not unlike that of Alan Garner: both are writers talented far more than most, but the books they have written—with a few exceptions— contain too many serious flaws. (pp. 180-83)

David Rees, "Long Ride through a Painted Desert— Virginia Hamilton," in his Painted Desert, Green Shade: Essays on Contemporary Writers of Fiction for Children and Young Adults, *The Horn Book Inc., 1984, pp. 168-84.*

M. C. HIGGINS, THE GREAT (1974)

They say the pity of youth is that it's wasted on the young. Since we're well into our thirties and because we love the stories of Virginia Hamilton we must agree. Before motherhood descended upon us we could curl up in a corner with *Zeely* or *The Planet of Junior Brown* and cry all alone remembering . . . wishing . . . hoping about a childhood of our dreams. Now we gather child, dog, and gerbils . . . around us . . . and share *M. C. Higgins, the Great*. Actually we're proud to share Virginia Hamilton with our family. They should know the good things.

M. C. Higgins is a very nice dude. He's just beginning to recognize girls as different from boys and basically worthy of kissing. But M. C. also has come into a recognition of responsibility. His family lives on Sarah's Mountain which, because of strip mining, is in danger of being deluged by the waste. M. C. doesn't quite understand that strip mining will forever change the countryside he has grown so used to but he does know his way of life is in danger. He dreams and ultimately plans a way to save his mountain.

The dream involves his mother. Banina Higgins has the best voice in the state and another dude with a tape recorder is coming to "take his mother's voice" and make her a star. M. C. is sure when the dude hears her sing that's exactly what he will do. But Ben Killburn isn't so sure. Ben is M. C.'s best friend though they have to keep that a secret since the Killburns are "strange people" and M. C.'s father, Jones, wants nothing to do with them.

Into M. C.'s and Ben's life comes Lurhetta, a girl who works all year during school so that she can roam the countryside in the summer. She is, as neither Ben nor M. C. are even likely to know, free. But with freedom comes always a price. The ability to take care of yourself, to follow your own wishes also compels you to travel alone. M. C. can leave Sarah's Mountain, can leave his stubborn father, can be free from watching his younger brothers and sisters but he will also be without roots. His great-grandmother Sarah had traveled to this mountain with a baby on her hip and the hounds of the slavemaster at her heels some hundred years ago. Could he, should he really turn that land over to those who only see the coal beneath . . . not the love . . . the sacrifice . . . the history the hill represents? . . . Mayo Cornelius Higgins makes the only decision a truly great person could make.

Once again Virginia Hamilton creates a world and invites us in. *M. C. Higgins, the Great* is not an adorable book, not a lived-happily-ever-after kind of story. It is warm, humane and hopeful and does what every book should do—creates characters with whom we can identify and for whom we care. M. C.'s plight may cause some to reconsider our acceptance of strip mining. Without extra coal some may be a bit cooler but with the extra coal many will be homeless and worse, rootless. Is that really fair? We're glad M. C. decided to build his wall with the headstones of his ancestors. Old Sarah gave her great-grandson not only the mountain but the ability to claim it. Virginia Hamilton has joined the forces of hope with the forces of dreams to forge a powerful story. We're glad Miss Hamilton is a writer. It makes the world just a little bit richer and our lives just a little bit warmer.

> *Nikki Giovanni, in a review of "M. C. Higgins, the Great," in* The New York Times Book Review, *September 22, 1974, p. 8.*

From her first novel, *Zeely,* onward through *M. C. Higgins,* Virginia Hamilton has been a mature and arresting writer; a storyteller of great originality and subtlety; a stylist; and a creator of rich, believable characters. It is amazing that a British publisher has waited this long to add her to its list. The explanations for this reticence are mystifying: "*very* American"; "language verging on the idiosyncratic"; "the black milieu is unfamiliar to English children", and so on. For the fact is that Hamilton is that rarest of authors—*an original*. It is perhaps the case that many of your young people will not understand her books. Those who do, however, will never forget them. There can be no better reason for publishing her.

M. C. Higgins tells a simple story artfully. . . . The sense of family feeling in the story is especially strong. Is it because the family lives apart from town life? Is it a "holy" family? Does poverty create family feeling in some while destroying it in others? In any event, this feeling appears in various ways in each of the family members—mother, father, M. C. and younger siblings. (p. 91)

Another remarkable facet of this book is its evocation of people in (as a part of, really) nature. M. C. and his mother come upon a doe as they walk in the hills:

> They had flushed the doe, coming on her blindly. She sprang up amidst the trees like a wind-up toy, swift and magical. Banina raised her hand as if to touch the deer's fluid shape and hold her wild motion.

Or again, when the two reach a lake that they think of as their own:

> M. C. felt warm sun on his back. Neither he nor Banina spoke, out of respect for the lake, for the dawn and the sun.

I'm not certain that the word innocent ever appears in *M. C. Higgins,* but the story is an exploration of the singularity in our society of innocence, not a naive, simple innocence but an informed innocence made out of choice. This kind of innocence means that a priority is placed on independence:

> It's just a way in the hills. . . . Whatever you want to say is fine. Most folks say what they want to say, but ask no questions.

And the independence explains all of the events in this glorious, inevitable story. (p. 92)

> *John Donovan, "American Dispatch," in* Signal, *No. 17, May, 1975, pp. 91-5.**

[*M. C. Higgins, the Great*] is a composite of rich interwoven themes, strengthened by vivid characterization and a deep sense of place. (p. 194)

There is magic in this book. Virginia Hamilton's style is mesmerizing, a combination of such poetic expressions as the description of a sunrise as "a brilliant gash ripped across the summit of Hall Mountain" and of such quaint mountain expressions as the remark Banina, M. C.'s lovely mother, makes about the mountain. She says it "must be what Sunday people call God Almighty. . . . High enough for heaven and older than anybody ever lived."

The symbols this author uses are also unique. M. C.'s forty-foot steel pole, his prize for swimming the Ohio River (the feat which he thinks gives him the right to the title "M. C. Higgins, the Great"), is unusual and significant, but its purpose is not quite clear. When M. C. climbs the pole and makes it move in "a slow, sweeping arc," he seems to have visionary glimpses of the past:

> As if past were present. . . . He sensed Sarah moving through undergrowth up the mountainside. . . . As if he were a ghost, waiting, and she, the living.

Again, the pole seems to be the pivot around which the whole story turns. Banina calls it "the marker for all of the dead," and, indeed, the bones of the ancestors are actually buried around the pole. Finally, it is the gravestones themselves, encased in the wall, that seem to be the cement that connects the living present to the past.

It is impossible to do justice to this many-faceted book. The beauty of the writing, the poetic imagery, the characters, each unique yet completely believable, and the original themes all make the reading of this book an unforgettable experience, and mark Virginia Hamilton as one of the most important of today's writers for children. (pp. 194-95)

> *Carol Vassallo, "A Miscellany: 'M. C. Higgins, the Great',"* in Children's Literature: Annual of the Modern Language Association Seminar on Children's Literature and The Children's Literature Association, *Vol. 4, 1975, pp. 194-95.*

M. C. Higgins, the Great was a landmark in several respects. Not only was the author able to convey a portion of black experience authentically, but she was able to do this in language and in narrative style that gives a reader a strong feeling for M. C.'s speech and his way of thinking. One librarian described it to me as stream-of-consciousness, which seems appropriate. The adult reader can recognize and appreciate Virginia Hamilton's creativity. It can be predicted, however, that the young reader may have difficulty with the book. And, indeed, the librarian reported the book as being "less popular" in her university-town library which draws many avid young readers.

One problem can occur as a consequence of telling M. C.'s story through his own mind's eye—M. C. becomes the audience for his own story. This in turn can become a problem for the young reader, who is used to, and has a tighter hold on, a more usual narrative form involving a setting, followed by certain actions and consequences. . . . From the opening words of *M. C.* we are running with him over terrain that catches and snags us, and we aren't sure where we are. This might not be a problem for the reader familiar with M. C.'s part of the country or his cultural group. But some young readers, particularly white, middle-class ones, may find themselves at a loss in trying to cope with an unfamiliar writing style, unfamiliar cultural group, and unfamiliar location all at the same time.

Schema theory suggests that we learn by attaching new information to schemata we already have about the world, and then by modifying our original schemata appropriately. What Adams and Collins (1977) describe as resource-limited processing can occur when a reader is too far out of her/his area of expertise and unable to make sense of the material. An adult might experience this in trying to comprehend a legal document. Children encounter some new material in any book they read, it is true, but it is material the child is able to accommodate because it is built on a familiar style of storytelling or a familiar setting or cultural group. All readers occasionally find themselves resource-limited. This is where the perceptive teacher

or librarian can be a help to the reader. By discussing with the child some basic traditions as they appear in this novel, bringing into play the reader's own knowledge of her/his own belief system, tying into folkloric information the reader already possesses, an appreciation of *M.C. Higgins, the Great* becomes more likely. (pp. 420-21)

[What] is the folklore, and what does it do for the novel? To answer this question, folklore collections were searched for parallels and variations of the lore discovered, but even more valuable was a telephone interview with author Virginia Hamilton who commented about particular beliefs in her book and where they had come from.

The two traditions that run through the book are the belief in witches and the use of traditional songs and song-types in a number of different situations. The basic belief in the book, which becomes one of its basic conflicts, concerns not only what a witch is and what it does, but also what physical characteristics a witch may be known by. From his parents, M. C. knows that the Killburns (Ben's family) are considered "witchy." The signs of their being witchy are found particularly in their red hair and in their six-digit fingers and toes. Jones tells M. C.,

> He, with skin so fair, he is near white. But hair is always thick and tight so you can tell, and always almost red. . . . For he is merino. Or witchy, as folks here always know him. . . .

To a young white reader, a witch may be the Halloween interpretation: white skin, dark hair, ugly, and dressed in black, with a broomstick and a black cat nearby. To this child, witches are make-believe; to M. C., they are real. His beliefs are easily collaborated in folklore collections, as in the *Frank C. Brown Collection of North Carolina Folklore* (VII, #5589, p. 112, collected in Texas): "A red-haired Negro is a witch. If he gives you a rabbit's foot, you have an all-powerful talisman against evil, and for good luck." Virginia Hamilton herself says,

> There was always a group of black people when I was a child called merinos. I don't know where the name comes from, but it has to do with having reddish hair and freckles and light skin. And you were never to trust a merino. Malcolm X was considered a merino by certain black people, and not trustworthy. It's an old, old superstition.

In M. C.'s belief system, if you were a witch, you had certain powers, among these the power of healing and of casting out devils. As an extension of this Ben reports that the Killburn men tried to heal the strip mining cuts in the mountain by laying hands on them. Witches also have the ability, according to M. C.'s beliefs, to mark people by touching them. . . .

Near the end of the novel, M. C. has caught a rabbit and killed it. When he returns to it after a visit to the Killburns, all its feet are missing. It is implied that the Killburns took them. Although the idea of a rabbit's foot being good luck is probably not new to any reader, possible special implications of its power in the hands of a witch have already been mentioned.

The belief about green-grass snakes in the book may be new to readers. Ben's father likes the snakes, but they have been misbehaving and are being punished by being kept in a box. N. N. Puckett in *Folk Beliefs of the Southern Negro* says, "such reptiles play a large role in Negro signs, and possibly represent a remnant of former voodoo snake worship" (1926,

p. 321). Add to that the Thompson *Motif-Index*'s mention of a "witch in form of snake" (1966, G211.8.1) and we begin to see how natural it is for Ben's father to have snakes in his barn, almost in the role of familiars.

In speaking to Hamilton, who had been reported in the *Horn Book* as having "absorbed the traditional lore and the story-telling inclination" of one side of her family . . . , it was interesting to find out what she was aware of as coming to her directly through oral transmission versus what she thought did not pass to her through oral tradition. About the mention of second sight in the book . . . , Hamilton said,

> Oh, that's just a device. It could come from anywhere. It's nothing specific out of my background. There's nobody that I know of, or anybody talked of, that had second sight.

In appraising the folklore in *M. C. Higgins, the Great,* we need to be aware not only of specific beliefs which motivate characters, but of the situations in which they occur. In real life, folklore is presented orally in varied ways. Sometimes it is a group presentation, with one person performing, followed by some type of audience response. Often, however, folklore is transmitted on a one-to-one basis. When two people have the opportunity to talk because they are relaxing or taking a rest from their work, or because their work does not take great concentration, the situation is right for the sharing of folklore. We see this in *M. C. Higgins* when Banina tells M. C. of her experience seeing Viola Killburn (Ben's mother) heal a child's leg. M. C. and his mother have stopped to rest in their climb to the mountain lake where they go for an early morning swim. In the presence of another person, the conversation probably would not have taken place. So it is in real life, when imparting strange or awkward information. The right situation, involving participants who are at ease with one another, contributes to the passing on of folklore.

Another example of a situation in which folklore is used is when the icemen (Ben's male relatives) appear at the Higgins' house. On this particular day Jones is present, and his wild behavior is a result of his fear that he may have to touch, or be touched by the Killburns' "witchy hands." His frantic reaction is entirely like that of a person confronted with a situation in which it appears he will have to break, or see broken, a taboo.

Let us turn to a consideration of the other important tradition in the book—the use of song. Folk songs figure prominently in *M. C. Higgins*. Banina's yodeling is a folk form of communicating. Harold Courlander in *Negro Folk Music* reports finding yodeling practiced in Nigeria, Haiti, Cuba, South Carolina and Alabama (1963, pp. 80-88). Hamilton states,

> Part of my family is from Kentucky. That was the way the mother called the children, by yodeling. Of course, it wasn't the same as the kind of way that I made very clear in *M. C.*—the mother using parts of their names, and so forth. In the hills, when people yodel, they have a particular sound, as I tried to express. They have a minor cadence, or beat, or something, that a family will recognize. When I was a child we did a little bit of that.

Other characters sing in *M. C. Higgins* besides Banina. Jones teaches M. C. an African song from great-grandmother Sarah.

Where does it come from, and what does it mean? Hamilton responds,

> It comes from one side of my family in a very curious way. I think it came down from white missionaries in Africa, who brought it back to the United States and sang it to black children in the hills. One branch of my family for generations has known that song.

Its meaning is unknown.

When Banina sings for the dude, among her songs are "Juba" and "Drinkin' of the Wine." It is not difficult to find variations of these traditional songs in folklore collections (Parrish 1942; Talley 1922; White 1928; Scarborough 1963). They would, of course, have particular meaning for children who were already familiar with one or more variations.

If we look at the situations in which the songs are presented, we realize their authentic nature. Banina sings the "ring song" with the children in a circle. She performs for the dude. She yodels as she climbs.

When we look at the folklore in *M. C. Higgins, the Great,* we see that it provides a key to understanding the characters and their belief systems upon which the conflict in the book is built. The folklore is essential to the book.

Adolescence is a time of transition. The boy is not ready to be a man, yet he is no longer a boy. This is made clear in *M. C. Higgins*. M.C. is not ready to completely give up his parents' beliefs in witches, yet he begins to question these beliefs. He begins to see through Lurhetta . . . that there are other possible explanations. When M. C. tells her that the Killburns "each have twelve fingers and twelve toes. And that witchy skin and that hair," . . . she replies, "People have all kinds of defects. A man is crippled in the legs—do you say he is 'witchy'?" . . . A part of M. C.'s already shaky belief system begins to crack. The implication of M. C.'s working openly with Ben at the end of the novel is that M. C. is in the process of changing parts of his belief system. His father's acceptance of that decision marks the way in which M. C. is passing to maturity. M. C. is a strongly individual character, yet a universal one. *M. C. Higgins, the Great* is a landmark in children's book publishing, not only as an authentic statement of a way of experiencing life that is both particular and universal, but as the finest example of a creative work for children that deals with a black experience so completely. (pp. 421-24)

Kathleen Scholl, "Black Traditions in 'M. C. Higgins, the Great'," in Language Arts, *Vol. 57, No. 4, April, 1980, pp. 420-24.*

Hamilton's intimacy with generations of black families and her interest in black history are evidenced in all her novels. . . . But [*M. C. Higgins, the Great*] is more than the story of the black and the poor; it is the story of all who survive painful obstacles to growth and self-actualization. (p. 202)

Hamilton's purpose in *M. C. Higgins, the Great* is to provide the reader with understanding of the human condition and of human competence to meet this condition. On the one hand, she mourns the situation of the poor and the powerless; on the other hand, she extols the human being himself. No one dies in the book. But M. C.'s efforts to stay alive, to preserve respect and meaning in life are central to the narrative.

The characters in the story are free and live in the North, but their roots are in slavery in the South. The main character,

Mayo Cornelius Higgins, is a teenager of uncommon curiosity and strength. He has concern with the need to survive on a physical level, with the need to love and be loved, to play, to master complex skills. That's a lot for a young man to worry about, but he is "M. C. Higgins, the Great."

The family is the principal institution through which needs are approached; family members work together for economic survival, they play together, and they love and care for each other. The mother holds the steady job; the father works only intermittently when he can find work, staying home the rest of the time to cook and care for his children. There is no ill feeling between spouses; there is on the contrary, expression of romantic love. When the two parents are home together, they care for the children together.

Satisfactions occur in the book through individual and family efforts. The main characters view themselves well, and they view people, their people, well. They are in control of their own lives even though they need to consider family, past and present, to plan for the future—for it is within the family that they find courage and determination to go on. (pp. 203-04)

Hamilton introduces in children's literature a strong new character, like herself, black and resolute in a white world. . . . [She pays] tribute to the child . . . by portraying a child of considerable complexity and ability. . . . (p. 204)

> *Mary Lystad, "1956-1975: 'But We Can Have / Lots of Good Fun That Is Funny!'" in her From Dr. Mather to Dr. Seuss: 200 Years of American Books for Children, Schenkman Books, Inc., 1980, pp. 179-205.**

Someone who accidentally read [Toni Morrison's] *Song of Solomon* as a children's novel or *M. C. Higgins, the Great* as an adult one might not be terribly surprised. Not only are they similar to each other, but *Song of Solomon* has qualities usually ascribed to children's fiction, qualities *M. C. Higgins* lacks. . . . [Readers] have fastened on the adult qualities of the children's novel and the childlike qualities of the adult one as the most noteworthy things about them. A critic suggests the unusual narrative stance of *M. C. Higgins* "can become a problem for the young reader, who is used to, and has a tighter hold on, a more usual narrative form . . ." [see excerpt above by Kathleen Scholl dated 1980], and a reviewer of *Song of Solomon* says its grisly events "are nearly deprived of their grisliness by the tone. It might be a folktale . . .", a form usually considered appropriate for children. These readers had expectations which these novels did not meet. I suspect someone who did read *M. C. Higgins* as an adult novel or *Song of Solomon* as one for children would still concentrate on their variance from the expected norm. The fact that one was written for children and one was not makes them markedly unlike each other.

"The father may soar / And the children may know their names"; the epigraph of *Song of Solomon* suggests themes which also appear in *M. C. Higgins,* but to quite different effect. In both novels, young black men feel blocked by their fathers. Milkman Dead more or less rejects his father; M. C. Higgins eventually accepts his. But Milkman must deny his father because his values are contemporary, urban, and white; M. C. must accept his father because his values are traditional, rural, and black— the values Milkman also accepts. I believe the different ways the two arrive at the same conclusion derive from our ideas about the difference between childhood and maturity. Since we believe that children want to rebel against parental values,

we like to tell them they will gain maturity by perceiving their parent's worth; adults, who have accepted mature values, sometimes see them as "shades of the prison-house" that blot out the light of their childhood innocence. As the protagonist of a children's novel, M. C. finds happiness in becoming mature. . . . (pp. 45-6)

Both novels associate childhood innocence with the past, and with traditional black culture. But *Song of Solomon* seems to reject contemporary white civilization, while *M. C. Higgins* tries to balance past and present, black and white, freedom and constraint. *M. C. Higgins* creates a complex balance between the values it first opposes, while *Song of Solomon* works at replacing one clearcut set of values with another. Milkman learns to trust simplicity, while M. C. must learn that things are more complicated than he thought. . . . Children's novels about children of all colours frequently end as *M. C. Higgins* does, with their protagonists' awakening realizations of their previous egocentricity; in children's novels, even black children have to grow up. Meanwhile, many adult novels concern their protagonists' unegocentric understanding of the real complexities of living with others—their lack of childish certainty. Since we value that certainty to the extent that we do not have it, literature written for adults inevitably values the childlike more than children's literature does.

Consequently, children's novels tend to have a different structural focus than adult ones. Since children's novels typically end with their protagonists' discovery of new values, they are often shaped like traditional quests. The protagonist leaves the security of home, or like M. C. Higgins, the security of childlike perception, and discovers a larger world outside. He returns home wiser; but since he does return home, he must fit together his old ideas and his new ones, and in doing so, realize the ambiguity of maturity. This is the "circular journey" which Jon Stott sees as a basic pattern of children's literature. Meanwhile, adult novels tend to be less quests for something different than analyses of life as it is already; characters who understand that there's no place *not* like home learn more about themselves where they already are. They do that by exploring the meaning of their experiences, and Jonathan Culler suggests that such explorations form patterns of binary opposites: "when two things are set in opposition to one another the reader is forced to explore qualitative similarities and differences, to make a connection so as to derive meaning from the disjunction." Since the meaning emerges from confusion—the ambiguity of maturity—the connections of resolution have a comparative simplicity. . . . (p. 46)

To generalize wildly: in children's books, things get better by getting more complex; in adult books they get better by getting less complex, more understandable. Children's books describe loss of innocence, adult books attempts to regain it. . . . Since children's books move out of egocentricity toward maturity, the question that shapes them is an old one: what will happen next? Will M. C. leave the mountain? Will Jones? Will M. C.'s mother get a recording contract? Will the spoil heap fall? While most adult novels do not ask the opposite question with the intensity of *Song of Solomon,* they usually imply it: what happened? what brought us to this pass? *Song of Solomon* moves forward by moving back—by finding explanations in the past for circumstances in the present.

C. S. Lewis once said that writing a children's novel "compels one to throw all the force of the book into what was done and said. It checks what a kind but discerning critic called 'the expository demon' in me." Like Lewis, most readers expect children's novels to tell a story above all else, to be organized as a series of unified actions—to have a plot; and we tend to expect adult novels to be filled with exposition, to be organized around *explanations* of what their events mean—to have a theme based on binary opposites. If Culler is right about expectations, we will find exactly what we want—and indeed, *M. C. Higgins* does offer a plot that focusses our attention on what will happen next, and *Song of Solomon* a set of binary opposites that provide explanations.

But the plot of *M. C. Higgins* is not very satisfying. When I taught this novel to students of children's literature, they disliked it, not just because so little happens in it, but because it thwarted their expectations of what might happen. It was not about a circus or a superhero, as the title led many of them to expect. M. C. does not fly; he does not even try and fail. M. C.'s mother does not become a recording star. M. C. meets a girl he likes, but she leaves without resolving his confusion about her. The spoil heap does not fall, nothing happens to prevent it from falling, and it is not shown conclusively that it will never fall; there is no confrontation with the strip miners. According to my students, the novel frittered away its opportunities for satisfying action amidst a welter of what they called "descriptions"; they saw it as a boringly overdetailed travelogue, a day in the life of M. C. Higgins.

The binary opposites to be found in *Song of Solomon* are not as unsatisfactory as the plot of *M. C. Higgins;* a close reading showed me how they organize the novel and make it meaningful. . . . But the binary opposites that explain events in *Song of Solomon* no more completely describe the novel than a summary of the plot describes *M. C. Higgins* as a whole. Despite our expectations that the children's novel tell a story and that the adult one have meaning, both of these novels offer something more, something that should perplex careful readers and demand further attention.

At one point, Hamilton tells us that M. C. Higgins is "overcome by the power of two separate thoughts"; in fact, her entire novel consists of a clear and careful counterpointing of opposed separate thoughts and images, centering around leaving and staying, freedom and constraint, growing up and staying young, tradition and modernity, past and future. My own literary training allows me to see such binary opposites with ease, and I had no trouble in finding them (usually embedded in what my students called descriptions) or in describing them to my students, in an attempt to make them appreciate the novel more. But my discussion did nothing to change their minds; if *they* needed help to understand it, they said, then what hope was there for mere children? Limited by their own structural expectations, they assumed children shared them, and rejected a book that did not meet them. (pp. 46-7)

When I taught *Song of Solomon* to a group of English majors a few weeks after my experience with *M. C. Higgins,* I was not surprised that they enjoyed the novel. But they were so busy ferreting out its meaning that they seemed not to have noticed that anything had happened in it at all. Like my children's literature students, these English majors were limited by their limited expectations of structure. My experience in teaching *M. C. Higgins* had made me so conscious of their silence on the subject of plot that I asked them about it. They agreed it was exciting, and that it held their attention completely; but beyond that they could say nothing. Their training as students of literature had rendered them incapable of discussing any sort of literary structure but binary opposites; they

had no language to describe a large part of their experience of the book.

The novel had another quality they could not deal with, which they called "magic"; but they were bothered by it enough to talk about it extensively. . . . My English majors were just as disturbed by the moments of fantasy in a primarily realistic novel as were my children's literature students by the apparent excess of description in *M. C. Higgins;* and they calmly accepted the sort of discussion of the novel's binary opposites that had merely confirmed my children's literature students' dislike of *M. C. Higgins.* Limited by their structural expectations, my students could cope neither with the childlike qualities of the adult novel nor the theoretically adult qualities of the children's novel.

Even worse, they could not see how these novels, which both have carefully constructed plots and carefully constructed patterns of binary opposites, fit those two structures together. An analysis of plot by itself, which merely maps out how a book excites attention, cannot suggest what readers should give their attention to once it has been excited. An analysis of binary opposites by themselves cannot explain how a novel makes us care about its theme, or even how meaning evolves from events. Patterns of binary opposites are purely two-dimensional until they resolve, and Frank Kermode rightly condemns "the questionable literary practice of calling literary structure *spatial.* We can distribute our fictions in time as well as in space, which is why we must avoid an easy translation from the one to the other." Since novels must combine the spatial order of binary opposites with the temporal order of events, a discussion of one is incomplete without a discussion of the other. It was only when my students' responses to these novels made me realize that and I tried to see how the two structures fit together in both novels that I began to realize how richly and intricately constructed they both are. (p. 47)

M. C. Higgins is constructed like a symphony in three movements, each following the same pattern but establishing a different mood and exploring a different aspect of the same central questions. The first movement presents clearcut oppositions, the second muddies them and shows their ambiguities, and the third resolves them; each movement occurs on a different day in M. C.'s life, and each comments on the others by establishing parallels between quite different events, people, and images.

In fact, both *Song of Solomon* and *M. C. Higgins* express their meaning exactly and most completely through the carefully chosen sequencing of their events. Despite the instructive way in which they express the limitations of the genres they belong to, both move past those limitations—but only for readers willing and able to see that. If we limit ourselves to patterns of binary opposites that resolve without ever evolving, we lose both the pleasure of stories for their own sake and the more satisfying perception of *how* stories make events meaningful. Even more sadly, our nostalgic conviction that the innocence of childhood is an unmixed blessing to be preserved at all cost lets us persuade ourselves that children need and can comprehend nothing more in literature than the pleasure of stories for their own sake; it also lets us deprive children of most of the true rewards of fiction. If perception of structural patterns is a learned competence, there is no reason why human beings of any age should not be taught it. Furthermore, parents and teachers who care enough about both children and literature to teach them that competence soon discover that children are eminently capable of learning it. (p. 48)

Perry Nodelman, *"The Limits of Structures: A Shorter Version of a Comparison between Toni Morrison's 'Song of Solomon' and Virginia Hamilton's 'M. C. Higgins, the Great',"* in Children's Literature Association Quarterly, Vol. 7, No. 3, Fall, 1982, pp. 45-8.*

ARILLA SUN DOWN (1976)

Virginia Hamilton likes dangerous edges. She tries things that might not work. Her books are experimental, different, strange. She runs bravely along the edges of cliffs.

Her characters also exist on the edges of things. Often they cross the border into adolescence, teeming out of childhood into the chancy independence of maturity with a bursting strength that sometimes brims over into violence. They are black, but their color is not what is most important about them. At Virginia Hamilton's best, her characters transcend race and youth, and grow larger until they are towering images of dignity and power.

In *Arilla Sun Down* the muscular young presence is Arilla's big brother Jack Sun Run. Sun skirts dangerous precipices. Bare-chested, splendid as an Indian warrior, he rears his horse, defying white policemen. And Arilla, too, bumps up against hostile boundaries. There is the bruising rivalry with her overpowering brother and the grinding chafe between black and red in the mixed inheritance of her family. . . .

Writers brave enough to take risks sometimes fail. *Arilla Sun Down* is not one grand ascending curve like Hamilton's *M. C. Higgins, the Great*. Perhaps too many things are piled too precariously on too many edges. There is too much talking, too much explaining and forced Indian imagery.

And there are things this reader couldn't quite believe. Arilla remembers her Indian origins by thinking back to her early childhood with a kind of feel-speech:

> Late in the big night and snow has no end. Taking me a long kind of time going to the hill.

So far, so good. But her memory also includes exact adult language, like the monologue of an old Indian woman:

> And women, Hohé, tough and poor. They talk tribal politics, you know, baby? . . . Tribal and individual.

Nor do I believe rebellious Jack Sun Run is an A-student. The contrast between the Indian reminiscences and the daily facts of contemporary suburban life is sometimes more grotesque than it is haunting and sad. It is hard to focus into one vision Jack Sun Run standing at attention in his war bonnet in his mother's dance studio and his mother performing as a mime in leotards.

But amid all this confusion two things are unforgettable, the stature of Jack Sun Run and Arilla's painful sense of insignificance beside him. . . . In the end she becomes his equal. After Sun falls disastrously from his horse, she bravely rescues him. Secretly, then, she abandons the Indian name of her childhood, Little Moon (the moon shines only by reflecting the sun), and gives herself the name which is the title of this book. . . .

This book is some trouble, but it's not ordinary and it's not dull. Virginia Hamilton's failed tries are more interesting than other people's tidy successes.

Jane Langton, in a review of "Arilla Sun Down," in The New York Times Book Review, October 31, 1976, p. 39.

The author states that the book originated from two well-springs of intense concern: a presumption of an Indian strain in her ancestry—her grandmother was reputed to be part-Cherokee—and her own personal situation as the mother in an interracial family. And in a curious way, the novel is doubly autobiographical, for in the narrative both mother and child reflect two phases of Virginia Hamilton's own life. . . . Dominating the book is the powerful figure of Arilla's teen-aged brother, Jack Sun Run, brilliant, defiant, and aloof—exulting in his "Amerind" birthright, with his headband on glossy black hair, his moccasins, and his superb horsemanship. . . .

The entire book is impressionistic, each of its bits and pieces carefully shaped and sculptured. Arilla's story is interspersed with flashbacks—vague recollections of sensations and happenings from her early childhood set down in floating, incomplete sentences; and each of the "re-memory" sequences slides seamlessly into the main fabric of current events. . . . Thus, the reader often comprehends the present in terms of the past.

Since the novel ends near the small Ohio town where it began, the structure—as the author points out—is circular. Moreover, a cyclical concept of continuity is stressed again and again, particularly by old James, the beloved full-blood whose Indian philosophy permeates the story: " 'On and on in a circle. For all time.' "

But the book makes enormous demands; the writing is often elliptical and oblique, and one wonders whether young people will persevere, seeing the story only through a glass darkly, as, indeed, Arilla herself perceives the world during much of the book. On the other hand, for those readers gifted with determination—or encouragement—the new work by a much-honored author will yield a unique experience.

Ethel L. Heins, in a review of "Arilla Sun Down," in The Horn Book Magazine, Vol. LII, No. 6, December, 1976, p. 611.

Virginia Hamilton, herself a descendant of slaves, is concerned with black identity. In *M. C. Higgins The Great* this concern is subtly explored in the history of the Higgins family. In *Arilla Sun Down* the concern is continued and deepened in the author's sophisticated treatment of intra-family relationships, the conflicts of adolescent choice, and sibling rivalry. Here the "interracial" Adams family is split between those who identify exclusively with one cultural component of their heritage against those who accept a shared collective interracial past. . . .

[In] spite of her self-possessed, glamorous brother, Arilla manages to grow. She even gains, in the tradition of her native American heritage, her second name—Sun Down—only to discover that she has grown into something more than that name can encompass: she has become independent, her interracial identity confirmed.

An equally strong theme of *Arilla Sun Down* is the ethnic identity of the family as a whole. This identity breaks through the narrative in Arilla's disjointed infant memories and in snatches of half-remembered conversations which all merge as the book progresses into an acceptance of the family's shared interracial character. The conflicts and compromises of this splendid family portrait fit alongside each individual member's pride in and growing awareness of their need for each other and of their common heritage.

Virginia Hamilton is an important chronicler of the black experience. She writes in an intense, understated narrative, interspersed with evocative flashbacks, the whole richly reflecting the different levels of this complex and powerful story. And, coming from a direction that is new and unfamiliar to most of us, *Arilla Sun Down* is a little culture shock all on its own: here there are no "ghetto" signposts, no bland apologia for the liberal conscience. In describing so perceptively this particular interracial family struggling with the choices thrown up by their heritage and the pressures of the moment, Virginia Hamilton has achieved a universal statement about people and their roots.

> *Rosemary Stones, "Pressures of the Past," in* The Times Literary Supplement, *No. 3915, March 25, 1977, p. 359.*

Although it is the relationship between sister and brother which directs the surface action of [*Arilla Sun Down*], the understanding between father and daughter goes deeper. The climax of the story is not the great rescue episode but a quieter scene in which Arilla is sent to bring back her apparently feckless father and discovers the conflicting stresses which send him back, from time to time, to renew himself among almost forgotten scenes. In understanding him, Arilla learns about herself . . . .

This is a subtle and a difficult book. The difficulty is increased by the writer's putting everything into Arilla's words, whether she is an intelligent and articulate twelve-year-old or a baby thinking in the idiom of the Indian. Despite the complexities the book is strangely compulsive. Mixed up teenagers may find here, in a fascinatingly distorted mirror, some of their own dilemmas, and perhaps a hint at solutions. This wise and eloquent book is entirely original in its subject and in its technique. It will haunt the imagination for a long time.

> *M. Crouch, in a review of "Arilla Sun Down," in* The Junior Bookshelf, *Vol. 41, No. 3, June, 1977, p. 177.*

The manner of a book can be superimposed or it can be integral to it, part of its argument and its unity. In a lecture delivered at the Library of Congress in November 1975 Virginia Hamilton discussed the close relationship of form and idea which makes each of her books such a fine aesthetic experience. . . . [She] makes the point that each book must have its own style, its own images, its own reality, and she decides that

> To write about a family unit in which some members are in the process of learning who they are and in which others are living a fiction they admire seemed to be the perfect sort of risk for me.

This kind of risk she took in *Arilla Sun Down*. It was a risk if only because the story of Arilla Adams . . . would inevitably be read by many as a problem novel about an inter-racial family. This theme, though, is not a general but a particular one in her book. Within the relationships between Arilla and her older brother Jack and her parents, racial influence on behaviour is only part of a complex of personal attachments and antagonisms. (pp. 3147-48)

Symbol and image are necessary in the expression of the complex brother and sister relationship no less than in the exploration of Arilla's changing perceptions of her mother, who needs to stay firm in her childhood environment, and her father whose nomadic impulses are suggested by the circular structure of the book; it begins with the five-year-old Arilla speeding dangerously down an ice slope behind her father on a sled and ends on the same slope when seven years later she fetches him from one of his wanderings. A geometrical pattern, a constant interaction of images and fugal variation of phrases and incidents (somewhat in the manner of Faulkner)—these are only some of the ways in which the characters in the book acquire their startling reality, eccentric perhaps (a word that Virginia Hamilton uses significantly in her lecture) but only because they are individuals.

I have said nothing of the evanescent dry humour in the book or the warmth and liveliness of the dialogue or the syntactical changes that mark Arilla's recollections from her running commentary on the present or the almost shocking brilliance of implied description (no less forceful in the birthday party scene than in the drama of the storm). I make no apology for recommending the young to take the book seriously, to read and re-read it; there is enough in it to fill out a score of fictions from writers who 'take up' the craft of fiction to produce tracts for the times or placebos for the reluctant reader. We have few real novelists for the young: Virginia Hamilton is one of the most rewarding and developing. (p. 3148)

> *Margery Fisher, in a review of "Arilla Sun Down," in* Growing Point, *Vol. 16, No. 2, July, 1977, pp. 3147-48.*

Arilla Sun Down is most certainly a courageous and aesthetically adventurous book, both in its innovative narrative technique and in its treatment of race and gender; Betsy Hearne has written that "Virginia Hamilton has heightened the standards for children's literature as few authors have" [see excerpt above in General Commentary dated 1980]. Hamilton writes most often about the black experience because, as she suggests in a comment quoted by Hearne, she feels that "the making of any fiction is foremost a self-viewing that becomes a force for life and living." In *Arilla Sun Down* the reader becomes immersed in the "self-viewing," questing, groping, first-person narrative of a Midwestern girl, black with some Amerindian blood, who must contend with an unusual family that pulls her in conflicting directions.

In her award-winning novel *M. C. Higgins, the Great,* Hamilton had presented her young protagonist M. C. as living in the patriarchal shadow of his powerful but, in some respects, morally blind father, Jones. After he encounters both New Woman in the person of young Lurhetta Outlaw and the traditional matriarchal values on Killburn Mound, M. C. acquires a more balanced and integrated sense of self—what some feminist critics have called "the androgynous self." He seems content to make home safe for every member of the family through his humble act of building a wall, rather than attempting to dominate the entire mountain on his forty-foot pole in the difficult patriarchal role of "M. C. Higgins, the Great." It is this kind of aggressive patriarchy—M. C. the Hunter, the conqueror of the earth—that, in its most extreme form, has resulted in the rape of the mountain by strip mining.

In *Arilla Sun Down,* Hamilton again reveals this "androgynous vision" of the self. In this novel she endorses liberation from excessively rigid gender norms that have imprisoned both men and women in the past. She shows that her character need not settle for confinement and enclosure. She need not be the "moon," a looking-glass reflection of her brother, who sees himself as the sun, and she can create richer, newer fictions for herself than even her storytelling mentor, James False Face, had dreamed or imagined. Hamilton's character Arilla reveals that integrity of the self lies in a movement away from sexual and racial polarization toward a state in which individual roles and modes of conduct may be freely chosen. Bathed and obscured by the too-brilliant radiance of Jack Sun Run, her proud, self-defined brother, Arilla must uncover her own light and let it shine. Arilla's attempt to recover her past experience through memory, to transcend power struggles with her brother and mother, and to create an identity through her own literary talent as she breaks out of fixed images of race and gender, enable her to aspire toward a wholeness of being that may be called androgynous.

Achieving identity, a true name, and a secure sense of self is perhaps more difficult for Arilla Adams than for most adolescents. She often feels overwhelmed and anxious. Her mother is a tall, beautiful, and powerful black dancer, who restricts and encloses Arilla excessively. Moreover, Lillian Adams forces her son, Jack Sun Run, to participate in restricting Arilla; a key scene in the novel shows Jack's tying Arilla to sumac trees. Jack in turn resents Arilla's presence since he sees her as an impediment to his freedom; he blames the mother for having wanted another baby. Arilla is quite literally blinded by her brother's presence. He calls her "Moon," the traditional symbol of the female among Native American peoples. Arilla firmly resists the attempts of Jack to fix her, to name and define her. Just as she has resisted dancing because she does not wish to be a shadow of her powerful mother, she also resists the names of "Moon Child" or "Moon Flower" because she does not wish to be a mere, diminished reflection of the Sun. Jack has apparently chosen his own identity—that of an assertive and charismatic "blood," a modern warrior, complete with knife between his teeth and his vitally powerful horse, Jeremiah. Arilla's father, Stone Father, apparently doesn't know who he is supposed to be; at times he suddenly disappears from his job and his family to go back to Cliffville. As Arilla observes,

> This is the queerest, dumbest family that ever there was. . . . A disappearing dad. A dancing mother. And a half-killed, crazy brother. That's it. So here I am.

Hamilton stresses her character's emotional distress through Arilla's experiences of confinement and suffocating enclosure on one hand, and out-of-control images of flight and freedom on the other. The first chapter of the novel is a stream-of-consciousness, disjointed narrative, depicting Arilla's experience of sledding down an icy slope toward a cliff-edge with her father. Night is her time, the Moon's time, and Arilla can hear her father's whoops of joyous freedom as he flies toward the cliff-edge, and possibly, death and oblivion. She flees from the confinement and enclosure she associates with her mother. To identify with the mother, for Arilla, then is to be enclosed, confined, and absorbed in her mother's power. (pp. 25-6)

The reader learns in the first chapter of the novel that Arilla's mother, Lillian Perry Adams, essentially rejects her husband's Amerindian culture. She becomes especially fearful when Arilla begins to "speak like an old one, like James False Face". . . . It is Arilla's appropriation of the ways of the storyteller that convinces Lillian that the family must get away from Cliffville. Moreover, in addition to confining Arilla, Lillian Adams tries

to remake her daughter in her own image: "Arilla, I have to admit that one of my great disappointments is the fact that you refuse to learn The Dance". . . . Lillian admits to Shy Woman, wife of James False Face, "I don't know much about your . . . your people". . . . "'No,' changing woman hard, 'you still don't. You don't want to'". . . . And in one key scene, Lillian argues with her son about his race. He is not a "blood," an Amerind, she says. He is "interracial," and what he wants to be doesn't matter; "It's what society says". . . .

It is especially telling that Lillian should fear Arilla's capacity for language, speech, and story, insisting instead that the girl should accept the mother's art in a diminished form. . . .

Lillian Adams, "the best looking, lightskinned woman in town," superb dancer and gifted mime artist, can create magic and illusion; through her art, she has created a magnetic personality and presence for herself, one which threatens to absorb her husband and her daughter. When she looks at Arilla, she apparently wishes to see only a diminished image of herself and her art; but unlike the weak, Snow White daughters in fairy tales, Arilla possesses an art, a creative potential, which must flower despite the dwarfing she feels in the shadow of her beautiful mother and the overpowering radiance of her brother.

To identify with her father, on the other hand, is for Arilla to experience a surfeit of freedom, flying out of control over the cliff into darkness, oblivion, nonbeing. The father seems to belong to the lost past: "Stone Father is a black wolf with fading moonshine in his eyes" who feels about himself that "what great wolf there was has long since fled these sorry bones". . . .

Arilla feels that all her experiences—her birthday, her horse, her name—are lost in Jack Sun Run's glory. Hamilton repeatedly portrays Jack against the sun, Arilla's upturned face blinded by his overpowering bronzed presence. Her efforts to shape and to define herself get lost in him. . . .

Throughout the narrative, Arilla is reminded through half-conscious memory that there is a mysterious and powerful dimension to her, just out of reach, hovering near consciousness, something she has forgotten. Repeatedly Arilla uses metaphors which suggest dark misty confusion. Being twelve, she says, is "like dangling at the end of a rope and not being able to let go". . . . (p. 26)

Even in her confused emotional state, though, Arilla is aware of "knowing things and not knowing how I know". . . . The sense that some elusive knowledge is within her is an idea Arilla expresses repeatedly:

> My head is like that. A flash of something clear, but the rest darkness. Nothing. Kind of scary. I get a scent of trees sometimes, and a flash of cool pale bark of a tree. I appear to be floating past it, back and forth. I get kind of weak, either with floating back and forth or with the scent of the tree. I wonder if somewhere, sometime, I have lived another life. . . .

Literally, this scene may refer to the incident when Jack Sun Run had tied his sister to the sumac trees, confining her in order to enjoy adventures on his own, or to her swinging in the trees. Symbolically, at least, this sense of having forgotten something is closely tied to Arilla's identity as storyteller and writer. In their study *The Madwoman in the Attic*, Sandra Gilbert and Susan Gubar stress the prevalence of blindness, claustrophobia, images of enclosure, and confusion about language among nineteenth-century women writers: "Many women writers manage to imply that the reason for such ignorance of language—as well as the reason for their deep sense of alienation and inescapable feeling of anomie—is that they have *forgotten* something." According to Gilbert and Gubar, these writers "have to fight their internalization of patriarchal strictures for even a faint trace memory of what they might have become." What they have forgotten and must recover is "their matrilineal heritage of literary strength, their female power." Indeed, this part of herself, the storytelling capacity, seems to be what Arilla has forgotten and what she must recover and reveal. At the same time, she looks for something new and strange in the future. As she skates in freedom, Arilla thinks, "Ahead of me, I think rolling I will come to something stroking that I have never come to before. Someday." . . .

This literary strength and knowledge comes to Arilla through disjointed, impressionistic memories of experiences with James False Face, the storyteller who names her "wordkeeper," who promises that one day she will keep the stories, and who reminds her, too, that it was a young woman who had brought the first stories and the law to the People. When James False Face dies, he admonishes her to live with honor and to remember who she is. For a time, however, Arilla forgets. (The fact that James keeps the stories but that his "false face" implies a Janus-like identity; his close connection with Arilla suggests an androgynous view of his art.) Experiencing herself as an absence, as something missing or forgotten, Arilla can define herself only negatively—a negation of her brother. When Jack Sun Run injures himself in an ice storm and Arilla must save his life, she thinks that she is "Arilla Sun Down." She also successfully completes the quest to bring home her father after one of his disappearing acts. During this journey back to Cliffville, Arilla recovers crucial lost knowledge about herself and her feelings toward her brother. She learns, for example, that Jack Sun Run had saved her from an icy death after she and her father had almost plunged over the side of the cliff. She sleds down the hill with her father again, but this time a fence at the bottom of the hill makes the ride safe. She is privileged to hear her father enacting his spiritual self as he howls like a wolf. Finally, she finds a trunk full of her father's treasures, emblems of his Native American culture: a silver bridle, a tomahawk, hides with painted scenes, leggings, belts with beadwork, and a pack of moccasins. Arilla convinces her father that he must bring the trunk home with them, that he must try to integrate past and present identities, that her mother must come to accept that part of her husband's life. Hamilton poignantly shows that the small girl Arilla helps her father to grow; the two of them grow together. Arilla finds that she cannot merely put on the identity and the name which James False-Face had created for her. She must put on her literary, word-keeping, and story-making power and use it to break out of the prison of past selves and to forge an entirely new one. Speeding down the superhighway with her dad, Arilla says that she will escape from the confinements and enclosures erected for her by Jack Sun Run and her mother; the "nomad" in her, she says, needs to skate free in the daylight on her own terms. And she thinks to herself about writing her autobiography: "I could have a name for myself more than Sun Down. It'd be what I gave myself for what I do that's all my own". . . .

In his massive study *The Masks of God*, Joseph Campbell explains that the patriarchal, anti-androgynous view is usually distinguished "by its setting apart of all pairs of opposites—male and female, life and death, true and false, good and evil." In Hamilton's novel, Arilla reaches far back into her Native

American cultural past through James False Face to apprehend new modes of being and knowing; she learns, for example, that time is "only going in a circle". . . . She learns that power for herself does not need to mean weakness and defeat for Jack Sun Run. And she realizes that she must skate into the future with her imagination in its newly-found power and freedom to imagine a time when names—"Indian," "Black," "Male," "Female,"—won't erect delimiting barriers and strictures to growth, and won't signal hateful power struggles between husbands and wives, between brothers and sisters. Carolyn Heilbrun has written that "androgyny suggests a spirit of reconciliation between the sexes . . . it suggests a full range of experience . . . a spectrum upon which human beings may freely choose their place." In *Arilla Sun Down*, Hamilton shows that such a spirit of reconciliation can help to heal gaps between cultures, races, and gender. (p. 27)

> *Anita Moss, "Frontiers of Gender in Children's Literature: Virginia Hamilton's 'Arilla Sun Down'," in* Children's Literature Association Quarterly, *Vol. 8, No. 4, Winter, 1983, pp. 25-7.*

JUSTICE AND HER BROTHERS (1978)

Virginia Hamilton is one of our great stylists, and in this story of eleven-year-old Tice (Justice) Douglass and her brothers, who are identical twins of thirteen, her prose carries readers through a slow beginning to a compelling and quickening movement of events that have a quality of inexorable force. Tice is afraid of one of the twins, Thomas, whose teasing has a cruelty and anger she cannot understand, while she feels that her other brother Lee (Levi) protects her. She begins to be aware that there is a strange empathy between the boys; it seems a telepathic communication. Then, guided by a neighbor who is psychic, Tice becomes aware of her own psychic powers—and as soon as she does, the full force of Tom's malevolence, the full disclosure of the brutal invasion he makes of his twin's mind, and the nature of the battle between them become evident. The story is fleshed out with other action (Tice's participation in a snake hunt) and other characters (warm relationships between Tice and her parents, who are supportive and strong) and with a vivid evocation of the rural setting. It concludes on a hopeful, if tantalizing note, as the three children and a fourth, son of the woman who has helped Tice find her powers, look to a future in which they will be together, knowing they are different from other people.

> *Zena Sutherland, in a review of "Justice and Her Brothers," in* Bulletin of the Center for Children's Books, *Vol. 32, No. 1, September, 1978, p. 9.*

Reading Virginia Hamilton is like being shot out of a cannon into the Milky Way. Sometimes just a phrase sends you off, an image or a scene, but invariably at the end of a book you marvel: look how high I've been *just on words!* Indeed such is the extraordinary quality of Miss Hamilton's imagination that her characters seem to have to go faster than other fictional characters just to keep up with her. . . .

Here is Miss Hamilton at her best, plunging her characters into unique situations in order to work out the ambivalence and antagonisms of family relationships which she understands so well. She reaches over the precipice and risks even more than usual when she gives the identicals the power of telepathic communication with each other. It is only when, towards the middle of the book, she extends (and even magnifies) this power to include Justice, her strange neighbor, Mrs. Jefferson, and her son, Dorian, that we wonder if this time the author may not have risked too much. The idea is a dazzling one—these five born in the wrong age, the first unit of a new people with new powers; the difficulty is that we see Miss Hamilton manipulating and maneuvering to get the idea across. The book is like an expertly crafted, highly original painting over which a surrealistic film has been tacked. The author has given herself a hard assignment, but even in the Milky Way, a reader doesn't want to see an author at work.

> *Jean Fritz, in a review of "Justice and Her Brothers," in* The New York Times Book Review, *December 17, 1978, p. 27.*

[*Justice and Her Brothers* is] a brilliant book, compulsively readable, but disturbing. There is little untrammeled action. Delight is dark. Is it suitable for 12-year-olds? I have to say no. The average child of this age will find it boringly serious. The more sensitive will be troubled by its convincing portrayal of mental malpractice, and could miss the key phrase spoken to Levi by Thomas: "I couldn't do any of this if you were ever strong enough to stop me." This is an extraordinary novel, but I believe it is for secure, intelligent, and tough-minded late teens and adults.

> *Clive Lawrance, in a review of "Justice and Her Brothers," in* The Christian Science Monitor, *March 12, 1979, p. B4.*

[*Justice and Her Brothers*] begins as a psychological study, then degenerates into a lengthy exercise on ESP. The book is unfocused, with plot and theme changing in midstream. Telepathic forays into the future and other psychic tricks do not divert from unsolved human problems. Tension generated by Ticey's twin brothers just dissipates, cheating fictional characters and readers alike.

> *Ruth M. Stein, in a review of "Justice and Her Brothers," in* Language Arts, *Vol. 56, No. 4, April, 1979, p. 444.*

Here is a black novelist using racial characteristics in a new, altogether fascinating way.... There is a slow and menacing build-up of tension as 11-year-old Justice talks to herself of her fears, almost as though the story were being told in the first person.... On the surface, we have merely seen a young sister trying desperately to keep up with her brothers and their friends.... But while the everyday story in its interestingly different setting comes alive with close realistic detail and Negro speech rhythms, we find ourselves in a Science Fiction world. Reassuringly, the balance of powers is restored for this world by Justice the Watcher and Dorian the Healer, all memories are wiped out for the present, in this world, and four ordinary children race off home at the end. Though the narrative may seem deceptively slow-moving at first, it is full of rewards, not least the good characterisation of family relationships, the style, and Justice's poetic vision of her surroundings.

> *M. Hobbs, in a review of "Justice and Her Brothers," in* The Junior Bookshelf, *Vol. 43, No. 4, August, 1979, p. 220.*

DUSTLAND (1980)

Like middle children the middle title of a trilogy often has special problems. It may seem to do little more than mark time between the intrigue of the first and the resolution of the last episodes. *Dustland* continues the story begun in *Justice and*

Her Brothers.... The action now occurs mainly in the future (or imaginary) world the four children enter. If the landscape owes something to Herbert's *Dune* (Chilton, 1965), the strange creatures, particularly a dog-like animal and a species of winged humanoid, are unique. Thomas imperils the group by running off, but the suspense is tainted by the general obscurity of his motives. Like the others, Thomas wants to go home: since he (and we) know running cannot get him there, his action seems aimless. It may be significant on the psychological level but works against the simple credibility of the plot. At the very end of the novel a new factor appears to mitigate the animosity Thomas feels towards Justice, but this solution has an unsatisfying air of *deus ex machina*. Readers who have persevered to this point probably have the patience to await the final answers. But the real subject of this novel, and it would appear, of the trilogy, is the nature of knowing and being—the old question of whether "reality" is a mere by-product of consciousness or has an independent existence outside the mind. Hamilton has revived the debate between the idealists and the materialists. Perhaps the winner, too, will be announced in the last installment.

> *Patricia Dooley, in a review of "Dustland," in* School Library Journal, *Vol. 26, No. 7, March, 1980, p. 140.*

Set aside your preconceptions; forget your notions of genres; put *Dustland* in the hands of a reading child who knows and cares nothing about literary categories. Then read it yourself.

Virginia Hamilton is a writer of rare depth and range. Her subjects, her stories, her style, continue to press forward and away from what she has written before. *Dustland* is an exception only because it follows *Justice and her Brothers* and ought to be read as part of the *Justice* cycle....

The struggle between Thomas and Justice, the recurring questions about the nature of reality, and the moral limits to which any individual may apply his or her unique powers, create a narrative tension in which character and idea become indivisible.

Young readers may be so spellbound with this book that they will taste the grit of Dustland for hours or days after the book is finished, but no one can close the book without a sense of being lifted, like the Slaker, beyond the dust into Hamilton's "enormous world of light."

> *Betty Levin, "Fantasy Journey for All Ages," in* The Christian Science Monitor, *May 12, 1980, p. B9.*

Virginia Hamilton once said of her writing, "'I am learning to go backward and forward in time with the feeling of simultaneousness.'" In the multilayered time fantasy, second in her proposed trilogy, she creates just that—a sense of the unity of time. As bits of information are revealed, her characters ponder fascinating conundrums about the relationships linking the past, the present, and the future.... The author's use of incomplete and staccato sentences helps to increase the tension and create often fragmentary pictures. Never a transparent writer, she has drawn subtle parallels between the characters of the children and those of the future beings. Although questioning the nature of survivors, survival itself is not the issue; when Justice says, about the Slakers, "'What matters is that they get a free chance to see what they can do,'" she is stating the theme of the book.

Celia H. Morris, in a review of ''Dustland,'' in The Horn Book Magazine, Vol. LVI, No. 3, June, 1980, p. 305.

The Watcher, the supposed influence for good, seems full of its own self-importance. To what purpose will all this power be put? The author's attempt to convey differing intelligences with slang language is annoying. The sentences come in short, staccato bursts. Good for heightening tension; bad for the reader trying to understand complicated imagery and unfamiliar creatures and settings. No progress is made throughout the book— no character development, no change in circumstances. The solution, if there is one, is no nearer than at the beginning.

Ultimately, the book has no focus. One scene, that is used as the cover illustration, is typical. Justice creates a 20 foot high image of her head on the road in front of them. It sits, ''an entertainment'' and Thomas embellishes it with his special brand of magic, but it means nothing, does nothing to advance the story line, and disappears never to be mentioned again. . . .

I would give [*Dustland*] the ''Shelf-Sitter Book of the Year'' award and predict that very few kids will pick it up, and less will like or understand it. If Hamilton's audience is still children, she has lost sight of them. (p. 32)

Diane G. Yates, in a review of ''Dustland,'' in Voice of Youth Advocates, Vol. 3, No. 3, August, 1980, pp. 31-2.

In *Justice and Her Brothers*, the first novel of her trilogy, Virginia Hamilton's character, Justice, is well drawn. She springs to life—impish, charming, witty and above all courageous in facing the challenges brought about by being the youngest among her parents' three children. She holds our affection even after finding herself endowed with the awesome responsibility of extrasensory powers. . . .

[In *Dustland*], Justice uses her extrasensory ability to guide her twin brothers, a friend named Dorian and herself (the four, called The Unit, all have extrasensory powers)—into a ''mind-jump.'' Leaving their bodies in the present, their minds have gone into the future to a place of endless gritty dust, which they name Dustland.

We meet several creatures there: The Worlmas—bullet-shaped creatures that suck up water and grow to three times their normal size so that their legs snap off; Miacis, who has a likeness to a dog, and like a dog is happy to find a master in Justice; Bambnua, a Slaker—a winged humanoid with an owl-like appearance and a pink bald head. In an attempt to probe the mysteries of Dustland, the unit communicates with these creatures through a process called ''mind-tracing.'' But one is never sure what they do learn.

The mind is trapped unless it has a body to incite. And the limitation of mind-tracing traps the novel—and its characters— in the morass of dust. Impish Justice dissolves into the dust, too, her mind becoming a senseless tyranny which traps her brothers and Dorian (as well as the reader) in a barren land. What can it gain her? Us? Anyone? When Bambnua flies off searching for ''an end,'' we hope for an end, too.

So desperately does this novel need the dynamics of conflict that when the conniving Thomas rips his mind away from the unit and goes racing across Dustland, we race along simply to relieve the monotony. Thomas becomes almost sympathetic, almost believable as a character. He at least is willing to struggle for *his* meaning. But even Thomas cannot hold our interest

completely. We know that what happens to him—to have meaning—must happen in the present, not the future. Any attempt to force a contradiction to this merely becomes confusing.

Justice is as confused about Dustland as we are:

> ''Why must this be *our* future?'' her mind asks. ''But if this is not *our* future, then whose is it? That creature's. Miacis'.''
>
> . . . this was not the unit's future. Yet it was the future of Dustland.
>
> *A* future, but not ours.
>
> All at once Justice felt tired.

Upon The Unit's return to the present, the immense potential of the novel becomes apparent. Mrs. Jefferson, Dorian's mother, has been standing over the four mindless bodies of the children, under a tree. . . .

The juxtaposition of the present with the future would have given the novel a center. It would have demanded conflict, heightened suspense, supplied the drama the novel is crying for. A greater urgency for the book to follow would have been created: The giant shadow stalking the present to take the unit off again, into the unknown.

Rosa Guy, ''Crossing the Threshold to a Twilit World,'' in Book World—The Washington Post, September 14, 1980, p. 6.

[The four children] are so scantily drawn as to evade the imagination. However assiduously we follow up clues and try to interpret allegories (even with recourse to *The New Testament*, Tolkien, or *Psychic News*), without a picture of the children, only available in *Dustland*'s precursor, *Justice and her Brothers* or towards the end of *Dustland* itself, we risk bewilderment and boredom. This is a great pity for if the two books had been combined the Dustland episode would have been absorbed into an intriguing whole.

In the earlier book we gradually become aware of the extrasensory powers of a family of three American, small-town, lower middle-class children and their friend Dorian. The unlikelihood of ESP, which is skilfully inserted into the main narrative, is acceptable to the sceptic and enhances rather than detracts from a delicate and adventurous story of sibling rivalry. It is easy to believe in the telepathic ''identicals'' (twins, Thomas and Levi), and Dorian who has healing powers and whose slovenly down-South mother, ''the Sensitive'', shows the heroine, ''singleton'' Justice how to come to terms with her extra dimension of perception. Parental attempts to understand their children's abnormal powers and adolescent quarrels, with the aid of common sense, folk adage and adult-education-class science, help keep the story on a knife edge of reality; at the same time we are prepared for the improbable.

Perhaps Miss Hamilton's original intention was one book. Perhaps her publishers may yet reissue *Justice and her Brothers* and *Dustland* under a single title. Such is the strength of her first book that if this should happen we would be in possession of a minor American classic. The Douglass children's ancestors are Huck Finn and Tom Sawyer. It is not just that they live in the same part of America, but they respond to life with the same verve and their cameraderie and pranks are reminiscent of some of the best of Twain's invention. Desegregation and the Space Age are opportunities for new kinds of adventures.

It should be mentioned that Miss Hamilton is a black writer, writing about, and surely to a certain extent for, black children. She can hardly fail to have absorbed the works of black writers such as Toni Morrison, yet at no point in *Justice and her Brothers* or *Dustland* does she allow racial issues to obtrude and her writing is the more powerful for this restraint. This is yet another reason to hope that the soft centre of *Dustland* may one day be encased in its appropriate shell.

Holly Eley, "Future Darkness," in The Times Literary Supplement, *No. 4042, September 19, 1980, p. 1024.*

JAHDU (1980)

> I'm a streak of light! I'm a trick-maker! I'm Jahdu just running through!

This free self-description is the first suggestion we get of Jahdu's identity, and it occurs after pages of Jahdu running along, shaking off his "Jahdu dust" and gathering it back into himself; trying to put a "wing-low bird" to sleep and then trying to change into the child Lee Edward but failing in both attempts because, as both bird and boy tell him, "you have lost something and you don't know it." Jahdu himself is absent from the pictures, and beginning readers who have not encountered him in Hamilton's previous stories [*The Time-Ago Tales of Jahdu* and *Time-Ago Lost: More Tales of Jahdu*] will have a hard time forming any picture of her elusive figment. Those who stick with the story will be treated to some rich and snappy dialogue between Jahdu and his shadow, and some highly imaginative, playfully mythic doings off beyond the horizon. There Jahdu confronts the pesky CIGAM, which turns out to be his own magic, spelled backwards and wrapped around his rebellious shadow. The adventure is related with a spell-binding profusion of imagery, rhythm, and impish exuberance, which makes it well worth trying. In the realms to which Hamilton transports them, children might miss the orienting presence of a companion that can be either seen (to the end, we glimpse only Jahdu's shadow and a pair of sandaled feet), defined (is he an imaginary boy, a spirit, or what?), or traced somewhere (there's no story-telling Mama Luka here, no background on the passing Lee Edwards). Elusive. (pp. 1354-55)

A review of "Jahdu," in Kirkus Reviews, *Vol. XLVIII, No. 20, October 15, 1980, pp. 1354-55.*

Curiously carved and lucent beads on a storyteller's chain, anecdotes about the great Jahdu . . . are linked to form a story for beginning readers. Although more simply written, the prose has the same lyric quality as Hamilton's first Jahdu tales. . . . Being Jahdu, he solves the situation and regains his power, in an ending that should satisfy readers; what may appeal to some readers even more, however, is the imagery Hamilton uses and the playfulness with which she invents words: "Don't get so pooft and pahft," Shadow says, and repeatedly Jahdu says, in moments of stress, "Woogily!"

Zena Sutherland, in a review of "Jahdu," in Bulletin of the Center for Children's Books, *Vol. 34, No. 3, November, 1980, p. 53.*

[Virginia Hamilton has written stories about Jahdu] for older readers; here she humorously breaks them down, using the repetition and simplicity called for by beginning readers. The language is well crafted, its rhythm becoming almost a chant sometimes, yet the dialogue is a lively use of the vernacular:

"'Woogily' said Jahdu. 'I'll have me some fun.'" Jahdu remains a magical mystery creature—neither the text nor Jerry Pinkney's pencil and mauve illustrations are specific in their descriptions of him—but his cocky personality shines through. A good change of pace for the genre. (pp. 64-5)

Nancy Palmer, in a review of "Jahdu," in School Library Journal, *Vol. 27, No. 4, December, 1980, pp. 64-5.*

THE GATHERING (1981)

In the last book of a science fiction trilogy (*Justice and Her Brothers, Dustland*) the four time travellers whose parapsychological powers have carried them into the strangeness of another culture unite to fight their final battle, combining their psychic force to defeat the dark Mal. Rescuing others, they have come to the domed land from which power emanates and learn that Dustland is the future of their own time; they return home to family love and security but know that they still have power, that their knowledge of the future is not in vain. This volume, as beautifully written and as intricate as its predecessor, is a bit slow in starting; for those who have not read *Dustland* the proliferation of strange creatures, strange names, and odd speech patterns may be cumbersome at first. The story gathers momentum, however, and comes to a sharp focus and strong action. What is perhaps most impressive about Hamilton's writing is her superb ability to fuse the mystical and the dramatic; like a skilled musician, she is in control of both the music and the instrument.

Zena Sutherland, in a review of "The Gathering," in Bulletin of the Center for Children's Books, *Vol. 34, No. 7, March, 1981, p. 134.*

In the third of Hamilton's *Justice* trilogy, Justice, her twin brothers Levi and Thomas and their friend Dorian merge to form "the unit," mind-travel to the future and lead the inhabitants of Dustland into the unknown regions beyond the power of Mal, the threatening presence that has imprisoned them in Dustland. In these regions, they discover through their psychic abilities a grim yet enlightening vision of mankind's legacy to the universe. Tightly constructed with unusual yet precise metaphoric combinations, the story offers an additional dimension to the familiar concepts of dreaming, thinking and communicating. While thematically the story touches on some complex and portentous questions regarding freedom and the cost of survival, Hamilton avoids a ponderous tone by staying in touch with the children's reactions and responses and by injecting moments of light humor, particularly when the future-beast Miacis expresses herself in the colorful vernacular she's picked up from reading Thomas' mind. Readers familiar with the first two books of the trilogy . . . will find it easier to envision the characters and the situation, but those who persevere past the confusing first few chapters will be rewarded with a gripping tale that blends elements of fantasy, science fiction and classic suspense.

Marilyn Kaye, in a review of "The Gathering," in School Library Journal, *Vol. 27, No. 8, April, 1981, p. 140.*

[*The Gathering* is] the final volume of Hamilton's thoughtful but disappointing *Justice* trilogy. . . . By the end of the third volume, . . . Hamilton has established a future world as the children find it, complete with a range of mutant and created creatures, philosophical challenges, and the alternative revolutionary and social arrangements so dear to future fantasy creators. But that is where we might expect to be at the end of volume one, and we arrive there through expository conversation. We never see the four childrens' powers satisfactorily fulfilled, or see the time their formation as the "first unit" foretold. We never actually see any crisis or confrontation in the tightly controlled domity; and we never actually see the questions raised by the society's Master Plan played out in action. (pp. 682-83)

A review of "The Gathering," in Kirkus Reviews, *Vol. XLIX, No. 11, June 1, 1981, pp. 682-83.*

[The journey] out of Dustland and into the city of the Colossus, can be taken as an actual journey, so powerful is the imagery which shadows forth these two countries of the future.... Equally, this is a journey into adolescence, an experience which stretches [the young people's] capacities almost unbearably before returning them to the safe affections of home. This is an experience of people as well as of new lands. While they find ways to help submissive, dog-formed Miacis and the desert mutants, ... Justice and the rest are working out their relationships to one another, finding ways to co-exist peacefully in human as well as in exacting philosophical terms. This third book in a remarkable trilogy draws to a conclusion a unique and challenging adventure in living, presented in plangent and testingly simple prose. (pp. 3944-45)

Margery Fisher, in a review of "The Gathering," in Growing Point, *Vol. 20, No. 3, September, 1981, pp. 3944-45.*

[**The Gathering**] might conveniently be called science fiction but is more accurately described as a poet's flight into the future, in the same vein as Marge Piercy's *Woman on the Edge of Time* though unfortunately not as successful. Justice Douglass, the heroine of the trilogy, is a preadolescent who lives with her family somewhere in the vicinity of Yellow Springs, Ohio (where the author herself and many of her other memorable characters also reside). Yellow Springs was once an important stop on the Underground Railroad, a route that serves as a kind of historical metaphor for Justice's spiritual journey into the future....

[In volume one of this series, the] scenes where the youngsters first test their extrasensory powers work well, mainly because the author manages to inject a bit of magic into the proceedings. In volume two, when Tom Douglass wants to demonstrate his telekinetic powers, he does so by summoning up a gigantic astral projection of—what else?—McDonald's golden arches.

Now, having followed Justice and company into the final stage of their wanderings, one arrives in the distant future expecting something more exotic than a McDonald's logo, but the rewards just aren't there. In volume three Justice hardly exists as an independent character; for much of the story she and her companions take the form of a disembodied mind-set called the "unit." Escaping the arid waste known as Dustland, the children finally make their way to something called a "domity"—a domed city in the desert run by a godlike super-computer, Colossus, and its cyborg-archangel, Celester. Through Colossus we finally learn how this strange world came to be, but the explanation is extremely perfunctory—no more than a sketchy summary of how Earth as we know it was finally exhausted by greed, pollution and nuclear warfare and then abandoned by the genetically superior humans remaining on

it, who sailed for distant stars and left the Colossus machine behind to clean up the mess.

This grim vision might be more impressive if only we could see what it means to Justice. Supposedly she has come into the future to deliver to Colossus a spiritual gift that will enable the machine to introduce an element of freedom into the cloned, drug-sedated kingdom it rules over. However, it's never clear how the gift will change things or what it costs Justice to give it.

Virginia Hamilton is basically such an intelligent writer that she manages to pull her readers along even when there's no clear destination, and for all I know there are youngsters out there who will see their way through those murky passages that seemed so opaque to me. Nevertheless, getting through the last two-thirds of this story is a bit like listening to a recitation of the fascinating things that happened on someone's acid trip. You'd have to have been there to appreciate how meaningful it was.

Nothing is more frustrating than a fantasy whose author has given up hope of putting her vision into words, and significantly, when Levi Douglass, safely back home, tries to describe his experiences to his parents, he's reduced to drawing pictures—pictures that we, of course, never see. Says Levi:

> "See, Dad, you really have to 'see' the Slaker domity to appreciate it. You have to see the whole process of change." ... They waited for him to go on. He was clearly excited, even inspired by it. But he would not go on.

Uh-huh.

Joyce Milton, in a review of "The Gathering," in The New York Times Book Review, *September 27, 1981, p. 36.*

The Gathering, volume three of Virginia Hamilton's alluring but incohesive trilogy, is an innovative book; likely to engender a spate of analysis from Black Studies Departments, it is difficult to understand and not easy to read....

H. G. Well's, Orwell's and Aldous Huxley's accounts of the hazards of a future in which man's obsession with scientific advancement has superseded his concern for humanity are all more accessible than **The Gathering**. But Virginia Hamilton's Colossus, the crippled computer which controls Domity with its smooth-running transport system, clement climate and tranquil, because drugged, inhabitants is not complacent.

Hope that the reconstruction of a free world may be possible is indicated by Justice's willingness to give her particularly sensitive psychic power to the Colossus, even though in so doing she may be marooned forever in the Crossover. With her power the Colossus may be able to contact the Starters and together they will rebuild a humanitarian, if imperfect, planet. More interestingly, the youthful packens, who have never wholly lost their independence, decide to return to and make the best of purgatorial Dustland.

Her depiction of the aftermath of holocaust is, once one has worked out how to follow the narrative, predictable; though the possibility of an optimistic solution, however distant and for however few, is refreshing. Oblique allusion to black folklore, traditional American children's books such as Frank Baum's *Wizard of Oz*, comics and junior science fiction annuals will not be easily followed by British children and one is often tempted to treat **The Gathering** as a treasure hunt. The arbitrary use of lower case personal pronouns and dated hip-phraseology ("Be tight, you . . . be tight me") are irritating red herrings rather than welcome clues.

But it is not easy to deal with the complicated genre of science-fictional allegory for children while at the same time encouraging black confidence. Among Virginia Hamilton's more inventive devices are the children's abolitionist and humanist surnames of Douglass and Jefferson—a clear encouragement to young blacks, though also possibly a warning against losing touch with their roots and becoming the strongest of Starters.

Holly Eley, "Building New Worlds," in The Times Literary Supplement, *No. 4103, November 20, 1981, p. 1362.*

SWEET WHISPERS, BROTHER RUSH (1982)

AUTHOR'S COMMENTARY

[*Hamilton received the* Boston Globe-Horn Book *Award for fiction in 1983 for* Sweet Whispers, Brother Rush. *The following excerpt is taken from her acceptance speech, which she delivered at a meeting of the New England Library Association on October 31, 1983.*]

I'm sure I've said more than once in a moment of expansiveness that *Sweet Whispers, Brother Rush* practically wrote itself. That is to say, from the safety and comfort of retrospection it feels that way.

I don't recall any hardships, any difficulties; I sailed through the writing of *Sweet Whispers* with perfect equanimity—and total loss of memory. I do remember it was written in two separate locations. Through a fall and a cold, dull winter in Ohio, with my longing for warm sun; and on through the springtime of another year and then on to an arid, blistering hot island in the Caribbean. (p. 25)

That was, I believe, my first experience in writing a book depicting an especially specific and stark way of life remote from my natural habitat, and in writing it in two locales that were not only different from each other but also from the book's milieu. What I learned from the experience is that I can write practically anywhere, under almost any conditions, and with no ill effects to the established story line. For what goes on in my writing mind would seem to be unalterable.

I think we all know that, no matter what the writer may or may not remember about the process, a book of fiction does not write itself. That's merely the way one tosses it off after it's done—oh, it practically wrote itself. There is a willfulness, a stubbornness, to keeping oneself in a steady groove that remains the same, day after day over many long months. Moodiness, tantrums, tears, exhaustion, cries for help are not acceptable behavior. I might stomp from my study and demand the family's attention as they lounge comfortably about the round lime oak coffee table, with: "Do any of you *people* realize how hard I work?" Maybe, just maybe, one of them might glance in my direction. "I've got my own problems," my sixteen-year-old is likely to say. "Mom, can I use your car tonight?" Husband asks, "Would you like some hot tea?" Careful to keep his eyes on his beloved *New York Times.*

A fiction writer is a prisoner used to solitary confinement. It's really not so bad. One isn't actually alone because one has a steadily growing number of people—characters—in one's head. The "head" people usually have problems and difficulties over which, one realizes, one can eventually exert control. One can

even get involved in the process of solving their problems without anybody knowing one is a busybody, a literary *yenta,* so to speak.

There are some rather odd things that occur in writing a book like *Sweet Whispers.* There are those of my books that I will become more deeply involved in than others. I'm not actually aware that the involvement is more profound. But I feel a sense of calm, of being exactly within whatever it is I am writing. *Sweet Whispers* is a kind of book in which, once the first paragraph was correct as I understood correct, I knew that I could work through the rest of it; it would be all right.

My only concern was that the reader wouldn't believe in the ghost, Brother Rush. It was a problem for me, of convincing myself that the ghost could stand alone. I worried whether a reader would be convinced of a circle of springtime in a ghostly hand through which young Teresa Pratt entered another time. It was the fear that readers might not believe which made me study the ghost concept, time and time again, as the book progressed. I almost threw out Rush and his springtime. But whenever I wrote about Tree, whatever she did, Rush was there beside her, whether she was aware of him or not. Whenever I wrote about her, I thought about and saw him. That condition never varied. And, finally, I was convinced that my ghost was right on.

First lesson for a writer: Trust the primary idea and the developing structure; trust one's instincts. And go with the flow, as the young people say. That means, of course, let the writer write. Let one's self go on ahead. Writing fictions means slowing down the mind long enough to allow the hands to type what is seen in one's head. Each time I try to explain the process, the words seem to take me farther away from it. But it has to do with being able to see the feelings of others in their physical movement toward or away from one another. I could see Tree's love for her brother Dab as clearly as I could see the innocent, kind light that shone from her eyes. The light always streamed in Dab's direction, never away from him. But these feelings are largely indescribable in words. They are generally too important for conversation or dialogue and best left to motion. It is an idea that concerns touching.

Tree is really outraged at and bereft from her brother's death because it is the first time in her life that someone she has touched is dead. I wanted to say that in the book. But it is a motion of hands touching shoulders—fingers clutching. Once one has physically touched someone who is alive, one cannot accept at first that the touch, the warmth from one body to another, is forever altered. It is not something that Tree would know how to say, but it is the basis of her rage. I know it is there in her and her brother's patient, sincere motion toward each other. It was their dance of life. And to have it end was to Tree Pratt an outrage.

After seventeen books I am able to see very well and interpret what goes on in my head. I do believe I think in terms of stories. Everything that goes on in me and around me that I perceive as fresh and new lends itself to story-making. I see stories in a series of pictures to which I add words. I change words. I string them together. The pictures move and are animated lots of times, but not all the time. It depends on what the character is doing or feeling, whether or not a great deal of movement takes place.

Brother Rush never moved. Not even when he was driving his car or standing by Vy's front porch. It was as though he were a cardboard cutout. And each time I saw him, he had been moved, all of him in one piece to another place. Even bouncing the baby was a series of still shots for me. I watch the things that go on inside my head, just as some people watch television. I have done that since childhood. Daydreaming out a window, I watched what went on within. It's a strange way to live. Writing, making the book, brings this self-viewing into reality.

Sweet Whispers, Brother Rush represents a turning point at which I discovered that I have many more voices than I realized. It freed me from a set view of what fiction could be for me. I had reached some sort of plateau in my thinking. I wanted to be more daring in my work. Say more. Reach a different level of life. Speak differently. I am rather conservative in my mental set, and it takes time for me to release myself. This book has done a great deal toward a further development in my literary life. I am thrilled that it has been given such recognition. Poor Dab can live on. Even the ghost will live on and on. More young readers can read about Tree Pratt now that there are two paperback [editions]. . . . I find that exciting.

After each new book I throw up my hands and say, "I can't do it anymore." I'm tired. Husband says, "Let's go for a long drive, a couple of days." I love to drive. You can get me to do practically anything if you put me behind the wheel of a big Detroit-built. He knows that. I love sleek, overblown, cartoonish cars, the kind that Rush and Tree loved so much. Husband was right, of course. I needed to get on the highway, to turn on the radio, and to feel the America that drives right by and that you drive by; to stop and look, to smell and taste that which is so much a part of my being. I love writing books about Americans. And other books down the American road. Above all—being black, being a woman—I am an American. I can't help writing that. I can't stop it, working out the American dream learned at my mother's knee. Wouldn't want to.

Thanks so much for this recognition of *Sweet Whispers, Brother Rush*. It's good inside, when something that started as a quite personal vision is so embraced to belong to us all. (pp. 25-8)

> *Virginia Hamilton, "Boston Globe-Horn Book Award Acceptance," in* The Horn Book Magazine, *Vol. LX, No. 1, February, 1984, pp. 24-8.*

Although this has a fantasy element, it is the realistic matrix that is most touching and most trenchant. Tree (Teresa) lives with, loves, and protects her brother Dab, who is a gentle, retarded seventeen, two years older than Tree. Their mother, Vy, supports them but must live away from them in order to do so; their father has long ago decamped. Tree repeatedly sees visions of Brother Rush, her mother's brother, and in those visions she sees the past, so that gradually she pieces together the tragic family history; the tragedy culminates, for Tree, in the death of her brother after Vy (a practical nurse) has recognized the symptoms of a hereditary disease, porphyria. Heartbroken, Tree decides to run away, but the counsel and love she gets from Vy, Vy's gentle and compassionate friend Silversmith, and the elderly woman Vy invites to stay with Tree make her realize that Dab's death was inevitable, that Vy—despite her faults—is doing the best she can, and that not having to take care of Dab means that she can have some of the freedom and friendship that she has had to live without. Hamilton's writing style is always distinctive, never easy reading; here the start has an element of obscurity, but it serves almost as does the obscurity in detective fiction, to lure rather than to discourage. The characters and their relationships are

drawn with strength and sensitivity, fusing and interacting with inevitability in a positive affirmation of the power of love, an affirmation for which Tree's visions serve as a contrapuntal theme.

> *Zena Sutherland, in a review of "Sweet Whispers, Brother Rush," in* Bulletin of the Center for Children's Books, *Vol. 35, No. 11, July-August, 1982, p. 207.*

Few writers of fiction for young people are as daring, inventive, and challenging to read—or to review—as Virginia Hamilton. Frankly making demands on her readers, she nevertheless expresses herself in a style essentially simple and concise—though often given to outbursts of intense feeling. And meeting those demands, the reader not only forgives but learns to enjoy her small lapses into obscurity, which a less subtle writer would find intolerable. (pp. 505-06)

Predictably, the author has not written a conventional ghost story [with *Sweet Whispers, Brother Rush*] . . . , for Brother Rush—the ghost—is the literary device that makes the flashbacks both possible and plausible.

Not until about one-third of the story has been told does M'Vy, a vibrant figure, make her dramatic appearance—soon to be followed by that of her "'man friend,'" the sensitive, wonderfully gentle Sylvester Wiley D. Smith, nicknamed Silversmith. By this time Tree had discovered, to her horror, that the melancholy Dab had been a severely abused child; and when his agonizing illness ended in death, the story rises to a passionate peak as Tree vented her fury and her frustrated love—before she could be calmed by reconciliation and the prospect of a less isolated, more natural life.

The characters are as complex, contradictory, and ambivalent as is life itself: sometimes weak, sometimes attractive, always fiercely human. And totally convincing is Tree's perception of the ghost. (p. 506)

> *Ethel L. Heins, in a review of "Sweet Whispers, Brother Rush," in* The Horn Book Magazine, *Vol. LVIII, No. 5, October, 1982, pp. 505-06.*

[In reading *Sweet Whispers, Brother Rush*] I felt an unusual tension. At times it seemed simply a very well-written young adult novel, in which a young person's problems are bravely faced and explained. When Brother Rush was on the scene, however, I felt in the presence of another kind of imagination altogether, that of a poetic visionary who, for instance, could see two black men riding off into eternity in a fancy car smelling of alcohol and cigars. The book could vaguely bore me and utterly astound me within the space of a single chapter.

Virginia Hamilton is obviously an author who is willing to take chances, not only with her story but also in her use of language; much of her novel is told in black slang and dialect that were not easy for this white reader to follow. Her dialogue seems accurate, however, and her descriptive writing is vivid and succinct. Hamilton has won many prizes for her fiction for young people; this novel will also be widely and justly praised. I can't help wishing, however, that she would release her remarkable imagination from the contrived situations of the conventional young adult novel. I would love to see where such an imagination might lead her.

> *David Guy, "Escaping from a World of Troubles," in* Book World—The Washington Post, *November 7, 1982, p. 14.*

The last time a first paragraph chilled my spine like this one, I was 16 years old, hunched over a copy of *Rebecca*. There are those who say that Virginia Hamilton is a great writer but that her books are hard to get into. This one is not. It fairly reaches off the first page to grab you, and once it's got you, it sets you spinning deeper and deeper into its story. Needless to say, this is not a conventional ghost story. In fact, the function of the ghost in this book is to provide 14-year-old Tree Pratt with a place from which to view her world. (p. 41)

The supernatural, the search for identity, the need to belong to a family and the pain of belonging, the encounter with death—Miss Hamilton has taken ideas that occur repeatedly in books for the young and bathed them in her unique black light. Her readers have come to expect stories peopled with almost mythic black characters, but in this book everyone we meet, including the ghost, is wonderfully human: Tree, in the depths of her grief, takes secret delight in the attentions of a young man; her mother, Vy, who, when young, abused her strange little boy, is able as a woman to care for him with efficiency and love but still cannot call him by his name; and Miss Cenithia Pricherd, in her pageboy wig, is the prickliest, most lovable bag lady you'd ever want to know. The language too is of Miss Hamilton's own special kind, which uses the speech forms of the young to enhance rather than restrict the music of the book.

There is no need for me to say anything to those fierce Hamilton fans who will leap joyfully into anything she writes. But to the more timid reader, young or old, who may feel inadequate to Miss Hamilton's always demanding fiction, I say: Just read the first page, just the first paragraph, of *Sweet Whispers, Brother Rush*. Then stop—if you can. (p. 56)

> *Katherine Paterson, "Family Visions," in* The New York Times Book Review, *November 14, 1982, pp. 41, 56.*

Sweet Whispers, Brother Rush (ain't that a dandy title?) is like a thoughtfully designed African American quilt. It is finely stitched, tightly constructed and rooted in cultural authenticity. Hamilton uses humor that is sometimes finely wrought into a sharp pathos. She clips the fabric of tragedy, turning it into an arresting applique that makes her handling and revelation of human error, of human inability to cope, of tragedy, memorable. She has an ability to combine narration and dialogue in a way that stamps her as a consummate storyteller.

The story turns on three elements: the strong, loving relationship between fourteen-year-old Tree (Teresa, the main character) and her older brother Dab, who is retarded for reasons that are revealed in a fascinating way, the task Tree has in caring for her brother during her mother's extended absences and the relationship Tree has with a marvelous ghost, Brother Rush.

The narratives left by those men and women who were slaves document that ghosts revealed themselves accompanied by light and/or right after a rush of warmth. And so it is that Tree can tell, in the old tradition, when Brother Rush is coming: "Sunshine with little warmth was what it was like." . . .

The characters, even those who appear briefly, are clearly drawn and convincing, though the behavior of Tree's mother Vy may be difficult to understand. What is Vy's motivation for being gone so often and for so long? We know through Tree that some of the training that makes her loving and responsible comes from Vy. We learn toward the end of the story

some of the reasons it was difficult for Vy to be at home in the way that we might feel she ought to be. Hamilton has not created a traditional, stereotypic, idealized mother. Is Vy's behavior insensitive? Understandable? Unforgiveable? Necessary? Like behavior in the "real world"—or too like the stereotypic "neglectful" Black mother?

Virginia Hamilton is a courageous writer, sure of her ability to deal in depth with sensitive topics: the heartache of children in the face of adult betrayal or great loss, the fear that spirals in one's stomach when one contemplates being alone in the world, the inability to do a simple thing that everyone else knows or thinks ought to be done easily, and the struggle of a teen-ager on her own to manage big responsibilities. The author has great understanding of her characters, and she provides the reader with a strong identification or awareness, even disagreement with, them that continues, even after the book's been closed for three or four weeks.

There are a few stitches that come loose, but only a very few. Hamilton's use of African American language is so well done. We're treated, for instance, to a Tree who is a competent and authentic user of the language and who reads—also competently—to Dab from Warren Miller's book, *Cool World*. Hamilton thus sends a clear message to all those who keep insisting that Black children can't be taught to read unless they speak something we keep insisting is standard English. At the same time, there are ambivalent messages about the importance of our language. Tree continually speaks to herself about correcting her speech, and, at one point, Vy sees herself as "guilty" when she uses African American language forms, as though it were a crime. One wishes that Hamilton's characters did not convey such negative messages about the language that she herself writes so beautifully. However, a novelist who is poet enough to write "Their walking was a day rhythm in the midst of quiet light" is one who can dispel most of the annoyance.

And though not everyone will agree with the resolution of certain of the conflicts, one is inclined to doff one's cap to a writer who demonstrates that she can write/tell a story about such critical life problems and powerful emotions with grace, skill and *seeming ease*.

> *Geraldine Wilson, in a review of "Sweet Whispers, Brother Rush," in* Interracial Books for Children Bulletin, *Vol. 14, Nos. 1 & 2, 1983, p. 32.*

THE MAGICAL ADVENTURES OF PRETTY PEARL (1983)

In a blend of fantasy, folklore, realism and even aspects of her own family history, Hamilton tells an allegorical story of black people through the late 19th Century. Pretty Pearl, a god child moved by the suffering of the captured slaves in Africa, comes down from on high on Mount Kenya with her powerful god brother, John de Conquer. Disguised as albatrosses, the gods travel with the slave ships to Georgia and lie low in southern soil for hundreds of years. Then, at the time of Reconstruction, Pretty Pearl goes among the people, armed with magic powers and powerful ancient spirits, but disguised as a human. She resides with the "inside folks," a self-sufficient community of fugitives from racism, who secretly live deep in the forests of southern Georgia, closely in touch with a remnant Cherokee band. Then, with the railroads and hunters coming nearer, the time comes for the people to leave their secret place: led by the Indians, they avoid the Ku Klux Klan strongholds and cross the Jordan to settle in Ohio. John Henry is Pretty Pearl's brother, a black giant spirit, wonderfully drawn as a laughing daredevil character who cannot help choosing the human way and will die challenging the machine. Like her brother, Pretty Pearl loses her magic power and becomes part of the human community—which grows strong with the spirits of the ancient gods among the people and with the power of their stories. This imaginative truth of enduring community is perfectly expressed in Hamilton's style, which moves from simple narrative to folk-knowledge of "nut, leaf and bark," to colloquial idiom and blues rhythms; her telling demonstrates that songs, tales and chants are rooted in the daily experience of "folks everywhere," and that language is a living force.

> Hazel Rochman, in a review of "The Magical Adventures of Pretty Pearl," in School Library Journal, Vol. 29, No. 8, April, 1983, p. 123.

The truth is that Virginia Hamilton has a magical imagination, although once again young readers will have to stretch their own to follow hers in this blend of mythology and realism. . . . The most important and involving part of the book is [Pretty Pearl's] experience with a secret black community (spiritually reminiscent of the commune in *M. C. Higgins the Great* . . .) hiding in the depths of a dwindling Georgia forest and helped to freedom from persecution by a remnant of Cherokee warriors. Interwoven with the story of Pearl's transition from god to human is the lively appearance of spirit creatures such as her rascally companion Dwahro, her wise older god-self Mother Pearl, and her giant god-hero brother John Henry, all well developed in proportion with the forest leader Black Salt and his "inside folks." This is an impressive and vivid work that gathers force slowly and by the end, surely. The panorama is such that more historical exposition than is fictionally manageable backdrops the details that usually spring Hamilton's situations to life; John Henry's personal choice between bound godhood and free death is much more moving than Old Canoe's description of the Trail of Tears, for instance, and more complex in terms of the individual/group identity that runs so strongly throughout the book. On the other hand, the roots of the past—brilliantly represented in ginseng and John de Conquer roots that are the dominant images of spiritual power—are artfully nurtured toward a fruitful future as mythology, history, and personality converge in the conclusion. In terms of black studies, literature, and language (the stylistic variation is both demanding and memorable), this offers rich depth for discussion among perceptive readers. (pp. 1034-35)

> Betsy Hearne, in a review of "The Magical Adventures of Pretty Pearl," in Booklist, Vol. 79, No. 15, April 1, 1983, pp. 1034-35.

Like other mythical characters, Pretty Pearl embarks on an arduous journey to test her strength of character. Along the way, universal and timeless truths are revealed. Readers also learn the history of a specific people, in this case American blacks.

Miss Hamilton's language draws heavily from black idiom and is rich and playful. "Everybody got nothin' to do!" Pretty Pearl complains about life on the Mountain. Later, fallen from grace, she becomes "not-so-pretty Pearl," a "god-forsaken chile!"

Myths generally comprise more than one theme. *Pretty Pearl* is no exception. Predominant, though, is the idea that how we live is who we become. When Pearl acts hatefully—like a human being—her punishment is to become one. When the spirit Dwahro, who starts out as a caricature of the high-stepping dude, interested only in fine clothes and good times,

behaves unselfishly, "actin' de best way a human is to act," he gets his "most solemn wish. To be a man. To be free." John Henry, the "famous steel-drivin' man," is Pearl's oldest brother and a god. In a deft display of what free will is and is not, he beats the new steam drill and gets to die like a man. "To be human," he says, "is about worth de whole world."

The truth is that the truth of any people touches us all. This novel can be read and understood on more than one level. What young readers may miss the first time around they will understand better the next. It is a book to be read and reread, and not only by children.

> Barbara Ann Porte, in a review of "The Magical Adventures of Pretty Pearl," in The New York Times Book Review, September 4, 1983, p. 14.

There are few authors who possess the literary talent that Virginia Hamilton is able to bring to her stories. **The Magical Adventures of Pretty Pearl** is marvelous fantasy, fascinating history; filled with poetic beauty and characters who are real. Hamilton is a gifted writer whose capabilities in evoking magic within the pages of books is without parallel. Her stories and characters are the kinds of which dreams are made. Unlike **Sweet Whispers, Brother Rush, The Magical Adventures of Pretty Pearl** requires a more literary, sophisticated audience. Readers need to bring at least an interest in African folklore fables, mythology and history to really get the full picture of this wonderful, indeed magical novel.

As you read **The Magical Adventures of Pretty Pearl,** the pictures brought to life by the text, the lyricism, the love of the story is evident. . . . I do not agree with some reviewers who designated this as a children's book. It certainly requires a maturity that only a small percentage of children would have. I am not certain that the message Hamilton imparts in this novel would necessarily appeal to children. Young adults and adults will enjoy more.

> Penny Parker, in a review of "The Magical Adventures of Pretty Pearl," in Voice of Youth Advocates, Vol. 6, No. 4, October, 1983, p. 215.

The Magical Adventures of Pretty Pearl, like much of Hamilton's writing, has the quality of a grand myth. It draws on fragments of stories heard in family and community, memories of African American childhood games and the much suppressed African roots of our culture. It also draws on stories of the slave and reconstruction eras with Black protagonists. These tales are still highly threatening to white society, so how they are retold is important. They require sensitive, artistic and respectful handling, and Hamilton does a fine job of meeting these criteria in a book that should serve as an inspiration for other African American writers. . . .

Symbolically, this is a creative retelling of the sojourn of African peoples in this country, what happened to them, and the spirits and traditions they brought with them that led to the creation of African American spirits and traditions.

There are a couple of areas of ambiguity. One is the repeated use of "them" or "they" or "who" that keeps the "darker people," as Hamilton calls them, enslaved. While it is important not to belabor this point to the detriment of the story, explicitness about the role of white slavers and slavemasters would have made that aspect of the history sharper. The misperceptions young people have about the history of slavery is breathtaking. In addition, Hamilton seems to be writing about an "outlyer community," one of the secret communities established by runaway slaves, but I wonder if the setting is clear enough for children.

And will children understand the "charred black shape hung from a limb of a poplar tree beside a smoldering cabin"? Pretty Pearl says that "Be my poor heart hangin there—yes, it is!" And it is *her* heart, it is my heart, it was my mother's heart as she struggled to tell me what lynching was. But she told me. Hamilton implies, but does not say explicitly, that what hung on the tree was a person. Children should be given the gift of fact. A tough assignment.

Nonetheless, Hamilton gives us many moments of prophetic clarity and she has given us a respectful approximation of the language forms that Black Americans used in the 19th Century. She's included *authentic* phrases and idioms and has done well with the structure and phrasing.

Don't miss *Pretty Pearl*! The book will provide you with magical spiritual moments, some belly laughs. But best, it will introduce you to some very serious African American ancestors and cultural archetypes who inhabit a great history we should all know much better. (p. 17)

> Geraldine L. Wilson, in a review of "The Magical Adventures of Pretty Pearl," in Interracial Books for Children Bulletin, Vol. 15, No. 5, 1984, pp. 17-18.

Few contemporary American writers for adults or children have explored the limits of narrative as courageously as Virginia Hamilton; the innovative stream-of-consciousness first chapter of *Arilla Sun Down*, the radically unexpected ending of *The Planet of Junior Brown* with its community of underground children who have found their own free space in the basement of an abandoned building; the richly textured prose of *M. C. Higgins the Great*—these are only a few of her achievements. Indeed many of Hamilton's novels for children and young adults have explored the nature of story and narrative itself, often celebrating the charmed circle of power drawn around tellers and listeners. In *The Magical Adventures of Pretty Pearl* Hamilton intricately weaves strands of African myth and folklore with social and family history to create a powerful tapestry which reveals what it is to be divine and mortal, mother and daughter, brother and sister, slave and free human being. Finally the narrative presents a powerful quest for black female identity as artist who is valued by the community. In telling the magical adventures of her memorable female hero, Hamilton incorporates folk poetry and song, using such typical Afro-American literary devices as repetition, call-and-response, and creative improvisation. Not the least of Hamilton's achievements in *The Magical Adventures of Pretty Pearl* is her use of intensely poetic prose rendered in a compelling black idiom.

Structurally *The Magical Adventures of Pretty Pearl* features a linear quest and a fall from innocence into painful experience. Born on Mount Kenya, Pretty Pearl, god chile, yearns to rescue suffering Africans from oppressive slavery. Pearl's older brother, the chief god on Mount Kenya (called Mount Highness), John de Conquer, warns Pearl not to leave the mountain.... (pp. 50-1)

Despite his reservations, John de Conquer, the most powerful god and giver of the magical folk herb, John de Conquer root, often called "King of the Forest," accompanies Pearl on part of her journey.... [He] hopes to teach Pearl that she must remember that she is a god and that she must not become involved in the human cycles of history.

Pearl, however, ... [is] anxious to work for the people. She challenges her brother. Why not free the people and take them back to Africa at once? John de Conquer patiently explains that, "De human life got to unfold and be written".... But Pearl is not satisfied; she thinks that her brother is just spoiled and used to having his own way. She becomes yet more impatient as she sees the former slaves without food, homes, employment, or education. Many of the people are murdered and terrorized by evil white Night Riders, the dreaded "Ku Kluck." Many more starve to death. Watching it all in anger, Pretty Pearl exclaims: "That's no kind of way to die.... You call that freedom?" ....

As Pretty Pearl readies herself to begin her quest to help the people, she makes up songs and stories, Hamilton's way of stressing that folklore, story, and song are important ways by which suffering human beings survive and even make art out of the direst human experience. Many of these songs come directly from the despairing hearts of the people.... (pp. 51-2)

At last John de Conquer agrees that Pretty Pearl must go into the forest and live like the people in order to help them. He also gives her several gifts as protective talismans: a magical necklace made of two strands of his strong black hair on which is strung a rich dark John de Conquer root and four spirits— the African *fula*-fa-fa (a woodpecker), the Hodag for a workhorse, the Hide-behind to "scare bad folks and enemies to death," and Dwahro, who can "feel and tell and know better than most".... These gifts, John de Conquer explains, must not be misused. Pearl must never part with her necklace and she must never use her spirits to hurt or to frighten human children out of spite or anger. The young female hero, once she is clothed in the kind of shift worn by human children, is now ready to begin her epic journey. She knows that her destination lies deep within the dark and mysterious forest. So it is that Pretty Pearl, happy and innocent god child, embarks upon her perilous way into the labyrinth of the human condition. Pretty Pearl is destined to fail one of her most important tests of character and to fall into the flawed state of humanity. Hamilton suggests finally, however, that Pearl's is a happy fall indeed. No longer immortal and divine, the human child nevertheless possesses divine gifts in the end: she has the gift and the power of storytelling and the joy of belonging to the human community.

In the course of her adventures Pearl must contend with Dwahro's rebellious nature. He begins his spiritual life as a singing, dancing "dude," who loves fine clothes and good times. Dwahro dislikes his status as spirit, wishes to be human, and particularly resents Pretty Pearl's authority over him.... To control Dwahro's restless spirit, ... Pretty Pearl uses chants and spells. (pp. 52-3)

Pretty Pearl's gifts for language, story, and song become an important way in which she comforts and inspires the suffering freed slaves:

> I'm goin' down that long, lonesome road,
> I'm goin' where those chilly winds don't blow....

The people take up Pearl's song and begin to hum; song and poetry enable them to endure. Pearl also serves as a namer in her community. (p. 53)

Eventually, as Pretty Pearl grows to feel more and more like a human child, she splits herself into two manifestations, creating a mother out of her own wishing and needing. Hence, Mother Pearl, Dwahro, and Pretty Pearl continue their journey through the dark forest of North Georgia. Before reaching the edenic community of "Promise," the place where a group of freed black people who call themselves the "inside folks" live, Mother Pearl teaches Dwahro some of the forest's secrets. She shows him how to fashion pottery from clay and how to glean yellow dye from black hickory bark, green from oak leaves, purple from pokeberry roots, indigo blue from maple bark, and even reveals to him such heavenly colors as *yennier, glamina,* and *uleena.* When paints, bowls, and brushes are all in order, Dwahro begins his first painting on Mother Pearl's apron: a picture of Mother Pearl herself next to a great yellow poplar. When he had finished the first painting, "he painted the scene again on the apron in the painting. And again. And again. When he was finally finished, he had a painting within a painting within a painting in a painting on Mother's apron". . . . This powerful and infinitely receding image mesmerizes three bandits who wish to terrorize and to murder the little party, an incident suggesting that Hamilton sees art itself as a potent mode of survival. Dwahro, the vain, blithe, and light-hearted dude, thus begins to grow into an artist. When he does so, he is ever so close to becoming truly human.

The inside folks of Promise, the community led by a strong black man, Black Salt, welcome Mother Pearl, Pretty Pearl, and Dwahro. This group of fugitives is protected by a band of Cherokees, in turn led by a kind and wise old chief, Old Canoe, who functions also as historian and storyteller. He reminds the inside folks of the "Trail of Tears" when so many of his people had died on the long journey west to Oklahoma; many black people also died on that journey, he says. Mother Pearl becomes the "mawmaw" woman for the community. While the other women labor in the fields or gather ginseng, Mother Pearl watches over the children, organizes them into groups to complete household chores, and stirs the pot of "King Gombo" to feed the people. Perhaps more important, she tells the children stories. She and Dwahro also teach them the use of herbs, roots, and the use of other good things from the forest, which emerges as a kind of sacred symbol, a sheltering place which also provides all things needed by the inside folks. Mother Pearl knows a song or a chant for every occasion. . . . Mother Pearl and Dwahro, then, help to make the community more secure and comfortable by helping to organize labor and by teaching arts and crafts, story, song, and dance.

Meanwhile Pretty Pearl begins to forget who she is. Increasingly her ways of knowing, seeing, and feeling become more and more human; she realizes that "she would likely enjoy herself best with humans if she allowed herself to discover and know the way they did". . . . Like any human child, Pearl sometimes becomes irritable and cranky. In an impulsive fit of spite and anger, she releases the hide-behind to frighten the children. In the process she also releases the *fula*-fa-fa and the hodag. As a result of her folly, Pearl loses her power and her divinity. The John de Conquer root shrivels and dies. Pearl herself falls sick, her hair and eyes losing their vitality and beauty. Pearl's famous brother, John Henry Roustabout, the steel driving giant, arrives in Promise to comfort his little sister. But even John Henry is powerless to help her.

As Pearl has fallen and lost her divine power, so the community of Promise begins to change from its edenic state of innocence. Old Canoe warns Black Salt and the other inside folks that the railroad is coming and that bird hunters are drawing ever nearer. Promise is no longer a haven and a free space deep within the forest. Sadly the people prepare to leave separately and to journey farther north in search of a home where they may at last be free and safe.

At last John de Conquer comes close to Promise to see Pretty Pearl. Mother Pearl, John Henry, and Dwahro can hear de Conquer's magical singing drum; Pearl can hear nothing now but the forest sounds. When he arrives, John de Conquer restores Pearl's beauty but not her divinity and not her immortality. John Henry, Pretty Pearl, and Dwahro have all become human. To be human is to assume mortality as well. John Henry's fate is to beat the steam drill and to leave an inspiring heroic legend for his people. In the long journey to find a new home, Black Salt and his family will look to Dwahro to give them spirit. With his prancing, dancing, and singing, Dwahro gives the people joy, makes them laugh, and shows them how to play. But Pretty Pearl gives them myth and story. She reminds them of who they are and where they came from. Proud and tall now, Pearl has inner vision and reveals the word. She tells how John Henry beat the steam drill and "'he die with two hammers in his hands'". . . . She reminds the people how John de Conquer fooled the slave owners and freed the people and how:

> "Anytime we need him hard, he hit that hypocrite. *Ta-ta-tum.* It singin' freedom. *Ta-ta-tum.* Teachin', 'Know him by de Conquer, secret root.' *Ta-ta-tum.* Him comin' home to us, hold us safe. *John de Conquer.*"

> "Yea, Lawd," the folks murmured, and sat there, satisfied, enjoying themselves. . . .

To find her own voice and to secure her identity, her own place within the community, Pretty Pearl must endure a painful but inevitable separation from both her mother and her brothers. Hamilton conveys Mother Pearl's pain at leaving her child with understated poignance. Mother protects her children as well as she can. She spreads her apron over them. She teaches Pearl her stories. She gives Black Salt a family name, "Perry" (Hamilton's family name). She then transforms herself into an albatross to return to Mount Kenya with John de Conquer. But she knows the pain Pretty Pearl faces in becoming human. Mother Pearl must bear the double sorrow of knowing that Pretty Pearl must assume her own pain and experience and that she, Mother, is finally powerless to shield her child. Most important, though, Mother Pearl and Pretty Pearl are one. As Adrienne Rich has written, in an important way women *are* their mothers and their grandmothers. Hence Hamilton's character, Sweet, in *Sweet Whispers, Brother Rush,* literally slides into her mother's skin in order to feel and to know her mother's experience. Pretty Pearl keeps the divine part of herself when Mother tells her the stories and makes her the keeper of the community's history. In making her potent myth about an Afro-American *hero* as opposed to the *hero,* Hamilton seems herself to reach far back into the mythical past to uncover the hidden and buried stories of black women. To tell this mythical story of the Mother, Hamilton has used the simplest folklore, "nut, leaf, and bark," as well as complex and sophisticated figuration. Her use of the black idiom resonates with the rhythms of the blues; her improvisations in narrative technique, her deft play with black language, her intricate weaving of dance, song, story, and chant resemble an accomplished jazz composition. . . . A powerful muse has allowed Virginia Hamilton to re-absorb and to re-express African and Afro-American myth and folklore. While many characteristics of *The Magical Adventures of Pretty Pearl* resemble the older myths, Hamilton has nevertheless created a powerful allegory for her own time and place. One of the most pervasive themes in African and Afro-American folk literature concerns the victory of the small and in some ways helpless character over force and oppression. Often in African myths even the high god himself is outwitted by the trickster hero, just as Pretty Pearl, Mother Pearl, and Dwahro outwit the bandits who wish to kill them.

In one important way, however, Hamilton has departed from a traditional pattern in her sources in order to create a myth appropriate for her own world. In African myths one of the most pervasive and persistent themes is the loss of paradise. This loss usually occurs because human beings lose a sense of comfort and unity when god removes himself. The gods in African myth do not usually concern themselves with human beings. Even the Trickster, who sometimes appears as a Primitive Prometheus, is not truly concerned with humanity. When his actions benefit human beings, it is usually accidental. *The Magical Adventures of Pretty Pearl* reverses this pattern. God is not a male and not powerful, but a small and vulnerable girl who loves human beings and who feels called to the world of experience and pain. Her divine fire is the fire of the imagination which she freely imparts to the human community in the form of the arts of song, story, and dance. Though Mother Pearl and John de Conquer depart for Mount Kenya in the end, they leave a deep and abiding part of themselves with the people. God and humanity, Hamilton affirms, are deeply implicated one with the other. The powerful vehicle for connecting divine and human beings is through art and creative human faculties. Pearl's storytelling is a public and communal occasion. Hers is an intensely dramatic art in which the audience participates in making the event. Hamilton thus celebrates the idea of community which lives strong and vibrant through the lively arts of story and song, just as the gods themselves live for the people in Pretty Pearl's stories. (pp. 53-7)

> *Anita Moss, "Mythical Narrative: Virginia Hamilton's 'The Magical Adventures of Pretty Pearl'," in* The Lion and the Unicorn, *Vol. 9, 1985, pp. 50-7.*

WILLIE BEA AND THE TIME THE MARTIANS LANDED (1983)

The focal point of an absorbing family story is its reaction to the now-famous Orson Welles broadcast that frightened so many people throughout the United States. Willie Bea is as credulous and convinced as are other members of her family, even though she hasn't heard the broadcast, because it's an adult (glamorous Aunt Leah, always dramatic) who brings the news that the Martians have landed in New Jersey. Hamilton uses the material with great skill, but—exciting as it is—the most impressive facet of the book is the vibrant, loving picture it draws of an extended black family. The story takes place in 1938 on Halloween, and most of the children and grandchildren of an Ohio farm family are gathered together for dinner, a time of cousins squabbling, sisters gossiping, grandmother calmly organizing, all the small events of a reunion under and through which are the sustaining love and security of family life. Willie Bea is a touching heroine, volatile and imaginative, protective toward her younger siblings, candid and intelligent. Like the book, she's a winner. (pp. 50-1)

> *Zena Sutherland, in a review of "Willie Bea and the Time the Martians Landed," in* Bulletin of the Center for Children's Books, *Vol. 37, No. 3, November, 1983, pp. 50-1.*

Hamilton's gallery of richly portrayed characters extends to one more: a girl old enough to take responsibility for all her cousins at the Sunday dinner, extended-family gathering that defines the first half of the book; a girl young enough to be overwhelmed with fear by some new harvesting equipment on the Halloween night in 1938 when Orson Welles featured his Martian invasion program, which dominates the second half of the book. The action here is fairly meandering, but the reactions are as perceptively drawn as ever. Dynamics among both adults and children are sharp and clearly detailed through conversation and episode both typical of the times and unique to the individuals. More than a story of one memorable day and night, this is a celebration of kinship ties, sometimes strained but ultimately strong, that will give contemporary importance to a historical setting.

> *Betsy Hearne, in a review of "Willie Bea and the Time the Martians Landed," in* Booklist, *Vol. 80, No. 5, November 1, 1983, p. 408.*

The Martians—of Orson Welles' famous 1938 broadcast—don't just queer Willie Bea's Halloween; they pretty much shatter Hamilton's keen, affecting drama of family relations.... [Waiting] for trick-or-treat time, Willie Bea entertains her little sister and brother with radio imitations (a wonderful, period- and child-true scene); she gets them ready, in make-do costumes and (scarey-to-themselves) makeup; and, then, descending in triumph—they find Aunt Leah, glamorously attired and escorted, shrieking that the world is coming to an end! What follows is mainly spook-farce and thematic manipulation—which will be read differently, moreover, by kids who've learned about the Orson Welles broadcast from the jacket (or elsewhere), and those who haven't.... In switching to special effects and juvenile-fiction platitudes, Hamilton undercuts the resonant descriptions and emotional cross-currents of her earlier, stage-worthy naturalism. For kids, it won't be fatal; but it is too bad. (pp. J-191-92)

> *A review of "Willie Bea and the Time the Martians Landed," in* Kirkus Reviews, *Vol. LI, No. 21, November 1, 1983, pp. J-191-92.*

Although the cover illustration is an unfortunate giveaway of the climax, our heroine's daring-do doesn't slip into the cornball, overly sentimentalized antics that spoil too many pre-teen books today. Author Virginia Hamilton once again saves the day for imaginative fiction with a finely crafted blend of once-in-a-lifetime escapades and everyday events.

Some young readers may stumble over the country dialects, and others probably won't appreciate Willie Bea's renditions of such popular radio shows of the day as "The Green Hornet" and "Little Orphan Annie." But overall, the sights and sounds, aromas, and impressions of rural Ohio—from homemade corn muffins to cool, springy green lawns—are among the details that contribute to the success of this remarkably effective story.

On one level, it's an unpredictable adventure. On another level, it's an intimate look at one extended black family that helps to remind us that all families have their share of characters.

What makes the Mills and Wing kinfolk so appealing is the unabashed affection they share with one another. At her grandparents' homestead, Willie Bea slices up pumpkin and lemon meringue pies for her younger cousins. At home she likes to feel her baby brother's hand in hers as they descend the darkened stairs together; when she spots her father returning from work, she puts on her Mary Janes to go out to meet him.

At the end of the book, when Aunt Leah leaves a surprise hanging on the back of Willie Bea's bedroom door—a store-bought Halloween costume—we can fully agree with the attached note that promises, "Wave your magic wand and anything can happen."

Diane Casselberry Manuel, "A Halloween Night to Remember," in The Christian Science Monitor, March 2, 1984, p. B7.

Much has been written about the panic that seized the nation when the Orson Welles broadcast of "The War of the Worlds" was heard on the radio and mistaken for an actual news report of Martians landing. Virginia Hamilton's extraordinary talent with language weaves a tale that extends beyond a simple description of the impact of the broadcast. It's a portrait of family life, with the interaction between neatly sketched, memorable characters revealing the full range of human emotions.

This is one of Miss Hamilton's most accessible books. Despite any unfamiliarity with the time and situation, readers will recognize the appealing protagonist's relationships with her relatives, her protective instincts toward her younger siblings, her rivalry with a nasty cousin. Willie Bea's own encounter with the "Martians" . . . lends drama and suspense to a charming story that rings with humor and warmth. . . .

Many critics and reviewers consider Miss Hamilton one of the most significant contemporary writers for children. She's been awarded just about every recognition in the field, including the Newbery Medal and the National Book Award. Her talent includes a demonstrated ability to illuminate the human experience in the context of black culture.

Some have said that her work is not always suitable for children and that the richness of her prose and the elaborate configurations and interactions of her plots put the story out of a child's reach. It is true that her intricate patterns of language and nontraditional plots suggest a refusal to condescend to any prescribed notion of a child's understanding. But her work is accessible to the intelligent and demanding young reader.

In *Willie Bea and the Time the Martians Landed,* the child's voice prevails as she encounters an unfamiliar situation and responds as a child would. The adult point of view never intrudes. The reader lives through Willie Bea's experiences with her, and the terror of the night becomes a shared adventure.

Miss Hamilton has a graceful way of evoking time and place without irrelevant or obvious detail. While the circumstances of the novel are historically essential to the plot, the emphasis, as in all her work, is on character and the workings of one special mind in a special circumstance.

Marilyn Kaye, in a review of "Willie Bea and the Time the Martians Landed," in The New York Times Book Review, March 18, 1984, p. 31.

A LITTLE LOVE (1984)

A novel that dignifies the term *teenage romance* casts four (black) characters so three-dimensionally that a reader will sense their presence almost physically. A slow, heavyset teenager with artistic hands and a flair for work in her food service major at a vocational high school, Sheema becomes obsessed by the thought of finding her father, who left home the day her mother died in childbirth. Sheema's boyfriend Forrest strongly supports her through difficult days at school and home, where the grandparents who have raised her seem to be deserting her now—her grandfather increasingly absent from home, her grandmother increasingly absentminded. The parallel relationships between the young couple (they secretly make love at night in Forrest's car) and the old one are touchingly detailed as both find new closeness through Sheema's rite of passage, a trip south with Forrest to confront her father. This book reaffirms the strength of young people and old people—ordinary people figuratively and sometimes literally hungry for love. The attentive development, rhythmic narrative in black English, and vivid scenes rival and extend Hamilton's crafting of *Sweet Whispers, Brother Rush.*

Betsy Hearne, in a review of "A Little Love," in Booklist, Vol. 80, No. 19, June 1, 1984, p. 1392.

Sheema is overweight, casual about her love affairs, and a slow student in school. Out of such unpromising material grows a memorable character whose thoughts, fears, and motives one comes to understand and respect. . . . Riding in her boyfriend's ancient Dodge, against a background of gas stations and drive-ins, Sheema looks for her father; yet, in its ultimate revelation of her own self-worth, the search acquires the dignity of a true quest. The author's finely tuned understanding of the rhythm and flow of black speech and her keen observation of the humdrum details of daily living lend richness and vitality to Sheema's story. The book explores her awakening consciousness as a black woman, and it paints, in a masterly mixture of humor and compassion, a compelling portrait of her grandparents. When Sheema finds her father and realizes what he might have contributed to her intellectual development, her anguish is a transcendant moment of understanding as is her final acceptance of her grandparents' limited aspirations but enduring affection. (pp. 597-98)

Ethel R. Twichell, in a review of "A Little Love," in The Horn Book Magazine, Vol. LX, No. 5, September-October, 1984, pp. 597-98.

Virginia Hamilton's prose in *A Little Love* is expertly crafted. It expresses the richness of Black English and, like excellent poetry, introduces endless images, metaphors and ideas with an economy of words. Moving easily between the world of Sheema's thoughts and feelings and the details of her daily life, Hamilton communicates the subtle shifts in Sheema's consciousness as she awakens to a sense of self. She also creates meaningful portraits of the rigors of attending vocational high school, of life with two aged adults, and of being lost and Black in a Southern town.

Sheema herself is one of the most original characters to spring to life in a young adult novel. Replete with inconsistencies, her integrity is unquestionable. . . . Like most of us, she is complex, wavering in self-awareness. And, like the most fortunate among us, she comes into her own with the support and love of those whom she loves.

Susan C. Griffith, "Novel Depicts Black Teens," in New Directions for Women, Vol. 13, No. 6, November-December, 1984, p. 19.

Virginia Hamilton always creates memorable characters in her well-told stories. In *A Little Love,* she once again writes of a solitary female teenager who "comes of age" through struggle in order to face some painful realities in her life. . . .

Insightful, reflective and, in the end, determined, Sheema makes progressively mature decisions—not without depression and anxiety—in preparation for her adult life which will come quickly.

As in some of Hamilton's previous books, the solitary young woman is cast opposite a strong, engaging male. This time, it's no ghost or cultural archetype. Forrest is a friendly, caring person, a fellow student who cares about Sheema and assists her in the process of learning to value herself and become self-confident. . . .

Sheema's quest to find her father, the shocking recognition that her grandparents are aging and her struggles to control her appetite and depression are well-done, often moving. Such struggles should be an inspiration to teenagers.

A few worries. Sheema is a "sexually active teen-ager," and Forrest is responsible for helping her face and curb her casual sexual encounters with a number of boys. (Whenever Forrest and Sheema "make love," Hamilton writes the phrase "a little love.") Given that simply *everybody* knows that teenagers are sexually active, does one simply write about all that exists or does one pose some challenging, creative alternatives to what many consider questionable behavior for youngsters? Forrest and Sheema's sexual activity is romantic, often clearly the refuge that both teenagers feel they need emotionally. As such it almost seems appropriate, but do we really approve of sexual behavior at a young age? (Moreover, the teenagers have almost no discussion about birth control.) . . .

Another problem. The text, with no countering statement, notes that Sheema didn't "like blowing out her hair, although it always made it look so much better." How can Black women with tightly curled, naturally springy hair counter such assaults? Such topics would make a great story. Meantime, read *A Little Love.*

> Geraldine L. Wilson, in a review of "A Little Love," in Interracial Books for Children Bulletin, Vol. 16, No. 4, 1985, p. 19.

A Little Love is a brilliant tightrope performance, in which third-person narrative and stream-of-consciousness are held in a delicate balance. . . .

There is no melodrama, no grand revelation. Simply a marvellously acute portrait of a girl and boy learning to rely on themselves, and on each other, related in a style which, like that for which Robert Louis Stevenson strove, "attains the highest degree of elegant and pregnant implication unobtrusively". Virginia Hamilton is responsive to the cadences and idioms of street talk embedded in the thoughts of a natural observer who has never learned to make connections. The story proceeds by oblique statement, and trivial incident so sharply felt that the reader is continually surprised by the sudden woundingness of everyday life. . . .

"Old-fashioned" Granmom and Granpop are tenderly and precisely observed; he with his need for little intrigues, she lapsing into a querulous inanition, living for the daily "soaps" on afternoon television. Sheema's slow realization that they are getting too old to cope is conveyed in a series of poignant vignettes which never tip into sentimentality. Of all the central characters only Sheema's father, when we finally meet him, seems rather thin; but, then, that is Sheema's impression too.

The scenes on the road are—perhaps because one compares them to so many other books and films—less immediate and compelling than those at school or at Sheema's grandparents' house. Nevertheless it is on the road that the special quality of the relationship shown in the earlier section is made plain. This is no teenage problem fiction; Sheema and Forrest's is a

real love, and it will last: "Have to marry you, you worry me so."

The limpid economy of this book, and the idiosyncratic exactness of its language, make one think of William Mayne. The book is open and accessible, but every word has been weighed and tested, and the syntax—for instance, the variation of tense—carries the emotional charge. Virginia Hamilton is highly regarded in America, but has yet to make an impact in Britain. The eloquent restraint of this humane and moving novel should change that.

> Neil Philip, "What You Ain't Never Known," in The Times Literary Supplement, No. 4300, August 30, 1985, p. 958.

Virginia Hamilton is never dogmatic or restrictive about her characters. We have to decide for ourselves why Sheema suddenly needs to find the father who had walked out after her mother died in bearing her. Perhaps she realises that she must find a way to be more independent of the old people, whose wayward behaviour seems at times frighteningly like senility. . . . The journey, central to the plot as it is, is described succinctly and with a shrewd eye to the extra difficulties that could beset two black teenagers travelling in a jalopy outside their own state; what matters more is the parallel journey of emotion as Sheema faces the fact that her father doesn't need her and that she can do without him. This is a wonderfully taut, rich picture of two young people, their love expressed in idiomatic, casual, poignant talk, their lack of experience as evident as their courage in moving outside the regular pattern of school and home. Once more Virginia Hamilton has broken the limitations of novels for teens by her extraordinarily rhythmic, compelling prose and her perceptive view of the tragi-comic business of growing up. (pp. 4525-26)

> Margery Fisher, in a review of "A Little Love," in Growing Point, Vol. 24, No. 4, November, 1985, pp. 4525-26.

JUNIUS OVER FAR (1985)

In Grandfather Jackabo's lilting Caribbean speech, the title means that his grandson is far away. The gentle old man, often confused, misses the son and grandson he has left in the States to return to the small and beautiful island of his youth. For most of the book the chapters alternate, written from Grandfather's viewpoint or from that of Junius. Each has his own concerns (the boy with a budding love affair, the man with the mysterious disappearance of a white man who is a distant relative and has been both companion and enemy). As Grandfather's letters sound increasingly confused, Junius decides he wants to go with his father to see what is wrong and to bring the old man home with them. The story gives adequate preparation for the dramatic conclusion (contraband, an arms cache, mercenaries, arrest) of events on the island and for the reunion of the three loving men of the family. Hamilton will never hurry her writing; because her tales unfold at their own pace and in her laminated style, her books are seldom easy to read. That is true here; although the writing is clear, it is deliberate in pace and nuance; it is also richly rewarding for its color, warmth, subtlety, and memorable characters.

> Zena Sutherland, in a review of "Junius Over Far," in Bulletin of the Center for Children's Books, Vol. 38, No. 8, April, 1985, p. 148.

This richly textured new novel by Virginia Hamilton has two memorable heroes, a setting of great beauty and the clear intention of enlarging black people's awareness of their past. . . . [Jackabo is] an imposing, emblematic figure in a monks'-cloth cloak, with his bamboo staff, touchingly human as he battles the onslaughts and indignities of age. . . .

[The] most enjoyable section of the book [comes after Jackabo is rescued]. Junius experiences the island in its splendor. He starts to become "an island mahn for true" while also gaining insights into its complex problems. This enables him to understand his father better, and the two draw closer.

It's all convincing, except the end. The idea that the black Rawlingses will now be able to take over the plantation and make it a vacation home seems more expressive of the author's longing than strictly probable.

Make of this what you will. But read the book with care. It's worth it. Mrs. Hamilton respects her art too much to restrict her exuberant vocabulary. Nor does she curtail needed exposition: As for descriptions, she glories in them. Reader, even if you usually tend to skip descriptions, try giving these their due. They will yield pleasure and an almost physical sense of being on that spectacular island "over far," right along with Junius.

> *Doris Orgel, in a review of "Junius Over Far," in* The New York Times Book Review, *April 7, 1985, p. 20.*

The novel has more dimensions than a plot outline can indicate: Junius' first love is sensitively developed, as is Jackabo's vividly described drifting between senility and reality. The dynamics between child, parents, and paternal grandfather are well handled; and those between the descendant of slave owners and the descendant of slaves are complex—a seesaw of name-calling, understanding, bitterness, and begrudging respect. In many ways an adult novel, this will challenge high school and perceptive junior high readers.

> *Betsy Hearne, in a review of "Junius Over Far," in* Booklist, *Vol. 81, No. 18, May 15, 1985, p. 1325.*

To the list of strong charcters denoted in *Zeely, M. C. Higgins, The Great* and *Sweet Whispers, Brother Rush,* Hamilton adds a new group. . . . It is the bond of love, respect, and charity cemented with perseverance which overcomes obstacles arising from shyness, loneliness, aging, and self-delusion in this excellent novel interlaced with the human conditions portrayed through family unity, student life, adventure, mystery, intrigue, folklore, romance, and poetry. A notable author provides another masterpiece to increase the value of every YA collection. (pp. 130-31)

> *Virginia B. Moore, in a review of "Junius Over Far," in* Voice of Youth Advocates, *Vol. 8, No. 2, June, 1985, pp. 130-31.*

As always, Virginia Hamilton explores fundamental and important themes through powerful descriptions, but the alternating settings and shifts from Caribbean dialect to standard narrative form may prove to be too difficult for all but the most tenacious readers. The book's principal interest lies not in the plot but in the gradual unfolding of the complex bonds that link generations, the provocative exploration of the relationship between Jackabo and Burtie, and the subtle balancing of a young boy's journey into manhood against an old man's journey toward eternity. The portrayal of the debilitating effects

of age is especially moving, but the perspective is as sophisticated as it is powerful. Like Hemingway's *Old Man and the Sea,* the novel not only requires a mature audience for full understanding but also demands rereading for full appreciation. (p. 564)

> *Mary M. Burns, in a review of "Junius Over Far," in* The Horn Book Magazine, *Vol. LXI, No. 5, September-October, 1985, pp. 563-64.*

THE PEOPLE COULD FLY: AMERICAN BLACK FOLK TALES (1985)

In her own voice, which is true to the original stories in all their variety, Hamilton retells 24 representative black folktales with immediacy and drama. The stories are organized into four sections: tales of animals; the supernatural; the real, extravagant, and fanciful; and freedom tales. There are famous stories, such as the Tar Baby . . . and also the less well known (including several tales brought to the U.S. by immigrants from the Cape Verde Islands off the coast of West Africa). Hamilton's introduction emphasizes the creativity of the slaves, whose stories combined their African heritage with the sorrow of their oppression, as they secretly and symbolically told one another their hopes and fears. At the end of each story a brief note discusses topics such as origin, variants, motifs, and symbolic meaning. A long bibliography lists adult collections and commentary. Many of the stories demand to be told or read aloud. They start directly and develop with exaggeration, comedy, horror, and wit: the ugly Hairy Man was

> coarse-hairy all over. His eyes burned red as fire. He had great big teeth, with spit all in his mouth and running down his chin.

They may end with a laugh or a shiver. The true slave narrative about rowing runaways across the Ohio River has a stark poetry: "we were so scared and it was so dark and we knew we could get caught and never get gone"; and Hamilton relates this to her grandfather's story of escape. The beautiful title story, both anguished and hopeful, is about those who flew away from brutality to freedom, and those who had to stay and who told the story. From *The House of Dies Drear* to *The Magical Adventures of Pretty Pearl,* Hamilton has made this folklore an integral part of her fiction. Now she tells the stories for themselves with a simple power that will make this a classic collection for all ages.

> *Hazel Rochman, in a review of "The People Could Fly: American Black Folk Tales," in* Booklist, *Vol. 81, No. 21, July, 1985, p. 1554.*

The combination of Newbery winner Hamilton and [Leo and Diane Dillon], two-time Caldecott Medalists, raises high expectations. It is especially noteworthy that they've combined their talents to present a collection of Black American tales— a folklore awesome in its richness, power and complexity. With all this in mind, we expect to find here nothing less than fire from the mountain. Though there is much to enjoy, and many parts are quite stirring (such as the title story), Hamilton has prepared a sampling of carefully and respectfully retold tales, not a living work of art.

A surprisingly facile introduction sets a restrained tone. And her forerunner, the complex figure of Joel Chandler Harris, is unfairly assessed. From reading Hamilton, one would not get the idea that Harris took enormous pains to reproduce the tales as he heard them, even when elements of the stories were incomprehensible to him. (p. 1088)

The final [section] ("Carrying the Running-Aways: And Other Slave Tales of Freedom") is by far the most effective for the contemporary reader; the best of these stories convey great heroism, beauty and nobility. Less rewarding are the fantasy tales (with the exception of **"Wiley, His Mama, and the Hairy Man"**), and the supernatural tales (although they frequently entertain, and several would be excellent as read-alouds). The animal tales move the reader the least, and are rather lifeless.

Hamilton's approximation of dialect speech is laudable for its readability. The Dillons have lent handsome black-and-white paintings to the work, but they seem posed and static. Still and all, this is a useful collection and a valuable undertaking. Though flawed, it brings a good sampling of lore from the past to a new generation of readers. (pp. 1088-89)

A review of "The People Could Fly: American Black Folk Tales," in Kirkus Reviews, *Vol. LIII, No. 19, October, 1985, pp. 1088-89.*

Over the years, Afro-American writers have retold these stories; some have even written their own versions, but seldom has this ancient literature been made available to younger readers. Fortunately, Virginia Hamilton, the distinguished children's author, has corrected this absence with her extraordinary and wonderful *The People Could Fly.*

The world depicted here is gruesome, but no more so than in the world's epics, the Bible, the cabala, the Icelandic sagas and the Homeric tales. People sell their grandmother's corpse for money. In the first section, "He Lion, Bruh Bear, and Bruh Rabbit," pride is dealt with by putting a boastful lion in high-risk contact with an armed huntsman. Entrapment strategies are used against thieves, as in the famous and eerie Tar Baby tale. In one tale, a wolf who steals milk from Aunt Fish-Horse (a manatee) is tortured before being drowned. In the most obvious racial allegory, a well-off family of alligators who don't know what Trouble is are given a deadly lesson by Bruh Rabbit, who has had much experience with Trouble.

The second part of Miss Hamilton's book is entitled "The Beautiful Girl of the Moon Tower and Other Tales of the Real, Extravagant, and Fanciful." Its narrative style is poetic and strange; the plots filled with surprises and deceptive twists, magic and riddles. They are all about humble lads, equipped only with confidence, who rise to the top of the feudalistic order by using conjure. . . .

The book's final section, "Carrying the Running-Aways and Other Slave Tales of Freedom," includes stories based on actual events, as well as fantastic tales. Arnold Gragston, a slave in Kentucky, tells of towing fugitives across the Ohio River to freedom. In other tales, slaves perform fantastic feats, solve riddles and amuse their masters in order to gain their freedom. In the last story, **"The People Could Fly,"** slaves escape by becoming airborne. . . .

[Miss Hamilton] has been successful in her efforts to write these tales in the Black English of the slave storytellers. Her scholarship is unobtrusive and intelligible. She has provided a glossary and notes concerning the origins of the tales and the different versions in other cultures. . . . *The People Could Fly* makes these tales available to another generation of readers. What an excellent present.

Ishmael Reed, "Allegories with Alligators," in The New York Times Book Review, *November 10, 1985, p. 38.*

Hamilton brings back to us, in fresh ways, one of the oldest storytelling traditions in our history. . . . Its tales of tricksters and transcendence have a political bite, but no pat political lessons, a deadpan irony without cheap tricks, the surrealism of the oppressed, in which the craziest things do happen. More than that, Hamilton has the language. She has found a way to write in a black English that escapes sounding like Uncle Remus, and imparts a poetry you'll never get from the Brothers Grimm. Some years ago, working as a book clerk, I saw plenty of middle-aged black customers, and some whites, buying *Roots* as a treasured keepsake, a monument to Afro-American survival. *The People Could Fly* has at least as many claims to be a source of pride. (p. 18)

Sean Wilentz, "On Reading to Children: Sweet Dreams Are Made of This," in VLS, *No. 41, December, 1985, pp. 1, 16-19.**

The People Could Fly is a solidly entertaining collection of folktales in dialect, well illustrated and splendidly told; but it does not represent, as its teller Virginia Hamilton seems to think, a body of testimony about what it was like to be black and unfree in America. She includes in the book some slaves' wish-fulfilment fantasies and also a "reality tale", about rowing runaway slaves across the Ohio River; she pays tribute to its superior reality with a signed postscript, as if all the other words in the book were not hers as well.

If a story depends for its force on historical fact, it isn't a folktale. There is something rather too much like historical pain in a passage like this:

> Sarah couldn't stand up straight any longer. She was too weak. The sun burned her face. The babe cried and cried, "Pity me, oh, pity me", say it sounded like. Sarah was so sad and starvin, she sat down in the row. "Get up, you black cow", called the Overseer. He pointed his hand, and the Driver's whip snarled round Sarah's legs. Her sack dress tore into rags. Her legs bled onto the earth. She couldn't get up.

In this story, **"The People Could Fly"**, the boundaries of reality and fantasy remain sharply demarcated. In a true folktale, like **"The Two Johns"**, the boundaries are fluid and pain is casual; someone killing your grandmother is only the middle term of an escalating series of trials you undergo, something that happens to you rather than to her.

A folktale betrays the times of its first telling or first popularity only in trace elements, like the magic spells of these stories, which are in a language that Hamilton presumes to be a garbled African, but cannot reconstitute.

It must be tempting to see in these stories the record of a particular painful history, but Hamilton does not make a convincing case. Slaves belonged to their masters very much as their cattle or horses did, and this leads her to detect identification on the teller's part with animals, which she describes as "highly unusual in the animal folklore genre". But anthropomorphism is such a basic mechanism of folklore, from Aesop all the way down to Richard Adams, that this sounds very much like special pleading.

Hamilton scolds Joel Chandler Harris (whose *Uncle Remus,* 1880, gave many Americans their first exposure to black folktales) for not "reproducing exactly the tales or their language" and for using "phonetic dialect as a literary device". Unfortunately no transcriber of oral lore, Hamilton included, has any choice in the matter. Since the tales do not exist in a final form, no reproduction can be exact, and the alternative to using dialect as a literary device is to abandon it.

Harris may have made too much of the quaintness of the tales he passed on, but Hamilton has a bias of her own: she chooses to see these stories as in some essential way exotic. This is understandable enough with some stories, where she has, so to speak, had to translate from Gullah English (originally Angola English); but she underplays any links between her tales and, say, their English relations. She traces the bogeyman Raw Head and Bloody Bones, in the story **"Little Eight John"**, back to a "slavery folk rhyme", but doesn't mention that Raw Head and Bloody Bones, who even puts in an appearance in *Ulysses,* has been used to frighten children since at least 1550.

Scholarship, then, is not Virginia Hamilton's strong point; but it hardly needs to be. Her tales get going with a splendid bland confidence. "Now, facts are facts", she will say, or "Let's talk about one time", or "Think a sea wave left this tell on the doorstep". The best tales hover between laughter and fear. Wolf, in **"Wolf and Birds and the Fish-Horse"** . . . starts as a stooge and a villain, but ends up almost as a tragic hero when Aunt Fish-Horse takes her revenge on him. . . .

A similar impressive balance is achieved by **"The Peculiar Such Thing"**, which also exploits dialect's affinity for vivid non-description. The details of the horror are delayed almost to the end of the story; M. R. James would surely have approved. The only comic element in the whole tale is the peculiar such thing's peculiar sing-song phrasing; but that is enough to intensify the reader's shivers.

Adam Mars-Jones, "Talk About One Time," in The Times Literary Supplement, *No. 4326, February 28, 1986, p. 230.*

The eminent black author's abiding interest in folklore has generated a highly significant collection. . . . [One] finds in the book a tar baby story and other slyly comic narratives about such characters as Bruh Rabbit, Bruh Fox, Bruh Alligator, and Bruh Deer. **"The Beautiful Girl of the Moon Tower,"** on the other hand, is an "exaggerated-reality" tale, an elegantly simple one of magic and love. **"The Two Johns"** is a variant not only of a well-known folk tale but of Hans Christian Andersen's "Big Claus and Little Claus"; and there is a lively version of the adventures of Wiley and the hairy man. **"John and the Devil's Daughter"** features the legendary hero John de Conquer, while **"Little Eight John"** is a mock-serious cautionary tale about a contrary little boy. A wonderful retelling of the American scary tale **"Better Wait till Martin Comes"** fits in nicely as does a rollicking version of the familiar **"Wicked John and the Devil."** In the final group the mood changes; the humor becomes somewhat sardonic, while anger, sorrow, and heroism lie beneath the surface of the poignant tales. **"Carrying the Running-Aways,"** a true story out of the author's own family history, is striking in its immediacy and realism. And the title story, while available in other collections, has nowhere else been recounted as movingly and memorably. Found in the book are many universal folkloric motifs—riddles, numerology, lies and exaggerations, magical transformations, and especially the triumph of the downtrodden over the powerful—which are overcast with black images and meanings. The author's notes, brief, informal, and illuminating, are sensibly placed at the end of each story. A few of the tales contain some dialect, and a racially allegorical Gullah story includes a glossary; but most of the tales are told in standard English of pungency and zest. (pp. 212-13)

Ethel L. Heins, in a review of "The People Could Fly: American Black Folktales," in The Horn Book Magazine, *Vol. LXII, No. 2, March-April, 1986, pp. 212-13.*

Erik Christian Haugaard

1923-

Danish author of fiction and translator.

Haugaard is regarded as a powerful storyteller and disciplined craftsman whose historical fiction for upper-grade readers usually features children coping with the horrors of war. Noted for his multilingual background and careful research, Haugaard uses accurate detail, relevant imagery, and poetic language to recreate the historical and cultural environments of such diverse periods as Viking Norway, feudal Japan, Cromwellian England, and Second World War Italy. Setting his epic tales in times of violent upheaval which challenge traditional values, he stresses the futility of war and the importance of human worth, compassion, and courage. Haugaard's protagonists, usually male adolescent orphans, reflect his indomitable faith that youth can prevail despite frequent encounters with adult betrayal, persecution, and death.

Critics acclaim Haugaard for the significance of his topics, the imaginative force of his language, and the vividness and authenticity of his settings. Although some reviewers point out that his child heroes sometimes sound too wise, most acknowledge that Haugaard's characters, including the secondary figures, are well drawn and that he treats his readers with uncommon respect. Commentators agree that Haugaard portrays history with the sensitivity of a poet while presenting timeless messages to his audience.

The Little Fishes **received the first** *Boston Globe-Horn Book* **Award for Excellence in Text in 1967.**

(See also *Something about the Author,* **Vol. 4;** *Contemporary Authors New Revision Series,* **Vol. 3; and** *Contemporary Authors,* **Vols. 5-8, rev. ed.)**

Courtesy of Erik Haugaard

AUTHOR'S COMMENTARY

Why is so much of children's literature inferior? There are, after all, very few children's classics. Fairy tales and folk tales were composed for grownups, and many of our favorite nursery rhymes were originally political quips. When we write for children, we hold doomsday over our own childhood, which is not only unpleasant but may even be dangerous. "Children are happy, for if I have not been happy once, then I cannot bear my present state." The little savages must have lived in paradise, and the knowledge of growing up expelled them. The baby's shoes, eternized in bronze, on the mantelshelf, once covered carefree feet. This picture of the child is still cherished in children's literature, not because it is true, but because it makes life bearable for the adult. Children's literature is meant to be read by children; but it is written, published, and bought by adults, who have a personal stake in the image of childhood. (p. 445)

What should children's books do? A book for a child ought to teach something, or articulate something which the child has, as yet, only felt. A children's book should be like a good grownups' book: an experience which enriches the reader. It should be a work of art and should be judged by that standard, for any lesser standard is an insult to its audience. There are

differences between the children's world and the grownups', and the writer should remember them, certainly. After all, the child has not reached his full physical development; nor is he free, in the sense that a grownup is free—or at least, has the possibility of being free.

It is easier to discuss what children's books should not be. They should not be based upon their creators' nostalgia for "paradise lost," nor upon the daydreams of children, in which ten-year-olds perform Herculean tasks; the latter produces the "yellow press" for children, which is no less contemptible than the one for adults.

The state of children's literature seems to me to be both worse and better than it was in my own childhood. Better for the obvious reason that there are many good writers writing for children (though I wish some of them had more respect for their readers). Worse because of the comic books and the speculation in cheap books for the birthday trade, which is encouraged by the fact that many adults spend less time choosing a book for their children than they do picking a soap for their washing machines.

If you ask a question and the answer given you is a lie, you would have been better served had you received no answer at all. Then, at least, you would have been free to speculate for yourself until you discovered an answer which satisfied you.

If you accept the lie and build on it, you will spend great effort and time propping up the walls for fear the building will fall upon you. If a child is fed on comic books and sugar-coated lies, unless he is a very extraordinary child, he will continue to have a taste for such drugs. Children will go from comic books to movie magazines, and from sentimental children's books to sentimental best sellers. (p. 446)

Erik Christian Haugaard, "A Writer Comments," in The Horn Book Magazine, Vol. XLIII, No. 4, August, 1967, pp. 444-46.

[In the following excerpt, Shelton L. Root, Jr. and M. Jean Green-law interview Haugaard on his youth, writing background, and some of his works.]

[Shelton L. Root, Jr. and M. Jean Greenlaw]: When did you start to write?

[Erik Christian Haugaard]: I made up stories long before I could write. In Denmark children do not begin school until they are seven years old. My parents told me that I used to call these stories "self" stories to distinguish them from the ones they read aloud to me.

[Interviewer]: Do you know why you made up these stories?

[Haugaard]: I think all children are forced to face at a very early age—certainly, before they can read—that there is an endless number of questions to which they are given no answers; or put off with a "just because," "that's the way things are," or "don't trouble yourself about that." . . . Then, I believe, the child with imagination tries to conceive of a world without hypocrisy and war. He or she probably does not succeed, but in the process of formulating the queries into pictures, he stumbles on the causes that make these questions answerless. At this point many children are satisfied, they identify with the grownups and share in their resignation. But the artistic child persists, at least partly because he is fascinated by the journey, he delights in his make believe world. . . . But wait, although there are escapist elements in it, I am not talking about escapism. The sensitive child does find it necessary to escape, but unless his fantasy is to become his enemy instead of his staunchest friend, he must take some part of reality with him, so that the transition is not too painful.

[Interviewer]: When did you decide that you were a writer?

[Haugaard]: When I started making a living at it. I was over forty by then.

[Interviewer]: Is that your definition of a writer: one who earns his living at it?

[Haugaard]: There is something in all of us that makes us want to earn our living at our art, which can be distinguished from writing for money. I think every writer knows what will sell and that it's just a matter of luck and good publicity which one of a hundred mediocrities—of good books—is on the best-seller list. I knew when I wrote *The Rider and His Horse* that I should have called it *The Fall of the Masada,* and I regret now that I didn't. But when that book was published, I had just returned from living on a kibbutz in Israel, where most of the members were survivors of concentration camps; and I thought it would be wrong of me to exploit the American Jewish public. *The Rider and His Horse* is the only one of my books that is out of print in the USA. The pride was false, but perhaps also I did not have faith enough in the book.

[Interviewer]: Do you think less of *The Rider and His Horse* than you do of your other books?

[Haugaard]: By no means! Probably more.

.[Interviewer]: But you just said—

[Haugaard]: I know. I know. I don't think any of my books are bad. Modesty is not one of my virtues or my faults. But we started by talking about my beginnings as a writer, my childhood hopes. Now, I should probably call them childish but I can't. I wanted to write like Conrad and I haven't succeeded. In fact I think that *The Rider and His Horse* is one of my best attempts to create literature. Although I am not Jewish, it is the most autobiographical of all my books. The story of an upper class boy who suddenly finds himself alone among the poor. . . . I became a farmhand when I was fifteen.

[Interviewer]: Yes, that experience seems to have been traumatic. You mention it often. Could you explain more specifically? You described your family as "wealthy," "bourgeois," "upper-middle class." Why did you go out to work on a farm?

[Haugaard]: They lost their money. . . . [The] idea of going to work on a farm was my own. At fifteen I was a rebel and a dropout. I was difficult, strongwilled, and an embarrassment, especially to my mother, who found it impossible to believe that anyone who did badly in school was not stupid. (pp. 551-52)

With all the advantages of a room of my own, an intellectual background, liberal parents, I had failed! There were no mitigating circumstances. It wasn't a sin, but certainly it was a shame. (p. 553)

When I was at home, I felt that I was a clod. I wasn't even a very good farmer. I was small for my age and not very strong.

[Interviewer]: Then you weren't the resourceful Guido of *The Little Fishes*?

[Haugaard]: Oh no! Guido was inspired by a beggar whom we met in Italy in the late 1950s. He was totally self-sufficient. Almost all the incidents in *The Little Fishes* are based on stories that my wife and I heard about what had happened in the area near Cassino during the Second World War. Most of them were told to us by Liliana and Menenio Codella, to whom the book is dedicated. Liliana had lived in the cave which is described in the final chapters of the book. A baby actually was born there. (pp. 553-54)

[Interviewer:] What about the main plot, the story of the journey from Naples to Cassino which Guido made with Anna and her little brother?

[Haugaard:] Oh, that was more or less my own; but it has its roots in reality. All the places exist, including the Roman bridge, "the magic road," and the water-mill. As I said, the beggar boy was someone we knew in southern Italy in 1959 or 1960. I shall have to call him "the real Guido" because I never knew his name. He came to our apartment every day for weeks. My wife fed him and gave him a few lira and sometimes clothes. One day, because it was snowing and he had on only a pair of old tennis shoes, she gave him a pair of ski boots. The following day, though it was still very cold, I met him in the marketplace wearing his tennis shoes again. We knew that he sold most of the clothes we gave him and that was all right. But it annoyed me to think that he had probably received almost nothing for a really fine pair of boots, especially since he had so much use for them himself. So I told him that I thought he'd been a fool. "But I didn't sell them!" he protested. "I don't believe you," I said. "Wait here," he ordered—"the real Guido'' was never polite. About twenty minutes later, he returned with a five-year-old boy who was wearing the boots tied to his legs to keep them on, for they were too big for him. ''My brother,'' he announced. ''I take good care of him.'' (p. 554)

[Interviewer:] I think we ought to get your chronology straight. I have you on a farm in Denmark at fifteen and in the Royal Canadian Air Force at twenty. I have heard you say that you believe that it is the experiences of one's youth that determine what one will write about. Those five years must have been crucial.

[Haugaard:] I am pretty bad at details like dates, but I know that I came to the United States in March of 1940, when I was seventeen. My brother and I sailed on the last ship to leave Danish waters before the German invasion. (p. 555)

Like driftwood, like any one of my own heroes, I was caught up, my choices limited and determined by events over which I had absolutely no control, or even understanding—though I wouldn't have admitted it then. . . . Being uprooted because of war, I suppose that is the basic situation in most of my books; but the themes vary. Only the very young are totally choiceless; that is one of the things that I was trying to say in *The Untold Tale.* Dag was only seven years old. He could not fend for himself as Guido had. Almost any adult—even the prostitute who beat him—was better than none. (p. 556)

[Interviewer:] How did you get started writing for chlidren?

[Haugaard:] I sent a manuscript to Houghton Mifflin called *The Last Heathen.* It was an adult novel about Earl Hakon of Norway who attempted to re-introduce the Norse religion a generation after his realm had been Christianized. Such folly fascinates me. The manuscript was returned with a letter that began: ''This is one of the most distinguished manuscripts Houghton Mifflin has received in a long time . . . ,'' then it went on to say that in spite of its distinction, the book wouldn't sell because there was no interest in the subject matter. A few days later came a letter from Mary K. Harmon, Houghton Mifflin's children's editor. She had also seen *The Last Heathen* and suggested that I might be able to write a children's book on the same theme. My opinion of American children's books was based on ignorance and hearsay, and I wasn't enthusiastic about the project; but then Mary K. sent me a copy of Scott O'Dell's *Island of the Blue Dolphins* to give me an idea of the kind of book she hoped I'd write. I was deeply impressed; if that's what she wanted, then it was certainly worth trying to do, and I started writing *Hakon of Rogen's Saga.*

[Interviewer:] How much does an editor have to do with your books?

[Haugaard:] With the actual writing, nothing at all. I am open to suggestions about additions or changes after the book is written, but I only appreciate them properly in retrospect. Mary K. and I disagreed about *A Slave's Tale,* and we decided to ask Ruth Hill Viguers to act as judge. She said that she understood Houghton Mifflin's reservations, nonetheless she felt that the book ought to be printed as I had written it, and it was. On other occasions I have been very grateful for criticism. Mary K. thought that *A Messenger for Parliament* was too confusing and demanded too much historical knowledge to be read by American children; still Houghton Mifflin was willing to publish it if I would add a few explanatory pages. This time I realized how much validity there was in the critique, and I rewrote the whole book. I am very glad I did. I think an author's

relationship with an editor is very much like a pregnant woman's with her doctor; it's highly important and very individual. What I want is constant encouragement. Praise, I can't get enough of it!

[Interviewer:] I understand that *A Messenger for Parliament* is the first volume of a trilogy about the English Civil War, a children's *War and Peace.* Did you have any particular reason for choosing this period of history?

[Haugaard:] I wanted to write a book about the Irish famine— I still do. But in order to understand anything that's happened in Ireland during the last three centuries, you have to know something about Cromwell's invasion. Once I got started studying the English Civil War, I was struck by how much that period resembled our own. (pp. 557-58)

[Interviewer:] Aren't you implying that history repeats itself?

[Haugaard:] I do believe that under similar circumstances, the stage is set for similar things to happen; but that they don't necessarily have to because what the players say and do still matters. And the more you know about the possible eventualities, the better equipped you are, at least, to prevent those which you consider the most catastrophic. I sometimes wonder whether those who advocate that children should be taught current events at the expense of history are aware that they are making them not more politically conscious but more manipulable. To isolate children in time is as crippling to their imagination as to isolate them in space is to their intellect.

[Interviewer:] Is that the reason you write historical fiction, to throw light on our own times?

[Haugaard:] Partly, I suppose. I probably write historical novels because they are the kind of books that I liked as a child. I found my own times dull; . . . I loved to daydream, I still do. When I am writing a book, I am totally immersed in the period. I want to know what my characters would be doing in every situation, even though I may have no reason to write about them. I talk about nothing else. (pp. 558-59)

[Interviewer:] That makes five periods in history that you must be an expert on: the Vikings, the American Civil War, the fall of Jerusalem—

[Haugaard:] Stop! I don't know a thing about any of them! I don't know how to explain it, but as soon as I have finished a book, I take down all the maps, and remove all the reference books; and somehow, as I tidy up my studio, I seem to sweep my mind clean at the same time. I sometimes cannot even recall the names of the characters in my books. I have such a very poor memory; that is one of the reasons that I did so badly in school. I suffer terribly because of it. You'll find above my typewriter not only Cromwell's dates, but those of my own hero, Oliver Cutter.

[Interviewer:] In *A Slave's Tale,* your protagonist is a girl. She stows away on a ship, she fights on a battlefield, she even kills a man. Was this your way of doing something for women's liberation?

[Haugaard:] Helga, the heroine of *A Slave's Tale,* was a Norse woman and they did bear arms as well as sail. For Scandinavian women, the conversion to Christianity was a step backwards. I really wouldn't consciously distort history, you know, even to prove my favorite theories. Writing any book is a matter of selection and that's where the self-deception usually takes place. Oh, there is some deliberate deletion, too. I think an author does have a responsibility towards society, especially when he is writing for children.... I think one should always aim at objectivity, aware, of course, that we'll never never achieve it. You know it's probably an excuse, but whenever I am truly trying to be truthful, about the good and beautiful, I find my mind filling up with clichés and platitudes. It's so much easier to be clever about what's wrong with the world than what's right.

[Interviewer:] You haven't mentioned *Orphans of the Wind*, and yet I understand that that was your romp.

[Haugaard:] I did enjoy writing it most. It's a sea story. My studio was filled with books about ships; there was a huge diagram on the wall with the name of every stick and sail. I love sailing. (p. 559)

> *Shelton L. Root, Jr. and M. Jean Greenlaw, "Pro-file: An Interview with Erik Christian Haugaard," in* Language Arts, *Vol. 56, No. 5, May, 1979, pp. 549-61.*

GENERAL COMMENTARY

RUTH HILL VIGUERS

Erik Haugaard's *Hakon of Rogen's Saga* . . . introduced one of the most important writers of the sixties to the United States.... *Hakon* and *A Slave's Tale* . . . are laid in Norway and in the seas about her islands at the end of the Viking period. Although the action is violent, brutal, and tragic, the stories are moving and often beautiful. Mr. Haugaard's third book, *Orphans of the Wind* . . . , is a thrilling adventure story laid at sea, in the Carolinas, and in Virginia during the first Battle of Bull Run. It is narrated by Jim, a deck boy on a British blockade runner, whose awakening to the meaning of slavery and of civil war is sharp and unforgettable.

Mr. Haugaard sets a high standard for books for today's young people. Always he has a story to tell, a powerful story that touches emotions and shows respect for his readers. And, deeply and completely integrated in his story, he has something to say that transcends didacticism, that leaves a residue of wisdom and compassion in the hearts of his readers. He accomplishes what is expected of the best novelists—a reflection of life that throws light upon humanity and the needs and desires of the human spirit. (p. 496)

> *Ruth Hill Viguers, "Quests, Survival, and the Ro-mance of History," in* A Critical History of Chil-dren's Literature *by Cornelia Meigs, Anne Thaxter Eaton, Elizabeth Nesbitt, and Ruth Hill Viguers, ed-ited by Cornelia Meigs, revised edition, Macmillan Publishing Company, 1969, pp. 484-510.*

SHELTON L. ROOT, JR. AND M. JEAN GREENLAW

When Houghton Mifflin published Erik Haugaard's first book, *Hakon of Rogen's Saga* . . . , it was evident that a writer of tremendous talent had arrived on the scene. His style matches his approach to historical fiction. He is a sure-footed storyteller who knows what he wants to say and says it with such perfectly cadenced prose that mood and theme are subtly reinforced without his style ever becoming obvious. Each of his books is informed by a wisdom that makes it profound, but never pe-dantic. (p. 549)

> *Shelton L. Root, Jr. and M. Jean Greenlaw, "Pro-file: An Interview with Erik Christian Haugaard," in* Language Arts, *Vol. 56, No. 5, May, 1979, pp. 549-61.*

LOIS R. KUZNETS

Erik Christian Haugaard is not only an historical novelist, but a truly international one. A Dane who writes in English and publishes in the United States, Haugaard began, in writing *Hakon of Rogen's Saga* and *A Slave's Tale,* with a Viking past that was part of his own Scandinavian heritage. Within a five-year period, however, he extended the range of his subjects to include British shipping to Civil War America (*Orphans of the Wind*), Southern Italy in World War II (*The Little Fishes*), and the fall of Jerusalem in the First Century A.D. (*The Rider and His Horse*). Then, after several years, Haugaard returned to Scandinavian history with *The Untold Tale,* set in seventeenth-century Denmark at war with Sweden. Now, branching out again, he is engaged on part three of a trilogy about Cromwell's England, the first two volumes of which have already appeared (*A Messenger for Parliament* and *Cromwell's Boy*).

Haugaard's reputation for careful research needs no defense: his books are of general interest for their faithful depiction of various epochs of Western history. But Haugaard, perhaps more than many historical writers, searches out not only the diverse but the universal in these historical moments: his books are not just glimpses of other days and worlds, but investi-gations of the human spirit under the most trying circum-stances. Throughout his works, Haugaard's choices of situa-tion, character, narrator, and image are significant, for they contribute not to the glorification of the powerful, but to the appreciation of the often neglected powerless. Generally, he sees the powerless as people who manage, despite all hin-drances, to make important moral decisions and to achieve emotional and spiritual growth that the powerful rarely per-ceive, understand, or attain.

This paper investigates the ways in which Haugaard's tech-niques and the choices and concerns common to his novels express and exemplify a basic philosophy of life. The following three quotations, each from a different book, express both poetically and implicitly the nature of the task he has set out for himself in writing about the powerless:

> For a moment we stood in silence. Then the screams, curses and moans of the wounded be-gan. This is the song of the battlefield that no one dares tell. . . .
>
> (*Hakon of Rogen's Saga*)
>
> Will no one ever listen to the sparrow's song and learn from it the truth the eagle flies too high to hear? . . .
>
> (*A Slave's Tale*)
>
> . . . I had read history too closely, read of Cae-sar and the Roman Empire. I had not noticed that in the books there were white spaces be-tween each line; the spaces are there to remind you of the unspoken, the unwritten truth. . . .
>
> (*The Little Fishes*)

In even a superficial reading of Haugaard's books, one clearly discerns that they are alike in general situation: all are about periods of extreme violence and armed conflict. Haugaard de-scribes the full horrors of these times, certainly more fully than we would like our children to experience them in life, or per-haps even in print. His confrontation of violence and its results has its purpose, however: it allows Haugaard to "sing," as stated in the quotation above, "the song of the battlefield that no one dares tell" and to write "the hitherto unspoken, unwritten truth'' ignored by standard histories, hoping someone will at last listen to the ''sparrow's song.''

War is truly Hell. Haugaard insists that no one, not even children—and not even in the interest of psychological protection—should ever be persuaded or permitted to think of war as fun and games. Haugaard, whose purpose is similar to Kurt Vonnegut's in *Slaughterhouse Five* (although his technique is very different), makes certain that violence is never attractive and never a matter of triumph. Says Rark, the slave mentor, to his young master, Hakon: ''Never brag of having slain a man, Hakon. Life is holy and even the foulest of men has been a child and worthy of love'''.... (pp. 62-3)

Haugaard consistently chooses to write about periods shown in historical perspective to be turning points in human thought and feeling, periods that mark the end of an era, forcing those born into them to reassess traditional values and ideas. For example, **Hakon of Rogen's Saga** and **A Slave's Tale** are, like certain of the original sagas that are their prototypes, basically concerned with the inadequacies and cruelties of a social organization based on individual or tribal revenge and with the dislocations inherent in the transition from the Old Gods to Christianity; *Orphans of the Wind* portrays the end of the last era of publicly acknowledged and supported slavery in the West and examines the moral question of economic association with it; **The Rider and His Horse** marks the dispersion of the Jewish people and their transition from a society of the sword to a society of the Book; **The Little Fishes,** although less clearly transitional, suggests the connection of Italian Fascism with an abortive attempt to resurrect the glory of the Roman Empire. But **The Little Fishes** and **The Untold Tale,** both of which might be seen as more pessimistic and despairing than Haugaard's other novels, are atypical and tend to emphasize the violent chaos rather than possible emerging values of their periods. Finally and most recently, the Cromwell books, with more emphasis on the issues and values for which at least some of the members of the opposing Royalist and Parliamentarian forces stood, might be considered to be again concerned with a transitional, as well as violent, period.

The choice of such periods permits Haugaard to consider not only outer conflict, but also inner conflict over the values that foster such violence. During such periods, in the midst of carnage and widespread disdain for the sacredness of the individual human being, it is, nevertheless, not historically anachronistic to find some atypical humanistic characters ''far ahead'' of their times. In at least his earlier works, Haugaard chooses to dwell on such characters and to emphasize their capacity to cherish other people's children. This becomes a central theme for Haugaard; understanding it is a prerequisite to knowing Haugaard's individual books and his works as a whole.

In Haugaard's first five books, he chooses to have the story told by a youthful narrator-protagonist and to depict one, and sometimes more, adult characters who represent the most humanistically advanced thought of their time. Significantly, these persons serve to some extent as mentors and protectors to the young narrators. In **Hakon,** we have Hakon's stepmother, Thora, and the Norman slave Rark; in **A Slave's Tale,** the freedman Rark and Magnus the Fair; in **Orphans of the Wind,** Rolf, the ship's cook; in **The Little Fishes,** Guido's mother and the former teacher, Luigi (alias Jason); and in **The Rider and His Horse,** Rabbi Simon.

The Untold Tale and the subsequent Cromwell trilogy seem to mark departures from this technique. The former is the tale of a young child, Dag, who fails to survive partly because the narrator, now an old man, has served as neither protector nor mentor; the Trilogy returns to a narrator, who is the center of his own story, but who is telling the tale with the retrospection of an old man who, in his youth, met with a number of adults, some of whom might have served as mentors; yet with none of them, even Cromwell, has an intimate relationship been established.

Haugaard's characterization of adults achieves a degree of complexity not often found in children's books. An underlying pacifism that requires Haugaard to depict the full horrors of war also requires that he, again like Vonnegut, create no traditional heroes—warriors or men who are so correct and strong that they can act unerringly for right and be successful in every situation. Haugaard shows that even the good and perceptive mentors are still not always able to live up to their finest perception. Occasionally, they are mistaken in their judgments, and they are themselves vulnerable. Finally, as noted above, **The Untold Tale** depicts an adult who fails miserably, despite his good intentions.

Yet, despite the complexity and vulnerability of Haugaard's adult characters, both his child characters and his child readers can usually tell which adults are to be trusted and honored in these books. Here we return to the central theme noted above: there is one test, implicit throughout, that distinguishes the better adults from the worse: Does the adult treat other people's children as though they were his own? I find the implications of that simple test both manifold and profound; it is fascinating to consider how that test works itself out in Haugaard's books.

Note that the narrators, in addition to being young, are—with the exception of David in **The Rider and His Horse**—all orphans or semi-orphans; all, including David, are between the ages of twelve and fifteen when the story takes place; and all, with the exception of Helga in **A Slave's Tale,** are boys. Even the elderly narrator of the Trilogy is seen throughout most of the first two books as his early adolescent, semi-orphaned self. (In *The Untold Tale,* the central protagonist, who is not the narrator, is also an orphan, but he is only seven.)

The orphaned state of most of these narrators removes them from parental protection and throws them on the mercy of society as a whole (not unlike many of Dickens' characters). The mercy of society does not rain upon these orphans very freely. Haugaard's view of society's failure to protect other people's children is most profoundly condemnatory in **The Little Fishes** and **The Untold Tale;** elsewhere, the orphan state of the narrators is significant because at least a few of the adults meet the test, and the narrators usually find some protection.

This is not the only purpose of the orphan state of the narrators in these works. It also provides (as the widespread phenomenon of the ''missing parent'' in children's literature often does) a testing ground not only for others, but also for the individual child himself. It is a means of growing up and finding himself, rather than just substituting protective parents. David, the eldest Haugaard protagonist-narrator, and the one who is not orphaned, but who chooses not to return to his parents after he escapes from thieves, exemplifies most clearly this aspect of the orphan condition: the search for an independent identity and the discovery of one's own potential power.

Nothing, one feels, in Haugaard's work is there by chance. His choice of young adolescents as his narrators, in terms of their very age, is a case in point. The pre-adolescent child can not survive alone, but the unprotected adolescent may be expected to at least live. Beyond this, for the older child, a positive benefit may result from an enforced independence—not mere survival, but inner development and growth. Early adolescents may also be expected to have the ability to be thoughtful about identity and the adult life ahead. The age of Haugaard's narrators furthers our willingness to believe in each story as one that passes through the narrator's consciousness.

It is the imagery above all in Haugaard's work that brings out the hidden strengths of the weak and the potential they possess to do *more than merely survive*. Two metaphors used to particularly striking advantage are the sparrow-eagle metaphor in *A Slave's Tale* and the big-fishes/little-fishes motif in *The Little Fishes*. In both books, the repeated use of the metaphor seems to move in a similar direction: the vulnerability of the youthful narrator is emphasized at first; then, as the book progresses, the meaning of the image itself changes, and hidden strengths are brought out in both the metaphor and the protagonist.

The sparrow metaphor in *A Slave's Tale* is introduced by Helga in the quotation that appears near the beginning of this paper. For her, it serves to establish the contrast between her obscurity as a slave and the glory of the eagle-like kings whose story everyone tells. One of the extraordinary aspects of the novel is the presentation of the psychic condition of slavery and of Helga's need, having been legally freed, to learn what it means not to be a slave. Unlike her broken mother, who, having lost her own will to live, cannot even love her daughter, Helga is able to make this transition. She figures out much for herself, but Magnus, her older suitor—who is eventually killed in battle—also serves as a mentor, helping her to understand the significance of her life. Magnus, in the course of the book, also makes the comparison between Helga's lot and a sparrow's. But when she replies that a sparrow's song is meaningless, he says, "... not meaningless; it is the song of the earth, the song of the seed breaking through the frost-hard ground, saying to the world, 'I want to live.'" And of the eagle, Magnus has this to say:

> It circles the air, so faraway from the earth that it no longer belongs to it. And if another eagle comes near it, it attacks, as if the whole sky were not large enough for two eagles. Men say, 'free as an eagle,' but that bird had made of the wide sky a cage even smaller than the kind we make of willow branches.

(pp. 63-6)

What he has to say of course reflects back on the earlier comparison between eagle and sparrow.

In *The Little Fishes*, a scornful German officer applies the little fishes image to the street children in Naples: "In the unclean waters live the little fishes". This image is cynically expanded by a frightening adult bully, whom Guido, the twelve-year old narrator, and his two younger charges, Anna and Mario, meet on the road: "'There are two kinds of people in the world; those who steal and those who are stolen from; the fishes in the sea and the fishermen who catch and eat them'". . . . But Guido is a little fish that is not eaten. His refusal to accept the bully's view of the world recalls what Magnus said about the eagle in Haugaard's earlier book. Here is Guido:

> ... what he said lingered in my mind, for somewhere I had heard those words before. . . .
> The German officer on the day that I had met Anna and Mario! He, too, had talked about fishes and compared human beings to them.

He, too, had thought of himself as a fisherman, or at least one of the big fish who ate the little ones. "They are strong men," I thought, "but they have no kindness and they wear themselves out, without ever having enjoyed the beauty of strength, which is to protect the weak, not to threaten them."

(pp. 66-7)

If both the sparrow-eagle and the little fishes metaphor bring out the initial powerlessness of the child narrator, they also are developed sufficiently in the course of the book to emphasize that the means by which these children survive and achieve some power are not entirely external; inner growth must also occur.

In Haugaard's worlds, not all the children survive, and the resilience of those who do will never excuse the neglect and brutality of adults, but will occasionally overcome it; the resulting invitation to the child reader to identify with the protagonist is an invitation to choose to be not just one's strongest, but one's *best* self.

Haugaard's concern with the importance of moral choices for both children and adults, even when they are relatively powerless, is, of course, still more of a lesson for the relatively powerful. As Guido says, the "beauty of strength" lies in its ability to protect the weak. It is fairly obvious that Haugaard usually chooses male narrators because he identifies with them. Beyond that immediate identification, however, Haugaard seems to recognize that the relative physical strength and worldly power of men must be tempered by virtues not always highly cultivated in the male sex—particularly the urge to nurture—in order for history not continually to repeat itself in its bloody way. The adult characters most often and complexly portrayed in Haugaard's books are also male; there, nurturing men, not traditional heroes, are the most highly honored. The virtue most highly honored in turn is not the traditional male *courage*, but the godly type of love for all that is the original meaning of *charity*.

Having now considered some of Haugaard's choices of situation, character, narrator, and image, one must again note that an outstanding general aspect of Haugaard's work is its concern for the universal in the historical and national. His sense of the value of every human being in whatever time and place is no doubt an essential component of Haugaard's fierce anti-war stance. But anti-war books have not traditionally been children's books, and one might well wonder why Haugaard, unlike Vonnegut, generally has chosen a mode accessible to both children and adults as "the best art-form for something (he had) to say" (to paraphrase C. S. Lewis).

In the children's book, Haugaard could, while writing the "unwritten truth," also sing "the sparrow's song" in its purest form and bring down to its most concrete and moving level the interrelationship of the fates of children and adults in diverse places and chaotic times. While showing children themselves as coping with—and developing in spite of—great cruelty and suffering, Haugaard gives all children both hope for the future and identification with the oppressed. At the same time, Haugaard's message, embodied in the "other people's children theme" is unequivocally clear: *every* child in *every* place and time is of *equal* value.

This message obviously challenges all other "isms"—racism, sexism, elitism, even nationalism—for Haugaard's internationalism goes beyond most to imply that to limit one's love and concern to the children of one's own family, or tribe, or even nation is an intolerable exclusiveness. Haugaard's artistic choices of situation, character, narrator, and image are strong and purposeful, supporting an internationalism that seems to me a philosophy worthy of profound respect, however difficult it is for us to measure up to it and however natural it seems to care only for "our own". (pp. 67-8)

> Lois R. Kuznets, "Other People's Children: Erik Haugaard's 'Untold Tales'," in Children's literature in education, Vol. 11, No. 2 (Summer), 1980, pp. 62-8.

ZENA SUTHERLAND, DIANNE L. MONSON, AND MAY HILL ARBUTHNOT

[*Hakon of Rogen's Saga*] is not a traditional saga but a realistic story taking place in the last days of the Vikings. . . . To Hakon, Rogen Island and his powerful father seem indestructible—but there is a bloody family battle and when it is over, Hakon is an orphan at the mercy of his treacherous uncle, who wants Rogen for his own. How Hakon suffers enslavement and brutal treatment, bides his time, finds a hideout in the mountain caves, mobilizes his few loyal men, and eventually takes Rogen again reads much like an old Norse saga. . . . In this book the Vikings are of heroic stature and the author clothes their story with nobility.

Its sequel, *A Slave's Tale* . . . , is told by the small slave girl Helga, to whom Hakon is like a beloved brother. Their affection ripens into love, but this is a minor facet of the story, which is primarily a tale of a voyage to Frankland in a longboat. The writing, in explication and dialogue as well as in the period details, vividly creates the historical milieu and has the sweep and cadence of a Norse epic.

The Rider and His Horse . . . is set in ancient Israel at the final battle between the Jews and Romans at Masada, while *The Untold Tale* . . . gives an all-too-clear picture of life for the poor in Denmark in the 1600s. Haugaard's heroes always face horror realistically and unflinchingly, and tragedy is as often the outcome as is triumph. In *A Messenger for Parliament* . . . a young man named for Oliver Cromwell tells his life story as a camp follower of the Parliamentary Army, in a story that vividly depicts the fierce allegiances of a divided country. (pp. 380-81)

> Zena Sutherland, Dianne L. Monson, and May Hill Arbuthnot, "Historical Fiction: 'Hakon of Rogen's Saga' and 'A Messenger for Parliament'," in their Children and Books, sixth edition, Scott, Foresman and Company, 1981, pp. 380-81.

BERNICE E. CULLINAN, WITH MARY K. KARRER AND ARLENE M. PILLAR

The cadences of an ancient saga permeate Erik Haugaard's novel *Hakon of Rogen's Saga* and its sequel *A Slave's Tale*. . . . Themes of slavery of the mind and slavery of power are interwoven in both stories. Haugaard states that he has not blunted his pen in writing for young people and asks to be judged by adult standards; even when judged by the highest standards, he succeeds. Readers savor the metaphorical language: disasters lurk behind each day, pride makes a poor shield. Images of the Vikings crystallize in such prose. (p. 340)

> Bernice E. Cullinan, with Mary K. Karrer and Arlene M. Pillar, "Historical Fiction and Biography," in their Literature and the Child, Harcourt Brace Jovanovich, Inc., 1981, pp. 329-82.*

HAKON OF ROGEN'S SAGA   (1963; British edition as *Hakon's Saga*)

AUTHOR'S COMMENTARY

In *Hakon of Rogen's Saga,* I have attempted to tell the story of a boy who lived at the end of the Viking period. It was not written for "youth," in the sense that I have blunted my pen before I started. I abhor those writers who have not the skill to keep the attention of adults, and therefore think themselves equipped to write for children. I have done my best, and I leave you to be my critic. (p. iv)

> Erik Christian Haugaard, in a preface to his Hakon of Rogen's Saga, Houghton Mifflin Company, 1963, pp. iii-iv.

Fresh and intensely interesting is a book by a Danish author, Erik Christian Haugaard. *Hakon of Rogen's Saga,* though not drawn from legend, is so infused with the feeling of the Norse sagas, and the author is so steeped in them and so completely at home in their settings, that the story has the atmosphere and conviction of a northern epic.

Hakon had not known a mother until he was eleven, when his father brought home a new wife, Thora; for a year the boy knew her gentle companionship and love. But Thora had been stolen, and her father did not rest long before he sent Rolf Blackbeard to avenge him and bring back his daughter. The battle left Hakon a complete orphan and his life in constant danger from an uncle determined to gain for himself Hakon's birthright, the rocky island of Rogen. The youth of the hero and the sympathy roused by the little slave girl Helga should make the story appealing to boys and girls of ten and eleven as well as to those of junior-high-school ages. The telling has directness and a clear line of plot which builds suspense and great excitement; and the style has the dignity and smoothness of a recital by an ancient sagateller. An absorbing, moving, and beautiful book. (pp. 272-73)

> Ruth Hill Viguers, "Two Heroes: 'Dietrich of Berne' and 'Hakon of Rogen's Saga'," in The Horn Book Magazine, Vol. XXXIX, No. 3, June, 1963, pp. 272-73.*

Realistic, vigorous, discerning story of a boy who grows into manhood through hardship and bloodshed. Hakon's affection for Helga, a slave girl helps to make this an adventure story for both boys and girls. . . . Exciting and beautiful prose with the flavor of the old sagas. Good characterization.

> Inger Boye, in a review of "Hakon of Rogen's Saga," in Library Journal, Vol. 88, No. 13, July, 1963, p. 2781.

The setting and the description of battle is very well done; one can really believe in this barren land surrounded by dangerous seas and influenced by the Gods. It is in his characterisation that the author fails, no one really "lives," least of all the young hero who speaks with the tongue of a wise old man. First person narratives are always more difficult for children to appreciate, but a first person who is as introspective as Hakon is at a grave disadvantage, and the author fails to portray youth successfully. (p. 315)

> A review of "Hakon's Saga," in The Junior Bookshelf, Vol. 28, No. 5, November, 1964, pp. 314-15.

The book is well written: Mr. Haugaard presents a convincing picture of hardship, love of battle and remoteness. But the book might be more suitable as a present for an individual child, rather than a library purchase. There is little 'history' in it, and the style would appeal to the able child rather than the average one.

> *James Falkner, in a review of "Hakon's Saga," in* The School Librarian and School Library Review, *Vol. 13, No. 1, March, 1965, p. 102.*

[*Hakon's Saga*] shows a humane spirit which may be anachronistic, but this is an essential element in a story whose economy, sincerity and eloquence make it one of the most memorable of the century. . . .

The grim little story is told relentlessly. Life is harsh and there is no pretence. What sustains Hakon, and the reader, is belief in a better life. . . . All the best historical novels are stories of change. The change in *Hakon's Saga* is a small one—a change of ruler in a tiny island—but it has importance because it represents a change of heart. The new Rogen will be well governed; it will also be a land without slaves. '"That is everyone's birthright, his freedom, and the gods have only one message to us, that we must live."' The message may seem oversimplified; the story, for all its brevity, is not at all simple. It has the naked splendour of great art. (p. 80)

> *Marcus Crouch, "The Abysm of Time," in his* The Nesbit Tradition: The Children's Novel in England 1945-1970, *Ernest Benn Limited, 1972, pp. 57-85.**

A SLAVE'S TALE (1965)

Hakon (the hero of Mr. Haugaard's fine novel, *Hakon of Rogen's Saga* . . .) and Helga, his foster sister who is a slave girl, lived in cruel Viking times. This tragically moving new story about them is told by an author who writes history like a poet. Helga is the narrator. Because she loves Hakon, she stows away on the boat which is to take him on a long voyage to return Rark, a former slave, to his home in Brittany. 24 men and three women set forth from Rogen; four return. Made wise by suffering, Helga writes of death and life, of her love and her fears, of the disasters and dangers encountered, the brutalities she sees and shares. And, not slighting the healing influences, she tells of the old gods of Norway and the strange new beliefs of the priests in Brittany, wryly adding that "Gods of peace will matter little so long as men worship the sword." The events are so absorbing, the emotions aroused so powerful that we hardly notice the skill with which the historical background is drawn, but it is splendidly imagined and convincing. A rare and fine historical novel.

> *Margaret Sherwood Libby, "Straightening Facts with Fiction," in* Book Week—The Sunday Herald Tribune, *May 30, 1965, p. 15.**

It is unusual for a Viking story to be told by a girl, and a slave girl at that. But this is a very unusual book. It is a sequel to *Hakon of Rogen's Saga*, but it stands independently and a reader need have no knowledge of the previous fine book. This book is as realistic, absorbing, and emotion-filled as its predecessor. . . .

[The journey to Rark's home is] full of adventure and rich in incident and characters. The conflict between paganism and the new religion of Christianity plays a large part. The author presents the new religion sympathetically, yet he does not rep-

resent all Christians as following Christ's teachings. Nor are all the pagans shown as bloodthirsty, misguided pirates. Men are ruled by similar passions everywhere—some by love, some by greed for gold, some by greed for power, some by wisdom—and the religion they profess doesn't necessarily change their basic natures. . . .

This book is basically a book of character studies: Helga—meek and good as the world sees her and seething with emotions she cannot articulate because she doesn't understand them; Hakon—just and peace-loving, but a strong commander and warrior, yet beset by doubts; Magnus—great-hearted, kind, strong, and loving, full of life and dying miserably for no reason and with a girl he doesn't even like; and Orm and Hjalte Gudbrandson and Rigmor, and all the rest of the ill-fated crew. This is memorable reading!

> *Phyllis Cohen, in a review of "A Slave's Tale," in* Young Readers Review, *Vol I, No. 10, June, 1965, p. 5.*

[This] stark, realistic tale of Norse life filled with war, death, love, adventure, and folklore brings the people and time vividly alive. . . . The beautiful style of writing, the understanding of what slavery and freedom mean to the human spirit, as well as a good plot, exciting and convincing, give distinction to this tale.

> *Clayton E. Kilpatrick, in a review of "A Slave's Tale," in* Library Journal, *Vol. 90, No. 12, June 15, 1965, p. 2894.*

So completely realized are even the minor characters that the treachery and cruelty which destroy them are the more devastatingly tragic. Much of the stark epic quality of *Hakon of Rogen's Saga* is here, but rising above it is a deeply felt message. When a Frankish priest aids Hakon's escape from his enemies to pay "a debt of honor, not as a priest of his god, for between his god and those who worship false gods, no peace can exist," Hakon answers, ". . . it would be far better if man took the bloody sword and called it his own; and to the gods gave the honor of those deeds done from love and the pitying heart." An absorbing, powerful story.

> *Ruth Hill Viguers, in a review of "A Slave's Tale," in* The Horn Book Magazine, *Vol. XLI, No. 4, August, 1965, p. 395.*

This tale of sea journeys and fights is shot with superstition and cruelty, but its main theme is one of loyalty, emphasised since the story is told by Helga, Hakon's foster-sister, freed by him to become his wife. A lively and eventful story with a crisp style that suits it well.

> *Margery Fisher, in a review of "A Slave's Tale," in* Growing Point, *Vol. 5, No. 5, November, 1966, p. 803.*

ORPHANS OF THE WIND (1966)

Jim was an orphan when his uncle sent him away to sea and "orphans of the wind" was his friend Rolf's explanation of all sailors. Eventually Jim learns that "Rolf was wrong: we were not 'orphans of the wind'; we were brothers of the earth, and the wind and the sea were our parents." Underscoring the story of how he came to this understanding is the emphasis on the importance of individual liberty which was so well demonstrated in the author's *Hakon of Rogen's Saga* . . . and *A*

Haugaard at his desk. Courtesy of Erik Haugaard.

Slave's Tale. . . . The point does not come off quite so well here, since it is indicated too often through asides rather than as an integral part of the plot. Nevertheless the adventure, which deals with sabotage aboard the supposedly Boston-bound ship, with its cargo of arms, its destruction off the Carolina coast, the struggle of Jim and his friends to reach land, and their attempt to escape enlistment in the Confederate Army and to join the Northern forces, is strong in itself. This is not the author's best but it is still an absorbing story with a stirring theme.

> *A review of "Orphans of the Wind," in* Virginia Kirkus' Service, *Vol. XXXIV, No. 9, May 1, 1966, p. 479.*

An orphan signing aboard ship is a commonplace opening for a sea story. But the wind is with Erik Haugaard. This is a powerful, absorbing tale with a finely honed plot and distinctive literary style. . . .

The reader's emotions are swept up in the boy's experiences, and the author's development of circumstance and character induces mounting suspense. Cruel, caustic Captain Mathews is wholly convincing, as is crazy Noah, the ship's carpenter, who spends his days quoting the Bible and, angered over the slavery issue, which is hotly contested in the fo'c'sle, sets the ship afire. Important touches, such as Jim's departure without

learning his shipmate's last names, or where they came from, is what lifts the tale to rare heights—for it's this way with men who go down to the sea in ships.

> *Polly Burroughs, in a review of "Orphans of the Wind," in* The New York Times Book Review, *July 31, 1966, p. 18.*

Behind the drama of life at sea with the fear and loneliness and the cruelty of both man and nature, a strong sense of elation and freedom is present in this author's stories, whether they are laid in the period of the ancient sagas or in the nineteenth century. . . . The part of the story that takes place on land and in American history may lack the subtlety of the seagoing chapters, but that is a minor matter. The whole has a particular eloquence which leaves a residue of wisdom. If it had not been for Jim's friend Rolf the cook, Jim's childish heart, struggling to evaluate the cruelties of past and present, might not so soon have been shocked into a humane awareness. (pp. 438-39)

> *Ruth Hill Viguers, in a review of "Orphans of the Wind," in* The Horn Book Magazine, *Vol. XLII, No. 4, August, 1966, pp. 438-39.*

[*Orphans of the Wind*] is a sea tale, in part, and in the best tradition of the genre, for Erik Haugaard writes with the easy self-confidence of the master. . . . The flavor and detail of life at sea is evoked in language that is swift, penetrating, and

poetic. The ship-board characters, while verging on the melodramatic, are nonetheless three-dimensional. . . . Mr. Haugaard is too wise to preach, yet a concern for the fundamental
tragedies of war, death, and slavery gives the story a significance beyond the purely historical.

> *Houston L. Maples, "Historical Novels," in* Book
> Week—The Sunday Herald Tribune, *August 14, 1966,
> p. 13.**

A somewhat confused and pretentious book, disappointing after
the stark grandeur and much clearer statements on freedom and
self-respect in *Hakon's Saga* and *A Slave's Tale.* The author's
intentions are obviously good but he seems to express them
much more clumsily in this tale of a Bristol boy on a sailing
ship bound for the American south with ammunition for the
Confederate forces. There are some interesting characters on
board though some of their conversation sounds most contrived—and surely no one a century ago, if ever, said "me
thinks" as two words?. . . In the last episode Jim is on a ship
bound for California and thinks "The world is good". Of
course he *is* only twelve but considering what he has seen in
the past this needs some qualification. . . . The author is plainly
concerned with things that matter but this time his message is
somewhat muddled.

> *A review of "Orphans of the Wind," in* The Junior
> Bookshelf, *Vol. 31, No. 6, December, 1967, p. 392.*

THE LITTLE FISHES (1967)

AUTHOR'S COMMENTARY

[*The following excerpt is taken from Haugaard's response upon
receiving the first* Boston Globe-Horn Book *Award for Excellence
in Text in October 1967.*]

All my books have had a purpose; they have had a rudder and
sails that could be set to steer a certain course. In each of them
I wished to express something specific—a significant comment
on humanity.

We have a fear of morality today, as if we lived in the times
of Puritan intolerance. The knowledge of evil which we gained
from the last war has made us suspect even the search for good.
The shadow of the concentration camps and the gas chambers
falls on our minds. We have stopped believing in the existence
of all abstractions; even Love and Justice, that to most of
humanity are realities, are to the majority of intellectuals, ab-
surdities. We do evil and good by chance; unknowingly we
fear the choice. We have made the discovery that much of our
morality was a double morality: false and hollow, the tree was
rotten. But we have neither cut down the tree nor planted a
new one; instead we have declared the tree an anachronism.

To me this possibility is an impossibility. Concepts of the good
and the perfect are natural to man; without them there is neither
art nor poetry. You can blind your eyes and say that it is always
night, but refusal to see will not change the course of the sun.
Because our philosophies and languages have been distorted
by politicians, there is no reason for us to give them up to their
tormentors.

In *The Little Fishes* I wanted to tell not only what happened
to the victims of war but also how a person could survive, how
in degradation he could refuse to be degraded. Our history
books tell about the victories and defeats of armies; I wanted
to tell about the defeat and victory of a human being.

> *Erik Haugaard, "A Thank You Note and a Credo,"
> in* The Horn Book Magazine, *Vol. XLIV, No. 1,
> February, 1968, p. 14.*

"In the unclean waters live the little fishes. Some are eaten;
most I believe. But some will escape." The prophecy of a
German officer, uttered in contempt, comes to pass in this
stark, sometimes ironic, novella of children in war [in Naples
of 1943]. . . . No melodrama here, much mature, sometimes
wry reflection (on the art of begging, on scars as "the story
of your life," on the incomprehensibility of war, on Fascism,
on man as neither good nor bad but having "the right to live"),
and a recurrent refrain at the beginning, "The scream of the
poor is not always just; but if you do not listen to it, then you
will never understand justice"; at the end, "It is understanding
that makes the difference between us and the animals. And
when you understand you can feel a kind of happiness even in
the worst misery." Uniquely powerful in circumstance and
piercing in analysis for a juvenile; it looks younger than it
should and may disturb some, but it's a must for the mature;
and they needn't be "readers."

> *A review of "The Little Fishes," in* Kirkus Service,
> *Vol. XXXV, No. 9, May 1, 1967, p. 565.*

This is the touching story of three Neapolitan waifs and their
struggle to survive the German occupation during World War II.
Guido, the narrator, is 12, Anna is 11 and her brother Mario,
4. All three beg for a living. Guido lives in a cave in the steep
part of Naples. His most prized possession is a torn woolen
mattress from a bombed house.

After a while, the three children decide to flee the shattered
city. They head north for Cassino and the hoped-for shelter of
the monastery. The second half of the book is their odyssey
on the road—and the trial by fire that waits at their journey's
end. Now the compassion and clarity are quite extraordinary.
Old for his years, ageless in the way he protects his weaker
comrades, Guido is exemplary, heroic even, as he finds ways
to survive in the midst of danger.

Sometimes his insights are more the author's than the child's:
("Everything leaves a little scar: both the good and the bad;
and when you grow up then the scars are the story of your
life." "My thoughts surprised me for I had never had thoughts
. . . that could make me love everything about me, everything
I saw.") But these are small flaws in an absorbing, dramatic
tale. Mostly, Danish author Erik Haugaard lets Guido tell his
tale in straightforward prose. . . . Here is war in one of its most
tragic aspects—the backwash of battle, and the terrors and the
trauma it inflicts on the young. (pp. 14, 16)

> *Bruce Wilkinson, in a review of "The Little Fishes,"
> in* The New York Times Book Review, *Part II, May
> 7, 1967, pp. 14, 16.*

Erik Haugaard wants to shock and startle the young with the
brutality, the wastefulness of war; but if he is uncompromising,
he is certainly not cynical. He does not show us children corrupted by a homeless life; rather, their essential innocence
provides the keynote of a sincere and brave story.

> *Margery Fisher, in a review of "The Little Fishes,"
> in* Growing Point, *Vol. 6, No. 9, April, 1968, p.
> 1090.*

[*Hakon's Saga* and *A Slave's Tale*] seemed so all-of-a-piece, the next [*Orphans of the Wind*] was relatively unimpressive—interesting, but diffuse, well-intentioned but rather scrambling. Now Mr. Haugaard has moved still nearer our own times and in this story of refugee children in the last war has gathered his forces to better effect, though the total impact is less than that made by his first two books. There is no doubt, however, that he is a brave man and a good one; his preoccupation throughout has been with war and peace, human dignity and kindness, a sense of values, so perhaps it is not altogether surprising that he sometimes loses in a struggle to get some particular aspect across in a way young readers can comprehend. He must be honoured for grappling with such a difficult subject as this, and playing fair with it, and it is good that in an age when children are still being rendered stateless overnight their contemporaries should have some comprehension of what this means in practical terms. . . . Having raised the question of "that secret in the faces of men" when they look at little girls, the author should perhaps have resolved it to some extent and not left it up in the air, but the other questions he raises about violence, honesty, loyalty and much else he handles very well, especially considering the difficulties he has made for himself by choosing to make Guido a somewhat "oblique philosopher" type. He makes us believe Guido is indeed an Italian peasant boy in the '40's, not a disguised American youth of the '60's, and the ideas he should stimulate in his readers' minds will still have universal importance in the '80's, so this is definitely a book to recommend. Amongst other assets, it contains a vivid picture of the Italian people and countryside in the early years of the war and shows the effect of occupation and attack on a civilian population, but it can be introduced honestly enough simply as a good story of three youngsters on their own, making their way in a not-altogether-hostile world.

> *A review of "The Little Fishes," in* The Junior Bookshelf, *Vol 32, No. 2, April, 1968, p. 113.*

Eloquently written, with many layers of meaning to ponder, this story will lead a youngster well along the road to appreciating good books. It deals with eternal verities: the need for a human being to develop and live by a code that includes responsibility to one's self and love and understanding of one's brothers. Because of the author's skill in placing these ideas within the dramatic turmoil of war, and at the same time as part of a child's understanding, this book is becoming a modern classic. (p. 245)

> *John Gillespie and Diana Lembo, "Appreciating Books," in their* Introducing Books: A Guide for the Middle Grades, *R. R. Bowker Company, 1970, pp. 234-62.**

THE RIDER AND HIS HORSE   (1968)

An accomplished writer is not limited by time and place if he understands the promptings of the human heart and mind. The author of *The Little Fishes*—a Dane, writing in English—has given new and significant life to an episode in Josephus' history of the conquest of the Jews by the Romans. The account in Josephus and the findings of recent archaeological investigations made at the Masada—a fort and palace built by King Herod among the cliffs and rocky formations overlooking the Dead Sea—have been activated in the story of David ben Joseph of Tyre.

The son of a merchant traveling in Palestine just after the destruction of Jerusalem, David—who at the age of fourteen is beginning to question the authority of his father's ideas—is captured by brigands, but escapes. Instead of seeking his father, he makes his way to Jerusalem, where he sees for himself the ruins of the city and the Temple. After a sojourn with Simon ben Judas, a scholar and sage, David finally seeks out the Masada, where the Zealots, led by Eleazar ben Ya'ir, are making a last stand against the Romans. When the Romans are finally ready to take the seemingly impregnable fortress, the Zealots cheat the conquerors by killing themselves and their families. But David, along with two women and two children, is left alive at the express command of the Zealot leader.

In terms of David's life and development, the dramatic and heroic ending of the novel takes on an added meaning. For a long time, David had been trying to find himself. Preferring the sea to a sedentary life, rejecting his training in traditional Hebrew and classical lore, he matures in experience. He witnesses brigandage, crucifixion, devastation, and heroism. He meets people with different answers to life: a scholar and a woman who believe in continuity; ascetic Essenes, who withdraw from the world; uncompromising Zealots; and Josephus himself, who appears at the beginning and the end of David's self-told story. In moments of stress and confusion, verses from Holy Writ take on a new meaning for him; and at the end of the novel, he (like Horatio in Shakespeare's *Hamlet*) realizes that he has been a witness of unusual deeds and that he must remain a witness to them.

The novel is masterfully constructed. The historical facts are made meaningful in the adolescent boy's encounter with them. His adventures, exciting in themselves, spring from his search for personal identity; and the final tragic meaning of the martyrdom of the Zealots becomes part of his maturing consciousness.

> *Paul Heins, in a review of "The Rider and His Horse," in* The Horn Book Magazine, *Vol. XLIV, No. 6, December, 1968, p. 675.*

Each one of Haugaard's historical books has been deeply felt and unusual in subject and structure; this tale of Masada is surely his most significant book so far. Young readers in their 'teens who are aware of the tragedy as well as the glory of nationalism may welcome this straight look at the Jewish past. The last stand of the Zealots at Masada and their mass suicide is seen from two points of view. . . . David's uncle, the historian Josephus, tries to pass on to the boy his cynical attitude to Eleazar, leader of the Zealots. Wisely the author leaves it to the reader to see that no heroic struggle is capable of simple or single analysis. From a literary point of view this book is superb. It has a narrative framework skilfully made to seem almost casual and thus compelling us to believe in David's wanderings and to accept the alternations of Hebrew and Roman attitudes as real and relevant. (p. 1393)

> *Margery Fisher, in a review of "The Rider and His Horse," in* Growing Point, *Vol. 8, No. 4, October, 1969, pp. 1392-93.*

This may not be the slowest-moving tale ever told in the modern idiom but it must be a qualifier. This, however, is the worst that may be said. . . . Mingled with [David's] wandering and captivity are thoughts and recollections which perhaps show the developing mind of a fourteen-year-old coming to terms with the adult world of conflict and cruelty but they seem at times too mature and disconnected for the same reader who will enjoy the tale for its setting and incident. The final chapter in which the Zealots cheat the conquerors by self-slaughter is well composed and will be a revelation of no mean order to those who know not the end. Not everyone's book but worth the time and concentration of deliberate reading. (pp. 387-88)

> *A review of "The Rider and His Horse," in* The Junior Bookshelf, *Vol. 33, No. 6, December, 1969, pp. 387-88.*

This is a fine but very demanding book. As in *The Little Fishes* Haugaard does not shirk the unpleasantness of war but neither does he misuse it, and here he gives an impressive and moving account of an adolescent's involvement in the stand made by the Jews against the Romans in AD 70. By showing the qualities which ensured their survival as a nation, he provides insight into the fierce nationalism of modern Israel. The impression of authenticity is achieved by a simple style and frequent quotation from Jewish literature. As an analysis of adolescence the book is also interesting. David's search for himself, his shrewd observation of adult hypocrisy, and his own transition from the cussed truthfulness of youth to the self-preserving circumspection of manhood is presented with insight and sympathy. The boy is sometimes greater than the man.

> *P. Robertson, in a review of "The Rider and His Horse," in* The School Librarian, *Vol. 13, No. 1, March, 1970, p. 80.*

THE UNTOLD TALE (1971)

[*The Untold Tale*] is set in Denmark early in the 17th century. Dag is a 7-year-old boy. His people are small tenant farmers on the king's land, and times are hard. On his way to the capital for help, the father freezes to death; at home the sick mother dies. In the stable the animals lie dead of starvation. The child sets out to find the king who will put everything right, and we accompany him across country to his own death.

Within this gloomy framework the action is lively and the characters various. The boy attaches himself to a series of grown-ups: Black Lars, the sympathetic outlaw; Peter, the maker of songs; and Bodil, the black-marketeering camp follower with her ragged, affectionate little daughter Kirsten. Grown-ups and children all are to some degree obsessed by the off-stage king. . . .

The author draws his people with some nice touches. My favorite character is Jens Bjornson, the commandant of Fort Christianopolis who lacks the ability for leadership. . . .

One feels the authority of the research. . . . [The] story moves well. I daresay I would have eaten it up when I was young, but then I ate up every bit of print in sight—the classic school girl romances and writing on the milk carton. Now that my appetite is smaller and I need delight to reward the effort of reading this book does not pay off.

The book is "historical" and this confers a solemnity on the characters. Seventeenth-century people laugh, just like you and me, but never at anything we think funny; and they tend to talk in proverbs: "Any news you bring is as welcome to me as a pair of fingernails are to a flea." (I'll wager that tidbit was translated from an early source where it had better rhythms; it doesn't fit into realistic writing.) Moreover the chronicler who tells this tale likes generalizations: "Weakness in a woman was far more attractive to [the man] than strength." Oh dear? Maybe it's true: I just wish he didn't speak his truths in such stilted language: "As a man needs to wash and cleanse his body, so does he at times need to cleanse his soul."

These are minor irritations. I think my main complaint is not against this book, which is a good enough example of a suspect category, the juvenile. It does bad things to writing.

When the great Lewis Carroll or the good E. B. White or the eternal tellers of fairy tales address children, even when Maurice Sendak is talking to the babies, they write for their own delight and choose the young to talk to because they are in touch with their own youth; their words reverberate infinitely.

But the writers of "juveniles" address themselves to the "juvenile market" and speak to the "juvenile" mind as if it were a foreigner, slowly and loudly so that they will be understood: Meanings are always single and can be picked off the top of the page and carried away. The child protagonists in these books are never children: Seven-year-old Dag "didn't distinguish between beautiful and ugly. In his veins still flowed so much mother's milk, that he divided up mankind only into good and evil." Even good literature is full of these wise children. I've never liked them. Their wisdom is always in grown-up terms. The wisdom of the 7-year-olds of my acquaintance is stronger, nuttier stuff.

Let the young read *The Untold Tale*. They'll probably like it. But if they are old enough to deal with its subject matter (including an illegitimate baby, a prostitute and a massacre) and can handle its adult vocabulary, they could be taking books off the shelves of world literature. If they don't understand everything let them carry away what happens to stick. That's what the rest of us do the rest of our lives.

> *Lore Segal, in a review of "The Untold Tale," in* The New York Times Book Review, *May 9, 1971, p. 8.*

As in the author's previous books, the background is seen as just another—albeit historically interesting—setting for the universal problems that bring pain and sorrow to men and children. The events are presented with powerful immediacy; the characters are vigorously delineated in their suffering, weakness, or evil; and their interrelationship with the times in which they live traces the design of their destiny.

> *Paul Heins, in a review of "The Untold Tale," in* The Horn Book Magazine, *Vol. XLVII, No. 3, June, 1971, p. 292.*

The landscapes and events are recorded with the precision of a camera in poetic, saga-style prose. With great delicacy, Haugaard delineates the emotional make-up of the people he portrays and brings even his secondary characters alive. . . . [This] tragic story will be a moving experience for any reader. (p. 128)

> *Nancy Berkowitz, in a review of "The Untold Tale," in* School Library Journal, *an appendix to* Library Journal, *Vol. 18, No. 1, September, 1971, pp. 127-28.*

A MESSENGER FOR PARLIAMENT (1976)

The lot of children in Haugaard's visions of wartime in history is harsh. Once more their victimization is a central theme, and his young protagonist, Oliver Cutter, steps stoically, if gingerly, through the chaos stirred up by the English civil war. The story unfolds in flashback as Oliver, now an aging Bostonian, looks back to his boyhood when the death of his mother and offhand abandonment by his father pushed him into the first waves of civil war. With his mother dead, Oliver and his father start out following the Parliamentary forces to make a living, but Oliver is separated from him at the looting of Worcester. A band of boys briefly becomes his family and one quick wit among them, Easy Jack, becomes Oliver's special friend. When the two boys find themselves on their own, it's Jack who wins them a home of sorts with a London printer who eventually sends them to Royalist Oxford with his pro-Parliament newspaper. Their contact there enlists them to carry a secret letter to Cromwell in Cambridge; this final journey proves both eventful and dangerous, with Jack being critically wounded by a highwayman and Oliver managing to evade Royalist pursuers to deliver the letter. A sequel is promised and that's a good thing, for though Haugaard's storytelling is articulate and his prose rich, the pace lulls and several plot terms seem too arbitrary in light of what's here—though their significance may well come clear with the projected installment.

> *Denise M. Wilms, in a review of "A Messenger for Parliament," in* Booklist, *Vol. 73, No. 4, October 15, 1976, p. 322.*

The story contains many of the traditional elements of the picaresque novel. It is as rewarding to read for its sententious, epigrammatic style as for its narrative; but the historical background of the bitter conflict is made perfectly clear. (p. 56)

> *Ethel L. Heins, in a review of " A Messenger for Parliament," in* The Horn Book Magazine, *Vol. LIII, No. 1, February, 1977, pp. 55-6.*

Haugaard does a fine job in this historical fiction, focusing attention on the vicissitudes of Oliver's life and on the ordinary people he meets but relating the lives of such people to the cross-currents and fierce allegiances of a divided country. The fictionalizing is used for fiction; Haugaard never falls into the pit of inventing adventures for the historical characters. The writing style had vigor, the plot is well-constructed and paced. (p. 126)

> *Zena Sutherland, in a review of "A Messenger for Parliament," in* Bulletin of the Center for Children's Books, *Vol. 30, No. 8, April, 1977, pp. 125-26.*

[*A Messenger for Parliament*] has the sense of excitement and the style that have made its prolific author internationally acclaimed. (p. 103)

As in all of the author's books, the nature and variety of humankind are explored through the eyes of a youngster. The complexities of the human condition are well illustrated. The insight shown by the author in revealing a young person's thoughts is startling. Also brilliantly expressed is the flavor of the historical period. The times are recreated in a crisp prose, the countryside so neatly described that one might even feel confident enough to walk the road from Oxford to Cambridge or tend bar in The Unicorn or do many of the other things the young hero does. The book provides an intriguing look at and an understanding of one brief historical moment on a foreign soil. (p. 105)

> *Diana L. Spirt, "Forming a View of the World," in her* Introducing More Books: A Guide for the Middle Grades, *R. R. Bowker Company, 1978, pp. 96-120.**

CROMWELL'S BOY (1978)

An extension of the story *A Messenger for Parliament* . . . about the thirteen-year-old orphan Oliver Cutter, chosen as a spy for General Cromwell because he is an excellent horseman and is clever enough to keep secrets. He develops an increasing interest in Faith Powers, whose advice he heeded in the previous story—that his love for her should not interfere with his opportunities to advance under Cromwell. The episodic narrative, with descriptions of lively skirmishes, increases in pace as Oliver makes an escape from Oxford with a stolen horse, bringing Faith to safety. Oliver is a strongly individualized character, a real boy not above prevarication for the cause. A style enriched with aphorisms and details enhances the color and atmosphere of the story without diminishing tension, although the book may demand an audience of superior young readers.

> *Virginia Haviland, in a review of "Cromwell's Boy," in* The Horn Book Magazine, *Vol. LIV, No. 6, December, 1978, p. 644.*

Haugaard's skill as a writer is obviously great; Oliver's character is drawn with both depth and sensitivity, and the world in which he lives is depicted with seemingly effortless conviction and detail which compare favorably to the time portraits drawn by such distinguished historical novelists as Rosemary Sutcliff and Henry Treece. Such grisly but fascinating asides as his description of a traveling toothpuller's activities on the village square, for example, make it seem almost possible that the book really is the work of Oliver himself as an old man, as it purports to be.

> *Chuck Schacht, in a review of "Cromwell's Boy," in* School Library Journal, *Vol. 25, No. 4, December, 1978, p. 60.*

There's more storytelling here than previously: the plot, along with Haugaard's dignified style and keen characterization, move the story along well, and historical information is never overpowering. The resulting life is welcome and makes this sequel superior to its predecessor.

> *Denise M. Wilms, in a review of "Cromwell's Boy," in* Booklist, *Vol. 75, No. 7, December 1, 1978, p. 616.*

Oliver's first person narration is flashbacked from "an age when it is difficult to be young, if my feet are cold"—what a refreshing way to say old age and make an English sentence stir again for adolescents who can't and won't read! Like the boy in Camelot commissioned by Arthur "to tell the story, strong and clear," the aging Oliver does just that. He frankly admits the Biblical story of Saul and David is his favorite, a fact mirrored in the way he lionizes English history's often vilified Oliver Cromwell. This appealing messenger-boy-turned-spy makes Cromwell if not a saint at least not the righteous Saint of the Puritan cause. Cromwell himself could have picked no better biographer than Oliver Cutter who puts a measure of humanity into the tragedy of Cromwell's war and its heroes. For once even I understood the English Civil War and delighted in the self-effacing but glowing *Cromwell's Boy* who puts for "those who do not know better," reality, not mere "secret meetings and nightly prowls" into spying and still makes it exciting. Children's literature is the richer and so are children of my age who read *Cromwell's Boy*.

> *Barbara Hoffman, in a review of "Cromwell's Boy," in* Best Sellers, *Vol. 38, No. 12, March, 1979, p. 407.*

Haugaard's forte is that he keeps sight of the individual amid the larger cause. Oliver's attempts to steal a horse become as important as his spying activities. The people who protect and threaten the picaresque hero attain three-dimensional stature through vigorous writing and first-class use of language. It seems the author plans to carry the protagonist to his old age in the Colonies. Somehow, I cannot reconcile the sad old man recapturing his past with the daring young man on horseback, however much one keeps faith with the other.

A review of "Cromwell's Boy," in Language Arts, *Vol. 56, No. 5, May, 1979, p. 547.*

CHASE ME, CATCH NOBODY! (1980)

On a school trip to Germany in 1937, 14-year-old Dane Erik Hansen is handed a batch of forged passports by a mysterious man who tells the boy where to take them when he leaves the ferry. After seeing the man arrested by the Nazi SS, Erik vows to deliver the passports. This he does, in the process becoming a target of a Nazi police hunt himself. His friend Nikolai, whose parents are Communist anti-Fascists, provides moral help and comic relief to Erik's close calls—and his teachers (one a Nazi-sympathizer and one a cautious and wise anti-Nazi) help him decide that getting involved is worth the risk. Erik finally escapes into Denmark with a half-Jewish German girl (who calls herself "Nobody") and Nikolai. The colorful characters in this action-packed story give Erik foils against which to define himself. Unfortunately, Haugaard . . . interjects many of his opinions and autobiographical adult perceptions into Erik's narration. Also, the title is awkward and cutesy (a pun on the name "Nobody") and some of the many German phrases used can be understood only by context. Nuances of Danish and German social class and political humor permeate the story. Some readers will have questions about this social/political milieu (not necessarily a bad thing), and many will find Erik's and Nikolai's rebellious heroics very admirable and absorbing reading.

Jack Forman, in a review of "Chase Me, Catch Nobody!" in School Library Journal, *Vol. 26, No. 8, April, 1980, p. 124.*

This is a good adventure story, but it's much more than that; it's an indictment of a cruel regime, and it is also a perceptive, smooth development of a growing political awareness on Erik's part, an awareness that stirs a sense of justice, an anger at injustice, a willingness to become involved, and that results in an impressive (and credible) display of courage and initiative. The story is strengthened by vivid characterization and relieved by some very funny dialogue and pranks among the group of boys.

Zena Sutherland, in a review of "Chase Me, Catch Nobody!" in Bulletin of the Center for Children's Books, *Vol. 33, No. 10, June, 1980, p. 191.*

The adventure-filled thriller, told with exactly the right overtones of schoolboy humor, evokes the political ambience of a historic time and place. The story is a departure for the author because of its pace and subject and will perhaps be more accessible to a broad audience than were some of his earlier novels. But it is characterized once again by fine word-crafting and attention to structure, which makes the aphoristic style both memorable and appropriate. Like the protagonist, the reader comes to appreciate that "the fact that someone else is a fool does not make you into a genius."

Mary M. Burns, in a review of "Chase Me, Catch Nobody!" in The Horn Book Magazine, *Vol. LVI, No. 3, June, 1980, p. 296.*

Much of the interest [of the first half of the story] derives from Haugaard's delightfully sharp, subtle portrayal, not only of the two boys' behavior, but also of the various shades of reaction to the Nazis on the part of the Danish boys and their two teachers. In the second half of the story, the characterization, though vivid, becomes broader, and the accent shifts to suspense. . . . It's a bit disappointing that the earlier moral-political-psychological facets become mere background to an international adventure. However, as in many such adventures, if readers accept the villains' predilection for circuitous maneuvers and the hero's choice of a lone and dangerous route, they'll be taken along on a breathless chase to the end.

A review of "Chase Me, Catch Nobody!" in Kirkus Reviews, *Vol. XLVIII, No. 15, August 1, 1980, p. 984.*

Despite its lively scenario, this novel is more than just another adventure yarn of The-Hardy-Boys-Best-The-Nazi-Juggernaut kind. Erik is a typical boy: proud and clumsy, caustic and confused, well-meaning and uncertain; "a bit of a snob" who tends to be impatient with his parents and his teachers. Though he must make many difficult choices, he is consistently denied the grandeur so many other heroes enjoy. (With their stolen rowboat slowly sinking, Erik decides to slide overboard into the fiord, sacrificing his life in order to save the lives of his friends. He releases his grip, only to find "the bottom was slimy mud. I was standing waist-deep in water.") The novel also dashes expectations in other, more searching ways. Early in the book, Erik muses on the fact that the tongue "so often says the very opposite of what you mean," as if it were "an inborn traitor." The novel's persistent concern with the problems of loyalty and self-knowledge elevates it above period romance. Erik learns that a teacher whose ironic anti-Nazi humour he has come to admire in fact lacks the courage of his witticisms; the reassurances Erik offers Isolde are undermined by his knowledge that the Danish police are returning to Germany Jews who have entered Denmark "illegally." The delicacy and understatement of which the author is capable are well conveyed in a throw-away remark in Erik's epilogue: "An unhappy time was in store for Denmark. A few years later, it was invaded by the Nazis. I could not imagine that Nikolai would not fight them could you?"

Within the narrow confines of the adventure story for children, Haugaard manages to be witty and sensitive and ironic. His story is consistently entertaining without ever ceasing to convey a sense of the complexity of human experience. This deft combination of serious theme and fast-paced adventure deserves—and richly repays—both our interest and our gratitude.

William Blackburn, in a review of "Chase Me, Catch Nobody!" in The World of Children's Books, *Vol. VI, 1981, p. 70.*

LEIF THE UNLUCKY (1982)

The abandoned Norse colony in Greenland in its tragic last days in the late 15th Century is the setting for Haugaard's fine new historical novel. Erik the Red had established the thriving colony 500 years before. But now only a few hundred people are left, decimated by epidemics and the increasingly severe cold; and in their terrible isolation "at the end of the world," where fragments of Christianity mix with the half-remembered Norse religion and the fierce sagas, the society is breaking down. With the adults defeated, sunk in their dreams of a glorious past and of a ship from Norway that will come to take them back, the struggle for survival is played out by the younger generation. In a situation reminiscent of *Lord of the Flies* (Paragon, 1959), the attempts of 15-year-old Leif to maintain community and cooperation are challenged by Egil and his band, who rule by violence and fear. Though he tries for some complexity of character and is careful to undermine the heroic view of physical combat, Haugaard is unable to depict Leif and his friends in much depth: the dialogue is stilted and the relationships are unconvincing. The book's power lies rather in the broad sweep of its subject: Haugaard evokes a natural landscape of beauty and terror, almost bare of vegetation and animal life, and with the always encroaching ice; he captures the malaise of the dying community with its ruined and abandoned farms. Even readers who do not normally like historical fiction will respond to this power struggle between young people in a harsh and desolate land.

> *Hazel Rochman, in a review of "Leif the Unlucky," in* School Library Journal, *Vol. 28, No. 7, March, 1982, p. 158.*

Haugaard's measured tones and preference for sage description have the effect of pushing readers to ponder his characters and their performance. There is much between the lines on matters of life, death, honor, and service. The story ends on a positive note, but the darker historical canvas betrays that optimism, and experienced Haugaard readers will recognize his theme of children coping in a world gone wrong.

> *Denise M. Wilms, in a review of "Leif the Unlucky," in* Booklist, *Vol. 78, No. 15, April 1, 1982, p. 1018.*

Haugaard writes commandingly of the last remnants of the Greenland colony in the early fifteenth century.... This primitive world is brought to vivid life in a story that is as effective in picturing the bleak desolation of the moribund colony as it is in creating strongly individual characters. There is a sense of doom and inevitability about the story, yet it has high drama and action; this has some of the major attributes of good historical fiction: vivid details of time and place, association with historical characters, and focus on fictional characters whose lives engage the reader. (pp. 207-08)

> *Zena Sutherland, in a review of "Leif the Unlucky," in* Bulletin of the Center for Children's Books, *Vol. 35, No. 11, July-August, 1982, pp. 207-08.*

[*Leif the Unlucky*] is a haunting tale, well told, filled with memorable characters old and young. That distant, shadowy time and place become sharp and alive. A perfect story to read aloud, and a fine one for those who enjoy reading and are good at it.

> *Nancy K. Johansen, in a review of "Leif the Unlucky," in* Language Arts, *Vol. 59, No. 7, October, 1982, p. 752.*

A BOY'S WILL (1983)

Although Haugaard's new novel is sometimes lax in construction—unaccountably switching the narrative viewpoint—it is a moving and tense story of divided loyalties. [Troy] Howell's drawings of the sea and the forlorn landscapes of the Irish coast in 1779 strongly illustrate Patrick's deeds. An orphan, Patrick

lives with his paternal grandfather, an unkind man who despises the boy's ''popish'' name and reviles Patrick's dead, penniless, Catholic mother. Is it this attitude, or Patrick's sympathy for the American fight for independence that urges him into a dangerous mission? He sets out in a small boat to warn Capt. Paul Jones when he hears his grandfather plotting with the British to ambush the rebel fleet, knowing that his homeland will be lost to him forever. The action is vividly described, right up to the bittersweet close.

> *A review of "A Boy's Will," in* Publishers Weekly, *Vol. 224, No. 17, October 21, 1983, p. 67.*

This has some historical interest and some action and suspense; it is less substantial and less polished than most of Haugaard's work, however, and is uneven in pace despite its brevity.

> *Zena Sutherland, in a review of "A Boy's Will," in* Bulletin of the Center for Children's Books, *Vol. 37, No. 5, January, 1984, p. 88.*

A lonely night vigil and a desperate race against his grandfather's larger, faster ship provide the action in what is essentially a short story.... Some of the vocabulary (''Now he deemed himself ready ...'') may be problematic, but characterization is simple and straightforward. The brevity ... will appeal to young readers. (pp. 71-2)

> *Gale Eaton, in a review of "A Boy's Will," in* School Library Journal, *Vol. 30, No. 6, February, 1984, pp. 71-2.*

THE SAMURAI'S TALE (1984)

After a year in Japan, immersed in Japanese life, history, and culture, Erik Christian Haugaard has written an absorbing novel about the chaotic samurai period during the sixteenth century, when noblemen ferociously fought one another in an attempt to seize complete control of their country. (p. 178)

[The author] is telling a story—an episodic adventure story—full of significant events; at the same time, he has written a psychological novel, delving into the hero's development and commenting on his turns of fortune. For the retrospective narrative, told by an old man in a village, is rich with the vividness and immediacy of the experiences of a boy as he grows up to be a young man of eighteen.

Perilously close to death when he was rescued at the age of four by the intercession of Lord Akiyama—an enemy samurai who ultimately became the boy's patron—Taro, the only surviving member of a defeated noble family, was first sent to work in a kitchen and later in the stables. Attaining the position of messenger, he was finally restored to the rank of samurai, having in the meantime cultivated the virtues of the class he had been born into. Sent on dangerous missions, playing an important part in the siege of a castle, and composing love lyrics to a young girl of noble blood, Taro felt he had come into his own.

But having established Taro's position in historical time, the author goes beyond the temporal and interpolates an extra dimension: He gives the young man a universal human aspect—the privilege of a writer using historical material creatively. Occasionally, for example, Taro soliloquizes.

> When I had been a poor boy working in the stable, or before that in the cookhouse with Togan, I had only one dream—to become a

samurai. Now I was one, even a trusted one . . . I was respected beyond my age; even older samurai treated me with respect . . . So, I said to myself, your dream has come true; the gods have heard you and have given you what you asked for. Yet you are not satisfied. Why is that? I smiled a little forlornly—it was strange to be sitting here in the night holding a conversation with myself. ''Because I was poor once,'' I whispered. ''Part of me still belongs in the cookhouse with Togan'' . . . I shall always be not one but two persons.

Taro's story follows a biographical pattern, each episode rounded out with the making of friends and the appearance of enemies; but, in the long run, with the defeat of Lord Akiyama the young man finds himself once again at the bottom rung of the ladder of fate. (pp. 178-79)

> *Paul Heins, in a review of ''The Samurai's Tale,'' in* The Horn Book Magazine, *Vol. LX, No. 2, April, 1984, pp. 178-79.*

The personal, episodic side of Taro's story is expertly played out against the complex historical backdrop of shifting hegemony in the Kai region of Japan. The richly imaged narrative . . . evokes not just the history but also the philosophy and morality of feudal Japan. The polysyllabic Japanese names are undeniably difficult to keep straight, but a list of characters helps. Those who give this the slow, attentive reading it merits will be rapidly absorbed by Haugaard's chronicle of far-reaching friendship and tragedy and will hope for the continuation that is hinted in the novel's final paragraphs. (p. 1116)

> *Karen Stang Hanley, in a review of ''The Samurai's Tale,'' in* Booklist, *Vol. 80, No. 15, April 1, 1984, pp. 1115-16.*

The characterization of Taro is excellent, and the elaborate samurai code and social structure of traditional Japan are well presented and explained. . . . The subject matter and intricacy of the relationships and loyalties in this fast-paced story will limit the appeal to mature and perceptive readers. It is a worthy addition to the list of excellent books set in feudal Japan, such as Katherine Paterson's *The Sign of the Chrysanthemum* (Crowell, 1973) and *The Master Puppeteer* (Crowell, 1975). . . .

> *Phyllis Ingram, in a review of ''The Samurai's Tale,'' in* School Library Journal, *Vol. 30, No. 9, May, 1984, p. 89.*

Of prominence in the story is the use of dialogue in first person which is crisp and clipped suggesting oriental language. It is refreshing to find a historical novel that does not use ''media-language,'' which is so common in today's stories, especially of the Indian cultures.

Mr. Haugaard's strength is in the analogies that he uses and the subtle use of setting and religious philosophies that permeate the plot. (p. 89)

> *A review of ''The Samurai's Tale,'' in* Language Arts, *Vol. 62, No. 1, January, 1985, pp. 88-9.*

Haugaard is never for the mass market. Yet his contribution to children's literature is ever constant. He never writes down to the reader, but rather draws the reader up into his work, challenging every step of the way. Thus the reader is rewarded handsomely for the time so generously spent in so vast a tale. And one looks forward with great anticipation to a (could be) sequel. It has long been this reviewer's feeling that if we do not support writers the caliber of Haugaard . . . what quality and poetic beauty will we be offered in its place?

> *Sally Ann Thompson, in a review of ''The Samurai's Tale,'' in* Catholic Library World, *Vol. 56, No. 8, March, 1985, p. 341.*

Kathryn Lasky (Knight)

1944-

American author of nonfiction, fiction, and picture books.

Lasky is a versatile and lyrical writer best known for her informational books for middle graders and novels for young adults. Her nonfiction, which contains photographs by her husband Christopher G. Knight, often centers on traditional crafts such as weaving and dollmaking while spotlighting their gifted practitioners. Transcending classification as how-to books, the works impart a sense of admiration for the artisan's skill and provide evidence of the author's extensive research. Lasky's novels—*The Night Journey, Beyond the Divide, Prank,* and *Home Free*—feature strong-willed protagonists and generally contain ethnic, historical, or religious elements which inspire or challenge the characters. Her picture books for younger readers focus on warm family relationships and include the photoessay *A Baby for Max,* which documents the reactions of Lasky's son to his mother's pregnancy and the arrival of a sister.

Critics commend Lasky for her eloquent, clear style, well-developed characterizations, and use of vivid imagery. Although reviewers occasionally fault her for wordiness, they consider Lasky a fluent writer who captures moods as well as facts in often poetic language.

The Weaver's Gift received the *Boston Globe-Horn Book* Award for Nonfiction in 1981 and *The Night Journey* won the National Jewish Book Award for Children in 1982. *Sugaring Time* was a Newbery Honor Book in 1984.

(See also *Something about the Author,* Vol. 13; *Contemporary Authors New Revision Series,* Vol. 11; and *Contemporary Authors,* Vols. 69-72.)

Photograph by Christopher Knight. Courtesy of Kathryn Lasky

AUTHOR'S COMMENTARY

I am not one of those artless fools who airily says about my writing, "Oh, I don't think about it; I just do it." It does me before I do it. There are no muses lurking around the Lasky-Knight household. There are interruptions. There is broken plumbing. There is a small boy who designs weaponry, everything from catapults to lasers, with a zeal that makes Caspar Weinberger look like a dove. There is a two-and-a-half-year-old girl. Her favorite activity is rearranging the contents of drawers and closets onto floors. Somehow all this is not inviting to the muse population. One look at our chaotic household and people say, "You don't need a muse; you need a cleaning lady."

So when I started to write about nonfiction, in my desperation I began where I used to eons ago—then I was a seventh-grader on a Sunday night, with a report due Monday morning on the Pleistocene Age. My route of research went something like this: First I went to the dictionary and looked up a definition. Webster really had a knack for providing material for desperate seventh-graders. Then I would proceed to the *World Book Encyclopedia.* If I was feeling very scholarly, I would persevere and take on the Mount Everest of research—*Encyclopaedia Britannica.* We did need a stepladder in our house to scale the lofty *Britannica* peaks. Rappelling back down, I would tremble at the thought of those thousands of tissue-thin pages and masses of fine print under my arm. I would silently curse the idiot who had set his mind to collecting all this information in the first place. But more often than not, I would skip the *Britannica* and go on to my final step in the research process: Bursting into my sister's room, I would fling myself on her bed and in anguish cry, "Quick, I need a first sentence about the Pleistocene Age!" Sometimes I would get one from her, and sometimes she'd tell me to get out. In the second case I would go to my mother, and that move could prove to be exceedingly frustrating. She would plunge right in and start tossing off opening sentences like a comedy writer searching for one-liners. Like all seventh-graders I considered the quality of my mother's thoughts stupid, boring, and embarrassing. I would roll my eyes and groan and wish that Ozzie and Harriet were my real parents.

So in looking for the answer as to how one writes nonfiction, I began as I had begun twenty-five years ago—by looking in the dictionary. I started getting a queasy feeling almost immediately as I turned to the *non* section of the dictionary and skimmed down the page—*noncommittal, nondescript, noneffective.* Indeed, I was feeling nearly negative by the time I came to *nonfiction*— which was defined as "prose work other than fiction." It sounded like nonbooks to me. I hate to be in the "other than" category. Well, I thought I'd better get serious; I've matured since seventh grade—supposedly. I've outgrown the dictionary. So I glanced at that established authority on children's literature, Lillian H. Smith and *The Unreluctant Years* (ALA). She states:

> In the telling of a story the author's whole mind and heart are necessarily engaged and his preoccupation is with the art of literature. This can only be a secondary consideration with the writer of an informational book. His interest must center in the special field of knowledge he is to present. . . . For this reason, informational books are infrequently literature and seldom do they survive the generation for which they were written.

I find this statement appalling. I always find it appalling when people tell me where my heart and mind are or are not. So I went elsewhere to find out exactly what I was devoting my time and energy to—not to mention my heart and brain. I picked up Rebecca Lukens's *A Critical Handbook of Children's Literature* (Scott, Foresman), and in "Nonfiction Defined" I looked for my road map, my crystal ball that told me what I had been doing. I was excited and confident. Within five minutes, however, I had run the gamut of emotions from excitement to horror. I was grateful that I had not read these guidelines earlier in my career, or certainly I never would have written informational books. But in reading these suggestions for aspiring nonfiction writers, it finally occurred to me what I do not do—and what I seek to do—in my writing.

The first guideline was that the successful "nonfiction writer is concerned with *facts first of all*." Therefore the writer must satisfy curiosity. To satisfy that curiosity the writer must avoid suggesting miracles. Wonder is fine, but miracles connote "mystery and the unknowable." I suppose that is where we get all those quaint titles like *The Wonderful World of Coral Asteroids*.

I do not agree that a satisfying experience in literature derives from knowing all the facts. This condition suggests to me a kind of mechanical mystery, a sort of soulless exploration of phenomena. That is not why I read books or why I think children read books. That idea suggests a notion of an almost totally explainable and knowable world. Miracle connotes mystery and the unknowable. I believe in miracle and mystery. The way in which Carole Bowling, the master dollmaker in *Dollmaker* . . . , paints the light in a doll's eyes is unknowable, a mystery. She could write down her paint formula, the brush size. There is probably a machine that could measure the length and number of every brush stroke. You could give all this information to other dollmakers, but they could not make the same doll. It would not be as good. Why, we don't know. It is a mystery, a miracle that has to do with talent but that is beyond explanation—a mystery which I chose not even to try to explain, but to deepen. I do not feel that in presenting such a mystery I have made an unsatisfying experience in literature.

Lawrence Pringle says that we must "acknowledge that the world is a complex place" and that there are not always absolute answers but that there is a continual search for the truth. I think he is correct and that for me in writing I am searching for the story among the truths, the facts, the lies, and the realities.

Another guideline from *A Critical Handbook* states that "there is no need for characterization . . . only occasionally does the

text evoke mood." This statement suggests that all nonfiction books take place in laboratories run by robots. In my own experience in writing I have always tried hard to listen, smell, and touch the place that I write about—especially if I am lucky enough to be there. I will never forget the smell of the lanolin vapors rising from the merino sheep's back under the heat lamp of the lambing pen in the barn that early March morning. Nor will I forget Carole Bowling, trembling and pale, as she made the mold of her doll's clay head. If the original were damaged, she would have to scrap two months of painstaking work. Feeling her tension, seeing her lips bitten white with apprehension—that is characterization. I am dealing with her character, her personality during the agonizing minutes as she unclamps the mold boards.

In *Puppeteer* . . . I dealt with a master puppeteer, Paul Vincent Davis. I watched Paul hard at work painting the faces on the puppets he had sculpted. Suddenly, Paul—a rather immense man, over two hundred fifty pounds, who certainly destroys any notions we have of little shriveled up toy-makers like Geppetto—sneezed, and ten puppets shivered and trembled. Light and dark played across their faces, and suddenly I could hear the muffled voices deep in their rubber throats trying to get out. Paul's hours of work were instantly drawn into focus for me. These puppets were not facsimiles of life; they were actors waiting for their voices, for their moves, and like the rest of us a chance at that little slip between two eternities that we call life. From my perspective as a writer, this moment was the single most important thing that happened in the studio that morning. I would devote a few sentences to the facts concerning his painting of the faces, but the real mystery that I would focus on would be the sneeze. What happens when a two hundred fifty pound puppeteer sneezes in his studio? That was where the tension was, the life and death drama, the mystery of a seemingly ordinary morning.

Sometimes I cannot be on site where a story is happening. In *Tall Ships* . . . I did not know what it really was like to be fourteen years old and dying to go to sea, to long to climb through the spidery ropes and spars of a full-rigged ship sailing on a strange sea. I knew the facts; I had spent a whole summer at the Peabody Museum in Salem going through archives. With my husband I had twice sailed the Atlantic Ocean in a ridiculously small boat, hating almost every minute of it. But why a fourteen-year-old like Andrew Pendleton and hundreds like him back in the nineteenth century would give their eye teeth to sail on a ship seemed beyond me. Then I read somewhere that Samuel Eliot Morison had said that history is one-tenth fact and nine-tenths imagination. So I started imagining. That meant forgetting who I was and the fact that while I was crossing the Atlantic Ocean, I would rather have been in Bloomingdale's. I had to imagine what it would have been like to be fourteen in the year 1856 in a one-street town in Maine. (pp. 527-31)

In the end I cannot agree with the attributes these two critics give to nonfiction. I have a fascination with the inexact and the unexplainable. I try to do as little explaining as possible, but I try to present my subject in some way so it will not lose what I have found to be or suspect to be its sacred dimension. I seem to seek a nonfactual kind of truth that focuses on certain aesthetic and psychological realities. Facts are quite cheap, but real stories are rare and expensive. If there was any special moment for me in the process of maple sugaring, it was one that I did not observe but could only imagine. When Don Lacey, exhausted from a day of sugaring, doctoring, and parenting, would sit alone in the sugarhouse until late at night, long past midnight, tending the arch. There is no bed, no radio, no real light to read by. "At night in the sugarhouse a person can only think and dream and tend the arch. But it doesn't matter, for it's a gentle darkness that smells like maple clouds and reminds you of a winter now gone and a spring just born." This passage is my favorite in the book. I think of it as a celebration of being alone, of being human and solitary at night.

The world is a very complicated place. I choose to present this complexity but not to analyze it. There are not always absolute answers, but there is a continual search for aspects of the truth. Stephen Jay Gould, who teaches evolutionary biology and the history of science at Harvard, is one of the most articulate voices in this century on the essential messiness of science, life, and nature. He is an eloquent and witty proponent of nature as a tinkerer and not, as he says, a "divine artificer." I am quite comfortable with this notion, a very different one, I might add, from what I was presented with as a budding and disastrous science student in school. Gould says that odd arrangements and funny solutions are the proof of evolution—paths, he says, that a sensible God would never tread but that a natural process constrained by history follows perforce. I am an idolator of insensible gods, for they are indeed the most sacred. In my books I am not concerned with messages, and I really do not care if readers remember a single fact. What I do hope is that they come away with a sense of joy—indeed celebration—about something they have sensed of the world in which they live. (p. 532)

> *Kathryn Lasky, "Reflections on Nonfiction," in* The Horn Book Magazine, *Vol. LXI, No. 5, September-October, 1985, pp. 527-32.*

I HAVE FOUR NAMES FOR MY GRANDFATHER (1976)

The four names, anticlimactically, are Poppy, Pop, Grandpa and Gramps—"But with all four names he's always the same grandfather for me." The rest of this tender, annotated photo album is just as expectable. We see the man and the boy running, fishing, planting flowers, inspecting a locomotive, etc., and we're told that "Grandpa and I play a lot" and that Gramp has four hats, makes funny faces, etc.—"But best of all when I am sad, he hugs me very close and says: 'I love you, Tom.'" As seen [in Christopher G. Knight's photographs], Tom and his grandfather are a happy pair, but their story is an exercise in banality.

> *A review of "I Have Four Names for My Grandfather," in* Kirkus Reviews, *Vol. XLIV, No. 13, July 1, 1976, p. 728.*

The pictures afford an interesting visual presentation for preschool and early elementary grade children, but the sensitivity and depth of feeling within the text are more suitable for middle grades and up. In fact, the adult audience will probably provide the most appreciative readership.

> *Barbara S. Wertheimer, in a review of "I Have Four Names for My Grandfather," in* Children's Book Review Service, *Vol. 5, No. 3, November, 1976, p. 22.*

Written from a child's point of view in a simple, direct style, this photo-essay sensitively treats the feelings of a young boy for his grandfather. The strength of the book lies in the compatibility of the text with the abundant photographs....

> *Andd Ward, in a review of "I Have Four Names for My Grandfather," in* School Library Journal, *Vol. 23, No. 3, November, 1976, p. 48.*

TUGBOATS NEVER SLEEP (1977)

Souped up with color photos and focusing, for young-reader involvement, on a boy who lives near Boston Harbor, this not only tells you less than Plowden's *Tugboat* (1976) but also lacks the genuine impact of the earlier book's strong black-and-white photos and intrinsically interesting text. Here we have the boy, Jason, musing at night about the tugs, viewing their blurred lights from his window, and rushing next morning . . . to board the *Cabot*. Once on board he greets the crew, then concentrates on Jimmy—who shows Jason how to make a clove hitch, tells how he "speaks rope" with non-English speaking deckhands, and delights him with a promise that he can tie up the tug next morning. . . . [You] never get to know the *Cabot* for all the attention to Jason; conversely, he never transcends his role as a "Let's Visit" device for viewing the tug.

> *A review of "Tugboats Never Sleep," in* Kirkus Reviews, *Vol. XLV, No. 14, July 15, 1977, p. 729.*

Not a book about tugboats and their work per se, as you might assume from the title; rather this is a poetic mood piece. . . . [There's] a touch of self-consciousness about the story, especially in the poetic thrusts toward the end. In sum, it's quiet and unassuming, but Jason's eager presence and the waterfront activity will exert an appeal, especially for young boat enthusiasts.

> *Denise M. Wilms, in a review of "Tugboats Never Sleep," in* Booklist, *Vol. 74, No. 4, October 15, 1977, p. 376.*

TALL SHIPS (1978)

"Operation Sail," the hit of the bicentenary, launches and concludes this slender volume—but the surprisingly substantial balance is a mini-history of American sailing on the high seas. "The goal," unromantically, "was to make a profit on each cargo and thus to increase the total profit of the enterprise." As evidence, Lasky provides an owner's cagey instructions to a captain—and mentions that many a lad was christened "Increase." Piquant asides, graphic examples, and plain speaking also freshen the discussion of trade goods (opium to China, slaves to the U.S., ice [!] to the West Indies); the rush to compete (hence designer Donald McKay's "peculiar concave prow lines and sharp-edged shapes"); the hard lot of a ship's "boy," the craft of sailmaker and carpenter; Nathaniel Bowditch's navigation-made-simple for ordinary seamen—and the complicated maneuver of "tacking." . . . In sum, an interesting, instructive, exceptionally well-integrated book that far outclasses both Colby's *Sailing Ships* (1970) and Adkins' *Wooden Ship* (1978)—in the latter instance because Lasky and Knight also give us the essentials of wooden-ship construction.

> *A review of "Tall Ships," in* Kirkus Reviews, *Vol. XLVIII, No. 3, February 1, 1979, p. 130.*

[*Tall Ships*] suffers from the lack of a firm hand at the tiller. The authors travel from America's place in the age of sail, to the China trade, to the New England genius for shipbuilding, to life aboard ship, and, finally, to the recent Bicentennial celebration involving these graceful crafts. The text is enlivened by excerpts from diaries and ships' logs but all are topics worthy of fuller development. A lovely browsing item but more pertinent information can be found in C. B. Colby's *Sailing Ships* (Coward, 1970), Jane D. Lyon's *Clipper Ships and Captains* (American Heritage, 1962), and Alfred Tamarin and Shirley Glubock's *Voyaging to Cathay* (Viking, 1976).

> *Barbara C. Campbell, in a review of ''Tall Ships,'' in* School Library Journal, *Vol. 25, No. 7, March, 1979, p. 141.*

Tall Ships is a short book, but this history of the 19th-century American sailing trade is surprisingly solid and consistently entertaining. Its success lies in its use of colorful anecdotes about the men who built, owned and sailed the tall ships. Almost everything is recalled with a story, and every story is an adventure.

Kathryn Lasky, its author, and Christopher Knight, her photographer husband, both sailors, have paid loving attention to historical details. . . .

Never mind the weak opening and close, which use the Bicentennial ''Operation Sail'' to get into and out of the subject. Like the sailing trade it describes, *Tall Ships* is a lively, instructive and satisfying work.

> *Peter Freedberger, in a review of ''Tall Ships,'' in* The New York Times Book Review, *March 18, 1979, p. 26.*

Occasionally a facet of the subject [of sailing] has treatment that seems inadequate (discussing the opium trade without mentioning the fact that it had been outlawed by the Chinese government, for example) but the coverage is quite good, the facts are accurate, the material often dramatic. . . . An index is appended.

> *Zena Sutherland, in a review of ''Tall Ships,'' in* Bulletin of the Center for Children's Books, *Vol. 32, No. 9, May, 1979, p. 157.*

MY ISLAND GRANDMA (1979)

My Island Grandma is a new-fashioned grandmother who ''has strong hands that hold me tight and safe in the cool deep water while I learn to swim.'' Who takes the little-girl narrator blueberry-picking (''I pretend that I am a little bear, just like the story Grandma read to me'') and takes her sailing (''We look up in the sky and find special shapes in the clouds''); who shows her a nest of eggs about to hatch (''that's the blood that comes with new life'') and shows her ''star pictures'' in the sky. The wonderment is, indeed, lightened with humor (''Speak English,'' Abbey retorts to a recital of constellations) but the whole is never more than a model experience composed of familiar ingredients. . . .

> *A review of ''My Island Grandma,'' in* Kirkus Reviews, *Vol. XLVIII, No. 7, April 1, 1979, p. 385.*

Abbey describes the joys of her island summer in a book that has no story line but depends on the charm of setting and incidents to appeal to the read-aloud audience. Through Abbey, Lasky gives a vivid picture of the island, the long days of summer, and the relationship between Abbey and her grandmother as they observe nature, take a lazy sail, have a swimming lesson, and enjoy cozy cookie-bakes. Abbey's parents (in a cabin near Grandma's) are conspicuously absent, and

astute young listeners will detect a few hints about behavior, but the whole is a sunny, bracing entity. . . .

> *Zena Sutherland, in a review of ''My Island Grandma,'' in* Bulletin of the Center for Children's Books, *Vol. 32, No. 11, July, 1979, p. 194.*

There is no plot per se; merely a listing of activities [Abbey and her grandmother] share. But the character of the incidents points to a bond that's deep and special. . . . This is low-key, but the feeling of warmth is steady, the mood tender.

> *Denise M. Wilms, in a review of ''My Island Grandma,'' in* Booklist, *Vol. 75, No. 21, July 1, 1979, p. 1580.*

THE WEAVER'S GIFT (1981)

Seven short, photo-illustrated chapters follow the ''almost magic'' process by which wool is sheared from the sheep, sorted, carded, spun and woven into a child's blanket. . . . With a text that leaves out nothing in the process . . . , this is not a how-to but a description that evokes the sights, sounds and textures of a homey, ancient art.

> *Patricia Homer, in a review of ''The Weaver's Gift,'' in* School Library Journal, *Vol. 27, No. 7, March, 1981, p. 147.*

Weaver Carolyn Frye lives with her school-principal husband on a small Vermont farm, where they raise sheep and she converts their wool to finished products. In clear, uneffusively lyrical text and photos, Lasky and Knight convey an understanding of, and appreciation for, her work and her art. . . . In recent years there have been other juvenile introductions to this basic sequence, but they are dull or feeble in comparison.

> *A review of ''The Weaver's Gift,'' in* Kirkus Reviews, *Vol. XLIX, No. 5, March 1, 1981, p. 286.*

Much detail on the traditional methods of preparing cloth is included in the text. The vantage point is close and generally effective, the whole a fine documentary of a dying art.

> *Judith Goldberger, in a review of ''The Weaver's Gift,'' in* Booklist, *Vol. 77, No. 17, May 1, 1981, p. 1197.*

The Weaver's Gift is a rare find. . . .

The author makes no effort to oversimplify the text, which is extremely well-written and factual and shows deep appreciation and respect for a woman and her trade. The reader gains a clear sense of the step-by-step weaving process. Children will learn not to take a finished product for granted, and their curiosity about other processes of making things will most surely be aroused.

The book has a strong female central character, who is helped by a supportive husband and by Rob Burroughs, a man who has been shearing sheep for over 50 years. Rob is a model of a competent older person who does valuable work.

The book can be read to pre-schoolers or by older children. It can be used for a research project on weaving, or as an example of one woman's productivity and contributions to society. It is a delightful book!

> *Jan M. Goodman, in a review of ''The Weaver's Gift,'' in* Interracial Books for Children Bulletin, *Vol. 12, Nos. 4 & 5, 1981, p. 38.*

The Weaver's Gift is essentially a picture book, but it should be included in middle and high school libraries. There is an increased interest in crafts, and the superb photographs combined with the clear and concise text carry the reader from the birth of a lamb through the completion of a wool blanket for a child. . . . The book engenders great respect for the finished product as well as for those who are willing to create their "gifts."

> *M. Jean Greenlaw, in a review of "The Weaver's Gift," in* Journal of Reading, *Vol. 25, No. 4, January, 1982, p. 389.*

THE NIGHT JOURNEY (1981)

Each afternoon 13-year-old Rachel spends time keeping her great-grandmother, Nana Sashie, company. This trial they both must endure turns into the highlight of their lives when Nana decides to share with Rachel the story of her family's escape from czarist Russia. Rather than telling Nana's story as a straight narrative, Lasky wisely Ping-Pongs the action between the past and the present. Just as Rachel must wait to hear the whole adventure, the reader too is tantalized, eager to hear more. The story has so many aspects that each person will come away with his own idea of what makes this book memorable. For some it will be the dramatic telling of how a nine-year-old girl's plan saved her family. Others will be intrigued by Rachel's multi-generational family sharing a home. Still others will be moved by the malevolent Wolf, the stranger who has his own dark reasons for helping the family escape. . . . A story to cherish. (pp. 439-40)

> *Ilene Cooper, in a review of "The Night Journey," in* Booklist, *Vol. 78, No. 6, November 15, 1981, pp. 439-40.*

The novel shifts back and forth from the dangerous journey out of Russia to Rachel's own casual, secure life at home and school. These transitions are handled with a smoothness that doesn't break the intrinsic tension of the story, and the contrast between the two lives demonstrates with poignant clarity the real meaning of freedom. The portrayal of warm, supportive families in both stories becomes a link between past and present.

> *Marilyn Kaye, in a review of "The Night Journey," in* School Library Journal, *Vol. 28, No. 5, January, 1982, p. 79.*

Rache's reflective afterword, looking back on [the time she spent with Nana Sashie] might well have been dispensed with. There are internal inconsistencies of tone too (the haunted Joe, in particular, is a bit much). But the shifts of milieu and mood are also inherent in Rache—and each will evoke a response in youngsters of her age.

> *A review of "The Night Journey," in* Kirkus Reviews, *Vol. L, No. 3, February 1, 1982, p. 136.*

Comparatively little fiction about this phase of Jewish history [late nineteenth-century czarist Russia] has been written for children, and the author has dealt skillfully with her plot. But while she writes her factual books in a clean, straightforward manner, her fictional style wants chastening; for her writing is marred by an excess of emotion and by repetitious, ornate metaphors. (pp. 166-67)

> *Ethel L. Heins, in a review of "The Night Journey," in* The Horn Book Magazine, *Vol. LVIII, No. 2, April, 1982, pp. 166-67.*

Amy Schwartz is rehearsing Ado Annie's show-stopper song, "I Caint Say No", for her school production of *Oklahoma*. That's all we hear of Amy in *The Night Journey*. She's hilariously hopeless. "You know why they gave me this part?" she whined. "They think I need a confidence builder." Amy is a great character; I wish we could have had more of her than this tempting picture masterfully sketched in a couple of pages. This richly funny interlude apart, the book is grimly serious, though great-grandmother Sashie . . . is skilfully and, in the widest sense of the word, humorously depicted. . . .

The discussions about the escape are more interesting, if not more exciting, than the escape itself. . . . And the encounters with the Imperial Tsarist soldiery, intended to make one's hair curl, are near bathetic. Less than satisfying too is the vagueness of the background of this Russian-Jewish family. They are an enlightened lot. What schooling, if any, did they have? Where did they get their, for those days, advanced ideas on dental hygiene? After all, severely restrictive Jewish "quotas" still existed within the Pale of Settlement.

> *Stephen Corrin, "Jewish Generations," in* The Times Educational Supplement, *No. 3464, November 19, 1982, p. 36.**

I read this book in one sitting and its essence remained during the two weeks before my second and slower reading. I was gripped and moved by it, though I wondered whether my reactions were over-influenced by the historical reality of pogroms and the Jews in Tsarist Russia. On reflection, I believe this to be a satisfying novel, if not without blemish, and I recommend it strongly.

Continuity and an intense sense of family are paramount. Great granddaughter hears from aged great grandmother shortly before her death of the family's escape from Russia. The structure of the narrative underlines this sense of continuity and the book is full of images which echo across time and back into Jewish history. The tormented figure of Wolf, who makes possible their escape, hidden in a wagon under crates of chickens, did not quite convince me even though his anguish remains in my memory. The major blemish lies in the dialogue: the idiom of the modern American family and that of the original family escaping from Russia are too closely related, and my reading was jarred by some expressions which taste too strongly of the late twentieth century. The family relationships both now and in the past, and across the years, are satisfying, as are young Sashie's sensations and emotions at the time of her exodus.

> *Peter Kennerley, in a review of "The Night Journey," in* The School Librarian, *Vol. 31, No. 2, June, 1983, p. 144.*

DOLLMAKER: THE EYELIGHT AND THE SHADOW (1981)

The doll maker's world is filled with measurements and calibrations, miniscule tools, and the desire to replicate in dolls the light in a child's eye. Lasky and Knight take readers on a photographic journey through the world of one particular doll maker, Carole Bowling, and the voyage is no less than amazing. Each step of the craft is painstakingly yet lovingly described, complementing Bowling's careful, at times tedious, work on a doll in the image of her son, Matthew. Lasky's prose can be forgiven its reverential heights; the workmanship she chronicles seems to deserve it.

> *Ilene Cooper, in a review of "Dollmaker: The Eye-light and the Shadow," in* Booklist, *Vol. 78, No. 11, February 1, 1982, p. 707.*

In the environs of Boston, a young woman named Carole Bowling makes lifelike, limited-edition dolls for collectors—and this is chiefly an evocation of that sensibility. (It has little to do, that is, with either the making of dolls generally or a child's conception of a doll.) Carole, we're told, came to her vocation by working "as a switchboard operator for [a] collector's answering-service." She was surrounded by dolls: "The expressions were exquisite—some with bemused half-smiles, the paperweight eyes slightly troubled, some flirty with glass-blown or painted eyes, some sober or tentative with enigmatic smiles, eyes staring out of another century, seeming almost to sense the future." The child who gets past a sentence like that—if such there be—will eventually find Carole painstakingly modeling the face of her six-year-old son Matthew . . . to achieve an exact, proportionate likeness. (Earlier we have heard also about "that child-light that is the soul of a real child's eye.") When she has her clay model, she makes a single mold and casts three or four heads with which to make two or three dolls (the figures are given differently at different points). "This will make the dolls *original*, rare, and unreplicable in quality." On the last page we see, indistinguishable from Matthew, a Matty doll. It's all slightly creepy—and very rarefied.

> *A review of "Dollmaker: The Eyelight and the Shadow," in* Kirkus Reviews, *Vol. L, No. 4, February 15, 1982, p. 204 [the excerpt of Kathryn Lasky's work used here was originally published in her* Dollmaker: The Eyelight and the Shadow, *Charles Scribner's Sons, 1981].*

The author gets inside of the dollmaker's craft to such an extent that not only is each step beautifully detailed, but the dollmaker's anxieties and concerns over her creation are expressed as well. Although a few steps are glossed over and not shown, we do see how the head is sculpted, a mold made, the head poured, the body made and wig and clothes sewed until the finished product looks like a miniature boy. Much as she did with weaving in *The Weaver's Gift* . . . , Lasky lifts the dollmaker's craft to an art. This is particularly apparent in her description of the dollmaker slowly, meticulously painting the doll's face. "The changes within an hour or two are barely discernible. . . . It is like trying to watch a rosebud bloom or a chrysalis turn into a butterfly." And like her earlier effort, this is also not a "how-to" book, but a description of a talented artist working. (pp. 148-49)

> *Patricia Homer, in a review of "Dollmaker: The Eyelight and the Shadow," in* School Library Journal, *Vol. 28, No. 7, March, 1982, pp. 148-49.*

JEM'S ISLAND (1982)

At home in Cleveland on a winter's night, Jem dreams about what the summer will hold. His family will be in Maine then, and he and his father—just the two of them—will load the kayak and camp overnight together. After months of waiting and preparing, the dream comes true. They pick their destination, paddle to the island, and sleep outdoors on a perfect trip which, Jem hopes, will provide the first of many more happy memories. Lasky, a remarkably versatile writer, is in a

quiet mood here, and though the episode on the kayak has the aura of adventure, the mood throughout is one of tranquility. . . . Still, in the midst of all this quietude is much information about navigation, survival, and other aspects of camping. Not for everyone, but those who love camping and canoeing will be taken.

> *Ilene Cooper, in a review of "Jem's Island," in* Booklist, *Vol. 79, No. 6, November 15, 1982, p. 446.*

Crisp, vivid writing conveys the sights, sounds, and smells of the Maine coast as the *Wasso* glided through the sea. The author is keenly aware of what would be important to a boy on such an adventure—eating authentic hardtack, finding a piece of driftwood shaped like a whale, camping on an unnamed island, and taking a "'night glide'" under a starry sky.

> *Kate M. Flanagan, in a review of "Jem's Island," in* The Horn Book Magazine, *Vol. LIX, No. 1, February, 1983, p. 45.*

From practice the summer before, through dreaming and planning over the winter, to the actual trip, the author catches the flavor of anticipation and excitement attendant with such adventure. No waves here; the narrative glides along smoothly. . . . The author has an excellent feel for the adventure, and draws sensory images of her own. If the story has no plot as such, it certainly expresses the dream inherent in every young person—to be old enough to live an adult adventure, and then to actually do it.

> *Nancy Ferrell, in a review of "Jem's Island," in* School Library Journal, *Vol. 29, No. 6, February, 1983, p. 78.*

SUGARING TIME (1983)

[Kathryn Lasky and Christopher G. Knight] visited a Vermont farm last year, one with plenty of children around, and recorded the whole operation of making maple syrup, from the tapping of the first tree to the final cleanup of equipment months later. The pictures are wonderful, the text pretty good. . . .

Although the text is too adult-poetic and too short on narrative to be fully satisfactory, there are sections that are excellently written, and the book is worth getting.

> *Noel Perrin, in a review of "Sugaring Time," in* The New York Times Book Review, *March 13, 1983, p. 29.*

The author and the photographer who collaborated so successfully on *The Weaver's Gift* . . . and *The Dollmaker* . . . combine their talents again in a book that celebrates, rather than just describes, another old craft. In vivid, clear, and at times even mouth-watering prose the author explains the steps involved in making maple syrup, from "breaking out" the sugar trails to grading the final product. The book chronicles the activities of the Lacey family during the March sugaring time on their Vermont farm, "when winter seems tired and spring is only a hoped-for thing." In the course of four weeks tapholes are drilled, buckets are hung, and sap is gathered and boiled in the sugarhouse while the temperature climbs and the place fills with maple fog. Detailed but not too technical, . . . the book is a fine testimony to "mud and greenness, sweetness and renewed life."

Lasky with her husband Christopher G. Knight, son Max, and daughter Meribah. Photograph by Marvin Lasky. Courtesy of Kathryn Lasky.

*Karen Jameyson, in a review of "Sugaring Time,"
in* The Horn Book Magazine, *Vol. LIX, No. 3, June, 1983, p. 323.*

Lasky's frame for the account, which has a narrative quality but is not fictionalized, is poetic but not prolix; it evokes both a sense of the changing seasons and a sense of the Lacey family's anticipation and—for all the hard work—pleasure. . . . This is informative and attractive, less formal and more anecdotal than the equally fine book for the same reading range, Elizabeth Gemming's *Maple Harvest: The Story of Maple Sugaring.*

*Zena Sutherland, in a review of "Sugaring Time,"
in* Bulletin of the Center for Children's Books, *Vol. 36, No. 11, July-August, 1983, p. 213.*

Sugaring Time is a blend of poetry and science which makes for a very enjoyable reading experience. You can almost hear the crunch of snow beneath the horses' feet, the sweet maple sap dripping into the buckets, and the roar of the fire in the sugarhouse. You can smell the muddy earth, wood smoke, and boiling sap. Kathryn Lasky involves *all* the reader's senses in her memorable description of the collecting and processing of maple sap in a small sugarbush in Vermont. . . . Young readers are sure to identify with the Lacey children as they help their parents at every step in the process. (p. 34)

The book is *not* a reference book—there are no page numbers, no index, no captions on the photographs. You will not find a specific chapter that explains the anatomy of a sugar maple tree and how it produces sap. Rather, this information is dispersed throughout the text. This is certainly not a fault. Although the descriptions are metaphoric, they are not inaccurate. The author and photographer were attempting to capture an essence, to convey a very positive relationship of man to his environment. They succeeded in creating a very beautiful, highly sensory, environmental education book! (p. 35)

*Martha T. Kane, in a review of "Sugaring Time,"
in* Appraisal: Science Books for Young People, *Vol. 17, No. 1, Winter, 1984, pp. 34-5.*

The author presents a remarkably clear picture of the process of making maple syrup. The text is distinctly sequenced with specific terms being clarified when used. Variety and appeal of descriptive words, sentence structure, and sugar terms heighten the reader's sense of being directly involved.

*Ronald A. Jobe, in a review of "Sugaring Time,"
in* Language Arts, *Vol. 61, No. 2, February, 1984, p. 183.*

The beauty and clarity of the expository writing, accompanied by informative, action-filled photographs excite readers' interest in Vermont maple-sugaring time. . . . The style is as clear and rich as "fancy" syrup. The author's perspective on the value of all living things, the seasons, work, and tradition provides a warm and satisfying framework for this presentation of information. The text, a model of good exposition, is also a positive stimulus to vocabulary building. . . . Contrasts between factual and interpretive statements are easily discovered and enjoyed.

> *Alice Naylor, in a review of "Sugaring Time," in* Language Arts, *Vol. 61, No. 5, September, 1984, p. 543.*

BEYOND THE DIVIDE (1983)

One of a large Amish family, Meribah decides to leave and go west with her father, who has been shunned by the rest of his family for breaking the strict Amish code. This is the story of that journey; it is preceded by a brief entry dated January, 1850, when Meribah, alone and starving in the Sierra wilderness, fights off two vultures so that she can eat some of the doe on which they had been feeding. The text moves back nine months, to describe Meribah's decision and the long, detailed journey in which she suffers the slow privations of the trek, is horrified by the rape and ensuing suicide of the one friend she's made, is bereaved when her father dies of a wound infection, is finally left alone and stranded. Rescued by a group of Yahi Indians, Meribah learns to love them and their way of life; by this time it is June of 1850 and she has decided she will go back, alone, to a fertile valley she had loved when the wagon train had halted there. An afterword explains that soon thereafter, the Yana (of which the Yahi were a tribe) had been exterminated by whites, and that in 1900 the last Yahi was found: Ishi, the last of his tribe. Lasky writes a vivid and stirring tale that takes the pseudo-romance out of westward migration; while the painstaking delineations of minor characters are interesting, they shift the focus from the protagonist, who is going through more than the physical trials of the journey, for she is learning to understand a range of people whose lifestyles and interests conflict with Amish mores. Despite the pace, an interesting story.

> *Zena Sutherland, in a review of "Beyond the Divide," in* Bulletin of the Center for Children's Books, *Vol. 36, No. 10, June, 1983, p. 192.*

The versatile Lasky has written a quintessential pioneer story, a piece so textured and rich that readers will remember it long after they've put it down. . . . If there can be too much of a good thing, it is Lasky's descriptions, which, while truly evocative, occasionally impede the story's flow. Meribah and her evolution from innocent to self-sufficient woman is finely drawn. Lasky's accomplishment of making the reader clearly see another era through the eyes of the person living out the adventure is bolstered by her extensive research, a hint of which is given in the afterword. An elegantly written tour de force.

> *Ilene Cooper, in a review of "Beyond the Divide," in* Booklist, *Vol. 79, No. 21, July, 1983, p. 1402.*

If it weren't for the fact that this novel suffers from none of the tedium of an actual diary, it would be easy to believe that *Beyond the Divide* derived directly from such a first-hand account. Reading it, you are sure you could physically follow the route of 14-year-old Meribah Simon and her father on their long journey from Pennsylvania west to California during the gold rush years of 1849 and 1850.

Miss Lasky has created a rather remarkable record of the joys and agonies of the trek for the members of the wagon train. Seen through Meribah's eyes, each character—and there are many—has a vivid personality that becomes more clearly defined as the wagon train moves through new terrain and meets some new difficulty. The result of the author's careful research is a very effective historical novel. In tone, the book is more historical than novelistic—having the calm directness admired in Miss Lasky's works of nonfiction—but that is all to the good; it enhances the sense of reality.

That feeling of reality breaks down at the end of the story when Meribah, orphaned and left alone in the wilderness, survives a winter through the kindness of a small tribe of Indians. After this, she chooses to become a child of nature, striking off alone rather than returning to the civilization she had once so sorely missed. This part of the novel, in which the Yana tribe is introduced, is the only one for which source documentation is given; it is also, curiously, the most passionate section. Consequently, it represents a double departure and brings an unfinished feeling to the novel as a whole.

Nevertheless, *Beyond the Divide* is engrossing, a strong presentation of what life must surely have been like for those amazing souls who crossed this vast country in its unsettled state so short a time ago.

> *Natalie Babbitt, in a review of "Beyond the Divide," in* The New York Times Book Review, *August 21, 1983, p. 26.*

Lasky does a beautiful job of developing Meribah's character as the pioneers move west. . . . Her struggle to keep her father alive, rebuild the wagon, and keep herself from dying offers some of the book's best scenes and shows Lasky's writing at its best.

Beyond the Divide has some of the tender qualities of the Laura Ingalls Wilder books. It also has the excellent characterization of a strong female with a will to survive that is reminiscent of Jean George's *Julie of the Wolves.* This story of the Old West looks at the struggle, fortitude, and courage of some of the Gold Rush emigrants. It also paints an unpleasant, but accurate, picture of the pioneers and their attacks on the Indians. Lasky's book is one of the finest historical novels I've read in a long time. It certainly ought to be considered for the Newbery Award. (p. 87)

> *Dick Abrahamson, "To Start the New Year Off Right," in* English Journal, *Vol. 73, No. 1, January, 1984, pp. 87-9.**

Beyond the Divide is a book with much to recommend it. Characterizations are vivid as this is as much a story of the people who went West as it is of the horrendous struggles they faced. The triumph of the human spirit, as well as the petty and sometimes evil actions of members of the wagon train, are made believable through the careful development of the characters as they encounter increasing perils. Setting is beautifully depicted through the device of Meribah's artistry. One is never tempted to skip to the "action," as much of the beauty of this book lies in understanding and living with the people on the trail. The major strength of the book is that it is a magnificent story. The westward movement is an integral part of American history and nature, and this book is the most gripping account of that time I have ever read.

The obvious use of this book is during a study of the time period. A more important use is in the reading and rereading of an author who polishes her phrasing until it gleams with the beauty of the gold that many of the people moving West sought. (pp. 70-1)

M. Jean Greenlaw, in a review of ''Beyond the Divide,'' in Language Arts, *Vol. 61, No. 1, January, 1984, pp. 70-1.*

PRANK (1984)

A member of an East Boston blue collar family, Birdie Flynn is disturbed when her brother Tim is picked up as one of three juveniles who have desecrated a local synagogue. Most of the story is concerned with Birdie's worry about Tim, her concern about her own future (she wants to be a writer and is working in a department store), and her deep and growing horror at everything she has read about the treatment of Jews in Germany. She sees, in Tim, a parallel to all those Nazis who said they merely watched (like Tim) but did nothing violent. Lasky has to an extent defeated her apparent purpose, to show how deeply the Holocaust can still affect young people; the defeat is caused by repetition and by overwriting—both too many tangential incidents and several peripheral characters who contribute little to the story.

Zena Sutherland, in a review of ''Prank,'' in Bulletin of the Center for Children's Books, *Vol. 37, No. 9, May, 1984, p. 168.*

While most of Lasky's characters are stereotypical, she uses them effectively, and readers will be provoked to think about their own situations in comparison or contrast with the Flynns'. As she has in her other books, Lasky combines powerful imagery and compelling situations. A fine writer continues to hone her craft.

Ilene Cooper, in a review of ''Prank,'' in Booklist, *Vol. 80, No. 17, May 1, 1984, p. 1250.*

A Boston synagogue is vandalized by Birdie Flynn's brother and two friends. Why did he do it and what was its effect on the persons involved? These two themes are hard to tackle in one book, but the author might have succeeded were it not for the wordiness of the text. East Boston is vividly described, presenting a seemingly hopeless picture of life in a low-income, Irish family. The characters are well-developed, the reasons behind the vandalism are explored, and we see the children struggling for self-respect and future happiness. . . . There is an important lesson to be learned here, but the long descriptive sequences and unnecessary language will discourage most readers.

Maxine Kamin, in a review of ''Prank,'' in Children's Book Review Service, *Vol. 12, No. 11, June, 1984, p. 117.*

This story starts slowly—I had to prod myself to pay attention to the characters. Which is a shame, because I wound up being pleased with the book's outcome, and hoping it might fall into the hands of a sensitive teenager.

Prank deals with anti-semitism in present day East Boston. Birdie Flynn's brother Timmy and a few friends deface a local synagogue. Through this simple but flagrant act, the reader watches the changes in Birdie's sudden awareness of the plight of the Jews during World War II, her brother's purposeless life and the Flynn Family's coming to terms with the maturization of their children. Quite a lot for one slim volume to

deal with; many adolescent novels don't even tackle one topic of such magnitude.

Kathryn Lasky does it well. She evokes the horror young Birdie feels as she researches the Nazi concentration camps fully to realize the implications of her brother's actions. She evokes the desolation young Timmy feels when everything he does goes wrong. And she does an admirable job projecting the puzzled faces of Birdie's and Timmy's parents around an awkward supper table as they try to reckon with the growth of their children beyond what they themselves could hope to be.

The jewel in this book is so subtle it may escape its audience. Lasky lays a careful path to compare the observers of the death camps to those of us who watch crimes happen and don't take the responsibility to stop them. (pp. 234-35)

Michele Carlo, in a review of ''Prank,'' in Best Sellers, *Vol. 44, No. 6, September, 1984, pp. 234-35.*

The ''prank'' of this story is not a simple, mischievous adolescent act: it involves the desecration of a synagogue. Timmy Flynn paints graffiti, his friends paint swastikas. It all adds up to anti-Semitism and when the results are witnessed by Mrs. Pearlowitz, a former Nazi concentration camp victim, the ''prank'' takes on terrible dimensions.

It is Timmy's sister Birdie who picks up on the anti-Semitic aspects of the ''prank.'' It is she who understands that the anti-Semitic statements said carelessly around the school and her own house may have influenced her brother. It is she who decides to find out about the Holocaust and reads a selection from *Night* by Elie Wiesel and excerpts from *Commandant of Auschwitz* by Rudolph Hoess. It is also through Birdie's eyes that we see her Boston Irish-Catholic family falling apart. Her mother and father are without hope, her brother and sisters are equally hopeless dropouts. The family is troubled, quarrelsome, self-deprecating and held together mainly by a TV set.

But after all this is spelled out for the reader, as if by magic the whole family changes. Birdie's sister, a battered wife, decides to obtain a divorce. Timmy, who has flunked almost every subject in school and is beaten by his father, suddenly signs up on a boat and looks forward to taking his third mate exam. Birdie's mother suddenly takes hold and defends her children. Her father feels sorry about knocking a tooth out of Timmy's mouth and becomes more understanding. The only one left in utter despair is Mrs. Pearlowitz, the concentration camp survivor who screams in anguish in the middle of the night.

In the last chapter, Birdie, who hopes to become a writer, recaps the events of this book in a brief story. She talks about the synagogue desecration and how her brother did it because it made him feel, very briefly, good—''He felt power.'' Afterwards he was sorry: ''He hadn't meant it.'' But the problem seems to be less the nature of his act than the fact that ''what he had become as a person was not real but a prank.'' And then she goes on to detail what a successful boat navigator he has become. After raising serious societal issues, the author ignores them, suggesting that anti-Semitism is due to troubled individuals rather than societal factors.

Lasky's characters are vital, her scenes dynamic. The Flynn family does come to life. The vandalizing of synagogues in the United States and the relationship of these acts to the Holocaust are vitally important topics. Yet, this book's weak plot development and poor construction lead one to feel that these important themes are exploited or, worse, trivialized. (pp. 7-8)

Albert V. Schwartz, in a review of "Prank," in Interracial Books for Children Bulletin, *Vol. 16, No. 1, 1985, pp. 7-8.*

A BABY FOR MAX (1984)

[This] is a modest photodocumentary about the advent of the couple's second child, as told by five-year-old Max. The text is easy enough for beginning independent readers but so simplified in tone and concept that it seems more appropriate for the preschool child. The book (text and pictures) describes Mom's pregnancy, the preparation—physical and emotional—for an addition to the family, hospital visits when little Meribah is born, and Max's reactions (the usual mingling of affection and resentment) at the hospital and later at home when the baby begins to respond. Not highly original, but pleasant and useful to assuage pangs of dethronement.

Zena Sutherland, in a review of "A Baby for Max," in Bulletin of the Center for Children's Books, *Vol. 37, No. 11, July, 1984, p. 208.*

Since Max is the narrator, some of the ideas expressed are the sort that adults may appreciate but which are inaccurate and may confuse youngsters: "[the unborn baby] kicks because it wants to get out." Even so, Max is more mature and less jealous than the little girl in Holland's *We Are Having a Baby* (Scribners, 1972), and his loving ways show that he is happy to take his role as big brother seriously.

Anne Osborn, in a review of "A Baby for Max," in School Library Journal, *Vol. 31, No. 2, October, 1984, p. 149.*

The book's personal quality and the fact that it presents a range of typical childhood reactions toward a new sibling give it high marks as a bibliotherapeutic tool. It's a likely pick for anyone coaching a preschooler through the emotional rigors of accepting a new contender around the house.

Denise M. Wilms, in a review of "A Baby for Max," in Booklist, *Vol. 81, No. 5, November 1, 1984, p. 369.*

In the words and feelings of young Max, the text is refreshingly delightful in its honest viewpoint. All the uncertainties, joys, fears, and frustrations of getting a baby sister are frankly spoken. Max has a remarkable awareness of his mother's tiredness, the baby kicking to be born, and his dad's pride in making a changing table. (pp. 287-88)

Highly commendable is the empathetic role of the parents who encourage Max to become part of the wondrous event.

"Some days I feel angry because everybody's talking all the time about Meribah." When a baby arrives, there are feelings which need to be recognized and dealt with. Readers, like Max, can develop a better understanding and sense of empathy. (p. 288)

Ronald A. Jobe, in a review of "A Baby for Max," in Language Arts, *Vol. 62, No. 3, March, 1985, pp. 287-88.*

PUPPETEER (1985)

Lasky, who evinced rapport with homier crafts and practitioners in *The Weaver's Gift* and *Sugaring Time*, shows a little more strain here: She never brings us very close to her puppeteer subject, 50-some-year-old Paul Vincent Davis of Boston's Puppet Show Place; and she tends to play up his profession, repeating the words "magic" and "magical," rather than allow whatever magic inheres in the material to present itself.

Nevertheless, there's much interest in this photo-chronicle of Paul's preparation for his one-man production of the Aladdin story. Readers see Paul solving a logistics problem by making the animals and background characters out of jigsaw-cut "flats," devising a puppet that can change onstage from a dwarf to a tall magician, and sculpting and casting heads for the puppets. Lasky also makes clear the work and adjustments required of a successful performer. . . .

Lasky does an effective job of meting out bits of the story and dialogue without subjecting readers to a chunk of text.

A review of "Puppeteer," in Kirkus Reviews, *Juvenile Issue, Vol. LIII, Nos. 5-10, May 15, 1985, p. 39.*

Photographs of excellent quality illustrate and extend the text of a book that is sequentially organized, balanced in coverage, and written with controlled admiration and zeal. . . . The book makes vivid the craftsmanship, the infinite attention to details, the rigors of practice, and the theatrical flair that go into creating a polished and dramatic illusion in a form of the performing arts that has always been especially popular with children. (pp. 209-10)

Zena Sutherland, in a review of "Puppeteer," in Bulletin of the Center for Children's Books, *Vol. 38, No. 11, July-August, 1985, pp. 209-10.*

The beauty of the puppets and the glimpses behind the curtain would be difficult to imagine without the photos. Yet it is the prose which pulls readers into the magical world of the puppeteer, giving insight into the artist's dedication. It reveals the tension that is building toward the performance, when the silent and still puppets who are "without voice or life, just bundles of exquisitely sewn fabric" are given "movement, words, and passion" by the puppeteer. This is a book which will create curiosity about its unique subject.

Lee Bock, in a review of "Puppeteer," in School Library Journal, *Vol. 31, No. 10, August, 1985, p. 67.*

HOME FREE (1985)

Here, a laudable attempt to preserve and cultivate wilderness areas takes on magical proportions.

Thoughtful, sensitive, 15-year-old Sam and his mother have moved to New England from the Midwest after the death of Sam's father. Sam is full of his loss, uncertain about his new home, worried about his grieving mom. Nearby lies the huge Quabbin Reservoir, once a valley containing several villages, now an "artificial" wilderness. Some townspeople want to turn the Quabbin into a recreational area; others want to encourage endangered bald eagles to nest and breed there. Environmentalists plan to raise eaglets at the Quabbin, then release them. In order to make a strong case for preservation, two eagles must return to breed. Sam becomes deeply involved with the mission to "eaglize" the Quabbin, allying himself with elderly Gus, passionate environmentalist and chief photographer for the state's Wildlife Division. Sam also befriends beautiful Lucy, a supposedly autistic orphan who has a special feeling for the eagles and for nature. Lucy is actually a ghost from the valley's lost past, which Sam "experiences" from the beginning of time through the last century and up to the 1930's, just before the valley's towns were destroyed. This journey through time and space occurs with the help of a magic eagle named Ilirah. Then the story concludes satisfactorily with the return of the eagles and, it seems, the reincarnation of Lucy.

The novel makes a fairly smooth transition from the real to the fantastic, thanks to a tone of mystical wonder that makes it clear from the beginning that something extraordinary will happen. Lasky also makes it possible for readers to feel Sam and Lucy's magical experiences. Teens are likely to not only enjoy the story but also come away with their environmental consciousness raised.

A review of "Home Free," in Kirkus Reviews, *Vol. LIII, No. 21, November 1, 1985, p. 1198.*

Enlivened by bright dialogue and luminous descriptions of natural phenomena, Lasky's new novel concerns a battle over the fate of a wilderness in Massachusetts. . . . Sam's relationship with Lucy adds deep dimensions to Lasky's unsentimentalized, beautifully written story.

A review of "Home Free," in Publishers Weekly, *Vol. 229, No. 2, January 10, 1986, p. 84.*

Few authors are as eloquent as Lasky and here the writing is often lyrical. Relationships are well developed too, but the story is overwritten and the plot moves much too slowly. The introduction of the fantasy element comes too late and seems to belong in another book. Nature lovers, especially those interested in endangered species, may find this of interest, but many readers drawn in by the haunting cover will be disappointed. (pp. 758-59)

Ilene Cooper, in a review of "Home Free," in Booklist, *Vol. 82, No. 10, January 15, 1986, pp. 758-59.*

Lasky is really writing three books here, a psychological novel, a time fantasy, and realistic fiction about human and natural cycles. Each story in itself is fascinating but doesn't always blend with the others. . . . While Sam's adjustment and relationships with his mother and the old man are well drawn, Lucy's quick recovery and absorption into Sam's household is problematic, as is her communication with the birds. By the same token, Sam's observations of the past are vivid, but the transitions confusing. An ambitious book, only partially successful.

A review of "Home Free," in Bulletin of the Center for Children's Books, *Vol. 39, No. 6, February, 1986, p. 112.*

Kevin Major

1949-

Canadian author and author/illustrator of fiction and editor.

Recognized as one of Canada's most promising and unconventional authors for young people, Major is regarded as an especially honest and insightful chronicler of adolescence; his three young adult novels—*Hold Fast, Far from Shore,* and *Thirty-Six Exposures*—have inspired both praise and controversy. Combining observations of his native Newfoundland with portraits of contemporary teenagers, Major considers such issues as conflict with authority, alienation, peer pressure, and family strife while stressing the reactions, survival, and growth of his male protagonists. Setting his works in small Newfoundland outports, Major utilizes varying narrative points of view while lacing his works with regional dialect; his inclusion of explicit language and frank references to drug use and sexuality have occasionally caused the books to be removed from Canadian library shelves. Underscoring Major's works, however, is his respect for Newfoundland and its strong core of moral values as well as a concern for the economic and cultural changes that have affected local family life. Also a photographer, Major contributed the illustrations to *Doryloads,* an anthology of Newfoundland art and literature that he edited.

Reviewers praise Major for creating works that transcend the format of the young adult novel through their literary quality, depth, believability, and relevance; Canadian critic Ann Johnston says that Major "has become the strongest voice from the East since Lucy Maud Montgomery created Anne Shirley." Commentators also consider Major's first novel, *Hold Fast,* as a cornerstone of Canadian children's literature and compare the book's main character to Huckleberry Finn and Holden Caulfield. Although some reviewers deplore the language and sexuality of Major's novels and note flaws in plot and structure, most observers laud Major as an important spokesperson for both Newfoundland and young people.

Major received the Canada Council Children's Literature Prize and the Canadian Library Association Book of the Year for Children Award in 1979 for *Hold Fast.*

(See also *Contemporary Literary Criticism,* Vol. 26; *Something about the Author,* Vol. 32; and *Contemporary Authors,* Vols. 97-100.)

AUTHOR'S COMMENTARY

[In telling stories to young people] I always make what to my mind is an important distinction—I write not for young people, but about young people. I do not feel my audience is limited to a particular age group, although I realize that the books have a special appeal to teenagers because the main character in each is a teenager. As a serious writer I give it my best creative shot, bringing all the energy I have to the effort, just as I would if the protagonists were adults. I despair of critics who feel such attention unworthy of the serious writer, just as I despair of writers who feel they must tone down their work for fear of criticism.

Courtesy of Kevin Major

I write for the pleasure of knowing that I have created something that others feel is of lasting worth to them. And that I may have given cause for people to reflect upon some aspect of their own lives or made them more understanding of the feelings and attitudes of others. I don't write only for entertainment, just as I don't read only for that. As Flannery O'Connor has said:

> The basis of art is truth. The person who aims after art in his work aims after truth, in an imaginative sense, no more and no less.

It is this sense of truth that has brought my work both its highest praise and its sharpest criticism. The comments about my work that I cherish the most are contained in some of the letters I have received from young people.

From a Grade 8 student in Sault Saint Marie:

> I have never read a book such as this, I like the way Michael and others talk because I can put my own voice in there and with most books you can't.

From high school students in Toronto:

> The characters in your books are very interesting, real and relatively funny. The basis of

the book is very real which makes the story more believeable as well as much more interesting.

The language seemed to be integrated in the teenage character, they spoke so freely. There was nothing covered up in any way. Those teenage characters that you've written about were just the average teenager.

(p. 15)

These letters as contrasted with these comments from a school librarian published recently in an Ontario newspaper:

Because of Major's propensity to use swear words in a not-too-subtle attempt to maintain readers' interest, I made the decision last year that his works would not "grace" the shelves of our school's library. While I can understand why Mr. Major feels that he should use the vocabulary he does, I am disappointed to learn that the Canada Council and the Canadian Association of Children's Librarians propagate such "literature".

I write this literature (without quotation marks) the way I do because, given the type of characters I've created, to do otherwise would be false and literature, after all, is one very important means by which we see how other people live. Their speech, their attitudes, their lifestyles, may be quite different from our own, but it is a vital part of our education to share in their lives. It makes us broader-minded, more tolerant individuals. If there are words that have the same impact and convey the same meaning as the ones I first write, but may be less offensive to some people, then I'll make the second choice. But other than that I make no attempt to tone down my writing for the sake of other people's concerns. If they don't want to read my work, fine, that is their choice. But neither should they deny others the opportunity to read it. We supposedly live in a free society, and it is an open traffic in ideas that makes us free.

I have known libraries, such as the one referred to in the letter, which refuse to carry my work. I have been asked by educators to rewrite *Hold Fast* into a so called "school" edition. I say, listen, and [the] strong language or sexual references used in my books are there because they are an integral part of the characters and story. And if the readers cannot take the characters to be believeable, how can I expect them to take seriously what I'm trying to say in the book?

Sex and strong language play no greater or no lesser a part in my work than they do in real life. The truth is both are preoccupations of adolescents as is their family life, school, their relationships with their friends. So why the great fear? (pp. 15-16)

As I said in the beginning, writing about young people is not a trivial undertaking. During adolescence we encounter the most deeply felt things in life—love, fear of rejection, death perhaps, and intense happiness. We often respond with greater emotion than at any other point in our lives. Adolescence is often a worrisome period of pressures—pressure to do well in school, to gain acceptance from friends, to cope with problems without the fund of experience that adults often take for granted.

As an author who has chosen to write about them, I feel a responsibility to young people to speak the truth. To say yes, all is not well in the world, that others have problems, just as

you have problems. And I feel equally the responsibilty to say that youth is a joyous time, so enjoy yourself.

I feel I have achieved the goal I have set for myself in writing my books when a young person makes comments such as this from a 12-year-old reviewer of *Far From Shore:*

I think Kevin Major writes that way to make his characters seem real and it certainly works for him. The book leaves me with the feeling that it all could have really happened.

(p. 16)

Kevin Major, "Challenged Materials: An Author's Perspective," in School Libraries in Canada, *Vol. 4, No. 3, Spring, 1984, pp. 15-16.*

Books in Canada: What led you to write young adult fiction?

Kevin Major: As a substitute teacher, I saw that young people were voraciously reading the new genre of American realistic young adult fiction by Judy Blume, Robert Cormier, and S. E. Hinton. Those novels seemed to have a wider appeal and readership than the traditional fiction aimed at young people—adventure and animal stories. Initially, I was attracted by the novels' directness, straightforward first-person narrations, and characters who were not idealized or old-fashioned. I saw that there were no comparable stories for a similar age group situated in Newfoundland, so I decided to write a story about young people growing up in the outports, dramatizing situations that would be relevant to their lives.

BiC: What features of young adult fiction appealed to you?

Major: Actually, a lot of the novels don't appeal to me at all. Certainly there are good writers of them, like Robert Cormier, but I find many of the novels shallow and too pre-packaged. The writers have a tendency to choose a highly topical problem, like anorexia nervosa or homosexuality, and then build a story around it. Novels should be relevant and readable in years to come—which I doubt many of them will be. As well, I'm dissatisfied with the way they are written. They frequently lack any strong feeling for character, being basically sociological problem novels. The writers make it too easy for the readers, don't challenge them enough. Young readers need to be exposed to more than one method of telling a story. Many of the novels rely too heavily on telling the story with a first-person narrator.

BiC: What are the experiences and issues of your readers that you want to address?

Major: Primarily, I want my books to be relevant to the experience of growing up in Newfoundland. Newfoundland society is in the midst of tremendous changes. The young are caught between the old traditional values of Newfoundland outport society and the onslaught of American popular culture. For those young people growing up in small communities, that struggle is causing stress and estrangement in the family structure. My novels dramatize the conflicts that have developed between parents and their children because of those changes. In a more general sense, the novels deal with the issues that confront all teenagers—family relationships, dealings with authority on a parental and societal level, the effects of peer pressure, experimentation with drugs, exploration of sexuality, contemplation of the future. However, the problems are never the focus of the novels. My emphasis is on how individual characters cope with the problems.

BiC: In each novel, you've used a different narrative point of view. Why?

Major: I'm always aware of not wanting to repeat myself. In changing the point of view I wanted to go beyond the standard stylistic conventions employed in young adult fiction. Often, young adult novels are quite simplistic in their approach to story-telling. My books, particularly the last two, require more involvement on the reader's part. I'm interested in the reader who is willing to take a little more time and effort.

BiC: The language in the novels is frank and your characters experiment with drugs and their sexuality. Have you encountered any censorship problems?

Major: Two years ago, I was scheduled to do a reading in Rainy River, Ont. A week before the reading, the chairman of the library board cancelled the reading without informing the other members of the board. He said that he considered passages of the books unsuitable for the young people of the community. There was an outcry from the Writers' Union and the Canadian Library Association. The reading was held when another board member provided his school for the reading. The irony of the situation was that no young people attended. I asked one of the board members where were the teenagers? He replied, "It's Friday night. They're probably out drinking." I found that amusing, considering the chairman's objection to characters drinking in my books.

There have been a number of instances where the books have been removed from library shelves. In one small library in Newfoundland, the principal wouldn't allow my books in the school library, because he thought the characters were too similar to teenagers in the community. My books are not listed on any of the novel lists put out by the Newfoundland Board of Education, which seems to me to be the most obvious place for them to be listed. Obversely, I have met librarians who have told me they are glad that there are novels that are portraying teenagers in a more realistic light and that are situated in Canada.

BiC: For teenagers, isn't the attraction of your novels, in part, the confirmation of their own experiences?

Major: Yes. What attracts young people to the books is that they have a feeling that others are experiencing similar problems, holding the same outlooks and attitudes. When we were growing up, there weren't books available that reconfirmed our experience in a realistic manner.

BiC: Do you anticipate any problems with *Thirty-Six Exposures* due to its explicit language and sexuality?

Major: No doubt. I think it will cause problems. As a writer whose main readership is 12 years old and up, one of the problems you have is that your readers don't purchase the books. The novels filter through adult hands. Adults are concerned that their children will try to emulate the characters' actions.

BiC: Isn't that concern diffused by the strong core of moral values held by your characters, despite the dilemmas they encounter?

Major: Yes, countering any so-called modern problems faced by the characters is their own strong sense of the traditional moral values of Newfoundland society.

BiC: Is there any significance to the fact that your characters are getting progressively older in your novels?

Major: At some critical point, I may turn to adult fiction. Since my characters have been getting older, it now seems a logical move. Add two more years to the age of the main character of my next novel and the protagonist will be 20, which I guess moves me into adult fiction. But really, I haven't decided as of yet. With the birth of my son I have been thinking about writing for a much younger audience. Right now, I'm thinking about adapting one of the books into a play, and about the plans to turn *Hold Fast* into a TV movie.

BiC: Do you plan to continue writing young adult fiction?

Major: I dislike being labelled a young adult novelist. I write about young people, not exclusively for them. I would hope that my books have an interest for adults. Adults with teenage children have told me that they enjoy the books in themselves and for the insights they give them into their children's thinking. A good novel, whether it is about someone five or 55, should be able to stand on its own. (pp. 24-5)

> *Sherie Posesorski, in an interview with Kevin Major, in* Books in Canada, *Vol. 13, No. 10, December, 1984, pp. 24-5.*

GENERAL COMMENTARY

JOHN MOSS

[Kevin Major is] among the best Canadian writers of his generation. In two years, with only two novels, he has established himself as a figure of singular importance in our literature. *Hold Fast* and his most recent work, *Far from Shore,* are for younger readers, but both refuse to bear the epithet "second-rank." In fact, Major defies many of the conventions of so-called children's literature. Characters swear in his novels, and break the law; people drink and have sexual experiences and sexual anxieties; people die and others grieve or are defiant. In prose that is exact and vivid, an equivalent in words to super-realism on the artist's canvas, the author describes life from an adolescent Newfoundlander's perspective. He has a superb command of outport dialect; he has a refined and highly engaging sense of narrative style, one that is uncannily appropriate to his narrator's personality. In *Hold Fast,* fourteen-year-old Michael recounts his own story with cheeky wit and irrepressible bravado. . . . It is a simple, honest story, with implications, even for very young readers, that are profound and complex. *Hold Fast* is a fine novel, a genuine work of literature in its own right.

> *John Moss, "Kevin Major," in his* A Reader's Guide to the Canadian Novel, *McClelland and Stewart, 1981, p. 340.*

RAYMOND E. JONES

[Kevin Major] has created distinctive fiction by combining local color and the universal problems of adolescence. Major is not, however, simply an author giving novelty or quaintness to the "problem novel," a form that usually chronicles the tribulations of the urban teenager. He is, in fact, quite critical of much adolescent fiction. . . .

In an attempt to avoid the limitations of the typical adolescent novel while still retaining its audience appeal, Major has tried to make the Newfoundland setting itself one source of conflict. Furthermore, he has emphasized psychology rather than sociology, character rather than topical problem. (p. 140)

Although Major occasionally stumbles, failing to provide a completely satisfying resolution of plot, his novels are accomplished performances. In each, the basic problem, the age and circumstance of the narrator, and the narrative technique are different; but when read in order, these novels reveal a consistent but perhaps darkening view of the problems of both regional life and contemporary adolescents.

Newfoundland outport life is somewhat idyllic in *Hold Fast.* For Michael, the fourteen-year-old narrator who has been orphaned by a drunk driver, life in the outport of Marten is simple and perpetually interesting. It is, furthermore, intimately tied to many good times outdoors, doing such traditional things as squidding with his father and grandfather, both of whom were very close to him.

The crowded urban world, dominated by materialism and such signs of American popular culture as Dairy Queens and Kentucky Fried Chicken stores, has no appeal for Michael. When he is sent to St. Albert to live with his dictatorial uncle, he discovers that he is an outsider, a "baywop," set apart by his habits of speech and his interest in nature. Instead of the familial warmth and the respect for individuals that typified life in Marten, he finds an obsession with possessions and conformity. His uncle, the blackest representative of urban materialism, lives in a modern house with every conceivable convenience, but he has none of the qualities that turn the materially poorer outport houses into true homes. He is so domineering and so lacking in respect for others that he alienates not only the orphan he has reluctantly taken into his house but also his own children.

The novel's action, although rather typical of the plots of many problem novels, subtly implies that traditional Newfoundland life gives Michael the moral and psychological values necessary for survival. Finding urban life intolerable, Michael runs away with his cousin. He is not, however, naive or foolish: Michael realizes that he cannot run away forever, but he wants to prove something. His rebellion is an assertion of his independent identity and his humanity. Staying in a park closed for the winter season, he uses the trapping skills learned in the outport to feed himself and his cousin. His actions illustrate the image implied by the book's title, an image that, unfortunately, is explained only on the jacket flap of the hardcover edition. There, Major is quoted as saying that his novel "is a plea for us Newfoundlanders to be like certain of the species of seaweed that inhabit our shores, which, when faced with the threat of being destroyed by forces they cannot control, evolve an appendage to hold them to the rocks, a holdfast."

The novel gives further subtle but overt support to this idea after Michael makes his way to Marten. He arrives to find that his beloved grandfather is dying. Because he has been running away from his loveless uncle's house and towards the true home inhabited by his grandfather, who obviously represents a traditional love of family and nature, nothing makes sense to him. . . . Thinking about the earlier loss of his parents, he feels devastatingly isolated, as he indicates in the only passage using the title phrase:

> I got nobody now here to help me. They're gone. And this is one time I don't figure there's enough of them left in me to hold fast. . . .

Michael does hold fast to his memories of his parents and grandfather, however, and his elderly aunt shows the traditional compassion and humanity of the outports by silently agreeing to let him remain with her. Involvement in life with his brother, aunt, and friends, and in rural activities like fixing a skidoo,

allows him to get control of his emotions. . . . Traditional life thus provides both solace and emotional growth.

Modern economic conditions have an even more devastating impact in *Far from Shore,* which is probably Major's best novel. This novel traces the tensions that develop when Christopher Slade's father becomes a victim of one of Newfoundland's most persistent problems, chronic unemployment. At first, Chris's father drinks excessively, spoiling such traditional family events as the Christmas Eve decorating of the tree. Realizing the toll his situation is taking on his family and his own self-respect, the father, like so many other Newfoundlanders, heads to Calgary to find a job.

With the father's necessary departure, Chris becomes a type, an example of the devastation caused by economic conditions. He is, that is, another victim of the collapse of traditional, stable family life. Left without the guidance, support, and visible love of his father, Chris loses interest in school, fails his grade, and succumbs to the temptations presented by the wild, heavy-drinking, fast crowd. Eventually, he gets into legal trouble, when the group breaks school windows while on a spree. . . . Given a chance to work as a counsellor at a church camp while awaiting trial, Chris again gets into trouble, this time for showing bad judgment by giving in to the wishes of a shy camper he had been trying to bring out of a social shell. The camper nearly dies when Chris foolishly takes a canoe out onto a large pond during heavy weather. As if this is not enough, Chris arrives home unexpectedly and discovers a man with his mother. Only the return of the father restores some sense of balance. That balance is, however, quite precarious, because the novel ends with the father searching for employment locally. The implication is that, unless he finds work, the family either will deteriorate or will have to move from Newfoundland.

The issue of social upheaval is also prominent in *Thirty-six Exposures,* but it is not quite as critical to the plot. It is brought in mainly through a dramatic performance that a group of students stage as a novel way of meeting the demands of a History assignment. Their presentation brings out something of the history of the province of Newfoundland, and more of the growing feeling of the young that they will have to leave their island home if they are ever to have a chance at secure employment and meaningful futures. The sense that the young must leave is also brought out by the novel's epilogue, a poem written by the central character explaining that he had to go to Europe to find himself.

One other episode has at least some bearing on the lot of Newfoundland's young. Trevor, who sees no future for himself, except for occasional fishing to qualify for unemployment insurance, dies in a car crash after a graduation party. Although his fate is typical of that of many teenagers on graduation night and, hence, is a presentation of a universal problem, it may also be a symbolic presentation of the despair and self destruction of the Island's young. In any case, except for the students' presentation and the conclusion, the influence of setting in this novel is not obviously distinguishable from that of any small, somewhat stifling community. When the novel is read as the final volume of a trilogy on the decay of traditional values, this fact alone makes this Major's most sombre use of local color.

In addition to providing an increasingly darkening view of regional life, Major's novels also show the increasingly complex problems of adolescence. Part of this is, of course, attributable to the fact that the protagonists in each of his novels have been getting older (Michael in *Hold Fast* has just turned 14, Chris Slade turns 16 during the course of *Far from Shore*, and Lorne in *Thirty-six Exposures* is 18). Naturally enough, questions of drinking, drugs, and sex become more prominent in each work. Such questions are to a large degree, however, the local color of adolescence: they give the works the background of authentic adolescent feelings and experiences against which the central characters struggle to comprehend their individuality. Nevertheless, Major's novels are not purely studies of character, and it is in the treatment of the problems that test character that they have their few weaknesses.

Basically, Major's treatment of the problems themselves becomes less satisfying as they multiply and as his novels become less traditional in format. *Hold Fast*, a straightforward first-person narrative, may seem slightly familiar as a running-away-from-the-unloving-house story, but it has no actual plotting flaws. The episodes are plausible, and the solution is satisfying in its refusal to insist that things will change in the house of the unloving uncle. In *Far from Shore*, however, a significant section of the novel is unnecessarily melodramatic. The sequence in which Chris gives in to the wish of the shy camper and nearly kills him, does show that Chris, in spite of his worsening reputation, has good intentions and is a good person at heart. The shifting points of view—although Chris is the predominant narrator, four more narrators provide their first-person perspective of events—further bring out both the failure of others to understand him and his own confusions about his motives. The episode is, though, too much of a stock device in an otherwise original and realistic story, too clearly a mechanism for getting Chris away so that his mother can contemplate having an affair.

The slight lapse in realistic focus and originality only slightly mars the superb counterpointing of viewpoints that makes *Far from Shore* such a richly rewarding novel. Major tries for a similiar counterpointing in *Thirty-six Exposures* by interspersing throughout the third-person narrative personal poems his narrator secretly writes. In *Thirty-six Exposures* the lapses in focus and plot are, however, nearly fatal. One of the central public issues in that novel is the protest against a teacher who is arbitrary and unfair in his treatment of his students. Lorne, idealistically committed to truth and fairness, leads a protest, even though adults try to convince him that he should ignore the situation because the teacher is retiring at the end of the year. Lorne prepares a valedictory address that will get him the revenge he wants by exposing and humiliating the teacher. At the last moment he changes it to something innocuously traditional and optimistic, because he learns that his grandmother and the teacher had once been lovers and are now going to get married.

This tawdry plot contrivance completely avoids the issues of students' rights and the morality of revenge that had been developed throughout the novel. It represents a failure of nerve on the part of the author—he has his central character do the "decent" thing without ever coming to an understanding of why he is doing it. Personal feelings often compromise principles in real life, but the circumstances here are so blatantly contrived that they don't even adequately demonstrate that unhappy truth. Furthermore, they deflect attention away from what Major himself declared was the central concern of his work, the way in which individuals cope with problems. One indication of the shallowness of the treatment here is that, unlike most of the significant events in Lorne's life, this one

doesn't even inspire him to write a poem exploring its private meaning.

Kevin Major's narrative approach is different in each of his novels, yet each book is a portrait that combines the subtle hues of local color with the stark lines of universal problems. As a result, the works are neither examples of quaint regionalism nor standard problem novels. They are, instead, entertaining and perceptive studies of adolescence itself—that time in which private feelings and public problems both terrify and exhilarate. Although they do appeal to adolescent Newfoundlanders, who find their experiences painted with honesty and compassion, they also offer rewards to adolescents elsewhere and even to adults. Major noted in his *Books in Canada* interview [see excerpt above in Author's Commentary] that many adults can "enjoy the books in themselves and for the insights they give them into their children's thinking". . . . As "books in themselves," *Hold Fast* and *Far from Shore* offer enough psychological insight and narrative freshness to make them significant literary achievements. Although *Thirty-six Exposures* is less successful, it does not significantly diminish the temptation to make a pun of the author's name. If he can maintain his strong sense of local color and universal problems while overcoming some of his plotting limitations, Kevin Major may indeed become a major author of adolescent life. (pp. 140-41)

Raymond E. Jones, "Local Color, Universal Problems: The Novels of Kevin Major," in Children's Literature Association Quarterly, Vol. 10, No. 3, Fall, 1985, pp. 140-41.

HOLD FAST (1978)

Hold Fast is a landmark in Canadian writing for young people. It reaches other, profounder places than most realistic writing meant for them. And it discovers Newfoundland as the source-spring of a major new talent. . . . [Here is] a stunningly perceptive novel of family life in the outport and the city in his native province, and of one young person at the centre of it.

Michael at 14 loses his parents in a car accident, and suddenly his world becomes an alien place. He has to cope with a double loss: first his parents' death, then leaving his outpost home, for he goes to live in a city hundreds of miles away with his unsympathetic uncle's family.

In the space of a fortnight Michael has to begin testing the strengths of his developing maturity. What has he learned about how to conduct his life, about what to expect of life, during his short span?

His reactions to the death of his parents are typical of those bereaved of loved ones. But he begins immediately to take on the responsibility for his own life and for his young brother's. He agrees that only his brother should live with his loving aunt and favoured grandfather to relieve their economic burdens. He knows that his uncle was held aloof by his father; even so Michael goes to live with this alienated family where he finds a despot at its head. His uncle's word is law and Michael comes under it now that he has joined them.

Michael is thrust into untenable circumstances, yet his free spirit prevails because he relies on the moral touchstones of his past. His ability to think through a problem creatively helps him to logical solutions and we get to know a young man of uncommon integrity.

Major creates a sympathetic, admirable character in Michael. His empathy for young people allows for genuine appreciation of Michael's intelligence and maturity that in turn prepares him to encompass solutions that Michael can see are possible—and we get to know an author of uncommon integrity.

The first person narrative is enhanced by the delightful Newfoundland dialect that hastens a feeling of intimacy and involvement in the reader. Michael has let us into his life. Soon we accept him as he is; then we become his admirers. When he cries for his parents, when he teaches his cousin to stand up against his tyrant-father, when he reminisces with his grandfather, when he first feels the stirrings of love for a girl, he is ever a person we care about.

Hold Fast stands with other indigenous novels of stature that have pictured Newfoundland for young readers: *The Adventures of Billy Topsail* by Norman Duncan, Erle Spencer's *Yo-Ho-Ho! a story of modern piracy and smuggling, Dangerous Cove* by John Hayes and *The Black Joke* by Farley Mowat. And *Hold Fast* holds its own among them beautifully.

> *Irma McDonough, in a review of "Hold Fast," in*
> In Review: Canadian Books for Children, *Vol. 12, No. 3, Summer, 1978, p. 70.*

It is, I suppose, decidedly unfair to compare the first novel of a young new writer with the acclaimed classic of a master storyteller, but Kevin Major's *Hold Fast* brought me so often into remembered contact with Mark Twain's *Huckleberry Finn* that a comparison (or at least a referential glossing) became unavoidable. Such a comparison, in fact, tells us much about Major's technique and purpose and, lest the reader be apprehensive on this point, does nothing to devalue this young Newfoundland author's achievement.

Anyone who has read *Huckleberry Finn* cannot, for example, fail to see just how much alike Huck Finn and Michael (Major's protagonist) are. Both are physical and spiritual orphans treading the hard road to self-awareness; Michael, like Huck, is unsure of himself, stubborn ("pig-headed" Michael calls it), given to lying and to fits of self-pity and remorse; and even when a degree of self-awareness is attained there is always that shadow of doubt. How similar they are, and how close Major comes to achieving Twain's poignancy through his first-person naive narrator can be seen in a juxtaposition of the key (climactic) passages in the novels. Huck Finn, in that famous bout with his conscience, comes to grips with his lying in this fashion:

> It was because my heart warn't right; it was because I warn't square; it was because I was playing double. I was letting on to give up sin, but away inside of me I was holding on to the biggest one of all. I was trying to make my mouth *say* I would do the right thing and the clean thing, and go and write to that nigger's owner and tell where he was; but deep down in me I knowed it was a lie . . .

Michael, after having hitched a ride with an old man (in a chapter which is both amusing and forceful), and having deceived him outrageously, states:

> The strangest kind of feeling started to come over me. I started to get mad at myself and ashamed that I lied like a real son-of-a-bitch to the old fellow the way I done. And when I was doing it I was getting the biggest kinda kick

out of it too. That made it worse. And I didn't just stop at a few lies to answer his questions, I went on and on cracking off the big ones and him believing it like it was the gospel truth.

> I tell you I didn't know what was getting into me.

> Guilt like that might seem stupid. Probably I'd never lay eyes on the old fellow again. But here I was making him feel sorry for us when he might a had all kinds of trouble of his own. His wife might a been real sick or something, for God's sake. And for no reason at all. I felt guilty as hell. I never lied as bad as that before. And shit, it was starting to louse up everything on the very first day. . . .

> See, I can certainly screw up things for myself. I made a vow then and there that if there was any more lies that I'd have to tell then they'd only be enough to get us off the hook. That was all. Not a word more.

"They'd only be enough to get us off the hook"; how typically Huck Finn that is.

Apart from the thematic similarity, other Twainian characteristics abound: Michael's cousin Curtis is a perfect foil, another Tom Sawyer; the first-person narrative (especially the employment of a naive narrator) is full of subtle ironies; Major's use of Newfoundland dialect, like Twain's innovative use of the southern dialect, offers a sense of immediacy and a control of tone. Major, in fact, is at his best in his execution of dialect and dialogue.

Now, all this does not mean that *Hold Fast* is a derivative novel, that Major has simply imitated Twain. Far from it. Indeed, the comparison serves to show that the major theme of *Huckleberry Finn* is not sacrosanct, that it can be restated with fresh insights that a new environment and age reveals new problems and new solutions, that the picaresque novel can still provide an exciting experience. The fact that *Hold Fast,* even though it reminds me so forcibly of *Huckleberry Finn,* absorbs my interest and abounds with originality means that it does succeed in its own right.

Many readers, of course, will never be reminded of Huck Finn and it is not necessary that they be so. *Hold Fast* is, on a literal level, the story of a Newfoundland boy (fourteen years old) who loses both parents in a car accident and who is forced to live with unpleasant relatives in a strange (almost hostile) town. . . . No amount of novelty . . . can compensate for his loss. Thus, when life becomes unbearable, Michael (taking his discontented cousin Curtis with him) decides to return home. But it is much more than a "returning"; it is his journey into manhood, into self-awareness, taken appropriately in a stolen car and interrupted by a "return to nature"—a few days spent under Rousseau-like conditions in the winter confines of a closed National Park catching rabbits (this is, incidentally, the best section in the book and Major's finest writing).

Thus, *Hold Fast* has a multi-dimensional appeal: those who are not impressed by or interested in my Twainian-thematic approach may read it for its insights into youthful grief, modern-day rebellion, confused teenage values, adult-child conflicts, Newfoundland dialect and ways of life; or Major's frankness may be your interest—certainly his description of Michael's wet dream (a very controlled and realistic bit of writing) will give rise to discussion, even denunciation. Surely a novel which offers such a variety of issues should not be overlooked. Especially since, though not a masterpiece, **Hold Fast** is such a well-written novel.

My only question is this: what will teenagers think of the novel? Is it entertaining and exciting enough (as *Huckleberry Finn* always is) to hold their attention? When Major is describing Michael's return, his theft of the car, his nights in the Park, he is almost as good as Twain himself—that section, as I've said, is both funny and tragic, spell-binding stuff. But, prior to that, when Michael is lamenting his condition, describing his relatives, their bitchiness, the excitement lags, the writing becomes pseudo-sociological. Perhaps, of course, I'm too sceptical (I'm a parent myself); I don't know. But it will be extremely enlightening to find out and I hope I will. (pp. 56-9)

> *R. G. Moyles, in a review of "Hold Fast," in* The World of Children's Books, *Vol. III, No. 2, Fall, 1978, pp. 56-9.*

There aren't many novels that connect a commercial American style and the special qualities of a Canadian region, but . . . [**Hold Fast**] does just that. It brings together the current mode of "young adult" novel as developed in the United States and the longings of Newfoundlanders for their past. In this sense it's a unique product of recent Canadian literature. . . .

Newfoundlanders realize that, spiritually, all that they possess is the tradition their ancestors left them: the tradition of the intimate and isolated fishing villages, the seal hunt, the special language that is so different from the English most of us speak. At the same time, they know that forces they can't control (including forces within themselves) are drawing them away from that tradition, into urbanization and a closer contact with mainland Canada.

This is an odd subject for a juvenile novel, but it is one of the subjects of **Hold Fast**. . . . Major stresses the contrasts between the authenticity of outport life—its close relation to nature, particularly in hunting and fishing—and the artificiality of the city. It's a romantic view, but one that everyone who knows Newfoundland, even slightly, will understand immediately.

Major also uses a written version of Newfoundland dialect to give his book regional atmosphere. Sometimes he expects too much of mainland readers: when he refers to people watching "the story" on TV he assumes we'll know that by this Newfoundlanders mean U.S. soap opera (many of us won't know). Most of the time, though, the dialect is both right and comprehensible. . . .

Hold Fast isn't entirely a tale of boyish innocence. The hero defies his elders, breaks the law, and even has a sex life. (p. 14)

Michael contains a bit of Holden Caulfield and a bit of Huckleberry Finn, but there is also something authentically Newfoundland about him. **Hold Fast** isn't in any sense a sophisticated novel, but it speaks honestly from a regional consciousness. (pp. 14-15)

> *Robert Fulford, "Capturing Newfoundland before It Goes Away," in* Saturday Night, *Vol. 93, No. 8, October, 1978, pp. 14-15.*

Hold Fast is a novel surrounded by death. It begins with the burial of Michael's parents, who have been killed in a car crash involving a drunken driver, and ends with his grandfather's death in sickness and old age. In between, we have the struggle of a fourteen-year-old boy to maintain his identity in a world of harshness, ignorance, and insensitivity. (p. 81)

Above all, Michael is a realist. . . . Although he runs away at several points in the novel, he quickly faces up to reality and is prepared to defend his position with stubbornness and sense, even if it means standing up to the tyrannous Uncle Ted or a bureaucratic bus driver after he has been abused by a drunken fellow passenger.

Michael is faced with other obstacles as well: his outport dialect is mocked by students at school in St. Albert. He has to defend himself in a fight which leads to a painful interview with the principal and subsequent suspension. Other problems are less insuperable: in a skilfully depicted episode, he copes maturely with his awakening sexuality and his attraction to girls.

We are firmly ensconced in Newfoundland and the most obvious contrast is between the hardy fishing village of Marten and the stereotyped middle-class neighbourhood in St. Albert. Yet, along the way we are given graphic glimpses of squid jigging and the art of snaring and skinning rabbits. We can enjoy Michael's descriptions of these activities and his pride in other aspects of Newfoundland. . . .

Hold Fast is divided into three sections, each of which contains the motif of escape and return to reality by the hero. The first escape is simply a brief but meaningful run to the seashore during the burial of his parents; the second, also brief, is a running away from the circumstances concerning Michael's fight with a classmate. The third escape, more elaborate and adventurous, is a kind of initiation rite into young manhood and an assertion of pride in his heritage when he "borrows" a car and survives by his wits for two wintry days in the washroom of a deserted campsite. These three escapes have considerable character-building power and when Michael is faced with his grandfather's death, there is no running away: "In the cemetery I watched the casket go into the ground, and never once did I move from the spot where I stood."

Probably what one notices most readily about this novel is the style of the hero-narrator. His colourful, earthy, rhythmic idiom may jar at first, but then it settles into warm, colloquial undulation. . . . The diction is salted with four-letter words too well known to fourteen-year-olds but there is an occasional arresting phrase which rolls out of the narrator just as naturally: "Downstairs, me and Brent walked in on a kitchenful of miserable silence." One wishes there were more of these.

A definite weakness in the novel is Kevin Major's delineation of adults. Admittedly, there is always a difficulty in portraying adults in children's books. Either they come off as weak, flat characters as in E. Nesbit's *The Treasure Seekers* or they are merely absent for the better part of the action as in Arthur Ransome's *We Didn't Mean to Go to Sea*. Quite obviously, Mr. Major sees adults in **Hold Fast** as symbolic destroyers of freedom and naturalness in human relations—qualities of life that are so precious to Michael. Whether it is the busdriver, the official at the airport, the principal or Uncle Ted, Michael must face a world of repression and red tape totally foreign to his upbringing. The only adult who can communicate with Michael is his grandfather, but they share only brief memories before being separated at the beginning. Yet, it is surely a falsification of reality—in this most realistic of novels—to view adults as a predictable series of Uncle Teds.

In spite of this stereotyping, the novel does work—and work admirably. Kevin Major, according to the note on the dust jacket, would have us believe that his novel "is a plea for us Newfoundlanders to be like certain of the species of seaweed that inhabit our shores, which, when faced with the threat of being destroyed by forces they cannot control, evolve an appendage to hold them to the rocks, a holdfast."

The message is not just for Newfoundlanders. The values emphasized here are some of the most significant and universal: pride in oneself and one's heritage, courage to express and hold to one's opinions, the necessity to find a balance between emotion and reason and to cultivate a fine sensitivity for others and absolute honesty in assessing social relations.

Hold Fast may be a novel surrounded by death, but it pulses with an unbounded love of life which is attractive and meaningful. (pp. 81-3)

        Gary H. Paterson, "Learning to Hold Fast," in Canadian Children's Literature: A Journal of Criticism and Review, *No. 14, 1979, pp. 81-3.*

Hold Fast has been criticized because Michael is ostensibly a juvenile delinquent. Yet, given what happens to him in the novel, his behaviour is understandable. One occasionally wishes he were not so arrogant but he is for the most part an engaging character.

One of the clear strengths of *Hold Fast* is its language. Michael expresses himself in an idiom completely natural for a teenage outport boy. This very accuracy has created a resistance to the work in some parts of the country; many schools do not use it, and one planned reading by the author in an Ontario library was cancelled. But teenagers need to read clear, unsentimental accounts of what they are dealing with in their own lives, not some glossed-over version of experience portraying them as the unrealistic creatures some adults would like them to be.

Hold Fast was written primarily for adolescents but adults can enjoy it too. [It] . . . richly deserves the many awards it has won. . . . Finally, Michael has been compared with Holden Caulfield and Huckleberry Finn, and I suspect that, like them, he will be around for a long, long time.

        Helen Porter, "'Hold Fast': A Retrospective Review," in Atlantic Provinces Book Review, *Vol. 10, Nos. 3 & 4, November & December, 1983, p. 18.*

Kevin Major's novel *Hold Fast* is a good example of a book that takes its narrative strength from a deep rooting in a particular place and its emotional conviction from the voice of a particular character. In terms of action we are in familiar young adult territory—that somber land of anger and alienation. (p. 99)

Although the plot is framed by death, the total effect of the book is actually one of energy and affirmation. Michael tells his own story in the universal unpolished and passionate voice of youth but, more important, in the lilt and cadence of Newfoundland speech.

Newfoundland English is sufficiently unique in vocabulary to merit its own dictionary, and *Hold Fast* is sprinkled with fine-tasting words—*scravelling, squid-jigging* and *boughwiffen*. But beyond the words themselves are the rhythms of the language. Here is Michael running away from his parents' grave:

> Run. Run, you crazy fool of a son. Run through the paths. Jump outa the way or them thoughts'll grab ya! Bring ya up all-standing. Choke ya. Take away your last livin breath, clean and holy.

In *Hold Fast* we have the egotistical, raw, first-person narrative that has become the formula for young adult fiction, but in place of the flat lingua franca of adolescence Michael tells his story in a language rich with the history and identity of his people.

The issue of diction has an important role to play in the action of the book as well. . . . [Michael's] frustrations are sharpened by the teasing he suffers because of his accent, and this teasing enrages Michael into an act of violence precipitating his flight into the bush. Mockery of his speech has created in the boy a deep dislocation in his sense of self-worth. In the few days that Michael and his cousin spend in an abandoned camp site, snaring rabbits and talking, the whole tone of the book changes. Energy is unleashed, and the same words that have been edged with despair and violence become exuberantly joyful. One of the most poignant moments occurs when the city-bred cousin begins to copy Michael's phrases. The narrative ends on a somber note, but the reader is confident that the reconstruction of Michael's life has begun. (pp. 99-100)

        Sarah Ellis, "News from the North," in The Horn Book Magazine, *Vol. LX, No. 1, February, 1984, pp. 99-103.**

FAR FROM SHORE   (1980)

Chris Slade is a teen-aged boy in a small town in Newfoundland. His father is out of work and drinking. His mother takes a job to support the family and falls for her boss. His sister hates everybody. Soap opera? Social worker's case history? No, it's not. The people in it are much too real.

Far from Shore is the story of what happens to a family when the work gives out. It's also the story of Chris, who, despite his strong Newfoundland speech, could be a teen-aged boy anywhere yearning for the security of a solid home, awkwardly pursuing the excitement of sex, stabbing at the adventure and responsibility of manhood. It begins on Christmas Eve when Father stumbles home drunk and crashes into the Christmas tree. Only Jennifer, lost in the self-pity of a broken romance, is entirely without sympathy. Mother is worried sick and Chris, bewildered but not knowing what else to do, shrugs and goes off to the midnight church service because it's his turn to serve communion.

Over the next couple of months things get worse. . . . And Chris begins to cave in.

Growing angry and morose, he loses his girlfriend, he fails his year and decides not to go back to school and he picks up with a crowd of older boys who have a car, lots of beer, and dope. The morning the cop comes to charge him with smashing windows in a nearby school he is too hung-over to remember whether he did it or not.

To the rescue comes Rev. Wheaton to offer a job as a junior counsellor at the church camp. (p. 21)

The book ends with the mother and father reconciled, Jennifer at university and Chris back at school. Father doesn't swear off drink completely, Jennifer doesn't become a sugar-sweet sister, and Chris sees no blinding light to turn his life around. But it's clear that the Slades are going to go on as a family and that Chris is ready to face the next crisis with a bit more wisdom than he faced this one with.

The book has flaws. For one thing its structure is awkward and often confusing. It's told from the points of view of all the major characters. The result is choppy. It's like the kind of television interview show that leaps from subject to subject until you get knots of frustration in your stomach trying to keep everyone straight.

And Major's strength is not story-telling. His plot is trite and the story doesn't flow. There are, in fact, a couple of abrupt shifts that really jar. The most serious one comes when Chris goes off to camp after his big binge. Like the *deus ex machina* of the Greek dramas Rev. Wheaton appears, plucks Chris out of his tight spot and drops him into a new milieu—and it might be a whole new story. Neither plot nor character development follow from what has gone before. It's almost as though the author had two plots in mind, couldn't decide which to use, and so used both.

But the weaknesses of plot do not destroy the book. This isn't just another fashionably slick tale of sex, violence, and drugs among young adults. It's an honest and deeply felt story. Kevin Major . . . cares so much about his characters that you find yourself at the edge of tears even while you're laughing or shaking your fist in frustration or outrage. And he writes well. His picture of life in Newfoundland is bright and sharp, not, thank God, that salty picaresque pastiche we mainlanders so often get to chuckle indulgently over. His portrait is a gutsy view of people you could really know (and want to). And Chris Slade is one of the most engaging young men you're apt to meet in modern fiction for the young. (pp. 22-3)

Far from Shore is a more ambitious book [than *Hold Fast*]. Major tries to explore more fully the relationships in a family. He fails because this is so much Chris's story that we get both too much and too little of the other characters. But even the failure is interesting in that the attempt provides a richness and a roundness not often found in books about kids in high school. Major understands people; he really knows kids. There are times when the teacher in him shows through too clearly but he puts his finger on the raw, heart-breaking quality of the adolescent so perfectly, so delicately, and so without that sense of the adult watching that too often mars work for the young, that young people are bound to respond to him with thanksgiving. (p. 23)

Janet Lunn, "Huck Finn in Newfoundland," in Books in Canada, *Vol. 9, No. 10, December, 1980, pp. 21-3.*

For those who like to think that family life is still more or less as it was on *Leave It to Beaver*, *Far From Shore* hits hard and low. For others, weary of the sensationalism of juvenile novels, Kevin Major's story is a brave look at how a tough period can harden a boy like a nut. The pressures on the Slade family are like a vise gripping a migraine. Some (as in Major's last novel, *Hold Fast*) come from the frustrations of life in a small Newfoundland outport—boredom, unemployment, a general yearning to be anyplace but home. But more often they are the pressures of a family that isn't sure it's a unit any longer, and the one who flounders most is 15-year-old Chris. A cocky, wisecracking kid—when Jennifer snarls, he considers tossing her "a chunk of raw meat to quiet her down"—he is snared by the dissatisfaction around him. . . .

Brilliantly, Major tackles his story in five voices—the four Slades, plus Rev. Wheaton, the camp director. They pass their story along like a hot potato, contradicting, misunderstanding and forgiving, until voices reverberate from the four corners of the house. When they finally come together, it's like the end of any family argument: you're pummelled and drained,

and you can't remember whose side you first took. Major has pulled powerfully at unwilling chords, making sense of the most confusing battleground there is. (p. 57)

Ann Johnston, "Tales to Keep the Nightlights Burning," in Maclean's Magazine, *Vol. 93, No. 50, December 15, 1980, pp. 52, 54, 56-8.* *

Kevin Major's second book fulfils the promise that was evident in *Hold Fast*. It is a satisfying literary experience that once again reveals Major's uncommon artistic integrity. . . .

But now his narrative technique is different. And his hero is older and has to face alternatives that shade off into grey, making the right one hard to choose. The larger world encroaches more decisively on Chris than it did on Michael in *Hold Fast* as Major deals with the results of large social issues like unemployment, alcoholism, infidelity and the hard decisions thrust on teen-agers these days. . . .

For all the stark realities he puts in his hero's way Major ends Chris's nine month journey toward maturity with hope for better days. This is not a romantic hope but one based on actual events in the story; Chris (and the reader) need this hope—and deserve it.

We hear five voices telling the story. In some cases there are four or five opinions on the same situation. Major deals deftly with Chris's turns and even his sister's; the three adults have believable though less rounded personalities, but their points of view are more stereotypical.

Major's strength lies in his absolute concentration on the story. He is psychologically and emotionally true to Chris and his destiny, and we believe him. The delayed climax only adds conviction to the plot—another new narrative technique.

If four letter words offend you do not even open this book. But, if how words are put together to tell a compelling story interests you, then you will want to read *Far from Shore*. Most middle teen-agers will want to read it too. (pp. 42-3)

Irma McDonough, in a review of "Far from Shore," in In Review: Canadian Books for Children, *Vol. 15, No. 1, February, 1981, pp. 42-3.*

The number of Canadian authors writing particularly for teenage boys is small and those who come readily to mind—Roderick Haig-Brown, Farley Mowat, and David Walker, for example—have generally confined themselves to adventure stories in which a young hero, blessed with endurance and luck, overcomes the obstacles of a wilderness setting and achieves recognition and reward. . . . [We] must recognise the need for well-written books that come to grips with contemporary social problems. . . . Conflicts must be introduced early, dialogue must take precedence over description, and there must be a central character with whom the reader can identify. There must also, I think, be a positive philosophical view that makes a connection between cause and effect and that accepts the possibility of a happy ending. Kevin Major's *Far From Shore* is a welcome contribution to an uncrowded field. (pp. 50-1)

The strength of *Far From Shore* lies in the author's ability to present each of the major characters sympathetically in spite of their shortcomings. Through the device of interior monologue, actions and attitudes are provided with an emotional frame of reference that makes them comprehensible. (p. 52)

The least convincingly portrayed character is Mrs. Slade who is caught between loyalty to her husband and concern for her children. . . . As a working mother myself, I find it hard to believe that Mrs. Slade would nonchalantly jettison her domestic responsibilities. Furthermore, her romantic involvement with her employer seems an unnecessary complication. But this is a small quibble in an otherwise convincingly plotted book.

Major's use of dialogue is particularly admirable both as a means of projecting character and as a device for conveying regional flavour. He catches the rhythms of Newfoundland speech without the peppering of apostrophes that has annoyed me in dialect stories ever since I encountered ''Brer Rabbit and the Tar Baby'' at an early age. Chris's language is also enlivened by the profanity that Salinger's *Catcher in the Rye* established as a means of expressing teenage turmoil. The deterioration of the boy's social relationships is marked by a corresponding increase in his use of four-letter words. . . . (pp. 52-3)

Kevin Major should also be commended for the fine balance which he strikes between social and economic determinism, on the one hand, and personal responsibility, on the other. It is not Chris's fault that, living in a depressed area, he cannot find a summer job. It is his fault that he chooses to waste his time in bad company. Havng drifted far from shore, both literally and figuratively, his recognition that ''Come right down to it and it was all my own friggin' fault'' indicates his new-found maturity. Major's social realism is essentially optimistic. Each of the characters has the opportunity of starting over. (p. 53)

Muriel Whitaker, ''Getting Loused Up in Newfoundland,'' in Canadian Children's Literature: A Journal of Criticism and Review, No. 22, 1981, pp. 50-3.

When Kevin Major's **Hold Fast** was published three years ago, it was rightly hailed as a milestone in Canadian children's book publishing. Major captured in stark, vivid, detail the violent, troubled life of a Newfoundland teenager. . . .

We approached [*Far From Shore*] with some trepidation, knowing that second novels can often be disappointing. However, we were not disappointed. (p. 29)

Showing a daring not often found in young novelists, Major has decided to tell **Far From Shore** from multiple points of view. Thus we see the reactions of each member of the family not only to the events that most concern them individually, but also to those touching each other. The reader thus becomes aware of relativity; no man, or woman, is an island.

Far From Shore belongs to the type of fiction known as social realism, the type of story which deals with the troubles experienced by children and adolescents growing up in the complex modern world. Too often, social realism can fall into mere didacticism or into a kind of clinical case study. And often, there are happy endings which seem forced: the central figure has faced his problems and mastered them and is ready to enter into a meaningful relationship with society.

Now **Far From Shore** does have a happy ending, of sorts. . . . However, the author does not allow either the readers or the characters to believe that everything will be perfect from now on. (pp. 29-30)

Major has written a good second novel. It isn't perfect: some of the swearing seems gratuitous, although not offensive; and the relationship between father and son might have been more fully developed. We await with great interest his third novel;

it should give a fairly clear indication of whether or not Major will fully develop the considerable talent that we find in his first two books. (p. 30)

Jon C. Stott, in a review of ''Far from Shore,'' in The World of Children's Books, Vol. VI, 1981, pp. 29-30.

A scathing witty review of this, Kevin Major's second novel, might be more appropriate. Mimicking his coarse inane language, with which I'm sure he intends to identify himself with lost youth, might have been more entertaining. But having spent nine earnest years in a middle school classroom, I could conjure nothing more than disgust from my pen.

My very sensibilities have been offended by this book—its creation by its author and its direction toward an innocent public by Delacorte Press. . . .

Chris is a fifteen year old semi-delinquent, his sister Jennifer is contrite and an over-achiever in school. Mother is overworked and permanently distraught. Father is picturesque, regularly vomiting all over his long johns after drinking binges.

The story tries to focus on Chris—his aimless alliances, his need for some direction in his life. And he might have been a valid subject were it not for his profuse and pointless profanity caused, without question, by Major's coarse and ineffective use of the English language in some attempt to evoke a colloquial tongue.

Examine as evidence:

> Where we go drinking is mostly down by the beach. It's a good place because there's no one to bother you. Tonight is the most I guess I ever seen here. Everybody's got the same idea— a good tear now that we're out of school. There's plenty of girls around. Of course a booze is no friggin good unless there's few girls to liven things up.

I do not deny that casual bad grammar, talk of drugs and drink have some appeal to young people. But Kevin Major's novel lacks even the most remote sense of any redeeming virtue.

The probability of this book eventually appearing on middle and high school library shelves greatly disturbs me. It is difficult to believe that Major's first novel, **Hold Fast,** received three major Canadian book awards or that it was chosen best book of 1980 by School Library Journal. It couldn't have been anything like this.

Michele Carlo, in a review of ''Far from Shore,'' in Best Sellers, Vol. 41, No. 10, January, 1982, p. 403.

THIRTY-SIX EXPOSURES (1984)

Major's 18-year-old central character in **Thirty-Six Exposures** must learn to deal with the anger and frustration that affect so many of today's young people, not only those in Newfoundland. . . .

Major, in **Thirty-Six Exposures,** has abandoned the first-person voice he used so effectively in his earlier novels. In his new book, he has kept his viewpoint right over the shoulder of his central character, but the third-person point of view lets us see too much of the large chip Lorne carries there.

Like the narrators of *Far From Shore* and *Hold Fast,* Lorne is angry. Unlike those narrators, however, his anger seems unnecessary at the outset and unresolved at the end. Major's use of third-person narration has distanced the reader from Lorne, lessening our sympathy for him: he is left at the end of the novel just as he was at the beginning—angry, lonely, and very private. And the reader doesn't care.

The problem that will strike many readers, however, is not that of the narrative but the treatment of sex and foul language in the book. Lorne struggles with impotence in Chapter 3, masturbates in Chapter 6, and doesn't quite achieve successful intercourse by Chapter 30. Lorne's best friend, Trevor, dots his conversations with that f-word often bandied about by teenagers but which rarely appears in young-adult print. In *Thirty-Six Exposures,* Major seems to be testing the limits of the young-adult genre. Fortunately, his treatment of frustrated adolescent sex and real adolescent language is honest. Unfortunately, honesty alone isn't likely to win *Thirty-Six Exposures* a place in our schools.

Each of the 36 chapters in the book offers a snapshot, marvellous in its detail but not connected to the others. The plot revolves around Lorne and his friend Trevor, Trevor's disciplinary problems with a history teacher, and a school strike led by Lorne that succeeds in getting his friend reinstated. The snapshots follow Lorne through to graduation, his rejection by his girlfriend, his frustrated sex with Gwen, and his climb with Trevor up a watertower to write "Graduated, eh?" with spray paint. That question marks the real ending of the book, one that chronicles the confusion and frustration of young people with limited dreams and limited options. The book's tragic ending seems like an afterthought: Major should have stopped at the watertower—his point had been made.

The flaws in Major's new book will bring some disappointment to his fans, though the controversy over its content may well keep the book in the public eye.

> *Paul Kropp, "Growing Up Is Hard to Do: Leaving the Boy Behind," in* Quill and Quire, *Vol. 50, No. 11, November, 1984, p. 18.**

Lorne's story is told in third-person narrative that from time to time segues into his first-person poems, which propel the action along and add an introspective perspective. The story is episodic, at times to a fault (perhaps an attempt to unfold it like frames from a roll of film); the writing style is spare; the dialogue, including a goodly dose of vulgar language, is natural; and characterizations—because of the story's construction—emerge in bits and pieces that eventually coalesce. Nevertheless, this is a compelling coming-of-age novel with a message: right or wrong, succeeding generations must do things their own way.

> *Sally Estes, in a review of "Thirty-Six Exposures," in* Booklist, *Vol. 81, No. 5, November 1, 1984, p. 361.*

Although Major's story suffers from several flaws, especially from a lack of character development, it would be interesting to analyze in a writing class. . . . [The] title is really a reference

to an interesting attempt at a writing style. The story is written in thirty-six choppy mostly disconnected chapters (exposures).

At first I found the style a bit difficult to follow, but once I realized what the author was doing, I found it an interesting approach. This style is not the problem. The problem is that in some respects the story lacks a focus.

Lorne, the major character, who will give his senior class valedictory, is involved in a class project which produces some surprising information about his grandmother. Lorne's group of friends includes the usual assortment of adolescents, including one, Trevor, whose future looks cloudy. What does the author do with Trevor? I think, unfortunately, the author chose an approach that is currently in vogue, the easy way out, used in movies for the teen market, like *The Outsiders,* by having Trevor meet with an unfortunate tragedy. . . .

Major's story has too much dependence on [strong language and sexual innuendoes] and as a result the story falls far short of Major's capabilities as a writer.

> *Jack Beidler, in a review of "Thirty-Six Exposures," in* Best Sellers, *Vol. 44, No. 11, February, 1985, p. 439.*

Thirty-Six Exposures runs the gamut of teen problems: conflicts with authority; guilt and confusion about sexual desires; the need for peer acceptance. . . . The plot, while not original, is fast paced, but the characters are not involving. The book has some strengths: teens will understand Lorne's rebellion, his desire to break away from his family, his use of profanity. However, there is a coldness in the development of the characters that leaves readers detached from Lorne and Trevor, and the abrupt ending is a let-down. A book that tries hard to be contemporary but is too forced to be completely successful. (pp. 85-6)

> *Ellen M. Fecher, in a review of "Thirty-Six Exposures," in* School Library Journal, *Vol. 31, No. 6, February, 1985, pp. 85-6.*

Rarely are books set in as interesting a locale as is this, but even the Canadian setting does not quite seem to salvage the story line. At the end, I still was not quite sure what the author's point was in writing the book. The plot line is fairly straightforward. . . . [We] meet several students working on a combined effort for their senior project, a romance here, a confrontation there, a surfacing relationship between Lorne's widowed grandmother and the unfair teacher, and the almost-obligatory auto accident ending in the death of one of the characters. Also present are several scenes of questionable nature; masturbation, sexual encounters, double-dating leading to a little bit of envious voyeurism—this type of material seems to be present only for the sake of attempting to appeal to the teenaged reader. For the most part, the scenes were tame, but still they may cause eyebrows to raise. Not a bad book, just not great.

> *John Lord, in a review of "Thirty-Six Exposures," in* Voice of Youth Advocates, *Vol 7, No. 6, February, 1985, p. 329.*

Jan(et Marjorie Brisland) Mark

1943-

English author of fiction and short stories.

One of England's most distinguished children's writers, Mark is recognized for her incisive prose, deft humor, and penetrating insight into the lives of her protagonists. Stylistically compared to William Mayne, she is best known for her first book, *Thunder and Lightnings,* a sensitive depiction of a growing friendship between two uniquely individual boys. Mark's often plotless stories for younger readers, middle graders, and young adults characteristically focus on episodes that illuminate friendship and other social relationships in Norfolk school and home settings. Generally centering on lonely children who experience life's injustices, her books evince careful research into such topics as World War II airplanes (*Thunder and Lightnings*), motorbikes (*Handles*), and trucks (*Trouble Half-Way*). The bittersweet realism that pervades Mark's works is accentuated in her bleaker and more sophisticated novels—*The Ennead, Divide and Rule,* and *Aquarius*—which explore political, religious, and emotional manipulation in other times.

Critics praise Mark's original characterizations, natural dialogue, and powerful descriptions while applauding her ability to unite literary and structural elements into a cohesive whole. Although she is faulted for the despairing messages of *The Ennead, Divide and Rule,* and *Aquarius,* the majority of reviewers consider Mark a perceptive and witty commentator on the concerns of children and young people.

In 1977, *Thunder and Lightnings* received the Carnegie Medal and a *Guardian* Commendation. In 1981, *Nothing to be Afraid Of* was highly commended by the Carnegie committee and earned a *Guardian* Special Prize. *Handles* won the Carnegie Medal in 1984 and *Trouble Half-Way* was a runner up for the *Guardian* Award in 1986.

(See also *Something about the Author,* Vol. 22 and *Contemporary Authors,* Vols. 93-96.)

AUTHOR'S COMMENTARY

A letter published in the *Guardian* last August indicated that certain children's books might be banned, or under threat of banning, from certain children's libraries. It is suggested elsewhere that children's publishing in this country [England] is blatantly racist. I learn from an article about my books that I am 'another talent lost through egoism and ill advice to the proper pursuit of producing superlative, *relevant* books for children' [see excerpt dated 1980 in General Commentary]. Evidently it is not my business to decide what I may write or, to look at the situation from another angle, there appears to be a number of people who feel that it is their business to decide what children may read.

This is nothing new, but is it a part of history that we would like to see repeat itself? In an article of my own, written in 1978, I remarked in passing, that I was lucky to have begun writing for children when I did, since I was benefiting from the considerable freedom achieved by other authors over the past twenty-five years. I'm not sure that I would say that so

confidently now, and while I don't quite foresee bonfires of kiddiporn in the streets, I reluctantly sense the pressure of an encroaching desire to intervene; as though the recent proliferation of books for children had run dangerously out of control. There are those who would like to control it.

There is an increasing tendency among some reviewers to devote their meagre column inches to rubbishing the books that fail to meet with their approval, instead of commending those that they admire. This grudging attitude is also, in a way, a self-indulgent one. In too many instances the book in question ceases to have any intrinsic worth and becomes merely a platform upon which the critic may perform.

Is any amount of intervention, interference, pressure; call it what you will, going to prevent children from getting at the reading matter that they want? If they are prevented from reading say, my nasty books in juvenile libraries, what will divert them from reading much nastier ones elsewhere? They have only to go into an adult library, or a bookshop. No angel with a fiery sword will be there to keep them out. I experienced my first brush with censorship when I was twelve. Deciding that I could no longer enter the children's library with undiminished dignity, I turned my attention to the tall bookcase at home. The height is relevant. It was furnished with books left behind by my father when he cantered out of our lives, and his tastes were catholic—so catholic that my mother felt obliged to place particular volumes on the top shelf, just below the ceiling and out of my reach. I was on my honour not to climb but she was out at work all day, and I climbed. It was a long shelf and the naughty books were relatively few, so the remaining space was occupied by works of a mainly innocuous nature, by authors who might have been alarmed at the company they were keeping. I did not know this and, supposing the top shelf to be all corruption, discovered unimagined aspects of vice. Alongside Henry Miller who was obviously very naughty indeed (and extremely tedious between the naughty bits) I found delightful stories by many distinguished writers. I wondered and wondered what filth they were so cunningly concealing in their limpid prose. One of them quoted a poem by Lovelace. I was suspicious of Lovelace for years.

As for the lower shelves, I left them untouched, and missed a good deal, thereby. If the interventionists do get their mitts on children's books, is anyone going to bother to look at what gets left behind? It is becoming apparent that the majority of children prefer reading paperbacks to hard backed books. I suspect that the majority of this majority would equally prefer to read nothing at all, than to read what is prescribed as good for them, and while I don't feel exhilarated by the discovery that a whole class of fourteen-year-olds is hooked on the vicarious horrors of *Jaws,* it is preferable to seeing them hooked on the more immediate horrors available to them in real life. They are unlikely to run wild in the streets as a result, gnawing the legs from innocent bystanders. A few years back, a youth on trial for a violent crime, pleaded that he had been influenced by reading *A Clockwork Orange.* Here is an opportunity to inveigh against the evil power of print, but a century or two earlier, two boys in similar circumstances were apprehended with copies of *The Beggar's Opera* in their pockets. I believe that this fact was forwarded at the time as a good reason for banning it.

Sed quis custodiet ipsos custodes? Lewis Carroll, who has had some debatable motives imputed to him in recent years, would have Bowdlerized Bowdler if he could. Bowdler dismayed him not by what he left out but by what he left in. When studying Chaucer for A level we noticed that some lines in that most harmless of fables, *The Nun's Priest's Tale,* were represented by a row of dots; for instance, Chanticleer's expressed desire to 'ride' upon Pertelote, were not their perch so narrow, and this after six years of biology lessons. Bees by all means, but not birds. We were not credited with curiosity, or the intelligence to go straight down to the library to look up the omissions in Skeat. Or had we not been considered at all? Were the dots to spare the teacher's blushes? And how she did blush when we told her, generously, what was missing. Bearing this in mind, might it not follow that those who seek to suppress a book for any reason (apart from the fact that it is so lacking in all qualities that it was not worth recommending in the first place—understandable given that shelf space is limited and money more so) are moved by the fear that if they do not, they will be thought to have set their seal of approval on it?

I was originally invited to give some indication of the way in which I thought my own writing might be going. To hell in a hand cart, by the look of it. I have been very well treated in my reviews; well enough to be able to regard the bad ones objectively even if I do feel they are cruelly inaccurate. The one that worries me is the one quoted earlier, which questions my right to choose what I write about. If I do not choose *who chooses for me*? If I find the human race a depressing spectacle,

must I disguise the fact when I write, or must I stop writing? I should like to make use of all the virtues if I found them readily observable, but the smiling villain is always with us, and a more stimulating subject than the sober saint. (pp. 8-9)

[Human] nastiness is not the monopoly of villains, and it is a manifestation that has engaged my attention. Come to think of it, I've not had much truck with villains, preferring the flawed and venal protagonists of traditional tragedy. The burden of their song is 'Anything for a quiet life' but of course, a quiet life is not what they get and they sink under the weight of their own inertia.

I am about to begin a novel with no villains at all, and I'm prepared to say no more than that, for a very good reason. In the autumn of 1979 I gave a talk to a conference of English advisers, and was afterwards asked what I intended to write next. I explained in some detail the outline and aims of the novel which I hoped to begin in the New Year—and did indeed begin. 'Oh,' said my questioner, 'do you usually know so much about it in advance?' and I was obliged to admit that I did not.

Now, this was very acute of him because, when I did begin work on it I was uneasy, and by the time I had completed 9,000 words it was only too clear that we were going to get no further. The manuscript is in a file, somewhere, and likely to remain there. What went wrong?

There were a number of external contributory factors, but the main setback—and who needs a setback on, as it were, the starting line?—was the fact that I knew too much before I began. I knew all about the main character, who was a poor stick, in retrospect, and all about what would happen to him. I had decided what he was going to do before I had discovered what he was like. Fatal; plot and character must interact and develop inseparably. My well-hatched plot had left me nothing to discover. There was no sense of quest. I write for a living, not for fun, as I sternly tell small children who ask if I have any other hobbies, but I do expect to enjoy it and for me, the element of enjoyment is furnished by the process of finding out about the people I am creating. Take *Divide and Rule,* for instance; had I known, when I began it, what was going to happen to Hanno, I doubt if I would have had the heart to set him off on his dreadful career. By the time I had finished I could see that his fate had been inevitable from the start, but it took me three drafts, 200,000 words, six months to realize it.

So, this time I am going to keep myself in the dark and if some reviewer comes along afterwards and says that I appear to have written it with my eyes shut, I shan't care. Well, yes, I shall: then. But I don't care now, I dare not care now, and this, I hope, may save my soul from the dread dead hand of the interventionist. If ever I start to worry about the kind of reviews a book will get while I am still writing it, then it will be time to shut up shop. (p. 10)

Jan Mark, "Something to Be Afraid Of," in English in Education, *Vol. 15, No. 1, Spring, 1981, pp. 8-10.*

[*In the following interview with Neil Philip, Mark comments on her view of religion, her involvement with schools and their use of children's literature, and the influence of William Mayne on her writing style.*]

Jan Mark's writing is in two modes; the intimate naturalism of her stories of school and home such as *Thunder and Lightnings* and the intense symbolism of her metaphysical thrillers such as *The Ennead.* The divide is sharp and intriguing. But there is an overriding theme: the uses of friendship. And whether in the consoling vein of the early or the despairing one of the later books, that theme is tinged with a sense of bitterness, loss, betrayal. That sense is tied up with a very harsh view of the ability of religion to offer either true solace or true hope. Blake's note to his *Four Zoas* could stand as the epigraph to all her work: ''The Christian Religion teaches that No Man is Indifferent to you, but that every one is Either your friend or your enemy; he must necessarily be either the one or the other, And that he will be equally profitable both ways if you treat him as he deserves.''

During a lengthy and pleasant conversation, I caught Jan Mark on the raw only once, when I questioned her about the bleak portrayal of religion in such novels as *The Ennead* and *Divide and Rule* and stories such as ''A Little Misunderstanding'' in her sprightly new collection *Feet*. . . . She told me, ''I find a great deal that's very detestable, especially in Christianity, and many other religions, but particularly Christianity, which is really the religion I'm using in *Divide and Rule,* the worst aspects of it.'' I asked if this revulsion stemmed from religion masking the individual's responsibility for his own actions (elsewhere in our conversation she attacked fantasies of good against evil, such as C. S. Lewis's overtly Christian Narnia sequence, for ''the abdication of personal responsibility''). ''It's partly that, but it's partly the uses to which people put religion. I mean the temple in *Divide and Rule* is just a vast job-creation scheme. It simply exists to employ the people who work there. Their only interest is in securing their future, and they form a cult quite cynically''. In the process the central character Hanno is slowly and deliberately driven insane. It is chilling for the reader of ''A Little Misunderstanding'' to register in Jan Mark's description of a boy at a fundamentalist meeting the self-same tone used to chart Hanno's fate.

Discussing the loose trilogy *The Ennead, Divide and Rule* and *Aquarius,* Jan Mark told me: ''The idea of manipulation is what I'm working on in all three books. Not only why we do it, but why do we allow it? How much capital do you think you can make out of allowing yourselves to be used? Some people can, some can't. Some people need to be the used half in a relationship, or feel that in fact in a subliminal way they are the controlling force.'' These thoughts are made manifest in *Aquarius* by a deliberate transgression of the implicit bond between writer and reader. The central character Viner is set up as the hero, and then the reader is alienated from him. ''I was trying something out there: I wanted to see how long the reader's sympathies remained with him. And what I thought would happen has happened: people will go to extraordinary lengths to justify what he does, because they thought from the start he was going to be the hero. I think what he does is completely unforgivable, but a lot of people don't . . . I've got no sympathy for him at all.''

Some may think that her exploration of such ideas by such techniques has taken the bulk of her writing outside the area in which it is useful to talk of a separate children's literature. Jan Mark herself talked of how enjoyable the ''trilogy'' was to write, ''perhaps because of the feeling that the possibilities are infinite, whereas the ones that deal with children are restricted by children's experience, which is limited—the children in the book rather than the children reading. The brightest child doesn't know much.'' . . .

On the other hand, she is also ''in and out of schools all the time'', on one-off visits as a writer and at the moment on a regular basis as part of her role as Fellow in Children's Lit-

erature in the Department of Education at Oxford Polytechnic. This is an experience she is finding ''very valuable'': ''One thing I'd forgotten is what it's like to be working with people. The input is non-stop. I'm almost over-stimulated there's so much going on . . . After eight hours a day alone with a typewriter for eight years it's a bit of a culture shock. But there's a lot coming out of it. It's already had an effect on the writing.''

Jan Mark was herself a teacher of Art and English in secondary schools, an experience she has drawn on directly in, for instance, the story ''Chutzpah'' in *Hairs in the Palm of the Hand*, and indirectly throughout her work. What is so refreshing about her writing both about and for children, and what places it for me above her work for an older audience, is the accuracy with which she reflects the real concerns of childhood; an accuracy born of careful observation. ''It's the best place to observe them from, the front of a classroom, or the back of a classroom.'' Memory of her own childhood also plays its part: the stories in *Nothing to be Afraid Of,* the strongest and most coherent of her collections, recall her own fifties upbringing in Ashford in Kent.

I asked her what she felt now about the use of literature in the classroom. ''There's too much emphasis on how to use it, I think. A lot of teachers, and reviewers, people who review for teachers, are too ready to discard a book because there's nothing you can do with it in class except read it . . . Something I thought of doing when I first went to the Poly, and which I'm determined to do now, was to make a list of what we call 'classroom classics': books that seem very popular in the classroom not because they're good, necessarily, but because they're safe. The teacher will try them out and discover it goes down well with third years, particularly the boys, and we all know how difficult they are to please, so they get a set in, and it's passed on to the next teacher who's responsible for that age group, and within a couple of years the whole third year is doing it every year, and doing projects on it, and last year's project work is still hanging from the ceiling . . . They become classics by inertia. There are a number of these: one's *The Goalkeeper's Revenge,* which is understandable because for about 20 years it was about the only collection of short stories for children available, *The Silver Sword,* the Narnia books, and I said laughingly to a lecturer I'm working with, 'I bet *Thunder and Lightnings* is going the same way,' and it is . . . *Thunder and Lightnings* is the book which sends up projects rotten, in fact there is an HMI who reads it around the country as an awful warning to teachers and students, and yet people do project work on it—on the aeroplanes. Well it's not about aeroplanes: as you said, it's about making friends.''

Thunder and Lightnings was her first book, though ''I'd never stopped writing from about the age of four onwards.'' It was written for the Penguin/Guardian competition, which it won. . . . The book established her immediately as a writer with a voice of her own, though the oblique restraint of the style clearly owed something to William Mayne. I quoted to her Margaret Meek's quip in *The Signal Review of Children's Books 1* that perhaps Mayne ''is Jan Mark's godfather'', and she laughed: ''He influenced me in a way to begin with. It was the courage to say exactly what you mean, go to any lengths. It's almost Biblical clarity in Mayne. It's so clear it looks convoluted. He will say exactly what he wants to say, and seeing somebody else do that gave me tremendous confidence to try and do the same thing.''

The key moment of Mayne's *Earthfasts* is when Keith recognizes that ''the lost places are in this world and belong to the people in it and are all that they have to call home''; it is a similar truth that Jan Mark's highly wrought fiction urges her readers to accept. The truth encapsulated in her belief that while "children spend most of their childhood either being frightened or frightening other children", "There's no need to frighten yourself after a bit."

Neil Philip, "Read Mark, Learn," in The Times Educational Supplement, No. 3492, June 3, 1983, p. 37.

[In the following interview from Books for Keeps, Mark discusses her approach to writing.]

[Jan Mark's] stature amongst English writers for children has grown with each new publication. . . . A measure of her stature is her nomination [in 1984] as the British entry for the international Hans Andersen award.

Few writers are as coherent as Jan Mark when talking about their intentions as a writer or more trenchant in their views about children as writers.

She makes clear distinctions about her work as a short story writer—a form she clearly enjoys returning to (**Nothing to Be Afraid Of, Hairs in the Palm of the Hand, Feet**); what she calls her 'observational' novels (**Thunder and Lightnings, Under the Autumn Garden, Handles**); and the 'heavies', her 'speculative' novels (**The Ennead, Divide and Rule, Aquarius**).

These distinctions depend for her much more upon the different demands of the short story and the novel rather than on the audience she's writing for—children or adults:

'Novels are linear but short stories aren't. The best analogy is the movie. A film is made up of thousands of still frames and if you isolate one frame, as with a paragraph in a novel, you learn very little. In a short story you're stopping the movie at one frame, isolating a particular moment, the seminal moment at which development begins to happen. It may be the moment when someone is jolted out of inertia and it's your job as a writer to justify the moment. In **"A Little Misunderstanding"** **(Feet)**, I deliberately chose that title because the boy entirely misconceived the situation and it's only at the very end that he realises what he's let himself in for. So in a short story, you've got to know the moment towards which you're working; . . . the end is in the beginning.'

Moving on to discuss her first two novels [**Thunder and Lightnings** and **Under the Autumn Garden**] and the latest **Handles**, Jan used a different analogy—that of the artist 'working from life'. **Handles** is a 'look at a relationship', a developing relationship—that between the eleven year old, bike-mad Erica and 'Elsie' Wainwright, the ex-teacher who runs a failing motor-cycle repair business:

'It's very episodic and, like **Thunder and Lightnings,** it's got no plot. It's a love-story—Erica is in love with 'Elsie'. It's the beginning of a sexual attraction which she doesn't understand. I doubt if many children would realise that or many adults— they're so conditioned to thinking that eleven year olds couldn't feel like that. Taken one way it's a very depressing book—it's certainly not light. But I'm not trying to make any points. I'm observing day-to-day situations. An adult would speculate— that Erica's probably not going to realise her dream and become a mechanic or that, 'Elsie's business will fail. I don't think a child would pick up the implications. . . .'

The novels in which she 'works from life' are all about children and the narrative is shaped by the child's perception of the world. They also impose their own demands on the writer:

'You owe it to the audience to provide a story. Children are not experienced in the way that adults are. They haven't got the equipment so you have to give them something more concrete to work on. There has to be something there other than hints, clues, allusions which you can expect a more experienced reader to pick up (as in **Aquarius**). I like writing about children. I don't want always to be writing about children. . . .'

So what about the novels, the three 'heavies', which are not 'about children'?—'In them, I'm setting up situations and inviting the reader to explore the situation along with the writer. They're for a sophisticated reader and they're deliberately written to discourage an unsophisticated reader. (p. 12)

'They are very literary and I don't like being explicit. I like to make the reader work hard. . . .'

There was a strong sense, too, in her remarks of a desire to go on to do new things:

'They (the "heavies") could get very much more self-indulgent. I didn't think so at the time but I think I'm coming dangerously close to covering the same ground by doing three books so similar in treatment.' . . .

Whatever she may have gained from the experience of working with student teachers [at Oxford Polytechnic], there can be little doubt about what they will have gained from her. She has encouraged them to write though she hasn't set up 'creative writing workshops'—'that's anathema'. Rather she's asked her students to write that they might better understand the demands teachers so thoughtlessly impose when they ask children to write fiction. It was here that the connection became clear between her own intentions as a writer and her work with children and students.

Her students, she remarked: 'have no confidence in their personal lives. Yet each one of them is uniquely qualified to write about themselves; . . . the first duty of a teacher is to convince the pupils of the immense value of what they know.'

This emphasis on the personal knowledge of the writer emerged again when Jan talked about how she researched her books. None of her readers can have failed to notice the expertise she shows—the knowledge of bikes, for example, which she displays through Erica in **Handles**. Authenticity and integrity are closely related in her writing.

'The research for **Handles** was more a matter of checking with living people. . . . I do myself like to know how things work. It is essential you know and you've got to let it show. It weakens the reader's confidence in the writer if you generalise and gloss over. You need to demand to be believed. Your knowledge gives you an authority which transmits itself to the reader.'

In talking about the novel she's working on at the moment [**Trouble Half-Way**], Jan gave an interesting insight into how the elements she'd described work out in practice. The raw materials are there in personal experience and her scrupulous observation of the world around her and these elements are transformed by her interest in 'looking at a relationship' at the point when it's beginning to develop.

'It's based partly on a trip I made with my brother who's a long distance lorry driver; . . . then I went to Rochdale to visit a school and I had to travel through Oldham from Manchester and I saw the cotton-mills. They've got names on, proper names, about 190 of them all with names. I linked this with the idea of the long distance lorry driver . . . a man who's still getting to know his stepdaughter. They're still at the stage of being fearfully polite to each other and he coaxes her to come with him up North in the lorry to see one of the mills that's got her name on it. That's the basis of the story. . . .'

At some point in the future we can also expect a picture book [*Out of the Oven*] illustrated by Antony Maitland. The starting point this time is not personal experience but an incident from Gorky's *My Childhood*—a story his grandmother tells of thousands of little furry, kitten-like devils being released one time when the oven door blew open. It's a story that Jan obviously relishes:

'It's quite unlike anything I've done. . . . I wasn't trying to make a new departure for picture books based on Russian classics. It's purely personal pleasure and a sort of perverted enjoyment of knowing it comes from such an unlikely source. I know four year olds won't give a damn where it came from but it amuses me to think I've got a picture book out of Gorky. And it's also the only animal story I've ever written. All the others have been about people. It's really about keeping a pet, featuring a responsible adult who says ''Put that back where you found it!'' In this case, it's a devil that's supposed to be going back into the oven. . . .'

Whatever we may expect from Jan Mark in the future we can be sure that she will go on resisting 'covering the same ground' to the despair, no doubt, of those same critics who wanted her to go on rewriting *Thunder and Lightnings*. It's her own 'personal pleasure' she'll be pursuing in her writing. Otherwise, as far as she's concerned 'the excitement would have gone out.' (p. 13)

> *"Authorgraph No. 25: Jan Mark,"* in Books for Keeps, *No. 25, March, 1984, pp. 12-13.*

GENERAL COMMENTARY

WINIFRED WHITEHEAD

When Jan Mark's first book for children, *Thunder and Lightnings,* was published in 1976, it attracted the penetrating comment from Philippa Pearce: 'A rich book; rich in human feeling; in response to the world around; in aptness of writing, always making the words a pleasure to read.' Now that Jan Mark has published six more books it is evident that this richness has also a variety and range which can attract a wide readership on many different levels.

For some, *Thunder and Lightnings* will remain the best book, because it seems comparatively straightforward, uncomplicated, an easy read. The story flows easily enough, centring around the friendship and everyday concerns of Andrew and Victor. Andrew is a newcomer to the Norfolk village of Pallingham, where Victor has lived all his life. . . . [Andrew] quickly comes to appreciate Victor's unquenchable personality, his quiet sense of humour, and his passion for aircraft, especially for the Lightnings still stationed at Coltishall, nearby. It is this passion which provides the main storyline. . . . (p. 32)

Behind the apparent simplicity, the everydayness of the story's events, and Victor's infectious enthusiasm for aircraft lies a penetrating analysis of the two boys and their lives. Both, initially, are loners at home and at school. Andrew's parents are reasonably sympathetic, good humoured and interested in

his affairs, but Andrew doesn't always recognise this. 'You couldn't see that I was afraid of going to school,' he says accusingly to his mother, towards the end of the novel.

> 'Oh yes, I could,' said Mum. 'That's why I made you start at once, instead of next term. You'd have been dead of fright by September. Now you know what to expect and you've got a friend to go back with.'
>
> 'Why didn't you say something then?' asked Andrew.
>
> 'I did,' said Mum. 'I said, 'The first day's always the worst,' and you thought it was a big con. If I'd tried to talk you round, you wouldn't have taken any notice. You were determined to hate it before you got there.'

His Mum's slightly detached penetration; her 'excessive' love of records and books; her use of long words like 'avionics'; her insistence that he take baby Edward out shopping; the friendly muddle of her housekeeping and her careless indifference to appearances are all trying to Andrew from time to time, but at least his home is a comfortable place, lively, interesting and amusing. Jan Mark's sense of humour is at its best in scenes at the Mitchells' home. Victor's home, on the other hand, horrifies Andrew. It is true that he has a warm retreat in his bedroom, where he does as he likes.

> It was just like walking into a spider's web. Dozens of pieces of cotton hung from the ceiling and on the ends of the cotton were model aeroplanes.

Like Victor himself, the room is fiercely individual; it defies even his mother's tidying up. Here Victor lies for hours, watching his planes, under the fifteen watt light which is his 'bomber's moon.' But the rest of the house is bleakly unwelcoming, and Andrew is consumed with an indignation and pity at Victor's lot which comes to a head when he sees Mrs Skelton's unreasonable anger over an accidentally soiled sheet.

> She looked at him, at Victor and at the sheet, then without saying anything, she smacked Victor hard, three times, across the side of the head. Victor rocked on his feet and put his hand to his head, but he said nothing either.
>
> Andrew was shocked by the silence of it. In his home any trouble was accompanied by much shouting and table-thumping, all over in a few moments because no one could ever get angry enough to keep it up.

'It wasn't fair,' Andrew says later to his own mother. 'Nothing's fair,' his Mum tells him. 'There's no such thing as fairness. It's a word made up to keep children quiet. When you discover it's a fraud then you're starting to grow up. The difference between you and Victor is that you're still finding out and he knows perfectly well already.' It is the 'knowing perfectly well already' that leads Victor to his dismissive attitude to school and learning. He begins to indicate this quite cheerfully, in an amusing scene in which he explains to Andrew how to set about project work.

> 'I do fish. Fish are easy. They're all the same shape. . . .'

'Don't you have to write anything?' asked Andrew.

'Yes, look, I wrote a bit back here. About every four pages will do,' said Victor. 'Miss Beale, she keep saying I ought to write more but she's glad when I don't. She's got to read it. Nobody can read my writing.'

This deliberate policy is born of a profound scepticism about his own worth; and is accompanied, also, by a shrewd thrust at the way in which school work can transform interest to boredom. Andrew naively remarks, 'I thought the whole point of the project was to do something you liked.' Victor knows better.

'Ah, yes,' said Victor. 'But it would be having to like aeroplanes instead of just liking them. Every time a Harrier went over I wouldn't be thinking, there goes a Harrier. I'd think, there goes my project. Then I wouldn't want to look at it. School's like measles. That spread.'

Behind this acute and perceptive comment lies, of course, a bitterly clearsighted awareness of the way his teachers, and his parents judge him. The bitterness becomes more explicit, later, when Andrew helpfully tries to encourage Victor to read about aircraft for himself.

'That's no good, you know,' he said. 'That's no good you trying to teach me anything. I'll never be any use. I don't even think I want to be. If you start being good at something, people expect you to be even better and then they get annoyed when you aren't. That's safer to seem a bit dafter than you are.'

The apparently cynical pessimism of this remark is, however, counterbalanced by Victor's unquenchable individualism and resilience, as is shown in the closing paragraph of the story. Here he sees what may be 'the last Lightning of all' in a spectacular last display of aerobatics. 'What a way to go out, eh?' he says, with 'his old and famous grin.' 'Whaaaaam!'. The book ends on this consoling note: Victor will not be put down.

Matthew, the eleven year old hero of *Under the Autumn Garden*, is also dogged by his school project: this time on local history. Unlike Victor he takes it seriously, at least to the extent of being determined to find something really interesting and original. This, as Victor could have foretold, is fatal. ('Ho,' said Victor, when Andrew expressed a similar desire to do something interesting. 'You'll come to a bad end, you will.') In face of opposition and discouragement from his mother and his teacher, then, Matthew stubbornly persists in digging under the garden, hoping desperately to find something to justify his activity. At first he is good humouredly assisted by an older boy, Paul Angel, but in the end Paul annexes the only promising 'find' and leaves Matthew to face his teacher empty-handed.

Although Matthew's dig provides the framework of the story, the real interest lies in the amusingly truthful portrayal of his changing—often fraught—relationships at home and at school, and in particular with Paul Angel and the various other members of this clannish family. (pp. 32-5)

There are many subtle undertones in this fine story, ripe for exploration: but even at surface level the book has plenty to offer. It is amusing, lively, perceptive, very close to life: Mat-thew's predicament should find an echo in most eleven year old readers.

The next two novels, though, are on a different plane altogether, decidedly for the more sophisticated older reader. The heroes of both books are older boys; Isaac is fifteen and Hanno eighteen, and they face a harsher and more intractable reality than the younger protagonists of the earlier books.

The Ennead takes places not in the familiar, homely setting of a Norfolk village, but in another galaxy altogether, on a strange bleak planet, Erato, some time in the distant future. Its hero, Isaac, is isolated in many different ways; he is the sole survivor of a now-dead planet, Orpheus; he has been rescued and adopted by Mr Swenson, who has also died; and he depends on the patronage of his half-brother, Theodore, who would willingly be rid of him. Erato, moreover, is a planet devoted to the doctrine of extreme self-interest; anyone who becomes unemployed, and therefore a liability, is immediately deported, even though the odds are against his surviving the journey to another planet. So Isaac is desperately trying to trick his way into a livelihood. Having succeeded at least for the time being, he tries in addition to relieve his own isolation by persuading Theodore to hire a sculptor, hoping thus to acquire a grateful, friendly protégé. Eleanor, unfortunately, as becomes a dedicated artist, is too fiercely individual to be humbly grateful, or even to conform to the requirements of Erato society. Isaac and his friend Moshe become involved with her in her stubborn nonconformity, until, finally, all three face deportation. . . . This is a powerful story, one which, though in such different terms, has obvious links with the themes of conflict and isolation implicit in the earlier books. But the ruthlessness which society can show to those who refuse to conform is horrifyingly cold, logical and relentless in *The Ennead:* it is a society which lacks all tenderness and understanding. Indeed it is for these very qualities that the three friends ultimately suffer; for their compassion and moral and artistic integrity.

Although at first sight the society of *Divide and Rule* seems less coldly self-interested than this, its effect on Hanno is quite as disastrous. This is a society which pays lipservice at least to a primitive religion, one which has passed beyond human sacrifice, but which still demands a symbolic year's service from an unwilling individual whom the god chooses. The hero, Hanno, a more than usually unwilling 'Shepherd', is chosen by a complicated ritual, and is then forced to remain a close prisoner in the Temple, serving a god in whose existence he does not even believe. His initial incredulity and rebellion are slowly subdued into unwilling conformity, but even this proves not enough to help him survive the year. The details of his servitude, his humiliations, his resentful chafing against his enforced idleness and isolation, and his rising panic and fear of the eventual outcome are powerfully described. One of the most bitterly ironic scenes is his brief visit home, to find what irreversible changes have occurred in his once relaxed and pleasantly undisciplined relationships with his family. The story moves inexorably, frighteningly, gathering momentum to the point at which he is required to take part in a vast deception intended to restore the failing faith of the people. Although he desperately tries to thwart the Temple plot, he is nevertheless cleverly jockeyed into the position they require, and then, having been made use of, relentlessly pushed aside, sick, destitute, speechless and apparently hopeless. Even his boat, symbolic of his old life, fails to sustain him. In this respect the story takes to its tragic conclusion Victor's sad remark: 'Everything go that you like best. That never come back.'

'Had I known when I began it,' said Jan Mark in a recent article [see excerpt dated 1981 in Author's Commentary] . . . 'what was going to happen to Hanno, I doubt if I would have had the heart to set him off on his dreadful career. By the time I had finished I could see that his fate had been inevitable from the start, but it took me three drafts, 200,000 words, six months to realise it.' As one reads the story one can see, not merely the inevitability of Hanno's fate, but that it has been in preparation longer than Jan Mark suggests. In all four novels written so far, widely different in setting, event, expected audience, the problem of the isolated individual, stubbornly battling his own way against odds, and in some measure bringing down upon himself his own consequent pain and retribution, has been a central preoccupation. But whereas Andrew, Victor and Matthew survive and learn from their mistakes, and even Isaac, Eleanor and Moshe go down fighting, unvanquished in spirit at least, at the end of this story Hanno is broken, defeated. Does this imply a reservation about *Divide and Rule* as a book for young people? Some critics have thought so, but Jan Mark has strongly defended her position in the article already mentioned.

Certainly it is a book in which, after all, the reader is passionately involved on Hanno's side against the inflexible fanatical dogma of the Temple Guardians. Jan Mark mobilises the reader's anger in a positive and constructive way against their narrow, arrogant certainty, as she had earlier directed it against the ruthless selfishness of Erato. At the same time she reveals clearly the individual's own complicity in his downfall, so that the reader, alongside the protagonist, is led to judge clearsightedly, to see that there can be no complacently reassuring and simplistic answer to the problems exposed. But there is no defeatism, partly because the societies portrayed are not yet, after all, our own, and partly because the attentive, close and intelligent reading, involvement and discussion which the story evokes are themselves an invitation to the hopefulness that comes from shared indignation. Hanno, one remembers, was on his own.

In addition to these stirring novels are three more recent books, a slight but amusing story for younger readers, and two books of short stories. Steven, the young hero of *The Short Voyage of the Albert Ross,* lives on the edge of a small town. Across the potato field lie the railway and the river, both forbidden but fascinating territory, in spite of the real and imaginary terrors which surround them. Steven's adventures there with the older hectoring and domineering John to contend with make a good story to read to six or seven year olds, with the possibility, then, for abler children to read the book for themselves.

Nothing to be Afraid Of is a delightful collection of stories, all very funny, but many with a macabre or sinister twist. The title story is an amusingly horrifying cautionary tale of four-year-old Robin, whose mother has so smothered him with care that he has become a featureless nonentity. (pp. 35-8)

What happens to him at Anthea's hands is vivid and unexpected. Then there is the story of 'Nule', a newel post at the bottom of the stairs which gradually takes on a menacing life; of William, whose uncompromising version of 'The Three Little Pigs' reflects his jealousy of the coming baby; and of Brenda, who is sent backwards and forwards between two hostile teachers like a shuttlecock. This would be a good book to read from, selectively, to children from eleven to fourteen, for although some of the protagonists are quite young, the subtly malicious flavour requires a sophisticated audience. *Hairs in the Palm of the Hand* contains two stories only. The first,

set in a boys' school, is a hilarious account of a bet laid on the number of minutes wasted in one week; the second, **'Chutzpah'**, tells how Eileen, a 'new girl' in a mixed comprehensive school, sets everyone by the ears with unsurpassable effrontery. The authenticity of detail and the penetrating wit at the expense of school life will be appreciated with wry smiles and delighted chuckles. In these stories fun and entertainment are unmixed with any sense of impending doom.

With such variety of stories so far, then, we wait expectantly for Jan Mark's next book. (pp. 38-9)

Winifred Whitehead, ''Jan Mark,'' in The Use of English, *Vol. 33, No. 2, Spring, 1982, pp. 32-9.*

JOHN ROWE TOWNSEND

Among British writers first published since 1973, the most interesting is Jan Mark. (p. 334)

Thunder and Lightnings is episodic; *Under the Autumn Garden* . . . has a storyline—a boy's search for relics of the past—but it is not much more than a thread running through the book, of which the main feature is again a sharp and witty perception of how children think and feel and relate to one another. With *The Ennead* . . . and *Divide and Rule* . . . , Jan Mark moved from our everyday world into imagined ones, and showed a bleaker side of her writing nature. In both of these books, individuals are defeated by cynically operated systems, but at least in *The Ennead* the human spirit goes down fighting and undiminished. . . . *Divide and Rule,* starker still, shows its hero still alive at the end but cast out by the system as a mere husk.

Aquarius . . . is possibly Jan Mark's bleakest book so far. . . . In this story, belief and morality and friendship are all uncertain and appear to be forever shifting; and the relationship between Viner and the failed Rain King, which is a main theme of the book, is profoundly ambiguous. While the ending is on an upturn, the general air is one of aridity and disillusionment. One feels that Jan Mark has journeyed to the farthest frontier of children's literature, and possibly across it. But the old humorous Jan Mark is very much alive in *Hairs in the Palm of the Hand* . . . , a pair of hilarious long-short stories about goings-on in school. (p. 335)

John Rowe Townsend, ''Since 1973 (i): Older Fiction,'' in his Written for Children: An Outline of English-Language Children's Literature, *second revised edition, J. B. Lippincott, 1983, pp. 329-40.**

AIDAN CHAMBERS

[There] are several children's writers whose short stories I always look forward to reading, and the one I . . . [want to talk about] is Jan Mark. . . . [*Nothing to Be Afraid Of*] indicated just how appropriate the [short story] form is for her talents. The collection is funny, uncomfortably accurate in its dialogue and in the persuasiveness of its narrative situations, and written throughout with the combination of an unflinchingly sharp eye for human foible and a detached sympathy for the underdog— even for rather unattractive underdogs—that makes fiction, in the hands of a writer of Jan Mark's outstanding quality, more potent than real life for the observing reader. And this volume is so coolly well judged for the nine-to-thirteen-year-olds that I wonder if someone didn't provoke Jan Mark by saying, ''I'll bet you can't write really catchy stories for pubescent youngsters—especially the ones who don't want to bother reading at all!'' If someone did, he or she lost the bet.

Nothing to Be Afraid Of is full of pawky rebels—quiet, shy rebels, some of them, but indomitable always. At one extreme there's flat-faced Robin in the title story who "was not anything much, except four years old, and he looked a lot younger; probably because nothing ever happened to him." Something does happen to him, though: His cousin Anthea tries her best to scare the living daylights out of this timid mouse—only to find the tables turned on her next morning when, after a terrified night, Robin asks to be taken back to the supposedly spooky places where Anthea tried to frighten him. At the other extreme is the usually submissive, always well-behaved twelve-year-old Brenda who is forced into such an excruciatingly cruel and all-too-true dilemma by rival schoolteachers using her as their shuttlecock that she solves the problem by giving up both of the out-of-school activities that give her pleasure—a protest neither teacher will ever notice or would care about if they did. (pp. 667-68)

[*Feet* is] a collection of four new stories and four reprinted from other anthologies, a book most likely to be enjoyed by eleven-to-sixteen-year-olds. *Feet* displays the mature work of a writer who has quarried a place of distinction for herself among British children's writers. The private hurts of adolescence provide the linking, thematic core of the book, the kinds of wounded love being the stories' shared subject. It is through the precision of the dialogue and by the perspicacity of the narrators' comparisons between event and image that the attention is held. A scalpel-sharp irony adds a dissecting humor. And each story employs an extended metaphor, generally signaled by the title, to provide what an actor would call "the through line" to the drama.

The title story, for example, uses a school tennis match—a sporting metaphor for the sport of adolescent love-games—and is told in the first person by Jane Turner, an inexperienced umpire who takes foot-faulting revenge (deliberately or, as she claims, only in the way of doing her job?) on a player for an unrequited teenaged crush. **"Posts and Telecommunications"** follows, an image for the distance between children and selfish parents and how they don't communicate. Isobel, her mother dead, isolated in boarding school, so hates telephones as a means of talking to her always professional father that she calls it *telephobia*, "not understanding," the narrator remarks, "its literal meaning which was more accurate than she knew." In the end Isobel, like Jane, takes her revenge, using her father's "ansafone" to do the job—emotional distance turned by telephone against her distant father. If she can't have her father's love, she'll make sure her father gets none, either.

Other stories use railway travel, a school play, music, an art school still life, and the perils of revivalist religion for their images. "The End of Childhood Innocence" could be the book's subtitle. What saves the stories from being as bitter and as dark as my summaries have perhaps made you think they are is that behind all of them is a vibrant mind informed by an inventive imagination taking all its cues from everyday realities but transforming our view of their darker side by an enlivening wit. Jan Mark is a life preserver in every sense. Reading her stories of private hurts makes all private hurts more bearable and less crushing.

In addition—and this is enough to give her distinction—what gives me as much pleasure as anything else about her work is the confident ease and the energy with which she tells her stories and achieves that primary element, the intermeshing unity of every feature. The language, the narrative voice, the plot, the sides of the characters she chooses to show, the thematic ideas, the way the plot dramatizes them, and the metaphoric structure that holds everything together and gives the

story its referential life and density of meaning: Everything is focused to a single beam as through a lens.

For my part, only one thing is lacking in Jan Mark's work. I wish she would explore her narrative techniques more than she does. Very rarely does she break out of the familiar mode of first or third person, consistently used, a chronological sequencing of the plot with perhaps a flashback here and there. And, as I say, she does all this with such confident assurance that I wonder why she doesn't try fresh treatments. Which is only to say that the writers who give you the most satisfaction are also the ones you are never satisfied with. (pp. 668-69)

One of the topics that preoccupies me constantly at present is the nature of narrative technique. Hence, I wonder about it in Jan Mark's work, because I admire her work very greatly. But, in fact, such a remark falls into the trap awaiting bad reviewers—the trap of writing about the book you would prefer to have read because you would prefer to have written it, rather than about the book the author produced. Technique is no problem for Jan Mark or for her readers; it is a problem only for me. (p. 670)

> *Aidan Chambers, "Letters From England: A Mark of Distinction," in* The Horn Book Magazine, *Vol. LX, No. 5, September-October, 1984, pp. 665-70.*

DAVID REES

[*The following excerpt is a slightly revised version of an essay that originally appeared in the September, 1981 issue of the* School Librarian.]

Few first novels have achieved such acclaim as Jan Mark's *Thunder and Lightnings.* . . . It is a remarkable book in many ways, but its huge critical success has ultimately done its writer a disservice by helping to obscure the very considerable merits of the rest of her work. One view of Jan Mark's novels, as expressed by Peter Hunt in his essay "Whatever Happened to Jan Mark?" [see excerpt above dated 1980], suggests that her progress has been downhill all the way, a descent into fashionable obscurity of meaning; that spontaneous, genuinely felt life has been edged out of her writing by contrived, conventional plots; that, somehow, winning the prizes turned her head and made her produce smart, pseudo-clever novels beloved only by some in-group of children's book people. This view of Jan Mark seems to me to be wholly wrong, and particularly irritating is the idea that winning literary awards is likely to divert an author of integrity from what he or she really should be doing. Robert Westall wrote, in 1979, that winning the Carnegie made *him* write "books for the children of publishers, librarians and the literary gent of The Times," and while this may well be a truthful statement about the stories that he wrote for a period following *The Machine-Gunners,* he is probably quite exceptional in having been influenced in such a manner. His comment is not valid as far as Jan Mark or other Carnegie winners are concerned.

The assessment by Peter Hunt of Jan Mark's books is a rather long-winded way of asking why she did not write another novel just like *Thunder and Lightnings*—a common enough complaint by readers of a book they have thoroughly enjoyed, who are disappointed to find that other stories by the same author do not encapsulate them in the same world. In fact, *Thunder and Lightnings* is unique; any attempt to repeat it would be disastrous. The development of the slightly uneasy friendship between the two central characters, Andrew and Victor, is beautifully done—the joyous surface of the book masks the underlying tensions and complexities, so that the reader is aware only at certain points that its theme is, to quote Andrew's mother—

> There's no such thing as fairness. It's a word made up to keep children quiet. When you discover it's a fraud, then you're starting to grow up.

That life is very often an unjust, unpleasant and bloody battleground, a struggle for the survival of the fittest, is the theme of all Jan Mark's novels; but in *Thunder and Lightnings* it is on the whole buried beneath a very rich texture of incident, anecdote, and detail about two contrasting households, school life, the patterns of living in rural Norfolk, aircraft, comic dialogue and characters, and some very evocative writing that varies from the poetic and sensuous to the amusingly grotesque:

> The house was long and low, lurking behind the bushes with its head down.

> At once, the little sound changed to a furious roar, so suddenly that he half expected to see the sky crazed all over like a cracked bowl.

> Bob had the kind of moustache that parrots could perch on and rarely said anything other than ''Bang on!''

> ''Yes, but that's not right to spoil a funeral,'' said Victor. ''After all, that's the last party you ever have.''

Thunder and Lightnings is an unusual book in that it is almost entirely without a plot; an extreme example, in fact, of a story that has no recognizable beginning, middle, and end. Its apparently disconnected events are a way, in fact, of showing the development of the friendship between Victor and Andrew, and the recurring motifs—the guinea-pigs, for instance, or Victor's attempts to draw, and, above all, the airplanes—are not only realistic details of the boys' lives but they act as metaphors for the different stages of their relationship. Andrew and Victor *are* the story, the essence of it:

> Wearing only a singlet and shorts, Victor looked unprotected, as if he had gone into battle without his armor. Possibly he felt unprotected too. Anyone who habitually went about wearing four or five layers of clothing was bound to feel at a loss when he took them off. If he was allowed to compete in his usual clothes, he might sweep the field, winning every event, if he weren't earthbound by the weight.

Here is Andrew, a very different kind of person, but also another loner:

> Then he found a lump on his neck and hoped that his tonsils might be swelling up, but he couldn't make them hurt, no matter how hard he prodded. He looked at his watch. It was a quarter to nine. He thought, in exactly twelve hours' time the bus will be stopping in Polthorpe and I shall be walking up the path into school. The very thought was enough to give him a clutching sort of pain, exactly where he thought his heart must be, but it passed away, almost before he had time to feel it. He went over to the window and looked out, kneeling on the floor with his chin wedged against the sill.

The difference between them is summed up by Victor's comment ''I don't want to learn things; I'd rather just find out.'' Andrew, on the other hand, is much happier doing what he is told to do. This kind of writing is similar to that of Paula Fox, who, in *Portrait of Ivan* and *The Stone-Faced Boy,* moves the plotless novel almost to the point where the author is in danger of losing the reader: there is a welter of extraneous detail and events that are, seemingly, not germane. Paula Fox, however, does manage to reassure us that she knows what she is doing; by the end of the story we know the relevance of that attention to detail and why certain incidents that seemed so unimportant at the time were included. But there are moments in *Thunder and Lightnings* when Jan Mark seems to be flying dangerously by the seat of her pants, moments when she really is unsure which direction the book is taking—what follows is there only because there has to be something—anything—that happens next. The two opening pages of chapter thirteen are a good example. What is happening sounds flat and inconsequential; the prose, accordingly, becomes clumsy. The description of the wind being ''like a mean child who jeered round corners and disappeared when you followed it'' is a feeble grasping after effect compared with, say, the scene in chapter eleven where the boys are looking at an ordnance map ''patterned all over with the ghostly bones of dead airfields.''

Thunder and Lightnings, good though it may be, *is* a first novel, and close examination of the text reveals uncertainties and weaknesses—the strained, too literary image; the incident that has no real purpose—that disappear in its successors. *Under the Autumn Garden* may be a less appealing book, but it is more subtle. Matthew, the central character, does not possess Andrew's cool intelligence, nor does he have Victor's attractive energy; there is less humor and what remains of it is more sardonic, and the adults are either unsympathetic or rather nasty. But there are very few weak moments in the writing. A house is described as having a ''roof like a quilt thrown over an unmade bed'' and Matthew at one point says ''She goes on, whaa-whaa-whaa, just like a chain saw.'' In this second apparently plotless novel, the author now seems to be in control of all the different elements. It isn't without story in quite the same way as *Thunder and Lightnings.* It consists of several small stories that illustrate the various areas of Matthew's life— the history project at school; the Bagnalls and their six cats; the attempt to establish the fact that Sir Oliver of Hoxenham really existed; the unhappy relationship with the children of the builder who is repairing the house next door. In each of these a crisis occurs, and Matthew, being a rather weak character who lacks sufficient inner resources and strengths to face trouble, comes almost to the point of breakdown. (This is exactly the same theme as *Divide and Rule,* but in the latter work Jan Mark explores it more powerfully.) Matthew in fact does not break down, and the ending of the book, with the discovery of Sir Oliver's ring, suggests a note of cautious optimism, of recovery.

This is symbolized very effectively by the hole Matthew has been digging, which is the most striking image in the book. Trying to uncover the garden and search for the remains of a medieval priory is a ridiculous thing to do, quite beyond the abilities of one boy, and it is not surprising that nobody will take him very seriously. As the novel progresses, however, the function of the hole becomes more metaphorical than actual—it is Matthew burying his head in the sand, hiding away from unpleasant realities. Indeed, for one brief moment, it becomes a sort of troglodyte dwelling, used by the horrible Angel girls as a house. They, too, are running away from reality, but, unfortunately, they cannot understand Matthew's problems, nor he theirs. Eventually the hole ceases to have any point as symbol or actuality, and Matthew is forbidden to dig in it any longer. By this stage he no longer cares—he has stopped running away. He suffers from having no outlet for his anger. "That's a good fuel, anger," Victor says in *Thunder and Lightnings*. So it may be, up to a point: Victor cannot respond angrily to his mother's unfair treatment of him, but at least he can come third in a race when the rest of the school laugh at him for entering it. Matthew is in a worse situation. He is thwarted at every turn, and, without the ability to hit back, he allows his anger and frustration to turn in on himself where it operates, of course, destructively.

As with its predecessor, the texture of *Under the Autumn Garden* is extremely rich. The patterns of rural life are once again part of the story—we are in the same village, and some of the characters in *Thunder and Lightnings* play minor roles in this novel. There is the same verbal dexterity, the point made in a few striking words:

> Matthew reflected that people were not, after all, interested in his school work. They were only interested in him doing it.

And a similar use is made of detail that is seemingly irrelevant, but which provides an illuminating comment on character and situation:

> The sands and the sea were empty: he walked down to the edge of the water and sat there, letting the buzz go out of his ears. A little flat dog minced along the sand, glanced at Matthew, and sat down a few yards away, courteously looking out to sea instead of grinning at him after the fashion of solitary dogs. After a while it got up and walked quietly away. He was almost sorry to see it go.
>
> It was such a gentlemanly dog.

Matthew is courteous, gentlemanly, "flat"—too much so: these attributes almost ruin him. It is interesting that this passage is the only point in the book where the sea is mentioned, and yet Matthew lives only a short distance from the beach. This is right, for he cannot yet find himself in the vast expanses that sea and sand imply; his head and his heart are buried in a hole.

If there is a weakness in *Under the Autumn Garden*, it is that neither the reader nor Matthew discover until almost the end of the book that Mrs. Angel has left home and abandoned her children. It is true that the story demands that this information be hidden from the reader, but there is no convincing reason why Matthew's parents should not tell him. This is the only moment when it is difficult to believe in what is happening, so that the ultimate disclosure of the fact seems artificially contrived. No such weakness is apparent in Jan Mark's third novel, *The Ennead*. At first sight, nothing more different from its predecessors could be imagined. Rural Norfolk has been replaced by life on Erato, a planet in a remote galaxy; we are in the future instead of the present; it is about adults, not children; it is science fiction rather than the expected children's novel, with a well-organized, fast-moving story-line, a plot instead of incidents, action instead of metaphor, image, and dense texture. But the themes of the book are a development of those explored in *Under the Autumn Garden*. Once again, *The Ennead* is a story about the struggle of the individual to remain alive, his integrity intact, in a wholly alien and hostile

society. Here, in a novel which is much more likely to be read by teenagers than younger children, it is possible to go further; there is no hope at the end: Eleanor, Moshe, and Isaac opt for an almost certain death rather than submit to the stultifying prurient mores of Erato. How much should one compromise in order to find a place in the world is a question *The Ennead* poses: how far should one conform to a morality that entirely ruins the good in people? Not at all, Jan Mark seems to be saying. Isaac, who has posed as a conformist for the whole of his life, has had most of his natural fellow-feeling destroyed; but not quite all: in helping Eleanor to escape from the wrath of the inhabitants of Epsilon, he knows he will suffer the same fate as she will. The one area of unselfishness left in him is his undoing.

The message is bleak, but not totally despairing. Moshe, Isaac and Eleanor have courage and a tremendous inner toughness; Moshe and Eleanor have dignity as well, and an ability to love. On Erato, where population control, dislike, suspicion, and minding everybody else's business are the norm, such people are particularly vulnerable. Even inspecting a mural is seen as an anti-social act:

> "What are you doing, looking at our wall?" Barnet demanded.
>
> "Isn't it meant to be looked at?"

Human love—particularly sexual love—is frowned on more than anything else:

> Isaac, like everyone else, cast about covertly for the said fornicator. Don't be seen not wondering. No name was ever mentioned on such occasions; the threat was enough. Whoever the message was for knew that it was for him.

One is reminded of the follies of extreme puritan theocracies such as that of the original settlers in New England and the witch-hunts that led to the tragedies in Salem; and indeed Eleanor is exposed and pursued almost as if she was a witch. (pp. 62-9)

But *The Ennead*, of course, is not a historical novel: it is about a future that has its seeds in our immediate present. It is a picture of what life may well be like in a world that becomes too obsessed with population control, a world in which we abdicate our responsibilities to ourselves and each other and hand our consciences over to some outside authority such as the Church or the State. . . . *The Ennead* is not a bleak novel in emphasizing the fact that without the capacity to love, to be unselfish, to have courage to continue to make our own moral decisions, we cease to be viable human beings, and that when Authority will not allow us to be viable human beings, we are better off dead.

Parts of *The Ennead* portray the struggle between the individual and the dictates of organized religion, and Jan Mark's fourth novel, *Divide and Rule*, is almost wholly concerned with this struggle. . . . We are, once more, in a strange alien world, remote in place and time, but precisely where and when we are not told. This doesn't matter; the vagueness helps to universalize the message: the points made can be applied to *any* theocratic society. The story concerns Hanno, an eighteen-year-old boy, who is chosen by an absurd ritualistic mumbo-jumbo—so old that any meaning and purpose it may have had has long since been lost—to be the temple Shepherd for one year. (pp. 69-70)

He is more sheep than shepherd, more body than brain. Indeed the author draws attention to this more than once by suggesting that his name is like the sound of a sheep bleating. The other famous Hanno in contemporary children's fiction is the gorilla in Lucy Boston's *A Stranger at Green Knowe,* and maybe a parallel is intended. Both Hannos are unfortunate victims of an alien environment; neither can cope, and Jan Mark's Hanno is, physically, a bit of a gorilla—a big, shambling youth of little intelligence.

The message is similar to that of *The Ennead.* State or Church will go to any lengths to make the individual conform, and those that can't or won't conform are eliminated. It is a more disturbing book than *The Ennead,* because Hanno, likeable though he is, lacks the qualities we see in Moshe and Eleanor. The scheming, plotting Isaac—a typical example of the reed who bends in the wind—would have had a very successful and enjoyable year in the temple, but Hanno cannot bend. One major difference from *The Ennead*—and this makes *Divide and Rule* a novel of even less hope than its predecessor—is that the author seems to be implying here that if we want to survive we must force ourselves, for a time, into a pretense of conforming. Individual and society in *Divide and Rule* are totally at loggerheads. Which brings us back to *Thunder and Lightnings* and Andrew's mother:

> There's no such thing as fairness. It's a word made up to keep children quiet. When you discover it's a fraud, then you're starting to grow up.

Adulthood, Jan Mark seems to be saying in all her books, is at best messy, at worst brutish and nasty; the growing up processes involve coming to terms with these facts and making of them what you will—but if you totally reject the demands of authority, however worthy and fine your motives may be, you won't be able to escape punishment.

Aquarius . . . is as harsh and bleak as its predecessors. Once again we are in an unnamed country at an unspecified date, though the technology of the inhabitants suggests a time no later than the early Middle Ages. The central character, Viner, gets his name from his craft—that of a water diviner—but he finds he is living in the wrong place; his village is subjected to constant rain and almost nonstop flooding. The local people think he actually causes the rain, and drive him away. On his travels he reaches a country where there is unprecedented drought; the wells are drying up, and all the efforts of Morning Light, the rain-maker and king, to produce water are useless. Viner, after finding several new wells, becomes popular and politically powerful, but he refuses an arranged marriage that would make him the monarch: he is sexually attracted to Morning Light, and guesses, rightly, that the rain-king's gifts are the opposite of what is supposed—he causes droughts. He abducts Morning Light (considerable physical violence is involved in this) and takes him back to his own village: Viner has now got what he wants—status among his *own* people, and the man he desires is his virtual prisoner. . . . (pp. 70-2)

This is not a book for the backward reader. The prose makes few compromises—adult vocabulary often densely packed with imagery, long complex sentences—but almost always it is an effective instrument:

> The bridge was thriftily built at the river's narrowest point within the village boundary, and that circumstance, coupled with the fact that the two piles which supported the centre span

forced the water into turbulent rapids, ensured that the bridge was under constant assault from the pressure of the torrent beneath it, the author of its own destruction.

We have come a long way from the apparent simplicity of *Thunder and Lightnings.*

Aquarius has a well-constructed absorbing narrative, full of memorable characters and exciting incident—one thinks in particular of the scenes in which people struggle for political power when the rain-king is known to be a broken man—and it has many fine descriptive passages dealing with landscape and weather. The landscape is entirely fictitious, but it is made very real: "Nightfall found him limping among rubble on a blasted hillside where nothing stood except the dead bracken that crisped and crinkled underfoot"—and there is from time to time a skillful use of simile that is terse and evocative: "holding his breath and trembling like the dry twigs all about him."

There is no happy future ahead, at the end of the book, for Viner's relationship with Morning Light. Morning Light now hates Viner more than any other living person. The message is that in struggling for status people manipulate and use one another to the extent that love can be totally destroyed; that those who get exactly what they want may do immense harm to others and lose their own humanity. Affection, Jan Mark is saying, contains the seeds of possessiveness, and possessiveness is the opposite of freedom, for both parties concerned.

Scarcely anyone writing today presents youth with a more somber picture of life than does Jan Mark. Sometimes the reader may feel that her novels go to an extreme beyond which it is not possible to venture in books for children and teenagers. This doesn't matter: the harsh truths of her vision of the world are infinitely preferable to the cozy pap that is sometimes served up for the young. (pp. 72-3)

> *David Rees, "No Such Thing as Fairness: Jan Mark," in his* Painted Desert, Green Shade: Essays on Contemporary Writers of Fiction for Children and Young Adults, *The Horn Book Inc., 1984, pp. 62-74.*

LANCE SALWAY

Nothing much happens in [*Handles,*] . . . but Jan Mark's incisive humour will keep the attention of persistent readers to the end, despite a palpable lack of plot to lead them along.

Jan Mark's talent works best within a briefer compass. Her shorter stories for younger readers, like the two hilarious school comedies in *Hairs in the Palm of the Hand* . . . , display her sly wit and mordant observation of character to full advantage. *Feet and Other Stories* . . . is a collection of stylish stories for older readers, deceptively simple in form but rich in precise exploration of character and situation. The themes range from parental selfishness to teenage relationships, and all are models of their kind. . . . [*Feet*] is well worth buying for '**Posts and Telecommunications**' alone—a witty, bitter tale that should make any prospective purchaser of a telephone answering machine think twice.

> *Lance Salway, "Fiction: 'Handles'," in* The Signal Review 2: A Selective Guide to Children's Books 1983, *edited by Nancy Chambers, The Thimble Press, 1984, p. 41.*

THUNDER AND LIGHTNINGS (1976)

[The] stylish grace and perspective of [*Thunder and Lightnings*] direct it towards anyone at all (over the age of nine or ten) who is interested in the stages of an unlikely friendship. Andrew, middle-class with a father working on computers and a mother till recently a librarian, collects racing-cars and is sorry to leave town life and Brands Hatch for a Norfolk village: cottagebred Victor, who lives down the lane with a cold, house-proud mother, is an ardent (and erudite) collector of model aeroplanes and is classed as ineducable at the village school. Unerringly selecting detail and setting scenes, Jan Mark shows with humour and a pervasive light irony how far the two boys are conditioned by social background and how far they are independent of it as individuals. She is supremely successful in the way she leads us from one facet to another of Victor's character. We see him embarking on his chosen school project for the fourth time ("Fish are easy. They're all the same shape"), making his unique, coltishly wise approaches to Andrew's baby brother, regarding with silent contempt a know-all motorist who wrongly identifies 'planes landing at Coltishall. The eyes of all the characters turn towards Victor. We watch with Andrew's parents, with Victor's outrageous mother and with cheerful Andrew, as the country boy, classified once and for all by his teachers, defies classification. This is a book to be read at a sitting with delighted recognition of its wit and style, to be read again with renewed admiration of the depth of its simplicities. . . . It now remains to hope that Jan Mark is not a one-book woman; somehow I am sure she is not. (pp. 2939-40)

Margery Fisher, in a review of "Thunder and Lightnings," in Growing Point, *Vol. 15, No. 3, September, 1976, pp. 2939-40.*

[*Thunder and Lightnings*] is a significant pointer to a new style in books for children of the wide age group we cater for in the junior school. The technique of the teller of tales is shifting; the stance of the author is somewhere other than above the readers' heads. The rhetoric is changing to be nearer the TV dialogue that lets the reader/listener fill in what used to be 'description'. Compare the opening of this book with Penelope Lively's *A Stitch in Time* . . . . Both begin with the end of a journey by car. The redundancy of Miss Lively's introduction is pared away almost to Mayne-like ellipsis in Mrs Mark, but the details stand out, crystal clear. . . .

[For] the first time for ages I'm intrigued by the positive estimation of readers by an author who undertakes a much subtler relationship of text and message for children younger than twelve, and who counts on their *good sense* (the best thing about the pre-logical stage) and sympathetic response. This is a most important book.

Margaret Meek, in a review of "Thunder and Lightnings," in The School Librarian, *Vol. 24, No. 3, September, 1976, p. 226.*

Jan Mark has given a vivid account of the relationship between two boys who find a common enthusiasm for aeroplanes—the Lightnings of the title. She has an unerring eye for the narrow-minded prejudices and obsessive cleanliness of the ambitious working classes and the slap-happy scruffiness of the professional middle classes—a reversal of the more usual presentation. But it is her understanding of Victor . . . [and Andrew] and the way the two boys are enriched by their friendship which makes the book such compulsive reading.

Valerie Alderson, in a review of "Thunder and Lightnings," in Children's Book Review, *Vol. VI, October, 1976, p. 39.*

Thunder and Lightnings is a book which sparkles with humour—sometimes gentle and sometimes irreverent, frequently at the expense of adults . . . : it is teachers and institutions that are the particular butt. . . .

[There] are a number of social and educational issues which the book will raise in the mind of the concerned teacher—issues similar, in many ways, to those of *A Kestrel for a Knave*, by Barry Hines—and the danger is that these will cloud the awareness of, and delight in, the other facets of *Thunder and Lightnings*. (p. 19)

The teacher will see at once the parallel with students he has taught who show no real absorption in any schoolwork, even when free to choose, but who may be extremely intelligent and knowledgeable about subjects they *are* interested in—yet one that is too private and precious to be "spoiled" by the school ethos. And the teacher will know the anxieties over how to reach that student and attempt to draw out some of that potential for his own sake, without appearing to intrude on his privacy. Such an awareness will enable the teacher to point out the factors in Victor's background which affect his attitudes and motivation. For Victor, there is no middle-class expectation of "doing well" for himself, either from his parents or in his own mind, and he has a quietly wry acceptance of the situation: when he and Andrew are working together on the project, and Andrew tries to encourage him to read, he says,

> That's no good you trying to teach me anything. I'll never be any use. I don't think I even want to be. If you start being good at something, people expect you to be even better and then they get annoyed when you aren't. That's safer to seem a bit dafter than you are.

And when their afternoon out is spoiled by his mother's punishment for his dropping a newly-laundered sheet in the dirt, he understands the way things are while Andrew is protesting at home, "It wasn't fair."

> "Nothing's fair," said Mum. "There's no such thing as fairness. It's a word made up to keep children quiet. When you discover it's a fraud then you're starting to grow up. The difference between you and Victor is that you're still finding out and he knows perfectly well already."

Where Andrew needs to be told that, Victor already has a quiet maturity in his understanding of the way the world works for people like himself, and a gently humorous acceptance of this. He has worked out the least troublesome way of dealing with the needs of life—such as projects which, for some reason, teachers will require him to do. Following on from Victor's point that fish are "easy," Andrew suggests worms:

> "Nothing could be easier than worms. Wiggle-wiggle-wiggle: all over in a second. Page one, worms are long and thin. Page two, worms are round."

> Victor began to grin . . . "I reckon you're catching on," he said. "Why don't you do worms?"

> "I want to do something interesting," said Andrew.

"Ho," said Victor. "You'll come to a bad end, you will."

And later, when Andrew asks him why he doesn't do a project on aeroplanes, after some thought Victor decides,

If I started doing that for school, I wouldn't be interested in them any more. I don't care about fish, so I don't mind doing them. . . . It would be having to like aeroplanes instead of just liking them. Every time a Harrier went over I wouldn't be thinking, there go a Harrier, I'd think, there goes my project. Then I wouldn't like to look at it. Schools's like measles. That spread.

Andrew suggests they might work on it together, but one of them would have to learn to draw:

"Not me," said Victor. "There you go, you see. Just like measles. As soon as you put anything down on paper you have to start learning something. I don't want to learn things, I'd rather just find out."

That may well be a salutary lesson for the teacher to learn, or be reminded of, but I suspect that most of his students will take it for granted.

Victor's acceptance is not born of cowed passivity, however. He has built up his defences against a hostile and incomprehending world where they are necessary: in the classroom, against teachers in an amiable sort of way; at home, he has the refuge of his room. His layers of clothing, too, are symbolic: like a traveller on some picaresque journey through life, he feels safer and happier when he is wearing all his clothes at once, and only in very secure circumstances will he remove an item. An exception, however, to this, and to his acceptance of others' view of him, is when he enters the mile race on Sports Day; looking very vulnerable in only singlet and shorts, he comes in third. When Andrew questions him, he comments "That take a long time to run a mile. I had time to think."

"I thought about how they were all expecting me to come last. They thought that was a joke, me running a mile," said Victor. "Old Skelton's soft in the head. Nothing between the ears. Brains in the feet. So I have, though, if that's what make me run."

Andrew looked sideways at him and saw that his everlasting grin was a little fiercer, a little less amiable, than usual. "Were you angry, then?"

"I suppose I was," said Victor. "That's a good fuel, anger."

It is the grinning, witty, sometimes angry side of Victor which will interest the student reader in him as a character, and he *is* a rounded, varied individual irrespective of his sociological or educational significance. (Like some of Dickens' characters, he may be formed by his background, but his personality is what delights.) It is interesting, in this light, again to compare *A Kestrel for a Knave:* if the scenes in the libraries in the two novels are compared, a significant difference emerges. Billy Casper, thwarted by the rules in his attempt to borrow a book, is baffled and depressed, and eventually resorts to stealing; a comment is made on the whole "system" of school, home, and institutions, and we as readers feel totally depressed at the

hopeless situation. Victor, faced with the same frustrating delay (the library will be closed by the time they've had their forms signed) and watched all the way out by the librarian, turns at the door and makes the "sign against the evil eye"—to Andrew's chagrin and our amusement. He is definitely a survivor. (And his name *is* Victor.)

Jan Mark's deadpan style and ear for dialogue, particularly Victor's quick comments (of Andrew's baby brother who wakes up making "angry, whirring noises," "This baby will self-destruct in five seconds;" when Andrew mentions that the Egyptians used to fill mummies up with "something else"— "sage and onion?'; and when the artist in the graveyard comments honestly on his drawing, "terrible," "It's easy to see you're not a teacher," said Victor. "If you were a teacher you'd say, 'That's awfully good, what is it?'") all contribute to this atmosphere of ultimate survival. Even though Victor's favourite aircraft, the Lightnings, are being phased out—the ultimate disappointment and loss in terms of what he values most—nevertheless we have a sense of triumph in the long, daring dive of the last one the boys are able to watch; and we feel, with Mrs. Mitchell, that perhaps he will transfer his enthusiasm, if not his allegiance, to another aircraft in time. (pp. 20-3)

> *Robbie March-Penney, "I Don't Want to Learn Things, I'd Rather Just Find Out: Jan Mark's 'Thunder and Lightnings',"* in Children's literature in education, *Vol. 10, No. 1 (Spring), 1979, pp. 18-24.*

[Andrew and Victor's] relationship is depicted with humor and subtlety; the story, though, is seriously weakened by an actionless plot and unnatural, moralizing dialogue. Young readers will find that most of the thunder and lightning has been taken from this tale, leaving a trail of invisible exhaust.

> *Jack Forman, in a review of "Thunder and Lightnings,"* in School Library Journal, *Vol. 25, No. 8, April, 1979, p. 70.*

Thunder and Lightnings is not a school story in the normal sense; little of it happens in school. Nor is it a story in the normal sense; little out of the ordinary happens. . . . (pp. 58-9)

The book's overt theme is coming to terms with transience: Victor's beloved Lightnings, which he is always cycling miles to see on local airfields, are being replaced by Jaguars. "Everything go. Everything go that you like best. That never come back," he says, in his dialect. The resolution of this problem is positive and unsentimental. But the book's lasting impression is the vivid contrast between Victor's silent, oppressive, obsessively clean home and Andrew's, which is noisy, lively, chaotic, and human. In fact, the book is a series of contrasts: between appearance and reality, official estimation and real worth, formal schooling and out-of-school learning, artificial projects and genuine interests, fear and love. It is rare for adults to count for much in children's books, but Andrew's Mum is a memorable, fully realised creation: witty, playful, wise, and caring. Andrew says, "Mum never says what she means. She says something different and you have to guess."

That is also partly true of Jan Mark's accomplished technique. For all her serious intent, she has a light touch, a flare for word play, and a warm sense of fun. She handles feelings with honesty and tact, and has a keen eye for significant detail in everyday things and events. Nothing extraordinary happens in this book—except for a little growth in understanding in ways which schools rarely wittingly provide. (p. 59)

Graham Hammond, in a review of "Thunder and Lightnings," in Children's literature in education, *Vol. 13, No. 2 (Summer), 1982, pp. 58-9.*

UNDER THE AUTUMN GARDEN   (1977)

Measuring a writer's latest work against her previous one always was a bore, as well as being unhelpful. A story is a story is a story. . . . So I'm glad I hadn't read *Thunder and Lightnings* when I picked up Jan Mark's second novel, for it stands up marvellously in its own right, both for adult and young readers. It's exciting to stumble across someone with such a talent for storytelling.

Matthew is a 10-year-old living in a Norfolk village. He's in trouble at school for not doing a history project, which he finds boring. His mum's a dinner lady at the school—so he's in trouble at home as well. On top of this, his house, garden and most of his waking hours are temporarily invaded by a wayward and motherless family of five children, whose builder father is renovating the house next door.

Matthew has his own history project—the cause of as well as the escape from many of his problems and anxieties. He digs in the overgrown garden next door in a determined search for relics from the medieval priory that once stood there. The story concerns his attempts to ward off the interferences of the other children, and to cope with the amusement, scepticism and indifference of most of the adults around him.

To Matthew, life begins to seem like a great conspiracy, abounding in casual put-downs and unjust rebuffs. People are not after all interested in his school work, he reflects, only in him doing it. Jan Mark tells the tale through his eyes with vivid economy and a wry assurance.

The novel's apparent simplicity and everydayness belies a richness of characterization, and a superb feel for the shape of a story. Matthew's small triumph at the end is believably apt. If there's a flaw, it's in the writer's evident relish for language, which just occasionally allows her to slip a rather adult perception into Matthew's vision.

Jonathan Croall, "Coping with Adults," in The Times Educational Supplement, *No. 3269, February 3, 1978, p. 36.*

The background outshines the foreground in this English novel. . . . [The] jackpot ending is unconvincing: Matthew casually finds a ring that he suspects belonged to Sir Oliver, village ghost. . . . The plot meanders and some of the characters drown in their own mannerisms, but the details of everyday life in rural England will give readers a feeling for the frugal, hardworking people enviably rich in traditions and community. Some of the language is unfamiliar but the author writes vividly, and her descriptions are pungent.

Marilyn R. Singer, in a review of "Under the Autumn Garden," in School Library Journal, *Vol. 26, No. 1, September, 1979, p. 144.*

[*Under the Autumn Garden* is] a book that is rich in characterization, sensitive to relationships among children, lightened by the humor of the dialogue and colored by local idiom. A gentle and perceptive story is distinctively English in flavor but its differences should present no barrier to enjoyment by children elsewhere.

Zena Sutherland, in a review of "Under the Autumn Garden," in Bulletin of the Center for Children's Books, *Vol. 33, No. 2, October, 1979, p. 32.*

Jan Mark's Norfolk people sound consistently right and once again her dialogue is richly funny without ever being facetious; *Under the Autumn Garden* . . . deals in small events with large implications, farce trembling on the edge of everyday tragedy: it deserves as many awards as her earlier *Thunder and Lightnings.*

Audrey Laski, "Innocent Naughtiness, Good Magic," in The Times Educational Supplement, *No. 3368, January 9, 1981, p. 23.**

Jan Mark has a reputation for creating slightly prickly, sometimes none too loveable characters, but this is what real people are, and set in her interesting and amusing plot they bring great life to the story. . . . Lots of unexpected twists and turns make a very amusing story.

Eileen A. Archer, in a review of "Under the Autumn Garden," in Book Window, *Vol. 8, No. 2, Spring, 1981, p. 25.*

THE ENNEAD   (1978)

[*The Ennead*] is science ficion set on an arid mining planet named Erato, member of a nine-planet system settled by colonists from a now dead Earth. The story is told from the viewpoint of 15-year-old Isaac, foster son of a dead trader, Swenson. Through trickery, Isaac has gotten himself appointed steward for the household of Swenson's son Theodore, eventually revealed as Isaac's half-brother. Isaac unwittingly disrupts the tightly controlled, status-conscious society of Erato when, to buttress his scheme for security and power, he imports a sculptor named Eleanor from the over-populated planet of Euterpe. But her devotion to her craft confuses Isaac and his friend Moshe, a gardener, is inspired by Eleanor to a show of defiance that leads to his banishment to Euterpe. Eleanor soon earns the same but manages to escape, and the end finds Isaac rushing to her aid and both of them facing almost certain death. The author's depiction of Erato is vivid. Unfortunately, the characters lack appeal; Moshe is shadowy until the end; Eleanor doesn't appear till the second third of the book; Isaac's weak and scheming personality is superbly rendered but will not attract young teens, and his turnabout at the end is not plausible.

Margaret A. Dorsey, in a review of "The Ennead," in School Library Journal, *Vol. 25, No. 2, October, 1978, p. 157.*

The Ennead has two ringing messages to put over—"This is what we are like" and "This is what we might be like if . . .". The two themes are neither mutually exclusive nor interchangeable, and in fact it is their juxtaposition that gives a structural and moral unity to a remarkable book. . . . The reader soon perceives, as Isaac realises only slowly and painfully, that Eleanor and her friend, the gardener Moshe, are in fact changing the boy, forcing him to sacrifice comfort and intrigue and stand with them against the bureaucracy and the deadening isolationism of the citizens of Epsilon. Analogies with our time are not hard to find in the events of the story—crypto-racism, the persecution of Jewish minorities, social greed, police corruption, the erosion of civil liberties—and these analogies are cunningly presented in terms of a world which, in spite of them, is utterly alien in appearance, atmosphere and ideology.

Jan Mark has gone further than any writer I know in the broad spectrum of space-fiction, except for André Norton, in suggesting a different *kind* of human nature. These are people, with arms, legs, eyes and speech like our own, but they are not like us, they are terrifyingly alien, their personalities shaped by cold, distance, stone. Through clipped, elliptical dialogue and sparse, precisely directed description, Jan Mark has given us a glimpse, a clear and challenging glimpse, of one possible direction for our species. (pp. 3413-14)

> *Margery Fisher, in a review of "The Ennead," in* Growing Point, *Vol. 17, No. 4, November, 1978, pp. 3413-14.*

[Ruth Nichols' *The Left-Handed Spirit* and Jan Mark's **The Ennead**] are, in effect, two pictures of strong women, one cast in the remote past and one in the remote future. Everything about each book—the style, the concepts, the syntax—fits its time period well, as least insofar as we have prescribed such a fitness, and both are very good indeed, even remarkable. (p. E1)

[**The Ennead**] moves quickly and its style, since it needn't heed precedent, is fresh and winning. It will be classed as science fiction but it isn't that, exactly, for it doesn't concern itself at all with the gadgetry and pageant of *Star Wars* or with the cosmic grandeur of *A Wrinkle In Time*. It is about people who will seem familiar to the reader, though they are stylized to an extent, and about a place which seems reasonable, now that we have photographs of the surface of the moon. There is no space-age jargon or machinery and there isn't a cliché in it anywhere. Instead, it is sharp, witty, and clean. In case you had begun to think that the language had yielded up all its treasures long since, read **The Ennead** and be reassured. The storyline is not new, the ending predictable and perhaps, the one genuine cliché, but the language is delicious throughout. (p. E2)

> *Natalie Babbitt, "Women of Distant Worlds," in* Book World—The Washington Post, *November 12, 1978, pp. E1-E2.**

Although **The Ennead** is superficially a science-fiction novel, it is essentially a book about people, about the ways in which we exploit each other and are exploited in our turn and the possibility of breaking out of the vicious circle of behaviour which this mutual exploitation creates. . . . The vision of the future and of human nature in **The Ennead** is a bleak one, and to read the book is to undergo an emotionally shattering experience. The reader is kept on the edge of his seat waiting for a redeeming miracle. None comes.

> *Neil Philip, "Against the Tide," in* The Times Educational Supplement, *No. 3308, November 24, 1978, p. 43.**

Jan Mark is a writer of great resource and greater potential, but who would have thought that she had a surprise of this magnitude up her sleeve? **The Ennead** is not only very different from her previous books, it belongs to quite a different league. (p. 56)

The tragic centrepiece of this magnificent story is not perhaps Isaac, certainly not Eleanor whose role is that of catalyst, but Moshe, the silent gardener of the neighbouring estate, whose mass of hair conceals a man of extreme beauty. Moshe is the archetypal Jew, the man born to suffering and to keeping alive the story of his people. He too goes down in the general ruin.

Only the conformers survive, and for them the future may not be long.

There is little for comfort here, only perhaps the lesson that integrity is its own reward. It is some indication of the power of her writing that Miss Mark leaves us exhilarated rather than depressed. As an exercise in detailed imagining **The Ennead** is indeed remarkable. Every detail of the ghastly world of Erato has been worked out consistently. The satire is sharp, the humour controlled and bitter. The book belongs not with conventional science-fiction but with *Utopia* and other records of lost opportunities. (p. 57)

> *M. Crouch, in a review of "The Ennead," in* The Junior Bookshelf, *Vol. 43, No. 1, February, 1979, pp. 56-7.*

[A] summary can give no idea of the book's mood, which is at once light, humorous and serious; of the subtlety with which the relationship between Isaac and Eleanor is portrayed; or of the skill with which the viciousness of the small protection-racket man, Gregor, and the sadism of the lazy policeman, are shown to be a pervasive influence without the tone of the book becoming corrosive. Jan Mark is definitely here to stay.

> *Norman Culpan, in a review of "The Ennead," in* The School Librarian, *Vol. 27, No. 1, March, 1979, p. 58.*

DIVIDE AND RULE (1979)

Jan Mark's disturbing **Divide and Rule** has much to say, and little of it palatable. It is a bleak, unhappy, difficult book, its concerns, the corruption of power and humanity's capacity for self-delusion, those of adolescents and adults rather than children. After the harsh power of **The Ennead, Divide and Rule,** in which an unscrupulous priestly caste use the sceptical Hanno for their own ends and then engineer his mental breakdown, seems thin, though assured. Its setting, a cross between that of Brian Aldiss's *Malacia Tapestry* and that of Peter Dickinson's *The Blue Hawk*, is unconvincing after the powerfully conceived planet of Erato in **The Ennead**, and instead of the balance of interest between three characters offered by that book **Divide and Rule** concentrates on one, Hanno. The other actors are faceless, and as a consequence the dialogue falters and becomes stilted on occasion.

Still, if it is slightly disappointing by the high standards Jan Mark has previously set, **Divide and Rule** has much to offer: a fine awareness of momentary perceptions, a thought-provoking examination of human motives, a well-drawn central character and an intensity of purpose which borders on the claustrophobic.

> *Neil Philip, "Stark Mountains, Haunted Valleys," in* The Times Educational Supplement, *No. 3312, November 30, 1979, p. 25.**

Hanno is the drop-out son of a well-to-do, fond family. He has chosen the drifting occupaton of waterman—"gone to the bad in a boat". The truth is that he has secret problems of seeing: though at the sunny opening of the story it is not clear if this is the whole reason for his taking to the river. He seems generally to be a nonconformist; certainly in the matter of religion. He avoids going to the temple, if he can; is impatient with the need to offer himself, the next day, as a candidate for the role of Shepherd. The chosen young man must spend a year in the temple—an unthinkable fate, acting as a sort of "coathanger, something to carry the sacred vestments". Hanno won't be chosen, of course: he is a convinced and, surely, obvious disbeliever. In any case, he has an appointment with Anise, the steadiest of his many unsteady girls.

It is a measure of Jan Mark's skill, but perhaps a cause of later dissatisfactions, that you do not ask yourself when and where this is happening. She creates an absorbing small model world. The choice does fall on Hanno. Even the tradition that the Shepherd must be unwilling hardly covers his stormy reluctance. But he is in the hands of the Guardians: rather as if the sulkiest rebel in the school were imprisoned for a year in the prefects' room. There are Handmaidens, too, but at least one of these, Hanno feels, might subject him to the unholiest of assaults. There is also Aram, the madman who leads a tolerated existence in the hinterland of the altar. Aram foretells his own death, without a mark upon him. He lives in a tent roofed with an old tapestry depicting an earlier tradition of the Shepherd being sacrificed at the year's end. . . .

Now, all this is very well done. The narrative has great energy: one is soon in a world of interlocking paranoias: a sort of lucid uncertainty as to the meaning of any event is finely suggested. But then the tempo increases, together with the sheer density of the tale. Aram is found dead: he has no mark upon him: it looks as though Hanno might be cast as the Ritual Murderer. He discovers that the Book, the bible of the faith, is (and clearly always has been) constantly rewritten.

He determines not to play his part in this: he will, in his final appearance as Shepherd, testify against it all. But even his refusals and rebellions, he finds, are capable of being written into the Book. He stumbles out, his year over, robbed of health, reason, family, identity and even pity. No one cares.

So in the end it turns out to be the beautifully told, unbearable tale of the destruction of an attractive, sane human being. It is at this point that one begins to wonder about that subtly undescribed society in which it all occurs. Given a theocracy that could produce Hanno, would it produce only Hanno? What are missing from this story, I think, are Hanno's allies. It is painfully unfair on its hero.

> *Edward Blishen, "Hanno's Choice," in* The Times Literary Supplement, *No. 4004, December 14, 1979, p. 122.*

It is something of a tour de force to create so hazy and yet so compelling an imaginary world as Hanno inhabits. There are echoes of every theocracy that ever ruled in this powerful story of an unwilling participant in the religious life of his society. . . .

Capital letters are much in use giving a pseudo esoteric flourish to the conversation and activities in the Temple with its Guardians, Handmaidens and Ritual Maniac who is given to declaiming prophecies rather like T. S. Eliot at his most cryptic.

> The day of the worm cometh, and the sand shall run and run through the glass on that day.

The vocabulary is rich, varied and biblical. It effectively gives substance to this unrecognisable world with its superstition-ridden people who are weighed down by the traditions to which they cling. The reader must cope with such lines as

> One courting couple, so closely wrapped that they seemed to be encinctured with a single endless arm . . .

Is it to be taken as an Allegory? It is certainly an unusual story which the average reader may find difficult to grasp and identify with despite its brilliant style. Hanno is very much the tragic hero who fights hopelessly against the fates. It may be realistic but it is certainly a very cruel story.

> *D. A. Young, in a review of "Divide and Rule," in* The Junior Bookshelf, *Vol. 44, No. 1, February, 1980, p. 32.*

Alien figures and bizarre scientific devices can in skilful hands give readers shocks of terror and of speculation, but ***Divide and Rule*** gets under one's skin by a brilliant and sombre manipulation of a world which at first seems totally familiar. . . . It is open to any reader to extract a message from the story—about brain-washing, about integrity, about meaningless ritual. The author remains detached yet obviously committed by virtue of the sheer brutal, concrete detail through which we watch Hanno's disintegration. Her prose, stark yet graceful, has never been more effective in making explicit statements of action and speech beneath which reverberate trenchant and necessary meanings. (pp. 3655-56)

> *Margery Fisher, in a review of "Divide and Rule," in* Growing Point, *Vol. 18, No. 6, March, 1980, pp. 3655-56.*

When the time comes for Jan Mark's work to be looked at as a whole, some notice, lengthier than this, will be taken of her as a fabulist. From the tight stringing of her dialogue in ***Thunder and lightnings*** and the clarity of the internal weather of the hero in ***Under the autumn garden*** she moved to the stranger landscape of ***The Ennead***. She now takes up the powerful theme of belief, and its concomitant construct, knowing and being known. (p. 59)

The telling is deceptively simple and restrained, with sinewy power. The temple floor is tiled with ceramic flowers which Hanno names as he walks, a garden litany of the world he has left outside. The temple guards are sketched in hard outline. Their talk is prophecy and threat blending with each other. The power lies in what isn't actually said, all the things that anthropologists say escape them when they encounter strange cultures. Hanno is all the time treading on the hells underneath, yet this is only guessed at by the reader. The power of withheld explanations, as in *The turn of the screw*, is tremendous. That's what stories can do, and Jan Mark knows how. But Ursula Le Guin has more experience and knows better. The genuinely mythic is the constant challenge to writers for the young, but Jan Mark, as fabulist, measures up to the task. (pp. 59, 61)

> *Margaret Meek, in a review of "Divide and Rule," in* The School Librarian, *Vol. 28, No. 1, March, 1980, pp. 59, 61.*

Hanno is compelled to spend a year serving in the Temple of a nameless past civilization. This is about all there is in the way of plot: the book is really a study in the gratuitous breaking of a free spirit, the destruction of a child-like innocent in the name of a god in whom he does not even believe. Religion is pilloried as empty, ruthless, and treacherously manipulative. It kills Aram bodily and demands the sacrifice of Hanno's soul. It is an appalling game, in which the rules unpredictably change or are concealed from the players altogether. The winners are those professional servants of the god who *make* the rules, creating a ritual and a deity to serve themselves. Mark stacks the deck: there are no truly spiritual characters in the book. The followers of religion are deluded, hypocritical, foolish or venal: their ugly qualities, moreover, are the result of belief. The story is told from Hanno's perspective, and his disintegration is convincing. Mark's orchestration of words and symbols, the deft touches of humor and irony, do not, however, lighten the oppressive gloom. Less depressing, more subtle examination of the deadening psychological effects and political power of religion and ritual can be found in Dickinson's *The Blue Hawk* (Atlantic: Little, 1976) and Le Guin's *The Tombs of Atuan* (Atheneum, 1971). (pp. 77-8)

> *Patricia Dooley, in a review of "Divide and Rule,"*
> in School Library Journal, *Vol. 26, No. 10, August,*
> *1980, pp. 77-8.*

THE SHORT VOYAGE OF THE 'ALBERT ROSS' (1980)

Steven is officially friendly with John, next-door-but-one, but John, larger and less sensitive, is turning into a bully, and when Steven laboriously converts an old door into a raft, John forces his way into the river adventure on his own terms, only to be mortified at the younger boy's unexpected belligerence. Selective detail and a precise use of words contribute to a setting which scarcely needs the prefatory map [by Gavin Rowe] for the reader to grasp it as a mental picture, while the antagonism of the boys, expressed in verbal insult and vigorous gesture, is triumphantly authentic. . . .

> *Margery Fisher, in a review of "The Short Voyage*
> *of the Albert Ross," in* Growing Point, *Vol. 19, No.*
> *2, July, 1980, p. 3738.*

As in the earlier novels, there are the pervasive mental maps, the masterly portrayal of shifting moods, the potential power within the commonplace. A deserted field is "a brown desert with sly serpents lurking behind every clod of earth. At any moment a heavy dinosaur might come lounging round the corner, leaving footprints like moon craters and clanking louder than a lorry load of milk churns". At its simplest level, as a narrative tale, it may not satisfy the younger reader; the more sophisticated will be challenged, as by fables. The best compliment is that Jan Mark's writing, in its artlessness, catches the stories that children the age of her leading characters write themselves: she always gives the child's eye view.

> *Colin Mills, "The Narrator's Voice," in* The Times
> Literary Supplement, *No. 4042, September 19, 1980,*
> *p. 1033.**

[*The Short Voyage of the Albert Ross*] has ideas very much bigger than its frame. . . .

The seventy pages of Jan Mark's little tale are deceptive. There is a wealth here of wisdom as well as observation, a tiny fragment of childhood captured and preserved in all its sharp detail. Gavin Rowe's line drawings are of the same kind, apparently simple but springing from close observation and profound understanding.

> *M. Crouch, in a review of "The Short Voyage of the*
> *Albert Ross," in* The Junior Bookshelf, *Vol. 44, No.*
> *6, December, 1980, p. 293.*

NOTHING TO BE AFRAID OF (1980)

Best books of 1980. *Nothing To Be Afraid Of* by Jan Mark . . . and *A Sense of Shame and other stories* by Jan Needle. . . . Set in what the blurb rather strangely describes as "those pretelevision days of the early Fifties", Jan Mark's latest consists of ten jewel-like stories. Her speciality is unusual small boys. There is Robin, whose "face was as pale and flat as a saucer of milk", and whose "eyes floated in it like drops of cod-liver oil" and Anthony, who was "thin and dark with little eyes like cold cinders", and whose "hair curled up at the front in horns". Jan Mark does not say "like" but "in horns". Every word talks with her.

"William's Version", in which William rightly corrects his Granny's version of the story of the three little pigs, is another small masterpiece. I know of no other writer whose combination of tenderness and assertiveness makes such irresistible reading.

> *John Horder, in a review of "Nothing to Be Afraid*
> *Of," in* Punch, *Vol. 279, No. 7310, December 10,*
> *1980, p. 1087.*

[*The following excerpt is from a review of* Nothing to Be Afraid Of *and* All Made of Fantasy, *an anthology of short stories edited by Marjorie and Jeremy Rowe.*]

Aunty Lynn goes to great lengths to make sure little Robin has nothing to be afraid of. His world is sanitized, safe, secure. Until Anthea takes him to the park. The good leopard, the bad leopard, the python tree, Poison Alley, the Fever Pit, the Greasy Witch, Frightful Corner, the Lavatory Demon, all the grisly delights of hyper-imaginative childhood horrors beset him. Aunty Lynn is as furious as it is genteel to be, but she cannot assuage the demons; and Robin does not want her to. It is sharply perceptive, acutely rendered, verbally precise and elegant, and most of all it is very funny. For in these 10 stories Jan Mark has regained control over the comic gift which distinguishes her *Thunder and Lightnings* as one of the very best children's novels of the seventies.

Her recent work—*The Ennead, Divide and Rule*—has been powerful but increasingly bleak, chilling, despairing. *Thunder and Lightnings* is a sad book but it is also a warm one, and it is from it that these stories, set unerringly in the early 1950s, take their tone. The Coronation Mob, a pair of scruffy tikes in army surplus, determine to break up a Coronation street party, but instead to their disgust win a prize for their unwitting impersonation of Hillary and Tensing conquering Everest. The narrator has wrapped herself in patriotic shades of muslin as "the Spirit of England"; as for the rest of her family, "Several people pointed out my brother as that dear little dragon. 'Tell them you're a frog', my mother kept hissing". It is father who awards the contentious prize.

Jan Mark's children are not the polite, self-reliant, resourceful family groups she satirizes in **"Marrow Hill"**: they are loners, and most of them are little terrors. Demonic Anthony ("eyes like cold cinders") horrifies the neighbourhood with his Bonfire Night guy, "Flabber"; **"William's Version"** gleefully sabotages his Granny's attempt to tell him a nice fairy tale.

Bloodthirsty Robin, who causes havoc in Helen Cresswell's "Snake in the Grass", the first and best story in the Chipping Norton Theatre's fund-raising anthology [*All Made of Fantasy*], is similarly untameable. Though Helen Cresswell's exuberant farce is deflated by Jan Mark's telling accuracy, there is no denying the verve of her comic creations. The other stories in *All Made of Fantasy* are disappointingly weak. . . .

Jan Mark's keen awareness of the rhythms of ordinary speech and of the interest in ordinary events marks the various contributors to *All Made of Fantasy*'s frantic efforts to interest their readers as wasted labour. While they strain to inject the strange, the magical, the funny, the significant into their stories, Jan Mark reveals them in all our lives.

Neil Philip, "Comic Horrors," in The Times Educational Supplement, *No. 3369, January 16, 1981, p. 34.**

What a fine writer this is! She may possibly look on this collection of short-stories as light-weight, but they all have the same qualities which give the highest distinction to her full-length novels.

Each of the ten tales is sharply individual. Each is enriched by the author's humour—although they are by no means exclusively funny—and by a clear, critical and tolerant observation. Take, for example, the first story which features Robin, a small boy so cossetted by his Mama that "when you picked him up you expected him to squelch, like a hot-water bottle full of half-set custard". Anthea, who comes from a very different stable, opens a door for Robin by the simple expedient of scaring him half out of his small wits. In another story William introduces Granny to a new version of the Three Little Pigs, and in another we meet Arthur, who knows all the answers. The last story, **"Nule,"** is likely to foster some rare and fruitful nightmares. But enough of particulars; here is the stuff for lasting enjoyment, read alone or in the family circle or even in the classroom.

M. Crouch, in a review of "Nothing to Be Afraid Of," in The Junior Bookshelf, *Vol. 45, No. 1, February, 1981, p. 22.*

It is always a luxury to read Jan Mark's books. **"Nothing to be afraid of"** is the first in a collection of ten stories set in the fifties, each radiating her unique charm and distinctive command of language. The characters are portrayed with an apt insight. The children are anarchic, irritating, sanctimonious, imaginative, irrepressible and real. Macabre Anthony, for instance: 'He was nine. He looked thirty but stunted.' Or Billy with shoes on the wrong feet: 'His mother was trying to cure his pigeon toes.' . . .

A wonderfully funny book, written with flair and sensitivity, which should, along with all Jan Mark's books, be in every classroom in the country. (p. 33)

Caroline Wynburne, in a review of "Nothing to Be Afraid Of," in The School Librarian, *Vol. 29, No. 1, March, 1981, pp. 33-4.*

Seven wickedly witty stories that capture, with uncanny accuracy, those dark areas of our universal experience where the sun of redemption never shines. Except a bleak, loveless, sardonic world whose misanthropic inhabitants seem to have been spawned under a rock. . . . What these gleefully ghastly characters have in common is a contentious distaste for each other and the conventions of the gloomy world they inhabit. Children detest other children ("I think you're a fat loony," said Anthony) and regard adults as distasteful curiosities (" 'I can see up your nose,' said William. 'It's all whiskery.' "). Adults occasionally return the favor. The stories are outrageously funny with their black humor, well crafted (except for a few disappointingly flat endings) and beautifully written . . . , although the diction is relentlessly British—unlikely to matter to any but those who refuse to read Sherlock Holmes because they don't know what a "gasogene" and a "tantalus" are. Those looking for something "healthy" and "edifying" will be appalled. But kids will be delighted—provided (and it's a big

provided) they are able to appreciate the ironies and subtleties of the stories.

Michael Cart, in a review of "Nothing to Be Afraid Of," in School Library Journal, *Vol. 28, No. 9, May, 1982, p. 72.*

HAIRS IN THE PALM OF THE HAND (1981)

Jan Mark is living proof that the best writing for children can also be the most popular. There is nothing in the two stories in *Hairs in the Palm of the Hand,* to bore, confuse or patronize the young; equally, there is nothing to pander to them. They are hilariously funny, meticulously observed, shaped with mature skill in economical, precise prose. The comedy derives from the observation; it is not a comedy of exaggeration, omission or alteration, but of structure: language, situation, character and concept harnessed to a clear vision. It is a comedy which strikes deep notes.

In **"Time and the Hour"** Martin's time and motion study of IX's week becomes the centre of a Machiavellian power struggle. When the class lay wagers on how much working time will be lost through trivial interruptions, Manipulative Addison bets that the class will *save* 15 minutes, and proceeds to ensure that this will be so. The punters' desperate time-wasting and time-saving ploys build a fine comic climax; and behind it all is a most subtle and penetrating understanding of the complex dynamics of the group. **"Time and the Hour"** is as elegantly turned as Wodehouse's "The Great Sermon Handicap."

"Chutzpah" moves from the boys' grammar school setting to a co-ed comprehensive. It is the first day of the new school year, and confusion reigns; even more so than usual. Behind most of the chaos—the girls' petition to be taught woodwork, the senior boys' sit-in in the Medical Room—is a cocky, streetwise girl sporting a t-shirt which reads WEST HAM FOR PRESIDENT. This is Eileen, a law unto herself. She picks and chooses which class to attend, cheeks the teachers, gives false names, won't wear school uniform. She just breezes about with an infuriating, enticing insouciance. Plaintive, tearful new-girl Lisa tags along, till she finds a friend more suited to her nerves. An attempt to introduce the two is hardly a success: "The friend sucked in a great wad of lower lip under her front teeth and tittered, ih-ih-ih-ih, like a ping-pong ball; let go of her lip and said, breathily, 'You're not supposed to wear trousers'."

These pictures of school life make Geoffrey Trease's 1952 school story "The Colorado Quest" in his new collection *A Wood in Moonlight* seem the pallid, conventional thing it is.

Neil Philip, "Don't Pander, Don't Patronize," in The Times Educational Supplement, *No. 3397, August 7, 1981, p. 17.**

Stories of school life and its hazards are steadily receiving more realistic and honest treatment than was the case even ten years ago. In these stories of events in two different schools, Jan Mark has struck a fresh note in humour and ingenuity and at the same time reminded us that schools are populated by human beings some of whom, at least, are individuals and not mere educational fodder, and that some teachers realise this more than might be thought. In **"Time and the Hour"**, an offbeat piece of research into time wasting leads to a secret wager whose outcome is decided by some very devious methods, though not, one is pleased to note, through villainy. In **"Chutzpah"** the nightmare of keeping tabs on everyone and everything in a large comprehensive school is demonstrated beautifully in the chaos caused on the first day of term by an enterprising, brash and cynically malicious girl who pretends to be a pupil but is in fact still on holiday from her own place of instruction. It is not that teachers or pupils are inherently gullible; the system, as anyone who has been part of it knows, is too unwieldy. Full marks.

A. R. Williams, in a review of "Hairs in the Palm of the Hand," in The Junior Bookshelf, *Vol. 45, No. 5, October, 1981, p. 214.*

Jan Mark's humour when it is focussed on schools may be warmer and kinder than Tim Kennermore's [in *The Fortunate Few*] but it is just as shrewd and searching. In **Hairs in the Palm of the Hand,** the running battle between Them and Us is exactly defined in two separate but analogous situations. . . . To an ounce of sense, a pound of nonsense—the recipe works well when it is in such capable hands. Any one of the escalating incidents could have happened in any one school: the sum of so many possibilities adds up to two rousing comedies, with not a word wasted and not an atom of their basic truth either.

Margery Fisher, in a review of "Hairs in the Palm of the Hand," in Growing Point, *Vol. 20, No. 4, November, 1981, p. 3970.*

AQUARIUS (1982)

"What did free men do, to demonstrate their freedom?" That question, asked in its early pages, reverberates throughout Jan Mark's new novel, *Aquarius,* which stylistically and thematically recalls her earlier books **The Ennead** and **Divide and Rule.** It is, like them, a sombre, taxing book: unmistakably the work of a writer of power and originality, but lacking in the easy flow and warmth of her fiction for younger children.

The very first sentence presents difficulties which many readers will not surmount. It reads, "The night the bridge collapsed for the third time in living memory, the population of the village fell by one, drowned, and rose by two, found clinging next morning to the remaining upright of the bridge." This is not only hard to take in cold, but its odd internal rhyme and dislocated rhythm are offputting. Later obstacles include, for instance, the introduction of a major character simply as a "prognathous youth", those who look up prognathous and discover it to mean "with a protruding lower jaw" will not be much wiser when the same character is then repeatedly referred to as chinless. And if the style is sometimes cumbersome, the story offers few familiar gripping points.

The main character Viner's "mystery" of water-divining is not prized in his home village, which is subject to constant flooding. He leaves and eventually reaches a land where water is desperately needed. A rain-king dances forlornly each day, summoning nothing but the contempt of his matriarchal queen. Viner's talent proves a way to respect, position, power. What he does with that power is the real subject of the book, which, like **The Ennead,** is essentially about emotional manipulation. Viner falls in love with Morning Light, the rain-king, but cannot recognize or admit the love; when he has the chance, he fails to do what free men do, to demonstrate their freedom, and instead steps out of one cage into another.

There is much in *Aquarius* to admire: the insidious way in which Jan Mark reveals her characters by documenting their moments of failure, of loss of nerve, of betrayal; her language, which, while it sometimes clogs, often attains a chilling beauty;

her ability to communicate the subtle ebb and flow of obedience and command in unequal and unstable relationships. But there is also much obscurity—for instance the meaning of the wasteland imagery, of the Gravesian fertility king theme, indeed of the water-divining itself—and, connected with this, a sense that the lands in which the story is set, with their bizarre extremities of flood and drought, exist only as a context for Viner and his anguish. Without him, they are nothing.

Neil Philip, "From the Wasteland," in The Times Educational Supplement, *No. 3441, June 11, 1982, p. 41.**

What makes a good story? Literary criticism can supply only a partial answer: there is, in the true purveyor of fiction, an x-factor which defies analysis. I can suggest reasons why I find *Aquarius* such a fine book, but they fall short of the absolute truth every time. I can, for instance, point to the structural virtues of the story. Narrative pattern is as important in a novel as it is in a piece of music, guiding and satisfying the reader, usually in a subliminal way. Jan Mark's new story is a particularly symmetrical one. Two extremes of climate are balanced—in the water-logged valley to which Viner . . . is washed with his mother on a flooded river, and in the distant land where civilisation is failing through drought and where his gift brings fame and fortune, but danger and perplexity as well. There is a necessary parallel in the way Rain King's servants blindfold Viner to take him to the half-ruinous palace, and the way Viner blindfolds the King, Morning Light, when in a cruel kind of friendship he forces him away from the desert land which he has failed to help with his ritual dancing and towards the sodden village which Viner believes he will save as a Sun King.

Within this very formal structure the story of two journeys and a dangerous sojourn takes what seems to be a rather leisurely, low-keyed course. Instead of dramatic climaxes and sensational set-pieces, there is a continuous ebb and flow of relationships; each of the characters in turn affects the moods and actions of the others, with Viner always as the focal point. The bored, malicious Queen erodes her consort's confidence with her bitter, feminist scorn; the king finds himself as a man when his daughter is born—but too late for his safety, enmeshed as he is in the dictates of a superstitious people; his two close associates, Cleaver and Hern, work out their individual interpretations of duty and loyalty, holding their precarious power as Viner locates wells and streams. Behind the brief, sharp indications of character lie powerful associations with legend, even with myth; Morning Light is in some senses the Sick King of the Waste Land, and these echoes add colour to Jan Mark's plain, direct, concrete prose.

Plain prose but by no means pallid. For one thing, there is a strong sense of rhythm in the sentence-patterns of description and dialogue and in the carefully arranged alternations of these elements. The articulate discussions in which Cleaver and Viner express their rather different concepts of friendship allow for sudden insights which alter the tone of seemingly simple dialogue. There are moments when description takes over, illuminating the appearance of a person (the King, for instance, seen all silver as he dances and later brown and commonplace) or a place (the huts and broken stone of the palace buildings, the ruined bridge in the drowned valley), and a picture leaps out of the pages. Locality, talk, movement, all contribute to the argument of the book, the celebration of friendship in many forms, containing as it does malice and affection, cruelty and kindness, perception and puzzlement. Like many tales of secondary worlds, this one teases the reader with hidden meanings and with an almost contradictory effect in the contrast between the anonymous atmospheres and rituals of legend and a kind of Piers Plowman sturdiness of dialogue and landscape. Behind everything is the mystery of it all. Who is Viner? Was he, as his specific name suggests, the true, destined Rain King? Had he drifted down, as an infant, from that drought-stricken land?

Add together technical excellence of narrative, character, description, combining to further an emotional theme, and you still have not identified or isolated that final story-teller's magic. What is it that holds the attention, quickens the imagination, in a perfectly plain paragraph like this:

> Unwilling to be thought a thief, even after he had gone, he laid aside most of the clothes that had been given to him, and selected only the warmest and thickest against his return to a colder climate. He rolled them tight and stuffed them into his brother's bait bag, with the bacon bone and the pot bottle which he filled with wine from the jar by his bed. With luck he might find something to eat as he passed by the kitchen, but food was the least of his worries. His only concern was to get away. He was used to hunger, and if he needed water, he knew how to get it. His last action was to take his divining rod from its hiding place from under the mattress and put it under his shirt. Then he blew out the light and crept onto the landing.

What is it in these words that activates the essential bond between author and reader? The gift to compel through words is mysterious, especially in the sphere of adventure fiction. Masefield had it, even at his most naïf and literal: Mary Stewart and Peter Dickinson have it, so had Buchan and Nevil Shute. Jan Mark, I suggest, should be added to this unwritten and important list. (pp. 3914-15)

> *Margery Fisher, in a review of "Aquarius," in* Growing Point, *Vol. 21, No. 2, July, 1982, pp. 3914-15.*

This is a well-made tale on the whole, with much good descriptive detail, good overall structure and some nicely humorous effects, especially early on. But the ending is unsatisfactory; there is too much bad blood between Viner and Morning Light, too much is unresolved. Viner is hard to identify with, inspiring neither liking, nor sympathy, nor respect. His occasional good impulses are just that—impulses, and both he and Morning Light are implausibly childish, sulky, thoughtless and ungracious. It would, certainly, be very dull if all children's stories were morally as black and white as *The Lord of the Rings*, but Viner's positively neurotic changes of moral mood prevent one from forming any sense of him as a real person. Altogether he is a very strange character to find in a children's story.

Nevertheless, the basic idea of *Aquarius* is a good one; there are some compelling moments. Perhaps the best indication of how good it is is the disappointment one feels when Jan Mark does not make more of Viner's aquarian progress round the parched realms of the rain king: one very much wants to hear more about the divining and the digging, the first water in the deepening trenches, the dry-lipped peasant astonishment, the wells and the gratitude; this is an opportunity missed.

> *Galen Strawson, "Rain Dancers," in* The Times Literary Supplement, *No. 4138, July 23, 1982, p. 791.*

The intentional manipulation of other people to attain, or retain, social status is the underlying theme of *Aquarius*, by Jan Mark. *Aquarius* is a mixture of fantasy and reality; the land where the story takes place is recognizable, yet it is not a realistic country. It is set in a time before the Industrial Revolution, but the customs are not recognizable. . . .

Aquarius has a well-constructed, absorbing narrative. The characters' manipulation of each other is so mutually accepted that it seems virtually a way of life. Even Viner, who desperately values the king's friendship, eventually manipulates his friends to further his own status.

The transition from a soggy, soaking wet village to a dry, hot, desertlike settlement is also very well handled. In fact, the reader is so mired in mud and water at the beginning of the book, there is a need to get away from the wringing-wet village:

> Everything was green. Grass grew on the thatch, moss on the windowsills, and a lush, indeterminate silkiness on the walls, under the blebs and running welts of water. Even the sheep, grazing aimlessly by the bridge, had vegetation on their backs, for as it flourished on the roofs so the grass grew abundantly in their waterlogged fleece.

Jan Mark's book is demanding: the prose tightly written, the sentences complex, the imagery exact and succinct. It does not condescend to its reader. Young readers will sympathize with Viner's alienation against his village and recognize his moral decline, but will probably cheer him on because he is taking charge of his own actions.

> *Lisa Lane, "Of Friendship and Manipulation," in* The Christian Science Monitor, *February 1, 1985, p. B5.*

Mainly science fantasy, the book also combines elements of the historical, adventure and human interest novel, but because of the science fantasy history aspect, this one may have limited initial appeal and will have to be introduced. Those who do read it will enjoy it; the writing is clear, concise and well-paced. Action is quick; description, while adequate, does not bog down the story. Balance between dialogue and imagery is also good. Mark is adept at evoking empathy for her characters, who are well-drawn and realistic. There are no absolute personalities here but combinations of desirable and undesirable that will provoke some thought.

> *Denise L. Moll, in a review of "Aquarius," in* School Library Journal, *Vol. 31, No. 8, April, 1985, p. 98.*

Mark has produced an interesting and unusual book: she handles well the language, settings, thematic patterns, and the development of the main character; all are complex and subtle, if somewhat repellant. In addition, its dearth of fantastic elements makes the tale seem more like a naturalistic novel than a fantasy story; but this is no book for those who love the magic of rings and wands.

On the other hand, some aspects of the novel may disappoint you: for so psychologically-oriented a story, there's relatively little attention to the characters other than Viner, so that their motivation remains rather obscure. Naturally enough, Viner has been warped by his suffering at the hands of people who fear and hate him, and his predominantly opportunistic motivation is properly complex. But the other characters call for more development so as to provide a corresponding setting for this dark jewel. This trouble also arises in Viner's attitudes when he takes captive and brutalizes Morning Light, someone for whom he feels fellowship and sympathy. Finally, I think, the novel's appeal will depend on your response to Mark's descriptions; her evocation of the mood, psychology, and politics of these cultures; and her intricate study of the central character. These have merits enough, of course, but *Aquarius* might well have been richer; and sometimes in the reading I wished it weren't so dry.

> *Len Hatfield, "Dry Fantasy," in* Fantasy Review, *Vol. 9, No. 6, June, 1985, p. 23.*

THE DEAD LETTER BOX (1982)

Louie and Glenda were best friends mainly because they were near neighbours but Louie hardly realised this until Glenda moved away and failed to play her part in Louie's ingenious arrangements for their continued relationship. ***The Dead Letter Box*** has a serious theme carried on extremely natural dialogue and light humour in a story with a neat shape. Louie's letterbox is the front slot in a certain story-book in the children's library—a book which, since it was last taken out more than four years before, seems safe enough. As Glenda fails to find the letter, it hardly matters that a newcomer, sympathising with an author who is apparently never read, upsets Louie's plan, especially as scholarly Jane invents a splendid new game which reduces the library to mild chaos. Jan Mark's sparkling, selective and notably concrete prose makes simplicity a virtue. . . .

We need far more books of this kind—alert, individual yet wholly accessible for children to cut their teeth on, once they are reading fluently, so that without realising it they acquire the rudiments of a sense of literary quality.

> *Margery Fisher, in a review of "The Dead Letter Box," in* Growing Point, *Vol. 21, No. 3, September, 1982, p. 3944.*

In this satisfying story there are the untaught lessons of literacy: about reading a book more than once, writing letters that don't say much, and those that do. The author's simple seeming surface moves back to significant depths of feeling. Read this one carefully and the young will do the same.

> *Margaret Meek, in a review of "The Dead Letter Box," in* The School Librarian, *Vol. 30, No. 3, September, 1982, p. 236.*

This is one of those rare books that not only engage seven to tens on the level of 'what happens next?', but holds within it some of the powerful ideas most of them are beginning to think about. . . .

You don't have to believe this, but the group of second year juniors I read this to involved themselves with the themes of this book for days . . . What does writing enable us to *do*? What's a true friend? All this, much more, Jan Mark's feeling for children's lives, lore and language—plus a character called Wayne who won't take his snorkel jacket off in class, make it one of the best so far this year.

> *Colin Mills, in a review of "The Dead Letter Box," in* Books for Keeps, *No. 23, November, 1983, p. 12.*

Jan Mark's ***The Dead Letter Box*** is based upon her precise observation of children's friendship and her penchant for slightly disordering official systems (the public library this time). I feel she is best writing for a slightly more sophisticated audience, but this can be well placed in the hands of a child who is just ready to break away from formula writing and listen for the individual voice of the author.

> *Mary Steele, "Younger Fiction: 'The Dead Letter Box'," in the* The Signal Review 1: A Selective Guide to Children's Books 1982, *edited by Nancy Chambers, The Thimble Press, 1983, p. 24.*

FEET AND OTHER STORIES (1983)

One envies the bright heaven of invention which can produce another collection of short stories so full of life and ironic observation of children, and adults, during the years of schooling. There is some quiet malice here and there which reminds the reader that children are not always nice even if they are not actually delinquent. Jane's revenge on the condescending tennis champion in **"Feet"**, and Isobel's revenge on an indifferent step-mother in **"Posts and Telecommunications"** are cases in point. There are two pretty 'courtships', amusingly abortive, in **"Enough is too much already"** and **"I was adored once too"**, the former with a vintage Hoffnung type plot into the bargain. The art class in **"Still life: remote control"** is just hilarious but still credible. Bert Kitchen's decorations are pleasing but Jan Mark needs no assistance in bringing her characters or their surroundings to life.

> *A. R. Williams, in a review of "Feet and Other Stories," in* The Junior Bookshelf, *Vol. 47, No. 3, June, 1983, p. 128.*

Jan Mark is formidably talented. She has a deft hand with a story line and a fine ear for dialogue. She can catch the likeness of a character, either in full-length portrait or rapid sketch. She plays on the English language like the infinitely subtle instrument it is. She can be marvellously funny, too. But her true originality, I think, lies less in these gifts than in her perceptions: she sees people and events freshly, through a highly individual eye.

Feet brings together eight short stories, four of which have been previously published in different collections. They are about young people and presumably "for" young people: adolescents rather than pre-teenagers. Some of them take an uncomfortably disenchanted view of adults: in **"Poor Darling"** Adam tries with pathetic desperation to find excuses for his selfish, snobbish mother; and when Isobel in **"Posts and Telecommunications"** takes a vicious revenge on her continually-absent father, the awful truth is that he's asked for it. Not that the youngsters themselves are idealised, but their misdeeds are of a kind to invite sympathy or mockery rather than disgust. They get off more lightly than their elders, as is only proper.

The title story, in which the handsome, horrid tennis champion of the school is deservedly wrong-footed, and **"Enough is Too Much Already"**, which tells how Maurice was kept from the disco by a chapter of cumulative accidents, are predominantly humorous, although there are wry undertones to each. But the best and most poignant story is **"I Was Adored Once Too."** Lone, unglamorous Birkett controls the lights at rehearsals of the school production of *Twelfth Night*. In his crow's-nest above the stage, he feels "as remote as God, operating the firmament." Then Juliet, with large, hopeful face and piledriver legs, insinuates herself admiringly into his eyrie and tries to help.

When the part of Sir Andrew Aguecheek is thrust upon Birkett at short notice, Juliet takes over the lighting, makes a botch, and is dismissed with ignominy. The rehearsal goes on. "I was adored once too," says Birkett in the part of the foolish knight. Sad for him; the line, as he has already reflected, is not funny. Sadder still, one thinks a few seconds later, for Juliet.

The other three stories are not, in my view, as good as the ones named; but Jan Mark is always readable, and is witty even when she isn't being funny. She is brilliantly good at catching the tones of voice of today's young, and wickedly good at catching those of teachers.

> *John Rowe Townsend, "Chapter of Accidents," in* The Times Educational Supplement, *No. 3492, June 3, 1983, p. 43.*

[Jan Mark's] stylish pieces are more concrete and more direct than Tim Kennemore's [in *Here tomorrow, gone today*] but at the same time they have more to offer in the way of swift character-drawing and particularised themes. Deft in structure, firm in the pursuit of that emphatic climax so valuable to the short-story form, they range from '**Still Life: Remote Control**', a subtly organised over-view of art students doing their own thing, to a bitter scrutiny of unpunished family selfishness in '**Poor Darling**', in which a railway carriage becomes a whole world of tensions. Young relationships are considered in '**I was adored once too**' and '**Enough is too much already**' in a school setting which, again, has wider implications. Behind each precisely described, briskly animated boy or girl we sense the presence of a presiding adult, pressing her point without interfering too obviously in the gyrations of her puppets. (p. 4100)

> *Margery Fisher, in a review of "Feet and Other Stories," in* Growing Point, *Vol. 22, No. 2, July, 1983, pp. 4099-4100.*

Jan Mark is an excellent, never predictable writer, mistress of both long and short stories. Not always easy to follow at first glance, her plots here finally succeed because of her acute ear for authentic dialogue and real feeling. Four of the eight stories have already appeared in anthologies, but it is still worth having them all together. Writing of this quality is rare enough either for children or adults, and when it is funny too, in between the quieter moments, it would be greedy to ask for anything more.

> *Nicholas Tucker, in a review of "Feet and Other Stories," in* Books for Your Children, *Vol. 19, No. 2, Summer, 1984, p. 14.*

Sophisticated, witty, beautifully crafted stories very much for older readers. . . . Most of the eight stories are to do with seeing through people (or not)—complex patterns of lack of understanding, deception, manipulation, realisation, explanation. But also, in most of them, you are not quite sure what has happened by the end and nor are the main characters. On the surface, all seems clear. If the story is a mirror, it isn't misted; but mirror reflections are reversed and anyway, what's behind the mirror . . .? . . . This book you can't do without. Give it to

Sixth Formers as well as Fourth and Fifth. I hope lots of adults will have a chance to read it too.

> *Terry Downie, in a review of "Feet and Other Stories," in* Books for Keeps, *No. 30, January, 1985, p. 11.*

HANDLES (1983)

Jan Mark's allusive method is seen at its glorious best in ***Handles***, a book with all the exuberance and originality of her first, prize-winning ***Thunder and Lightnings***, with a tighter structure and broader terms of reference in regard to places and people. The plot is simple, even hackneyed. A schoolgirl of thirteen or so living in Norwich is sent to spend three weeks of the summer holidays with relations in a small Norfolk village. The routine of the market garden becomes tedious and Cousin Robert's rudeness exacerbating. Far from appreciating the peace of rural life, Erica longs for city noise and, above all, for the motor-bikes she has lovingly observed for years—for, awkwardly, she wants to be a motor mechanic as passionately as her older brother wants to be a nurse. This is a book about names and passwords, about the way a lively and determined girl finds friendship in a workshop, oily and chaotic, governed by its relaxed, humorous, philosophical owner. Elsie's unsuitable feminine handle marks the identity that suits him in his work-escape from a socially pretentious wife: the handle Erica claims after a casual comment on her rain-gear, the 'Dreaded Yellow Jelly Mould', stands for her joy at being allowed to help in repairing and restoring classic machines. Providing and defining handles is one of Jan Mark's most valuable gifts. The characters in the story live in speech and emerge as unmistakable individuals from their backgrounds. This tale of a holiday that offers Erica pleasure and pain, growth and self-knowledge, is described with verbal wit, with affectionate perception, with pictorial precision and an unerring dramatic instinct making each scene intensely active. It is a jewel of a book. (pp. 4186-87)

> *Margery Fisher, in a review of "Handles," in* Growing Point, *Vol. 22, No. 5, January, 1984, pp. 4186-87.*

Erica wants to be a motor-cycle mechanic—which to her dad would be "almost as unnatural as men having babies". Her brother Craig wants to be a nurse. It sounds like the beginning of a heavy lump of anti-sexist fiction. Don't groan; Jan Mark is much too subtle to perpetrate anything like that. She knows that sex-stereotyping is not a simple self-contained evil but an aspect of something much broader. ***Handles*** is shot through with the tensions between what people are and what they are expected to be.

Why *handles*? A handle is a descriptive nickname. . . . Unlike a given name, a handle defines you. It could even help you to know what you are. Erica, working her way into the tatty motorcycle repair shop whose proprietor has a name for everybody and everything, longs to earn a handle for herself.

I have almost outlined the plot without even trying. There isn't much of one. It is quite a light book. . . .

It's a graceful, witty book, a pleasure to read, and not as slight in theme as in acion. It's technically convincing, too; though I suspect that in the end it will appeal more to the bookish than to the bike-ish. Names and naming recur all the way through, but there is one creature in the story that doesn't have a name: the much-loved boar of Ted Hales, pigkeeper. "Name?" says

Ted. "He hent got a name. What'd he want a name for? He don't get letters."

> *John Rowe Townsend, "Nicknames," in* The Times Educational Supplement, *No. 3524, January 13, 1984, p. 38.*

It becomes more and more difficult to do justice to Jan Mark's writing without quoting substantial portions of what she has written. As an adult one realises one is being admitted to the world of a highly literate humorist and it only occasionally crosses one's mind that some of the humour may be too subtle for potential readers.... There is no plot to speak of: Erica arrives, participates, and departs. In between, the reader meets a gallery of original characters such as only Jan Mark consistently mounts. You don't want the book to end, which is not quite the same thing as not wanting to put it down. (pp. 34-5)

> *A. R. Williams, in a review of "Handles," in* The Junior Bookshelf, *Vol. 48, No. 1, February, 1984, pp. 34-5.*

This is a sharply funny book with a potently serious side which questions prescribed attitudes to male/female roles and the way in which we attach 'handles' to people. Jan Mark is nudging cultural assumptions and exploring and showing a whole range of pre-adolescent feelings with a most assured lightness of touch. One award winner which many children will enjoy and from which they could take away a great deal.

> *David Bennett, in a review of "Handles," in* Books for Keeps, *No. 32, May, 1985, p. 10.*

Handles is about Erica Timperley's quest for self-discovery. It is also about role models and love and growing up, but Erica never bandies such words about, nor does the author, Jan Mark. Erica, a sensible girl with a passion for the insides of motorcycles, accomplishes her puberty rites with laconic good nature and fortitude....

With this, ... Jan Mark stretches the range of children's books. Along with writers like Betty Levin, John Rowe Townsend and Robert Cormier, she provides for young people the combination of fine prose and strong realism generally reserved for adults. Especially praiseworthy is the glossary at the end of the book: "FAG ENDS—Cigarette butts," "NOBBLE—Interfere with." This is a far better solution to the language problem than losing all foreign flavor by substituting American for English words.

> *Jane Langton, in a review of "Handles," in* The New York Times Book Review, *July 28, 1985, p. 25.*

The plot is full of descriptive background details which slow down the action. Readers who are accustomed to the absorbing stories and slick dialogue of Blume or Gilson will find the excessive narrative and British speech patterns to be stumbling blocks, even though the book has a glossary explaining British terms. Still, Erica remains an interesting young lady, with a mind of her own, who learns to use her cleverness to make the best of a rather unpleasant situation, while the amusingly bizarre behavior of characters such as Robert and Elsie might intrigue young readers.

> *Phyllis Graves, in a review of "Handles," in* School Library Journal, *Vol. 31, No. 10, August, 1985, p. 78.*

AT THE SIGN OF THE DOG AND ROCKET (1985)

This story is in the realist tradition of the author's **Thunder and Lightnings** and **Hairs in the palm of the hand.** It is set in provincial Kent and the heroine is an ordinary school leaver. What makes her interesting is the degree of responsibility thrust upon her in running her parents' pub, while her mother is away and her father incapacitated; a teenage version of the 'absent parent' situation, popular in children's books. But here, life is real, a work routine has to be followed, and difficult relationships made to work. As always, Jan Mark enlivens her account of everyday life with well-drawn, rounded characters, gives us information (in this case, fascinating details of behind-the-bar life), and embellishes a simple prose with original touches. The book should appeal to the reader nearing school-leaving age, but also to a younger age group. Their only complaint might be the lack of a neat ending, but in this it is indeed true to life.

> *Joyce Banks, in a review of "At the Sign of the Dog and Rocket," in* The School Librarian, *Vol. 33, No. 2, June, 1985, p. 163.*

TROUBLE HALF-WAY (1985)

Readers who've admired Jan Mark's knowledge of aeroplanes and motor-bikes won't be surprised to find that she knows quite a bit about trucking, too.

There's more to it than the externals of the trip, of course. What's happening, partly, is that Amy is getting to know and accept the stepfather to whom she's previously been hostile. The journey is an ingenious device for accelerating what would really be a long-term development. Capable, commonsense Richard wins his way to Amy's affection: an achievement signalled by her casual reference to him on the next-to-last page as "my dad".

That's not all. Amy (who is child, not teenager) is a chip off Mum's block: cautious and self-preserving. For her the journey is away from suburban narrowness and towards independence. Richard has promised to show her, as the goal of the trip, a cotton mill called AMY, with her name on the side in huge letters. In the event, she has to get there on her own when he is immobilized by the breakdown of the truck. I would guess that the mill called Amy has a symbolic meaning: as a citadel of self, perhaps. There's surely an echo here of the archetypal quest story, in which the hero, though receiving help along the way, must complete the last stage of the quest alone.

So a slight, light structure is carrying quite a bit of weight; carrying it gracefully, as you might expect. This is not the greatest of Jan Mark's books, but neither does it let her down.

> *John Rowe Townsend, "Truckers' Luck," in* The Times Educational Supplement, *No. 3597, June 7, 1985, p. 54.*

"There might be fog" is Amy Calver's immediate response to the prospect of a journey. "Suppose the engine blows up?" Amy's mother's world, focused on the Gravesend estate where the streets are named after Second World War aircraft, is governed by a strict code of "niceness". For Amy's mother, the family ironing pile includes, naturally and honourably, the baby's nappies, Amy's school socks and her new husband's non-iron shirts.

The stepfather, Richard, seems a surprising second choice for the young widow. A long-distance lorry driver, he comes from the "life's too short" school, postponing household chores, the only untidy presence in an immaculate kitchen. So when Amy's mother and baby sister are swiftly removed by a family emergency, leaving Richard and Amy awkwardly together, he reaches for the Chinese take away and she regards the impromptu meal as the collapse of civilized values.

Trouble Half-way charts Amy's progress from the rather prissy girl of the book's opening, suspicious of everything untried, to a more confident and risk-taking individual who has acquired some basis for making her own comparisons. In the course of her journey she also comes to know and to appreciate her stepfather: an embarrassed mumble is all the name she can give him when she starts out; by the penultimate page it's "my dad said . . .". The vehicle—literally—for Amy's exploration is the HGV packed with badly-made furniture which Richard spends his working life delivering. A reluctant passenger, she is drawn into a kind of camping adventure in this down-to-earth environment.

> Mum would have a fit if she knew where Amy was now, under a dustsheet in a sleeping bag on a camp bed in a filthy old Luton in a lorry park in a back street in Cheltenham. Amy realized, little by little, that Mum's reluctance to let her travel with Richard had nothing to do with heavy traffic and freezing fog, missing school and the gymnastics—or very little: it was dirt.

Amy learns that a Gravesend accent in Cheltenham sounds to the locals like Australian. What is "the main road" to her is, matter-of-factly, the A2 in a wider world. Up North ("near the top, somewhere, wasn't it, just before Scotland?") appears to be full of aliens who amazingly regard her as the foreigner; and yet, to Amy's surprise, they turn out to be very much like everyone else. In fact, the universe does not pivot on Hurricane Crescent, and it is a bigger and yet less alarming place than she had been brought up to believe.

Jan Mark negotiates Amy's development economically and with wit. She has a warm touch with the contemporary settings, from genteel tea shop to transport cafe, and she presents the collision of expectations between the child and adult, between the vital importance of being Reserve in the gymnastics as against the necessity of a week's wage, with an affectionate and illuminating neutrality. *Trouble Half-way* is likely to be an encouraging version too of the step-relationship to children's eyes. If there is for adult readers the submerged question of whether a sexual element links the two generations, strengthened by the far-off echo of Humbert Humbert's long car-drive, that is surely a minor problem for Amy. Jan Mark takes a realistic and admirably balanced line on such confusing topics. She deals lightly with the unease that the stepfather-daughter association can raise for outsiders ("*Don't* go telling people I'm not your dad"). She makes clear that Amy is no nymphet but that the girl has to learn to distinguish between not talking to one kind of strangers and taking on others in order to reach the benefits of transaction with the human race.

> *Joanna Motion, "The Lure of the Road," in* The Times Literary Supplement, *No. 4288, June 7, 1985, p. 650.*

Jan Mark never labours her points but allows them to become apparent through casual chat and terse narrative. Sparing with words, she selects them to make the necessary impact and to fill out a picture of an immediate, recognisable world in which

her characters stand out as breathing, unmistakeable individuals. . . .

Compact in structure, sharp in portraiture, activated by a humane and sympathetic comic genius, Jan Mark's new book offers a fine insight into the way chance can operate at a moment when a girl is ready to consider new possibilities in life.

> *Margery Fisher, in a review of "Trouble Halfway," in* Growing Point, *Vol. 24, No. 2, July, 1985, p. 4456.*

I'm not sure, at the end, that [Amy] has changed much, but then Jan Mark is a realist who estimates children's chances of survival in terms of a sense of humour and the language that goes with it. Thus the conversations are splendid, the incidental awarenesses well up to standard, but the motivations are thin and conventional this time. The young stepfather is more interesting than the heroine. The best details are about eating, washing and what it feels like for someone from Gravesend to go to Manchester. Readers always find their culture confirmed by Jan Mark and that's a great bonus. (p. 356)

> *Margaret Meek, in a review of "Trouble Half-Way," in* The School Librarian, *Vol. 33, No. 4, December, 1985, pp. 355-56.*

Anyone who enjoys the English countryside will enjoy this gentle story of a girl traveling through it on a journey of self-discovery. But American children may not have the patience to motor through the many unknown British towns with Amy and Richard. The story is replete with regional references and Britishisms, some but not all of which are explained in a glossary at the back of the book. A charmingly told story, but rough going for American readers.

> *A review of "Trouble Half-Way," in* Kirkus Reviews, *Vol. LIV, No. 3, February 1, 1986, p. 210.*

A British book with universal appeal. . . . Amy and Richard are three-dimensional characters, each somewhat insecure in their dealings with the other, and readers will relish the gradual strengthening of their relationship. There are some Briticisms, but they will not be a deterrent to most American readers, and the glossary is helpful. An enjoyable story with touches of humor that contains much wisdom about human nature.

> *Sylvia S. Marantz, in a review of "Trouble Half-Way," in* School Library Journal, *Vol. 32, No. 9, May, 1986, p. 95.*

FRANKIE'S HAT (1986)

There are three unusual stories about teenagers in this new book by Carnegie Medal winner Jan Mark. In *Frankie's Hat* itself, the 17 year old heroine with a husband and baby is confronted by a reminder of her carefree past when her 12 year old sister comes to stay. To make matters worse, Frankie's husband is away on a course, it is her birthday, and practically all her presents only confirm her role of responsible domesticity. An unexpected offer of a free day in town brings back earlier perspectives. The outsize hat, bought in a second-hand shop and more outrageously embellished as the day wears on, becomes a symbol for her lost past but at the end of the day she is happy to ascribe its ownership without sentimentality to her younger sister, confirming her own new role. In the second story Yo-Yo eventually has to face the fact that her new "boyfriend'' is really more in tune with her younger brother and his pet rat. The final story is concerned with the ''insubstantial grievance'' that Ronda and her mother somehow feel towards Chloe, the business woman whose flat her mother cleans each morning. Chloe carefully avoids any reference to ''dailies'' or ''little treasures'' and would like to be known by her Christian name (which Ronda's mother resists)—but there is a vast chasm between her world of plenty and the way Ronda's family lives. Although Ronda never quite pinpoints the reasons for her irritation she nevertheless stumbles upon an unusual way of ''getting her own back''.

Jan Mark's characterization is at the same time entertaining and totally convincing and the sharpness of both dialogue and narrative turn essentially simple plots into a compelling and thought-provoking read.

> *J. Nicholls, in a review of ''Frankie's Hat,'' in* The Junior Bookshelf, *Vol. 50, No. 2, April, 1986, p. 79.*

[**Frankie's Hat**] is undeniably well-meaning and relevant. . . . [The title story concerns Frankie's] well-deserved and sympathetically presented escape from the restraints of her marriage and from a birthday distinguished, with some rather tawdry

realism, by her husband's present of ''a slow cooker with an odour-filter in the lid''.

The emphasis on the kitchen is found, too, in the story **''It Wasn't Me''**. . . . The story tries to come to terms with the inequalities of the relationship between Chloe and Dianne (and Ronda), admitting that the latter two have some ''insubstantial grievance'' about Chloe, who is resplendent and apparently leisured in her broderie anglaise housecoat; but it is a little heavy-handed in its message; and Ronda's brief moments of fantasy do little to lift the depressing atmosphere.

> *Emma Letley, ''Teen Dreams,'' in* The Times Literary Supplement, *No. 4338, May 23, 1986, p. 574.**

Humour is an important reason for Jan Mark's popularity with the young—a very genuine humour resting in a strong sense of the ridiculous and using absurd situations to imply something about people's behaviour. The three stories in **Frankie's Hat** show her crisp style and shrewd common sense to good advantage. . . . Nothing is overdone here, everything is crystal clear; behind a glorious sense of comedy.

> *Margery Fisher, in a review of ''Frankie's Hat,'' in* Growing Point, *Vol. 25, No. 1, May, 1986, p. 4625.*

Mercer Mayer

1943-

American author/illustrator and author of picture books and reteller.

A prolific and popular author, Mayer is recognized for his versatility, humor, and artistic skill. Noted as one of the first creators of wordless picture books, he is responsible for a variety of works—pure nonsense, droll fantasy, realistic stories, and retellings of familiar folktales. Mayer is perhaps best known for the funny, half-fearsome creatures which appear throughout his stories as well as for his textless adventures about a boy, a dog, and a frog. Many of Mayer's works reflect his sensitivity to children and his understanding of their world; his whimsical treatment of such issues as fear of the dark, jealousy, rebellion, and relationships with fathers and older brothers also demonstrates an awareness of what makes young readers laugh. As both writer and illustrator, Mayer brings an unconventional approach to his books. Utilizing language that can be spare or rich, slang-filled or sophisticated, he adds original twists to traditional literary formulas and embellishes his retellings by assembling unrelated sources and rearranging their contents. Mayer's illustrations also cover a wide range of artistic styles, from precise line drawings and subtle watercolors to lavish, tapestried paintings; his predilection for diversity is also evidenced by Mayer's use of varied formats.

Mayer is acclaimed for the lively action, witty charm, and captivating qualities of his books as well as for the verve and detail of his illustrations. Although critics consistently object to the excessive influence of Maurice Sendak on Mayer and disapprove of the techniques he uses to compose his retellings, most observers acknowledge Mayer as a superior entertainer who has the gift of relating easily to readers and nonreaders alike.

Mayer has received numerous awards for his illustrations.

(See also *Something about the Author*, Vols. 16, 32 and *Contemporary Authors*, Vols. 85-88.)

A BOY, A DOG, AND A FROG (1967)

There are, from an adult point of view, three stories inherent in this small book that small children can invent, as well, of course, as the story the author-illustrator has told of the meeting of boy, dog and frog. Small children with their larger than adult imaginations will probably find more. This adult's obvious criticism: the illustrations are Maurice Sendak imitations, but at least Mercer Mayer showed great judgment—he chose a giant to imitate. (pp. 74-5)

> *A review of "A Boy, a Dog and a Frog," in* Publishers Weekly, *Vol. 192, No. 8, August 21, 1967, pp. 74-5.*

This is a small . . . story-without-words for which the proper review ideograph might be a sugar-coated slapstick. The pictures are delicately detailed line drawings with an old-fashioned aura. . . . The illustrations are quite pleasant to contemplate, but they do not stimulate invention and imagination to the same

extent as Ruth Carroll's *What Whiskers Did*. Nevertheless, it is good reading readiness material.

> *Elinor Cullen, in a review of "A Boy, a Dog and a Frog," in* School Library Journal, *an appendix to* Library Journal, *Vol. 14, No. 2, October, 1967, p. 165.*

"What is the use of a book without pictures?" Alice asked. Going to the opposite extreme this season are four books [*A Boy, a Dog and a Frog; A Taste of Carrot* by Bill Hoest; *Dog* by Ellie Simmons; and *The Naughty Bird* by Peter Wezel]—all pictures and no words. The best is *A Boy, a Dog and a Frog* because Mercer Mayer so capably balances reality and absurdity. Here, a boy and his dog try to catch a frog; instead both get dunked. Another try and the dog is caught, neatly folded inside the fish net. Mercer expresses the boy's frustration with economy—a shaking fist—and the range of emotions the frog experiences, bafflement, annoyance, amusement, melancholy and, finally, joy, with a few deft pen strokes.

> *George A. Woods, in a review of "A Boy, a Dog and a Frog," in* The New York Times Book Review, *November 26, 1967, p. 62.*

This is a delightful picture book. Without any text, a fairly complicated adventure of a small boy is completely presented.

The illustrations require no elaboration. Little ones will be especially pleased since this is a book that they can "read" all by themselves. . . .

There is just enough detail to present some challenge without discouraging small children. The pen and ink drawings are wonderfully graphic and informative. This, coupled with the 5½" x 4½" format make this book a perfect treat for the very young. It is most heartily recommended for all picture book collections. . . .

Besides being great fun, nursery and kindergarten teachers will find it useful in a variety of ways.

> *Robert Cohen, in a review of "A Boy, a Dog and a Frog," in* Young Readers Review, *Vol. IV, No. 4, December, 1967, p. 12.*

Most of the wordless books are more or less agile variations on the formula of self-contained, immediately apprehensible action—action that is comprehensible just because it matches expectations or directly confounds them. One of the first, Mercer Mayer's *A Boy, a Dog, and a Frog* . . . , is a convenient example. Slapstick and melodrama, scaled and toned down, are as natural to them as to the old comic sequences (or, for that matter, to silent films) and hardly less so is cumulative action: the Mounting Disaster. Quasi-realistic, they substitute for the story-in-words; and in most cases they are slight, with nothing to convey that extends beyond their covers. (p. 540)

> *Barbara Bader, "Away from Words," in her* American Picture Books from Noah's Ark to the Beast Within, *Macmillan Publishing Company, 1976, pp. 525-43.**

THERE'S A NIGHTMARE IN MY CLOSET (1968; British edition as *There's a Nightmare in My Cupboard*)

"Hitch your wagon to a star" is one thing, but this is ridiculous—this picture book which is the latest of Mercer Mayer's sincerest form of flattery of Maurice Sendak. Mr. Mayer's illustrations are not only (pallid) imitations of Mr. Sendak's, his story is a (pallid) repetition of Mr. Sendak's *Where the Wild Things Are*. A combination that doesn't make another *Where the Wild Things Are*, but just another (pallid) picture book.

> *A review of "There's a Nightmare in My Closet," in* Publishers Weekly, *Vol. 193, No. 14, April 1, 1968, p. 39.*

There's a nightmare—and it's *real:* a bat-eared, buck-toothed monster who might be an escapee from Dr. Seuss. Creeping out of the closet toward the little boy's bed, he's three parts scarey, one part worried; backing away from the little boy's popgun, he becomes a big crybaby; tucked into bed with the little boy, he looks ludicrous. "I suppose there's another nightmare in my closet, but my bed's not big enough for three," says little boy, dropping off . . . while another bewhiskered creature peers around the closet door. For a book that's meant to calm a child, it's a rather peculiar message, and *as* a book this is just another instance of the current affection for Wild Things (with a look uncomfortably like the original). The trembling monster is funny enough in himself but his role is that of the ubiquitous reluctant dragon. A dubious equation, a small gasp of a story.

> *A review of "There's a Nightmare in My Closet," in* Kirkus Service, *Vol. XXXVI, No. 8, April 15, 1968, p. 456.*

This is a magnificently funny book! Children and their parents will really get a good laugh. . . .

[When the story is] combined with the superb illustrations the young readers and pre-schoolers will be completely captured.

Though this book is rather different from Mr. Mayer's excellent *A Boy, a Dog and a Frog* . . . it should prove quite as popular. The young boy reminds one of Max from Sendak's *Where the Wild Things Are;* his nightmare, though somewhat familiar to a wild thing in superficial grotesqueness, lacks terrible claws and is adorably pathetic. This is somewhat similar to Beman Lord's *A Monster's Visit* but is for younger children and is much, much funnier. This is a book that must be seen to be fully appreciated.

> *Phyllis Cohen, in a review of "There's a Nightmare in My Closet," in* Young Readers Review, *Vol. IV, No. 10, June, 1968, p. 10.*

Childhood fear of the dark and the resulting exercise in imaginative exaggeration are given that special Mercer Mayer treatment in this dryly humorous fantasy. Young children will easily empathize with the boy and can be comforted by his experience. . . . While the book recalls aspects of Sendak's *Where the Wild Things Are,* comparison would not be fair; this is bibliotherapeutic in intent, and judged by other fear-of-the-dark picture books, it has the merits of sensitivity and comedy.

> *Doris Solomon, in a review of "There's a Nightmare in My Closet," in* Library Journal, *Vol. 93, No. 12, June 15, 1968, p. 2534.*

To say this title is not popular with parents and children would be untrue, and the illustrations are perfect for the tone of this dryly humorous fantasy. The violence, however, makes me uncomfortable, and the sight of a coy little guy in an army helmet and pajamas is not appealing to me.

> *Enid Davis, "Picture Books: 'There's a Nightmare in My Closet'," in her* The Liberty Cap: A Catalogue of Non-Sexist Materials for Children, *Academy Press Limited, 1977, p. 76.*

Maurice Sendak's *Where the Wild Things Are* and Mercer Mayer's *There's a Nightmare in My Closet* share several qualities. They were both written and illustrated by one person. In each the protagonist is a young boy who, when he speaks, speaks in the imperative, in an attempt to control a strong emotion. They both turn that emotion into a manageable image: the boy in *Nightmare* comes to grips with his fear by confronting and controlling a good-natured creature, while the boy in *Wild Things* confronts his anger (and himself) by traveling to a magical place where he controls a band of mischievous creatures. And finally, the books are both set in a night which ends with the child's successful mastery of his problem.

But even though these books have much in common, they differ stylistically. By "style" I am referring to four aspects: the arrangement of text and illustrations on the page; the structure of the text; the structure of the illustrations; and the relationship between the text and illustrations.

The arrangement of text and illustration depends on a distinction between page and panel. The term "panel" refers to two facing pages linked by a common text and/or drawing, or to

From A Boy, a Dog and a Frog, *written and illustrated by Mercer Mayer. The Dial Press, 1967.*
Copyright © 1967 by Mercer Mayer. All rights reserved. Reproduced by permission of the publisher,
Dial Books for Young Readers.

one page with an independent text and/or drawing. *Wild Things* has nineteen panels, and *Nightmare* has twenty. (p. 122)

Sendak always works in two-page panels, while Mayer fluctuates between one-page and two-page panels. The only thing they share is the two-page drawing without text; Mayer uses this device to end his story with an image, while Sendak ends his story with bare text.

The choice of format should be linked to the story. *Nightmare*'s first double-page panel is a view of the boy's room in which the boy announces that "There used to be a nightmare in my closet" (panel 1). On the left page looms the closet door representing the unknown, while on the right page is the safety of the boy's bed. Each of the eight double-page panels depends on this same scene. The mystery of that closet is reinforced not only by its separation but by the text, which occurs on the right page with the boy. As the boy describes first his habit of sleeping with the closet door shut, and then his decision to "get rid of my nightmare once and for all" (panel 7), the single-page panels are used to focus attention on the characters. For instance, in panels 5 and 6 the boy first looks out over the end of his bed to announce "When I was safe in bed, I'd peek . . ." and then ducks beneath the covers to admit "sometimes." Similarly, in panels 13 and 14 the boy stands in a small green rectangle, arms crossed with a frown, claiming "I was mad . . ." and then melts into a smile, "but not too mad." This distinction between the broad room and the close up of character is not consistent, however, because in three of the single-page panels the boy or nightmare-creature confronts the closet door. For example, in panel 3 the boy pushes the door—"I

always closed the closet door"—and in panels 10 and 11 in front of an open door the boy threatens a frightened creature. Despite this inconsistency, however, Mayer reinforces the confrontation of creature and boy in panels 9-16 with an exclusive dependence on single-page, staccato panels. In panels 9 and 10 the boy catches the creature—"Quickly I turned on the light and caught him sitting at the foot of my bed. / 'Go away, Nightmare, or I'll shoot you,' I said."—and in panels 15 and 16, after short bursts of shooting, crying, and anger, the text stretches out again to restore calm—"'Nightmare, be quiet or you'll wake Mommy and Daddy,' I said. / He wouldn't stop crying so I took him by the hand. . . ." The final double-page panels relieve the tension, as the boy tucks the creature in bed and they await yet another nightmare from the closet together.

In *Wild Things*, Sendak's format is more closely linked to the story. The early separation of text and drawing gradually broadens to a full two-page panel in panel 9 when the boy arrives at where the wild things are. The panels shrink again when he leaves in panel 17 to return to his own room. This consistency, noticed by most reviewers of the book, reinforces the correspondence between the boy's power in the place he creates and his lack of power in his room. (p. 123)

Sendak's sentences are longer than Mayer's, and, even if we consider independent clauses (which many critics believe to be a better gauge of style than sentences), his clauses are almost twice as long as Mayer's. Furthermore, Sendak's text has as many subordinate clauses as independent ones, and most of the words are in subordinate constituents (adverbial clauses, relative clauses, appositives, and so on). In contrast, Mayer's text has almost twice as many independent clauses as subordinate ones, and most of his words fall into main clauses. . . . Sendak uses five relative clauses or their remnants to qualify nouns, whereas Mayer never uses a relative clause or appositive in his text. Both texts go on to use adverbials of time and place, infinitives, participial phrases, and nominal complements to tie subordinate material into the sentence. Both texts also move clauses to the front of the sentence. Adverbial clauses or phrases (particularly of time and place) introduce several sentences in both texts, but Sendak's introductory material is usually longer, as in the case in the first and second panels of his story, in which the entire text is a subordinate adverbial of time which pushes the subject "his mother" back to the third panel: "The night Max wore his wolf suit and made mischief of one kind / and another / his mother called him 'WILD THING!'" In two instances Mayer uses long quoted material initially and then ends the sentence with the main subject and verb "I said." This movement of clauses before the subject is the only kind of movement in both texts. The other constituents are where they are expected to be.

While both texts use coordination to tie clauses and phrases together, it is the principal means of introducing material and moving from one idea to another in *Wild Things*. Sendak even begins four of his sentences with conjunctions (three *ands* and a *but*) to further emphasize this dependency. And whenever more than two constituents are combined, the conjunction (in both texts) is used between all the constituents as in "The wild things roared . . . *and* gnashed . . . *and* rolled . . . *and* showed. . . but Max stepped . . . *and* waved . . . *and* sailed back . . ." (emphasis is mine). Furthermore, if we look at the repetition of words in the texts, the same pattern emerges. In *Wild Things* there are several instances of repeated words within one panel of each other, from "wild things" to "their terrible" to the repetition of the verb "grew." Such repetition occurs only twice in *Nightmare*. (pp. 123-24)

The repetition of particular words can reveal not only thematic tendencies but also organizational patterns. For example, most of Mayer's nouns refer to the narrator "I," the nightmare, the closet, and the bed. Sendak's nouns refer to the protagonist "Max," and the wild things, but he also weaves an intricate and subtle pattern of correspondences. The notion of eating something, for instance, begins with the boy's threat to eat his mother, then he is sent to bed without eating anything, then he sends the wild things to bed without their supper, then he smells good things to eat, then the wild things threaten to eat him, till finally he returns to his room where his supper (and not his mother) is waiting for him. Another correspondence is the use of inanimate pronouns or body parts to refer to the monsters. . . . One final series of correspondences developed by Sendak's diction depends on temporal and spatial words. The story begins with "the night," travels through "night and day," and then returns to the night. The progression from night to year, which is reversed and repeated when Max returns, parallels this movement: "and sailed back over a year and in and out of weeks through a day / and into the night of his very own room" (panels 17 and 18). The spatial movement from Max's room to the forest to the ocean coincides with the temporal movement, and distances Max in time and space until he can smell, from the world he left, his supper and return to his room.

The two texts differ in verb choice as well as noun choice. Sendak continues to develop and extend correspondences between the boy and the wild things by repeating verbs. For instance, if Max "made" mischief, was "called" a wild thing, "will eat up" his mother, and "was sent" to bed without supper early in the story, then later the wild things also "made" him king, "called" him the most wild thing, "will eat" Max up, and "are sent" to bed without supper. Max's threat "I'LL EAT YOU UP!" becomes in the mouths of the creatures a pleading for him to stay, "Oh please don't go—we'll eat you up we love you so!" In Mayer's text, there is no such lexical reinforcement of the extended metaphor. When the creature becomes child-like and cries or is tucked into the bed, there were no previous references to the boy crying or being tucked in to create a link either in experience or expectation.

Besides the repetition of nouns or verbs, the images they evoke in the reader are a powerful tool with which to reinforce or create meaning. In *Wild Things*, except for *vines* and *rumpus*, the nouns are fairly ordinary and their modifiers (*terrible*, *wild*, *good*, *private*, and so on) are uneventful. The verbs, on the other hand, touch some of the senses. We can hear the differences between *roared* and *gnashed* or feel *tumbled* and *rolled* or hear the pitch difference between *called* or *cried* and the more neutral *said*. In *Nightmare* there are no adjectives except for *closet*, which modifies door, and very little sensual evocation. *Peek* may give a better sense of *look* (as *staring* or *blinking* did in *Wild Things*), and *creeping* has rich connotations, but for the most part the word choice is usual.

Beside the denotative and connotative meanings of each word in our language, each carries as well restrictions on its use which can contribute to the creation of a metaphor. For instance, the verb *eat* carries a requirement that it must have an animate subject and an edible object, so that the sentence "My car eats gas" violates these restrictions. However, we can propose a metaphorical reading for the sentence because in other aspects—ingestion, necessity, excretion, and so on—that verb's meanings and restrictions can be assigned to *car* and *gas*.

In the same way, to say that there is "a nightmare in my closet" violates the restrictions of *nightmare* (that it is a creation of our mind and exists, if anywhere, in our imagination). Now "nightmare" = "concrete object": this new object is never described in the text (only named "Nightmare"), but it is illustrated in the panels. In the text, however, the object creeps, sits at the foot of the bed, cries, and is tucked in bed. Since a nightmare cannot do any of these things, the reader must struggle to interpret these metaphors: what can creep, sit, cry, and get tucked in? Children. Thus, the nightmare is described in language used to describe a frightened child, and the metaphor creates a link (where word choice did not) between the object of fear and the child.

In *Wild Things*, on the other hand, we wait until the fourth panel before any indication of a lexical violation. There, a forest begins to grow in Max's room. This violation of the restrictions of the word *room* and the subsequent description of ceiling and walls—"his ceiling hung with vines and the walls became the world all around" (panel 6)—creates not a metaphor but a conceit. Since it is impossible for the walls to become the world, we struggle to explain the contradiction, in much the same way we struggle with the conceits of seventeenth-century metaphysical poets. This struggle with place is complemented by a struggle with time, for Max sails "through night and day and in and out of weeks and almost over a year" (panel 8). These prepositions create the expectation that their objects will be nouns of place, not those of time. Thus, from the beginning of Max's adventure, violations of place and time are used to separate Max and the reader from the "real" world and isolate him in dream or fantasy. No such separation occurs in *Nightmare,* where the confrontation with the creature is very much part of the child's actual world.

The metaphors of "room = world" and "time = place" break down when Max smells something actual; he then once again sails back through time into the reality of his room. This journey motif allows Sendak to separate the boy from the wild things, which exist only in that nether world, unnamed and uncharted. Mayer, on the other hand, turns the boy's fear into a concrete object which remains very close to the boy. Which is the best strategy for dealing with our emotions must remain for psychologists to debate.

As the following chart reveals, the style and content of the illustrations in these books also create different structural relationships:

Panel	*Wild Things*	*Nightmare*
1	Max	room
2	Max	bed
3	room	closet
4	room	room
5	room	bed
6	world	bed
7	sea	room
8	sea	room
9	where . . . (shore)	bed
10	where . . .	closet
11	where . . .	closet
12	where . . .	creature
13	where . . .	boy
14	where . . .	boy
15	where . . .	creature
16	where . . . (shore)	creature
17	sea	room
18	room	room
19		room
20		room

Each arc links panels which are essentially the same basic scene, except for changes in coloring, light, position of characters, or other details. For instance, panels 3 and 18 of *Wild Things* are essentially the same view of the boy's room while panels 4 and 5 are revised views of the room as it changes to the "world outside." These arcs illustrate how both texts foreground the experience of the protagonist—either journey or confrontation—and then return the boy to the room where it all began. For Sendak, however, this movement is controlled and symmetrical, so that the dissolution of panels from room to sea to shore to where-the-wild-things-are is recapitulated as the boy emerges from the experience. In Mayer's book, on the other hand, images of bed and closet door which had been part of the boy's "real" world recur in the experiential phase of the story, so that the return to the room in panel 17 is not as dramatic. In this way, the pattern of illustrations parallels the differences between the two experiences which I discussed earlier. If the boy's struggle in *Nightmare* is not separated from the "real" world, then this ebb and flow of images corresponds to the blending of real and imagined. There is no going and coming; dream and real coexist for the child and share an equal importance.

Mayer's drawings depend on a mixture of light green, orange, and brown washes and inked contours or textures over them.

The room, which occupies 40% of the panels, is divided in half, with the closet and bureau on the left page and the window and bed on the right. The closet is given emphasis over other objects by its size, being a bit taller than the bureau next to it. The window is draped with a still smaller white curtain which billows out into the room, revealing in each panel a white moon in a green sky. Then, finally, in this left to right reading, the white of the pillow and sheets and the white of the boy's face complete the progression from large door to boy. The room is detailed with military toys—gun, cannon, army helmet, toy soldiers, bugle, fighter plane—which at first lie about on the bed and floor, but in later panels are put to use by the boy. For instance, in panel 7 the boy is wearing the helmet, holding the gun, and, with a confident expression for the first time, is bunkered behind his pillow with cannon and toy soldier before him. The creature is introduced in panel 8, as it sneaks on tiptoe out of the closet in the dark. The panel is awash in darker greens and browns and the creature is as tall as the room, green with extensive cross-hatching (as is the entire panel). However, this creature is more goofy than frightening; no claws, sharp teeth, or mean eyes characterize its physique. So when the boy turns on the light and sees a pink creature with green dots, droopy eyes, and a sad expression squatting on the bed post wringing his hands, he smiles and, in the very next panel, forgets his fear and threatens the poor cowering creature.

In this confrontation between nightmare and boy, the linear composition of the room gives way to a close-up of the characters in which the boy and creature mingle. This shift begins in panel 9, where the creature, sitting hunched over at the edge of the bed, and the boy, leaning back with gun and right leg extended, complete between them an oval shape—the eye traveling from the details of one round to the other and back again. This oval is recreated in the following two panels, as it stretches into a more oblique shape, is lost when the panels focus in on creature and boy alone, and then is resurrected in panel 15, where the boy is now leaning forward, motioning to the creature to be quiet as it leans back crying. The oval collapses in panel 16 when the boy touches the monster for the first time, grabbing him by the finger and pulling him to bed. The creature and boy are now one line stretching from the top left corner of the panel to the lower right, dribbling off to fallen helmet and discarded gun. The visual metaphor created by this composition is obvious: the boy and creature dancing in the circle and finally merging are one. That correspondence is reinforced by the literary metaphor of "nightmare = child," which I discussed earlier, and is consistent with the depiction of the creature sucking its finger and mimicking the expressions of the boy in the last four panels of the story, as they both get into bed and wait for yet another nightmare. (pp. 124-25)

Unlike the creature in *Nightmare* whose description is determined only by the drawings, Sendak's wild things must have the terrible teeth, yellow eyes and claws referred to in the text. And they do. But in addition, the wild things look like Max: many have horns or ears and long talons or claws which mirror the pointy ears and animal paws of Max's wolf suit. Besides their appearance the wild things repeat Max's gestures. Each of the two-page panels share a compounding compositional style (panels 8-15). In each Max and the wild things line up across the page gesturing, dancing, swinging from trees, marching, sleeping, and so on. This neat repetition of each creature modifying just a bit here or there the gesture or attitude of its neighbor reinforces the link between all of them and Max. Furthermore, just as Mayer linked boy and creature with

Quickly I turned on the light and caught him
sitting at the foot of my bed.

From There's a Nightmare in My Closet, *written and illustrated by Mercer Mayer. The Dial Press, 1968. Copyright © 1968 by Mercer Mayer. All rights reserved. Reproduced by permission of the publisher, Dial Books for
Young Readers.*

literary *and* visual metaphors, Sendak uses compounding and
repetition both as literary and visual devices to bind the characters together.

Another difference between the creatures of *Wild Things* and
Nightmare is the tension which exists in Sendak's drawings, a
tension which does not develop in Mayer's. The cover of Mayer's book shows a creature's eye peeking out of a closet and
a worried boy on a tricycle. This drawing does not reflect the
passive character of the creature in the story, but gives instead
the impression of danger. Similarly, Sendak's cover (a single
sleeping wild thing sitting in a grove of trees with an empty
boat moored near by) does not reflect the threatening postures
or expressions of the creatures in the story. Even though Max
is taming the wild things in panel 10, one last creature in line
lurks in the bushes to the right. Even though Max is king in
panel 11, one last creature to the right sits behind a tree with
a more sinister smile than the rest. In each panel (except,
possibly, for the one where they are asleep) one of the wild
things seems a bit less restrained, a bit nastier than the rest.
This tension gives Max's triumph more credibility. His har-
nessing of the potential dangers of sharp claws and teeth gives
the story more drama than the boy's triumph in *Nightmare* over
an almost toothless, goofy-faced, clawless creature which cow-
ers and cries too easily.

The drawings of each of these books complement the text of
each panel in one of three ways. They can provide an example
by explaining or giving details for a general statement in the
text. They can provide a setting which does not deal with any
specific statement in the text, but establishes a general scene.
Finally, they can provide an illustration reproducing some statement in the text. In most instances, both authors depend on
illustration to support the text of a panel. But Sendak uses his
drawings as examples in almost 20% of the panels and ignores
setting, while Mayer uses his drawings to establish setting in
almost 10% of his panels, and ignores example. (p. 126)

The text and drawings of both these stories attempt to develop
correspondences which reinforce the central theme. In *Nightmare* the boy manages to control his fear by frightening the
creature into submission. He turns the weapon of fear—here
made concrete by the toys of war—against the creature to
subdue him. The creature, though never established in the
illustrations as a threat, is characterized in the literary and visual
metaphors as a child, if not the boy himself. The boy then is
in the precarious position of using such extraordinary measures
against a harmless child. In contrast, the text and drawings of
Wild Things contribute to a subtle crescendo of mastery as the
boy controls the wild things, and then a decrescendo as he
returns to his room. As the size of the drawings increases and
then shrinks, all sorts of other developments, such as the metaphors of time and place, the topics of the illustrations, the
compounding style of both text and drawing, also expand and
contract, drawing us into this ordered, controlled experience.
The entire enterprise—text, drawings, printing, story—becomes one metaphor for Max's going and coming. For he does
not control his anger with a weapon (the hammers and forks
he uses in the opening panels are left behind); rather he exerts
his will and manages the wild things in that place, in himself,
so that in the last drawing he can remove the hood of his wolf
suit and sleepily scratch his head, child-like for the first time.
Just as Max's parents controlled him by their authority, so he
controls his anger through his own will. So Sendak controls
us subtly, structurally, covertly.

This contrast of control by management or intimidation lies at
the heart of the distinction I am proposing between the interplay
of content and style in these two books. A comparison of the
two reveals that *Where the Wild Things Are* is an excellent
book because every aspect of it—drawings, layout, and story—
contributes to the central theme of control. Each facet of the
book's style reinforces another, so that the experience of the
book for the reader emulates Max's experience. Thus, the artist
gives no explicit moral, and the reader, no matter of what age,
is left without a lesson. Like the wild things, which become
Max's playmates, we are drawn into the experience unconscious of the artist's manipulation. We are conscious only of
pleasure because patterns such as coordination, expansion and
contraction, and repetition manage our responses as Max manages both the wild things and his own anger. (pp. 126-27)

> *Paul G. Arakelian, "Text and Illustration: A Stylistic
> Analysis of Books by Sendak and Mayer," in* Chil-
> dren's Literature Association Quarterly, *Vol. 10, No.
> 3, Fall, 1985, pp. 122-27.**

IF I HAD . . .   (1968)

If we had every printed *If I Had . . .* wish, we couldn't ask for
anything more; but this tyke has a singular paranoi-ance: everybody picks on him (and his dog). He'd like a gorilla to

scare off the big boys at school, an alligator to keep them away in the water, a lion to look after his puppy, a snake to frighten little sister away from his toys, a porcupine to save his seat at the movies. All he has is . . . ''a big brother—and he's almost as good.'' The porcupine pillow has possibilities but the others exemplify revenge by brute force. And the steel-spectacled *schlemiel* protected by a football-padded brother is a stereotype that won't encourage timid souls to think better of themselves or stand up for themselves.

> *A review of "If I Had . . . ," in* Kirkus Service, *Vol. XXXVI, No. 15, August 1, 1968, p. 813.*

The other side of the sibling-rivalry coin, this slight book has a youngster pondering how a pet gorilla, alligator, lion, or porcupine would keep the neighborhood bullies at bay. . . . The pictures are the thing here—a properly boyish bespectacled narrator and a fine tongue-in-cheek ferociousness for his fantasized menagerie.

> *Clifford A. Ridley, in a review of "If I Had . . . ," in* The National Observer, *November 3, 1969, p. 21.*

TERRIBLE TROLL   (1968)

Though children may be captured momentarily by its abbreviated story line and its jaunty hero, this book will be most appreciated by adults. A small boy imagines that he and his cat serve as squires to a medieval knight, assisting him to slay dragons, champion distressed damsels and, disastrously, to seek out a troll. Their adventures are told in spare text and elaborately detailed three-color drawings. Relying heavily on sight gags to project the story's humor, the author-artist juxtaposes details from the hero's real and fantasy worlds—i.e., radiators in a baronial hall. Since these anachronisms and the exaggeratedly Gothic architecture shown are essentially adult in appeal, it seems unlikely that most children will be particularly amused by them and, indeed, there is no guarantee that very young children would even notice the double-dating details. In addition, the surprise ending in which the troll, rather than the knight, is victorious and the boy's sheepish admission that ''I'm glad I don't live a thousand years ago'' seem more an adult snicker at childish activity than a wholeheartedly humorous approach to be enjoyed by children themselves.

> *Elva Harmon, in a review of "Terrible Troll," in* School Library Journal, *an appendix to* Library Journal, *Vol. 15, No. 5, January, 1969, p. 60.*

I AM A HUNTER   (1969)

An imaginative treatment of an imaginative, rebellious little boy that doesn't provide the usual safe home-free ending that security-conscious young children may need. In a very attractive book that features one sentence of text per each double-page spread, Mr. Mayer presents a little hero who fights an enormous snake (the garden hose), overcomes a giant (piled up trash cans), eats like a cave man, and plays sea captain in his bath, throughout meeting only disapproval from his elders, who are depicted as frustrating Philistines. In the end, he simply sails away in his bath-tub, leaving his puzzled parents knee-deep in water. Though the expressive pen-and-ink sketches washed with pastel colors are remarkably clever, the book suffers in comparison to Sendak's *Where the Wild Things Are* (Harper, 1963), which handles a similar theme of childhood

rebellion but includes a realistic aftermath that shows its young hero returning from his daydream.

> *Mary Ann Wentroth, in a review of "I Am a Hunter," in* School Library Journal, *an appendix to* Library Journal, *Vol. 15, No. 8, April, 1969, p. 104.*

FROG, WHERE ARE YOU?   (1969)

Again friend frog is the come-on, as boy and dog search for him, stirring up a hornet's nest—and other troubles—before finding him near the pond, the proud father (assuming it's *he*) of a new family: in his place, boy takes home one of the babies. There's less light mockery than in the first, and a narrower range of expression generally—just action and reaction. But lively and easy enough to follow without words of explanation (if you assume also that the babies are flash-born).

> *A review of "Frog, Where Are You?" in* Kirkus Reviews, *Vol. XXXVII, No. 17, September 1, 1969, p. 925.*

[*Frog, Where Are You?*] is a delight from the first page when frog responds on a moonlit night to the call of an age-old song, to the last when a disgruntled offspring whose jumping is not yet accomplished, sounds what must be a discordant note. Though the bravely-booted boy carries the tune . . . , the dog provides some fine accompaniment as he searches for frog in his own way. Throughout, the expression of emotions is remarkably succinct.

> *Ingeborg Boudreau, in a review of "Frog, Where Are You?" in* The New York Times Book Review, *October 26, 1969, p. 44.*

A small book, its story told in pictures (one or two here really are worth a thousand words) and the plot easily comprehensible to the very young pre-reader. . . . [The] illustrations show one silly situation after another with just the sort of humor small children love (boy clinging to branches discovers he is draped between the prongs of a deer's antlers). The ending is satisfying, and a general air of cheerful nonsense pervades all.

> *Zena Sutherland, in a review of "Frog, Where Are You?" in* Bulletin of the Center for Children's Books, *Vol. 23, No. 5, January, 1970, p. 85.*

The charm of this pocket-size title lies in Mr. Mayer's detailed, humor-filled illustrations. The book is a fine impetus to imaginative story-telling—the different adventures of the three main characters are depicted with a subtlety that requires close attention to pictorial detail.

> *Marjorie Lewis, in a review of "Frog, Where Are You?" in* School Library Journal, *an appendix to* Library Journal, *Vol. 16, No. 8, April, 1970, p. 111.*

A SPECIAL TRICK   (1970)

It's all a matter of words, the words in the magician's dictionary that Elroy picks up when he's cleaning the tent hoping to be taught some tricks. ''Bing-dong-galaplop-bee-there,'' muttered inadvertently brings forth a monstrous six-eyed galaplop: a frantic ''Airis fare o farethee air. Fillthee air with hoppen hare'' replaces him with rabbits the size of big pigs; and so it goes until all is gone—including the tent and Elroy's pants—except the book. Which, read until dawn, yields the words to reverse all spells. The tent is reassembled, the pants reappear

. . . and Elroy retains the power to turn his bed into a winged pony at will, next to which the magician's promised "special trick"—producing a lollipop—is piffle. There's no special magic about the story either, just a dollop of wish fulfillment and a lexicon of mumbo-jumbo. Plus pictures in the shades of Rick Schreiter.

> *A review of "A Special Trick," in* Kirkus Reviews, *Vol. XXXVIII, No. 4, February 15, 1970, p. 170.*

If Maurice Sendak hadn't created *Where the Wild Things Are, A Special Trick* would be a rather spectacular book. As it is, Mercer's title, for a slightly older audience, seems unbecomingly imitative, but is still enjoyable and probably useful in elementary school libraries. The detailed pictures are interesting and competently done. Monsters abound, but are controlled by the words culled from a magician's handbook; this ability of Elroy's to control his environment may offer some children encouragement and be good for them to read about.

> *Jane M. Sepmeier, in a review of "A Special Trick," in* School Library Journal, *an appendix to* Library Journal, *Vol. 16, No. 9, May, 1970, p. 61.*

The author takes a familiar story, gives it an original twist, tells it with wit and humor and illustrates it in detailed full-color paintings. What more can a reader ask?

> *Amy Kellman, in a review of "A Special Trick," in* Grade Teacher, *Vol. 88, No. 1, September, 1970, p. 161.*

A rollicking sorcerer's apprentice type of fantasy. . . . Fairly scary in places and the usual concluding hint that it was all a dream may not be quite enough for an overimaginative four-year-old, but some will revel in the horrific.

> *Brigitte Weeks, in a review of "A Special Trick," in* Book World—The Washington Post, *September 19, 1976, p. H4.*

MINE (with Marianna Mayer, 1970)

Whimsical black-and-white line drawings illustrate the concepts of "mine" and "yours" for viewers through the actions of a grabby little boy. He tries to take such things as bones, dolls, fish, etc. away from their owners but is rebuffed in his attempts. Finally returning to the mess and clutter of his own room, he proclaims it "mine"; but when his mother presents him with broom and dustpan and says "yours," he woefully accepts these too, acknowledging (in smaller print) "mine." The alterations in the type size of "yours" and "mine" (the sole text) are apt, but the episodes of grabbiness are unevenly humorous and mothers may be more easily amused by some of the incidents than children will be.

> *Marian L. Strickland, in a review of "Mine!" in* School Library Journal, *an appendix to* Library Journal, *Vol. 17, No. 6, February, 1971, p. 49.*

In this selfish world of today where the idea of "Mine" and "Yours" is so little respected, parents and teachers alike should welcome this clever little book. They will consider it a "must" for both home and school library. It drives its lesson home effectively by employing persons and things encountered in the child's environment. The picture style of the book carries the idea so that little explanation is needed.

> *Sister Mary Henry, in a review of "Mine," in* Catholic Library World, *Vol. 42, No. 7, March, 1971, p. 459.*

A BOY, A DOG, A FROG, AND A FRIEND (with Marianna Mayer, 1971)

Again, no words—but this time a little explanation would be in order. A big nuisance of a turtle has made off with the boy's fishing rod, bitten the dog's paw, pulled him into the water by his tail, and, after being followed by the frog, has disappeared, only to reappear floating on his back. Is it so strange for a turtle to float? Not to most children, who'll think the boy poling the turtle toward shore really strange. Somehow or other, sooner (for some) or later (for others), it all gets straightened out: the boy, the dog and the frog, thinking the turtle dead, are about to bury him when he rights himself and there is general rejoicing. There'll be questions . . . and those about being buried alive parents might wish hadn't been raised.

> *A review of "A Boy, a Dog, a Frog and a Friend," in* Kirkus Reviews, *Vol. XXXIX, No. 5, March 1, 1971, p. 231.*

In *A Boy, A Dog, A Frog and A Friend* . . . , Mercer and Marianna Mayer prove that they are as adept as ever at telling a story without a single word. Yet, somehow they manage to fill their book not only with action but with feeling too. . . . Now a fishing trip and a series of minor mishaps introduce a new friend, an equally child-pleasing one.

> *Pamela Marsh, "From Frog to Friend," in* The Christian Science Monitor, *May 6, 1971, p. B5.**

Skillfully executed sepia-toned line drawings not only capture the excitement of an early morning fishing trip interrupted by an uninvited hard-shelled guest but also convey a sense of childlike wonder and response to the unexpected in a manner which is neither stereotyped nor sentimental. A small book, but one with potential for enlarging the "reader's" sympathetic reactions to the human comedy.

> *Mary M. Burns, in a review of "A Boy, a Dog, a Frog and a Friend," in* The Horn Book Magazine, *Vol. XLVII, No. 3, June, 1971, p. 279.*

The Mayers may be slipping into formula with this follow-up to *A Boy, a Dog and a Frog* and *Frog, Where Are You?* but the appeal of their latest picture story without words is undeniable. Of course, readers will have to understand death in order to appreciate the turtle's hoax. In fact it's a deceptively violent little world that the Mayers depict. But there is no blood, no harm done.

> *Christopher Lehmann-Haupt, in a review of "A Boy, a Dog, a Frog and a Friend," in* The New York Times, *December 14, 1971, p. 43.*

THE QUEEN ALWAYS WANTED TO DANCE (1971)

. . . so the King, deeming it unqueenly, banned dancing altogether; she took to singing in its place (and every place, including the chicken coop), so the King forbid that too. "Now," she smiled secretively, "you've gone too far," and "even in libraries, where no one is supposed to talk, people whispered" it. To make a longish story short, everyone is soon in jail having a ball—except the Queen, who arrests herself, and the woebegone King, who finally does the same, the next day changing the law. It's the sort of thing Jay Williams might make sport of though his plots are usually cleverer; here it simply collapses of its own crudity. The pictures—sh-sh!—bear a coarse resemblance to Sendak, conjuring up visions of a graph-papered world.

> *A review of "The Queen Always Wanted to Dance,"*
> *in* Kirkus Reviews, *Vol. XXXIX, No. 7, April 1,*
> *1971, p. 358.*

Mercer Mayer's irreverent tale about a domestic tiff which turns into a national crisis is madcap in mood. It can be taken as a superb bit of nonsense, or given deeper shades of meaning. "'You have made this kingdom a much better place to live in since you put everyone in jail, Your Majesty,' said the people who thought singing and dancing were a silly waste of time."

> *Jennifer Smith, "A Little Sense, a Little Nonsense,"*
> *in* The Christian Science Monitor, *June 26, 1971, p.*
> *B7.*

The text is cleverly repetitive and contains phrases listeners will delight in repeating. The illustrations, though subdued in color, are quite humorous. Unfortunately, some of the pictures covering two-page spreads do not illustrate the immediately preceding paragraphs, which may prove confusing to young children.

> *Gail A. Furnas, in a review of "The Queen Always*
> *Wanted to Dance," in* Library Journal, *Vol. 96, No.*
> *13, July, 1971, p. 2358.*

BUBBLE BUBBLE (1973)

Mercer Mayer is an author-illustrator who never lets his audience down, and they will appreciate this silly, wordless book

Mayer with two of his characters, "Little Monster"® and "Professor Wormbog." Courtesy of Mercer Mayer.

too. It's all about the fantasy creatures a small boy blows up when he buys a bubble pipe. . . . Book and pictures are superior entertainment for the nonreader, and the reader, as well.

> *A review of "Bubble Bubble," in* Publishers Weekly,
> *Vol. 203, No. 12, March 19, 1973, p. 71.*

Mayer's typical watercolor illustrations carry this story-without-words. . . . The qualities of soap bubbles are well captured—they float, reflect rainbow colors, and burst when touched. The book is a good size (5¾" x 6") for young children to handle, and libraries trying to build a collection of textless books will want to add this one.

> *Lillian Canzler, in a review of "Bubble Bubble," in*
> Library Journal, *Vol. 98, No. 13, July, 1973, p.*
> *2188.*

Mr. Mayer has drawn so many children's illustrations by now that he tends to fall back on clichés he himself once invented. . . . Still, this story in pictures of a boy and his magic bubble-maker seems to me unusually charming, and reminds me of the first time I ever looked at Mr. Mayer's work.

> *Christopher Lehmann-Haupt, in a review of "Bubble*
> *Bubble," in* The New York Times Book Review,
> *December 10, 1973, p. 35.*

MRS. BEGGS AND THE WIZARD (1973)

Mysterious events materialize at Mrs. Beggs' boarding house when Z. P. Alabasium, "wizard extraordinaire," rents a room. The wizard is outwitted with a Beggs' brand of witchcraft, but creepier consequences ensue. Kids love **Mrs. Beggs and the Wizard,** so be prepared for enthusiastic outbursts from the audience. The text is witty and unpredictable, synchronized with fantastic illustrations and chock-full of the strangest creatures imaginable. Don't read too fast; there's wizardry to see and hear.

> *Leslie Bodine, in a review of "Mrs. Beggs and the*
> *Wizard," in* Children's Book Review Service, *Vol.*
> *2, No. 4, December, 1973, p. 26.*

[After Mrs. Beggs routs the evil Alabasium,] the plot takes a surprising turn in a book which lovers of the absurd can enjoy again and again. It's hard to say which is more fun, the story or the *fin de siècle* artwork.

> *A review of "Mrs. Beggs and the Wizard," in* Pub-
> lishers Weekly, *Vol. 204, No. 25, December 17,*
> *1973, p. 38.*

The delightful text tells just enough and lets the illustrations extend the story, e.g., a gargantuan monster lurks behind Mrs. Beggs' bedroom which the landlady who only "heard strange noises" cannot see. The detailed and colorful drawings conjure up creatures silly enough not to be absolutely frightening, although they are reminiscent of Sendak's "Wild Things." (pp. 41-2)

> *Kristin E. Hammond, in a review of "Mrs. Beggs*
> *and the Wizard," in* School Library Journal, *an ap-*
> *pendix to* Library Journal, *Vol. 20, No. 5, January,*
> *1974, pp. 41-2.*

FROG GOES TO DINNER   (1974)

The boy's family goes out to dinner at a "Fancy Restaurant" thus giving the ubiquitous stowaway frog a chance to run riot in unusually elegant surroundings. He wastes no time—jumping down an orchestra member's saxophone, popping out from under a lady's salad, and giving one startled diner a great big kiss. Even when dressed for a night on the town, Mayer's people have the same baggy attire and top-heavy, jowled visages that make their double takes so arresting; on our part, we could follow frog's by now predictable antics with our eyes closed. (pp. 738-39)

> *A review of "Frog Goes to Dinner," in* Kirkus Reviews, *Vol. XLII, No. 14, July 15, 1974, pp. 738-39.*

Although similar in format and style to the earlier wordless picture books in the series, this story is less subtle than its predecessors—closer to farce than to comedy. But Frog, who has been endowed by his creator with infinite charm, continues to be irresistibly funny.

> *Mary M. Burns, in a review of "Frog Goes to Dinner," in* The Horn Book Magazine, *Vol. L, No. 6, December, 1974, p. 685.*

The drawings are funny indeed, and the book passes with flying colors the test for wordless stories: the plot is crystal-clear. Animals, action, humor, disruption—what more could any child want? (p. 83)

> *Zena Sutherland, in a review of "Frog Goes to Dinner," in* Bulletin of the Center for Children's Books, *Vol. 28, No. 5, January, 1975, pp. 82-3.*

TWO MORAL TALES; TWO MORE MORAL TALES   (1974)

If not profoundly moral, these wordless fables at least are imaginative proofs of the truism that bears will be bears . . . as well as pigs, pigs . . . foxes, foxes . . . and eggs, soon enough, chicks. In the two strongest episodes a pair of pigs spruce up for a motorcar outing that ends at the local wallow and a bear, who had been quite pleased with his ragtag clothing, turns the tables on a well tailored goat who makes fun of him; all four (printed two to a volume in "turnabout" style—that is, upside down from each other beginning at opposite covers) rely on Mayer's cleverly anthropomorphized animal caricatures. And they succeed because he matches their slight humorous content with an appropriately modest physical format. The visual whimsys are more to the point than that eternally gerplunking *Frog* . . . , and those morals—admittedly more in line with folk wisdom than existential philosophy—won't cause pre-readers any problems. (pp. 873-74)

> *A review of "Two Moral Tales" and "Two More Moral Tales," in* Kirkus Reviews, *Vol. XLII, No. 16, August 15, 1974, pp. 873-74.*

Follow the wordless story of a bear that dresses in rags, then forcibly trades clothes with a dapper goat that dares to make fun of him. Then turn the tiny book over, start from the front, and chuckle over the odd-looking bird that discards his top hat, sees it being used for a nest, dons it, and finds an egg hatching on his head. The stories in the second book are funnier and no more moral. . . . Mayer's black-and-white drawings are less careful and more sparing in humorous detail than some of his other books, but are funny enough to carry off a pleasant gimmick.

> *A review of "Two Moral Tales" and "Two More Moral Tales," in* The Booklist, *Vol. 71, No. 3, October 1, 1974, p. 178.*

The gay Mercer Mayer style consists of animal actions and antics with human foibles. . . . The morals are not pointed or overly obvious, so they can be interpreted in several ways. Children, parents, and teachers who really enjoy stories without words will find much to do with these action-illustrated tales.

> *Annette C. Blank, in a review of "Two Moral Tales" and "Two More Moral Tales," in* Children's Book Review Service, *Vol. 3, No. 4, December, 1974, p. 27.*

ONE MONSTER AFTER ANOTHER   (1974)

Sally Ann's letter to Lucy Jane changes paws as a thieving Stamp-Collecting Trollusk is robbed by a Letter-Eating Bombanat that is caught by a Bombanat-Munching Grumley in the Ocean of Bubbley Goo. From Grumley to a sea captain the letter goes, but a Typhoonigator sucks up all and deposits the letter on the Edge of Nowhere. Eventually, Sally Ann's letter, which expresses her boredom with everyday living, reaches its destination, but not before the sequence becomes more convoluted. The clunky text is saved by large Mayer illustrations in a full range of resplendently unsavory colors. This book will appease insatiable appetites for monster-fare, if only for a while.

> *A review of "One Monster after Another," in* The Booklist, *Vol. 71, No. 2, September 15, 1974, p. 101.*

For any library with frequent requests for "monster books," this oversize volume is a must. It is filled with several of the most loveable creatures ever created, and should delight rather than frighten even the youngest devotee of demons and dragons. . . . The size of the book (12″ x 10½″) plus a text which begs to be read aloud puts this at the top of the list for story-hours. On the other hand, the illustrations, brimming with humorous details, allow for close scrutiny by individual children as well. (pp. 308-09)

> *Barbara Dill, in review of "One Monster after Another," in* Wilson Library Bulletin, *Vol. 49, No. 4, December, 1974, pp. 308-09.*

The oversize pages afford Mayer a big canvas for a series of monsters in the Sendak tradition, and the illustrations have some nice touches of nonsense, but the story proliferates into rather tedious absurdity, with too many variations on the same theme.

> *Zena Sutherland, in a review of "One Monster after Another," in* Bulletin of the Center for Children's Books, *Vol. 28, No. 10, June, 1975, p. 164.*

The author relies on the monsters' names to carry the meager plot. They occur once, often twice, in every sentence: "The Stamp collecting Trollusk stole the letter and gabbled away with a smirk on his snerk." The cuteness is imitative of the worst of Seuss; the drawings, though competent and well-composed, are imitative of Sendak.

All of the actors in this adventure are male; the only females are Sally Ann and her friend, and the ironic point is that they're totally unaware of all that's been going on. . . . Being generous, the book has about five "good" pages and even by Golden Book standards, that's not a bargain. . . . (p. 5)

Marcia Newfield, "Golden Books with Tinsel Contents," in Interracial Books for Children Bulletin, Vol. 6, Nos. 5 & 6, 1975, pp. 5-6.

Since colours and monster-expressions are heavily indebted to Sendak, and name-styles to Dr. Seuss, it is difficult to detach oneself and give due credit where this book deserves it. There is real humour in the crowded details of American roadsides with lurking monsters, or gnome-like sailors and startled fishes, and fine overall design. . . . The endpapers are particularly attractive.

M. Hobbs, in a review of "One Monster after Another," in The Junior Bookshelf, *Vol. 41, No. 1, February, 1977, p. 16.*

YOU'RE THE SCAREDY-CAT (1974)

The big and ugly green garbage can monster is yet another bastard offspring of the Wild Things and it must be said that this fellow—with his bat ears, blunt cut hairdo and improbable pink nose—won't scare anyone except older brother, who invents him to enliven an impromptu night of backyard camping and then mistakes a friendly scavenging sheepdog for the creature of his own imagination. Younger brothers will recognize big brother for the nursery con man that he is and enjoy seeing him fooled; other observers will recognize an uncomfortable lot of resemblances to other nighttime escapades and other artists—similarities which make the green garbage can monster even less scarifying than he is at first meeting.

A review of "You're the Scaredy-Cat," in Kirkus Reviews, *Vol. XLII, No. 18, September 15, 1974, p. 1005.*

Using little text, Mercer Mayer's colorful drawings tell most of the story; and although his unscary monster looks like those in his other books—*There's a Nightmare in My Closet* . . . , *Mrs. Beggs and the Wizard* . . .—the humor is fresh and right on target for young readers.

Kristin E. Hammond, in a review of "You're the Scaredy-Cat," in School Library Journal, *an appendix to* Library Journal, *Vol. 21, No. 4, December, 1974, p. 38.*

A nicely sustained monologue half-tells the story, and the pictures do the rest. . . . The monster is reminiscent of Sendak, but the frowsty children are pure Mayer, the scope of the tale is just right for a young audience, and humor in the situation and the pictures is not overstated. (pp. 96-7)

Zena Sutherland, in a review of "You're the Scaredy-Cat," in Bulletin of the Center for Children's Books, *Vol. 28, No. 6, February, 1975, pp. 96-7.*

Mercer Mayer is clearly a disciple of Maurice Sendak and attempts to conjure fantasy out of a convincing everyday world—but he lacks Sendak's sure and brilliant touch. . . . The monster [in *You're the Scaredy-Cat*] is charming in a suitably frightening way (Sendak again), and children who see the point might like it and find it funny.

Virginia Makins, "Buns and Comforters," in The Times Educational Supplement, *No. 3258, November 18, 1977, p. 32.**

ONE FROG TOO MANY (with Marianna Mayer, 1975)

One can only go so far with amphibian acrobatics and mute double takes so it's easy to see why this new arrival . . . might well be one frog too many. Of course jealousy provides the perfect occasion for big frog to make outrageous faces—naughty and chagrined in turn—and his obvious appeal to human acting-out siblings will bounce him right into the playroom.

A review of "One Frog Too Many," in Kirkus Reviews, *Vol. XLIII, No. 16, August 15, 1975, p. 912.*

A new addition to the wordless *A Boy, A Dog, and a Frog* series, and more charming and humorous than ever. Frog does his best to rid himself of the newest member—another frog. His efforts meet with disapproval and failure. In the end he seems happy to have another frog in the family. Especially appropriate for all young children experiencing pangs of jealousy over a new sibling, this book will elicit chuckles from all children and adults who "read" through it.

Judy Resnick, in a review of "One Frog Too Many," in Children's Book Review Service, *Vol. 4, No. 1, September, 1975, p. 2.*

One Frog Too Many is a beautifully illustrated, wordless book which has as its central theme the issue of jealousy and how group pressure is used to force the protagonist, Frog, to conform. One day, Boy receives a surprise package, out of which pops a baby frog. . . . Frog number one is not too happy about this newcomer, and the remainder of the book focuses on his hostility and the group's reaction to it.

Finally, the group punishes Frog by leaving him behind while they go out for a raft ride. In an act of defiance and desperation, Frog jumps on the raft and kicks Little Frog overboard. Failing to recover Little Frog, the group goes home heartbroken and fully contemptuous of Frog. Little Frog's sudden and unexplained reappearance and the subsequent truce that is reached between the two frogs is very unrealistic. The seriousness of the issues at hand—jealousy, insecurity and the group's punitive approach—are glossed over. Frog's ultimate "acceptance" of Little Frog is more an expression of guilt and submission to group pressure than of healthy adjustment.

The jacket cover summary of the story describes as "hilarious" Frog's efforts "to rid himself of this invader" and promises that "the story and its comical drawings will have young children laughing aloud through many readings." If the expression of human feelings (jealousy and fear in this case) in individualistic and destructive acts is something to be viewed as light entertainment for children, this reviewer seriously questions what kinds of people we adults are trying to mold. (pp. 62-3)

"The Analyses: 'One Frog Too Many'," in Human—and Anti-Human—Values in Children's Books: A Content Rating Instrument for Educators and Concerned Parents, *edited by the Council on Interracial Books for Children, Inc., Racism and Sexism Resource Center for Educators, 1976, pp. 62-3.*

Even though this is a wordless picture book, it can be read aloud, in a fashion. As young children become used to the idea that a sequence of pictures tells a story, they will be more able to give their own verbal descriptions of what they see, eventually producing a sort of story line.

Responses that may be developed are, first and foremost, emotional involvement with the story told through pictures. Enjoyment is the key response. Some children will understand the story in terms of their own experiences with jealousy toward a new brother or sister. Frog's wicked delight in the mishaps he creates for the young frog is a familiar experience for many children. With a little help, they may begin to interpret the story, making some inferences about the need for Frog's change of heart and acceptance of the newcomer when he hops in through the window. Emotional involvement comes, of course, through the pictures and is a direct result of appreciation of them. Children may show some form of empathy for the characters. They may also begin to develop readiness for literary response to a plot structure based on conflict and resolution from experiences in "reading" a wordless picture book like this one. Picture interpretation and inference about the happenings provide important pre-reading experiences.

Because the pictures are small and have many details that children will enjoy, they should be used with a single child or, at most, two or three. A good way to get a child involved with the story is to read the title and ask the child to look at the cover picture to find out what seems to be the trouble between the two frogs. With that preview, you might just let the child move from page to page. Some children will tell the story out loud as it unfolds on the page. Others will simply make comments about details in the pictures. If the child is unfamiliar with picture reading, you may want to "read" a book first, then let the child "read" another one to you. To encourage children to make more inferences about the picture on page one, you might ask what could possibly be in the box and why the box has holes in it. To start children thinking about the problem situation in the plot, ask them to notice the expression on Frog's face in pictures two and three. Why does he look so unhappy? As the plot develops and Frog's treatment of the newcomer becomes more unkind, you can ask children what causes Frog to behave as he does. Ask, too, whether they have ever felt the way Frog feels. Some children will spontaneously respond to the ending by expressing relief that the small frog finds his way back and that Frog accepts him this time. You may want to ask whether the ending is a good one. How else could the story end? What ending would they prefer? (pp. 561-62)

> *May Hill Arbuthnot and Zena Sutherland, "Introducing Literature to Children," in their* Children and Books, *fifth edition, Scott, Foresman and Company, 1977, pp. 556-79.**

AH-CHOO (1976)

Having done *A Boy, a Dog and a Frog* to death, Mayer resorts to an allergic elephant in what the publishers announce as the first of a new series. The elephant's initial sneeze blows over a shack; for this he's taken to court where he sneezes again, knocking over the judge (an owl). Thus on to jail where—you guessed it—he sneezes off the door. There's also a little mouse carrying around the flowers that are causing all the sneezes, and, in the end, there's an allergic female hippopotamus with whom the elephant walks off, beating out his hippo jail guard. For some, all those elephant tears, smirks, scowls and blowing about might substitute for action as well as for words, but they leave us cold. Stifle it.

> *A review of "Ah-Choo," in* Kirkus Reviews, *Vol. XLIV, No. 5, March 1, 1976, p. 253.*

There is an amusing contrast between the book's miniscule size and the enormity of its main character—an allergy-ridden elephant. . . . As usual, Mayer's wordless picture book offers droll humor in its expressive pen-and-ink drawings, and young "readers" will appreciate the exaggerated situations and the easily-assimilated story line.

> *Cynthia Percak Infantino, in a review of "Ah-Choo," in* School Library Journal, *Vol. 22, No. 9, May, 1976, p. 52.*

LIZA LOU AND THE YELLER BELLY SWAMP (1976)

Patched and perky, Mayer's googley-eyed little Liza Lou could be a much younger, black Daisy Mae—and no doubt some will see her as a female Sambo. But Mayer saves his real efforts for the Swamp Haunt, Witch, Gobblygook and hoofed devil that threaten the little girl during her jaunts through the Yeller Belly Swamp. This specialist in terrible trolls and nightmares in closets outdoes himself with these pimpled noses, creepy claws, beast-like haunches, and general ugliness. Characteristically, he borrows from Brer Rabbit for the clever ruses with which Liza Lou outsmarts the monsters and from Hansel and Gretel for her disposal of the witch. You'll have more than one reason to be leery of this, even though you can't deny a gruesome fascination.

> *A review of "Liza Lou and the Yeller Belly Swamp," in* Kirkus Reviews, *Vol. XLIV, No. 8, April 15, 1976, p. 464.*

Mayer has borrowed freely from Brer Rabbit's tricks on Brer Fox: "Burn me, hang me, skin me alive—just don't throw me in that briar patch" becomes "boil *me* in your big pot of water if you must, and chew on my bones as much as you like. But please, oh please, don't . . ." and so on through several rounds. There's even Gretel's oven trick on the witch. But his book is a lot of fun anyway. It has a kick-up-your-heels quality—there's never any question about who's going to have the last laugh on all those dumb monsters. Cheeky Liza Lou . . . is in the prime of her confidence dealing with confederate haunts, warty-nosed witches, slithery gobblygooks, and even the devil himself, while her relatives and the local parson offer a supportive all-black cast. The illustrations show forceful proportion, lively expression, and energetic color with a few unexpectedly quiet flora-fauna backdrops peeking through.

> *Betsy Hearne, in a review of "Liza Lou and the Yeller Belly Swamp," in* Booklist, *Vol. 73, No. 1, September 1, 1976, p. 40.*

Mayer's book is fun to read. Cornball chants, hyperbole and words like "lickety-split" and "skedaddle" spice the text. Lush full-color illustrations are bold enough to accommodate the overdrawn horrors Liza Lou meets. Her cheesecake poses suit the art's florid beauty.

> *Jane Resh Thomas, in a review of "Liza Lou and the Yeller Belly Swamp," in* The New York Times Book Review, *September 19, 1976, p. 18.*

An intrepid little Black heroine is the only strong feature of this story set in the deep rural South. . . . The text limps (especially the verses), and the illustrations, complete with exaggerated features, bare feet, patched clothing, bandanas and crinkly hair, seem stereotypic.

> *Gertrude B. Herman, in a review of "Liza Lou and the Yeller Belly Swamp," in* School Library Journal, *Vol. 23, No. 3, November, 1976, p. 50.*

[As] lively entertainment, ***Liza Lou and the Yeller Belly Swamp*** is the prize of the [five books reviewed, which also include Petronella Breinburg's *Shawn's Red Bike,* Lucille Clifton's *Everett Anderson's Friend,* Ianthe Thomas's *My Street's a Morning Cool Street,* and Arnold Adoff's *Tell Me That I'm Black*]. Written in conventional sentence structures, but with studied colloquialisms and slang, the piece is constructed as a medley of parodies.

Liza Lou, our heroine, is sent on an errand to Gramma's house with "a tote bag full of sweet potatoes" because the old lady is "feeling a mite poorly." Just as the reader settles for the Little Red Riding Hood touch, the author shifts to a Brer Rabbit tone with the entry of Mr. Swamp Haunt, who is as white as any ghost would be, and who is still wearing his Confederate Army hat. Liza Lou outsmarts him with a briar patch routine and is ready for her next encounter with a Caucasian witch. Remembering her Hansel and Gretel, no doubt, "Liza Lou pushed that old swamp witch SPLAT into the pot of boiling water."

Mr. Gobblygook (baby pink) fared no better than his infamous counterpart in the Billy Goats Gruff. When the "rickety old swamp bridge began to creak and sway" . . . "the slithery gobblygook sank—GLUB! GLUB—back into the mucky goo where he belonged." For an encore, our ingenious and brassy Liza Lou entices a reddish-white devil (turned fly) into her little brown jug. Beyond that point shades of Aladdin's Lamp fade, for the parson's wife gives the devil his due with a fly swatter.

In keeping with the mimetic motif, the excellent illustrations of Liza Lou herself have more than a slight resemblance to Maurice Sendak's little people. The background pictures are so teeming with graphic cliche that they border kitsch. Nevertheless, they work well with the text, and the whole package amounts to a good-natured spoof that should amuse readers young and old. (pp. 947-48)

Mary Agnes Taylor, in a review of "Liza Lou and the Yeller Belly Swamp," in The Reading Teacher, *Vol. 30, No. 8, May, 1977, pp. 947-48.*

It is no secret that children adore monster tales and will love these fantastic swamp scenes, lush with fauna, flora, and nasty creatures. *However:* there is something not quite right in the portrayal of Liza and her home. Liza is a pretty little girl with a variety of short sundresses. But each dress is more ragged and patched than the last. Momma, the cottage curtains, the rag doll, etc. are equally tattered. I question the need for all this shabbiness. What must have seemed "cute" to Mr. Mayer looks suspiciously "pickaninny" to me. The Southern dialect and Liza's pet (which I mistook to be a large, pink rat) sadly interfere with the portrayal of a young Black heroine.

Enid Davis, "Picture Books: 'Liza Lou and the Yeller Belly Swamp'," in her The Liberty Cap: A Catalogue of Non-Sexist Materials for Children, *Academy Press Limited, 1977, p. 76.*

HICCUP (1976)

In the wake of **Ah-choo** . . ., Mayer's hippo duo take to a rowboat, where she begins to hiccup and he, gleefully, to douse, smack, and scare her to a cure. The predictable spill (and splash) is followed by just as predictable a switch when, once landed, he gets the hiccups and she seizes the chance to get her own back. We can't imagine even the pictures keeping this afloat, though Mayer's gross, googly-eyed buffoons in scanty finery might amuse others.

> *A review of "Hiccup," in* Kirkus Reviews, *Vol. XLIV, No. 17, September 1, 1976, p. 971.*

[Like Mayer's **Ah-Choo,**] *Hiccup* tackles a familiar malady. The wordless story proceeds in rapid-fire fashion: two hippos' pleasant afternoon boat ride is marred by the lady's bout with the hiccups. Enraged by her companion's attempts to cure her by dumping her overboard, she gets a chance to pay him back when he comes down with the hiccups. With a look that is positively wicked, she triumphantly bonks him on the head with her parasol, tosses him into the water and, adding insult to injury, sticks her tongue out at him. The crisp pen-and-ink drawings are packed with humor and vibrance, and the range of hippo facial expressions is truly superb. Sheer fun!

> *Cynthia Percak Infantino, in a review of "Hiccup," in* School Library Journal, *Vol. 23, No. 4, December, 1976, p. 50.*

One of the best kinds of books for reading to children is the kind that they want to read to you the second time around; you just grunt appreciately at the punch lines, and doze. Here's a perfect example of the genre. . . . [The] plot is too silly to be described, but the kids will laugh and so will you.

> *Michael T. Malloy, "Yes, Virginia, There Are . . . : Let's Hear It for Blood and Gore," in* The National Observer, *December 25, 1976, p. 14.**

PROFESSOR WORMBOG IN SEARCH FOR THE ZIPPERUMP-A-ZOO (1976)

Professor Wormbog collected beasties—every kind from *A* to *Y*. It should have been *A* to *Z*, but unfortunately he did not have a Zipperump-a-Zoo. So the professor decided to try to catch one. . . . Finally, very tired and disappointed, Professor Wormbog went home, where he quickly fell asleep thinking, "I guess I'll never have a Zipperump-a-Zoo of my very own." But while the text ends there the story doesn't, and children will delight in seeing the last double-page spread and realizing they know something the professor will probably never find out.

Mayer has brought together an engaging group of creatures—most of a pleasant nature. Children should enjoy trying to identify them as they appear throughout the story by flipping back to Wormbog's illustrated chart that lists alphabetically his entire collection. The book is oversize and the illustrations are in full color, but it would still be best to use this with small groups or one child, because each page is full of humorous details that older readers, especially, will not want to miss. This might be an interesting leadoff to have children create their own kinds of collections from *A* to *Z*. (pp. 312-13)

> *Barbara Dill, in a review of "Professor Wormbog in Search for the Zipperump-a-Zoo," in* Wilson Library Bulletin, *Vol. 51, No. 4, December, 1976, pp. 312-13.*

[**Professor Wormbog in Search for the Zipper-ump-a-Zoo** is identical] in format and tone to the author's oversized **One Monster After Another.** . . . The wild conglomeration of monsters and people (in garish colors outlined in black) presents a cluttered appearance light-years away from his meticulously-etched and subtly humorous "boy, dog, and frog" stories. Naturally, this book will be eagerly snatched up by monster-loving children, but more artful monsters can be found in Sendak's classic *Where the Wild Things Are* (Harper, 1963), Zemach's *The Judge* (Farrar, 1969), and Peet's *Cyrus the Unsinkable Sea Serpent* (Houghton, 1975).

> *Cynthia Percak Infantino, in a review of "Professor Wormbog in Search for the Zipper-ump-a-Zoo," in* School Library Journal, *Vol. 24, No. 1, September, 1977, p. 111.*

LITTLE MONSTER'S WORD BOOK (1977)

Richard Scarry, move over. Mercer Mayer has a word book. But instead of pigs and rabbits and kittens there are kerplop-puses and trollusks and zipperump-a-zoos here. Hundreds of objects are named in sections on games, weather, holidays, even feelings and "first times."

The attraction of the book is that Mercer Mayer remembers what it was like to be a little kid—the dopey things you did, what appealed to your funny bone—and he's captured it all on paper, in both words and pictures.

This is a book with which lots of little people are going to spend many happy hours.

> *Barbara Karlin, in a review of "Little Monster's Word Book," in* West Coast Review of Books, *Vol. 3, No. 5, September, 1977, p. 55.*

Little Monster's Word Book is an example of what *not* to impose on pre-school children. The pictures are too cluttered and confusing, the vocabulary too advanced for early reading skills, and the monsters, although not scary, are not attractive either.

> *Sally Cartwright, "How Many Hopping Bunnies Can You Count?" in* The Christian Science Monitor, *November 2, 1977, p. B4.**

JUST ME AND MY DAD (1977)

A little boy and his father go camping together. Once they are settled in their campsite, the boy sets about launching their canoe—and sinks it. Father and son go fishing, and the boy cooks their catch—which is stolen by a bear. Father and son dine on scrambled eggs. After dinner, the boy roundly frightens his father with ghost stories—but takes care to hug him so he'll feel better. Then they settle in their tent for a good night's sleep. The illustrations of this little boy's first-person narrative add much to a very simple text. They show, for example, that the characters are whimsical, furry animals. But they show too how understated the child's account is: when, for instance, he tells us, "I pitched the tent," we see him ensnared hopelessly in ropes, poles, and canvas. Above all, they show his adoring admiration for his father, who is a model of patience throughout.

> *Sharon Spredemann Dreyer, "Annotations: 'Just Me and My Dad'," in her* The Bookfinder, a Guide to Children's Literature about the Needs and Problems of Youth Aged 2-15: Annotations of Books Published

1975 through 1978, Vol. 2, *American Guidance Service, Inc., 1981, No. 447.*

LITTLE MONSTER AT WORK (1978)

"What will I be when I grow up," asks Mayer's homely-cute Little Monster, and so his grandfather takes him round to a circus, a medical center, a farmer's market, an airport, the moon, and other places where Little Monster can try out road building, TV work, science, crafts, the fast-food business . . . much as Mayer himself tries on different styles. Having worked his way through Sendak he is now playing Richard Scarry, this time with a bustling, label-filled double page for every field of endeavor. Mayer throws in some dopey one-liners ("Take me to your monster") and adult recognition gags (a submarine captain asks "Have you seen the White Whale," Gene Shalit pans a movie on TV); but even though the pages are a-jumble with monsters all busily at work, they convey no sense of vitality.

> *A review of "Little Monster at Work," in* Kirkus Reviews, *Vol. XLVI, No. 17, September 1, 1978, p. 947.*

APPELARD AND LIVERWURST (1978)

Appelard and Liverwurst, though similar to the scores of picture books about hippopotamuses, rhinoceroses, and Loch Ness-type monsters in incongruous circumstances, is better than most.

When a tornado scatters a circus troupe, a baby rhino, Liverwurst, ends up substituting for farmer Appelard's mule; the result is a bumper crop, which frees Appelard and his few scrawny animals to join the circus. The book is teeming with additional plot: Liverwurst gets excited by a cartload of mushrooms and smashes up the townfolk's vegetable stands on market day; he's imprisoned; his mother has been looking for him all the while and demolishes Appelard's farmhouse and the county jail in her search; a Civil War cannon is dragged out of the museum for protection.

The style is appropriately homespun, colloquial, laconic—excellent for reading aloud. (pp. 178-79)

> *Olga Richard and Donnarae MacCann, in a review of "Appelard and Liverwurst," in* Wilson Library Bulletin, *Vol. 53, No. 2, October, 1978, pp. 178-79.**

LITTLE MONSTER AT HOME; LITTLE MONSTER AT SCHOOL; LITTLE MONSTER'S ALPHABET BOOK; LITTLE MONSTER'S BEDTIME BOOK; LITTLE MONSTER'S COUNTING BOOK; LITTLE MONSTER'S NEIGHBORHOOD (1978)

Sticking with his established bevy of beasts, Mayer has risked monster overkill in these six books, all starring Little Monster and friends. The first finds *Little Monster at Home* giving a guided tour, cellar to attic, and relating each room's functions. . . . *At School,* Little Monster takes part in typical kindergarten activities, eventually befriending the class misfit, Yally. The . . . *Alphabet Book* includes "A . . . a brown, grumpy apple"; "D . . . a dragon"; "J . . . a jester"; etc. The . . . *Bedtime Book* contains rhymes about the Croonies, the Peevish, the Typhoonigator, and the Useless. The . . . *Counting Book,* the best of the series, counts items up to 21, and . . . *Neighborhood* takes readers through Little Monster's section of town, visiting his secret clubhouse, the Grithix Gas Station, church,

and the park. All are illustrated in Mayer's now-familiar style, and while the characters and formats may be a bit worn, they still merit consideration because of the popularity they are bound to enjoy.

> *Hayden Atwood, in a review of "Little Monster at Home" and others, in* School Library Journal, *Vol. 25, No. 7, March, 1979, p. 127.*

LITTLE MONSTER'S MOTHER GOOSE (1979)

Legions of kids who dote on monsters should give Mayer's new book little time to rest on the shelf. In full-color pictures, he illustrates the successes of a road-company Mother Goose tour with the grand dame electing Little Monster as star player. Increasing the fun are asides, before and after the productions, in which the troupers talk, argue and discuss their roles, etc. Acted out are nursery rhymes and they're the big surprise. Nearly all are delightfully fresh, not those every child already knows. Even the familiar ones get a twist, such as "Trollusk, be nimble, / Trollusk, be quick, / Trollusk, jump over the candlestick," or this, replacing the mouse in "Hickory, dickory, dock" with an eerie Croonie.

> *A review of "Little Monster's Mother Goose," in* Publishers Weekly, *Vol. 216, No. 2, July 9, 1979, p. 105.*

It is perfectly understandable that our age should seek a counter to the perceived sweetness and irrelevance of the Mother Goose rhymes we customarily purvey to little children—rhymes whose original social or political zing has faded to a scholarly rustle. This offering from Mercer Mayer is not that book, monster or no monster. In a subplot device of doubtful utility, the eponymous Little Monster plays lead in a sort of extended Mother Goose Play with skits or tableaus depicting various rhymes, mostly unfamiliar, some partially rewritten. There is nothing very monstrous about any of this, and although Mr. Mayer's rather coarse, spiky and busy drawings are full of by-play and wisecracks, it is hard to imagine why anyone would prefer this version to either a traditional Mother Goose (such as those by Marguerite De Angeli, Raymond Briggs or Alice and Martin Provensen) or a truly subversive rendering like that of Charles Addams or (for older readers) Frederick Winsor's *Space Child's Mother Goose.*

> *Georgess McHargue, in a review of "Little Monster's Mother Goose," in* The New York Times Book Review, *September 16, 1979, p. 32.*

What is this constant urge to redo [Mother Goose's] visage and reimagine all her favorite companions? There is a precedent, to be sure, since the original rhymes contained timely political and social commentary. Multitudes of versifiers (myself included) have transported Mother Goose into urban traffic, space-age rockets, even feminist frameworks, and illustrators from the Victorian age to the Doonesbury era have drawn and cornered her. (p. 15)

Once in a while, an illustrator is inspired and the familiar chants take on an energy and verve that we had been lulled into losing. Sometimes, though, the exercise comes across as a make-work project for an idling artist or as a set of crass cash-register jingles. One senses then that there has been a puffing attempt to trade on the reputation of the artist, the result of in-house memos suggesting that maybe this package could sell like Sendak or be a bargain Briggs.

From East of the Sun & West of the Moon, *written and illustrated by Mercer Mayer. Four Winds Press, 1980. Copyright © 1980 by Mercer Mayer. All rights reserved. Reproduced with permission of Four Winds Press, an imprint of Macmillan Publishing Company.*

One such attempt is Mercer Mayer's *Little Monster's Mother Goose*. It resembles nothing so much as a Saturday morning cartoon show commercial. Granted, today's children are tube-tested babies rather than ready readers, but must editors, as the adults in charge, sink to the lowest channel denominator? Are our prime resource, the nation's young, to be brainwashed for a society of binary ethics: the Off or On button and no other, two choices that are really none—either the book that comes on like a TV box or no book at all? *Little Monster* is a fearsome portent, particularly since Mercer Mayer has been a felicitous illustrator-author of many award-winning books for children. *Little Monster's Mother Goose* is monstrous indeed; crude and schlocky, with anachronistic humor that doesn't work.

Examples can be found on just about every page. Here is one of the least offensive: to supplement the weather quatrain "Evening red and morning gray, / Send the traveller on the way; / Evening gray and morning red, / Bring the rain upon his head," a cartoon figure exclaims, "Say, buddy, you're all wet!" (Incidentally, the figure bears a startling spin-off resemblance to one of the creatures from *Where the Wild Things Are*.) Another page offers the superb text

> When I was a little boy
> I had but little wit;

'Tis a long time ago,
And I have no more yet;
Nor ever, ever shall
Until I die,
For the longer I live
The more fool am I.

A creature comments on this, "That boy is the producer's son." Anyone for canned laugh-tracks? (pp. 15, 23)

> *Eve Merriam, "Mother Goosed," in Book World—The Washington Post, November 11, 1979, pp. 15, 23.*

EAST OF THE SUN AND WEST OF THE MOON (1980)

Under the title of the well-known Norwegian folktale . . . , there is here presented a pastiche of Mercer Mayer's creation—part "Frog Prince," part "East of the Sun," part compounded of other familiar motifs, part unfolklike invention. The daughter of a prosperous farmer declines all her suitors. Her father's fortunes fail; she has to forage for food; "Who"—she frets—"will have me now?" Her mother sends her on a journey to the South Wind's spring to fetch water for her languishing father; and when she finds the spring clouded over, she agrees to grant a frog three wishes if he will uncloud it. But she balks at his second wish—that she become his bride—and, when he persists, hurls him against a wall . . . whereupon he turns into a handsome youth bound in marriage (like the white bear/ enchanted prince of "East of the Moon") to a long-nosed troll princess—from whom *our* farmer's daughter proceeds to save him (by some similar, some different means). The parts don't hang together; the whole has no emotional weight (certainly nothing comparable to the original farmer's daughter's attachment to the white bear); and were it clearly and properly labeled a new story, there's no reason why anyone should give it a second glance.

> *A review of "East of the Sun and West of the Moon,"* in Kirkus Reviews, *Vol. XLVIII, No. 19, October 1, 1980, p. 1295.*

Despite the identical title, this is emphatically *not* the famous Norwegian fairy tale. . . . The text is a pastiche of several whole folk tales, altered to fit together to enforce morals so shockingly absent from the originals. . . . [Whereas] in Grimm the girl's violent resistance to the frog produces the happy ending, here she is punished for her aversion, and the transformation of frog to prince merely takes us to the final portion, loosely based on the above-mentioned Norwegian tale. Gone, however, are many of the best things in that tale: the White Bear, the aged women and their golden objects, the climactic washing of the white shirt. The Cupid and Psyche motif is no longer recognizable. The illustrations are in Mayer's richest vein, but the heroine is so mournful and consumptive-looking she hardly seems equal either to her tasks or her eventual happiness. Although Mayer's sources are German and Norwegian, his setting is evidently Russian. The figure of the North Wind . . . is taken from Michaelangelo's God the Father on the Sistine ceiling. One wonders why.

> *Patricia Dooley, in a review of "East of the Sun & West of the Moon,"* in School Library Journal, *Vol. 27, No. 3, November, 1980, p. 77.*

The narrative is smooth and those not concerned with authenticity in their folklore will find an adventurous journey. Illustrations, boldly executed with rich use of color and careful attention to detail, add still more cross-cultural motifs, from the Sistine Chapel to Russian iconography, but are graphically gripping.

> *Barbara Elleman, "East of the Sun & West of the Moon,"* in Booklist, *Vol. 77, No. 5, November 1, 1980, p. 407.*

Mercer Mayer's version of *East of the Sun and West of the Moon* is another of his visual tours de force much like his *Beauty and the Beast* of several years ago. When Mayer is "on," as he is in quite a few of the illustrations in this volume, he has the ability to take the reader's breath away. The translucent colors of his pictures, his meticulous sense of detail, the extraordinary feeling he has for his characters—whether they are his romantic portraits of the maiden or the nightmarish demons who capture the prince and lurk in the shadows of the troll's castle—all these, and many other elements in his illustrations, give his work its unmistakable signature. One wants to touch his pictures. They are so convincing, so lifelike. Mayer's illustrations are so good, in fact, that for all practical purposes they dominate his story line. Mayer has not simply reprocessed the tale. In his version he combines elements from "The Frog Prince" and his own fantasy. It would have been

better if Mayer had not introduced these new characters and motifs. While they are legitimate liberties that he has taken, they also tend to overload the story with too many new elements, losing at times the simple lines of the original story.

Clearly, Mayer's metier is that of an illustrator—one who can be bold and tender, earthy and ethereal. Still, he needs to have his exquisite visual talent coupled with more fully realized and poetic texts. Then the poetry of his own art would be fully complemented, as it deserves to be.

> *John Cech, "Glimpses of Fairy Realms and Fantasies,"* in The Christian Science Monitor, *January 12, 1981, p. B11.*

LIVERWURST IS MISSING (1981)

This story begins before the beginning: the background of the front-matter pages (dedication page, etc.) show three trench-coated thugs sneaking up on the Zanzibus Circus. By the light of the full moon they lure away Liverwurst, the baby rhinosterwurst. . . . Appelard and his farm friends . . . are off in pursuit. Do you like Indians and cavalry to the rescue? Child campers in on the adventure? A villain, representative of fast-food pollution and capitalism run amok? They are all here, sketched in almost adult prose, descriptive but easy to understand. . . . This is a whimsical and clever adaptation of an old formula.

> *Elizabeth Holtze, in a review of "Liverwurst Is Missing,"* in School Library Journal, *Vol. 28, No. 4, December, 1981, p. 54.*

Suspense, wild antics, and lots of action make up this zany fantasy. The "good triumphs over evil" plot is fairly predictable, but middle graders should enjoy the hectic pace. . . . [Both] author and illustrator [Steven Kellogg] must have had great fun dreaming up the humorous subtleties, which will appeal to adults who read the story aloud. Mother Rhinoceros is particularly well portrayed, from her ferociousness in battle to the emotional reunion with her baby. Purists may object to the stereotype of the Indians, and, as a language purist, I would feel more comfortable calling Liverwurst a rhinoceros, rather than a rhinosterwurst. Children have enough trouble with language as it is.

> *Beverly Woods, in a review of "Liverwurst Is Missing,"* in Children's Book Review Service, *Vol. 10, No. 7, February, 1982, p. 63.*

THE SLEEPING BEAUTY (1984)

All Sleeping Beauty stories share essential common elements, but Mercer Mayer has taken some liberties with his retelling. Interesting embellishments in the beginning of the story are nicely balanced by more complicated trials and temptations thrown up to the prince who awakens Sleeping Beauty. The characters in the full-color illustrations have the heavy tresses, long fingers, and elegant faces of Mayer's *Beauty and the Beast* though the background is not so richly detailed. Unfortunately, all the women tend to look alike and the costumes are not always a consistent indication of identity.

> *Gretchen S. Baldauf, in a review of "The Sleeping Beauty,"* in Children's Book Review Service, *Vol. 13, No. 3, November, 1984, p. 28.*

Mayer's retelling is yet another more elaborate version of this tale, one that adds characters and events but, unfortunately, subtracts much of the simple magic of the Brothers Grimm. There is too much explaining. A fairy tale is a skeleton that each listener fleshes out, and children don't need to be told the rationalization for a servant's mischief or the reason for the thicket's wonderous growth. Such verbal fat serves only to inhibit the imagination. The visualization is traditional: full-page, full-color scenes face the pages of text. Mayer uses his transparent washes and thin black lines to create a romantic never-never land whose carved wall reliefs and furniture suggest a Celtic medievalism. The ogre looms from Rackham-gnarled trees, skeletons laugh with full sets of teeth, and the griffin is appropriately puppy-doggish when patted by the hero. In brief, the pictures have a direct appeal and serve quite well to visualize many of the events. But they lack the mystery to go beyond surface qualities because everything seems so antiseptic, especially when compared to Trina Schart Hyman's dynamic humanism (Little, 1977).

> Kenneth Marantz, in a review of "The Sleeping Beauty," in School Library Journal, Vol. 31, No. 3, November, 1984, p. 113.

Mayer contributes an entirely new, enchanting lection to the classic fairy tale, placing it among the ancient Celts and giving an intriguingly different slant to the finale. The paintings are magnificent, their lush hues emphasizing dramatic events as well as the details showing the characters' habiliments, ceremonial accessories, etc.

> A review of "The Sleeping Beauty," in Publishers Weekly, Vol. 226, No. 22, November 30, 1984. p. 92.

Romantic and stylized, restrainedly erotic in the Aubrey Beardsley vein, this has beautifully detailed paintings. The artist's adaptation of the text (nowhere in book or jacket attributed to the Grimms) is florid and elaborate, more an embroidery for adult folklorists (including Celtic motifs) than a narrative for children, although the curse/long sleep/awakening by a kiss still carry the burden of the tale.

> Zena Sutherland, in a review of "The Sleeping Beauty," in Bulletin of the Center for Children's Books, Vol. 38, No. 4, December, 1984, p. 65.

[Mr. Mayer's edition of *The Sleeping Beauty*] includes a gratuitous prologue in which a silver owl blesses the barren queen with a child. The prince now must conquer not merely a wall of thorns but an ogre and a griffin as well, and it is revealed in the end that he is actually the son of the evil "Blue Faerie." Whatever the new book is, it is *not* "The Sleeping Beauty." Such revision can only frustrate children when they eventually encounter the traditional versions of these favorites.

> Michael Patrick Hearn, "The Emperor's New Clothes: Revising Children's Classics," in The New York Times Book Review, August 11, 1985, p. 21.*

TINK GOES FISHING: TINKA BAKES A CAKE; TUK TAKES A TRIP; TEEP AND BEEP GO TO SLEEP (TINY TINK! TONK! TALES) (1984)

Four brightly colored, short, fat board books are sure to please the smallest readers. In *TINK Goes Fishing, TINKA Bakes a Cake, TUK Takes a Trip, and TEEP and BEEP Go To Sleep*, the odd little Tink Tonk people, who come equipped with Tink Tonk-shaped pets, toys and houses go about their kindergarten-level appointed rounds. The tiny storylets are quite banal in themselves, but the weird, angular print-out people and the brilliant illustrations, as well as the most attractive format, will certainly please small novelty-seekers.

> Joan McGrath, in a review of "Tink Goes Fishing" and others, in Emergency Librarian, Vol. 12, No. 3, January-February, 1985, p. 44.

In this series of board books, developed to accompany a software package, the angular, awkward characters look as if they are made up of brightly colored graph squares. None of the four stories is complex or exciting. In the first, two characters cannot sleep, so they read, play games and finally realize the cause of their insomnia. When they locate their missing Tinky-bears, *Teep and Beep Go to Sleep. Tink Goes Fishing* and he has a long, hard day. When he finally does catch a fish, he realizes how hungry he is. This one does have an amusing twist at the end—they all (including the fish) rush home and have pizza for supper. *Tinka Bakes a Cake* for her friend Tink—with a little help from their friends and after many mishaps and several trips to the grocery store. In *Tuk Takes a Trip*, Tuk packs his toothpaste, pajamas, pillow and favorite toys to go on a trip—to his friend's house next door. These stories have been told before, and the use of graph characters to get on the computer bandwagon does not make them unusual enough to tell again. (pp. 79-80)

> Martha L. White, in a review of "Teep and Beep Go to Sleep" and others, in School Library Journal, Vol. 31, No. 9, May, 1985, pp. 79-80.

Robert M(arshall) McClung

1916-

American author/illustrator and author of nonfiction, picture books, and fiction.

McClung is the creator of science books in the fields of natural history, conservation, and ecology for children from preschool through high school. Presenting his facts most often within an appealing, easy-to-read fictional framework accompanied by color-washed line drawings, McClung reflects his unsentimental regard for living creatures and an ability to individualize subjects and dramatize natural events without recourse to anthropomorphism. Noted for the clarity and accuracy of his texts, McClung is the author of two major series for younger readers on vanishing wildlife and the life cycles of insects, birds, and animals. The latter series also relates the creatures being profiled to neighboring wildlife and to background flora and fauna. Formerly the Curator of Mammals and Birds at the Bronx Zoo, McClung provides middle graders with an authoritative reference tool in his introductory *How They Live* series, while his extensively researched trilogy—*Lost Wild America, Lost Wild Worlds*, and *Vanishing Wildlife of Latin America*—offers young adults a comprehensive background on the endangered species of the world. His only biography, *The True Adventures of Grizzly Adams*, furnishes a realistic portrait of the famed hunter and evokes a vivid picture of frontier America.

Critics praise McClung for the amount of information he incorporates into his works and for his skill in translating facts into entertaining stories. Although some observers point out that his illustrations need adjustment in scale, most reviewers find McClung's plentiful drawings to be a helpful and charming extension of the text. Commentators regard McClung not only as a knowledgeable and enthusiastic guide to the out-of-doors, but as an eloquent champion of conservation.

In addition to several other prizes, McClung received the Eva L. Gordon Award in 1966 for his outstanding achievement in nature literature.

(See also *Something about the Author*, Vol. 2; *Contemporary Authors New Revision Series*, Vol. 6; *Contemporary Authors*, Vols. 13-16, rev. ed.; and *Authors in the News*, Vol. 2.)

GENERAL COMMENTARY

SCIENCE BOOKS

McClung's little natural history books about individual species are always accurate scientifically, his paintings and drawings are personifications of beauty and realism, and the combination is an interesting and readable book. . . . No matter how many similar books a child may have read, or a library may own, there's always appetite and space for McClung's newest.

A review of "Redbird: The Story of a Cardinal," in Science Books, Vol. 4, No. 1, May, 1968, p. 50.

LILLIAN N. GERHARDT

McClung's books are consistently good instructors. His tested technique imparts information through supportive anecdotes of

Photograph by Carl Sherman. Courtesy of Robert M. McClung

the believe-it-or-not sort that attract middle graders; his short books, clearly illustrated in line drawings, are never guilty of telling readers more than they'd really care to know. . . .

Lillian N. Gerhardt, in a review of "Mice, Moose, and Men: How Their Populations Rise and Fall," in School Library Journal, *an appendix to* Library Journal, *Vol. 20, No. 3, November, 1973, p. 52.*

REBECCA J. LUKENS

[Robert McClung is] successful at weaving facts of nature into narrative form. In a factually accurate narrative called *Possum*, McClung faces the reality of the possum's life. We follow a family of nine babies and discover that they are easy prey; one is caught by a fox, another by a great horned owl, a third by a rattlesnake, another by a giant snapping turtle, and a fifth is run over as it crosses the road. These are the facts of life in the possums' world: nine babies, four survivors. Within the narrative form, *Possum* remains factually accurate. A more ambitious purpose unifies McClung's *Samson, Last of the California Grizzlies*. In this vivid narrative account, Samson, to satisfy the frontiersmen's craving for excitement, is pitted against Diablo the bull:

> The crowd roared as the two great beasts tangled again. Samson crouched low trying to seize the bull's head in his huge paws, while Diablo

thrust his horns downward in a deadly twisting sweep. As Samson rolled sideways to parry the blow, the tip of one of the bull's horns caught in a link of the chain that held the bear. There was a sudden loud snap as the chain broke, and Samson rolled free.

Here is a verifiable narrative of action on the frontier; there is sympathy for the two struggling animals forced to fight till death, but there is no sentimental distortion. (pp. 188-89)

> *Rebecca J. Lukens, "Nonfiction: Informational Books," in her* A Critical Handbook of Children's Literature, *Scott, Foresman and Company, 1976, pp. 185-97.**

MAY HILL ARBUTHNOT AND ZENA SUTHERLAND

McClung, a prolific author in his field, has written sympathetically but without sentimentality of all kinds of wildlife. He manages to be thorough, but not dry, and weaves a story without anthropomorphism into his factual approach. Threaded through all of his work is the persistent theme of good conservation practices, and his very early work **Spike; The Story of a Whitetail Deer** . . . is a fine illustration of this. In it, the reader is exposed to the illegal practice of hunters shining a flashlight at night to attract deer. His books for younger children have . . . clear, simple writing that never descends to over-simplification. In **Shag, Last of the Plains Buffalo** . . . , the author documents the savage slaughter of the buffalo as the white men drove westward with their guns and railroad tracks. **Honker; The Story of a Wild Goose** . . . and **Black Jack; Last of the Big Alligators** . . . , which contains an afterword about the alligator being an endangered species of American wildlife, continue the conservation story.

While McClung's illustrations are not always labeled, they are always accurate and well placed in relation to textual references. His ability to write for different age levels is evident in comparing **Sea Star** . . . , which is written in concise prose, and **Gypsy Moth** . . . , which is detailed enough for adult readers; at both levels the writing is lucid and the information accurate. An excellent book on animal camouflage, **How Animals Hide** . . . uses color photographs, showing examples of protective adaptation far better than any drawing could. (pp. 458-59)

> *May Hill Arbuthnot and Zena Sutherland, "Informational Books: 'Thor; Last of the Sperm Whales',"" in their* Children and Books, *fifth edition, Scott, Foresman and Company, 1977, pp. 458-59.*

WINGS IN THE WOODS (1948)

Young fiction with a natural science background. Dan, ten years old and full of natural boy curiosity, discovers a world populated by butterflies and moths. Family and farm interest keeps the story from bogging down in technicalities, and wide margins, pleasant illustrations and large, clear type have definite fourth and fifth grade appeal. Nor will sixth and seventh grades scorn such a book, where moth hunts become almost as exciting as the tracking of an African lion.

> *Siddie Joe Johnson, in a review of "Wings in the Woods," in* Library Journal, *Vol. 73, No. 14, August, 1948, p. 1098.*

A simply written but slow-moving story of a ten-year-old boy's first year on a farm. . . . The bitter antagonism between brothers

seems unnecessary and unfounded; however, the book may be useful in introducing the subject of moths and butterflies to prospective hobbyists.

> *A review of "Wings in the Woods," in* The Booklist, *Vol. 45, No. 2, September 15, 1948, p. 38.*

Dan has his very human failings, and part of his profit from the year on the farm was learning to live with other people. There is reality in the story and a feeling of country life, and it is a book that will encourage young readers to observe at first hand for themselves. The author's drawings are excellent.

> *Anne Thaxter Eaton, "Year on a Farm," in* The Christian Science Monitor, *December 16, 1948, p. 19.*

SPHINX: THE STORY OF A CATERPILLAR   (1949)

An assistant in the Department of Mammals and Birds at the N.Y. Zoological Park has presented in story form the life span of a caterpillar. With a real gift for writing for young children, he makes of the facts a fascinating story. [The] . . . charming black-and-white drawings, enhanced by the addition of green, show each step in the caterpillar's development to its maturity as a moth. Recommended for school libraries and natural history groups.

> *Jane F. Kennedy, in a review of "Sphinx: The Story of a Caterpillar," in* Library Journal, *Vol. 74, No. 17, October 1, 1949, p. 1465.*

[This short book] is an established classic of its type. . . . The text is clear, accurate, and interesting to read. . . . Intended for the six to ten year old reader, **Sphinx** provides a charming and scientifically accurate introduction to insect metamorphosis and balance in nature.

> *A. H. Drummond, Jr., in a review of "Sphinx: The Story of a Caterpillar," in* Appraisal: Science Books for Young People, *Vol. 15, No. 1, Winter, 1982, p. 43.*

[Each] stage of growth is accurately and simply described. The balance of nature is touched on by including the demise of three caterpillars by predation and parasitation as well as by mentioning slugs, birds, and rabbits also vying for food. There are a few minor points of criticism: The term "grub" is usually reserved for beetle larvae and is not applied to the larvae of other orders of insects. . . . [The word] "peavine" is written as one word. . . . This is an interesting, informative book to read to nursery or primary students and to be followed by appropriate discussion and activities.

> *Sister Edna Demanche, in a review of "Sphinx: The Story of a Caterpillar," in* Science Books & Films, *Vol. 17, No. 4, March-April, 1982, p. 216.*

RUBY THROAT: THE STORY OF A HUMMING BIRD (1950)

In this simple authentic nature book [the hummingbird] is brought into steady view for our closer acquaintance. Here is described a typical year in the life of a hummingbird. First we are introduced to the parents, then Young Ruby Throat is born in North America and we watch him develop into a swift flyer and, when occasion arises, a fierce fighter. We follow Ruby Throat on his winter migration to Central America—at a speed of more than fifty miles an hour—and back again to his birthplace in the springtime, ready to set up housekeeping on his own. Large type and the author's pleasingly colored illustrations help to make this an attractive book.

> *Irene Smith, "Hummingbird's Year," in* The New York Times Book Review, *October 15, 1950, p. 42.*

Here is a companion volume to this naturalist's book, **Sphinx: The Story of a Caterpillar.** Again, in simple text, in engaging style, he makes facts exciting for the youngest readers. The presentation, with large type and many pictures, is admirable. . . .

The pictures are both exact and charming, many touched with colors. It makes another fine introduction to nature study, for families, schools and libraries to share.

> *Louise S. Bechtel, in a review of "Ruby Throat: The Story of a Humming Bird," in* New York Herald Tribune Book Review, *October 29, 1950, p. 18.*

STRIPE: THE STORY OF A CHIPMUNK (1951)

A springtime-to-springtime story of the life of a chipmunk, told in a simple, understated style. [It] . . . relies for its appeal on natural fact rather than on animal characterization. Stripe's birth, nest life, his first introduction to the world, friends and terrible enemies, his building and tunnelling and some narrow escapes comprise a lively picture of the average life of this busy little beast. The black and white sketches by the author are accurate and appealing, but the two color illustrations are garish and off-register.

> *A review of "Stripe: The Story of a Chipmunk," in* Virginia Kirkus' Bookshop Service, *Vol. XIX, No. 14, July 15, 1951, p. 348.*

Another welcome easy-to-read nature book. The author . . . not only gives information in a readable style, but with illustrations in color and black and white brings to life this material. . . . Heartily recommended for third, fourth, and fifth grades.

> *Florence M. Hensey, in a review of "Stripe: The Story of a Chipmunk," in* Library Journal, *Vol. 76, No. 14, August, 1951, p. 1233.*

SPIKE: THE STORY OF A WHITETAIL DEER (1952)

Fall is good forest time and careful young nature watchers can look for Spike as he appears half way through this spring-to-spring chronicle of his life. Along the lines of the other books (**Stripe: The Story of a Chipmunk, Sphinx: The Story of a Caterpillar**) the author takes Spike and his mother on a seasonal round of living and learning that includes feeding on the lily pads, romping in the meadow and a full share of escapes— from hunters, a rattlesnake, a forest fire, birds of prey and so forth. In the fall they meet Spike's father who stays with them for a while presumably to bring on the new fawn. Two more things about the book: it is far less humanized than Jane Tompkins' *The Black Bear Twins;* it adheres to the cyclical and emotional patterns in Salten's *Bambi.* The author's illustrations are at times out of scale but have qualities of depth and softness which enhance the deer world.

> *A review of "Spike: The Story of a Whitetail Deer," in* Virginia Kirkus' Bookshop Service, *Vol. XX, No. 13, July 1, 1952, p. 367.*

The style is easy enough for most third grade readers to handle alone. The material is interesting and would have had a wide range of usefulness, especially for remedial reading, except that it is printed in the size type that is usually found in primers and will seem babyish for many readers who might otherwise have enjoyed the subject.

> *A review of "Spike: The Story of a Whitetail Deer," in* Bulletin of the Children's Book Center, *Vol. VI, No. 1, September, 1952, p. 7.*

A year in the life of a fawn is here presented in dramatic style and illustrated with lively black-and-white wash drawings by the author. Spike's forest neighbors, shown against a background of ferns, flowers, and trees share the interest of the story. . . . [This] is as valuable to children's collections as the author's earlier books.

> *Elizabeth Hodges, in a review of "Spike: The Story of a Whitetail Deer," in* Library Journal, *Vol. 77, No. 18, October 15, 1952, p. 1823.*

TIGER: THE STORY OF A SWALLOWTAIL BUTTERFLY (1953)

Here is the wonderful story of one complete cycle in the life of the swallowtail butterfly. Told in simple text and suitably illustrated with pencil sketches and color wash paintings by the author, it will appeal to any child between the ages of six and ten. Recommended for all libraries.

> *Elsie T. Dobbins, in a review of "Tiger: The Story of a Swallowtail Butterfly," in* Library Journal, *Vol. 78, No. 15, September 1, 1953, p. 1436.*

Similar in format to the author's earlier attractive and popular nature books, this is a clearly presented picture of the life cycle of a butterfly. Although simply written and very easily read, it nevertheless contains a great deal of information in its large type and many pictures in green, yellow and black. The teachers in my summer school course in Children's Books were especially enthusiastic about it.

> *Jennie D. Lindquist, in a review of "Tiger: The Story of a Swallowtail Butterfly," in* The Horn Book Magazine, *Vol. XXIX, No. 5, October, 1953, p. 363.*

[Mr. McClung] has made five handsome, slim, easy-reading picture books about creatures for younger children. This, the sixth, is lovely to look at, with its brilliant yellow butterfly winging across the pages. The short text, though simply written, is full of exact information which should lure children of about seven to ten to watch butterflies with much keener eyes, and to think of them as even more miraculous than they seem when skimming over the garden.

> *A review of "Tiger: The Story of a Swallowtail Butterfly," in* New York Herald Tribune Book Review, *November 15, 1953, p. 24.*

BUFO: THE STORY OF A TOAD (1954)

A good portrait of a pretty special character—this helpful garden toad—as any gardener or marauder knows. Robert Mc-Clung's simple text and finely detailed brown and green pictures tell the life cycle of this insect consumer. From tadpole to toad, Bufo's traits emerge,—an ever-flipping tongue, an exuding poison that thwarts threats to his safety, and so on.

These second and third grade true nature stories are popular and McClung manages to escape the obvious.

> *A review of "Bufo," in* Virginia Kirkus' Bookshop Service, *Vol. XXII, No. 13, July 1, 1954, p. 389.*

When a child first notices the funny old toad in his yard or garden, or first sees his dog making a face when he catches a toad, he should hear read aloud this delightful, short nature book. At seven or eight he can read its big type alone. For any age up to ten, its, many pictures, explicit and charming, half in two colors, will spur curiosity about a familiar creature, the wonderful way it is born, its usefulness in the world of nature. . . . Mr. McClung's attractive introductory books are proving very popular for nursery and kindergarten age.

> *Louise S. Bechtel, in a review of "Bufo: The Story of a Toad," in* New York Herald Tribune Book Review, *October 10, 1954, p. 10.*

Robert McClung's books are always a welcome addition to any library shelf. The text and illustrations are simple and bold, and the scientific information is accurate.

Bufo, the Story of a Toad further confirms the opinion that all of Mr. McClung's books are consistently good. The information is given in story form without any sugar-coating, writing down, or sentimentality. It is direct and clear—clear enough to be understood by the child of five or six, to be read with understanding by the seven- to nine-year-olds—yet meaty enough to inform and entertain an older child.

The excellent illustrations fit in so smoothly with the text as to seem a running part of it.

> *Margaret Mahon, in a review of "Bufo: The Story of a Toad," in* The Saturday Review, *New York, Vol. XXXVII, No. 46, November 13, 1954, p. 82.*

As in his earlier easy-to-read nature books, the author . . . handles his subject with useful detail and makes it entertaining. The many pictures in a sunny green and brown are full of movement and, illustrating many kinds of plant and animal life as well as Bufo's own life cycle, will attract even those young readers who might not seek a book on this subject.

> *Virginia Haviland, in a review of "Bufo: The Story of a Toad," in* The Horn Book Magazine, *Vol. XXX, No. 6, December, 1954, p. 438.*

VULCAN: THE STORY OF A BALD EAGLE   (1955)

A nicely written life cycle story . . . takes a North American eagle through the years from birth until it has reached the age of 22. The natural events in Vulcan's life are exciting, and there is a good sense of the course of nature as animals kill and flee—for survival. There is interesting material too, on the eagle's body structure and habits, the lifetime mates, brood raising and so forth.

> *A review of "Vulcan, the Story of a Bald Eagle," in* Virginia Kirkus' Service, *Vol. XXIII, No. 13, July 1, 1955, p. 419.*

The fictionized life cycle of the bald eagle is described for 7-9-year-olds. Death is dealt with so casually as not to offend the sensitive child. . . . A worthy addition to the author's other nature books for young readers.

> *Juanita Walker, in a review of "Vulcan: The Story of a Bald Eagle," in* Junior Libraries, *an appendix to* Library Journal, *Vol. 2, No. 2, October 15, 1955, p. 132.*

MAJOR: THE STORY OF A BLACK BEAR   (1956)

The life of a black bear through the seasons from the time he was a helpless newborn cub eight inches long until his fourth year when he fought a rival for a mate. Accurate information presented in an easy-to-read narrative and clear, agreeable drawings, without humanizing the animals.

> *A review of "Major: The Story of a Black Bear," in* The Booklist, *Vol. 52, No. 15, April 1, 1956, p. 320.*

Major is a winning little black bear whose exciting story . . . is well told by an experienced naturalist. **Major, the Story of a Black Bear** . . . packs an astonishing amount of information into its 64 large-print pages abundantly illustrated by its author. . . . [Mr. McClung] is a natural story teller, with a flair for making a child feel he knows the animals as friends.

> *Millicent Taylor, "Bird and Animal Tales," in* The Christian Science Monitor, *May 10, 1956, p. 15.**

Major and his twin sister have many delightful adventures which will appeal to children in grades 3 to 5. The text is written in a simple direct manner with careful regard for the accuracy of the facts of the life-cycle and habits of the black bear. Lively black and white illustrations.

> *Elizabeth F. Grave, in a review of "Major: The Story of a Black Bear," in* Library Journal, *Vol. 81, No. 11, June 1, 1956, p. 1550.*

GREEN DARNER: THE STORY OF A DRAGONFLY   (1956)

Similar in format and treatment to the author's books about the toad, humming bird, and other creatures. It is unfortunate, however, that the title seems to reiterate a superstitious fear of generations of children, though it is exploded in the book. Mr. McClung's detailed drawings enhance the simply told but accurate text.

> *Agnes Krarup, in a review of "Green Darner: The Story of a Dragonfly," in* Junior Libraries, *an appendix to* Library Journal, *Vol. 3, No. 2, October 15, 1956, p. 128.*

We never want to miss any of Robert McClung's life stories for the primaries. . . . They are accurate and beautiful. In **Green Darner: The Story of a Dragon Fly** . . . , we read in large print and simple sentences about his life, and see in bold gray and green and blue drawings his environment, his neighbors, his enemies and his prey. (p. 30)

> *"Bountiful Nature's Infinite Variety," in* New York Herald Tribune Book Review, *November 18, 1956, pp. 30, 32.**

[The text] is poetic, yet accurate enough in its descriptions of the various animals living in and around a pond. Mr. McClung is successful in emphasizing the beauties of the dragonfly and in dispelling many harmful myths about the insect. Any teacher who takes his/her class on a field trip to a pond or has an aquarium in the classroom will greatly appreciate this book as a reference.

From Green Darner: The Story of a Dragonfly, *written and illustrated by Robert M. McClung. Morrow, 1956. Copyright © 1956 by Robert M. McClung. All rights reserved. Reprinted by permission of the author.*

> *Martha T. Kane, in a review of "Green Darner: The Story of a Dragonfly," in* Appraisal: Children's Science Books, *Vol. 13, No. 3, Fall, 1980, p. 46.*

The text describes the complete life cycle of an insect that is both fascinating and fearsome to some youngsters because of the stories told about it (dragonflies will *not* sew your ears shut!). The format and the fictionalized text will make this more appealing as recreational reading than for school reports. There is no index or table of contents. Children in grades three and up will read this alone; younger children will find it a good lap book to share with a parent. Those writing reports may prefer to use chapters in the author's *Aquatic Insects and How They Live* . . . , or Hilda Simon's *Dragonflies* (Viking, 1972), but libraries will want to own all three of these titles.

> *Susan S. Sullivan, in a review of "Green Darner: The Story of a Dragonfly," in* Appraisal: Children's Science Books, *Vol. 13, No. 3, Fall, 1980, p. 46.*

LEAPER: THE STORY OF AN ATLANTIC SALMON   (1957)

The history of the salmon is especially interesting and though it is matter-of-factly told, the slight personalization of Leaper has the effect of heightening the drama. Illustrated by the author with soft wash drawings which are accurate in a general manner rather than closely detailed.

> *A review of "Leaper," in* Virginia Kirkus' Service, *Vol. XXV, No. 3, February 1, 1957, p. 77.*

Another interesting life cycle story. . . . The frankness in the description of mating on one page in the book should be noted by the librarian in case there might be objection by parents. Excellent book for pleasure reading or social studies. . . . Recommended for all libraries.

> *Gladys Conklin, in a review of "Leaper: The Story of an Atlantic Salmon," in* Junior Libraries, *an appendix to* Library Journal, *Vol. 3, No. 9, May 15, 1957, p. 30.*

The salmon is a good subject for a life-cycle story and Mr. McClung makes Leaper an excellent addition to his growing company of fascinating wild creatures. The easy-to-read text and the lively sketches of Leaper, through various stages of development and busily escaping from other species of wildlife and traps, nets, and lines, together describe an adventurous career.

> *Virginia Haviland, in a review of "Leaper, the Story of an Atlantic Salmon," in* The Horn Book Magazine, *Vol. XXXIII, No. 4, August, 1957, p. 315.*

LUNA: THE STORY OF A MOTH   (1957)

This excellent life-cycle story does for our giant silk moths what the author's *Tiger* does for butterflies. The beautiful luna, both as moth and caterpillar, is shown in color. Other moths and small creatures of the woods are pictured. . . . Second-graders will enjoy this book, also fourth- and fifth-graders interested in insects. Recommended for all libraries.

> *Gladys Conklin, in a review of "Luna: The Story of a Moth," in* Junior Libraries, *an appendix to* Library Journal, *Vol. 4, No. 2, October 15, 1957, p. 148.*

A beautiful and poetic treatment of the life cycle of this lovely great green moth fairy is written in narrative form for the six-to-tens. It skillfully brings in the whole background of Luna's habitat, both flora and fauna. Each page or double page is effectively designed with type and decoration as a unit, and the information, told simply enough for younger children, is authentic enough for any age.

> *Millicent Taylor, "At Home with Birds, Beavers, Moths, and Whales," in* The Christian Science Monitor, *November 7, 1957, p. 18.**

WHOOPING CRANE   (1959)

The drama of the Whooping Crane . . . is portrayed with unique feeling in this book by the prolific Robert McClung. Using the fictional device of a year in the life of two birds—their migration, their mating, their separation, and their ultimate reuniting—the entire cycle of the Whooping Crane's life and the problems with which they are urgently faced becomes dramatically apparent. A touching story which sounds a note of caution to those interested in the protection and preservation of American wildlife.

> *A review of "Whooping Crane," in* Virginia Kirkus' Service, *Vol. XXVII, No. 3, February 1, 1959, p. 90.*

This simple book by a popular writer of easy nature stories is a well-written . . . account of the whooping crane's habits and struggle against extinction. For younger readers than those of Lippincott's *Old Bill*, it has neither the detail nor tense dramatic quality of the latter. Both are worth having, particularly, since the public is being educated to recognize and protect the few survivors of these great American birds.

> *Julia J. Brody, in a review of "Whooping Crane," in* Junior Libraries, *an appendix to* Library Journal, *Vol. 5, No. 8, April, 1959, p. 44.*

Even a stark, factual account of the tall white bird that has become almost a symbol of man's determination to allow no more wildlife to disappear would be worth while. But Robert McClung's book is more than that. His story of Whooper and his mate and their migration to Canada is told in words near poetry, and . . . it should help to fire the enthusiasm of 8-12's.

> *Pamela Marsh, "Widening Horizons," in* The Christian Science Monitor, *April 9, 1959, p. 15.**

The delicate balance of nature and the important role of conservationists in helping to maintain it are indicated. The story has action and suspense, but naming the birds 'Whooper' and 'Grue' and 'Rusty' seems unfortunate.

> *Margaret Warren Brown, in a review of "Whooping Crane," in* The Horn Book Magazine, *Vol. XXXV, No. 3, June, 1959, p. 209.*

OTUS: THE STORY OF A SCREECH OWL   (1959)

Another in the series of life cycle books is this excellent story of a screech owl. The naming of Robert McClung's owl is his one concession to sentimentality in this depiction of the necessary brutality which is part of the pattern of animal survival. Taken from Otus' conception, through his own mating, one witnesses the killing of smaller animals by the owls as well as the destruction of members of the owl family by their natural enemies. Lloyd Sandford's illustrations are dramatic and capture the intense concentrations with which Robert McClung . . . handles the life cycle.

> *A review of "Otus: The Story of a Screech Owl," in* Virginia Kirkus' Service, *Vol. XXVII, No. 17, September 1, 1959, p. 651.*

Direct, simple writing; accurate and without sentimentality, this is as satisfying as are the previous books by McClung. . . . Only the name personalizes Otus, and the use of the same name for the baby owl who recapitulates the cycle is a most effective device. Good nature writing.

> *A review of "Otus: The Story of a Screech Owl," in* Bulletin of the Children's Book Center, *Vol. XIII, No. 7, March, 1960, p. 117.*

SHAG: LAST OF THE PLAINS BUFFALO   (1960)

This is the story of Shag, a bull buffalo. It is also the story of all the Plains Buffalo and their near extinction in the last decades of the nineteenth century by ruthless men, machines and natural phenomena. Leader of his herd, Shag watches the number of his followers diminish, but with the nobility native to his species, he refuses to submit to the forces that would destroy him. Finally, . . . the lonely and formidable animal is granted sanctuary by the game laws which the government provides. Robert McClung . . . evokes a mood of nobility which makes this book memorable both as a study of American plain life, a new facet of conservation and as the portrayal of immense animal dignity.

> *A review of "Shag, Last of the Plains Buffalo," in* Virginia Kirkus' Service, *Vol. XXVIII, No. 14, July 15, 1960, p. 560.*

Mr. McClung has again written an appealing, sympathetic, informative life-cycle book. Shag, born in 1869, when great herds of buffalo roamed the plains, lives to see them decimated by man. Well-written. . . .

> *May C. Ihnken, in a review of "Shag, Last of the Plains Buffalo," in* Junior Libraries, *an appendix to* Library Journal, *Vol. 7, No. 1, September, 1960, p. 72.*

MAMMALS AND HOW THEY LIVE   (1963)

A general review of the animal kingdom is given with a brief look at mammalian characteristics, evolution, simple biology, habitats, and behavior. This is an introductory book for younger children and includes a helpful list of mammalian orders with examples of each. Pertinent photographs accompany an easily read and understandable text.

> *Robert E. Roth, in a review of "Mammals and How They Live," in* School Library Journal, *an appendix to* Library Journal, *Vol. 10, No. 3, November, 1963, p. 69.*

[Robert McClung] writes informally and simply, without giving the impression that he is writing down to his audience. A book of this length [83 p.] might have profited from less variety and more depth, but **Mammals** is a reasonably informative, if crowded primer.

> *Leonard Engel, in a review of "Mammals and How They Live," in* The New York Times Book Review, *January 26, 1964, p. 26.*

SCREAMER: LAST OF THE EASTERN PANTHERS   (1964)

Stories about cats have a built-in appeal, and can be used to introduce a child to less-familiar nature lore. **Screamer: Last of the Eastern Panthers** . . . is among the best. . . . [It] is a fictionalized account of a mountain lion born in Pennsylvania in 1885, when its kind (along with the passenger pigeon) was vanishing. Without sentimentality the story speeds along and generates a sincere interest in the welfare of the big cat, as well as an understanding of its natural role in the mountain forest. (p. 37)

> *Lorus Milne and Margery Milne, "Natural Touches," in* The New York Times Book Review, *Part II, May 10, 1964, pp. 6, 37.**

SPOTTED SALAMANDER   (1964)

In the latest of a number of animal histories by this author, the mating habits, growth and development, and characteristics of the salamander are well presented as a kind of factual material which can be easily read by beginning readers. Some confusion may arise from the use of the generic name spotted salamander and the proper name Spotted Salamander applied to several denizens. The pictures are as precise and accurate as the text.

> *A review of "Spotted Salamander," in* Virginia Kirkus' Service, *Vol. XXXII, No. 13, July 1, 1964, p. 592.*

From Spotted Salamander, *written and illustrated by Robert M. McClung. Morrow, 1964. Copyright © 1964 by Robert M. McClung. All rights reserved. Reprinted by permission of the author.*

The naturalist, creator of many life-cycle studies, is skillful in providing information through striking illustration as well as in factual text. The spotted salamander, whose year-round cycle chiefly fills this account, is seen also in association with the newt, the red eft, and the lizard. Their resemblance, even in miniature, to the dinosaur type endows them with a special attractiveness for children. Concluding the book is a two-page directive for the keeping of salamanders as "interesting" pets. . . . [The] spirited wash pictures of many swimming creatures are effective both in black and white and in the scenes with green, blue, and yellow added.

> *Virginia Haviland, in a review of "Spotted Salamander," in* The Horn Book Magazine, *Vol. XL, No. 5, October, 1964, p. 512.*

When the sample baby (the child may be slightly confused between spotted salamander *mere* and spotted salamander *fils,* since both have the same name) grows legs and lungs and leaves the water for the cool moist world of the forest floor, he takes a walk. He sheds his skin and he meets his relatives, somewhat pointless encounters, since (a) nothing happens, and (b) by this time there is almost too much information.

> *Nora Magid, "Trailing along with Nature," in* Book Week—New York Herald Tribune, *November 1, 1964, p. 37.**

HONKER: THE STORY OF A WILD GOOSE   (1965)

Mr. McClung's excellent titles on the life cycles of various birds and animals are notable for their accuracy and his ability to personalize the bird or animal without resorting to anthropomorphizing. Honker is a leading gander in a flock of Canada geese. With his mate Branta, Honker raises his families and leads his fellows through the danger-filled long distance migrations down the Mississippi flyways. One flight south found the geese in a National Wildlife Refuge. The protective program of the U.S. Fish and Wildlife Service is fully outlined, especially in relation to hunting and bird health checks. . . . [This has a] smoothly written text.

> *A review of "Honker: The Story of a Wild Goose," in* Virginia Kirkus' Service, *Vol. XXXIII, No. 2, January 15, 1965, p. 60.*

Mr. McClung's appealing narrative of Honker and his mate Branta . . . will help 8-12's understand these interesting and beautiful birds. . . . Mr. McClung's accurate nature books need no introduction—another is always welcome.

> *Millicent Taylor, "On the Wildlife Side," in* The Christian Science Monitor, *May 6, 1965, p. 3B.**

Smoother and more sophisticated [than Alice Goudey's *Here Comes the Cottontails*] is Robert McClung's **Honker,** an absorbing nature story related with disarming delicacy. . . . Bob Hines's sensitive charcoal sketches reflect the author's own love for his subject.

> *Polly Burroughs, in a review of "Honker: The Story of a Wild Goose," in* The New York Times Book Review, *May 16, 1965, p. 42.*

A skillful weaving of unadorned facts into an engrossing adventure of a year in the life of a Canada goose. Even a hardhearted hunter would be apt to have doubts about his avocation were he to read about Honker and his family running "the gauntlet of the guns." Handsome illustrations complement this beautifully written story.

> *Joseph Howard, in a review of "Honker," in* Childhood Education, *Vol. 42, No. 3 (November, 1965), p. 182.*

CATERPILLARS AND HOW THEY LIVE   (1965)

An easily read, factual text and clear drawings describe the physical characteristics and life of the caterpillar, its struggle for survival, and its usefulness or harmfulness to man. A final chapter offers helpful suggestions for raising caterpillars. (pp. 97, 100)

> *A review of "Caterpillars and How They Live," in* The Booklist and Subscription Books Bulletin, *Vol. 62, No. 2, September 15, 1965, pp. 97, 100.*

An index would have been helpful. *Caterpillars* by Dorothy Sterling (Doubleday 1961) has a great deal more material, a good index and most of the caterpillars are shown in color. Most libraries can use both books.

> *Gladys Conklin, in a review of "Caterpillars and How They Live," in* School Library Journal, *an appendix to* Library Journal, *Vol. 12, No. 2, October, 1965, p. 232.*

LADYBUG (1966)

The author has produced many excellent animal studies for young readers. As in many books of this kind, this traces the life cycle of the subject by following the events occurring to one ladybug during the space of a year. Particular emphasis is on how the ladybug preys on insect pests, like aphids. The text also indicates how it protects itself where it lives, its different varieties, and the related species. The illustrations by the author are among his best, some are in black and white but most are attractively tinted in green and red; they are detailed and accurate and pleasing to view too.

> *A review of "Ladybug," in* Virginia Kirkus' Service, *Vol. XXXIV, No. 5, March 1, 1966, p. 246.*

In remarkably few and simple words, the author tells much about the life histories of the ladybug and other insects, with principal emphasis on their diets and the ecological effects of predation. His illustrations, though attractive and adequate, are not as precise as his text, and in a few cases the lack of labels may cause difficulty for some young readers. The final two pages set in smaller type, tell how the familiar rhyme, "Ladybug, ladybug, fly away home . . ." originated.

> *A review of "Ladybug," in* Science Books, *Vol. 2, No. 1, May, 1966, p. 45.*

Ladybug is filled with facts about a cherished insect. Her reproduction habits, methods of attack, close relatives, and appearance are carefully delineated in word and picture. This is an excellent reference book.

> *Carolyn H. Lavender, "On the Trail of Animals," in* The New York Times Book Review, *Part II, May 8, 1966, p. 43.**

Factual style and informative illustrations comprise a life-cycle presentation acceptable to older children, but the print and vocabulary are right for younger readers. Concluding are notes on the ladybug in history and in folklore.

> *Priscilla Landis Moulton, in a review of "Ladybug," in* The Horn Book Magazine, *Vol. XLII, No. 3, June, 1966, p. 321.*

THE SWIFT DEER (1966)

The Swift Deer covers the entire family—our eastern whitetails . . . , western mule deer, elk, moose, reindeer and their exotic kin. Elementary science books sometimes bog down in clichés and a stupefying mass of detail, but not this one. The author has chosen his facts carefully and has interesting things to tell.

> *Paul Walker, in a review of "The Swift Deer," in* The New York Times Book Review, *May 29, 1966, p. 16.*

A good general account of the natural history of deer is presented without either sentimentality or overly stressing the sportsman's attitude. . . . North American deer are emphasized but other important species are covered. The book contains a surprising amount of information, presented in readable style, covering a range of topics from the discovery of Pére David's deer to reindeer herding and white-tail overabundance.

> *A review of "The Swift Deer," in* Science Books, *Vol. 2, No. 2, September, 1966, p. 133.*

[Mr. McClung] presents his accurate knowledge of the history and life of all North American deer in an easy to read, well-arranged book. . . . There is an excellent chapter on deer antlers and how they differ from the horns of other cloven-hoofed animals. The author chooses his facts carefully and tells them well. He uses proper scientific terms and classifies the deer by kingdom, phylum, class, order, family, genus, and species. There is a good index.

> *Dorothy I. Comfort, in a review of "The Swift Deer," in* Appraisal: Children's Science Books, *Vol. 1, No. 3, Fall, 1968, p. 17.*

MOTHS AND BUTTERFLIES AND HOW THEY LIVE   (1966)

[A] brief but careful study of how butterflies and moths fly, eat, reproduce, and struggle to survive. Detailed line drawings and diagrams enlarge the text and often explain better than words; for example, the excellent drawing of a butterfly proboscis both curled and extended and the four types of butterfly and moth antennae shown together on one page. Thirty identified species are shown and the final chapter deals with hunting and collecting specimens. This is a good book for the beginner interested in this subject.

> *Gladys Conklin, in a review of "Moths and Butterflies and How They Live," in* School Library Journal, *an appendix to* Library Journal, *Vol. 13, No. 2, October, 1966, p. 233.*

A wealth of information is presented. . . . The style is so easy and informative that many 8-12's should read this book just for pleasure. Serious young students will find here all they need to start them out on the study of lepidoptera—all 100,000 different species.

> *Marian Sorenson, "Of Birds, Beasts, Beetles and Butterflies," in* The Christian Science Monitor, *November 3, 1966, p. B11.**

In a text which is a pleasure to read, the information which is given about moths and butterflies includes how and where to find them, and how to continue one's studies *and* let them live. This is a remarkable book for ease of reading, for the accurate facts, and the clear illustrations it presents.

> *Ethel R. Ambach, in a review of "Moths and Butterflies and How They Live," in* Appraisal: Children's Science Books, *Vol. 1, No. 1, Winter, 1967, p. 9.*

A companion to *Caterpillars and How They Live,* this small volume contains much accurate information. Structure is explained in terms of function; suggestions for observations are offered; there are directions for collecting. One of the book's strong values is the many black and white drawings which are an integral part of the presentation. Written simply, this is an effective and delightful introduction to the second largest order of insects.

> *Beryl Robinson, in a review of "Moths and Butterflies and How They Live," in* Appraisal: Children's Science Books, *Vol. 1, No. 1, Winter, 1967, p. 9.*

HORSESHOE CRAB (1967)

[The] horseshoe crab is of special interest because of its age. Large print and detailed drawings which elucidate the textual description will attract the young reader; the explicit explanation of the crab's life cycle, enlivened with guest appearances by a young boy and many ocean dwellers, will hold even those without a native affinity for natural history. A short afterword points out the importance of this particular crab as a prehistoric creature and the need for its conservation. Horseshoe crabs are fascinating, mainly thanks to Mr. McClung—in short, an excellent product.

A review of "Horseshoe Crab," in Kirkus Service, *Vol. XXXV, No. 6, March 15, 1967, p. 346.*

This book may have value as a reference source on this rather obscure creature, but it has shortcomings. Though the text is technically accurate, the drawings would be vastly improved by closer attention to scale and the addition of color, both of which are very important when identifying these shore creatures in their natural habitat.

Fred Geis, in a review of "Horseshoe Crab," in Appraisal: Children's Science Books, *Vol. 1, No. 2, Spring, 1968, p. 10.*

BLACK JACK: LAST OF THE BIG ALLIGATORS   (1967)

A fictionized account of the life of an alligator in the Okefenokee Swamp. In an uninspired style of writing, biological details are mixed with Black Jack's wanderings through the swamp. The repetition of eating, sleeping, and mating patterns does not make exciting reading as presented here, despite attempts to personalize Black Jack, giving him memory, thoughts, and feeling. The threats of poachers and drought provide the more interesting episodes of the book.... [The] same information about alligators is presented better in such books as Herbert Zim's *Alligators and Crocodiles* (Morrow) and Clarence Hylander's *Animals in Armor* (Macmillan).

Joan Lear Sher, in a review of "Black Jack: Last of the Big Alligators," in School Library Journal, *an appendix to* Library Journal, *Vol. 14, No. 3, November, 1967, p. 69.*

[*Black Jack* and Mary Adrian's *The American Alligator*] are handled in straightforward, unembossed prose. The authors offer detailed descriptions of the swamp and its wildlife. Though the stories of Black Jack and Gator could have been more "tail lashing," the real value of these books is in the information presented. (p. 53)

Mel Watkins, in a review of "Black Jack: Last of the Big Alligators" and "The American Alligator," in The New York Times Book Review, *Part II, November 5, 1967, pp. 52-3.**

Observations of McClung and information from references are combined in this account of Old Min, a mother alligator, and Black Jack, one of her offspring.... Anthropomorphism is repugnant in natural history writing for children. There is a thoughtful afterword on the need for conservation....

A review of "Black Jack: Last of the Big Alligators," in Science Books, *Vol. 3, No. 3, December, 1967, p. 242.*

REDBIRD: THE STORY OF A CARDINAL   (1968)

Never mind that his coat is Redbird's chief distinction, that a year in his life is much the same as a year in the life of many other birds—Mr. McClung exploits his good looks, the comparative pallor of his mate, and the peckish pink into ubiquitous brown of their offspring to make a visually effective family chronicle. Being McClung, it's bound to be informative and well-paced, with enough reminders of danger—routing a rival male cardinal, losing one baby to a grackle, driving off a cat and a blue jay—to keep interest keen. Don't consider this a definitive book on cardinals; consider it rather an introduction to fine-feathered courtship and child care, surprisingly warm despite its modesty and deliberation.

A review of "Redbird: The Story of a Cardinal," in Kirkus Service, *Vol. XXXVI, No. 7, April 1, 1968, p. 399.*

The science teacher in the early elementary grades will welcome this delightful volume about the cardinal. It is simply written but scientifically correct with illustrations that dovetail the text beautifully. There is great appeal for any bird lover.

Sister Marie O'Donnell, in a review of "Redbird," in Catholic Library World, *Vol. 40, No. 2, October, 1968, p. 145.*

The life cycle, habits, and behavior of the cardinal are accurately described in easily read text and in attractive black-and-white or colored illustrations on every page. The straightforward account is as lively and appealing as a book of fiction. . . .

The Booklist and Subscription Books Bulletin, "Pure Sciences: 'Redbird: The Story of a Cardinal'," in Books for Children: 1967-1968, American Library Association. *1968, p. 33.*

Although written in a very readable style for young people of pre-school or lower elementary grade level, this account of the family activities of a pair of cardinals is remarkably detailed and accurate. The courtship and establishment of territory are well covered, and the dangers inherent in raising the young birds are clearly revealed. Such a study of an individual species should surely make the Redbird a more distinct personality to the young bird watcher. A minor weakness is the coloration of some of the birds depicted. The female cardinal is never an over-all pink. (pp. 17-18)

Douglas B. Sands, in a review of "Redbird: The Story of a Cardinal," in Appraisal: Children's Science Books, *Vol. 2, No. 2, Spring, 1969, pp. 17-18.*

LOST WILD AMERICA: THE STORY OF OUR EXTINCT AND VANISHING WILDLIFE   (1969)

This volume seems to have everything to make it appeal to young readers except desire. The accounts are informative and researched, written with care.... But it will take a student with existing interest to pick up the volume, or a teacher who will recommend the book. The current nation-wide interest in conservation may help, but the volume will remain one that needs to be brought to the attention of the student if it is to have a good effect.

A review of "Lost Wild America: The Story of Our Extinct and Vanishing Wildlife," in Best Sellers, *Vol. 29, No. 5, June 1, 1969, p. 101.*

A thorough and sobering account of wild life in America, from the earliest times to the present. The author diligently and systematically traces the unfortunate effects man has had upon nature through ruthless slaughter and disregard for environ-

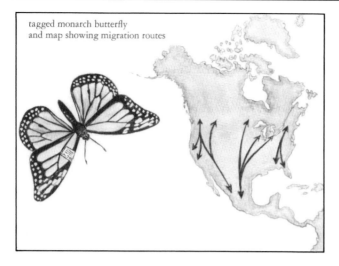

tagged monarch butterfly
and map showing migration routes

From Moths and Butterflies and How They Live, *written and illustrated by Robert M. McClung. Morrow, 1966. Copyright © 1966 by Robert M. McClung. All rights reserved. Reprinted by permission of the author.*

mental relationships. The book enumerates the wildlife victims, those which became extinct, those which were enabled to make a comeback, and those whose fate hangs in the balance. The human animal is also shown to be threatened by a growing population and intensification of technology which, unless drastic steps are taken, may make our earth an unfit place to live. Good line drawings [by Bob Hines], excellent index and extensive bibliography along with the mature, objective text make this a significant book and a good companion for Laycock's less advanced, more optimistic *America's Endangered Wildlife* (Norton, 1968).

> *Elizabeth F. Grave, in a review of "Lost Wild America: The Story of Our Extinct and Vanishing Wildlife," in* School Library Journal, *an appendix to* Library Journal, *Vol. 16, No. 1, September, 1969, p. 169.*

Vignettes of about 70 extinct or endangered animal species are narrated here with excellent chapters on current problems in environmental quality control. . . . The book and its bibliography could serve many students as a stimulating start in a research project on wildlife management or concerning the influence of man on other species. Unfortunately, the interesting facts cited in the historical accounts of a species are not cited as to source, which may impede any skeptical researcher. The historical theme of man's domination of his environment is done quite well. Problems of conservation legislation and details of range management are exposed. The book also demonstrates the natural events leading to extinction, such as migration of predators, submergence of off-shore islands, and restricted distribution. Most biology courses or related general science courses could use the book. Some passages, such as that on the passenger pigeon, arouse curiosity as to how these animals managed to evade extinction at the hands of predators (other than human). The book can stimulate excellent class discussions on evolution, as well as conservation. There is room for disagreement on some of the suggested causes of decrease in population size, which should allow the book to fit into a discovery or process oriented course, such as BSCS [Biological Sciences Curriculum Study]. There is a good index.

> *A review of "Lost Wild America: The Story of Our Extinct and Vanishing Wildlife," in* Science Books, *Vol. 5, No. 2, September, 1969, p. 181.*

This thoroughly researched survey is the most comprehensive and the most detailed of the several recent publications on vanishing wildlife. . . . Reference value enhanced by selected, extensive bibliography and excellent index.

> *A review of "Lost Wild America: The Story of Our Extinct and Vanishing Wildlife," in* The Booklist, *Vol. 66, No. 1, September 1, 1969, p. 56.*

BLAZE: THE STORY OF A STRIPED SKUNK (1969)

In Robert McClung's flat account of a skunk's comings and goings and her manner of raising her young, she sounds—except for her notoriously-scented spray—much like any other animal: although reference is made to her going out in the evening, the point that she's nocturnal is never made; neither, though she's not shown as aggressive, is it said that she's uniquely amiable. A child would be hard put to discern these distinguishing traits or to find anything particularly interesting about the skunk per se. There's a Lilo Hess photo-profile in the offing, plus Zistel's *Dangerous Year* as a backstop, but of course neither duplicates McClung's large print, brief text practicality where that's a prime consideration.

> *A review of "Blaze: The Story of a Striped Skunk," in* Kirkus Reviews, *Vol. XXXVII, No. 17, September 1, 1969, p. 934.*

Beginning readers can follow the striped skunk, Blaze, through one year of her life. She bears her young, teaches them to hunt, and meets some natural enemies during the course of the story. The child will learn about a skunk's living and eating habits, and how the mother cares for the young. The anthropomorphism does not detract from the story, and may serve further to interest the young reader. The author's own illustrations effectively add to this tale of one skunk and her family.

> *A review of "Blaze: The Story of a Striped Skunk," in* Science Books, *Vol. 5, No. 3, December, 1969, p. 257.*

The very elementary looking format . . . is deceiving because the vocabulary is difficult and the sentences extremely complex. The author attempts to glorify nature in a poetic style that just sounds awkward and flat. His illustrations, in color and black and white, are pleasant and lifelike.

> *Trevelyn Jones, in a review of "Blaze: The Story of a Striped Skunk," in* School Library Journal, *an appendix to* Library Journal, *Vol. 16, No. 9, May, 1970, p. 90.*

AQUATIC INSECTS AND HOW THEY LIVE (1970)

This is the most inclusive, easy-to-use book available on the subject for this age group, similar in appearance and presentation to McClung's other books. The author starts out by discussing "Insects and Water" generally, with regard to anatomy, breathing in water, eggs, and movement. Then, specific insect groups are considered. . . . The last chapter, on the collection of aquatic insects, is followed by a "Key to Adult and Immature Aquatic Insects," and by a good index. Clear illustrations adequate for identification purposes are placed in the margins next to corresponding verbal descriptions. The text is specific; subject headings subdivide the chapters—just what students appreciate when doing reference work.

> *Jane Austin, in a review of "Aquatic Insects and How They Live," in* School Library Journal, *an appendix to* Library Journal, *Vol. 17, No. 3, November, 1970, p. 109.*

A brief but interesting and well-organized account is presented of water insects, with a good description of larval forms. . . . Numerous illustrations . . . are well placed and helpful, and much information is presented in a clear, easy-to-read style, although one or two omissions detract from the value of the book: The pupal stage, mentioned frequently, is not explained; and the reader is left with the erroneous impression that all riffle beetle larvae are water pennies. A brief bibliography and a glossary which would include pronunciation of such terms as *haltere* would be a help to young readers.

> *A review of "Aquatic Insects and How They Live," in* Science Books, *Vol. 6, No. 3, December, 1970, p. 241.*

Mr. McClung presents his subject well-organized, clearly illustrated, and easy to comprehend. The book is about perfect for the intended reader encompassing a good format with sharp line drawings that clarify the well-researched text. Here is a thorough study of aquatic fresh water insects by identification, stages of development, and life in or out of the water. The author gives advice on insect collecting and tells how to record observations. The book is a valuable reference tool.

> *Dorothy Comfort, in a review of "Aquatic Insects and How They Live," in* Appraisal: Children's Science Books, *Vol. 4, No. 2, Spring, 1971, p. 24.*

THOR: LAST OF THE SPERM WHALES (1971)

Compact, consistently informative, broadly aware, this is McClung at his characteristic best. A vignette of the *Essex* sunk by a maddened sperm whale splays out into the heyday and decline of Yankee whaling, while Thor's life spans the resurgence of commercial whaling to the point—the present point—of overkill; subsumed also, via his chance encounters, are the traits and the fate of other types of whale. . . . Thor is himself and the many, which makes this unique among the young books on the subject.

> *A review of "Thor: Last of the Sperm Whales," in* Kirkus Reviews, *Vol. XXXIX, No. 7, April 1, 1971, p. 374.*

The life cycle, not quite completed, of a sperm whale is described in narrative form; although given a name, **Thor** is not fictionalized. . . . Direct and informative, the book is yet another example of the competence and ability that make McClung one of the most dependable science writers for children.

> *Zena Sutherland, in a review of "Thor: Last of the Sperm Whales," in* Bulletin of the Center for Children's Books, *Vol. 25, No. 5, January, 1972, p. 76.*

BEES, WASPS, AND HORNETS, AND HOW THEY LIVE (1971)

Some of the better-known hymenoptera . . . , perceptively examined in a smoothly informative survey. Though bees are covered more extensively elsewhere, McClung's introduction to their remarkable social organization is clear and consistently

interesting. The wasps fare even better, in a section twice as long that is no routine catalog but manages to say something fresh and specific about each of 16 types. . . . Like McClung's other insect books, this is a natural choice.

> *A review of "Bees, Wasps, and Hornets and How They Live," in* Kirkus Reviews, *Vol. XXXIX, No. 16, August 15, 1971, p. 879.*

Another excellent McClung title. Unlike most children's books on bees, wasps and hornets which accent the social species, this largely concerns the essential biology of the solitary species of *hymenoptera*. Packed with relevant information, easy to read, it has the plus of a pleasing format and well-captioned, detailed illustrations.

> *A. C. Haman, in a review of "Bees, Wasps, and Hornets and How They Live," in* School Library Journal, *an appendix to* Library Journal, *Vol. 18, No. 2, October, 1971, p. 125.*

McClung gives an excellent introduction to the order with simple but comprehensive notes on characteristics, evolution, habitats, life cycles, and food habits for beginning students in nature studies. Parasitic wasps, solitary wasps, social wasps, and bees are discussed with excellent illustrations. This book is written with clear language and accurate illustrations and is highly recommended for elementary school children.

> *A review of "Bees, Wasps, and Hornets and How They Live," in* Science Books, *Vol. 7, No. 4, March, 1972, p. 312.*

Pre-checked by zoology professor Dr. William B. Nutting of the University of Massachusetts, the similarities and differences of structure, habits and life roles of these insects are described in one of the best of Mr. McClung's nature titles. Technical names and terms are used throughout but they are well clarified within the text and the facts and descriptions are fascinating. The drawings and diagrams seem accurate with enough references to scale to make the varying sizes clear. There is a good index. There is no bibliography but there are references in the text to outstanding writers in the field like Fabre and Maeterlinck. (pp. 23-4)

> *Marianna H. Rowe, in a review of "Bees, Wasps, and Hornets and How They Live," in* Appraisal: Children's Science Books, *Vol. 5, No. 2, Spring, 1972, pp. 23-4.*

Written with lucid simplicity, this is . . . authoritative in both the writing and in the carefully detailed drawings. . . . All of the material is interesting, but the communications system of the bee and the fact that bees are more useful to men than are other members of the order makes the section on bees particularly valuable.

> *Zena Sutherland, in a review of "Bees, Wasps, and Hornets, and How They Live," in* Bulletin of the Center for Children's Books, *Vol. 25, No. 10, June, 1972, p. 159.*

SCOOP: LAST OF THE BROWN PELICANS (1972)

Considering the number of species threatened with extinction, the continuance of McClung's Vanishing Animals series seems assured. Now we learn with dismay that the brown pelican is making a last stand in Florida. Scoop, their representative, has a hard enough life as it is . . . , but the real villain is DDT which causes his mate's eggs to be impossibly thin-shelled. McClung states Scoop's case with expert economy, and as the susceptibility to DDT is shared by other types of birds as well, his advocacy deserves a wide audience. The somewhat unfinished look of the black and white illustrations may be attributed to the fact that they were completed by the author after Lloyd Sandford's death.

> *A review of "Scoop: Last of the Brown Pelicans,"* in Kirkus Reviews, *Vol. XL, No. 7, April 1, 1972, p. 407.*

McClung, a well-known author of wildlife books for children, has been successful primarily because each book is an in-depth study of a related group of animals or of an individual species. Into each one he successfully weaves a story line that enlivens the factual information, yet induces no anthropomorphisms.... There is an assessment of the pelican population of various areas, and information is provided on the research and conservation activities of state and federal agencies.

> *A review of "Scoop: Last of the Brown Pelicans,"* in Science Books, *Vol. 8, No. 2, September, 1972, p. 155.*

In his usual clear, concise style, a well-known nature writer traces the life cycle and environmental hazards of the brown pelican through the experiences of an individual male bird. Well illustrated with black-and-white drawings, the book provides pertinent information on an endangered species as well as authoritative bird lore.

> *A review of "Scoop: Last of the Brown Pelicans,"* in The Booklist, *Vol. 69, No. 6, November 15, 1972, p. 302.*

SAMSON: LAST OF THE CALIFORNIA GRIZZLIES   (1973)

In describing the life cycle of the fictional Samson, McClung has incorporated some bits of California history, but he focuses primarily on the animal's behavior patterns: his life as a cub and a yearling, mating, stalking his prey, avoiding the hated man-smell. There is no anthropomorphism here, but the story has real drama as the huge grizzly is hunted by a man he has mauled, trapped, used in a bear-and-bull fight, and escapes to the Sierras; the last incident is based on a newspaper account of such an event. The writing is straightforward, informative, and fictionalized only enough to give impact. (pp. 12-13)

> *Zena Sutherland, in a review of "Samson: Last of the California Grizzlies,"* in Bulletin of the Center for Children's Books, *Vol. 27, No. 1, September, 1973, pp. 12-13.*

As in his previous books, McClung establishes respect for animal life while presenting factual information within a fictionalized framework. This story is about a grizzly bear, a subject which appeals to children, and the plot effectively builds to a moving climax in which man's cruelty to wildlife is shown in an ugly bear-and-bull fight. The author's straightforward, informative note at the end points out the irony of California's use of the grizzly on their state flag after having exterminated the animal.... [The] story will arouse reader sympathy with its creditable, thought-provoking message about man's relationship to wildlife.

> *Margaret Bush, in a review of "Samson: Last of the California Grizzlies,"* in School Library Journal, *an*

appendix to Library Journal, *Vol. 20, No. 1, September, 1973, p. 131.*

An exciting story of the birth, life, capture, torture and escape of a grizzly bear.... Even though you might be sixty-eight instead of eight, do not pick up this book unless you are ready to read it from cover to cover.

> *Ruth Ann G. Butler, in a review of "Samson: Last of the California Grizzlies,"* in Appraisal: Children's Science Books, *Vol. 7, No. 1, Winter, 1974, p. 26.*

MICE, MOOSE, AND MEN: HOW THEIR POPULATIONS RISE AND FALL   (1973)

[*Mice, Moose, and Men: How Their Populations Rise and Fall*], added to [McClung's] many other titles ..., provides an excellent supplementary collection for beginning study units in natural history, conservation, and ecology. Here, he surveys the reasons for explosions in various animals' population cycles, the natural resources of weather, water, and food supply that dictate—and control—these rises and falls in numbers. A sound last chapter equates the phenomenon with human population/over population. Top-notch teaching in print.

> *Lillian N. Gerhardt, in a review of "Mice, Moose, and Men: How Their Populations Rise and Fall,"* in School Library Journal, *an appendix to* Library Journal, *Vol. 20, No. 3, November, 1973, p. 52.*

In a clear and well-organized text, McClung describes the cycles of population growth and decline.... Lucid and objective, this is a good overview of a complex problem of our time. A divided bibliography and an index are appended.

> *Zena Sutherland, in a review of "Mice, Moose, and Men: How Their Populations Rise and Fall,"* in Bulletin of the Center for Children's Books, *Vol. 27, No. 10, June, 1974, p. 160.*

GYPSY MOTH: ITS HISTORY IN AMERICA   (1974)

As an introduction to the gypsy moth *per se* this study suffers from insufficiently detailed illustrations, and even after studying the appendix on "insect pests often mistaken for gypsy moths," a reader probably still could not identify a gypsy moth if he saw one. Nevertheless this is a useful overview of progress in insect control—one which raises the important question of whether the side effects of extermination may not sometimes become more dangerous than the pests themselves.

> *A review of "Gypsy Moth: Its History in America,"* in Kirkus Reviews, *Vol. XLII, No. 17, September 1, 1974, p. 947.*

McClung is careful not to depict the gypsy moth as an "evil" enemy while he reveals at length research and action programs directed against this vegetation-eater. Despite dull, gray-and-white illustrations, this succeeds as a relevant treatise on ecological study. Descriptions of insect pests mistaken for gypsy moths and some suggestions of adult material for further reading are appended. (p. 345)

> *A review of "Gypsy Moth: Its History in America,"* in The Booklist, *Vol. 71, No. 6, November 15, 1974, pp. 344-45.*

Thorough coverage of the gypsy moth.... The history and difficulties in fighting the species . . . as well as the problems of maintaining ecological balance are well integrated into the smoothly written text. Well-placed pen-and-wash drawings enhance the pleasant format.

> *Margaret Bush, in a review of "Gypsy Moth: Its History in America," in* School Library Journal, *Vol. 21, No. 7, March, 1975, p. 98.*

The author researched classic gypsy moth literature that dates to the 1890's as well as recent USDA Forest Service information, and has made a well-balanced presentation of an ecological dilemma. A particularly good feature of the book is the appendix. In it insects often mistaken for the gypsy moth are described and discussed. Children in upper elementary and middle schools should read this book, for it is an excellent example of interesting natural history that communicates a scientific attitude.

> *J. J. Padalino, in a review of "Gypsy Moth: Its History in America," in* Appraisal: Children's Science Books, *Vol. 8, No. 3, Fall, 1975, p. 21.*

SEA STAR (1975)

Using his usual format—simple story form and competent pen-and-ink drawings frequently washed with gray—McClung introduces the life cycle and behavior of the common starfish. He describes the dangers from other animals that share the sea

star's waters, and concludes with two pages about related echinoderms which are pictured on the end pages. The presentation is bland but does cover more material than either Hurd's *Starfish* (Crowell, 1962) or Silverstein's *Star in the Sea* (Warne, 1969).

> *Margaret Bush, in a review of "Sea Star," in* School Library Journal, *Vol. 22, No. 2, October, 1975, p. 100.*

Throughout, the viewpoint is strictly that of an observer, and the information is authentic and adequate. Almost half the page space is taken up by illustrations, both color and black and white, showing starfish and other echinoderms in their environments and in various activities and stages of growth. A teacher could use this book as an introduction to ecology, for the emphasis is on relationships among living things and the environment. However, it would be an unusual child who would read this book without some special incentive, such as a visit to a seashore, or a nature class on echinoderms. (p. 40)

> *Grace Eldering, in a review of "Sea Star," in* Science Books & Films, *Vol. XII, No. 1, May, 1976, pp. 40-1.*

Once again, McClung has written and illustrated a book which will hold the attention of young readers while it informs and fascinates.... Particularly good are descriptions of tidewater life—birds, fish, other invertebrates—which show the interrelationships of animals, emphasizing (though not stating) the

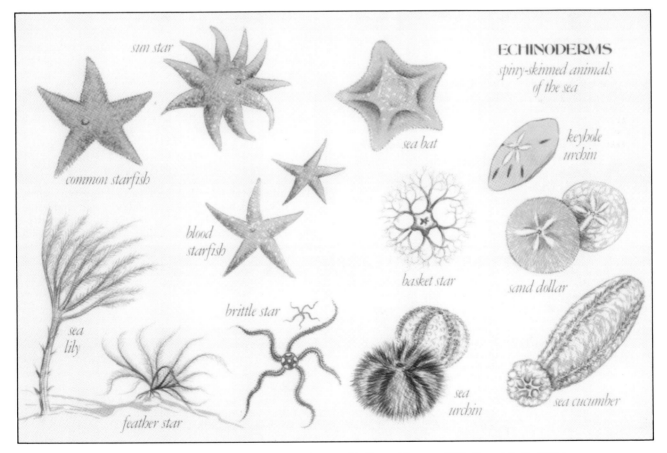

From Sea Star, *written and illustrated by Robert M. McClung. Morrow, 1975. Copyright © 1975 by Robert M. McClung. All rights reserved. Reprinted by permission of the author.*

ecological approach. The last two pages give biological information on echinoderms. Endpaper illustrations are helpful.

> *Frances Doughty, in a review of "Sea Star," in* Appraisal: Children's Science Books, *Vol. 9, No. 3, Fall, 1976, p. 29.*

Children on or near seashores may be motivated to read **Sea Star;** others will probably not find it useful or interesting, since it is mostly descriptive on some natural history of this animal. Young readers are denied one of the most striking characteristics of sea stars, their beautiful and varied colors. The line drawings used do not communicate well. The content is accurate and the type, sentences, and paragraph organization make this a very easy-to-read book. A star fish is carnivorous and the text does an excellent job of explaining its food and foraging habits. The life cycle, growth, and development, and problems of survival constitute most of the book. Other topics include regeneration and body characteristics. . . . No index.

> *John R. Pancella, in a review of "Sea Star," in* Appraisal: Children's Science Books, *Vol. 9, No. 3, Fall, 1976, p. 29.*

LOST WILD WORLDS: THE STORY OF EXTINCT AND VANISHING WILDLIFE OF THE EASTERN HEMISPHERE (1976)

McClung's skillfully written, convincing and alarming book will be offered as adult reading as well as for teenagers. Plainly, the author is a man who cares . . . about the results of humans' dereliction of duty as stewards of the earth. From the time when our ancestors, 15,000 years ago, reduced the woolly mammoth to extinction right up to the present, people have been killing off animals and growing things as if the riches of the earth were inexhaustible.

> *A review of "Lost Wild World: The Story of Extinct and Vanishing Wildlife of the Eastern Hemisphere," in* Publishers Weekly, *Vol. 210, No. 4, July 26, 1976, p. 79.*

A comprehensive, but rather adult, historical and geographic account of extinct and vanishing wild life in the Eastern Hemisphere. It is difficult to visualize even an avid young conservationist wading through this treatise from cover to cover. However, it is an excellent source book for the reference shelf.

> *George Barr, in a review of "Lost Wild Worlds: The Story of Extinct and Vanishing Wildlife of the Eastern Hemisphere," in* Children's Book Review Service, *Vol. 5, No. 5, January, 1977, p. 48.*

Unfortunately, trying to cover the entire Eastern Hemisphere in one volume has forced McClung to greatly compress his material. . . . The popular style of the text and approach make **Lost Wild Worlds** suitable for public libraries and especially for browsing and YA collections.

> *Murray S. Martin, in a review of "Lost Wild Worlds: The Story of Extinct and Vanishing Wildlife of the Eastern Hemisphere," in* Library Journal, *Vol. 102, No. 3, February 1, 1977, p. 398.*

Robert McClung provides a welcome source of information on the status of over fifty species of animals—primarily mammals, but also some well-known birds and a few reptiles. They are discussed by geographical area: Europe, Asia, Africa, Indian Ocean islands, Australia, New Zealand, and the Malay Ar-

chipelago. For each region the author briefly outlines the first appearance and the history of man's activities and describes the ensuing effects on the animals' habitats. Following are discussions of selected species. . . . The author collates interesting fragments of knowledge concerning the species; especially valuable are his estimates of present population size, information often difficult for children to find. A concluding section for each region mentions other endangered species and indicates the local governments' degree of conservation awareness. Because the book deals with the subject generally and specifically it can be picked up at any point and should be useful not only as a reference volume but for general reading on the animal depletion caused by man.

> *Sarah Gagné, in a review of "Lost Wild Worlds: The Story of Extinct and Vanishing Wildlife of the Eastern Hemisphere," in* The Horn Book Magazine, *Vol. LIII, No. 3, June, 1977, p. 339.*

In this highly readable account of . . . extinct and vanishing animals . . . , McClung presents conservation in a historical perspective. Wars, explorations and their protagonists, and the more recent research and conservation efforts in the field and in the zoological gardens are combined into lively and engaging stories about the animals. This book is a companion to the author's **Lost Wild America** . . . and performs a similar role of informing and alerting the reader to the history of wildlife destruction and to the various practices used to help endangered wildlife. . . . McClung lists the magazines and periodicals dealing with wildlife conservation, as well as selected books and articles to complement each chapter. Additional references are also provided for further study. The index is compact but adequate. This book will serve as a useful reference to students considering careers in conservation, wildlife management and zoo biology. It will provide interesting hours of straight reading or browsing to all animal lovers.

> *Sophie Jakowska, in a review of "Lost Wild Worlds: The Story of Extinct and Vanishing Wildlife of the Eastern Hemisphere," in* Science Books & Films, *Vol. XIII, No. 2, September, 1977, p. 82.*

PEEPER: FIRST VOICE OF SPRING (1977)

[The] direct and lucid text follows one tiny frog through its life cycle. McClung writes with authority and simplicity, giving a picture of the ecological balance of the peeper's environment as well as an explanation of the stages of its life and reproductive processes.

> *Zena Sutherland, in a review of "Peeper: First Voice of Spring," in* Bulletin of the Center for Children's Books, *Vol. 31, No. 5, January, 1978, p. 82.*

Meticulous pen-and-ink drawings [by Carol Lerner] together with concise wording make this account about the tree frog, hyla crucifer or spring peeper, an outstanding book. The environment of the pond and seasonal changes as they affect the hyla's development are described and pictured accurately and with appreciation. (pp. 198, 200)

> *Phyllis G. Sidorsky, in a review of "Peeper: First Voice of Spring," in* Childhood Education, *Vol. 54, No. 4 (February, 1978), pp. 198, 200.*

[The] text and illustration . . . are both accurate and inviting. . . .

[This] book gives [the reader] straight information and facts that hold together in a meaningful way for children.

The book is suggested for ages six to ten, but some of the vocabulary (such as fertilized, oxygen, developing, deposited, succession, and algae) is difficult for first graders.

> *Sally Cartwright, "Of Mice and Boys (Frogs, Too),"*
> *in The Christian Science Monitor, May 3, 1978, p.*
> *B5.**

The rebirth of the woods in the spring is the topic of this beautifully illustrated, . . . well-written book. . . . [The] tree frog's life cycle is beautifully described, stressing the dangers to survival, but with the understanding that these risks are a part of the balance of nature. This is a lovely book for home and school use. Most second graders would be able to read it by themselves.

> *Martha Sanders, in a review of "Peeper: First Voice*
> *of Spring," in Science Books & Films, Vol. XIV,*
> *No. 2, September, 1978, p. 112.*

HUNTED MAMMALS OF THE SEA (1978)

McClung's thorough research and skillful writing result in a fine examination of man's exploitation of sea animals for such products as oil, meat, hides, furs, and ivory. McClung discusses ways in which the use and misuse of the ocean and its inhabitants have upset the natural environment, endangering or eliminating species of whales, otter, seals, sea-cows, and walruses. . . . He also provides an up-to-date account of conservation efforts and legislation (or the disturbing lack thereof). Coverage is shorter and simpler than in McClung's **Lost Wild America** . . . and **Lost Wild Worlds** . . . and more clearly focused than in J. J. McCoy's *A Sea of Troubles* (Seabury, 1975).

> *Margaret Bush, in a review of "Hunted Mammals*
> *of the Sea," in School Library Journal, Vol. 25, No.*
> *1, September, 1978, p. 161.*

Few ecology causes have generated as much emotional heat and smoke as the plight of marine mammals: whale hunts, accidental drownings of dolphins in tuna nets, the clubbing of baby fur seals. So it is both a relief and a delight to find this an intelligent, concerned book which avoids the easy emotionalism often surrounding endangered species. . . . The balanced, thoughtful presentation is also highly readable, and is recommended for any collection which needs information on marine life or on endangered animals. There is a list of common and scientific names, a bibliography, and an index, as well as a chart of whale species, characteristics, and status; my only complaint about the book is that similar charts for the other animals should have been included.

> *Daphne Ann Hamilton, in a review of "Hunted Mam-*
> *mals of the Sea," in Appraisal: Children's Science*
> *Books, Vol. 12, No. 1, Winter, 1979, p. 26.*

Mr. McClung has prepared a comprehensive, absorbing account, at times sensitive, at other times brutally frank, of the life of sea mammals. . . . Studies, research reports, population facts and figures, and historical events are documented. Acknowledgements include the contributions of noted zoologists and naturalists. There is a selected bibliography of nearly fifty general and technical references. A detailed index is included which even uses scientific names. The theme throughout is one of an appeal for conservation and protection. Current efforts are described for these ends. There are convincing arguments in favor of saving endangered species for education, natural history research, recreation, and for their pure aesthetic beauty. This is a beautifully written reference for a school library or personal library of species preservation enthusiasts. (pp. 26-7)

> *John R. Pancella, in a review of "Hunted Mammals*
> *of the Sea," in Appraisal: Children's Science Books,*
> *Vol. 12, No. 1, Winter, 1979, pp. 26-7.*

Both scholarly and readable, **Hunted Mammals of the Sea** is a major book that compares well with the author's **Lost Wild Worlds: The Story of Extinct and Vanishing Wildlife of the Eastern Hemisphere**. . . . Natural history is discussed, but equal emphasis is given to conservation: man's hunting of sea animals and an estimation of the surviving populations. To obtain some of these facts in other places would take hours of searching in more technical literature. [This is] an excellent source for student research.

> *Sarah Gagné, in a review of "Hunted Mammals of*
> *the Sea," in The Horn Book Magazine, Vol. LV,*
> *No. 1, February, 1979, p. 94.*

Text allotted to the various species is proportional to current interest in the animals by North Americans. . . . Carefully and pleasantly written, balanced, up to date and factual, the book is also well designed and printed. There is a well-chosen bibliography. . . . (pp. 89-90)

> *Victor B. Scheffer, in a review of "Hunted Mammals*
> *of the Sea," in Science Books & Films, Vol. XV,*
> *No. 2, September, 1979, pp. 89-90.*

AMERICA'S ENDANGERED BIRDS: PROGRAMS AND PEOPLE WORKING TO SAVE THEM (1979)

The author gives equal space to opposing factions advocating either raising flocks in captivity or preserving the birds in the wild, explaining the advantages and problems of each view without favoring either side. This covers endangered species of birds thoroughly and extensively but is so loaded with facts and statistics that it is rough going even for readers interested in the topic.

> *Karen Ritter, in a review of "America's Endangered*
> *Birds: Programs and People Working to Save Them,"*
> *in School Library Journal, Vol. 26, No. 2, October,*
> *1979, p. 160.*

A book notable for being both enjoyable to read and useful as a reference work. (The author was similarly successful in two recent books, **Lost Wild Worlds** and **Hunted Mammals of the Sea**.) . . . So many facts are integrated into the book, one senses the author has a great deal of firsthand knowledge.

> *Sarah Gagné, in a review of "America's Endangered*
> *Birds: Programs and People Working to Save Them,"*
> *in The Horn Book Magazine, Vol. LVI, No. 1, Feb-*
> *ruary, 1980, p. 85.*

The lengths to which a man will go for a bird could be the theme of this detailed and carefully documented report. . . . Despite the extremity of the efforts, this hasn't the cause-centered readability of McClung's **Hunted Mammals of the Sea** . . . , but it is solidly informative—and valuable for its positive orientation.

A review of "America's Endangered Birds: Programs and People Working to Save Them," in Kirkus Reviews, *Vol. XLVIII, No. 3, February 1, 1980, p. 139.*

"Sixty-seven birds native to the United States are in danger of extinction." The urgency of saving them throbs through McClung's clear, objective prose. Here is yet another well-done McClung book on vanishing wildlife. . . . [Maps], index, bibliography, and a scientific glossary make this book a useful research tool for junior high and up.

> *Ruth S. Beebe, in a review of "America's Endangered Birds: Programs and People Working to Save Them," in* Appraisal: Children's Science Books, *Vol. 13, No. 3, Fall, 1980, p. 45.*

Much painstaking research has gone into the production of this excellent volume. . . . The maps showing migration routes, habitats, and ranges are most helpful. . . . The author has written many books on this and related subjects. This is one of his best. (pp. 45-6)

> *Glenn O. Bough, in a review of "America's Endangered Birds: Programs and People Working to Save Them," in* Appraisal: Children's Science Books, *Vol. 13, No. 3, Fall, 1980, pp. 45-6.*

SNAKES: THEIR PLACE IN THE SUN (1979)

Mr. McClung, a noted environmentalist, has written a very interesting book about snakes and their place in the balance of nature for young students. All the basic facts of their life style are here, plus the fascinating explanation of how their unique jaws permit them to swallow their food whole, how they shed their skin, and how they hibernate in winter. . . . Although there are many more elegant books about snakes on the market, this small book has just the right amount of detail and information for this age group with simple enough vocabulary for all.

> *Sallie Hope Erhard, in a review of "Snakes: Their Place in the Sun," in* Appraisal: Children's Science Books, *Vol. 13, No. 2, Spring, 1980, p. 48.*

This is an excellent introduction to how snakes fit into communities of living things. . . . The text is simple and understandable, but never dull or dry. . . . This is a book to recommend to children for their enjoyment as well as for the understanding they will gain from it.

> *Seymour Simon, in a review of "Snakes: Their Place in the Sun," in* Appraisal: Children's Science Books, *Vol. 13, No. 2, Spring, 1980, p. 48.*

A major focus of the book is an explanation of the snake's role in the food chain. Eating habits are emphasized . . . but not overdramatized. The snake, in turn, is sometimes eaten. . . . The popularity of the subject and the responsible and informed presentation will ensure steady use in most libraries.

> *Margaret Bush, in a review of "Snakes: Their Place in the Sun," in* School Library Journal, *Vol. 27, No. 1, September, 1980, p. 75.*

The publisher's claim that this is a "book to blow away the myths" is not justified. . . . The author's attempt to show [the snake's] ecological importance is the least effective section—it is repetitious and oblique. Nevertheless, elementary school libraries should consider this, especially if their coverage of snakes is inadequate.

> *Howard J. Stein, in a review of "Snakes: Their Place in the Sun," in* Science Books & Films, *Vol. 16, No. 1, September-October, 1980, p. 33.*

THE AMAZING EGG (1980)

McClung broadens readers' understanding of the role of the egg in the growth process as he elaborates on a host of egg-bearing and/or egg-laying species' methods of mating and nurturing the unborn and unhatched. Each chapter provides considerable detail, both in the text and through many careful black-and-white drawings. While not inspired, the writing is well organized, the text serviceable.

> *Judith Goldberger, in a review of "The Amazing Egg," in* Booklist, *Vol. 77, No. 12, February 15, 1981, p. 810.*

[*The Amazing Egg*] is a clear, straightforward, suitably-illustrated compendium of information, although without the detail or thought-provoking interest of Dorothy Patent's books on the different animal groups ". . . and How They Reproduce."

> *A review of "The Amazing Egg," in* Kirkus Reviews, *Vol. XLIX, No. 4, February 15, 1981, p. 217.*

Small pencil drawings and diagrams are generally useful in helping readers visualize some of the animals and processes described and include some particularly interesting life-size comparisons of eggs. Margaret Cosgrove's attractive and well-written *Eggs and What Happens Inside Them* (Dodd, 1966) covers very similar material, but McClung's book is informative, and the subject has not been treated copiously at this level.

> *Margaret Bush, in a review of "The Amazing Egg," in* School Library Journal, *Vol. 27, No. 8, April, 1981, p. 128.*

McClung writes in a straightforward, lucid style, with good organization of material and good integration of text and illustrations; the latter are soft, accurately detailed pencil drawings. . . . Nothing new here, but it's an exemplary science book, with broad coverage and authoritative tone; the appended index has been carefully compiled.

> *Zena Sutherland, in a review of "The Amazing Egg," in* Bulletin of the Center for Children's Books, *Vol. 34, No. 9, May, 1981, p. 176.*

A readable description of the production and development of the eggs of fish, amphibians, mammals, insects, birds and reptiles. Each scientific term is defined when introduced; nonetheless, a glossary would have been helpful. Black-and-white drawings, while useful, should provide a scale for comparison. In spite of these drawbacks, it is a worthwhile addition to the science collection.

> *Phyllis G. Sidorsky, in a review of "The Amazing Egg," in* Childhood Education, *Vol. 58, No. 1 (September-October, 1981), p. 51.*

VANISHING WILDLIFE OF LATIN AMERICA (1981)

Discerning and thoughtful, this exploration of the endangered species of the Caribbean, South America, and the Galápagos

From Spike: The Story of a Whitetail Deer, *written and illustrated by Robert M. McClung. Morrow, 1952. Copyright © 1952 by Robert M. McClung. All rights reserved. Reprinted by permission of the author.*

Islands completes McClung's trilogy (*Lost Wild America, Lost Wild Worlds*) on the current status of the world's wildlife. Geographically divided, the individual chapters briefly discuss the history of the area, chronicle specific vanishing creatures, and relate the factors affecting this course of events. The author lends authority to his material with numerous facts and statistics, yet provides a readable presentation through inclusion of fascinating information about the wide, and often unusual variety of native wildlife.

> *Barbara Elleman, in a review of "Vanishing Wildlife of Latin America," in* Booklist, *Vol. 77, No. 20, June 15, 1981, p. 1346.*

The book is well written and highly informative about many species whose unusual characteristics will be new to young readers in the United States. An extensive bibliography, an index, and outline maps of the areas covered are included. . . . Because there is so much content, the book, along with its companion titles, [*Lost Wild America* and *Lost Wild Worlds*], will probably serve best as a reference. (p. 28)

> *A. H. Drummond, in a review of "Vanishing Wildlife of Latin America," in* Appraisal: Science Books for Young People, *Vol. 14, No. 3, Fall, 1981, pp. 28-9.*

Robert McClung has written another of his outstanding books on the status of wildlife in different parts of the world. . . . An outstanding source for student reports, the book is easily read, up-to-date, and thorough. A prognosis for the future is given

at the end of each chapter. Interesting stories are incorporated. . . . (pp. 558-59)

> *Sarah Gagné, in a review of "Vanishing Wildlife of Latin America," in* The Horn Book Magazine, *Vol. LVII, No. 5, October, 1981, pp. 558-59.*

RAJPUR: LAST OF THE BENGAL TIGERS (1982)

Although told in narrative form, the story of Rajpur is based on known facts about the habits and habitat of the Bengal tiger; there is little personification and no anthropomorphism. It begins with Rajpur as a cub, learning to hunt by following his mother's example and learning about the predators he should avoid. Meeting his first rival, Rajpur goes off to find a new territory in the Himalayan hills, where he meets and courts a mate and starts a family. Guarding his mate when she is caught in a trap, he is taken by a team of scientists, drugged and tagged, and left to recover; because of the dwindling numbers of tigers, the area has been declared a wildlife reserve. The illustrations [by Irene Brady], in earth colors and orange, are dramatic but repetitive; the text is informative, slow-moving but relieved by moments of action and danger.

> *Zena Sutherland, in a review of "Rajpur, Last of the Bengal Tigers," in* Bulletin of the Center for Children's Books, *Vol. 36, No. 2, October, 1982, p. 31.*

Though Rajpur is not the last of the Bengal tigers, despite the title, he is one of the remnant of a once populous species. Handsome tiger-tone illustrations complement the extremely readable, sympathetic narration in this unusually well-made book.

> *George Gleason, in a review of "Rajpur: Last of the Bengal Tigers," in* School Library Journal, *Vol. 29, No. 3, November, 1982, p. 102.*

As in his many other appealing books McClung uses the life cycle format. . . . McClung traces [Rajpur's] life against a brilliant, teeming jungle background without a trace of anthropomorphism. The book is an eloquent plea for protecting this magnificent animal and his surroundings. . . . *The Tiger, Its Life in the Wild,* by George B. Schaller and Millicent E. Selsam (Harper, 1969) an equally excellent book, is more useful for research. *Rajpur* however, will appear to a younger audience of animal lovers.

> *Ruth S. Beebe, in a review of "Rajpur, Last of the Bengal Tigers," in* Appraisal: Science Books for Young People, *Vol. 16, No. 2, Spring-Summer, 1983, p. 36.*

Robert McClung may be the best interpreter of natural science now writing for young people. *Rajpur* does nothing to diminish that reputation. . . . Habitat encroachment and hunting, two principal factors in the species' fragile status, are vividly represented through the deaths of Rajpur's father and an injured man-killer. Rajpur finds protection in a reserve, and in a useful appendix McClung details current conservation efforts.

McClung is a fluid, graceful writer who makes the young tiger fairly leap off the page.

> *Don Lessem, in a review of "Rajpur, Last of the Bengal Tigers," in* Appraisal: Science Books for Young People, *Vol. 16, No. 2, Spring-Summer, 1983, p. 36.*

MYSTERIES OF MIGRATION (1983)

This perfunctory survey of migration covers both seasonal and once-in-a-lifetime animal treks. A few general statements about migration of birds, mammals, fish and amphibians, and insects preface a closer look at migratory patterns of one or two species in each group. McClung also talks briefly about nomads, animals that move constantly, and discusses how animal migrations can be traced. The five maps are well executed and very useful.... Although some long and unfamiliar words are used in the text (*leptocephali*, for one), there is no pronunciation guide.... [A] serviceable volume for collections needing brief supplementary material on animal migration.

> *Karen Stang Hanley, in a review of "Mysteries of Migration," in* Booklist, *Vol. 79, No. 21, July, 1983, p. 1403.*

Filling the gap between Swift's *Animal Travelers* (Greenwillow, 1977) and Jarman's *Atlas of Animal Migration* (Crowell, 1974), McClung provides a brief overview of why some animals, such as the Arctic tern, the Northern fur seal, the Pacific salmon and the American eel, migrate and others, such as army ants and mountain lions, do not.... Maps indicate migration routes and summer and winter nesting grounds. The information given is only enough to whet the appetite, but no bibliography is included.

> *Olive Hull, in a review of "Mysteries of Migration," in* School Library Journal, *Vol. 29, No. 10, August, 1983, p. 68.*

The discussion of spring migration includes the generalized statement: "Whales begin to travel northward to summer feeding grounds in Arctic waters."... This statement is applicable to the migration of the gray whale, but it is inappropriate for whales that feed in the Antarctic. Migration routes are clearly illustrated. The sentences are short, and the language is clear. A great deal of information is concisely presented in only 65 pages....

> *Theodore C. Byerley, in a review of "Mysteries of Migration," in* Science Books & Films, *Vol. 19, No. 1, September-October, 1983, p. 34.*

As usual Robert McClung has done a marvelous job. The text is written in a light and lucid manner.... This very attractive, easy to read, well-indexed book is a worthwhile purchase. Similar in amount of information is Jacquelyn Berrill's *Wonders of Animal Migration* (Dodd, Mead, 1964). There are several other titles that delve more deeply into the subject.

> *Althea L. Philips, in a review of "Mysteries of Migration," in* Appraisal: Science Books for Young People, *Vol. 16, No. 3, Fall, 1983, p. 40.*

GORILLA (1984)

McClung tells the story of a small gorilla band living on the Virunga Volcanoes of central Africa, focusing particularly on the experiences of young Beni through his first two years of life. He describes daily life and family relationships and the tragedy of human exploitation which has placed the species in probable permanent danger. A very moving portion of the book describes the entrapment and brutal slaying of much of Beni's family group by poachers. McClung deftly recreates the habitat and life experience of the gorillas; he draws on the written works of George Schaller and Dian Fossey and at the end of his story includes a final chapter on the efforts of scientists and African governments to protect the remaining gorillas.... [There] is a bibliography of sources by the major scientists who have studied gorillas. Kay McDearmon's *Gorillas* (Dodd, 1979) provides a factual approach and a bit more information for the same audience, but McClung's sobering account will have a long-lasting impact on animal lovers.

> *Margaret Bush, in a review of "Gorilla," in* School Library Journal, *Vol. 31, No. 5, January, 1985, p. 77.*

Science and nature writer McClung continues his successful profiles of endangered animals both as species and individuals with this affecting narrative about a young mountain gorilla.... Through McClung's smooth text and [Irene] Brady's skillful pencil drawings, readers are familiarized with the characteristics and habits of these reclusive animals.... Though fictitious, the treatment has a documentary flavor and is partly based on findings of Dian Fossey and other gorilla observers. An essay containing additional information about the species is appended along with a brief bibliography.

> *Karen Stang Hanley, in a review of "Gorilla," in* Booklist, *Vol. 81, No. 10, January 15, 1985, p. 719.*

Gorilla provides an accurate and interesting account of the natural history of gorillas in a fictional format, with a heavy emphasis on the continuing exploitation of this species by humans.... The book is an eloquent statement of the gorilla's precarious position in Africa and at the same time conveys a wealth of information about the animal's natural history. The story is well written....

> *Timothy D. Johnston, in a review of "Gorilla," in* Science Books & Films, *Vol. 20, No. 5, May-June, 1985, p. 309.*

This account of African mountain gorillas is as engrossing as any fiction. At first, the strong story line plus the naming of all the animals suggests anthropomorphism, but very soon it's apparent that both features are good vehicles for organizing the wealth of natural history in this short book.

A look at Dian Fossey's *Gorillas in the Mist* (Houghton Mifflin, 1983) assures us that naming each member of a gorilla band is the only reliable way to keep them all straight when scientists are working in the field. As for the story line, there is genuine drama in the lives of these endangered creatures whose habits mirror our own in so many ways.

Fossey and others are listed in an excellent short bibliography at the end of the book. There is also an appendix called The History of an Endangered Species.... There is no index.

> *Lavinia C. Demos, in a review of "Gorilla," in* Appraisal: Science Books for Young People, *Vol. 18, No. 3, Summer, 1985, p. 22.*

THE TRUE ADVENTURES OF GRIZZLY ADAMS (1985)

This biography will dash the TV image of Grizzly Adams. Unlike his fictionalized TV counterpart, the real Adams was a violent hunter who readily killed unnecessarily. He captured young animals by cruelly killing the mother and tamed his bear cubs by force. Hunters will enjoy reading about Adams's exploits, but the book itself is somewhat choppy. The bulk of the text is a series of incidents loosely strung together by mediocre narrative. One is left with impressions of Adams, not a clear picture or understanding of the man.

> *Susan H. Williamson, in a review of "The True Adventures of Grizzly Adams," in* The Book Report, *Vol. 4, No. 3, November-December, 1985, p. 43.*

Using Adams's own accounts, contemporary magazine and newspaper articles, and several biographies as sources, the author has composed a portrait which is quite different from the saintly animal lover depicted on the silver screen. . . . The author does not hide Adams's brutal, though never wanton, shooting of the females to obtain their young, nor the harsh methods he used in training. Independent, fearless, and eccentric, Adams personifies the scrambling, hustling, rough and ready image of gold rush frontiersman. The good, solid account of Adams's adventures brings him into a more accurate focus but in no way diminishes his skill in hunting, his respect for the animals he both killed and trained, and his incredible toughness. Notes and a list of sources accompany the text. The much-needed maps will facilitate following Adams's travels. Index. (pp. 751-52)

> *Ethel R. Twichell, in a review of "The True Adventures of Grizzly Adams," in* The Horn Book Magazine, *Vol. LXI, No. 6, November-December, 1985, pp. 751-52.*

Adams' contradictory character is well caught: the crude humor, the occasional cruelty, the penchant for lying, along with the loyalty, courage, and persistence that studded his actions. The problems with the book stem from repetition of similar hunting experiences and from awkward writing, particularly a noticeable overuse of gerunds to begin sentences, or the occasional clumsy phrase ("He had seldom seen a man with so much courage and guts.") Nevertheless, the book is soundly researched and documented, with helpful notes, bibliography, and a number of old prints and woodcuts. It will have special appeal for boys who are tired of reading about the honesty of George Washington.

> *A review of "The True Adventures of Grizzly Adams," in* Bulletin of the Center for Children's Books, *Vol. 39, No. 4, December, 1985, p. 72.*

McClung's description of Grizzly and his wilderness life will appeal to those youngsters who have an interest in the early American frontier. There are good descriptions of hunting/trapping the animals, treating wounds and encounters with the Indians. I especially enjoyed the sections, though brief, describing his dealings with P. T. Barnum. Good supplement for history of the American Frontier. (p. 334)

> *Anne Frost, in a review of "The True Adventures of Grizzly Adams," in* Voice of Youth Advocates, *Vol. 8, No. 5, December, 1985, pp. 333-34.*

Susan Beth Pfeffer

1948-

American author of fiction.

Pfeffer creates realistic fiction that features a variety of contemporary settings and topics popular with teens and preteens, including reluctant readers. Her young adult novels explore themes ranging from issues like suicide, divorce, and censorship to romantic glimpses into the world of fashion models, beauty queens, and television actresses. In her tales for younger readers, Pfeffer considers subjects which are meaningful to her audience, such as friendship, earning money, keeping secrets, and speaking in public. Her one picture book, *Awful Evelina*, is a humorous fantasy about a dreaded encounter with a mean cousin. Known for creating well-crafted and swiftly paced narratives, Pfeffer generally portrays believable characters who solve their problems with initiative and imagination.

Critics praise Pfeffer's natural dialogue and ability to treat serious topics with understanding and humor. Although some reviewers find her characterizations superficial and her endings predictable, they admire Pfeffer's perceptive handling of emotions and relationships and commend the values of self-reliance, courage, and common sense that her works affirm.

Pfeffer has won numerous child- and adult-selected awards.

(See also *Something about the Author*, Vol. 4 and *Contemporary Authors*, Vols. 29-32, rev. ed.)

GENERAL COMMENTARY

SARA SLOAN

I'm not quite sure why *Marly the Kid* is such a popular book with somewhat below-grade readers. . . . The character of 15-year-old Marly as developed by Pfeffer is undoubtedly part of the book's attraction.

Marly the Kid is basically the story of a high-school girl who follows her older sister's lead and runs away from a smothering, nagging mother. Marly's destination is her traveling-salesman father and her idealized stepmother, a teacher. Marly gets along well in her new home, has a crush on her male English teacher, gets suspended from school and generally leads the type of life which many of the book's readers would like to lead. Marly is depicted as a fun-loving, basically serious person who sticks up for her rights. When Marly is suspended from school for alleged rudeness to an abusive social-studies teacher she refuses to apologize to him until he is also forced to apologize to her. At the conclusion of the book, Marly states that her next battle will be challenging the custom that says that all cheerleaders have to be pretty. . . .

The book has a minimum of characters, most of whom are well developed. The sentences are primarily simple and the chapters average about 15 pages.

Marly is the sequel to *The Beauty Queen* but is definitely readable alone. *The Beauty Queen* centers around an older sister who has just graduated from high school. Marly is mentioned only in passing. *The Beauty Queen* has more characters, a

slightly more involved plot and has not acquired a large word-of-mouth following. It is generally read by readers who want to "find out more about Marly." *The Beauty Queen*'s plot deals with the title character being forced by her mother to enter a regional beauty contest, which she wins. At the urging of her boy friend she runs away before the state contest to pursue a lead about an acting job. . . .

About David is the story of a high-school boy, David, who kills his parents and then himself and the effect his actions have on the lives of his contemporaries and their families in a wealthy suburb. It is told through Lynn, his next-door neighbor. There is a large number of characters and a shift in form from narration to conversation and back throughout the book. This may make it difficult for the poorer reader to follow.

> *Sara Sloan, in a review of "Marly the Kid," "The Beauty Queen," and "About David," in* The High/ Low Report, *Vol. 2, No. 6, February, 1981, p. 4.*

JUST MORGAN   (1970)

To open with "My parents died early in May of my ninth-grade year at Fairfield" is to promise a Story, and Morgan comes through. She was parentless even when she wasn't and grieves only hollowly—but she plays the bereaved orphan not dishonestly when she aches for some reaction from her more willing than able guardian Uncle Tom. Meeting Village-y Ronnie who's slated for Fairfield too and dating Jimmie (pimply, but a Boy), Morgan rallies—till roommate Trinck hits New York, the personification of boarding school's in-crowd viciousness. The question of allegiance arises (Ronnie vs. the withering Trinck) and the problem of insecurity (feeling *de trop* with Uncle Tom) persists. But both are resolved as naturally as they evolved in a lightly perceptive scenario that's neither honeyed nor bitter. *Just Morgan*'s just about right.

> *A review of "Just Morgan," in* Kirkus Reviews, *Vol. XXXVIII, No. 5, March 1, 1970, p. 249.*

An honest story with interesting and wholly credible people, the book is particularly distinguished by the natural quality of the dialogue and the complete avoidance of formula situations.

> *Zena Sutherland, in a review of "Just Morgan," in* Saturday Review, *Vol. LIII, No. 19, May 9, 1970, p. 47.*

There's lots of fast, fresh, often very funny dialogue in this book. Its characters, both teen-age and adult, are interesting, individual and hip. Its author is 22 years old. That she writes convincingly of youth is not as remarkable as her understanding of subtle relationships and her insight into motivations. Miss Pfeffer instructs as well as amuses. (p. 16)

The scenes between [Morgan and her Uncle Tom] in which dating is an issue are among the best in the book....

[This is a] funny, worthwhile novel. (p. 18)

> *Robin Davies, in a review of "Just Morgan," in* The New York Times Book Review, *Part II, May 24, 1970, pp. 16, 18.*

Pleasant fiction for girls, with interesting characters, negligible plotting, and a low-key, if clichéd, lesson in choosing friendship over social pressure.... [Assorted] appealing characters (Morgan's first boyfriend, a new girlfriend, her cousin Josh, her uncle's secretary) contribute to Morgan's pleasures and pains in growing up—all in a deftly authored light manner that should win Morgan many friends among young teen readers.

> *Margaret A. Dorsey, in a review of "Just Morgan," in* School Library Journal, *an appendix to* Library Journal, *Vol. 17, No. 1, September, 1970, p. 176.*

Susan Pfeffer provides an excellent interpretation of adolescent uncertainties about physical attractiveness and verbal ability. *Just Morgan* is ideal reading for a younger adolescent girl who wants to explore romantic other worlds. Morgan Goodstone would be a very good friend!

> *John W. Conner, in a review of "Just Morgan," in* English Journal, *Vol. 61, No. 1, January, 1972, p. 138.*

BETTER THAN ALL RIGHT (1972)

All too often this is no more than a chance for Iris Levin to show off her jejune sophistication in contrast to her parentally sheltered 14 year-old cousin Caryn whom she's expected to keep company during a resort summer in upstate New York. In Shelly, whose conversation is dominated by his future commitment to an elusive community of the guilty called Mudlark College, Iris meets her verbal match. The two trade stagy monologues on their respective parents' colorful pasts and their own psyches (scarred in Shelly's case by a suicided older brother) and, in moments that come as a welcome relief from all that talk, sneak off for a shared joint, some quick, quiet lovemaking or a few pages of Dickens. Flashes of brittle wit illuminate banter which can only excite the admiration of less self-assured teenagers, but there are too few glimpses of Iris' underlying vulnerability and too many facile resemblances to other casualties of fictional divorces. As Iris packs her bags for greener pastures—miffed at the rejection of Caryn's parents and Shelly's self-indulgent fantasies of suicide—it's hard to share her own estimation that she's doing much better than all right.

> *A review of "Better Than All Right," in* Kirkus Reviews, *Vol. XL, No. 14, July 15, 1972, p. 808.*

Lonely, misunderstood teenagers and confused, inept parents who frequently divorce and remarry are the focus of Susan Pfeffer's latest novel. As in the author's *Just Morgan* ... teenagers lead disrupted, unstable lives, but here there is no joy in living—only oppression and isolation.... Reader interest is momentarily sparked when Iris's boyfriend reveals the inadvertent death of his brother, but this is the only insight into the wooden characters. Despite the author's attempt to use words currently fashionable among young adults, the conversations sound stilted, unnatural, and contrived. *Better Than All Right* goes beyond realism to espouse the philosophy that there can be no pleasure, only an avoidance of pain.

> *Phyllis Cantor, in a review of "Better Than All Right," in* School Library Journal, *an appendix to* Library Journal, *Vol. 19, No. 7, March, 1973, p. 119.*

RAINBOWS AND FIREWORKS (1973)

Susan Pfeffer's book faces the problem of much contemporary fiction. She creates a background that is radical. The situation is unique—artistic parents who write pornography, their children who are independent and free-thinking. The book made me quite uncomfortable in its attempt at non-conformism. The story deals with sophisticated ideologies while the writing remains condescending. Who is Ms. Pfeffer addressing? A ten-year-old or myself? We are bombarded with schizophrenia, college drop-outs, the hypocrisy of wealth, Socialism, and much more. We are left with a feeling that Ms. Pfeffer has much to say, but in stressing the intellectual didactic, the reading becomes too self-conscious.

> *Marianne Jacobbi, in a review of "Rainbows and Fireworks," in* Children's Book Review Service, *Vol. 1, No. 11, July, 1973, p. 74.*

The slickness of the writing is compensated for by the freshness of the situation and characters in this light, fast-moving novel about a pleasantly Bohemian family.... The dialogue is generally glib, but the characters do say some good things: e.g., Mr. Reisman says that he's proud of his daughters, "But not because they're lovely," implying that it's because of what they are and do instead. Moreover, the twins seem like together human beings and show a good amount of independence without it becoming the issue it seems to be in many teenage novels.

> *Marilyn R. Singer, in a review of "Rainbows & Fireworks," in* School Library Journal, *an appendix to* Library Journal, *Vol. 20, No. 1, September, 1973, p. 148.*

THE BEAUTY QUEEN (1974)

At eighteen, Katherine (Kit) Carson is a cool customer, well on her way to an acting career and able, rather against her better judgment, to project just the right note of sincerity to beauty contest judges and officials. Unfortunately Katherine retains the same sort of composure throughout her first-person account of her career as a reluctant beauty queen, and though she rejects the beauty pageant mentality (as much for its no-talent tackiness as for its values) and has a minor crisis over the realization that her beauty may have been an important factor in winning acting roles, Katherine is so obviously and confidently "a winner" that her resignation from the competition really does not seem to be much of a sacrifice. The satire on the beauty contest business is good, but could have been much sharper; this is obviously the Miss America contest, but it is never named as such, and none of Katherine's fellow contestants are waging the kind of semi-professional campaigns that are common among potential Miss Americas. Besides, it's just hard to believe that a relatively sophisticated eighteen-year-old, especially one with a theatrical background, could have been so unconscious of her looks and their impact on others. Katherine is courageous in her final decision to pursue her career on her own terms, kind to her plump younger sister, understanding of her pushy mother's anxieties, and entertainingly caustic on the subject of her family's money troubles and the contest's hypocrisy—but none of this adds up to more than a moderately convincing performance.

> *A review of "The Beauty Queen," in* Kirkus Reviews, *Vol. XLII, No. 9, May 1, 1974, p. 489.*

Katherine Carson is out of high school and into the theater, in a small way, far enough to assure herself that the only goal for her is to become a real professional. But her mother has other plans. . . . It's hard to believe the book—Kit is just too good to be true—but it's persuasively written, entertaining and can be taken as a lesson in values.

> *A review of "The Beauty Queen," in* Publishers Weekly, *Vol. 205, No. 23, June 10, 1974, p. 41.*

Although I don't think this book will ever win the Newbery Medal, I do think it has something to offer to teenage readers: a fresh plot, for one thing; fast-moving, easy-to-read, well-written prose for another; and a character who is interesting throughout, though not always credible. I think this is timely enough to be read and enjoyed by young teenagers who have just about had it with teenage problems.

> *Susan Zaretsky, in a review of "The Beauty Queen," in* Children's Book Review Service, *Vol. 2, No. 12, August, 1974, p. 111.*

[Selectors who used **Just Morgan**] with satisfied readers are in for a letdown with this dull novel. . . . The predictable ending and one-dimensional characters make this a totally forgettable performance.

> *Bonnie R. Wheatley, in a review of "The Beauty Queen," in* School Library Journal, *an appendix to* Library Journal, *Vol. 21, No. 1, September, 1974, p. 110.*

The backstage scenes of the beauty contest are interesting, the dialogue is natural and often pungent, and Kit is a sympathetic character, but it is Mom who steals the show; Pfeffer's portrayal of a tired, embittered, divorced woman whose ambition precludes compassion is biting.

> *Zena Sutherland, in a review of "The Beauty Queen," in* Bulletin of the Center for Children's Books, *Vol. 28, No. 3, November, 1974, p. 51.*

WHATEVER WORDS YOU WANT TO HEAR (1974)

Almost entirely in dialogue and in a tone of near clinical dispassion, Paula tells of her meeting with nice Jonny Stapleton and his fucked up brother Jordan who forces her on their first date to choose between them, and of her no-strings summer affair with rude, attractive Jordan just before she is to enter Princeton. . . . On completion the story leaves an odd impression of honesty without depth or even insight, despite extensive evidence (convincing enough on a case history level) linking both Paula's and Jordan's behavior to that of their parents. Still, all those probing personal conversations have a sort of voyeuristic fascination and, often, a brittle smart directness that less articulate girls will envy. And though Jordan is unusually nasty, many girls' first experiences with love and sex are probably just this unromantic; thus it's gratifying to meet a young heroine who takes it with equanimity.

> *A review of "Whatever Words You Want to Hear," in* Kirkus Reviews, *Vol. XLII, No. 15, August 1, 1974, p. 811.*

Ms. Pfeffer is a natural storyteller with an acute ear. In Jordan she has drawn a realistic picture of a troubled young man's inability to give of himself, even when he has the understanding patience of the girl who loves him. And Paula learns that, when two people talk, their words sometimes hide what they are really trying to say. The novel should find an empathetic audience.

> *A review of "Whatever Words You Want to Hear," in* Publishers Weekly, *Vol. 206, No. 13, September 23, 1974, p. 155.*

Realistic novels that are poorly written need a sensational plot or controversial material to keep young readers awake. Pfeffer doesn't provide any—just plenty of "heavy talk," and a contemporary setting for an old-fashioned teenage romance. . . . An unmemorable book.

> *Joyce W. Smothers, in a review of "Whatever Words You Want to Hear," in* Children's Book Review Service, *Vol. 3, No. 2, October, 1974, p. 16.*

Paula regards her feelings for [Jordan] and her first sexual experiences with chilly detachment; conversations between Paula and Jordan are incredibly glib; and Paula's way of relating to people is to psych them out. A few teenagers may be taken in by Paula's cool, but discerning readers will find the story unrealistic.

> *Linda R. Silver, in a review of "Whatever Words You Want to Hear," in* School Library Journal, *an appendix to* Library Journal, *Vol. 21, No. 4, December, 1974, p. 47.*

MARLY THE KID (1975)

[The sequel to **The Beauty Queen**] is even better, with more variation to the story line, excellent characterization, and an almost faultless ear for dialogue. Marly, whose beautiful older sister had run off to escape, in part, their mother's vitriolic tongue, follows suit. Kit had gone west to join a theater group; Marly turns up on her father's doorstep and is welcomed by him and by her stepmother, Sally. (No stereotypical situation, this.) It is Sally, even more than Marly's supportive father, who helps Marly adjust to her new life and who comes to Marly's aid when she gets in trouble for being too outspoken at school. No dramatic ending, but a cheerful and realistic note of encouragement as plump, plain Marly gains insight and perspective about herself. (pp. 182-83)

> *Zena Sutherland, in a review of "Marly the Kid,"* in Bulletin of the Center for Children's Books, *Vol. 28, No. 11, July-August, 1975, pp. 182-83.*

[Except] for Pfeffer's tendency to talk down to her readers (there's a long classroom discussion of Gerard Manley Hopkins which reveals how much she prides herself on being able to COMMUNICATE), the dialogue is sharp and spontaneous and Marly's self-dissatisfaction is realistically drawn.

> *A review of "Marly the Kid,"* in Kirkus Reviews, *Vol. XLIII, No. 15, August 1, 1975, p. 857.*

One of [this book's] best features is its contrasting of "sensitive" and "insensitive" male and female figures. The opposition between caring men (Marly's father and Mr. Hughes) and offensive ones (Mr. Marshall) and between shrewish women (Marly's mother) and more rational ones (Sally) breaks down the monolithic image of male and female character traits, as does Marly's decision to live with her father. As Marly comes to recognize, her mother is not, however, all bad. A nurse, she is independent and assertive. As Sally reminds Marly, "You had to get your big mouth from somebody, and I guess you got it from Adele . . . and since you seem to be enjoying it, you should thank her for making you a fighter." Indeed, the focus of the book is the process through which Marly achieves a balanced personality, learning to assert herself effectively without being offensive by integrating the best qualities of two women—her mother and her step-mother.

The story also makes other valuable distinctions: between good education and bad, between true love and "the crush" and between glamour and integrity. One factor, however, remains unclear: Why does Marly choose to direct her new-found assertiveness towards an individual challenge (the glamorous cheerleader image) while refusing to join the student review board for which she seems so well prepared by her experience? In the end we suspect that Marly may still be motivated by envy of her sister's beauty. (p. 8)

> *Lynne Rosenthal, in a review of "Marly the Kid,"* in Interracial Books for Children Bulletin, *Vol. 6, No. 8, 1975, pp. 7-8.*

Pfeffer makes a convincing portrayal of some well-known adolescent traits with one small but important exception: she convinces the reader at one point that Marly doesn't just have a crush on her handsome English teacher—she's truly in love. Shortly thereafter we find Marly's forgotten the whole thing. But Marly herself is an intriguing character. She's fat but not obsessed with dieting, and she doesn't even realize she's a feisty person till someone tells her. A conscientiously low reading level without the often-attendant simplification of ideas makes this title a versatile one. (pp. 582-83)

> *A review of "Marly the Kid,"* in The Booklist, *Vol. 72, No. 8, December 15, 1975, pp. 582-83.*

KID POWER   (1977)

Janie Golden's mother is laid off from her job; the bikes that Janie and her sister want are now an impossibility unless each earns half of the cost herself. Janie starts Kid Power, no job too big or too small. In the process of developing Kid Power, Janie discovers the intricacies of tackling a job and doing it well, and of getting along with people. Although the discussions in the book tend to lapse into clichés and smack of cant, the story is interesting and should encourage young readers to use their own abilities in various endeavors.

> *Anne Devereaux Jordan, in a review of "Kid Power,"* in Children's Book Review Service, *Vol. 6, No. 2, October, 1977, p. 19.*

Fiscal cutbacks and family budget worries set the scene for this comic novel featuring a heroine who is something of a female Great Brain. . . . The characters here—parents with tempers and a sense of humor, friends and neighbors with idiosyncracies—are alive and individual, and this makes a refreshing change from the somber viewpoint of most contemporary problem novels.

> *Christine McDonnell, in a review of "Kid Power,"* in School Library Journal, *Vol. 24, No. 3, November, 1977, p. 62.*

Janie tells the story convincingly, her descriptions of assignments are varied and interesting, and the Kid Power incidents are balanced by material about family and friends. The characterization is adequate, the relationships are perceptively depicted, and the dialogue is natural and often amusing.

> *Zena Sutherland, in a review of "Kid Power,"* in Bulletin of the Center for Children's Books, *Vol. 31, No. 5, January, 1978, p. 85.*

Through *Kid Power* Janie learns so much about people, problems, money, and herself, she almost loses her best friend and her self-respect—but not quite. There's a sense of humor in the text and a lilting, full-flavored view of eleven-year-old Janie. A delightful and understanding vignette by Susan Beth Pfeffer for younger and older readers, too.

> *Barbara Ann Kyle, in a review of "Kid Power,"* in The Babbling Bookworm, *Vol. 6, No. 1, February, 1978, p. 4.*

STARRING PETER AND LEIGH: A NOVEL   (1979)

Transplanted from Los Angeles to a suburban Long Island environment as a willing retiree from a career as a child actress, 16-year-old Leigh Thorpe settles down to join her mother, new stepfather, and 17-year-old hemophiliac stepbrother Peter. With help from the invalided Peter, Leigh begins the all-American teenager's existence she's acted on the screen but never lived, and at the same time helps Peter over a difficult period in his life. But the special affinity she feels for her craft never quite disappears and predictably, when a summer stock role alongside her father opens up, she decides to give acting another try. A touch of romance and a likable, uncomplicated set of characters offset the obvious, celluloid story line, making this hold up well as a less demanding change of pace from heavy teenage realism.

> *A review of "Starring Peter and Leigh: A Novel,"* in Booklist, *Vol. 75, No. 19, June 1, 1979, p. 1486.*

Pfeffer makes Leigh a believable and sympathetic character, and the relationship between her and Peter forceful; other characters and relationships are depicted with skill and perception, particularly those between young people and adults. There is a reflection of many universal problems of adolescence in Leigh's groping for self-understanding and her indecision about a career, as well as in her feelings of obligation toward her father, who can only have a part in the new play if his daughter stars with him. Although Peter has an uncomfortable relationship with his mother, in every way the story implies a mature adjustment to stepparents; in fact, perhaps the major appeals of the story for teenage readers may be the warmth and respect in familial relationships and the easy, bantering tone of much of the dialogue. (p. 199)

> *Zena Sutherland, in a review of "Starring Peter and Leigh," in* Bulletin of the Center for Children's Books, *Vol. 32, No. 11, July-August, 1979, pp. 198-99.*

Can a successful teenage Hollywood TV actress hope to lead a normal life on Long Island with her mother, new stepfather, and stepbrother (who also happens to be a hemophiliac)? Even if the question were intriguing, the conflicts and their resolutions are predictably trite. Unfortunately, Pfeffer seldom rises above romantic comic book stereotypes, and her young heroine comes off more plastic than flesh and blood.

> *Violet H. Harada, in a review of "Starring Peter and Leigh," in* Children's Book Review Service, *Vol. 7, No. 14, August, 1979, p. 139.*

The dialogue and repartee are engaging in this lightweight, breezy junior novel. The writing is generally slick, fast paced, and likely to stimulate the daydreams of star-struck adolescent readers. The characters, by and large, have the same dimensionality as those in television soaps. This frothy romance is both enlivened and weakened by Peter's characterization, an unconvincing portrayal of a boy troubled by fears but with compensating qualities as well—tenacity, social savvy, and determination. Although compassion is generated for his problem, he is depicted as an attractive, romantic youth, his wheelchair notwithstanding. The hero's disorder is apparently serious enough to exclude him from school, but this presentation emphasizes his illness as inconvenient, rather than debilitating, and one that additionally gives him an aura of glamour. (p. 357)

> *Barbara H. Baskin and Karen H. Harris, "An Annotated Guide to Juvenile Fiction Portraying the Disabled, 1976-1981: 'Starring Peter and Leigh'," in their* More Notes from a Different Drummer: A Guide to Juvenile Fiction Portraying the Disabled, *R. R. Bowker Company, 1984, pp. 356-57.*

Although few readers will be able to identify with Leigh's specific plight—that of choosing between a regulated home life and a career as a successful actress—many will sympathize with her wish to be accepted by her peers, her search for stability, and her undefined love for her stepbrother. Although the story line at times seems shallow and the heroine's first-person narration is less than sparkling, themes are clearly developed and the hemophiliac Peter is an interesting character. His guilt and alienation resulting from his parents' divorce are not explored in great depth. But Leigh's philosophical, almost jaunty, attitude toward her parents' breakup certainly presents the case that divorce is something to which teenagers can adjust. The dialogue includes some profanity.

> *Sharon Spredemann Dreyer, "Annotations: 'Starring Peter and Leigh'," in her* The Bookfinder, When Kids Need Books: Annotations of Books Published 1979 through 1982, *American Guidance Service, 1985, p. 287.*

AWFUL EVELINA (1979)

This picture book attempts to deal with a child's reluctance to visit a cousin whom she does not like at all. It takes us through a series of dreamlike avoidances that Meredith creates in her imagination on her way to the hated Evelina's house. . . . The text tries to express warmth, anger, understanding, and a whole range of emotions but it is too simplistic.

> *Joan Huenemann Michie, in a review of "Awful Evelina," in* School Library Journal, *Vol. 26, No. 3, November, 1979, p. 69.*

The lessons are told with enough humor to be palatable, even entertaining; the writing style has an easy flow for the read-aloud audience; although so much time is spent in this brief story on Meredith's imagined . . . crises and the final episode seems almost abrupt, those sequences do provide variety and humor.

> *Zena Sutherland, in a review of "Awful Evelina," in* Bulletin of the Center for Children's Books, *Vol. 33, No. 4, December, 1979, p. 79.*

Many children will identify with the plight of a child forced to play with someone who is mean to her. They will be relieved along with Meredith that Cousin Evelina has matured enough to be a nicer person. . . . The humor in the unfolding of the plot and in Meredith's fantasies prevents the tale from becoming didactic.

> *Sharon Spredemann Dreyer, "Annotations: 'Awful Evelina'," in her* The Bookfinder, When Kids Need Books: Annotations of Books Published 1979 through 1982, *American Guidance Service, 1985, p. 286.*

JUST BETWEEN US (1980)

Cass, who tells the story, knows that she has irritated more than one person by repeating something they've told her, not a fact they've asked to be kept secret, but one that she ought to have had enough discretion to keep to herself. Prompted by her best friend's anger, Cass embarks on a behavior conditioning program: any day she keeps a secret (without being told it's a secret) for ten days, she gets a dollar. It works, and Cass uses her new knowledge to help bridge a gap between her two best friends, one of whom has been especially hostile toward the other. The development is believable but uneven in pace, especially toward the end of the story; characterization and writing style are competent, but this has less cohesion and impact than Pfeffer's books for older readers.

> *Zena Sutherland, in a review of "Just between Us," in* Bulletin of the Center for Children's Books, *Vol. 33, No. 9, May, 1980, p. 180.*

[Though the resolution] is effected a bit too swiftly, Pfeffer has most certainly constructed an intriguing plot line centering around a neglected but very real pre-teen dilemma.

> *C. Nordhielm Wooldridge, in a review of "Just between Us," in* School Library Journal, *Vol. 26, No. 10, August, 1980, p. 69.*

Pfeffer leaves her semi-sophisticated teenagers behind in this younger, slighter story of sixth-grader Cass' inability to keep a secret. . . . Pfeffer gets more mileage than might be expected from Cass' early failures and growing success. . . . A problem-solving story with a life of its own.

> *A review of "Just between Us," in* Kirkus Reviews, *Vol. XLVIII, No. 17, September 1, 1980, p. 1164.*

ABOUT DAVID (1980)

About David is a curious book and, curiously, it may be a very good book for teen-agers. It is a rare high school that isn't rocked by tragedy, by an untimely death or an awful accident, during the years it takes one to pass through it. Thus, for many, a period of shock and its attendant grief are prerequisites to graduation. *About David* deals with this rite of passage for seventeen-year-old Lynn.

Lynn's closest friend is David. Page one has Lynn coming upon the immediate aftermath, the rotating red lights and the crush of onlookers, of David's momentous act. David's momentous act is also a momentary one; he has killed the father and mother who adopted and raised him and, after a short pause, himself.

About David, then, is really about Lynn. It is her introspective account of what this act means, of how it affects her friends in the senior class and most notably herself. Most of Lynn's account carries the half-numb sensation of emerging from anesthesia. Groggily she, and we, along with her, thrash toward understanding and a tentative grip on normality. The book concludes with just that, Lynn's tentative grip on normality. It is a fitting, genuine conclusion.

A teen-ager would not be likely to want to read many books with *About David's* theme or impact, but this volume serves well. With luck it may add a measure of empathy, some slight understanding of grief and how it passes, a touch of humanity, to its teen readers.

> *John Lansingh Bennett, in a review of "About David," in* Best Sellers, *Vol. 40, No. 8, November, 1980, p. 303.*

[Lynn] comes to understand why David did what he did . . . and that's where the flaw of the book is: the focus on David, his motivation, Lynn's adjustment to both the loss and the murder-suicide, is so strong that such matters as a new boy at school, or a college entrance interview, seem interruptions rather than development; the unfolding of David's motivation has suspense and impact, and it overbalances the material about Lynn too much to merge with it even though some of the material has to do with her missing David.

> *Zena Sutherland, in a review of "About David," in* Bulletin of the Center for Children's Books, *Vol. 34, No. 3, November, 1980, p. 61.*

[*About David* is] melodrama all the way. . . . No matter how flamboyant the circumstances, this is a healthier picture of suicide than Fran Arrick's *Tunnel Vision,* in which the dead boy emerges as somewhat heroic. Here suicide is seen as a psychopathology that harms the lives of all those around the self-destroyer. Pfeffer's previous books have been well crafted, extremely readable, but a bit on the frothy side. The strength of *About David* may augur a new dimension to her talent.

> *Patty Campbell, in a review of "About David," in* Wilson Library Bulletin, *Vol. 55, No. 4, December, 1980, p. 292.*

[This] reader at least would have preferred to learn more "about David" and his family. One feels that the author has worked very conscientiously to develop her story without sensationalism, but in the process her characters have become so smoothed over that they are little more than mouthpieces for predictable attitudes. Though it was surely intended to do much more, *About David* finally achieves the same appeal as soap opera—it democratizes suffering, so that everyone's problems are made to seem equally important and, in the end, equally banal.

> *Joyce Milton, in a review of "About David," in* The New York Times Book Review, *February 1, 1981, p. 28.*

[*About David*] is a very different kind of story [from Fran Arrick's *Tunnel Vision*]—more conventional but many people feel better because it doesn't appear to vaguely condone suicide as an alternative. . . . [The thrust of *About David*] is how people tolerate dreadful things as long as the niceties are observed, which is very different from the point of view in *Tunnel Vision.* But I think it is a very compelling book as well. Neither of these, I think, are necessarily great works of art, but they are more than just sociological novels. There's a seriousness of purpose that I think kids recognize. . . .

I think they're very accessible books, told without literary artistry except in their construction. The construction is extraordinarily good in both, in my view. (p. 103)

> *George Nicholson, "Children's Book Publishing: An Interview with George Nicholson," in* The Lion and the Unicorn, *Vol. 5, 1981, pp. 89-107.*

WHAT DO YOU DO WHEN YOUR MOUTH WON'T OPEN? (1981)

Pfeffer has given us another delightful story. This one concerns twelve-year-old Reesa, whose phobia about speaking in public finally ends when she has to represent her school in an essay contest. Young teens will surely enjoy this lively, entertaining story; it's solid in content and has enough fun and humor to hold the attention. Probably lots of kids will identify with Reesa's problems and cheer her strength and perseverance.

> *Glenda Broughton, in a review of "What Do You Do When Your Mouth Won't Open?" in* Children's Book Review Service, *Vol. 9, No. 8, March, 1981, p. 69.*

Reesa tells the story believably, and her efforts to get over her phobia (with the help of a sympathetic psychologist) in two weeks are equally convincing. . . . The story ends with Reesa's successful reading (no prize) after a deft build-up of suspense. Good pace, good style, and a perceptive handling of characters and relationships are the strong points of a story that may touch many readers who have shared Reesa's fears in varying degrees.

> *Zena Sutherland, in a review of "What Do You Do When Your Mouth Won't Open?" in* Bulletin of the Center for Children's Books, *Vol. 34, No. 8, April, 1981, p. 159.*

Aside from some minor incidents involving a jealous older sister, the plot is a bit lean and very predictable. Still it is nicely told, and Pfeffer again explores a problem not often confronted in fiction for young people.

> *C. Nordhielm Wooldridge, in a review of "What Do You Do When Your Mouth Won't Open?" in School Library Journal, Vol. 27, No. 9, May, 1981, p. 68.*

The book is contrived for a one-track situation, but the characters are natural and the protagonist's personal triumph over a phobia is all the more real for not resulting in the usual first-prize ending.

> *Betsy Hearne, in a review of "What Do You Do When Your Mouth Won't Open?" in Booklist, Vol. 77, Nos. 22 & 23, July 15 & August, 1981, p. 1449.*

Here is a clever, entertaining story with some practical suggestions for overcoming a fear of speaking before an audience. . . .

It is refreshing to find adult women portrayed in a variety of career roles—as a psychologist, a copywriter for an advertising agency and a school principal. (It's also nice to see another school principal named Mr. Sanchez.) Although the characterizations are somewhat shallow, the psychological techniques are graphically and accurately described in terms that should be easily understandable and helpful to most young readers.

In a gooey, sentimental ending, Reesa ad libs a speech extolling the virtues of the U.S., Franklin D. Roosevelt and the ability to change. But overall this book offers sound insights into a problem that is familiar to everyone.

> *Lauri Johnson, in a review of "What Do You Do When Your Mouth Won't Open?" in Interracial Books for Children Bulletin, Vol. 13, Nos. 4 & 5, 1982, p. 28.*

[This is a] lively first-person narrative. Although it seems odd that Reesa has never gotten help from parents or teachers and must seek it out herself, her encounters with the psychologist are convincing and the book's other relationships and situations ring true. (p. 289)

> *Sharon Spredemann Dreyer, "Annotations: 'What Do You Do When Your Mouth Won't Open?'" in her The Bookfinder, When Kids Need Books: Annotations of Books Published 1979 through 1982, American Guidance Service, 1985, pp. 288-89.*

A MATTER OF PRINCIPLE: A NOVEL (1982)

Provoked by the restrictive policies of their high school, a group of bright juniors publish an underground newspaper. The conservative school principal—enraged by the outspoken articles and a vulgar, mean-spirited cartoon—threatens the students with suspension. Honor student Becca Holtz, believing their rights have been violated, persuades her co-workers to join her in a legal battle—a fight for freedom of the press. Becca's conflict over a matter of principle gives her several surprises about her own motives and also about the strengths in the people she dislikes and the weaknesses in the people she loves. The characters are solid, and each deals with trouble in a credible manner. Pfeffer's writing is well paced, and her observation of young people's fears and foibles is astute.

> *Wendy Dellett, in a review of "A Matter of Principle," in School Library Journal, Vol. 28, No. 9, May, 1982, p. 74.*

Sometimes a simple story can be told in very ordinary words, yet be important because of the meaning it contains. . . . Susan Beth Pfeffer tells an excellent parable. If readers compare this work with her previous offerings (***Just Between Us, Starring Peter and Leigh, About David***), they will find all her books tell simple, almost predictable stories that stress character development. (p. 121)

Pfeffer deals with interesting questions in this work. May something be legal yet wrong to do? How do these teenagers hold up under the stresses created by this situation? How about the parents involved? the friends of these students? the student body? the principal? the teacher? How many of these students learned anything from all this?

Pfeffer handles very delicately an incident in which Ken, in mental exasperation, tries to persuade his equally beleaguered girl friend Becca to make love to him. She gently refuses only because of fear of pregnancy. I selected five high school students to read this section, and none of them drew any morally objectionable conclusions from it. Neither did I.

This book is a positive—and excellent—contribution to high school literature, and particularly attractive for slower readers. (pp. 121-22)

> *Michael M. Dudek, in a review of "A Matter of Principle," in Best Sellers, Vol. 42, No. 3, June, 1982, pp. 121-22.*

With lively dialogue and careful pacing, the author shows the realistic, human side of a battle of ideals as well as individual priorities to which each student ultimately feels responsible. As in ***About David*** . . . , she has explored a highly charged situation in a level-headed and intelligent manner without sacrificing dramatic tension or a sense of story.

> *Karen M. Klockner, in a review of "A Matter of Principle: A Novel," in The Horn Book Magazine, Vol. LVIII, No. 4, August, 1982, p. 416.*

With an admitted bias toward the issues raised in the book, I still think Pfeffer does her usually well-crafted job, without just making all the kids and adults one-dimensional mouthpieces for various points of view like so many of Hentoff's novels do. There are wonderful booktalk possibilities—the confrontation with the principal, the final courtroom scene when Becca takes the stand, various confrontations with her family and friends who do and do not cave in to personal or parental pressure. Also, within the first-person formula Pfeffer manages to point out that being well-off helps a lot when you take a stand, and that Becca's stand is not the only one is viable one. I think this is a provocative, carefully written book, which examines serious Constitutional issues in a way which makes them meaningful to those most concerned, the kids themselves.

> *Mary K. Chelton, in a review of "Matter of Principle," in Voice of Youth Advocates, Vol. 5, No. 3, August, 1982, p. 35.*

Pfeffer shows with precision and feeling just what effect fighting a battle for a cause may have on individuals, their friends and families. A price is paid, literally and figuratively and some are in better positions than others to pay that price. So, the ideas and the characters involved in this story are complex and will encourage YA readers to think about what they might be willing to fight for and how difficult that fight may be. Any teachers of political science courses might like to consider this as supplementary reading; it is a book that will interest most YA readers.

> *A review of "A Matter of Principle," in* Kliatt Young Adult Paperback Book Guide, *Vol. XVII, No. 6, September, 1983, p. 18.*

This book deals with the First Amendment rights of high school students to exercise freedom of the press in publishing an underground newspaper. Although the book makes some good points, it has serious drawbacks. (p. 35)

The author's style at times is trite, the characters lack depth, and dialogue is sometimes stilted. Problems with teenage alcoholism and decisions about sex are treated quite cursorily, and there is no analysis of how your socio-economic situation determines your ability to take risks and fight for your rights. What we see is the story of a group of rich kids who can afford to stand up for a matter of principle—after they have printed an inappropriately sexist and insulting cartoon about their teacher. (pp. 35-6)

> *Jan M. Goodman, in a review of "A Matter of Principle," in* Interracial Books for Children Bulletin, *Vol. 14, Nos. 7 & 8, 1983, pp. 35-6.*

STARTING WITH MELODIE (1982)

This story of the fallout from parental divorce is told from the viewpoint of the teenage child's best friend—which allows us to sympathize with the victim but spares us the worst of her misery. As the parents are a famous actress and a big director, both of them theatrical and on-stage even in their private fights, it also allows us to see the tempest as something of a show. Friend Elaine, who tells the story, has . . . a stable family she comes to appreciate for their support of Melodie and Melodie's little sister Lissa. . . . Despite the potential for comedy, this never becomes really funny or really moving; but at least it moves along, with enough friends and family members bouncing off each other to keep it in motion.

> *A review of "Starting with Melodie," in* Kirkus Reviews, *Vol. L, No. 20, October 15, 1982, p. 1159.*

Nothing earthshaking here, it's all familiar territory, but this story skips along easily, making it a quick, enjoyable read. Characterizations are overblown but amusing. Elaine and Melodie, both 15, seem more like 12, which will make the book more popular with middle-graders than older readers.

> *Ilene Cooper, in a review of "Starting with Melodie," in* Booklist, *Vol. 79, No. 7, December 1, 1982, p. 502.*

While Pfeffer's newest title isn't as original or serious as some of her previous books, and perhaps the resolution of problems is a trifle pat, the light, wholesome, easily-read story will be enjoyed by young teens. Some traces of humor run throughout the book. The adolescent characters seem much younger than their 15 years. All parents are portrayed as well-meaning people trying to do their best for their children.

> *Susan Rosenkoetter, in a review of "Starting with Melodie," in* School Library Journal, *Vol. 29, No. 7, March, 1983, p. 196.*

The book has believable characters and the family problem is handled with insight; the writing style is smooth, the plot rather tepid save for one episode in which Melodie's eight-year-old

sister runs away, creating a modicum of suspense until she's found asleep in Elaine's mother's car.

> *Zena Sutherland, in a review of "Starting with Melodie," in* Bulletin of the Center for Children's Books, *Vol. 36, No. 11, July-August, 1983, p. 217.*

This first-person story brings likeable characters into strong relationships and builds considerable sympathy for children who are victims of divorce. Although Elaine and Melodie are sometimes characterized as younger than they are supposed to be, the story resolves itself realistically.

> *Sharon Spredemann Dreyer, "Annotations: 'Starting with Melodie'," in her* The Bookfinder, When Kids Need Books: Annotations of Books Published 1979 through 1982, *American Guidance Service, 1985, p. 288.*

COURAGE, DANA (1983)

Twelve-year-old Dana is as surprised as anyone else when she risks her life to save a small child who's in the path of a car; Dana, who tells the story, is timid, fearful about many things. Delighted by her achievement, she becomes a bore and her best friend tells her so. To prove her courage, she goes to a graveyard at night; on the way home she sees a classmate spray-painting graffiti on the school wall and signing the initials of the class bully who's been persecuting him. The dilemma for Dana, who dislikes the bully, is whether to report what she knows. Again, Dana shows courage, and this time she's supported by her friend and her older sister Jean. And Jean's very large boy friend. The book explores a situation and experience many children share, and does so with insight and humor; the writing style is lively, with excellent dialogue, and the depth and warmth of family relationships buttress a good story of peer relations and attitudes. (pp. 156-57)

> *Zena Sutherland, in a review of "Courage, Dana," in* Bulletin of the Center for Children's Books, *Vol. 36, No. 8, April, 1983, pp. 156-57.*

Pfeffer's Dana is a sprightly heroine, and there are enough curves and flip-flops in the story to keep readers' interest. Its messages about honesty and bravery could be tucked a bit more discreetly into the story, but overall this is good entertainment with some meat to it.

> *Ilene Cooper, in a review of "Courage, Dana," in* Booklist, *Vol. 79, No. 16, April 15, 1983, p. 1097.*

The author not only provides excitement for her readers, but tries to get them to take a look at the meaning of courage. Ms. Pfeffer writes with charm, and this book will certainly appeal to youngsters. (p. 104)

> *Christine Boutrass, in a review of "Courage Dana," in* Children's Book Review Service, *Vol. II, No. 10, May, 1983, pp. 103-04.*

Pfeffer is expert at presenting child-size problems without sermonizing. Her characters, while not complex, are attractive: Dana and Sharon are as giggly as most seventh graders, even when facing serious problems. A cut above most light fiction, this should be as popular as *What Do You Do When Your Mouth Won't Open* . . . [and *Just Between Us*].

*Caroline S. Parr, in a review of "Courage, Dana,"
in* School Library Journal, *Vol. 29, No. 9, May,
1983, p. 76.*

TRUTH OR DARE (1984)

Cathy, just starting junior high and missing her two best friends
who have transferred, begins a campaign to get Jessica to like
her, since Jessica is pretty, intelligent, and obviously destined
to be a leader in junior high. Jessica is interested in Cathy's
brother Paul, who's devoted to ballet, but she barely responds
to Cathy's overtures. What Cathy learns, as she ignores other
friends in order to cultivate snobbish Jessica, is that she's made
a big mistake. This is not an unusual theme, but it's thoughtfully treated; the combination of a sound writing style, sturdy
characterization, and a theme balanced by other facets (family
relationships, for example) gives the story strength and substance.

*Zena Sutherland, in a review of "Truth or Dare,"
in* Bulletin of the Center for Children's Books, *Vol.
37, No. 9, May, 1984, p. 172.*

Many a reader will identify with one or more of the kinds of
friendship etched in this easily digested first-person novel that
packs a powerful punch with its insights about what friends
should be to each other. . . . Pfeffer has a sure, sensitive eye
for the dynamics of young friendships, and although the novel
is at times overcrowded, it should be a popular selection, especially with pre-junior-high girls. (pp. 1400-01)

*Karen Stang Hanley, in a review of "Truth or Dare,"
in* Booklist, *Vol. 80, No. 19, June 1, 1984, pp.
1400-01.*

In a thoughtful novel the issue of friendship, especially serious
to young people, is explored in several ways. . . . The dialogue
rings true, and the story is convincing; many a young person
will recognize the pains and anguishes of early adolescence.

*Ann A. Flowers, in a review of "Truth or Dare,"
in* The Horn Book Magazine, *Vol. LX, No. 4, August,
1984, p. 469.*

Readers, who will quickly grow to dislike Cathy's patently
shallow intentions, will rapidly sense the not-so-subtle lesson
being developed here (the cost of Cathy's obsession mounts in
terms of friends and self-esteem lost). Although the simplist-
ically-presented theme and its obvious resolution could have
hit readers like a ton of bricks, Pfeffer maintains an element
of suspense as readers wait for Jessica's topple from the ped-
estal and Cathy's come-uppance. . . . The characters, as well
as their families and school lives, are believable, well developed and timely without being trendy. A lesson well learned
in a credible story and setting.

*Catherine vanSonnenerg, in a review of "Truth or
Dare,"" in* School Library Journal, *Vol. 31, No. 2,
October, 1984, p. 160.*

FANTASY SUMMER (1984)

Four young women have been selected, in an annual competition, to spend the summer working and learning at the New
York offices of *Image,* a magazine for adolescents. Robin,
who is the photography intern, is the protagonist, and the personalities of the other girls as well as the events for the summer

(including romantic interests) are seen primarily from her viewpoint. The setting should appeal to readers; the problems and
interests are universal if not world-shaking. This hasn't the
depth and polish of most Pfeffer books, but it is believable,
adequate in characterization if trivialized in plot, and capably
written. (pp. 33-4)

*Zena Sutherland, in a review of "Fantasy Summer,"
in* Bulletin of the Center for Children's Books, *Vol.
38, No. 2, October, 1984, pp. 33-4.*

The most interesting of the sub-plots is Robin's coming to
terms with her grief over her older and "perfect" sister Caro's
death in a car accident, although this strand could have been
worked more skillfully into the plot.

Teen girls will probably enjoy submerging themselves in the
fantasy world of *Fantasy Summer* and may overlook some of
the glaring weaknesses. On the negative side, though, it seemed
just too coincidental that two cousins, Robin and Annie, would
be selected from a field of 7,000 applicants. Torey's abject
poverty and endless allusions to it grew tiresome, as well as
unbelievable. Ashley's altering of the cover picture seemed too
extreme even for her. Not a bad book and probably adequate
for leisure reading, but it was disappointing that Pfeffer didn't
make the effort to insure that the story was smooth and well-
integrated, and that the characters were a bit more believable.

*Brooke Selby Dillon, in a review of "Fantasy Sum-
mer," in* Voice of Youth Advocates, *Vol. 7, No. 4,
October, 1984, p. 198.*

[The] plot churns ahead leaving parties, interviews, television
appearances and such in its wake, but readers won't take any
of it or any of the characters really seriously. Perhaps it's just
that too much happens too quickly, perhaps it's that Pfeffer
tells us what her characters are feeling instead of showing us.
Still, pre-teenage girls will probably enjoy the featherweight
romance and glamour, and there's nothing to give offense to
the morals squad. This is the first of a projected series which
won't win any literary prizes and undoubtedly wasn't intended
to.

*Miriam Lang Budin, in a review of "Fantasy Sum-
mer," in* School Library Journal, *Vol. 31, No. 3,
November, 1984, p. 136.*

PAPER DOLLS (1984)

Bored with school (algebra) and with her ordinary life (loving
mother and stepfather in suburban Long Island), 16-year-old
Laurie Caswell has a fantasy come true: by an extraordinary
stroke of luck she gets a chance to try out as a model, and
enters the world of the teen model she admires and envies:
Taryn Blake. . . . Based on a made-for-TV movie (the pilot for
a new television series), Pfeffer's novel explores an unhappy
and somewhat exploitative side of high-fashion modeling for
teenagers. It is seen, through Laurie's and Taryn's eyes, as a
world in which innocence as well as sexual experience are
simply commodities. The plot moves briskly, and if the characters other than Laurie and Taryn are narrowly drawn, younger
teenage readers will be too caught up in the story to mind.

Kathie Meizner, in a review of "Paper Dolls," in
School Library Journal, *Vol. 31, No. 3, November,
1984, p. 136.*

[Laurie Caswell] wants glamour, fame and wealth (who doesn't?). . . . A bit predictable; not up to Pfeffer's usual; *The Beauty Queen* has more depth, but young YA females will enjoy. Certainly a step up from the soapy romances. . . .

> *Carole A. Barham, in a review of "Paper Dolls," in* Voice of Youth Advocates, *Vol. 7, No. 6, February, 1985, p. 330.*

KID POWER STRIKES BACK (1984)

The problems of the small businessperson are faced by Janie Golden as she tries to match up her friends and employment in a service called Kid Power. In this second book about "Kid Power", Janie tackles snow shoveling, assisting older citizens, and the threat of another snow removal team that tries to wrestle her customers. The story moves briskly and the characters are adequately developed; not great literature, but pleasant reading.

> *Barbara Baker, in a review of "Kid Power Strikes Back," in* Children's Book Review Service, *Vol. 13, No. 6, Winter Supplement, 1985, p. 64.*

Readers unfamiliar with Pfeffer's earlier book may have trouble sorting out the various characters, but the story is bright and fast-paced and the dialogue is witty. The main characters are nicely drawn, except for Johnny Richards, who sounds as though he came from a 1940s gangster movie. The relationship between Janie, her parents and older sister Carol is almost idealized, yet it still rings true. And if the story wraps up a shade too neatly with an unconvincing coincidence or two—well, it's still a lot of fun.

> *Kathleen Brachmann, in a review of "Kid Power Strikes Back," in* School Library Journal, *Vol. 31, No. 5, January, 1985, p. 78.*

The plot is busy; mixed in with the Kid Power story lines are the problems of Janie's family as individuals and as a group. Most of these complications add to the story's richness, however, striking a good balance between Janie's "career" and her home life. This not only gives kids a spunky heroine with which to identify, but also provides them with money-raising ideas of their own.

> *Ilene Cooper, in a review of "Kid Power Strikes Back," in* Booklist, *Vol. 81, No. 10, January 15, 1985, p. 722.*

PRIME TIME (1985)

Six teenagers in Hollywood audition for roles in *Prime Time,* a new weekly TV series. The story is centered on Miranda, a student from Massachusetts with no acting experience, and T. J., a former child star trying to make a comeback. The success of each is dependent upon the others, since the director is looking for a new group of stars who will work as an ensemble. All six have problems with their parents, tension in dealing with each other and doubts about their ability to become stars. The story moves along at a fast pace. This first book in the ["Make Me a Star"] series will appeal to teens looking for lightweight reading. They may find that reading about television is better than watching it.

> *Constance Allen, in a review of "Prime Time," in* School Library Journal, *Vol. 32, No. 2, October, 1985, p. 186.*

TAKE TWO AND . . . ROLLING! (1985)

Pfeffer continues the saga, begun in *Prime Time* . . . , of six teenagers featured in a weekly television soap. Central to this volume is Molly—tough, little and lonely—a child star who has spent most of her life on the road. She has landed a plum part and is on her way to becoming a star. But for Molly stardom is a means to other goals in her life—namely, a normal home with two parents in it. The parents in this book are a sorry lot, but no one tops Molly's mother, who agrees to live with her daughter only if Molly will get her a job on the series—at the price of giving up her social life. Molly swallows her pride and begs a job for her mother—at the price of giving up her social life. Molly concludes that since even family love has its price, self-interest will be her future guide. Pretty cynical for a 14 year old. One of the better examples of recent fiction reflecting show-biz hype.

> *Betty Ann Porter, in a review of "Take Two and . . . Rolling!" in* School Library Journal, *Vol. 32, No. 3, November, 1985, p. 100.*

Alice (Rose Twitchell) Provensen

1918-

Martin (Elias) Provensen

1916-

American author/illustrators of picture books, editors, and illustrators.

Creators of diverse, rich illustrations for almost forty years, the Provensens are highly regarded for their artistic integrity and proficiency as well as their succinct, informative texts. Their picture books on nature, science, and historic figures generally feature clear, stylized paintings and reveal an astute observation and attention to compositional elements. Noted for their charm and realism, the Provensens' engaging accounts of life at their country home—such as *Our Animal Friends at Maple Hill Farm*, *The Year at Maple Hill Farm*, and *An Owl and Three Pussycats*—portray distinctly personalized animals with unsentimental affection. *The Glorious Flight*, which wryly relates pilot Louis Blériot's successful crossing of the English Channel in 1909 despite numerous disasters, led the Provensens to continue their fascination with flying machines, European history, and human determination in the lavish pop-up book *Leonardo da Vinci*.

Critics hail the Provensens' works for the originality and excellence of their overall design. Although a few observers point out examples of sexual and ethnic stereotyping in their illustrations, they admire the authors' ability to instruct without overt didacticism. Reviewers appreciate the warmth and humor of the Provensens' entertaining style, and agree that the husband and wife team share a perceptive awareness of what appeals to children.

The Provensens have won many awards for their art. *A Visit to William Blake's Inn* was a Caldecott Honor Book and recipient of the *Boston Globe-Horn Book* Award for Illustration in 1982; *The Glorious Flight* received the Caldecott Medal in 1984.

(See also *Something about the Author*, Vol. 9; *Contemporary Authors New Revision Series*, Vol. 5; and *Contemporary Authors*, Vols. 53-56.)

AUTHORS' COMMENTARY

We have been working together for so long that it has ceased to be a question of *who* does *what*. In any given finished illustration one of us may have done the first sketch, the other may have painted what we hoped was to have been a finished picture. It almost always has to be done over several times; we pass it back and forth between us until we are both satisfied. It is a happy collaboration. If one sometimes reaches a degree of frustration, there is a certain joy in giving up and saying, "Here, *you* do this one." Since we are not competing with each other but rather are working toward the same goal, we are delighted if one of us can paint the better picture....

In the case of the books we have written as well as illustrated, the final text is often written after the drawings are completely visualized. There are advantages to writing one's own text. It saves much redundancy. There is no need for us to say, "A boy in a red hat was walking down a country road." We can easily draw the scene and allow the text to function as a counterpoint to it.

> *Alice Provensen and Martin Provensen, "Alice and Martin Provensen," a promotional piece by the Viking Press, 1983.*

[*The following excerpt is from an interview with Martin Provensen conducted by Nancy Willard, author of the Newbery-winning* A Visit to William Blake's Inn *(1981).*]

[Nancy Willard]: Martin, what are some of the first books you remember?

[Martin Provensen]: The first books I remember were those my grandmother had on her farm in Iowa. She had the Doré Bible and *The Pilgrim's Progress* and *Don Quixote*. So I was raised on some extraordinarily remarkable books. As for books written for children, there was *Alice in Wonderland* of course. And then a series of books passed through my hands, most of the illustrators of which I've forgotten. But I do remember a book called *The Poppy Seed Cakes* [by Margery Clark].

[NW]: I loved that book, too.

[MP]: When I was older, a group of books that meant a lot to me—and I still admire them—were the animal stories illustrated by Charles Livingston Bull. He drew animals very realistically, brilliantly, with a great deal of knowledge and skill.... When I was slightly older, I discovered Rackham and Dulac. And there was Kay Nielsen, who illustrated Danish fairy tales, and whom I got to know at Disney Studios many years later.... All these books were very important to me.

[NW]: When did you go to work at Disney Studios?

[MP]: After I'd gone to Berkeley and UCLA, I went to Disney's for one summer—this was in 1936—and I took a job for seventeen dollars a week. Not so bad in those days. I didn't like it very much and they didn't like me either. I was fired. I then went over to a place called "Harmon-Ising" for six or seven months. They folded after I arrived. But I made several very good friends there, and when they went to the Disney Studio, they took me with them as excess baggage. I was lucky; when I'd first worked there, I was in the animation department, which I never would have liked.... Animation is extraordinarily difficult and tedious—wonderful really, but it just didn't suit me. So I went into the story department, which I did like.

[NW]: I believe that kind of work has trained a good many illustrators.

[MP]: It was ideal training for book illustrating. Year after year, we would sit together in a sort of assembly line to do story boards, which were really walls of drawings. . . . It was great training because we'd be given a sequence, the barest outline, just a thread of narrative, and then it was up to us to improvise on this theme. . . .

[NW]: I can see, especially in the books about Maple Hill Farm, that some of the pages are organized like a sequence on film. A series of frames.

[MP]: When Alice was working in the film business, she started out as an animator. So she had the animation experience I didn't have, which we certainly use in our books: that concept of sequence and time, which is the essence of filmmaking. (p. 174)

[NW]: In *A Horse and A Hound, A Goat and A Gander,* you have one page which shows John the dog running to the right of the page at the top, then to the left just below it, and finally, at the bottom he finds the little girl hiding in the grass. Three images of the same subject in a single illustration. . . .

[MP]: There's no way to beat that way of telling a story, short of going into film. As long as you're committed to static drawings on a page, or a double spread, you simply can't improve that concept. (p. 175)

[NW]: So many of your books deal with time, with the seasons, and you find so many different ways of showing time other than the obvious one—just turning the page.

[MP]: The fact that both Alice and I worked in film for years may be more important to us than we realize. I should also add that we both love the great Oriental scrolls. As you wind the scroll, you watch episode after episode. Such an enchanting change from turning the pages of a book.

[NW]: So the story really is continuous. The way life is.

[MP]: Yes, we've always longed at least to hint at that in a book. We try to capture as much of that as possible. We've not yet done it to our own satisfaction. We're still trying to find a way. . . .

[NW]: [You] use the line for continuity.

[MP]: Yes, we do. Pull is terribly important in a book. If you don't capture the reader and make him want to turn the page and see what comes next, you've lost him before you've begun. . . .

[NW]: How can you make a book look authentic and not pedantic? I know a lot of research [goes into some of your books], but they never look labored over.

[MP]: I suppose when a book works well, the material isn't something one has rushed to the library and done a lot of research about. In our case, when a book works well, it's because we're using material that we've loved, or been attracted to, for a great many years. So we start out with some concept that is usually quite strong, and what we really have to do is check nuance and detail. It isn't as if one starts from scratch. We make a rough outline of the book. (pp. 175-76)

[NW]: How do you and Alice work together on a book?

[MP]: Well, I like to remind everyone who asks us this question that books, throughout their history, were often illustrated by a group of people. (p. 176)

[NW]: So your books are a collaboration in which you can't tell what you did and what Alice did?

[MP]: We don't worry about it. It's a matter of having confidence in your mutual understanding of what the goal is and how you want the book to look. I don't know how common this arrangement is now, but it's not something anyone invented today. The tradition has always been there.

[NW]: What goes into the design of a book? (p. 178)

[MP]: [You] read the text to get a sense of what it is, and then you think about the shape of the book—whether it should be vertical or horizontal—you think of the weight of the type, and the amount of type you should have on each page to balance the illustrations. Naturally, the younger the reader, the larger the print. (pp. 178-79)

[NW]: When do you hand-letter a text rather than have it set in type?

[MP]: We use hand-lettering for capitals or titles when we want a stepping stone between the typography and the illustrations. . . . On jacket covers we often use hand-lettering. Alice has a great feeling for this sort of work. So the physical character of books is very important to us. You have to start with the fact that the book is a *thing*. And yet it isn't a thing, because if you look at a book at midnight with no lights on, you turn this object over in your hands and what is it? It is as mysterious as a bat, it is a peculiar object that you can't really describe at all.

[NW]: Comparing books to bats—that delights me! In your books you are never very far from animals. Did you grow up with a lot of animals?

[MP]: No, not really, but both Alice and I love animals. Most children adore animals, and some adults never outgrow this passion. I think we fit into that category, as you can see by the way we live.

[NW]: When did you move to Maple Hill Farm?

[MP]: Thirty years ago. (p. 179)

[NW]: Are all the animals in your books animals you've lived with here?

[MP]: Yes. Almost all. Over thirty years, we've had a lot of animals because they live so short a span. We've never had cows; we brought in cows from the neighbors. That's poetic license. But we have had most of the others.

[NW]: I've always loved the names of the animals in your books. Evil Murdoch, Potato, Eggnog, Willow.

[MP]: Karen, our daughter, named a lot of the animals. She didn't intend them to be cute. She chose those names because that's the way the animals struck her. And we recognized the names as right, so we kept them. She still names most of our animals.

[NW]: Have you any favorite animals? Animals that you especially like to draw? I notice that you put a great many cats into your books.

From An Owl and Three Pussycats, *written and illustrated by Alice and Martin Provensen. Atheneum, 1981. Copyright © 1981 by Alice and Martin Provensen. All rights reserved. Reprinted with the permission of Atheneum Publishers. In Canada by Jonathan Cape Ltd, on behalf of the authors.*

[MP]: Well, I suppose we do have favorites, but all animals are fascinating to us. We'd like to have all sorts of animals if we could. You know, we just did a book about an owl that we had for a year. The more you relate to animals and the more you're around them, the more you develop a love for them. Animals are—for me, and I think for Alice too—guides to the unknown. And what guides they are! Wasn't it Einstein who said that the mysterious is the most wonderful thing a human being can know?

I profoundly believe this. Einstein goes on to say that the mysterious is the basis of all art and all science and certainly all religion. I believe everything that makes life truly enchanting grows out of the quality of mystery. And I feel that animals are not simply cute and adorable, but much more than that. For example, we have a cat who is maddening because she brings us corpses of animals. She kills and deposits the creatures here in the kitchen. I just spent the morning scraping guts off the floor in here, and I didn't particularly enjoy it. But this is an aspect of the animal that you can't deny or change. The cat doesn't understand that we don't enjoy her offerings.

[NW]: Was it you who told me once that cats bring their masters these offerings because they are trying to teach us how to hunt?

[MP]: What else? Certainly these offerings are gifts too. Dogs and cats form strong bonds with people. And lots of animals can be imprinted, as you know, so that they regard people as their parents. Ducks, for example. But certain dogs and cats form extraordinary attachments to people.

[NW]: What especially interests me in your drawings of cats is how often they are shown looking out of the drawing at the reader. I could only find one cat, in your Mother Goose book, that was seen in profile. The cats in your illustrations have such presence.

[MP]: Well, they are fascinating and alluring beings.

[NW]: You devote a couple of pages in *The Year At Maple Hill Farm* to the problems of getting animals to take medicine. And in *A Horse and A Hound, A Goat and A Gander,* isn't there a picture of Evil Murdoch at the veterinarian's?

[MP]: We went through it all. You can't make that stuff up. (pp. 180-81)

[NW]: It's like helping a member of the family.

[MP]: I would hate to think that we are overly sentimental in our relationships with animals. We do recognize that animals are animals, and we find their presence rewarding. We also recognize that some people don't. . . . But I do think animals have a great deal to teach people. (p. 182)

> Nancy Willard, "The Birds and the Beasts Were There: An Interview with Martin Provensen," in The Lion and the Unicorn, *Vol. 7, 1983 & Vol. 8, 1984, pp. 171-83.*

THE ANIMAL FAIR (1952)

This is pure enchantment. Stories and poems, plays and puzzles, far too varied and interesting to describe briefly. It will entertain and instruct you 'All about birds' or 'Camouflage'. You can even learn 'How to recognize a wolf in the forest'. (Little Red Riding Hood please note.) Eights to tens will delight in Young Noah, Maud the Talking Horse, and the Reformed Fox to mention but a few. Not only are the stories so good, but the illustrations are gorgeous in the true sense. It is worth buying for these alone. A real winner at the price.

> *H. Millington, in a review of "The Animal Fair,"*
> *in* The School Librarian and School Library Review,
> *Vol. 11, No. 4, March, 1963, p. 431.*

KAREN'S CURIOSITY; KAREN'S OPPOSITES (1963)

[In *Karen's Opposites*] Alice and Martin Provensen interpret pictorially and in simple rhyme such elementary pairs of contrasting words as in and out, whisper and shout, up and down, lost and found. "A puddle is SHALLOW. / A well is DEEP. / My dolls are AWAKE. / Sh-h-h, mine are ASLEEP." Captivatingly cheerful pen and color-wash drawings accompany the text, which, though modest, is emphatic and direct, resulting in a very charming simplicity. Its companion volume, *Karen's Curiosity* . . . , which imitates a child's inquisitiveness about the world and nature, is less successful. "What does that do?" a little girl asks about a cow. The answer is "Gives milk and says moo-o-o." To "Why is a tree?" the response is "for birds to be." Other questions are posed ("Is rain made of water? Is a mother a daughter?") without answers. It's a little too forcedly cute to pass muster. (p. 5)

> *George A. Woods, "A Growly Bear, Lovely Lioness—And Fun," in* The New York Times Book Review, *May 12, 1963, pp. 4-5.*

Engaging pictures [in *Karen's Curiosity*] accompany a whimsical rhyming text that is sometimes charming and occasionally affords opportunities for confusion. "What are those? A row

of toes. How many is four? How much is more? Is rain made of water? Is a mother a daughter?" Occasionally the illustrations add to the possibilities for confusion; for example, the page that asks "How many is four?" shows a child holding up fingers (not four, in either hand) and shows three rabbits. Sometimes the questions are answered, sometimes not. There is a humor and an appeal in the childlike questioning that is more likely to be appreciated by adults than by the small child to whom this is very ordinary conversation.

. . . . .

[*Karen's Opposites* is a] companion volume to *Karen's Curiosity;* here two small girls engage in diverse activities, at times noting opposites in what both are doing (both eating a hot dog, then eating cold ice cream) and at times each doing the opposite from the other (one whispers, one shouts). The pictures have a charming simplicity; the text is a bit more consistent than in the title reviewed above, although the illustrations here do not always clarify the text. In neither book is the "Karen" of the title identified.

> *Zena Sutherland, in a review of "Karen's Curiosity"*
> *and "Karen's Opposites," in* Bulletin of the Center
> for Children's Books, *Vol. XVI, No. 11, July-August,*
> *1963, p. 180.*

Two delightfully rhymed and illustrated books for very young children: not stories, but collections of thoughts and fancies which will turn into many and endless stories for an imaginative child. Excellent for the new reader, or for the still younger read-to.

> *Timothy Rogers, in a review of "Karen's Curiosity"*
> *and "Karen's Opposites," in* The School Librarian
> and School Library Review, *Vol. 13, No. 1, March,*
> *1965, p. 127.*

WHAT IS A COLOR? (1967)

An oversize book that attempts, as several others have done, to identify colors by association with familiar—or, unfortu-

From Karen's Opposites, *written and illustrated by A. and M. Provensen. Golden Press, 1963.* © *1963*
Western Publishing Company, Inc. Used by permission of Western Publishing Company, Inc.

nately, not familiar enough—objects. Sometimes the identification is straightforward: "Spring is green. Leaves on green apple trees are green." Sometimes it is not: "The greenest thing of anything is being underwater." Sometimes the text is confusing: "Eyes know what a color is." The rebus technique is used in the text—but not consistently. Some of the lines are amusing or evocative, but as a book of color labeling, the text is weak. The illustrations, on the other hand, are quite lovely; full-page or double-page pictures, one for each color, are suffused with humor and vigor.

> *Zena Sutherland, in a review of "What Is a Color?"*
> *in* Bulletin of the Center for Children's Books, *Vol.*
> *21, No. 2, October, 1967, p. 31.*

Designed for the preschool age, with large, boldly painted pictures and rhythmic text sprinkled with small, appropriately colored drawings of the objects mentioned, this oversize volume celebrates the delights of color in everyday things. The lighthearted presentation offers much help in forming color concepts, without ever becoming pedantic.

> *A review of "What Is a Color?," in* The Booklist
> and Subscription Books Bulletin, *Vol. 64, No. 10,*
> *January 15, 1968, p. 594.*

WHO'S IN THE EGG? (1970)

The Miss in this outsize volume is thinking about eggs—all kinds—and she comes up with a surprising variety: scrambled, boiled, Easter, freckled and speckled, China, darning, nest eggs but most especially eggs in a nest. That's the point here: a good natured look at nature and some of the life that comes from eggs (humans are not included!). In the Provensens' text and illustrations there are children peering inside hummingbird nests, falling into ponds as they look for fish and frog eggs, running from wasps, touring the zoo to see duckbill platypus, ostrich and tortoise eggs, tripping the museum for the sight of dinosaur eggs.

The book is an early lesson in science done in a very casual, charming manner. The full-page illustrations are like colorful, weathered frescoes. Geese fleshed with brush strokes of black and brown almost seem to waddle toward you; cats with orange and yellow fur sit smugly, saucily. The Provensens? With paint and brush they are a couple of very good eggs.

> *George A. Woods, in a review of "Who's in the*
> *Egg?" in* The New York Times Book Review, *March*
> *22, 1970, p. 26.*

Big, big pages afford the Provensens a splendid opportunity to fill space with color and movement, so that the book has visual appeal and can be used (with the loss of detail on some pages) with a group to advantage. The text, however, has several flaws that weaken the book considerably. Some of the animals are shown in their natural habitat (wasps in a nest) and some in artificial surroundings (ants in an exhibit case, on the page with the wasps' nest). Most of the animals are correctly named including extinct species, but "Dead old Steg-o-DINE-o-saurs, Gee-o-Gorgo-BRONT-o-saurs . . ." is followed by "Sad and sorry, Saurus. Al-lo-SAUR-us!" Various children romp through the pages noting different kinds of eggs. Sometimes the children speak, sometimes the creatures do, sometimes the text is impersonal; this can be very confusing, especially when there is no clear line of demarcation: "What kind of eggs are they? Who put them there? Hummingbirds!

We laid them there. Don't frighten us away." The book ends with chicks popping out of a basketful of eggs carried by a child. The idea that there are all kinds of eggs beginning life has been presented more forcefully and more interestingly in quite a few books.

> *Zena Sutherland, in a review of "Who's in the Egg?"*
> *in* Bulletin of the Center for Children's Books, *Vol.*
> *24, No. 1, September, 1970, p. 18.*

Eggs are full of surprises, as young children will discover from the Provensens' charming picture book. Certainly not a story-hour choice, this cheerful assemblage of casually introduced information about different kinds of present and prehistoric animal eggs will have its most appropriate use as a read-aloud to an intent pre-schooler. The simple words: e.g., 'What are these? Are they eggs?" "They are my eggs. Frogs lay eggs"; large size . . . ; and whimsically insouciant text insure its appeal for early readers. The Provensens' watercolors are stand-outs, each and every one.

> *Cary M. Ormond, in a review of "Who's in the*
> *Egg?" in* School Library Journal, *an appendix to*
> Library Journal, *Vol. 17, No. 3, November, 1970,*
> *p. 102.*

PLAY ON WORDS (1972)

Having built a highly successful career on the premise that two illustrators are better than one, the veteran husband-and-wife team of Alice and Martin Provensen has achieved another happy amalgam of droll pictures and minimal text in ***Play on Words***. . . . Any curious child above the age of two will be gently nudged toward the joys of reading by exposure to this paean to the eccentricities of sounds, words and phrases in English. Jazzily animated homonyms and irreverent portraits of oddball words like "clamoring" and "yammering" are only a couple of its delights. It is the sort of unassuming book children 3 to 8 will return to again and again. (pp. 44, 47)

> *Selma Lanes, "Picture Books: Pretty Things," in*
> The New York Times Book Review, *Part II, No-*
> *vember 5, 1972, pp. 44, 47.**

The title is somewhat misleading, since this is less a play on words than a collection of words—some of which are not really words but sounds—or words that sound alike, begin with the same letter, or are words within a word (elf, sew, low, etc. can be found in the word "flowers") or that are grouped, like words referring to time. The pictures are bright and busy, some mod and some conventional, with some instances of words that depend on the pictures: one page, for example, is headed "Noisy Words," and shows a "clamoring" and a "yammering"—a group of clams and a plate of yams. There is humor in some of the pages, an element of game-playing that will appeal to some readers, and the introduction of some concepts, but the whole is pretty hodgepodge, and the format—an oversize flat—better gauged to the picture book audience than the independent reader who might enjoy the visual humor.

> *Zena Sutherland, in a review of "Play on Words,"*
> *in* Bulletin of the Center for Children's Books, *Vol.*
> *27, No. 1, September, 1973, p. 16.*

A junior thesaurus, encouraging mental alertness in an amusing way. Each spread contains a fresh idea. On one headed by the word "flowers", names are seen as part of an object—a snail forms the word "slow", a water-can trickles out "blow" and so on. There are pages of onomatopoeic words, of homonyms, of names of vehicles, a rousing set of noise-words beginning with Y (yoicks, yelp, yip and others). Broadly comic pictures enforce and sometimes actually make the point, in an exhilarating vocabulary-stretcher.

> *Margery Fisher, in a review of "Play on Words,"*
> in Growing Point, *Vol. 13, No. 6, December, 1974,*
> *p. 2538.*

Although at first sight this might seem to be a book solely for the beginner reader, it is on the whole more suitable for those who have acquired the first skills of reading and writing. The author-artists have taken certain words and letters and exploited them in their various sounds and meanings in gay and rumbustious pictures. The book begins with sounds made by various letters, such as T R S and Z, goes on to words with the same pronunciation but different spellings and meanings, and from then on continues to exploit in playful mood a variety of words in a diversity of ways, including puzzle pictures. The treatment is unusual and effective, and the author's initial explanation of something of the meaning of language forms a useful introduction to their intent and lays emphasis—an emphasis too seldom made—upon the excitement of language. The whole is unique and original, and its illustrations lend an extra fascination to the subject. Beginner readers will gain something from the pictures and the elementary sections of the book, but it certainly should not be confined to that lowest age group. An attractive, intriguing and very desirable book, which should arouse and sharpen a child's awareness of words in a new way.

> *E. A. Astbury, in a review of "Play on Words," in*
> The Junior Bookshelf, *Vol. 38, No. 6, December,*
> *1974, p. 355.*

MY LITTLE HEN (1973)

With many a flourish of elegant handwriting, Alice and Martin Provensen record the career of *My Little Hen* . . . The pictures, in muted color, all smile.

The events are set out as in a family photo-album, and show Mrs. Parker, her daughter Emily, Etta the hen, and Etta's fluffy yellow chick Neddy. After running dire risks with a dog, a cat, and some ducklings, Neddy is eventually renamed Netta; it has carelessly matured into a pullet instead of a cockerel. This lack of cooperation does not disturb Emily; she loves both Etta and Netta, and all their progeny.

Gentle, humorous, accomplished, restrained, this one should please preschoolers and their immediate seniors.

> *Neil Millar, "Adrift in a Box of Biscuits and Other*
> *Animal Stories," in* The Christian Science Monitor,
> *November 7, 1973, p. B2.*

A story for the very young is just substantial enough for the audience and is illustrated with pictures in frames, in the style of a family album; some of the text is, indeed, written as captions to the pictures. . . . The pictures are less static than the format might imply, with Neddy teasing the dog, the dog looking sheepish and funny, the cat being rebuffed by Neddy's indignant mother, and a last picture of dozens of yellow chicks, all descendants of the original little hen.

> *Zena Sutherland, in a review of "My Little Hen,"*
> in Bulletin of the Center for Children's Books, *Vol.*
> *27, No. 5, January, 1974, p. 84.*

The very appealing illustrations and the family album-like way in which they are presented on each page, make this a delightful and attractive picture book. The colours are clear but delicate, an overall brown being highlighted here and there by splashes of brighter colours, and each is confined to a suitable shape or form on a palely mottled background. . . . All the characters express feeling and personality and although not fully introduced or integrated into the story by the text are sufficiently well delineated to impress themselves upon and to enliven thought in a young reader. Artistry, sympathy and humour combine to please and charm. The very short text is in script form and therefore not suitable for the young reader to read for himself, but it is a book either to be shared by adult and child and then left to stir a child's imagination in various ways, or for the stimulation to come from the pictures alone. (pp. 203-04)

> *E. A. Astbury, in a review of "My Little Hen," in*
> The Junior Bookshelf, *Vol. 38, No. 4, August, 1974,*
> *pp. 203-04.*

OUR ANIMAL FRIENDS AT MAPLE HILL FARM (1974)

[*Our Animal Friends at Maple Hill Farm* is] very satisfying, like a weekend at the farm. We get to know all the domestic animals—cats, dogs, horses, pigs, chickens, their names and personalities—as well as the neighbors' animals past and present and some of the wildlife from the ants that march in file to the garbage can and the moths that flutter around the outside light at night to the other nocturnal visitors, raccoons, skunks and possums. The Provensens haven't scrubbed everything clean for young visitors either. The house needs paint, there are cowpies in the driveway, Max the cat leaves gifts of guts and tails and chipmunk heads on the doorstep, another cat has a reputation for throwing up and a fox carries away one of the roosters—thank goodness it wasn't Lovelace or Pola Negri. There's little finesse to the Provensens' renderings of people in the watercolor illustrations but the animals are a colorful barnyard lot and have all the grace and power of a horse in mid-gallop.

> *George A. Woods, "Up and Down, In and Out, and*
> *All About," in* The New York Times Book Review,
> *September 8, 1974, p. 8.**

The animal inhabitants of Maple Hill Farm are humorously described and illustrated in a way that subtly gives the reader a lot of information about their characteristics, habits, and personalities as well as their relationships with other animals and people. Children will delight in the names and nicknames given the animals and the antics in which they become involved. Despite the humorous appeal of the text, the facts about animal behavior ring quite true.

> *Lois K. Nichols, in a review of "Our Animal Friends*
> *at Maple Hill Farm," in* Children's Book Review
> Service, *Vol. 3, No. 2, October, 1974, p. 10.*

The Provensens use the Richard Scarry approach of scattering sentences and paragraphs all over the pages in between appealing drawings large and small. Based on their own real farm in New York, the book is a fine entertainment for children aged 3 to 6.

> *David K. Willis, "The Nursery Visits the Farm," in*
> The Christian Science Monitor, *November 6, 1974,*
> *p. 10.*

Surprise, surprise. How often does one find an oversize book with animal-filled pages and no story line at all that is fun to read? Well, here it is. All of the animals at Maple Hill Farm have personalities, and they are described with humor in the captions for the several-to-many pictures on each page.... Periodically, after describing the vagaries of a group of animals, the authors say kindly "Oh, well, no horse is perfect ..." or "That's the trouble with geese, who otherwise are nearly perfect," after divulging the fact that they are greedy, grabby, grouchy, etc. Even the animals' names are fun. And the pictures are delightful: bright, lively, and drawn with affectionate humor.

> *Zena Sutherland, in a review of "Our Animal Friends at Maple Hill Farm," in* Bulletin of the Center for Children's Books, *Vol. 28, No. 4, December, 1974, p. 67.*

[This is a] delightful book by the 1984 Caldecott Medal winners. Charming, clear colour illustrations and informal but informative text describe the habits and personalities of all the different animals on Maple Hill Farm. There is plenty to look at, plenty to listen to and plenty to talk about, either with a young child on a knee or a group of young children in a playgroup or infant class.... [This] is a book to return to again and again.

> *J. Nicholls, in a review of "Our Animal Friends at Maple Hill Farm," in* The Junior Bookshelf, *Vol. 49, No. 3, June, 1985, p. 123.*

A BOOK OF SEASONS (1976)

Each of the four seasons is depicted with colorful pictures and descriptions. In the winter sections, the authors discuss the feel and odors of cold weather, the need for mittens, etc., and the illustrations show snow activities (shoveling, sled riding). Activities and sights of spring, such as flowers blooming and wind, are illustrated and discussed in a pleasant, realistic manner. The fun aspects of summer (laying in the grass, gardening) and fall (playing in leaves, going for walks) are also shown, and then readers are taken through another summer and spring. Spring is described as the earth's birthday which comes again and again and again. Color is nicely used to project a real sense of each season. The book is especially good for preschool readers because the pictures encompass three-quarters of each page thus allowing children to see pictured the descriptions being read. Also useful to teach primary graders about various aspects of the seasons.

> *Sue Hall, in a review of "A Book of Seasons," in* Science Books & Films, *Vol. XII, No. 3, December, 1976, p. 159.*

[*In 1982,* A Book of Seasons *was translated into Spanish as* El libro de las estaciones.]

If one were to list these four slim, 8"-square bilingual books [including *A Book of Seasons,* Stan and Jan Berenstain's *The Berenstain Bears' New Baby,* P. D. Eastman's *Big Dog . . . Little Dog,* and Harry McNaught's *500 Words to Grow On*] in qualitative order, the Provensens' *A Book of Seasons* would get top billing, for although the prose is insipid ("Winter is here. Put on your boots," and the like), the double-page illustrations encompassing placid rural scenes and sundry seasonal activities (making maple syrup, sledding, etc.) are thoroughly captivating in glowing colors and deftly limned details.

> *Daisy Kouzel, in a review of "El libro de las estaciones/A Book of Seasons," in* School Library Journal, *Vol. 29, No. 1, September, 1982, p. 103.*

Young children looking at this little book will certainly see that white children—both boys and girls—have fun in all weather. There is not a brown, black or other person of color in a single illustration. The children depicted are also all "perfectly" built. None even wears eye-glasses. How unreal!

> *"A review of "El libro de las estaciones/A Book of Seasons," in* Interracial Books for Children Bulletin, *Vol. 14, Nos. 7 & 8, 1983, p. 37.*

THE YEAR AT MAPLE HILL FARM (1978)

An American picture book about farm animals in each month of the year. All the animals are recognizable and the backgrounds are suitably anonymous. This is a very satisfying though quiet book because of its well organised text and layout. Content of the pictures is amusing but the main attraction is the reassuring way it nails down the months of the year, the seasons, and the well defined incidents within them. . . .

> *A review of "The Year at Maple Hill Farm," in* Books for Your Children, *Vol. 13, No. 3, Summer, 1978, p. 14.*

It is possible to be romantically misleading about the country without being positively inaccurate. *The Year at Maple Hill Farm* is an attractive book, its simple text linking boxed pictures in appealing colours showing "what happens during one year on a farm". With the exception of one or two details (pumpkins in October, a deep porch round the farmhouse), this American procession of the seasons will transplant easily enough to Europe, with geese laying in April, children skating, riding, watching the pig going to market on a lorry. But there is a Christmas-card air about the winter scenes and the animals, though presented straight, have somewhat knowing human expressions on their faces. I think any child who has ever mucked out a stable or collected open-range eggs in the rain will feel a certain mental reservation while enjoying the simple calendar-cliché march of the seasons.

> *Margery Fisher, in a review of "The Year at Maple Hill Farm," in* Growing Point, *Vol. 17, No. 3, September, 1978, p. 3384.*

It seems a long time since we in this country had a new Provensen picturebook. This one is well worth waiting for. As usual they do not waste time inventing a story to match the pictures, but simply present the passage of a single year in the country. . . . Most of the material is universal and almost timeless.

The pages are crammed with fascinating detail, calling for long and absorbed study, without detriment to the finely balanced design. Alongside runs a quiet but highly individual and humorous commentary, painting in word as in colour and line the passage of a single year. On the last page it all begins again, and I suspect that many readers will go straight back to the beginning for another run. A lovely book which should prove to have lasting qualities.

> *M. Crouch, in a review of "The Year at Maple Hill Farm," in* The Junior Bookshelf, *Vol. 42, No. 5, October, 1978, p. 252.*

During their distinguished partnership the Provensens have written and illustrated many beautiful and prize-winning books. Here is one of their loveliest, in sparkling colors. The bright jacket hints at the treasures inside as it depicts each month on the front and the four seasons on the back. A generously detailed text and lavish paintings take readers into the lives of country children as they help feed the animals in cold January but enjoy skating parties and other recreations in the wintertime. Each month following is chock full of tasks as well as play for farm families, wholly involved with nature. Those privileged to experience this book (grownups and the young) are sure to be convinced that country life has special rewards.

> *A review of "The Year at Maple Hill Farm," in* Publishers Weekly, *Vol. 215, No. 5, January 29, 1979, p. 114.*

A HORSE AND A HOUND, A GOAT AND A GANDER (1979)

A faintly whimsical series of vignettes of certain animals belonging to Maple Hill Farm—Bashful the horse, John the bloodhound, the recalcitrant Goat Dear and the bad-tempered goose Evil Murdoch, whose predilection for hub-caps leads to his downfall. Mildly off-naturalistic pictures allow facial expressions to the animals, and bright, engaging colours go some way to make up for the stodgily contrived nature of the text.

> *Margery Fisher, in a review of "A Horse and Hound a Goat and a Gander," in* Growing Point, *Vol. 18, No. 4, November, 1979, p. 3611.*

[*A horse and a hound a goat and a gander*] is not exactly a story, being fixed in the descriptive present tense, yet it holds the attention in the manner of story. We are introduced to various animals on the farm . . . and somehow these animals are presented as wholly convincing and authentic characters without anthropomorphism, sentimentality or cliché. Young children will find this a most attractive and informative introduction to farm animals. The artwork is clear, accurate and gently humorous, of a quality that is good enough for both the pre-literate and the sophisticated to browse through and admire.

> *Aidan Warlow, in a review of "A Horse and a Hound a Goat and a Gander," in* The School Librarian, *Vol. 28, No. 2, June, 1980, p. 142.*

[The Provensens'] draftsmanship and prose are as fluent as ever, and children will certainly learn a lot, quite unsentimentally, about the habits of the eponymous barnyard beasts. But

From A Horse and a Hound, a Goat and a Gander, *written and illustrated by Alice and Martin Provensen. Jonathan Cape, 1979. © by Alice and Martin Provensen. Reprinted with the permission of Atheneum Publishers. In Canada by Jonathan Cape Ltd, on behalf of the authors.*

I confess I've grown too familiar with the cast of characters and feel that the Provensens have too: there's an uncharacteristic slackness to both the text and images. Innocuous, where they formerly have been delightful—see *Our Animal Friends at Maple Hill Farm.*

> George A. Woods, in a review of "A Horse and a Hound, a Goat and a Gander," in The New York Times Book Review, November 9, 1980, p. 65.

This oversize book . . . is not quite as funny as the first nor as varied, but it is nevertheless engaging in its gentle humor and in the unsentimental affection with which it describes several distinctive animals. The four creatures of the title have distinctive personalities, and in each case the Provensens give some facts about them. . . . The text is slight, but it gives a real impression of some of the pleasures of living with pets.

> Zena Sutherland, in a review of "A Horse and a Hound, a Goat and a Gander," in Bulletin of the Center for Children's Books, Vol. 34, No. 5, January, 1981, p. 100.

AN OWL AND THREE PUSSYCATS (1981)

Very high praise . . . for *An Owl and Three Pussycats* by Alice and Martin Provensen. . . . Here, their characteristic clear clean style, witty yet child-angled, is allied to an excellent theme and text. The title hints at Lear—but No; these little tales or episodes are about three children on a farm and their experiences with certain young animals. A baby owl, found after a

storm, is taken in, fed, taught to fly and forage, and is finally set free. "You can't own an owl." For a while, though, it flies to them when they call. Three little kittens of totally different background—a waif, a Siamese, and the barn cat's baby—start life together in the house. But a cat is its own creature too. A splendid book: funny, serious, informing, beautifully observed.

> Naomi Lewis, "Beyond Our Wildest Dreams," in The Times Educational Supplement, No. 3389, June 5, 1981, p. 36.*

Homey details of family life on a farm along with the mischief and antics of young pets are portrayed in an abundance of warmly colored drawings on large pages. . . . Though there is a flatness of writing and drawing styles and little development of plot, the Provensens are adept at designing attractive pages, selecting subjects widely appealing to children and conveying a sense of authentic knowledge of their subject matter—in this case the manner and behavior of the rescued owl and the growing kittens. Younger children are apt to pore over the pleasantly detailed pictures; beginning readers will find satisfying food for thought; and viewers of all ages will enjoy the humorous individuality of the animals.

> Margaret Bush, in a review of "An Owl and Three Pussycats," in School Library Journal, Vol. 28, No. 1, September, 1981, p. 113.

The oversize pages accommodate many drawings each . . . ; the line, composition, color, and humor of the pictures are as engaging as ever. . . . The writing is breezy and affectionate, but neither the style nor the substance is impressive.

> *Zena Sutherland, in a review of "An Owl and Three Pussycats," in* Bulletin of the Center for Children's Books, *Vol. 35, No. 6, February, 1982, p. 114.*

THE GLORIOUS FLIGHT: ACROSS THE CHANNEL WITH LOUIS BLÉRIOT JULY 25, 1909 (1983)

AUTHORS' COMMENTARY

While we were growing up during the years of the Great Depression, our families moved from town to town all over America. We would stay a year or two or three and then move on. The one constant which we both discovered by some rare good fortune was the Library. That there were libraries with things about them that did not change, no matter where they were—Chicago, New York, Minneapolis, Boston, Washington, wherever—was a great comfort.

The clear light, the big tables, the books with their smell of paper and glue, the secret stacks like an Aladdin's cave full of gold, and the quiet, gentle librarians made the library a reassuring and inviting place.

Separately, we learned to find our way about the shelves and to discover the treasures there—P. G. Wodehouse (all forty volumes), Gene Stratton Porter and the magic of the Limberlost, the travel books—Richard Halliburton, Carl Akeley, Osa and Martin Johnson. We discovered the adventure stories of Rafael Sabatini and Talbot Mundy and Percival Christopher Wren. And we discovered the books in the art section. In those days art books had few color plates, but how hungrily we stared at those there were! (pp. 444-45)

In the course of growing up, our paths must have crossed many times—in Chicago, in Los Angeles, in school, in museums—but we did not meet until we were both working in the same animation studio during the Second World War. Now we often wonder if we couldn't have been sitting across from one another at one of those library tables so long ago.

Since books and libraries are very much a part of both of our lives, it is not perhaps so surprising that the similar experiences we had in our youth led us to find a common profession. The question we are most often asked is "How do you work together?" Everyone asks this of us because the stereotyped image of an artist is that of a lonely, starving figure working in a garret. People have forgotten that the first book illustrators, the illuminators of the Middle Ages, worked in concert—one

From The Glorious Flight: Across the Channel with Louis Blériot July 25, 1909, *written and illustrated by Alice and Martin Provensen. The Viking Press, 1983. Copyright © 1983 by Alice and Martin Provensen. All rights reserved. Reprinted by permission of Viking Penguin Inc.*

to paint the flowers, another to paint the figures, still another to do the background and the text. All through the Renaissance, artists' studios were little factories. The masters and their apprentices turned out marriage chests or murals, altar pieces or portraits, supplying the demand.

In any kind of work there is a great sense of support in having someone beside you whose skill and judgment you trust. It is true of bookmaking. There are so many decisions to be made—the page size, the choice of type, the paper, and the fitting of the pictures to the text. *We* start with the words. The story sets the style. No matter how fine the illustrations, unless they enhance the text, they fail. And we have had our failures. They are painful but valuable. Nothing teaches one so well as a mistake.

Little by little we learned something of the art of bookmaking—how to design not just a page but a whole book so it moves, so it is a unity. Our work in the animation studios taught us the concept of flow, linking one picture to another.

During our years at Golden Press, Pierre Martinot and Martin Connell and Frank Metz taught us the mechanics of signatures, binding, typography, and color separation. Later there were the designers, Grace Clark and Barbara Hennessy, who with enormous patience were able to translate our first roughs into feasible, affordable formats—teaching us the art of the possible.

There was and is so much to learn. The balance of light and dark in relation to type, all the complications and delights of color, the agony of the first printed proofs. It has taken us years of practicing the art even to begin to understand its complexity.

Making books for children is one of the very few areas left where old ways of working still apply. You have time to plan, to discard, to choose between alternatives, to explore possible solutions. Time, for artists of our temperament, is a necessity.

Although we admire the incredibly accomplished technique that is used in some book illustration, we do not try for too much polish, too facile a style. We like pictures that are a little clumsy, a little rough and lacking in finish. Children's drawings seem to us to be marvelous. If only we could draw like that!

We draw and paint to express our joy and excitement in life and to communicate our feelings to children in the most direct and effective way. This is the essential problem for us—to find the right, the inevitable, pictures and words that say what we want to say. But illustrating a book involves two things that do not always go together. To keep the flatness of the page and the abstract design (without which the book falls apart) and at the same time to illustrate the story line are the primary considerations. It is exciting to try to find a new solution for each new book.

The mechanics of bookmaking can be taught and learned, but we believe that children's book writers and illustrators are born, not made. First, there must be a great drive, a need to draw and write for children—for the child in oneself. This is not the part of bookmaking one can learn; it is something one must have.

Too, there is something odd about spending your whole life in front of a piece of paper. Perhaps it is because of this oddness that most artists have an impulse toward working in secret, almost as if there were something subversive in the act of drawing and painting an image. The painter Degas said he painted a picture "in the same spirit as a criminal committing a crime." Given then these difficulties and strangenesses, it is easy to wonder at the ability of artists, especially husbands and wives, to work together.

The early artisans and architects, illuminators and scribes are, by and large, anonymous. It was the work that counted, not the personality of its maker. It is still the work that counts, and some artists have always found a way to join their individual styles and skills. Georges Braque, writing of the first days of cubism, said that he and Picasso "were roped together like mountain climbers to try and scale the peaks before us." To make a children's book may be a smaller mountain, but for us each new book is a new challenge. The form, the style, the spirit of one particular unique book must have something that touches our inner selves—that in some small way speaks for us both. Otherwise, no matter how fine the artwork, no matter how clever the writing, it is just another book.

For us *The Glorious Flight* is not just another book.

Our fascination with airplanes and the magic of flight began with the flying circuses performed above dusty fields on the outskirts of the midwestern cities where we lived. Martin learned to fly, not too many years ago, at an airfield famous for its fleet of World War I aircraft, an experience which served to intensify our interest in early planes.

In telling the story of Louis Blériot and the first flight across the English Channel in a powered aircraft, we wanted to capture for children some of the incredible daring of the first days of flying when men in fragile boxes made of sticks and wire and linen lurched off cow pastures all over the world. They did not last long, those good old days. Men learned very fast. By 1914 quite efficient airplanes were gearing up for the war to be fought in the air. But there were a brief few years from about 1900 to 1910 when the amateur aviators and aircraft designers reigned supreme. The Wright brothers, Wilbur and Orville, were in the vanguard. At Kitty Hawk in 1903 they successfully flew the first powered airplane for a flight of eight hundred fifty-two feet in fifty-nine seconds. We know their glory.

The man who flew the English Channel in 1909, Louis Blériot, is not well known to Americans. He was a lovable, wonderful man as well as one of the great pioneers of aviation. Unskilled as a pilot, untutored as a designer (there were no teachers), he had to learn in the air. He was incredibly brave and enormously ingenious. His contraptions flapped, skipped, and sailed ponderously into that new element—the sky. If we caught just a flash of that great moment in our book about Papa Blériot, we consider ourselves lucky.

It has been suggested by some reviewers that *The Glorious Flight* has a message—"If at first you don't succeed, try, try again." This moral may be inherent in our story, but it was not a conscious intention. Rather, we wanted to write the story of a man with a passionate obsession to create something new, the successes and failures in his work toward that goal, and the moment of triumph that rewarded him.

For us, making new children's books is equally obsessive. . . . (pp.445-48)

Alice Provensen and Martin Provensen, "Caldecott Medal Acceptance," in The Horn Book Magazine, *Vol. LX, No. 4, August, 1984, pp. 444-48.*

One day in 1901, Louis Blériot, a French automobile-accessories magnate, looked up and saw the first airship to move through the sky over his city. The image became an obsession, and soon Blériot was producing his own planes. His first efforts landed crumpled on the ground or in the water. After each attempt, Blériot was a bit more bruised and battered, but none of this quenched his desire to fly. Finally, after building a successful airplane, he heard of a contest being held by a London newspaper offering £1,000 to anyone who could fly across the English Channel. On July 25, 1909, in the eleventh plane he designed and built himself, Blériot took off in bad weather and landed in Dover 37 minutes later. The Provensens have taken this information, available in any encyclopedia, personalized it by having one of Blériot's children narrate the events, added magnificent illustrations, and thus transformed the facts into a vibrant piece of history. The primitive-style artwork, which features continually changing perspectives and charming details of early-twentieth-century France, totally absorbs the reader. Many of the spreads sweep across two pages, giving an unbroken flow to the pictures that is especially effective in the flying scenes. There are touches of understated humor, as well, both in the text and in the artwork. Note Blériot's unchanging expression, whether he's crashing in the water or landing successfully in England. Cheers for Blériot, cheers for the Provensens. (pp. 418-19)

> *A review of "The Glorious Flight: Across the Channel with Louis Blériot," in* Booklist, *Vol. 80, No. 5, November 1, 1983, pp. 418-19.*

The text is succinct, caption-like in its directness and brevity: "It all began one morning." And, at the end: "Truly, it was a glorious flight." But the paintings that provide the visual narration add the necessary texture and tone to this marriage. This is vintage Provensen. Somehow, they manage to maintain a firm hand on their characteristic style . . . and yet are able to infuse their pictures with qualities of time and place that make each book fresh. Here, considerable care has been taken to represent the many flying machines accurately, to capture the costumes and street scenes of the turn-of-the-century France. The artists tend to eschew excess modeling, so figures and houses seem almost doll-like, as if frozen. Thus there is a strong emphasis on the pictorial compositions. With only a couple of exceptions, these pictures are double spreads—long rectangles that are ideal spaces for a book about things that must move through long distances.

> *Kenneth Marantz, in a review of "The Glorious Flight across the Channel with Louis Blériot," in* School Library Journal, *Vol. 30, No. 4, December, 1983, p. 68.*

What more can one ask of a book than it be visually stunning, entertainingly written, and informative, and true? The restrained, dry humor of the simple but sophisticated text makes the story of Bleriot's long struggle to build a machine that would fly a joy, and the paintings are striking in color and composition. . . . How his family, which had seen him off, manages to be at the scene of his triumphant landing is a moot point, but it is probable that few readers will object. A smashing success for Papa and for the Provensens.

> *Zena Sutherland, in a review of "The Glorious Flight," in* Bulletin of the Center for Children's Books, *Vol. 37, No. 5, January, 1984, p. 96.*

The Provensens are among the last of the great generation of husband/wife picture-book partnerships. They have been around

now for more than 35 years and show no signs of tiring or of losing their freshness and bubble. . . . Plenty of artists could have had fun with [Bleriot's] various designs, but it takes the Provensens to relate technology to its human originators. . . . The little story is presented against a series of charming land-and skyscapes. A quiet, modest book this, but a perfect example of how a picture-book should be made, in attention to detail and in subordination to an overall design. It could not be bettered.

> *M. Crouch, in a review of "The Glorious Flight," in* The Junior Bookshelf, *Vol. 48, No. 3, June, 1984, p. 120.*

How do picture book illustrators "perform" a collaboration? Does Martin Provensen, for example, say to Alice Provensen, "Hurry up! I can't do my part until yours gets dry?" Alice has explained that their method resembles that of ancient scribes and scriveners. They pass a drawing back and forth, adding and removing different portions, until both are satisfied. They both aim for directness and simplicity—a deceptively spontaneous-looking style.

The Provensens' Caldecott prize-winning book this year, **The Glorious Flight; Across the Channel with Louis Blériot,** expresses these aims. While characters are understated and backgrounds restrained, there is a stunning treatment of sky, water, and ground areas in soft, grayed shades of ochre, umber, blue, and green. A subtle but highly varied and rich background is achieved; it strengthens the design without interfering with the foreground.

The figures are stylized, simplified, and massed into mosaic-like clusters. Objects throughout are defined as light shapes against dark, or dark against light. At times a dark foreground object partially fades into a background shape in an intricate play of shapes and shades, as in some of the crowd scenes and family portraits. Faces stare blankly out at the viewer as if the excitement of this historic technical feat—or perhaps the discomfort of cultural nonconformity—has a numbing effect. The Provensens use their great design sense to underscore the paradox, to offset this aura of ambivalence about flying in 1909.

The first picture establishes the overall style. We have a bird's-eye view of a breakfast table, but not all objects share this particular perspective. The plates are round, as if we are looking straight down, but Papa Blériot is seen straight on, face front, and the chairs at the side tilt strangely. Flowers and fruit are treated with intricate detail, while members of the family are given less precise definition. In short, the artists are playing an interesting game with perspective, and it is all done with exceptional savvy. . . .

The text has a purely whimsical tone. On-the-spot immediacy is evoked with the use of the present tense, but no solemnity is implied. . . . A little technological bungling is discounted. When Papa runs down a vegetable cart, everyone is invited to a café to toast one another, to toast the squashed pumpkins, to toast the blimp-like vehicle that has distracted Papa. "Everyone is happy," write the Provensens. Nothing can dampen the pleasures of science.

> *Donnarae MacCann and Olga Richard, in a review of "The Glorious Flight: Across the Channel with Louis Blériot," in* Wilson Library Bulletin, *Vol. 58, No. 10, June, 1984, p. 738.*

This well-written and beautifully illustrated book chronicles the life of Louis Blériot, one of the great pioneers of aviation.

From Leonardo da Vinci: The Artist, Inventor, Scientist in Three-Dimensional, Movable Pictures, *written and illustrated by A. & M. Provensen. The Viking Press, 1984. Copyright © 1984 by Alice and Martin Provensen. All rights reserved. Reprinted by permission of Viking Penguin Inc.*

Children will enjoy it for many reasons, including the fact that flight fascinates them. . . . This book, well researched by the authors and their acknowledged assistants, is accurate history with a nice foreign flavor. Exposure to the development of Blériot's various aircraft should provide children with a sense of the stages one needs to go through to perfect a product. The soft-color illustrations are finely detailed and capture the feeling of the story. In summary, children and parents will be delighted by this book: it is easy to read, it gives children some background about the forerunners of the airplanes they see or ride in today, and it contains the valuable message that hard work and determination do pay off.

Carol L. Reiner, in a review of "The Glorious Flight: Across the Channel with Louis Blériot," in Science Books & Films, *Vol. 20, No. 2, November-December, 1984, p. 98.*

LEONARDO DA VINCI: THE ARTIST, INVENTOR, SCIENTIST IN THREE-DIMENSIONAL, MOVABLE PICTURES (1984)

AUTHORS' COMMENTARY

We used the pop-up technique for the child's Leonardo, first, because Leonardo's many inventions lent themselves to such treatment; second, because the pop-up form might help children accept a subject that might otherwise seem too remote—the inventions and artistic achievement of a fifteenth century Italian master.

We picked Leonardo da Vinci, I think, because we had just done a book on the early days of flight, and of course, Leonardo had almost invented the airplane and had devoted countless hours to the analysis of flight, in birds, in models of helicopters and ornithopters.

As far as is known, none of his experiments were successful, largely because of the lack of an adequate power source. But his intuitions were very close to the mark.

Also, all people who draw and paint owe a debt to Leonardo—who advanced the professional tools of the artist: perspective, the illusion of volume through light and shade; anatomy, the anatomy of plants, animals, sky and clouds—the intensive study of geometry in plastic art. All these aspects of graphic representation were enormously advanced by Leonardo.

We hope that our little book will awaken some child's interest in this marvelous man, who is as alive today as he was in the fifteenth century. Art changes, but unlike science, it does not really become more true or more profound, with new discovery. It alters as it mirrors its own time, and sometimes it can prophesy. Certainly, this is true of Leonardo da Vinci.

> *Martin Provensen, "On the Writing of 'Leonardo da Vinci'," in* Language Arts, *Vol. 62, No. 4, April, 1985, p. 426.*

The notion [of a three-dimensional Leonardo da Vinci] seems ludicrously tasteless, but it should be said that this book's artistry is exquisite and that every pop-up makes a point. The Provensens have shown themselves to be cool, sensitive portrayers of worlds that are slightly remote—the fantastic creatures and simple culture of *The Shaker Abecedarius*, the month-by-month chronicle of *The Year at Maple Hill Farm*—and here the poise and excited, inquiring spirit of 15th-century Florence is vividly captured. Birds flash through the sky, a primitive flying-machine lumbers unsuccessfully from the ground, an apprentice perches with makeshift wings on top of a perspectivised tower, while Leonardo scans the heavens.

The two most striking effects stay flat on the page; with a pull of a ribbon, a pair of circles dissolves: a Leonardo drawing turns into a collage of architectural, anatomical and nature sketches; Leonardo experimenting turns into a gory picture of the monster he painted on a round shield. It is only a pity that with all this skill the text, very brief and whimsical in tone, should be so inadequate: 'Gifted though he was, Leonardo had one great weakness. His imagination made him impatient, and it was hard for him to finish anything . . . ' The *Mona Lisa* isn't exactly unfinished (though from the final pop-up panorama in the book, it's difficult to see how Leonardo kept his eye on the subject). (p. 27)

> *William Henry Holmes, "Frog in Paris—Problems at Home," in* The Listener, *Vol. 112, No. 2886, November 29, 1984, pp. 27-8.*

This entertaining—but factually inaccurate—pop-up is extraordinary in its artwork [by the Provensens] and paper engineering [by John Strejan]. Scenes such as Leonardo's visit to the Florentine bird market are full of details drawn from Renaissance life and they are done in warm earth tones in an appealing and intricate style. The moving pictures include a beautiful roundel which changes from a view of Leonardo sketching to an array of sketches of his scientific works. Unfortunately the book is marred by an imprecise text. It begins by setting the scene in Florence in 1492 and describes Leonardo's daily life and two of his inventions. Then his work on the Sforza horse which began in 1493 is described. Next the story of how Leonardo fashioned a fearsome dragon is mentioned but this "legend" about Leonardo is usually attributed to his youth and not to his middle years. The year 1492 is again cited for his astrological discoveries and his labors on a painting which disappears because "the wall was as porous as a sponge." Although not titled, this is an allusion to the *Battle of Anghiari* (1503-06), which failed because of Leonardo's experimental painting technique. The text concludes by stating that "he painted the Mona Lisa instead." This abrupt ending is misleading, as according to Vasari he was painting the Mona Lisa at the same time that he received the commission for the *Battle of Anghiari*. It also leaves the unfortunate impression that his career ended then, whereas he continued with his remarkable discoveries until his death in 1519. As a toy book, *Leonardo da Vinci* is a success, but as an introduction to his life, it is flawed. Students needing research information would find Sach's *Leonardo and His World* (Silver Burdett, 1980) more useful.

> *Lorraine Douglas, in a review of "Leonardo da Vinci," in* School Library Journal, *Vol. 31, No. 5, January, 1985, p. 67.*

This book upsets me. In my view it trivialises Leonardo da Vinci's genius. The illustrations are stylised, using pop-ups (which do not look very robust) to create some entertainment effects quite out of sympathy with Leonardo's paintings (of which only the Mona Lisa is reproduced). Some of Leonardo's wonderful drawings and specimens of his unusual handwriting are used for mere decoration. The commentary, a catalogue of his varied skills and major projects, is at times trite. Leonardo the man simply doesn't come through. My reference books indicate that the part of the text relating to the fresco of the Battle of Anghiari is inaccurate. The paint did not sink in the wall. It refused to dry, and when braziers were brought in, it proceeded to drip down. The last sentence, 'So he painted the Mona Lisa instead', is the final agony. (pp. 149-50)

> *Stewart Scott, in a review of "Leonardo da Vinci," in* The School Librarian, *Vol. 33, No. 2, June, 1985, pp. 149-50.*

This book is six double-page panels with three-dimensional "stand-ups," turnable diagrams that reveal two scenes each, and an ingenious lift-and-pull page that illustrates da Vinci's flying machine. Terse, entertaining text on each page describes the man and his various activities in art, invention, engineering, and astronomy. Adults will enjoy buying this book for their favorite children, ages 8-14, and then working through it with them. The text can be read by seventh graders, but younger children will need help in order to learn what each working drawing depicts. The narrative portrays da Vinci as a genius with new ideas in many fields but also as someone with some very human failings, such as impatience and a lack of perseverance. This book is a technical masterpiece; each manipulative piece works well, and each is unique. Although classroom use by unsupervised children will shorten the book's life considerably, it would be a treasure for repeated browsing by individual owners. The format and spritely prose somehow embody the very spirit of Leonardo da Vinci. It looks like something he could have written. (pp. 35-6)

> *Mary B. Harbeck, in a review of "Leonardo da Vinci: The Artist, Inventor, Scientist," in* Science Books & Films, *Vol. 21, No. 1, September-October, 1985, pp. 35-6.*

TOWN AND COUNTRY (1985)

A portfolio of isolated impressions, stylized abstractions based on years of living in urban and rural communities. The city scenes of this large book are set vertically, in double-page spreads, with text in relatively thin white strips. The country half is made up of a variety of thick and thin horizontal bands. In both instances the text acts as expanded captions for the detail-packed scenes and typically puts into simple sentences what has been much more poetically expressed in paint. In other words, this is a book for looking, with lots of eye-roaming over pages that reflect the artists' memories, sandpapered by time to appear more idyllic than real. In the town, the Provensens pick up on the vehicles in rush hour, on the wonderful panoply of storefronts, billboards and building façades. People become multicolored accents in these visually activated tapestries. They don't have the vitality of Sasek's *"This Is . . ."* series of world capitals (Macmillan) nor the "guess who"

From Town and Country, *written and illustrated by Alice and Martin Provensen. Crown, 1985. Copyright © 1984 by Alice and Martin Provensen. Used by permission of Crown Publishers, Inc.*

character of Anno's *Journeys* (Philomel). But there is that sense of just-rightness to the design of each spread that has characterized most of the books from this pair of artists. The country half is necessarily visually more peaceful. Landscapes rather than buildings characterize these scenes. But they are also filled with carefully rendered buildings (farm and village) and gaggles of geese, flocks of sheep and a herd of multi-hued bovines coming to the barn at eveningtide. Without a narrative, these scenes can't have the zip of the authors' *A Glorious Flight*. . . . But it is an attractive assemblage.

> *Kenneth Marantz, in a review of "Town & Country,"*
> *in* School Library Journal, *Vol. 31, No. 8, April, 1985, p. 82.*

This book's richly detailed contrast of urban and rural America will unite many of its older readers in moments of time remembered: the classic architecture of Symphony Hall standing indignantly next to the frenetically lighted billboard of a rock concert; or the relentlessly pragmatic offense of a pneumatic drill vs. the aesthetic self-indulgence of a nearby restaurant. The country, too, has its energy and demands, and even noise, along with its very different images of pastoral quiet and simplicity. For young readers the book gives a provocative and distilled taste of the offerings of each environment.

So what more could one ask besides a comprehensive overview of two incredibly different modes of life—both so beautifully and realistically illustrated?

Perhaps a little more to discover, a little more poetic focusing on the particular. There doesn't seem to be much for the reader to do except identify and classify various objects and experiences in the text and illustration. The reader isn't enticed enough to enter into the multifaceted activities of these two worlds.

It's not that this worthy and highly commendable endeavor is anything less than what it wants to be: It's a magnificent success within its own design. Rather, it's that in the authors' desire to cover everything, they run the risk of lapsing into sheer listmaking when opportunities exist to tell even more in some particular image or text.

An engaging humor and a sense of the writer's voice do come forth in the text as a whole. They tell us that children learn basically the same things in country and city schools—but if you knock a ball over a fence in the country, "the only one who might mind will be a cow," whereas in the city, "you not only make someone angry, but you will probably lose [it]."

Putting aside the ways in which greater lyricism and imagination might have come into play, this book gets an "A" for sheer bigness of vision. It shows an honest ear for what interests children, and makes for an excellent, deft, intelligent piece of reading. By the time one gets through the contrasting depictions of urban and rural life, the overall feeling is one of very considerable immersion in the two great poles of human life.

> *Darian Scott, "City, Country: A Look at Contrasts,"
> in* The Christian Science Monitor, *April 5, 1985, p.
> B4.*

Large-scale, luxuriant paintings depict an imposing array of cityscapes and bucolic country scenes that collectively build an impressive album of city and country life. The text is largely descriptive, elaborating on what it is like to live in an urban area or in more rural surroundings. The city is depicted as teeming with life and color: "The whole city hums like a hive of bees. It would be fun to spend all of your time in the streets just looking and listening." And while the country is quieter, it too has its pace: "You can feel the thunder in the distance. You can hear the haybaler clank as the men hurry to bring in the hay before it rains" (an inadvertent bit of stereotyping here; there are plenty of farm women who have also rushed to save the hay from a rainstorm). The pictures are rich in color and detail. Clay tones and a matte-like finish modulate the brighter hues that spark the busy expanses. There is much to look at and, for younger readers still forming notions of life-styles, lots of observations to make.

> *Denise M. Wilms, in a review of "Town and Country,"
> in* Booklist, *Vol. 81, No. 16, April 15, 1985, p. 1200.*

The text speaks directly; it is generous but not wordy, eagerly explicative rather than narrative. Refusing to be constrained by verbal statements, however, the artwork soars with an energetic imagination of its own. Still displaying a fine disdain for perspective, the Provensens have created illustrations that are less decoratively stylized than those in many of their previous books and that are more precisely representational, with sharp images and a use of handsome, modulating full color. The juxtaposition of structures, objects, and people—especially in the urban scenes—makes for crowded but never confusing pictures; skyscrapers, schools, bridges, vehicles, stores, theaters, eating places, illuminated signs, ethnic diversity, and masses of human beings all add to the cheerful visual cacophony, while parks and museums offer more serene attractions.

Recalling American primitive painting of the nineteenth century, the rural panoramas stress the ever-changing beauty of the pastoral countryside as well as the busyness of farm and small-town life. A pleasing variety in the placement of text and illustrations and the interludes of quiet vignettes among the large-size pictures combine to relieve the eye and to lessen the impact of the book's ample dimensions. (pp. 328-29)

> *Ethel L. Heins, in a review of "Town and Country,"
> in* The Horn Book Magazine, *Vol. LXI, No. 3, May-
> June, 1985, pp. 328-29.*

The jacket bills **Town and Country** as a book that "introduces children to the sights, sounds and good times to be found wherever one may live in America." . . .

The text explains that big city populations include white people, Black people, brown people. Unfortunately, though, the book not only goes no further—it goes backwards. Its main failure is that the illustrations, which are lavish, depict various groups in horrendously stereotypical ways: an East Indian wears turban and jodhpurs; an Italian is dressed as a waiter, an Asian wears clog-like shoes, etc. Moreover, all the various groups are shown running "native" restaurants. (Two notable exceptions: there is no kosher food store—though one is mentioned in the text— nor a Black-run one. There *is* a "Seoul Food" store, thereby providing the double opportunity to take note of Koreans, albeit restaurant-operating ones, and point up the omission of Blacks.) A similar sensitivity regarding cultural issues is evident in the book's depiction of a "San Gennario"—rather than San Gennaro—festival.

The countryside, on the other hand, is depicted as populated only by whites. To be sure, the illustrations are technically skillful (as are those on big-city living). But by putting such bucolic scenes off-limits to all but whites, the artists miss an opportunity to show country life as it really is.

In short, the book makes two offensive points: ethnic groups in cities stick to cooking, and they are banned from country living. Definitely not a book to be recommended.

> *Emily Leinster, in a review of "Town & Country,"
> in* Interracial Books for Children Bulletin, *Vol. 16,
> No. 7, 1985, p. 18.*

Robert Louis (Balfour) Stevenson

1850-1894

(Born Robert Lewis Balfour Stevenson; also wrote under the pseudonym of Captain George North) Scottish novelist and poet.

The following entry presents criticism of Stevenson's *A Child's Garden of Verses*.

Renowned for his novels and short stories for adults and young people, Stevenson made a significant contribution to literature for the very young with his poetry collection *A Child's Garden of Verses*. The sixty-four poems introduced a new aspect to the genre by presenting the world of childhood—both real and imaginary—from the child's point of view. By describing his young narrator both at play and in solitary pursuits, Stevenson captured the interests, thoughts, and emotions of children in succinct rhymes and infectious rhythms. Underscoring the basically autobiographical poems are the immediacy and accuracy of Stevenson's memories and the simplicity and technical skill with which he fashioned them into verse. Stevenson began writing *A Child's Garden* in 1881 after reading Mrs. Sale Barker's verses for Kate Greenaway's *Birthday Book for Children;* "these are very nice rhymes," he said, "and I don't think such verses would be so difficult to do." Completing the main part of the book in 1883, Stevenson had it privately printed under the title *Penny Whistles*. The final version, which contained twenty-five additional poems, appeared as *A Child's Garden of Verses* in 1885. Appealing to both imaginative children and nostalgic adults, the poems have been frequently reprinted and are often set to music. *A Child's Garden* is now recognized as a classic of children's poetry and is usually considered the most successful example of Stevenson's poetic output.

Over the last century, critics have continually lauded *A Child's Garden of Verses* for its eloquence, honesty, and humor. Although some reviewers disfavor the poems which express adult sophistication and ethnocentrism, most praise Stevenson for his understanding of children and commend his genius in recollecting and articulating their feelings.

(See also *CLR*, Vol. 10; *Nineteenth-Century Literature Criticism*, Vol. 5; *Yesterday's Authors of Books for Children*, Vol. 2; and *Dictionary of Literary Biography*, Vol. 18: *Victorian Novelists after 1885.*)

AUTHOR'S COMMENTARY

[*Stevenson's essay "Child's Play," which originally appeared in* the Cornhill Magazine *in 1878, is considered by many critics to provide the philosophical basis for* A Child's Garden of Verses. *In* Chambers' Cyclopedia of English Literature, *J. W. Mackail notes that* A Child's Garden *is "as decisive and important a success in its own field of literature as* Treasure Island *had been two years before. The field was in this case almost wholly new; the* Child's Garden *may be said not only to have founded a new school, but to have opened up a new side of life, and to be a substantial contribution towards the theory of human development and the science of psychology. The essay called "Child's Play" . . . had broken ground in this direction, with singular delicacy and depth of insight." In the following excerpt from that essay, Ste-*

venson describes the child's need for play activity—"'making-believe'," he writes, "is the gist of his whole life"—and speculates on the attitudes of children towards adults.]

If a grown man does not like eating and drinking and exercise, if he is not something positive in his tastes, it means he has a feeble body and should have some medicine; but children may be pure spirits, if they will, and take their enjoyment in a world of moonshine. Sensation does not count for so much in our first years as afterwards; something of the swaddling numbness of infancy clings about us; we see and touch and hear through a sort of golden mist. Children, for instance, are able enough to see, but they have no great faculty for looking; they do not use their eyes for the pleasure of using them, but for by-ends of their own; and the things I call to mind seeing most vividly, were not beautiful in themselves, but merely interesting or enviable to me as I thought they might be turned to practical account in play. Nor is the sense of touch so clean and poignant in children as it is in a man. If you will turn over your old memories, I think the sensations of this sort you remember will be somewhat vague, and come to not much more than a blunt, general sense of heat on summer days, or a blunt, general sense of well-being in bed. And here, of course, you will understand pleasurable sensations; for overmastering pain—the most deadly and tragical element in life, and the true commander of man's soul and body—alas! pain has its own way with all of us; it breaks in, a rude visitant, upon the fairy garden where the child wanders in a dream, no less surely than it rules upon the field of battle, or sends the immortal war-god whimpering to his father; and innocence, no more than philosophy, can protect us from this sting. As for taste, when we bear in mind the excesses of unmitigated sugar which delight a youthful palate, "it is surely no very cynical asperity" to think taste a character of the maturer growth. Smell and hearing are perhaps more developed; I remember many scents, many voices, and a great deal of spring singing in the woods. But hearing is capable of vast improvement as a means of pleasure; and there is all the world between gaping wonderment at the jargon of birds, and the emotion with which a man listens to articulate music.

At the same time, and step by step with this increase in the definition and intensity of what we feel which accompanies our growing age, another change takes place in the sphere of intellect, by which all things are transformed and seen through theories and associations as through colored windows. The pleasure of surprise is passed away; sugar-loaves and water-carts seem mighty tame to encounter; and we walk the streets to make romances and to sociologize. Nor must we deny that a good many of us walk them solely for the purposes of transit or in the interest of a livelier digestion. These, indeed, may look back with mingled thoughts upon their childhood, but the rest are in a better case; they know more than when they were children, they understand better, their desires and sympathies answer more nimbly to the provocation of the senses, and their minds are brimming with interest as they go about the world.

According to my contention, this is a flight to which children can not rise. They are wheeled in perambulators or dragged about by nurses in a pleasing stupor. A vague, faint, abiding wonderment possesses them. Here and there some specially remarkable circumstance, such as a water-cart or a guardsman, fairly penetrates into the seat of thought and calls them, for half a moment, out of themselves; and you may see them, still towed forward sideways by the inexorable nurse as by a sort of destiny, but still staring at the bright object in their wake. It may be some minutes before another such moving spectacle reawakens them to the world in which they dwell. For other children, they almost invariably show some intelligent sympathy. "There is a fine fellow making mud pies," they seem to say; "that I can understand, there is some sense in mud pies." But the doings of their elders, unless where they are speakingly picturesque or recommend themselves by the quality of being easily imitable, they let them go over their heads (as we say) without the least regard. If it were not for this perpetual imitation, we should be tempted to fancy they despised us outright, or only considered us in the light of creatures brutally strong and brutally silly; among whom they condescended to dwell in obedience like a philosopher at a barbarous court. (pp. 126-28)

We grown people can tell ourselves a story, give and take strokes until the bucklers ring, ride far and fast, marry, fall, and die; all the while sitting quietly by the fire or lying prone in bed. This is exactly what a child can not do, or does not do, at least, when he can find anything else. He works all with lay figures and stage properties. When his story comes to the fighting, he must rise, get something by way of a sword and have a set-to with a piece of furniture, until he is out of breath. When he comes to ride with the king's pardon, he must bestride a chair, which he will so hurry and belabor and on which he will so furiously demean himself, that the messenger will ar-

rive, if not bloody with spurring, at least fiery red with haste. If his romance involves an accident upon a cliff, he must clamber in person about the chest of drawers and fall bodily upon the carpet, before his imagination is satisfied. Lead soldiers, dolls, all toys, in short, are in the same category and answer the same end. Nothing can stagger a child's faith; he accepts the clumsiest substitutes and can swallow the most staring incongruities. The chair he has just been besieging as a castle, or valiantly cutting to the ground as a dragon, is taken away for the accommodation of a morning visitor, and he is nothing abashed; he can skirmish by the hour with a stationary coal-scuttle; in the midst of the enchanted pleasance, he can see, without sensible shock, the gardener soberly digging potatoes for the day's dinner. He can make abstraction of whatever does not fit into his fable; and he puts his eyes into his pocket, just as we hold our noses in an unsavory lane. And so it is, that although the ways of children cross with those of their elders in a hundred places daily, they never go in the same direction nor so much as lie in the same element. So may the telegraph wires intersect the line of the high-road, or so might a landscape painter and a bagman visit the same country, and yet move in different worlds.

People struck with these spectacles, cry aloud about the power of imagination in the young. Indeed there may be two words to that. It is, in some ways, but a pedestrian fancy that the child exhibits. It is the grown people who make the nursery stories; all the children do, is jealously to preserve the text. . . . "On a cold and frosty morning," gives a good instance of the artistic taste in children. And this need for overt action and lay figures testifies to a defect in the child's imagination which prevents him from carrying out his novels in the privacy of his own heart. He does not yet know enough of the world and men. His experience is incomplete. That stage-wardrobe and scene-room that we call the memory is so ill provided, that he can overtake few combinations and body out few stories, to his own content, without some external aid. He is at the experimental stage; he is not sure how one would feel in certain circumstances; to make sure, he must come as near trying it as his means permit. And so here is young heroism with a wooden sword, and mothers practise their kind vocation over a bit of jointed stick. It may be laughable enough just now; but it is these same people and these same thoughts, that not long hence, when they are on the theatre of life, will make you weep and tremble. For children think very much the same thoughts and dream the same dreams as bearded men and marriageable women. No one is more romantic. Fame and honor, the love of young men and the love of mothers, the business man's pleasure in method, all these and others they anticipate and rehearse in their play hours. Upon us, who are further advanced and fairly dealing with the threads of destiny, they only glance from time to time to glean a hint for their own mimetic reproduction. Two children playing at soldiers are far more interesting to each other than one of the scarlet beings whom both are busy imitating. This is perhaps the greatest oddity of all. "Art for art" is their motto; and the doings of grown folk are only interesting as the raw material for play. Not Théophile Gautier, not Flaubert, can look more callously upon life, or rate the reproduction more highly over the reality; and they will parody an execution, a deathbed, or the funeral of the young man of Nain, with all the cheerfulness in the world.

The true parallel for play is not to be found, of course, in conscious art, which, though it be derived from play, is itself an abstract, impersonal thing, and depends largely upon philosophical interests beyond the scope of childhood. It is when we make castles in the air and personate the leading character in our own romances, that we return to the spirit of our first years. Only, there are several reasons why the spirit is no longer so agreeable to indulge. Nowadays, when we admit this personal element into our divagations we are apt to stir up uncomfortable and sorrowful memories, and remind ourselves sharply of old wounds. Our day-dreams can no longer lie all in the air like a story in the *Arabian Nights;* they read to us rather like the history of a period in which we ourselves had taken part, where we come across many unfortunate passages and find our own conduct smartly reprimanded. And then the child, mind you, acts his parts. He does not merely repeat them to himself; he leaps, he runs, and sets the blood agog over all his body. And so his play breathes him; and he no sooner assumes a passion than he gives it vent. Alas! when we betake ourselves to our intellectual form of play, sitting quietly by the fire or lying prone in bed, we rouse many hot feelings for which we can find no outlet. Substitutes are not acceptable to the mature mind, which desires the thing itself; and even to rehearse a triumphant dialogue with one's enemy, although it is perhaps the most satisfactory piece of play still left within our reach, is not entirely satisfying, and is even apt to lead to a visit and an interview which may be the reverse of triumphant after all.

In the child's world of dim sensation, play is all in all. "Making believe" is the gist of his whole life, and he can not so much as take a walk except in character. I could not learn my alphabet without some suitable *mise-èn-scène*, and had to act a business man in an office before I could sit down to my book. Will you kindly question your memory, and find out how much you did, work or pleasure, in good faith and soberness, and for how much you had to cheat yourself with some invention? I remember, as though it were yesterday, the expansion of spirit, the dignity and self-reliance, that came with a pair of mustachios in burnt cork, even when there was none to see. Children are even content to forego what we call the realities, and prefer the shadow to the substance. When they might be speaking intelligibly together, they chatter senseless gibberish by the hour, and are quite happy because they are making believe to speak French. [Even] the imperious appetite of hunger suffers itself to be gulled and led by the nose with the fag end of an old song. And it goes deeper than this: when children are together even a meal is felt as an interruption in the business of life; and they must find some imaginative sanction, and tell themselves some sort of story, to account for, to color, to render entertaining, the simple processes of eating and drinking. What wonderful fancies I have heard evolved out of the pattern upon tea-cups!—from which there followed a code of rules and a whole world of excitement, until tea-drinking began to take rank as a game. When my cousin and I took our porridge of a morning, we had a device to enliven the course of the meal. He ate his with sugar, and explained it to be a country continually buried under snow. I took mine with milk, and explained it to be a country suffering gradual inundation. You can imagine us exchanging bulletins; how here was an island still unsubmerged, here a valley not yet covered with snow; what inventions were made; how his population lived in cabins on perches and travelled on stilts, and how mine was always in boats; how the interest grew furious, as the last corner of safe ground was cut off on all sides and grew smaller every moment; and how, in fine, the food was of altogether secondary importance, and might even have been nauseous, so long as we seasoned it with these dreams. But perhaps the most exciting moments I ever had over a meal, were in the case of calves'

feet jelly. It was hardly possible not to believe—and you may be sure, so far from trying, I did all I could to favor the illusion—that some part of it was hollow, and that sooner or later my spoon would lay open the secret tabernacle of the golden rock. There, might some miniature *Red Beard* await his hour; there, might one find the treasures of the *Forty Thieves,* and bewildered Cassim beating about the walls. And so I quarried on slowly, with bated breath, savoring the interest. Believe me, I had little palate left for the jelly; and though I preferred the taste when I took cream with it, I used often to go without, because the cream dimmed the transparent fractures.

Even with games, this spirit is authoritative with right-minded children. It is thus that hide-and-seek has so pre-eminent a sovereignty, for it is the wellspring of romance, and the actions and the excitement to which it gives rise lend themselves to almost any sort of fable. (pp. 129-34)

To think of such a frame of mind, is to become disquieted about the bringing up of children. Surely they dwell in a mythological epoch, and are not the contemporaries of their parents. What can they think of them? what can they make of these bearded or petticoated giants who look down upon their games? who move upon a cloudy Olympus, following unknown designs apart from rational enjoyment? who profess the tenderest solicitude for children, and yet every now and again reach down out of their altitude and terribly vindicate the prerogatives of age? Off goes the child, corporally smarting, but morally rebellious. Were there ever such unthinkable deities as parents? I would give a great deal to know what, in nine cases out of ten, is the child's unvarnished feeling. A sense of past cajolery; a sense of personal attraction, at best very feeble; above all, I should imagine, a sense of terror for the untried residue of mankind; go to make up the attraction that he feels. No wonder, poor little heart, with such a weltering world in front of him, if he clings to the hand he knows! The dread irrationality of the whole affair, as it seems to children, is a thing we are all too ready to forget. "O, why," I remember passionately wondering, "why can we not all be happy and devote ourselves to play?" And when children do philosophize, I believe it is usually to very much the same purpose.

One thing, at least, comes very clearly out of these considerations; that whatever we are to expect at the hands of children, it should not be any peddling exactitude about matters of fact. They walk in a vain show, and among mists and rainbows; they are passionate after dreams and unconcerned about realities; speech is a difficult art not wholly learned; and there is nothing in their own tastes or purposes to teach them what we mean by abstract truthfulness. When a bad writer is inexact, even if he can look back on half a century of years, we charge him with incompetence and not with dishonesty. And why not extend the same allowance to imperfect speakers? Let a stockbroker be dead stupid about poetry, or a poet inexact in the details of business, and we excuse them heartily from blame. But show us a miserable, unbreeched, human entity, whose whole profession it is to take a tub for a fortified town and a shaving-brush for the deadly stiletto, and who passes three-fourths of his time in a dream and the rest in open self-deception, and we expect him to be as nice upon a matter of fact as a scientific expert bearing evidence. Upon my heart, I think it less than decent. You do not consider how little the child sees, or how swift he is to weave what he has seen into bewildering fiction; and that he cares no more for what you call truth, than you for a gingerbread dragoon.

I am reminded, as I write, that the child is very inquiring as to the precise truth of stories. But indeed this is a very different matter, and one bound up with the subject of play, and the precise amount of playfulness, or playability, to be looked for in the world. Many such burning questions must arise in the course of nursery education. Among the fauna of this planet, which already embraces the pretty soldier and the terrifying Irish beggarman, is, or is not, the child to expect a Bluebeard or a Cormoran? Is he, or is he not, to look out for magicians, kindly and potent? May he, or may he not, reasonably hope to be cast away upon a desert island, or turned to such diminutive proportions that he can live on equal terms with his lead soldiery, and go a cruise in his own toy schooner? Surely all these are practical questions to a neophyte entering upon life with a view to play. Precision upon such a point, the child can understand. But if you merely ask him of his past behavior, as to who threw such a stone, for instance, or struck such and such a match; or whether he had looked into a parcel or gone by a forbidden path—why, he can see no moment in the inquiry, and it is ten to one, he has already half forgotten and half bemused himself with subsequent imaginings.

It would be easy to leave them to their native cloudland, where they figure so prettily—pretty like flowers and innocent like dogs. They will come out of their gardens soon enough, and have to go into offices and the witness-box. Spare them yet a while, O conscientious parent! Let them doze among their playthings yet a little! for who knows what a rough, warfaring existence lies before them in the future? (pp. 134-37)

Robert Louis Stevenson, "Child's Play," in his Virginibus Puerisque and Other Papers; Memories and Portraits; Familiar Studies of Men and Books, *Charles Scribner's Sons, 1910, pp. 125-37.*

[*Stevenson often corresponded with Edmund Gosse, an English poet, critic, and man of letters who introduced the works of Henrik Ibsen to the English-speaking public and is considered a primary champion of Stevenson's literary reputation. The following excerpt is taken from a letter that Stevenson wrote to Gosse announcing the publication of* A Child's Garden of Verses; *Stevenson's comment that the verses "seem to have . . . a kind of childish treble note that sounds in my ears freshly; not song, . . . but a child's voice" is echoed by many critics.*]

I have now published on 101 small pages 'The Complete Proof of Mr. R. L. Stevenson's Incapacity to Write Verse', in a series of graduated examples with table of contents. I think I shall issue a companion volume of exercises: 'Analyse this poem. Collect and communicate the ugly words. Distinguish and condemn the *chevilles*. State Mr. Stevenson's faults of taste in regard to the measure. What reasons can you gather from this example for your behalf that Mr. S. is unable to write any other measure?'

They look ghastly in the cold light of print; but there is something nice in the little ragged regiment for all—the blackguards seem to me to smile, to have a kind of childish treble note that sounds in my ears freshly; not song, if you will, but a child's voice.

Robert Louis Stevenson, in an extract from a letter to Edmund Gosse on March 12, 1885, in Robert Louis Stevenson: The Critical Heritage, *edited by Paul Maixner, Routledge & Kegan Paul, 1981, p. 147.*

THE SATURDAY REVIEW, LONDON

[*When* The Saturday Review *published an unsigned review of* A Child's Garden of Verses, *the English poet, editor, and critic W. E. Henley wrote to Stevenson that this assessment might "hurt the book damnably" due to the critic's insistence that the poems fail to appeal equally to children and adults. As the following excerpt indicates, the reviewer also notes that Stevenson's volume "deserves to have plenty of readers, both young and old."*]

To write good verse for children where children are the only readers written for is no easy feat; to write such children's verse as may delight adults also is more difficult still. Mr. Robert Louis Stevenson, as much of his prose work has shown, is more than commonly well equipped with the qualities which make for success in either of these endeavours; yet we cannot say that in the volume before us he has been entirely successful. That simplicity of diction which is essential to such writing he has nearly always at command; the "force of statement"—we can find no less prosaic phrase to describe what we mean—which is characteristic of so much children's talk when it is at once intelligent and unaffected, in this also he is not wanting. Again, he has a quick and vivid fancy, with much power of picturesque description, and he can be humorous and tender, not only by turns, which is common enough, but at the same time. Nor can he be said to have neglected or inexpertly used the various gifts which he possesses. In this volume there is an abundance of graceful fancy, much of it admirably expressed. Some of its lyrics would undoubtedly delight any child

Stevenson with his mother, Margaret Stevenson.

old enough to take delight in such things at all; while others, again, will undoubtedly be read with pleasure by its elders. What we look for, however, in a book of this sort, though perhaps it is putting our requirements too high, is the combination of the two kinds of attraction in the same pieces. The highest point attainable in writing of this description is only attained when what may be called the surface-motive of the lyric or the prose-story is sufficient in itself to charm the child, while the adult sense of humour can enjoy the undercurrent of thought or meaning with a relish proportioned to the completeness of its concealment from the younger reader. This point, however, is rarely attained in Mr. Stevenson's verse. He has added to his difficulties—if also to his opportunities—by writing throughout in the person of the child. It is the child's thoughts, fancies, pleasures, ambitions—in short, the child's record of impressions and criticism of life—as given from its own lips; and it is, of course, extremely hard to maintain the requisite tone of *naïveté* in these touches, which are meant to appeal to the appreciation of its elders. The infantile humour or pathos cannot help appearing at times to be too conscious of itself.

We regret that considerations of space forbid us to illustrate with any fulness the points we have noted, but they are of the kind which at once strike any critical reader. No such reader, we imagine, can fail to observe how this faint undertone of self-consciousness just mars the effect of such an otherwise exquisite little piece as **"My Kingdom"** . . . or of the closing stanzas of the **"Dumb Soldier"** . . . We get it in—

> I called the little pool a sea,
> The little hills were big to me,
> For I am very small.

And we get it again in—

> Alas! and as my home I neared,
> How very big my nurse appeared.

This is not the child, but the "grown-up" speaking through the mouth of the child. Sometimes, indeed, the youthful voice is made to talk "old" with humour and appropriateness, as—

> The child that is not clean and neat,
> With lots of toys and things to eat,
> He is a naughty child, I'm sure—
> Or else his dear papa is poor.

It is easy to imagine a child picking up the idea conveyed in this last line from his elders, among whom the conversation has perhaps turned more often upon the worldly circumstances of "papas" in general than the philosophic mind would approve; and the sudden clash of the mystical and rationalistic theories of human unhappiness, without any suspicion of their incongruity, is delightfully fraught with the unconscious humour of childhood. **"Foreign Children,"** again, is good, though the lines, "You must often as you trod, Have wearied *not* to be abroad," meaning, "You must often have felt bored at being abroad," is unfortunately ambiguous, and would equally apply to a foreign child languishing under exile in England, which, of course, as the whole context shows, is the very reverse of what Mr. Stevenson means. Perhaps the most successful of all the poems in maintaining the child-attitude throughout is **"The Gardener"**. . . . But Mr. Stevenson would have done well to have rejected such trivialities as **"Auntie's Skirts"** and **"Rain,"** which are unworthy of any but a very young child indeed. And generally we should be disposed to say that the book would have been the better for being short-

ened. Sixty-four flower-beds are too many for a ***Child's Garden of Verses;*** we can hardly help tiring of such often-repeated specimens of what from the nature of the case must be a very limited order of horticulture. We are unwilling, however, to take leave of a volume in many respects so attractive as this with words of fault-finding. Considered merely as verse, and without any reference to its special claim upon the young, one may linger with pleasure upon many of its pages. For picturesque touches of observation, and for spirited workmanship, the five stanzas of **"Summer Sun"** surpass anything perhaps in the volume; **"Night and Day"** has merit enough to atone almost for the barbarous rhyme ("valleys" and "allies") with which it concludes; and the **"Envoys"** at the end of the book are full of grace and pathos, that **"To Minnie"** in particular possessing indescribable tenderness and charm. On the whole, and despite the shortcomings we have felt obliged to notice, Mr. Stevenson's book deserves to have plenty of readers, both young and old.

> *A review of "A Child's Garden of Verses," in* The Saturday Review, *London, Vol. LIX, No. 1534, March 21, 1885, p. 394.*

THE SPECTATOR

Mr. R. L. Stevenson has as good an idea of children and their favourite notions as any English writer of our time. His ***Treasure Island*** is the delight of all children, big and little, who love adventure in its simplest and most vivid forms; and he has just proved, in his ***Child's Garden of Verses*** that he understands equally well the imaginative world of children still smaller than those for whose delight ***Treasure Island*** was probably written. Nevertheless, he seems to us to fall into some confusion between two very different things indeed,—the verse which children might be supposed to write, and the verse which they would delight to read. In his ***Child's Garden of Verses*** he gives us a good many specimens of verses, of which the best you could say would be that a bright child might have written them, but which for that very reason no bright child would value, except indeed as his own productions. For example, the following **"Happy Thought"** . . . is hardly a thought which would make any child happy, unless from triumph at having given birth to a rhyme:—

> The world is so full of a number of things.
> I'm sure we should all be as happy as kings.

That is merely puerile, and you will never find children pleased at what is merely puerile. It is the same with **"Looking Forward"**. . . .

> When I am grown to man's estate
> I shall be very proud and great.
> And tell the other girls and boys
> Not to meddle with my toys.

That, again, expresses a very common puerile feeling in a decidedly puerile manner, and therefore it is not the sort of verse in which children would take pleasure. And of this puerile verse, though Mr. Stevenson knows better than to give us nothing else, there is a great deal too much for so small a volume as this,—a great deal too much that might really have been written by such a child as Mr. Stevenson himself once was, and which expresses nothing but frank, childish thoughts. Now, we are far from saying that children condemn verse because it is not poetry. On the contrary, they often take a great fancy to the prosaic verses written for them by older people,—witness the popularity a generation or two ago of the "Original Poems," by Jane Taylor, of Ongar. But then bad as most of the "Original Poems" were, considered as poems, they contained lively delineations of incident and character such as no child could have written. . . . Now, in the verses in Mr. R. L. Stevenson's volume, which we have described as verses which a smart boy might have written, there is no such force of graving. Like the specimens we have given, they have the mark of the child's experience without anything at all but the rhyme to distinguish them in form from the language in which a lively boy would have been apt to express that experience. But to find favour with children, verse needs a good deal more than this. Undoubtedly it must embody the child's feeling, but it must embody it in a form far beyond the reach of a child's power of expression,—in other words, in a form to give no less, or even more, vividness to the mere record of that feeling than the original feeling itself would have carried with it at the time it was present in all its force to the child's mind. Mr. Stevenson himself gives us ample opportunity of illustrating what we mean. Take, for example, [the] admirable little poem on the Wind. . . . That is not only a true poem, but a poem that expresses the child's wonder at the invisible force of the wind in words which, though simple enough, are far beyond the compass of a child's imagination. The burden, taken alone, is a whole world above the range of the child's thought. Again, the very form of the question,—

> O you that are so strong and cold,
> O blower, are you young or old?

is a form that would never occur to a child. He would never address the wind merely in the second person, nor without giving it the name of "wind" by which he knows it; and the mere fact of this direct address to an invisible and unknown power into the nature of which the questioner is inquiring, carries a sense of mystery which would excite the child's sense of wonder and lift him above the puerile level. Or, again, take [the] admirable little poem on a child's march to bed in the winter night, and notice how far beyond the child's power of expression is the verse, though it exactly touches the heart of an imaginative child's feeling. . . . What a force of vision there is in the lines:—

> All round the candle the crooked shadows come
> And go marching along up the stair.

How vividly that crookedness of the shadows, as they leaped from the wall to the ceiling, or from the floor to the wall, as the light changed its position, used to impress us as children, and yet how impossible it would have been for us to give to that half-shivering sense of the fearfulness of shadows, a voice so lively and yet so sensitive as this. Or, again, take [the] bright little picture of the advantages of birds over boys, conveyed in verses of almost birdlike simplicity and buoyancy. . . . What child could have written that? and, indeed, we may well ask what child could have written any sort of verse in which children would delight? What the child looks for to rouse his imagination, is some extension of his own experience, either in the direction of more living detail, or in the direction of a more buoyant imagination. No child would think of calling the songs of the birds "musical speeches;" and the very use of that expression widens his enjoyment of the bird's song, and brings it nearer to his heart. This is what Mr. Stevenson can do for the child when he will. But it is not by simply fitting a child's thought with rhymes that he can do it, but rather by fitting a child's feelings with wings. And when he does this he is delightful. For example, how he lifts the child's inarti-

culate thought into the heavens, when he sings of the dumb soldier whom the child is supposed to have buried in the grass:—

> He has seen the starry hours
> And the springing of the flowers;
> And the fairy things that pass
> In the forests of the grass.
>
> In the silence he has heard
> Talking bee and ladybird,
> And the butterfly has flown
> O'er him as he lay alone.
>
> Not a word will he disclose,
> Not a word of all he knows.
> I must lay him on the shelf,
> And make-up the tale myself.

But the child, though he might have made-up the tale himself, could never have made it up in that language of the heart which betrays the nice discernment at once what to say and what to omit. The child could never have spoken of "the forests of the grass," or have realised the lonely rapture of listening to "the talking-bee and ladybird," though that is what he might have tried dimly to express. No, Mr. Stevenson may be sure that those of his rhymes—and they are too many,—which a lively boy might have made, will never seize hold of children, while those of his poems which give the force of mature vision and emotion to childish feelings, will be as popular with children as even his romance of piracy itself. (pp. 382-83)

> *"Mr. R. L. Stevenson's Verse for Children," in* The Spectator, *Vol. 58, No. 2960, March 21, 1885, pp. 382-83.*

WILLIAM ARCHER

[*A Scottish dramatist and critic, Archer is best known as one of the earliest and most important translators of Henrik Ibsen's plays and as a drama critic of the London stage. In the November, 1885 issue of* Time, *Archer published "Robert Louis Stevenson: His Style and His Thought," an essay which is considered the first general assessment of Stevenson's work. In the following excerpt from Archer's review of* A Child's Garden of Verses *in the March 24, 1885 issue of the* Pall Mall Gazette, *he calls Stevenson "an artist in words, a man of alert, open-eyed sanity, . . . keenly alive to [childhood's] human grace and pathos, its fantastic gravity, its logical inconsequence, its exquisite egoism." Archer's comments prompted a letter of thanks from Stevenson, who wrote, "I am a man* blasé *to injudicious praise (though I hope some of it may be judicious too), but I have to thank you for THE BEST CRITICISM I EVER HAD; and am therefore, dear Mr. Archer, the most grateful critickee now extant."*]

The child is father to the man, and the Robert Louis Stevenson of to-day clearly takes after his father as figured for us in this delightful little book. It is autobiographical rather than dramatic. Mr. Stevenson does not attempt a many-sided view of child life, does not seek to depict varieties of child character, but sets himself to reflect the moods of one particular child, well known to him. He takes an Inland Voyage up the river of Memory, and sketches with his clear, crisp, vivid touch a few of his adventures and experiences. He draws with charming simplicity, yet in the selection of his subjects we trace the irony of self-conscious manhood, and here and there we find a touch in which the artist does not quite conceal his art. This is merely repeating in other words that he does not care to be consistently dramatic. 'These are my starry solitudes,' is a literary phrase, and so is

> I saw the dimpling river pass,
> And be the sky's blue looking-glass.
> [From **"Foreign Lands"**]

A child might conceivably say 'dimpled river,' or if the idea occurred to him at all would probably invent an adjective and say 'dimply;' but the participial epithet is a verse-writer's trick. Little disputable turns of this sort occur now and then; but, as Mr. Stevenson makes no professions, we can at worst maintain that they are inconsistent with his general practice.

In *Virginibus Puerisque* there is an essay on Child's Play which should be read as a preface to this booklet [see first excerpt above in Author's Commentary]. Its first line explains what many readers of the *Garden* must find noteworthy, if not absolutely strange, the persistent dwelling on the sunny aspect of childhood, with scarcely a hint of its night side. 'The regret we have for our childhood is not wholly justifiable,' says Mr. Stevenson, assuming as universal a feeling which in many minds is non-existent. He admits further on that 'innocence, no more than philosophy, can protect us from the sting of pain,' but this sting sends no discordant cries through his 'Songs of Innocence.' The child is the very same cheerful stoic whom we admire in the man—a philosopher who does not attempt to bring pain and evil into harmony with any system, but simply disregards and ignores them. On looking up a little poem which dwelt in our memory as illustrating this frame of mind, we find, curiously enough, that it is headed **"System"**:

> Every night my prayers I say,
> And get my dinner every day;
> And every day that I've been good
> I get an orange after food.
>
> The child that is not clean and neat,
> With lots of toys and things to eat,
> He is a naughty child, I'm sure—
> Or else his dear papa is poor.

That is enough; to inquire further were to inquire too curiously; a good child will be satisfied with proximate causes, and not rack his brains and worry his elders with questions as to the ultimate reasons of things. A few pages more and we come to the following **"Happy Thought"** into which is compressed the whole of Mr. Stevenson's gospel:—

> The world is so full of a number of things,
> I'm sure we should all be as happy as kings.

For the better enforcement of this maxim he has written several volumes which are not the least among the 'number of things' we Englishmen of to-day may be happy over. Were we not a perverse generation we should no doubt dance with a will to such resolutely cheerful piping; but, alas! even in this 'brave gymnasium, full of sea-bathing and horse exercise, and bracing, manly virtues,' the best we can do is to be about as happy—as kings.

Thoughts of Blake will inevitably intrude themselves upon readers of Mr. Stevenson's verses, but they should at once be banished as impertinent. The two men are on different planes. Their ends are different, their means are different. Blake is a poet who now and then rises to a poignant note beyond Mr. Stevenson's compass as it is above his ambition. Mr. Stevenson is a humourist and an artist in words, a man of alert, open-eyed sanity, unconcerned as to the mystery of childhood, but

keenly alive to its human grace and pathos, its fantastic gravity, its logical inconsequence, its exquisite egoism. Moreover, Mr. Stevenson's child, unlike Blake's children, is distinctly an agnostic. He says his prayers, but it is with no 'petitionary vehemence.' He does not seem even to indulge in the fetishism which is the first spiritual experience of so many children. It is the unhappy child who is a metaphysician, and is 'cradled into scepticism by wrong,' or into fetish worship, as the case may be. Mr. Stevenson knows nothing of the fierce rebellions, the agonized doubts as to the existence of justice, human or divine, which mar the music of childhood for so many; or if he realizes their existence, he relegates them to that other life, the life of pain, terror, and weariness, into which it is part of his philosophy to look as seldom as possible. . . . (pp. 155-57)

> William Archer, *"Unsigned Review, 'Pall Mall Gazette', March 1885,"* in Robert Louis Stevenson: The Critical Heritage, *edited by Paul Maixner, Routledge & Kegan Paul, 1981, pp. 154-57.*

H. C. BUNNER

It is rather hard, when once a man's youth has been renewed for him like the eagle's, and he has been led into green pastures such as cows and children only enjoy to the full—it is rather hard to snatch him back by the ear to this dull grown-up world,

Pencil sketch by Stevenson of his childhood nurse, Alison Cunningham ("Cummy"), to whom he dedicated A Child's Garden of Verses.

and to explain to him that it wasn't true after all, that he has only been making believe, under the guidance of an able adult magician—that he is no child, but a dull, mechanic, responsible man, and that he must sit down and write a notice commendatory of the skill of the able magician.

We know the magician of old. Under his spell we have seen the life of mediaeval France awaken for us, growing as warm, as real, as true, as—well, as our mosaic-working novelists and story-tellers don't make the life of to-day. And we have seen him turn this staid nineteenth century into a time of wild intrigue and mad adventure and high-hearted chivalry. . . .

But we never suspected that he had the power to unseal the tender springs of childhood's inborn poetry, and set them flowing in the sight of all men to tell to the world that secret which we each one of us, once upon a time, guarded so jealously: the secret of our dear playfellow who could not be seen or heard or felt of with our hands; but only be *thought* and *dreamed;* and whom, since then, we have learned to call Fancy. What a secret it was! It made the whole world glad and fair and desirable to us. And yet we scarcely dared whisper it to the older people, or even to the best of our comrades. You see, other people were likely to laugh, and nothing scared our playmate away like laughing at him.

But here is this Scotch magician making a child of himself for our benefit. And at first we look on, and smile at his childlike antics and oddities of expression, and say: ''How true! very accurate, indeed.'' And pretty soon we have ceased smiling and commenting, and before long we are children too, doing it all, thinking it all, being it all; and we know that it is true with a truth of which we do not often get glimpses. (p. 103)

We should all be grateful to our magician. But, like all true magicians, he has something more to do than merely to make us laugh and wonder. His art has a stronger hold on nature. Were he only the bright and clever man of talent, who does the bright and clever thing that a man may do with his talent, it would be easy enough to dismiss him with a hatful of thanks and compliments. But we who have read the half dozen books which he has given us must see clearly that we have to deal, not with talent, but with that strange and precious thing which we call genius. If he does no more than he has done—and he gives every sign and promise of doing more—Robert Louis Stevenson is one of these men whom we have to label with the name of genius. And the mission of genius, however it reveal itself, is sad at bottom. There is much in this book that we may teach to the children, at our side; there is much that we may smile over, remembering the childhood from which we grew; but there is also something there that hints of the stifled childhood in us that never grew up; something that touches us with a deep, half-understood, wholly unspeakable grief. (p. 104)

> *H. C. Bunner, ''Mr. Stevenson's Child's Verses,''*
> *in* The Book Buyer, *n.s. Vol. II, No. 4, May, 1885,*
> *pp. 103-04.*

EDMUND GOSSE

The *Child's Garden of Verses* has now been published long enough to enable us to make a calm consideration of its merits. When it was fresh, opinion was divided, as it always is about a new strong thing, between those who, in Mr. Longfellow's phrase about the little girl, think it very, very good, and those who think it is horrid. After reading the new book, the *Underwoods,* we come back to *A Child's Garden* with a clearer sense of the writer's intention, and a wider experience of his poetical outlook upon life. The later book helps us to comprehend the former; there is the same sincerity, the same buoyant simplicity, the same curiously candid and confidential attitude of mind. If any one doubted that Mr. Stevenson was putting his own childish memories into verse in the first book, all doubt must cease in reading the second book, where the experiences, although those of an adult, have exactly the same convincing air of candour. The first thing which struck the reader of *A Child's Garden* was the extraordinary clearness and precision with which the immature fancies of eager childhood were reproduced in it. People whose own childish memories had become very vague, and whose recollections of their games and dreams were hazy in the extreme, asked themselves how far this poet's visions were inspired by real memory and how far by invention. The new book sets that question at rest. (pp. 624-25)

We now perceive that it is not invention, but memory of an extraordinarily vivid kind, patiently directed to little things, and charged with imagination; and we turn back with increased interest to *A Child's Garden,* assured that it gives us a unique thing, a transcript of that child-mind which we have all possessed and enjoyed, but of which no one, except Mr. Stevenson, seems to have carried away a photograph. (p. 625)

Nothing is so hopelessly lost, so utterly volatile, as the fancies of our childhood. But Mr. Stevenson, alone amongst us all, appears to have kept daguerreotypes of the whole series of his childish sensations. Except the late Mrs. Ewing he seems to be without a rival in this branch of memory as applied to literature. (p. 626)

Many authors have achieved brilliant success in describing children, in verbally caressing them, in amusing, in instructing them; but only two, Mrs. Ewing in prose, and Mr. Stevenson in verse, have sat down with them without disturbing their fancies, and have looked into the world of 'make-believe' with the children's own eyes. If Victor Hugo should visit the nursery, every head of hair ought to be brushed, every pinafore be clean, and nurse must certainly be present, as well as mamma. But Mrs. Ewing or Mr. Stevenson might lead a long romp in the attic when nurse was out shopping, and not a child in the house should know that a grown-up person had been there. (p. 628)

> *Edmund Gosse, ''Mr. R. L. Stevenson as a Poet,''*
> *in* Longman's Magazine, *Vol. X, No. LX, October,*
> *1887, pp. 623-31.*

J. M. BARRIE

The key-note of all Mr. Stevenson's writings is his indifference, so far as his books are concerned, to the affairs of life and death on which their minds are chiefly set. Whether man has an immortal soul interests him as an artist not a whit: what is to come of man troubles him as little as where man came from. He is a warm, genial writer, yet this is so strange as to seem inhuman. His philosophy is that we are but as the lighthearted birds. This is our moment of being; let us play the intoxicating game of life beautifully, artistically, before we fall dead from the tree. We all know it is only in his books that Mr. Stevenson can live this life. The cry is to arms; spears glisten in the sun; see the brave bark riding joyously on the waves, the black flag, the dash of red color twisting round a mountain-side. Alas! the drummer lies on a couch beating his drum. It is a pathetic picture, less true to fact now, one rejoices to know, than it was recently. A common theory is that Mr. Stevenson dreams an ideal life to escape from his own sufferings. This sentimental plea suits very well. The noticeable thing, however, is that the grotesque, the uncanny, holds his soul; his brain will only follow a colored clew. The result is that he is chiefly picturesque, and, to those who want more than art for art's sake, never satisfying. Fascinating as his verses are, artless in the perfection of art, they take no reader a step forward. The children of whom he sings so sweetly are cherubs without souls. (pp. 123-24)

> *J. M. Barrie, "Robert Louis Stevenson," in his* An Edinburgh Eleven: Pencil Portraits from College Life, *Lovell, Coryell & Company, 1888, pp. 117-28.*

S. R. CROCKETT

[*A Scottish novelist and author of children's books, Crockett is perhaps best known for his historical romances* The Raiders *(1894) and* The Black Douglas *(1899) as well as for his juveniles* Sweetheart Travellers *(1895) and* Sir Toady Lion *(1897). Crockett admired Stevenson and dedicated* The Stickit Minister *(1893) to him; Stevenson returned the favor with his poem "To S. R. Crockett," which was posthumously published in 1896.*]

[When Mr. Stevenson] writes of himself, how supremely excellent is the reading. It is good even when he does it intentionally, as in *Portraits and Memories*. It is better still when he sings it, as in his *Child's Garden*. He is irresistible to every lonely child who reads and thrills, and reads again to find his past recovered for him with effortless ease. It is a book never long out of my hands, for only in it and in my dreams when I am touched with fever, do I grasp the long, long thoughts of a lonely child and a hill-wandering boy—thoughts I never told to any; yet which Mr. Stevenson tells over again to me as if he read them off a printed page. (p. 110)

> *S. R. Crockett, "Mr. Stevenson's Books," in* The Bookman, *London, Vol. VII, No. 40, January, 1895, pp. 109-11.*

THE SPECTATOR

We believe that the chief, perhaps the only, element of poetry which Mr. Stevenson lacks is that note of inevitability which all true poetry possesses,—the note which makes us understand what Milton meant when he spoke of—

> The Muse that lends
> Her nightly visitations unimplored;

or what was in Mr. Watson's mind when he speaks of the poet—

> Who finds, not fashions, his numbers.

It is this note of inevitability, again, which makes us feel that the exact thought, or rather mood, expressed by the poet has and could have no expression but in poetry,—that poetry alone would give the true emotional representation of the writer's thought. Now in neither respect do we meet with this inevitability in Mr. Stevenson's verse. We feel, to begin with, most distinctly that he has fashioned, not found, his verses, and indeed his inspiration. Still more do we find the lack of inevitability when we consider whether poetry alone could have given expression to the mood of the creator. Seldom, if ever, can we say that verse, and verse alone, could have been used to represent what he desired to represent. Mr. Stevenson's poetry could not, perhaps, have been expressed better in prose, but certainly as well. There is nothing that seems to proclaim it as poetry through and through, or as unthinkable in prose. Curiously enough, we see this even in Mr. Stevenson's most successful set of poems, *A Child's Garden of Verses*. The art

is charming, but it is not inevitable poetry, but merely an extraordinarily clever analysis of a child's mental attitude towards the external world set forth in a semi-dramatic form. A prose essay would not have done the work so originally, but still it could have done it. . . .

It is, indeed, a real relief to find the illustrations [by Mr. Charles Robinson] so pleasant, for the book is after all one of rare merit. To turn its pages was almost enough to make the present writer regret that he had assailed Mr. Stevenson's claim to be poet, and to retract all he had written. But, after all, poetry is poetry, and *A Child's Garden of Verses,* though it shows us the working of a child's mind by a delicious artifice of baby-rhymes, is not poetry, but merely very delicate criticism and analysis. *C'est magnifique, mais ce n'est pas la guerre.* Because we like poetry and because we like Mr. Stevenson's verse, we must not assume that they are one and the same thing. No; poetry is something different from all this. (p. 88)

> *"Mr. Stevenson's Poetry," in* The Spectator, *Vol. 76, No. 3525, January 18, 1896, pp. 87-8.*

E. V. LUCAS

How many of us there are who have been kept from the right attitude towards certain poems for no other reason than that in our young days we were incessantly called upon to learn or to admire them! If, however, we had been given a volume of verse of the kind we were ready to enjoy, which . . . had *stood for* poetry in our minds, we should have known no such barrier. Such a volume should entertain throughout—it should offer legend, narrative, and fun. It should be as gay as it could be made, compatible with technical excellency.

The Child's Anthology would not be easy to compile. On the other hand the editor setting about to prepare a book likely, by the emphasis which it laid upon the blessedness of the state of childhood, to turn mature thoughts very pleasantly, if somewhat regretfully, down the backward way, would find an abundance of fields in which to glean. And he would find, too, that several sources from which, at the first blush, one would think to borrow largely for the Child's Anthology are suitable only for the Grown-up's. There is, preeminently, Robert Louis Stevenson's *Child's Garden of Verses*. Only the other day no less a critic than Mr. Traill was remarking upon the gain to the British nursery afforded by this book, and yet our ideal editor for young readers would take not more than a mere sip from its pages. He would hold that it is not a child's book at all; he would hold that it is essentially matter for men and women, and is not to be opened until we are on the other and less delightful side of that phase of life of which it tells. To hand the book to children, he would say, and bid them learn it, is to manufacture so many second-hand Stevensons. Every child, more or less intelligently, does this kind of thing for itself, and in Heaven's name keep it original! *A Child's Garden of Verses,* however, may as well keep its reputation as a nursery classic, for it thus remains one of those books which parents buy for their children in order that they may read them themselves. Every Christmas there is a wave of such reflex generosity.

A Child's Garden of Verses is the ideal field for the Grown-up's harvester. It stands alone. There is nothing like it, so intimate, so simply truthful, in our language, in any language. Herein the poet . . . has accomplished that most difficult of feats: he has recaptured in maturity the thoughts, ambitions, purposes, hopes, fears, philosophy of the child. . . . It is our joy, as we listen, to recapture them too. To say "Such an one was I," "Just so did I behave," "I also hunted behind the sofa back.'' The man of genius who can draw from his charmed reader a genuine ''I also,'' is assured of a niche in the heart. The *Child's Garden of Verses* is one of those books which inspire the feeling—almost the passion—of gratitude. As we read our eyes are a little moist—with satisfaction. . . . As we read, years fall away, wrinkles are smoothed out, the envious crow removes his foot, world-knowledge so bitterly acquired evanesces, and once again the man is a child at play, and a bird is singing in his heart as of old.

I said just now that in reading these verses, we can exclaim ''I also.'' But that was a slight exaggeration. Only a very few readers could honestly say that, for the Stevenson child is a child of genius, removed from the ordinary child by a wide gulf. It is true that a philosopher has recorded his belief that every child has genius; but, even if that be so, there are degrees. It is given to few to possess the wisdom and imaginings of this little gardener. The difference between the child of genius and the ordinary child may be illustrated by quotation. The ordinary child, impelled to verse in the presence of a cow, remarks,

> Thank you, pretty cow, that made
> Pleasant milk to soak my bread,
> Every day and every night,
> Warm and sweet and fresh and white;

and so on. The child of genius says,

> The friendly cow, all red and white,
> I love with all my heart;
> She gives me cream with all her might,
> To eat with apple tart.

And take these lines, called **''System''** (noting what an advantage it is when child and man collaborate in a book about children—the child gives the essence and the man the titles):—

> Every night my prayers I say,
> And get my dinner every day,
> And every day that I've been good,
> I get an orange after food.
>
> The child that is not clean and neat,
> With lots of toys and things to eat,
> He is a naughty child, I'm sure!
> Or else his dear papa is poor.

The first seven lines might conceivably have been written by any average young rhymer. In the last—such a sweet reservation!—we have the child of genius again. And there is vision in this description of fairy land, as a place—

> Where all the children dine at five,
> And all the playthings come alive;

and in the thought as he launches his boats,

> Away down the river,
> A hundred miles or more,
> Other little children
> Shall bring my boats ashore

vision that would be impossible to the ordinary child. Similarly in this pronouncement on **''The Whole Duty of Children,''** the genius is in the last line:—

> A child should always say what's true,
> And speak when he is spoken to,
> And behave mannerly at table:
> At least as far as he is able.

But, with all deference to Mr. Traill, this is not food for young readers. The fact that Mr. Stevenson is always on the side of the nurses does not make him a writer for the nursery. To press poetry into the service of the disciplinarian is to mistake its function. What could be more delightful to read than this optimistic **''Thought,''** with its humorous vagueness—

> The world is so full of a number of things,
> I'm sure we should all be as happy as kings.

—and yet how disenchanting would it be to hear the sentiment uttered by one's own little son! These things should remain implicit in childhood; and when expressed, expressed by deeds, not words.

One reflection that occurs and recurs in childhood, and should be illustrated in the Grown-up's Anthology, finds no prominent place in Mr. Stevenson's pages: the unreason of grown-up people. The spectacle of their elders wasting their opportunities for enjoyment troubles most children. (pp. 393-95)

For the best make-believe poems, which would constitute a large section of the Grown-up's Anthology, we must go again to the *Child's Garden;* there the standard is once more set. Look, for example, at the **''Land of Story Books.''** (p. 395)

I cannot find anywhere else such intimate treatment of this side of child life. . . . [Mr. Stevenson] has had many imitators, but none of them have succeeded in capturing anything but the form. And among other writers of verse, who preceded him, or have made no conscious attempts to work on similar lines, none impresses and convinces as he. (p. 396)

> *E. V. Lucas, ''Some Notes on Poetry for Children,'' in* The Fortnightly Review, *n.s. Vol. LX, No. CCCLVII, September, 1896, pp. 391-407.*

EDMUND GOSSE

[*Child's Garden of Verses*] first made Stevenson known to the world as a poet and as a student of childhood. It is necessary to remind ourselves that twelve years ago Stevenson's name was not one to conjure with, as it is now. His friends were as timid as hens about this new experiment of their duckling's; they hesitated and doubted to the last. Nor was it only they who doubted. The poet himself had fearful qualms. . . .

The book, therefore, was somewhat timidly published; but there was no doubt about the authenticity of the voice, and Stevenson was accepted at once as one of the rare writers of genius about childhood. And then it was that Mr Swinburne chilled my blood by denying to the verses all appreciation of childhood! The explanation was, no doubt, that Mr Swinburne—whose rapture in the helpless charm of infancy is so marked that he cannot pass a cradle without peeping in, while the sirens sing for him behind the curtain of every wandering perambulator—felt at once that Stevenson had experienced nothing of this particular fascination of the genus Child. It is true, I think; Stevenson did experience nothing of it; but he possessed another and a still rarer quality. He retained, in extraordinary freshness, the memory of himself as a child. Most persons have a very vague recollection of what they themselves really felt and hoped for at the age of eight; they try to reproduce their impressions, and the experience of five mingles with that of fifteen. But Stevenson had no cloudiness of memory; he knew exactly what he had gone through. 'I remember,' he said, 'as though it were yesterday, the expansion of spirit, the dignity and self-reliance that came with a pair of moustachios in burnt cork, even when there was none to see' [see excerpt in Author's Commentary dated 1910]. He himself, as we soon divined, was the child whose emotions and adventures were described in the *Child's Garden of Verses.* But it was not so readily discovered that there was much of the grown-up Stevenson in some of those pretty confessions. Every one recollects and delights in **'The Land of Counterpane,'** which begins:

> When I was sick, and lay abed,
> I had two pillows at my head,
> And all my toys beside me lay
> To keep me happy all the day.

All this, we may say, is the imaginative experience of a sick child. But, to the very close of Stevenson's life, he was accustomed to make up adventures as he lay in bed very still, forbidden to speak or move, propped up on pillows, with the world of fancy before him. He had retained a great deal of the temperament of a child, and it was his philosophy to encourage it. In his dreary passages of bed, when his illness was more than commonly heavy upon him, he used to contrive little amusements for himself. He played on the flute, or he modelled little figures and groups in clay. But he could not always be doing this; and when his fingers were tired he lay gazing down on the white world which covered him, and imagined that armies were marching over the hills on his knees, or ships coming to anchor between the blanket and the sheet. Towards the end of his life he complained that he could not care any more about the Land of Counterpane; and to those who knew him best this seemed quite a serious sign of impaired vitality.

My conclusion, then, would be that, in the years I knew him, if Stevenson expressed much interest in children, it was mainly for the sake of their fathers and mothers; but that after a while he began to take a very great delight in summoning back to his clear recollection the panic fears and adventurous pleasures of his own early youth, thus becoming, in his portraiture of himself, the consummate painter of one species of child. (p. 451)

> *Edmund Gosse, "Stevenson's Relations with Children," in* Chamber's Journal, *Vol. II, No. 81, June 17, 1899, pp. 449-51.*

LLOYD OSBOURNE

[*An American novelist, playwright, and short story writer, Osbourne collaborated with Stevenson on three novels:* The Wrong Box *(1889),* The Wrecker *(1892), and* The Ebb-Tide *(1894). He was also Stevenson's stepson and the inspiration for* Treasure Island *(1883)* [see CLR, Vol. 10]. *As Osbourne notes in an unexcerpted portion of his 1901 introduction to* A Child's Garden of Verses, *critics often projected that Stevenson "gained his insight and appreciation into childhood by a constant contact with children, . . . listening to the confidences they were so ready to pour into his ear." In the following excerpt, Osbourne refutes this assumption and definitely identifies Stevenson as the subject and narrator of* A Child's Garden of Verses, *noting that "it is in this extraordinarily exact recollection of his childhood that we find the most compelling proof of his genius."*]

The child of the *Child's Garden* was Stevenson himself. The plays were his plays; the dreams were his dreams; the fears and fantasies were all his own. It is in this extraordinarily exact recollection of his childhood that we find the most compelling proof of his genius. We have all been children, but how few of us can recall our infancy with the intensity, the passion, the exquisite humor and pathos of Stevenson! We are reminded in every line of what each one of us has long ago forgotten. We live again in the world of make-believe—of bears and pirates, Indians, hunters and privateers. We tremble and we laugh with the inconsequent acceptance of all that comes, whether perishing in the wreck or glorying in sausages for tea. (pp. xiii-xiv)

> *Lloyd Osbourne, in an introduction to* A Child's Garden of Verses *by Robert Louis Stevenson, Charles Scribner's Sons, 1901, pp. xi-xxiv.*

H. BELLYSE BAILDON

This book has the enormous advantage of being unique, so far as I know, in English literature. There are enough of verses *for* children and *about* children, but none that represent childhood so accurately, as seen from the adult standpoint, and yet still perfectly remembered and understood. Reading this book we live our childhood over again. The child-psychology is so startlingly exact, that it brings back to us much that we had otherwise forgotten and lost. We see again our own tiny figure in short frocks, and, with a delicate humour and exquisite regret, we ourselves re-enact the joys and sorrows of child-life. . . . Stevenson retained much of the child in his nature; his recollections of his childhood seem miraculously lucid and sharp, and he positively never lapses from childish *naïveté.* Stevenson is always, in the best sense of the word, an impressionist. That is, he draws things, not as he knows them to be on reflection, but as they appear to him, and that is the method of a child. Here, for instance, is an excellent piece of impressionism:—

> The Dog and the Plough, and the Hunter and all,
> And the star of the sailor, and Mars.
> These shone in the sky, and *the pail by the wall*
> *Would be half full of water and stars.*

To the child the stars in the bucket are as real as the stars in the sky, and this is impressionism, to render a thing just as it appears to the senses, and it is this quality in Stevenson that often gives his descriptive touches such startling force and vividness. (pp. 116-17)

> *H. Bellyse Baildon, in his* Robert Louis Stevenson: A Life Study in Criticism, *A. Wessels Company, 1901, 244 p.*

LAFCADIO HEARN

[*Considered one of modern America's leading prose impressionists, Hearn was a short story and novella writer, critic, essayist, journalist, and translator. His essays on Japanese culture, such as* Glimpses of Unfamiliar Japan, Out of the East, *and* Kokoro, *are recognized as having influenced Western perceptions of the Orient. Also a teacher, Hearn was a professor of the history of English literature at the University of Tokyo. The following excerpt is taken from a lecture written down by one of Hearn's students between September 1900 and March 1903 and given here without any revision from Hearn himself.*]

[Stevenson] did not have the art of poetry to any marked degree. His *Songs of Travel* will not live. But his *Child's Garden of Verses* is likely to live for a very long time—not because it is even good poetry as to form, but because it possesses the same qualities of truth to nature and beautiful but simple feeling which distinguishes his other imaginative work. For instance, consider those verses of **"The Wind":—**

> I saw you toss the kites on high,
> And blow the birds about the sky;
> And all around I heard you pass,
> Like ladies' skirts across the grass. . . .
>
> I saw the different things you did;
> But always you yourself you hid:
> I felt you push, I heard you call;

I could not see yourself at all—
    O wind, a-blowing all day long,
    O wind, that sings so loud a song!

Now this may not be poetry, as form goes; but it represents exactly what a child feels, when he first begins to think about the mysterious and ghostly thing which we call wind. He hears it; he feels it push him—and yet he never can see it. Is it a ghost?—or an animal?—or what is it? There are many charming things like this in the *Child's Garden of Verses* which can not die. (pp. 790-91)

> *Lafcadio Hearn, "Victorian Fiction," in his* A History of English Literature in a Series of Lectures, *Vol. II, edited by R. Tanabe and T. Ochiai, The Hokuseido Press, 1927, pp. 735-809.*

FRANK SWINNERTON

[*Swinnerton was an English novelist and critic whose* R. L. Stevenson: A Critical Study *(1914) is recognized as perhaps the best and most controversial twentieth-century criticism on Stevenson. After the book's publication, fewer critics defined Stevenson as a major writer. In the following excerpt, however, Swinnerton calls* A Child's Garden of Verses *"a secondary nursery classic."*]

In *A Child's Garden of Verses* Stevenson was doing a thing which had never really been done before. There are nursery rhymes which crystallise children's ideas; but this book actually shows, in what we must believe to be an extraordinarily happy way, the working of a particular child mind over a great variety of matters. Its excellence is due to the fact that Stevenson's young days, lonely as some of them had been, had never lacked interest, had always been full of those simple and direct pleasures of incident and encounter and memory which happy children enjoy. The world had been full of a number of things; and the memory of those things had abided. It was the memory of a fanciful rather than an imaginative childhood, a childhood of superstitions and sports, of a buried tin soldier and of the pleasant land of play; but we must not forget that such poems as **"My Treasures"**, poor in some of their lines, are finely imaginative reconstructions, the naïveté of which prevents many readers from estimating their quality. So with **"The Unseen Playmate"**, which, although it is a poem for grown-ups, reveals an understanding of a most important fact in children's games far more profound than are the pretentious and unconvincing lines to R. A. M. Stevenson in *Underwoods*. Even if the idea of **"The Unseen Playmate"** may be the idea of a grown-up pretending, the writing of this, as of the other verses, is almost without lapse, charmingly simple and natural. I believe it is a fact that children appreciate and even delight in *A Child's Garden of Verses,* not merely at the bidding of their parents, but as a normal manifestation of taste. This in itself would be a proof that the book is already a secondary nursery classic. For our present purpose, if that does not seem rather an overbearing way of valuing a book so slight in form, it is sufficient to say that Stevenson's success here was due to the fact that he was legitimately using the memory of actual experience. Too many of his serious, or grown-up, poems show their models; too many of them flow undistinguished by any truly poetic quality; too many of them are experiments in metre or rhyme, such as one may write for fun, but never for free circulation. The *Child's Garden of Verses* alone . . . exhibits a strict harmony of design with performance. Its dedication to Stevenson's nurse, Alison Cunningham, serves only to make the book more complete. (pp. 97-8)

Frank Swinnerton, in his R. L. Stevenson: A Critical Study, *1914. Reprint by Mitchell Kennerley, 1915, 215 p.*

ALFRED NOYES

In the *Child's Garden of Verses* we have a perfect example . . . of how the poet can use small things to symbolize and shadow forth greater things. We find him there selecting the very simplest and clearest and best words; toiling, like his own monkish scribe, to give his thought just that lucidity which at last reflects, like a mountain-pool, a corner of blue heaven. But because there is no sign of effort, it is supposed by the unintelligent to be achieved without pains, and because it is so crystal-clear that it takes the infinite to its heart, it is supposed by turbid and shallow minds to be without any depth at all.

It may at first appear that the little poem with which he opens the *Child's Garden* is but a very small pail of clear water:

> I have to go to bed and see
> The birds still hopping on the tree,
> Or hear the grown-up people's feet
> Still going past me in the street.

I do not want to touch it with any more significance than it will bear; but does not a star begin to be reflected, faintly and tremulously, in that small pail of clear water when it is recalled that Tusitala himself was destined to leave, a little early, the life and the art that he loved so well.

> And does it not seem hard to you,
> When all the sky is clear and blue,
> And I should like so much to play,
> To have to go to bed by day?

It is clear enough that much is represented in little by the shadow-march of the **"North-West Passage"**. It is familiar enough as a child's poem. Consider it, for a moment, from our own point of view, here in a little lighted room, on a little planet, flying through the immensities of the universe:

> All round the house is the jet-black night,
>   It stares through the window-pane;
> It crawls in the corners, hiding from the light,
>   And it moves with the moving flame.
>
> Now my little heart goes a-beating like a drum
>   With the breath of the Bogie in my hair;
> And all round the candle the crookéd shadows come
>   And go marching along up the stair.
>
> The shadow of the balusters, the shadow of the lamp,
>   The shadow of the child that goes to bed—
> All the wicked shadows coming, tramp—tramp—tramp,
>   With the black night overhead.

The book is full of good-nights and good-byes. The Unseen Playmate is in it; and there is even—so great is the magic of its art—a reduction to its very simplest terms of the greatest of all political problems. Half the wars of the world would have been avoided if, in our individual lives and in our national lives, we all fully understood the exquisite elfin satire of one poem in the *Child's Garden of Verses*—the poem on foreign children. . . . (pp. 107-08)

There is all the pathos of human aspiration, I had almost said the pathos of human religion, in the last stanza of **"The Lamplighter"**, which deliberately in its first line adopts the fallacy which Voltaire satirized in *Candide,* and deliberately uses in

The Manse at Colinton, Scotland. Owned by Stevenson's grandfather, the Reverend Lewis Balfour, the Manse included the original "child's garden" which Stevenson later immortalized. Until he was ten, Stevenson spent his summer holidays here playing with his cousins, who figure in several of the verses.

its last line a cadence that, delicately as it is touched in, has unmistakable undertones:

> For we are very lucky, with a lamp before the door,
> And Leerie stops to light it as he lights so many more;
> And oh! before you hurry by with ladder and with light,
> O Leerie, see a little child and nod to him to-night.

These child-poems, in fact, illustrate Stevenson's peculiar gift of self-limitation. He writes always like a man who is telling tales to children. Sometimes it is a kind of self-parody, masking behind a half-smile the more serious thoughts that he would hesitate to wear upon his sleeve. (p. 109)

> Alfred Noyes, "Stevenson," in his Some Aspects of Modern Poetry, *Frederick A. Stokes Company, 1924, pp. 96-117.*

H. W. GARROD

A good many people, I know, are offended, in [Stevenson's] poetry, by nothing so much as by what they feel to be its *pretended* naturalness. I think them stupid; but I so far follow them that I recognize the degree to which a particular kind of make-believe colours all Stevenson's poetry. I am not thinking merely of the *Child's Garden of Verses*. No doubt, a Child's Garden of Verses would be best made by children, if children

could make as good verses as grown-up people. But they cannot; and the pretended naturalness of the *Child's Garden* has no greater element of pretence than accompanies any other attempt at communication between grown-ups and children. This genre Stevenson created; whether a valid and enduring one, I am not sure. At least he is as successful in it as his imitators. The *Child's Garden of Verses* was his first book of verse; and here at least his genius for make-believe exercises itself without offence. But I have the suspicion that the book could have been written only by some one who had first learned to be a child late in life; that in it Stevenson is, in fact, trying to recapture a nature from which circumstance had excluded him. He was an ailing child; and from an ailing childhood he passed to an ailing boyhood, youth, and manhood. For children, boys, young men, pirates, soldiers, and sailors, for all naturally healthy life, Stevenson had an affection the more real because, in each successive stage of his own development, the body plucked him back from the desire of the mind. When he dramatizes these characters, or some of them, in his novels, he does well with them. But in his poetry, which is rarely impersonal, his preoccupation with this kind of life takes, often, a strained expression. Loving it intensely, he can recapture it only by indulging the same kind of make-believe speech and sentiment as he employs to capture childhood in the *Child's*

Garden. The world of all his poetry becomes something of a garden-world, accordingly, and is to that extent, and in that sense, a sham world. . . . A sham optimist he was; and it is only one of a number of shams. He shammed happy; he shammed well; he shammed young and piratical; he shammed the natural man. But it is all the shamming of a heroical invalidism; and as such gains, perhaps, in poetry, as much as it loses, by being found out. (pp. 184-85)

H. W. Garrod, "The Poetry of R. L. Stevenson," in his The Profession of Poetry and Other Lectures, *Oxford at the Clarendon Press, Oxford, 1929, pp. 179-93.*

MAY HILL ARBUTHNOT

There was nothing comparable to these verses when they were written, no literary precedents, even though Stevenson himself said that the idea for his book came to him while he was glancing over one of Kate Greenaway's little books. *A Child's Garden of Verses* goes far beyond Greenaway at her best, both in its reflection of the child's point of view and in its poetry. (p. 106)

Not all these poems are for children; a few of them are merely about children or are adult reminiscences of childhood. Such poems creep into almost every collection of juvenile poetry but are nevertheless to be avoided; for example, Stevenson's **"Keepsake Mill," "Whole Duty of Children,"** and the rarely included **"To Any Reader"** and **"To Willie and Henrietta."**

With these exceptions, no careful reading of the poems can fail to leave you impressed with the author's genuine understanding of children. . . . His children get up shivering with cold on winter mornings; they yearn to travel; they discover the sea miraculously filling up their holes on the beach; they struggle with table manners; they have a deep respect for "System," an orderly world; they enjoy good days and bad ones, mostly good; they can't understand why the gardener doesn't want "to play at Indian wars" with them; they watch for the lamplighter; they wonder why they can't see the wind; and they enjoy a world of play and a world of the imagination as well. Children's interest in tiny things is found not only in **"The Little Land"** but over and over again in other verses. Here are real children, many-sided and with many interests.

Especially true to child life are the poems involving dramatic play. Imagination transfers a clothes basket into a boat. Climbing up in the cherry tree, the child glimpses not merely the next-door garden but foreign lands and even fairyland. . . . The poems bristle with the properties and imaginative transformations of that arch magician, the child of about four to seven years old.

People have complained that this child of the *Verses* is a solitary child, and they have read into the poems some of the pathos of the sick Louis. But if you study these verses, you will find several children playing pirates in the **"Pirate Story"**; building ships together in **"A Good Play"**; being "mountaineers" in **"The Hayloft"**; crawling "through the breach in the wall of the garden" to **"Keepsake Mill"**; tramping round the village in the **"Marching Song"** with Johnnie, Willie, Peter, and "great commander Jane"; and in **"Northwest Passage,"** facing together the "long black passage up to bed." These give us a fair proportion of other children and of social play. They emphasize also the healthy, normal play activities of healthy children. Nothing of the invalid here!

Perhaps the largest group of poems under a single general classification is made up of those concerned with night. What an imaginative group it is, and sometimes scary too: **"Young Night Thought," "My Bed Is a Boat," "The Land of Story-Books," "Night and Day," "The Moon," "Windy Nights," "Shadow March," "The Land of Nod," "Escape at Bedtime," "Good-Night,"** and **"In Port."** Of these, **"Escape at Bedtime"** is one of the most interesting because of its glimpse of starry skies. . . . There are two poems in this night group which are also notable for their rhythm. **"Shadow March"** has as perfect marching time as any music by Sousa, but it is an eerie, frightening march of bogies and shadows, not to be used before the children are seven or eight years old and stout enough to stand it. Less scary and still finer is that pounding gallop called [**"Windy Nights"**:]

Whenever the moon and stars are set,
  Whenever the wind is high,*
All night long in the dark and wet,
  A man goes riding by.*
Late in the night when the fires are out,
Why does he gallop and gallop about?*

Whenever the trees are crying aloud,
  And ships are tossed at sea,*
By, on the highway, low and loud,
  By at the gallop goes he;*
By at the gallop he goes, and then
By he comes back at the gallop again.*

Keep on saying "the gallop again, the gallop again, by he comes back at the gallop again," and you will feel yourself galloping, too. Notice in the starred lines the silent beat after the last word exactly like a rest in music. This probably calls for a little explanation. Read the poem aloud, tapping the meter with your finger, just as a metronome beats out the time of music. You discover the silent beat immediately, and you discover also how it enhances the galloping rhythm, even though you were unconscious of it. **"Windy Nights"** is a masterly bit of music-with-words, fine enough for older children to say in verse choirs and for any child to enjoy recalling when, snug in his bed, he listens to a great storm that sets the trees to "crying aloud."

Another fine example of the use of rhythm to suggest the subject is **"From a Railway Carriage."** Notice that the verse has the tempo and the driving speed of the train. (pp. 107-09)

These examples of rhythm illustrate another of the outstanding qualities in Stevenson's *Child's Garden of Verses:* the poems are markedly lyrical. Of course, numbers of them have been set to music, but they sing anyway, without benefit of notes. Take the concluding line of **"A Good Boy":** "And hear the thrushes singing in the lilacs round the lawn." It does sing, doesn't it? Or read the familiar [**"Singing"**]. . . . Or listen to the refrain in [**"The Wind"**]. . . . Go through page after page of these poems and you'll find them singing in your memory with their own melody. One of the most lyrical of them all is [**"Where Go the Boats?"**:]

Dark brown is the river,
  Golden is the sand.
It flows along forever,
  With trees on either hand.

Green leaves a-floating,
  Castles of the foam,

Boats of mine a-boating—
  Where will all come home?

On goes the river
  And out past the mill,
Away down the valley,
  Away down the hill.

Away down the river,
  A hundred miles or more,
Other little children
  Shall bring my boats ashore.

Notice the slow, smooth-flowing melody of the first two verses, like the flow of the river. In the third verse, the repetition of "Away" gives an impetus to the lines as if the current were really flowing faster and carrying the boats farther until, abruptly, as if in a little eddy, the boats come to anchor in the last two lines. Except that the poem has no gaiety, the smooth glide of the lines suggests the flowing melody of "The Moldau," by Smetana.

Stevenson was evidently fond of the poem pattern which seems to begin close at hand and go farther and farther away. He uses it again effectively in ["Foreign Lands"]. . . . In this, the child's vision is limited at first to the next-door gardens, but it widens until he glimpses, imaginatively, the sea and the magic road to fairyland. (pp. 110-11)

Although teachers and mothers who were raised on *A Child's Garden of Verses* may feel that the verses are overfamiliar, they must not forget that these poems are new to each generation of children. **"The Cow," "My Shadow," "The Swing," "Winter-time,"** and **"Time to Rise,"** in addition to the verses already quoted, are perennial favorites, and children should not miss them. New poets of childhood may make their contributions, but Robert Louis Stevenson has left to young children a legacy of small lyrics, just their size. (p. 111)

> *May Hill Arbuthnot, "Poetry of the Child's World," in her* Children and Books, *Scott, Foresman and Company, 1947, pp. 100-30.**

DAVID DAICHES

[*An English-born Scottish critic and educator, Daiches is considered a pioneer in reassessing Stevenson's life and career following the relative critical neglect caused by Frank Swinnerton's* R. L. Stevenson: A Critical Study *(1914) [see excerpt dated 1923]. Daiches is often credited with sparking a renewed interest in Stevenson and a more positive approach to his work. In the following excerpt, Daiches discusses the background and themes of* A Child's Garden of Verses.]

The poems of *A Child's Garden of Verses* are almost all attempts to capture some particular and clearly remembered childhood mood or scene, and their effectiveness depends on the extent to which they succeed in doing this. The idea was suggested by Kate Greenaway's *Birthday Book for Children,* but Stevenson's essentially autobiographical poems draw their real inspiration from his own memories. The childhood moods expressed in the poems are fairly limited in number; the same ones recur frequently, establishing principal *motifs* which run through the collection. And the scenes familiar to his childhood similarly recur, though not mentioned by name—the garden of his grandfather's manse at Colinton, his parents' house at 17 Heriot Row, and the cottage at Swanston; and all the sights and sounds of the Edinburgh of the late 1850's and early 1860's.

Stevenson was a sickly child, and as he lay in bed with one of his numerous childhood illnesses he would be forced to

depend largely on his imagination for his entertainment. **"The Land of Counterpane"** was all too familiar to him, and the imaginative qualities which this familiarity helped him to cultivate stood him in good stead throughout his childhood and beyond. All his daily activities as a small boy were transmuted into significant and exciting episodes. Travel was a theme that haunted him continually: the river flowing on through unvisited regions to the sea; the road winding away into the unknown—these are recurring symbols, so that even his bed becomes a boat in which to sail away to foreign parts. . . . (pp. 174-75)

This travel theme is found again and again in *A Child's Garden of Verses.* We see it in one of its more elemental forms in **"Foreign Lands":**

Up into the cherry tree
Who should climb but little me?
I held the trunk with both my hands
And looked abroad on foreign lands. . . .

I saw the dimpling river pass
And be the sky's blue looking-glass;
The dusty roads go up and down
With people tramping into town.

And then the child's ambition:

If I could find a higher tree
Farther and farther I should see,
To where the grown-up river slips
Into the sea among the ships. . . .

The simple metrical scheme and the straightforward, concrete imagery convey with great purity the child's view of the world and its activities. We see it again when he writes of sailing paper boats down the stream. . . . (p. 176)

The sense of the world's diversity, the exciting realization of the fact that at any given moment all sorts of different things are happening in all sorts of different places, was continually impressing [Stevenson] as a child. . . . (p. 177)

The idea of a map as the symbol of travel and adventure, which Stevenson used so effectively in *Treasure Island,* underlies many of these poems. The countryside as seen from a tree-top, the thin line of the river winding its way through ever further off places into the distant sea, is a favourite image: we hardly need Stevenson's use of the balloon in *St. Ives* to remind us that had he lived in the age of aviation he would have delighted in the idea of the countryside as viewed from an airplane. (pp. 177-78)

The theme of adventure is naturally closely linked to that of travel:

Where shall we adventure, to-day that we're afloat,
  Wary of the weather and steering by a star?
Will it be to Africa, a-steering of the boat,
  To Providence, or Babylon, or off to Malabar?

Occasionally a note of adult sophistication creeps into the travel poems:

I should like to rise and go
Where the golden apples grow. . . .

but more often the childhood attitude is remembered and captured:

We built a ship upon the stairs
All made of the back-bedroom chairs,

And filled it full of sofa pillows
To go a-sailing on the billows.

We took a saw and several nails,
And water in the nursery pails;
And Tom said, "Let us also take
An apple and a slice of cake;"—
Which was enough for Tom and me
To go a-sailing on, till tea.

To be at home and yet to enjoy the thrill of travel—this was one of the ideals of Stevenson's childhood. . . . **"From a Railway Carriage,"** describing an experience which neatly combines comfort with adventure, is thus a poem of particular interest. The child sits still and is carried through the map. (pp. 178-79)

Throughout these poems can be found the sights and sounds of the Edinburgh of Stevenson's childhood, as they impinged on the mind of a child. In the summer time, it is the trees and flowers of Colinton Manse and the long light evenings when "I have to go to bed by day." In the winter, it is the warm fireside interior contrasted with the chill dark outside; the lamplighter going on his rounds as the early dusk descends; the indistinct sound of grown-ups talking by the lamplight as the child lies in bed upstairs or hunts imaginary wild animals behind the sofa; the howling wind racing round the city on a stormy night. Stevenson was very sensitive to the changes the different seasons brought to his native city: the two extremes were the sunny "garden days" of mid-summer and the cosy winter interiors:

Sing a song of seasons!
Something bright in all!
Flowers in the summer,
Fires in the fall!

The poems of the **Garden** show an equal lingering over the garden days of summer and the "happy chimney-corner days" of winter: there is "something bright in all" the seasons, and always in describing them he emphasizes specific images drawn from his own childhood memories:

The lamps now glitter down the street;
Faintly sound the falling feet;
And the blue even slowly falls
About the garden trees and walls.

Now in the falling of the gloom
The red fire paints the empty room:
And warmly on the roof it looks,
And flickers on the backs of books.

This is in the true Scottish poetic tradition: Henryson, Dunbar, Fergusson and Burns all excelled in the painting of interiors, and though Stevenson has not the technical skill or the intense poetic imagination of his predecessors, confining himself as he does to the deliberately restricted area of childhood reminiscence, it is impossible not to be struck by this general resemblance. . . . Family resemblance that runs through all these Scottish poets, so different though they are in so many fundamental respects, must be attributed, perhaps, to the northern climate, which emphasizes the difference between the comfortable fireside within and the bleak weather outside. Like Stevenson's, theirs is the poetry of people who live indoors most of the year, and in whose life the contrast between interiors and exteriors is constantly being driven home. Only Stevenson, whose Colinton days gave him the opportunity to enjoy to the full the brief but memorable outdoor life that a Scottish summer makes possible, adds to these traditional themes that of the wild Edinburgh garden, with all its opportunities for childhood adventure. Later, the moorland and the seacoast were to provide very different open-air experiences, which left their mark on much of his fiction.

The **Child's Garden** thus represents a deliberate attempt on Stevenson's part to recapture the sights, sounds and emotions of his childhood, made at the time when the peace he had finally achieved with his family sent him back to explore those recollections which hitherto he had, in some degree, been forced to suppress. The atmosphere of his early home life, the affectionate care of his nurse Alison Cunningham, . . . and above all the essential quality of the city in which he grew up, are all to be found here. Stevenson was perfectly conscious of the nature of his achievement in these poems. They were written, as he said in the "envoy" addressed to his mother, "for love of unforgotten times." And behind all the poems lies the poignant sense of days of innocence for ever over:

But do not think you can at all,
By knocking on the window, call
That child to hear you. He intent
Is all on his play-business bent.
He does not hear; he will not look,
Nor yet be lured out of this book.
For long ago, the truth to say,
He has grown up and gone away,
And it is but a child of air
That lingers in the garden there.

(pp. 179-82)

The morality of these poems is the somewhat prim morality a child will adopt in those rare moments when, self-satisfied and at peace with his environment, he indulges in a complacent feeling of virtue. Stevenson, affectionately reconciled with his family after a long series of unhappy crises, sees himself as the little boy who has decided to be good. There is thus a "goody-goody" note in many of these poems which sounds hypocritical, but which in fact represents fairly accurately, though in a deliberately simplified form, Stevenson's mood when he began working on the collection:

It is very nice to think
The world is full of meat and drink,
With little children saying grace
In every Christian kind of place.

And yet the underlying emotion of these verses is an adult one, deriving from adult reminiscence. Anyone who compares the **Garden** with its twentieth century English counterpart—A. A. Milne's *When We Were Very Young* and *Now We Are Six*—will notice this at once. Except for the occasional intrusion of a sophisticated note when dealing with the world of nature. . . . Milne's poems seem to derive almost entirely from interested observation of a child's behavior and moods, not, as with Stevenson, from passionately retained personal recollection.

The versification in the **Child's Garden** is technically quite accomplished, though on a fairly simple level. Short, simply constructed stanzas, alternating or couplet rhymes, lines varying in length to correspond in a fairly direct way with the nature of the subject—these features enable Stevenson to cope adequately with his subject-matter and at the same time keep all the poetic devices on a level at which they can be readily appreciated by a young reader. The book is, in fact, first-rate children's poetry—that is, poetry which uses the devices of the poet naively, not sentimentally or corruptly. Good children's poetry is distinguished from bad by the avoidance of sentimental clichés which so many writers of children's verses seem to consider essential to this species of writing, and is distinguished from adult poetry by its use on a lower or simpler level of the techniques employed with greater subtlety in "full-grown" literature. The underlying emotion which we have noted in Stevenson's poems of childhood is not noticeable as an adult sophistication depriving the poems of their simplicity; it acts as a sort of cohesive agent, giving form and unity to the individual poems and to the collection as a whole, and thus adds to, rather than detracts from, the effective presentation of the theme. (pp. 182-84)

David Daiches, in his Robert Louis Stevenson, *New Directions Books, 1947, 196 p.*

DENNIS BUTTS

Stevenson's genius lies in his ability to interpret, in simple terms, childhood's moods: and many are autobiographical. . . . It was Stevenson's peculiar achievement to evoke the sights and sounds of his childhood [at Colinton Manse] or in Edinburgh in summer and winter, outdoors and indoors, with almost total recall. More than this, Stevenson actualises with great realism not merely the nature of the experiences, but the effect of them upon the mind of a young child. **'My Shadow,' 'Bed in Summer,' 'The Lamplighter', 'The Swing,** and **'From a Railway Carriage'** are all good examples of this group of poems, of which **'The Hayloft'** may be taken as representative:

> Through all the pleasant meadow-side
> The grass grew shoulder-high,
> Till the shining scythes went far and wide
> And cut it down to dry.
>
> These green and sweetly smelling drops
> They led in waggons home;
> And they piled them here in mountain tops
> For mountaineers to roam.
>
> Here is Mount Clear, Mount Rusty-Nail,
> Mount Eagle and Mount High;—
> The mice that in these mountains dwell,
> No happier are than I!
>
> O what a joy to clamber there,
> O what a place to play,
> With the sweet, the dim, the dusty air,
> The happy hills of hay.

If we find the note of happiness a little self-conscious at the close here, it is as well to set against that the real achievement of the poem, the fastidiousness with which the visual and olfactory senses are stirred ('shining', 'green', 'dim', 'dusty'), the delicately-poised metaphor of 'drops of hay', and the imaginative extension in the third verse which successfully recreates a new and wholesome experience. The atmosphere is so definite and infectious that the adult reader even today, when hay is seldom scythed or carted loose and even if he has never been in a hayloft, is forced to recall from his own childhood some similarly happy summer's day.

It may be, however, that Stevenson's most lasting success as a children's poet will come from his ability to show how naturally a young child uses creative imagination in what is called 'play'. The number of poems he wrote about this theme, **'Young Night Thoughts', 'Pirate Story', 'Foreign Lands', 'The Land of Counterpane', 'Marching Song', 'My Bed is a Boat',** is considerable, and they as readily evoke the *imaginative* ex-

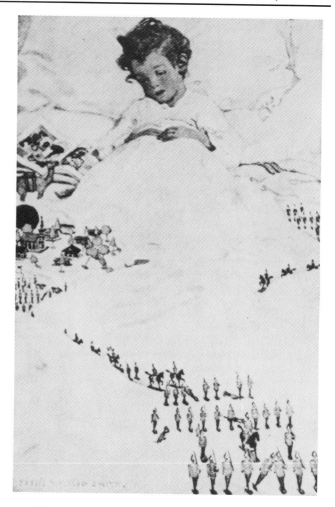

"The Land of Counterpane." Illustration by Jessie Wilcox Smith for the 1905 Scribners edition of A Child's Garden of Verses. *An American artist, Smith created paintings that are among the most beloved representations of Stevenson's poems.*

periences of children as elsewhere Stevenson interprets their *real* observations and experiences. (pp. 48-50)

Dennis Butts, in his R. L. Stevenson, *Henry Z. Walck, Incorporated, 1966, 72 p.*

ANNE THAXTER EATON

[*A Child's Garden of Verses*] was poetry that children read or heard or repeated for pleasure, because it told of the things that were nearest them, it appealed to their instinctive taste, the poet realizing that the unspoiled child was himself poetic. That children at once and for all time took this book to their hearts is a proof of the understanding of this great children's poet.

If we look into the matter more deeply, if we ask why adults also get so much from it, we see that the power of this collection of simple verses lies in the fact that it offers, not a glimpse, but the whole contour of the child's hidden world. It shows the life that a child lives within himself and takes so completely for granted that he seldom speaks of it, usually because he cannot. In later days he recollects brief moments of sharp impression, he responds gratefully to anything which reminds him of that which he had forgotten. Stevenson has here recaptured not only a part, but the whole of that hidden life, and has set those recollections forth in just the terms that children would use, could they put them into words at all. Here are the quaint conceits and errors, the imaginative interpretation of that region which is beyond their experience, all the unquestioning philosophy that has to do with home and parents and "being good." Not only the interesting and, when one is once reminded of them, the entirely familiar recollections are here: "In winter I get up at night," "My bed is like a little boat," "I have a little shadow that goes in and out with me." There is also that deeper experience which reaches into the invented world of adventure which every child must have. (p. 270)

Or we have the world of wonder about him. . . .

A child's imaginings not only explore the whole of his experience and beyond, they are creative also; wherever there is a need, imagination can fill it. . . . Last of all, to make the round complete, there is the child's simplified version of the knowledge that there is full partnership between duty and happiness. (p. 271)

That which so many other children's poets have tried to reach and rediscover, Stevenson has brought together in its entirety and has presented us with his small but perfect nosegay gathered in the child's own garden. (p. 272)

> *Anne Thaxter Eaton, "Poetry for Children in the Nineteenth Century," in* A Critical History of Children's Literature *by Cornelia Meigs, Anne Thaxter Eaton, Elizabeth Nesbitt, and Ruth Hill Viguers, edited by Cornelia Meigs, revised edition, Macmillan Company, 1969, pp. 263-72.**

EDWIN MORGAN

[*The following excerpt is taken from a lecture given in 1970.*]

Parents and children are . . . not an unexpected theme to find in Stevenson, and the poems in *A Child's Garden of Verses* . . . fit very well into his preoccupations. They have been described as about rather than for children, though some children do like them. Reading them today, one can see them as looking straight forward to Ian Hamilton Finlay, who has many affinities with Stevenson's period and whose pre-concrete poems particularly have many of the same qualities as *A Child's Garden of Verses*. I am thinking especially of Stevenson's **'My Bed is a Boat'**, **'The Lamplighter'**, **'The Cow'**, **'Singing'**, and **'Rain'**, all of which have not only the sort of subjects Mr. Finlay likes but also the same not-quite-innocent eye asking us humorously and gently to look at simple things.

> The rain is raining all around,
> It falls on field and tree,
> It rains on the umbrellas here,
> And on the ships at sea. . . .

Opinions have varied about this part of Stevenson's work, especially as he also wrote a mass of self-confessedly light verse for which no poetic claims were to be made. The *Child's Garden* poems seem to me to have great charm, and not to be light verse in a pejorative sense. . . . Are they all, however, boats and rain and cows and lamplighters? Is everything in this garden lovely? There are a surprising number of soldiers and guns and battles around. 'Now, with my little gun, I crawl / All in the dark along the wall' . . . What is Stevenson doing with his little gun? In another poem, called **'The Dumb Soldier'**, he tells a very fey tale of how he buried one of his lead soldiers underground in the lawn, and means some day to dig him up again to ask him what it was like lying alone in the

dark of the earth. And when, in another poem, he looks for pictures in the fire, what does Stevenson's child see? Armies and burning cities.

> Armies march by tower and spire
> Of cities blazing, in the fire;
> Till as I gaze with staring eyes,
> The armies fade, the lustre dies.
>
> Then once again the glow returns;
> Again the phantom city burns;
> And down the red-hot valley, lo!
> The phantom armies marching go!
>
> Blinking embers, tell me true
> Where are those armies marching to,
> And what the burning city is
> That crumbles in your furnaces! . . .

Every boy, perhaps, plays with soldiers and sees armies in the fire. But there does seem something particular, something underlined, in these poems of Stevenson's—notably the one where he buries the unresisting soldier in the lawn. It was not for nothing that A. E. Housman found himself so strongly attracted to Stevenson, and looking at it from a wider angle one can think back to George MacBeth's remark about the 'love of clandestine violence'. (pp. 39-40)

> *Edwin Morgan, "The Poetry of Robert Louis Stevenson," in* Scottish Literary Journal, *Vol. 1, No. 2, December, 1974, pp. 29-44.*

IRVING S. SAPOSNIK

Perhaps more listened to than read, and often sung, Stevenson's lyrics play upon the ear with a familiarity which has made them a traditional landmark in growing up. Recalling meaningful moments of childhood, their wide appeal is not entirely unlike that of Stevenson's other children's literature—*Treasure Island, Black Arrow,* and *Kidnapped*—since all are based upon his belief that "children think very much the same thoughts and dream the same dreams as bearded men and marriageable women" [see first excerpt above in Author's Commentary]. . . . This belief does not mean that children are merely miniature correspondences of their elders nor that adults conduct their lives with childish anticipation; rather, it indicates that in each life, no matter at what age, there exists some amount of play, some desire to leap over an all-too-pervasive reality into a realm of unlimited possibility. In creating poetry out of his childhood experiences, Stevenson fashions an order of experience whose basis is dream and whose direction is beyond. As the child is to the adult, so too are his compulsions preliminary movements in a never-ending journey out of the self. The poems of childhood are never lost because they are ever repeated. Deservedly the most popular of Stevenson's poems—their verse quality alone insures this—his childhood poems express what his other poems merely suggest, that "In spite of our wisdom / And sensible talking, / We on our feet must go / Plodding and walking" (**"Nest Eggs"** . . .). (p. 55)

Among the memorable qualities of *A Child's Garden of Verses* is the child who "speaks" most of the poems. That he is a child is most important because he speaks to children from their point of view; and, as he speaks with an immediacy unknown in other children's poetry, he imparts a sense of burdensome care and imaginative flight. Not totally identifiable with Stevenson, he nonetheless shares many of his sensibilities. Often alone and lonely, afraid and yet curious of the world about him, frightened by many of its fleeting shadows, longing to travel beyond his limited confines, the child has almost the dimensions of a fictional character lightly sketched in a "narrative" whose line is spiral rather than horizontal.

A child of well-to-do parents, he is cared for by a nurse ("**My Kingdom**"), and he lives in a large house ("**North-West Passage**") whose shadows frequently play havoc with his vivid imagination. Though he sometimes plays with others, he is most often dependent upon his own abilities. Usually confined to the walled family garden (even in his one visit to the seashore he is pretty much a solitary reveler), he frequently remains in bed ("**The Land of Counterpane**"); and he imagines it to be his portal at evening and his haven at morn ("**My Bed is a Boat**"). Inquisitive as well as introspective, he often thinks of other children either by comparing his daily activities with theirs ("**The Sun's Travels**") or by sailing his boats down the umbilical river from which "Other little children / Shall bring my boats ashore" ("**Where Go the Boats?**"), or by viewing them with a smug self-satisfaction which Stevenson treats with gentle irony ("**Foreign Children**").

The poems of this sensitive and lonely narrator follow in a familiar and carefully ordered succession. Divided into three sections—the title section contains forty-one poems; nine poems, under the heading "The Child Alone"; and a concluding eight poems, under "Garden Days"—the verses balance each other so that the suggestions of one poem are repeated with slight variation in order to emphasize the constant iteration of like emotion. Accordingly, "**The Little Land**" of the second section parallels "**Foreign Lands**" of the first, while "**Night and Day**" of the third provides a slight but firm echo of both. Again, "**Summer Sun**" in the concluding section recalls "**The Sun's Travels**" of the opening part. Occasionally, poems within individual sections compare and contrast with one another. So "**My Kingdom**" and "**The Land of Story-Books**" of the third section express the child's isolation in an adult world whose restrictions impair imaginative release, while "**Whole Duty of Children**" and "**System**" in the first section reveal the necessary distinction between spiritual will and physical possibility. Similarly, successive poems often reinforce initial attitudes, and so there appear poems on sleep, play, propriety, travel, and nature, each offering its suggestion of unappeasable loneliness.

Not only are the subjects of the poem thus repeated, but identical symbols occur with suggestive frequency. The house, the garden, the wall suggest limitation, something to leave behind or look beyond; darkness, night, the moon, and the wind bring to mind mystery, fright, and an eerie sense of ambiguous freedom. Conversely, the bed, daylight, the swing, the river represent release, the playful leap into the land "where the golden apples grow." By using suggestive imagery, Stevenson is able to maintain and reinforce the alternating emotions of self-centeredness and self-transcendence, the prevailing concordance of childhood delight and simultaneous sadness. Placing his child-narrator in a world from which he is often painfully apart, Stevenson creates a childhood equivalent of universal experience, a miniature gem of Victorian sensibility which speaks pointedly to the isolation of modern life.

Carefully ordered, delicately balanced, intensely subjective, *A Child's Garden of Verses* represents a landmark in children's poetry. Neither didactic nor whimsical, neither Isaac Watts nor Walter De La Mare, Stevenson's poems reconstruct the delicate fancy and persistent longing of children as no other poems have ever done. As a symbol of childhood visions and adult aspirations, Stevenson's child is a dreamer whose dreams constitute

a necessity for child and adult alike. Probing his own childhood memories, Stevenson creates a persona who stands midway between childish desire and adult regret; he is a singer of "New Songs of Innocence" (he once thought of using this title) who cautiously anticipates the experience to come. (pp. 55-7)

Irving S. Saposnik, in his Robert Louis Stevenson, *Twayne Publishers, Inc., 1974, 164 p.*

REBECCA LUKENS

It is past time to take a hard look at *A Child's Garden of Verses*, to apply to that classic the criteria of poetry—compactness, figurativeness, rhythm and sound patterns, and emotional intensity.

But first, a few concessions.

Some children may still play pirates; many set their boats afloat on tiny streams, and play with toy figures on the bedspread—though rarely with lead soldiers upon the counterpane. They march to tunes, but not always martial ones. They marvel at adults, but far less often at "nursie's" kindness, or the transformation brought about by lamplighters. They prefer the adventures of the astronaut, or even the clatter of the trash collectors below their windows. Most certainly children still love to go up in the swing, and to wonder at their shadows that shrink, then grow, then even disappear. And no one will ever be blase about how in every empty cup, "the sea came up / till it could come no more."

Once we put behind us, however, the fact that we first heard the verses read to us by attentive adults, we see them more objectively. Even the most casual critic is aware of the cliches, the lack of compactness, the plethora of throwaway words: "All in the pleasant open air, / All in the pleasant light of day"; "It is very nice to think"; "As plain as day before my eye" (to rhyme with "by"); "Must we to bed, indeed? Well, then, / Let us arise and go like men." Even children parading to music are drably described: "All carrying different kinds of things."

Stevenson's verses lack intensity; they are grayed with abstract and non-sensory adjectives like "merry," "pleasant," "jolly," and "sweet." Although children do "rise," "leave," and "come," the most frequently used verbs are forms of "to be." For variation Stevenson lapses into verbal antiques like "fare," "dwell," or "put by," just perhaps the terms used by Victorian children. Such bland wordiness shows no conviction that children lose themselves in play. The idea of making a ship upon the stairs, for example, is all that lingers from that verse. Nothing that is vivid remains, for no true experience is recounted: "We had the best of plays."

Rhythm and sound patterns are equally disappointing. Ignoring the use of rhythm and sound to enhance and intensify meaning, Stevenson's regular beat plods along in solemn iambs. More than that, to create lines of equal length, he pads the lines, resorting to empty words like those in "**The Moon.**" "But all of the things that belong to the day / Cuddle to sleep to be out of her way."

Not only do words exist only for regular da-dah / da-dah / da-dah meter—a solemn choice for scenes of play—but the verses of *A Child's Garden* are also forced into rhyme. In "**Travel**" we read that eastern cities for miles about "Are with mosque and minaret / Among sandy gardens set," and later on, "Where in jungles, near and far, / Man-devouring tigers are." The verse closes with "And flowers and children close their eyes / Till up in the morning the sun shall rise." Ignoring phonetic intensives, onomatopoeia and other devices of sound, Stevenson's verse exemplifies a condescending attitude toward poetry for children. It has two qualities—rhythm, regular and obvious, and rhyme in *abab* or *aabb* patterns. To fulfill these obligations, he does anything, forcing lines into the most banal of rhymes: sings / things; trees / sees; Japan / man; Spain / rain (**"Singing"**).

Perhaps for those who still cling to Stevenson's collection as the best for children, it was their only book of poems in childhood. Perhaps they surround that book with subliminal memories of a parent's lap, and a parent's voice. At the time, the rhythm and rhyme may have seemed to them sheer music. There may be still another reason for fond memories of the *Garden*. As adults look back, these verses may be the way they too remember childhood; clouded in nostalgia, adults may think they recall pleasant, jolly, sweet, nice, perhaps even merry days. They may have forgotten the excitement, the momentary fury, or the total immersion in play that characterizes real childhood and real play.

But Stevenson does not depict childhood. He looks back and thinks he recalls it. Sentimentality is rampant; a speaking child says he "loves" the friendly cow "with all my heart." The verse-maker's recollection in **"A Thought"** is surely a contrivance of adult memory.

> It is very nice to think
> The world is full of meat and drink.
> With little children saying grace
> In every Christian kind of place.

Does a true child, not a reminiscing adult, embarking on a sea voyage say, "Let us also take / An apple and a slice of cake"? Surely it was a grown Mr. Stevenson feeling instructive, who said,

> The world is so full of a number of things,
> I'm sure we should all be as happy as kings.

The real child who climbs the cherry tree and looks "abroad on foreign lands" (a nice name for what's next door, it's true), is far more aware of what he can see from the new perch than the "little me" who climbs up to see

> the next door garden lie,
> Adorned with flowers, before my eye,
> And many pleasant places more
> Than I had never seen before.

The regular metrics of Stevenson's didactic verses never fail to bring up the child properly. He says his prayers, gets his dinner, and is rewarded with an orange. But

> The child that is not clean and neat,
> With lots of toys and things to eat,
> He is a naughty child, I'm sure—
> Or else his dear papa is poor.

These self-righteous and condescending comments are labeled **"System."** The child in **"A Good Boy"** who has been "happy all the day,"never saying "an ugly word" but smiling and sticking to play, is downright unnatural. He knows that he's been good and won't forget his prayer, but he is sadly misinformed if he thinks such monastic behavior will assure him that "no ugly dream shall fright my mind, no ugly sight my eyes." Other didacticisms exist. To grow "great and stately,"

children must "walk sedately"—impossible task. They must be "bright and quiet,"

> And content with simple diet;
> And remain, through all bewild'ring,
> Innocent and honest children.

Children are told constantly to "be happy," happy in heart and face and play, and thus to grow to be kings or sages (**"Good and Bad Children"**). Being unruly or eating "unduly" (neat euphemism for gluttony) results in the best lines of the preachy piece: Such children grow up "hated, as their age increases, / By their nephews and their nieces."

Condescension toward other children exists elsewhere in a number of Stevenson's verses, but most flagrantly in **"Foreign Children,"** about children of other lands who have seen remarkable things like lions, scarlet trees, ostrich eggs, and turtles turned off their legs. The speaker, "fed on proper meat," smugly asks if the Little Indian, Sioux or Crow, the little frosty Eskimo, or the little Turk or "Japanee" doesn't wish "that you were me?"

We must admit, however, that Stevenson knows *that* children play; *how* they play, he has forgotten. And just occasionally he captures in terse and connotative language what is truly happening. The rhythm of **"From a Railway Carriage"** races the verse along. "Painted stations whistle by," a child clambers and scrambles "gathering brambles," a cart runs away in the road, "lumping along with man and load." **"My Treasures,"** despite its slow pace created by unnecessary words, does show the little mound of childhood keepsakes: the fool's gold, the whittled whistle, the hand-made chisel, and the nuts hidden beside the lead soldiers.

But Stevenson's lines rarely show the intensity and figurativeness we expect in poetry and find even in Mother Goose, which is rich with the joyous foolishness of folk and game rhymes. The verses of *Garden* are thoughts of a grown man remembering in a rosy haze what it was like to be a child, recalling the admonitions spoken to him, and believing they did become parts of his childhood pleasures. (pp. 49-53)

Rebecca Lukens, "Stevenson's 'Garden': Verse Is Verse," in The Lion and the Unicorn, *Vol. 4, No. 2, Winter, 1980-81, pp. 49-55.*

JOHN GOLDTHWAITE

In *A Child's Garden of Verses* Stevenson looks out at the world as he imagined he did as a child. He studies it while swinging above the garden wall, or climbing a cherry tree, or peering out the window of a railway car. What he sees is not the real world but the world of his story books, where 'the dusty roads go up and down' and where, for our entertainment, live the 'Little Indian, Sioux or Crow, / Little Frosty Eskimo'. *A Child's Garden* confuses, as if Stevenson could not always distinguish the one from the other, the true sentiment with the false, and nostalgia with accurate recall. What *is* real about the book, however, is his desire for the world. When he writes of his longing to travel through 'forests, hot as fire, / Wide as England', there is no false note being struck. This is how a child does daydream and how he might make up the world from the lines and colours on maps found in the drawing room. However much Stevenson may veer from a child's true perception from verse to verse, at the centre of the book is a real vision of the world, and his voice as he tells us about this world he sees is the voice of a man who couldn't wait to be joined with it, and went. (pp. 165-66)

John Goldthwaite, "The Black Rabbit: Part Two,"
in Signal, *No. 48, September, 1985, pp. 148-67.**

JOHN CECH

Stevenson touched that capacity for visionary flight that the young child discovers and that ultimately saves him (and his imagination) from the "hard" facts of living with adults—like their sending him "to bed by day." Perhaps because he was a sickly child and spent many days indoors, Stevenson cultivated a strong sense for how one can "escape" through the imagination. . . .

Though there are a few Victorian clinkers in the collection (like **"Foreign Children"**), the poems are remarkably free of the doggerel preachiness that marked so much of the verse that was served up to children in the latter part of the 19th century. But these poems are different; they are about the things of a child's life—digging holes at the seashore, playing, listening to the sounds, sights and smells of things, singing, exploring, and above all, observing. Whatever its few dated shortcomings may be, this remains one of the most important books of poetry for children that we have. (p. 20)

John Cech, "A Palette of Picture Books," in Book
World—The Washington Post, *November 10, 1985,
pp. 19-20.**

JUDITH NICHOLLS

Children's poetry has come a long way since the first publication a hundred years ago of Robert Louis Stevenson's *A child's garden of verses.* On the surface there is an obvious century's difference between this sometimes quaint, sometimes moralising medley of Victorian children's verse and the wide variety of specially written poetry available today. The fact that the book has been reprinted on so many occasions and can today be found on the lists of at least eight different publishers poses an interesting question: just who is buying these books?

At first consideration it seems possible that the purchasers might frequently be adults, nostalgic for their own childhood. . . . Another possible explanation is that RLS can clearly be seen as 'poetry' even to those who would never normally seek out poetry unless as a gift for some doting niece or grandson. Neither of these explanations, however, accounts for the steady appearance of a good handful of these little verses in many modern anthologies for children.

To browse through *A child's garden of verses* after a gap of several decades is rather like hearing a forgotten Shakespeare play and being struck by the familiarity of lines which have crept into our common language. Mention the collection itself and there may be very few nods of recognition; mention a line from **'Windy nights'** or **'My shadow'** or **'From a railway carriage'** and anyone at all familiar with children's poetry is likely to respond. (p. 306)

'These are rhymes, jingles; I don't go in for eternity and the three unities', wrote RLS. Nowadays we demand more from children's poetry than regular end-rhymes and an obvious rhythm, regardless of subject-matter. There are plenty of verses here which belong to the world of *Little women*, of buttered crumpets and 'honey-still-for-tea':

> How do you like to go up in a swing,
> Up in the air so blue?

> Oh, I do think it the pleasantest thing
> Ever a child can do!

Hardly the poetry to 'nudge us from comfort'; rather to be taken with buttered toast on a friendly knee by the fireside— much as RLS himself would have done with his nurse, 'Sitting safe in nursery nooks, Reading picture story-books'.

We have long lost the leisured age of Stevenson's childhood and it is interesting that children's poety has changed to some degree in the way in which film conventions have changed: the audience is required to be much more active in filling the gaps as the omissions grow. Stevenson's 'Land of story-books,' and 'Land of counterpane' are lands where the distinctions between what is happening to the child in 'reality' and what happens in his imagination are clearly spelt out in a way that is seen far less frequently today. It's not just a question of development from simile towards metaphor but rather involves a whole new directness of approach which has little to do with any idea of regurgitating classical forms with supposedly child-suited content.

We have moved from the general towards the highly specific and to spell out borderlines between reality and imagination would be regarded as a distraction as well as a detraction from the subject in hand, which is the development of the child through the development of his imagination. Compare Stevenson's approach to Autumn:

> Sing a song of seasons!
> Something bright in all!
> Flowers in the summer,
> Fires in the fall!

with the immediacy of the opening of Ted Hughes's 'Autumn song':

> There came a day that caught the summer
> Wrung its neck
> Plucked it
> And ate it.

> Now what shall I do with the trees?
> The day said, the day said.

(pp. 306-07)

The best Stevenson poems are often the simplest—as in the lovely child's-eye observation of **'Auntie's skirts'**:

> Whenever Auntie moves around,
> Her dresses make a curious sound;
> They trail behind her up the floor,
> And trundle after through the door,

or those like **'From a railway carriage'** or **'Windy nights'**, where rhythm complements meaning rather than imposes upon it:

> Whenever the moon and stars are set,
> Whenever the wind is high,
> All night long in the dark and wet,
> A man goes riding by.
> Late in the night when the fires are out,
> Why does he gallop and gallop about?

Verses like these have a timeless quality which will continue to ensure their survival in the anthologies of the future.

A child's garden of verses is a far cry from the vigorous style and content of *Treasure Island,* written around the same time as the first batch of these verses. . . . RLS's first reaction to the published poems was that they looked 'ghastly' in the cold light of print. [see excerpt above in Author's Commentary dated 1885]. Nevertheless, he had to admit that they seemed to have 'a kind of childish treble note that sounds in my ears freshly—not song, if you will, but a child's voice.' It is perhaps that clear child's voice which has made many of them still worthy of enjoyment one hundred years on. (p. 308)

> *Judith Nicholls, "Where the Golden Apples Grow . . . A New Look at 'A Child's Garden of Verses'," in* The School Librarian, *Vol. 33, No. 4, December, 1985, pp. 306-08.*

Todd Strasser

1950?-

(Also writes under the pseudonym of Morton Rhue) American author of fiction.

Strasser is a writer of fast-paced realistic fiction for teen and preteen boys. Combining romance with humor, he captures the attention of his readers by focusing on their concerns, fears, and goals in stories that reflect his familiarity with adolescent home and school life. Strasser's timely works utilize settings ranging from the suburban drug scene and the world of rock and roll to the restricted horizons of a young leukemia victim. The earthy language and sexual incidents in Strasser's books cause him to be a controversial figure among educators and community members; however, his relevant subjects and readable prose make him popular with youth of both sexes.

Reviewers commend Strasser for his well-defined, likeable protagonists, believable settings, and natural dialogue, as well as for the swift, easy pace of his narratives. Although his works are occasionally faulted for superficial plots and shallow characterizations, Strasser is praised for his handling of controversial subjects without resorting to sensationalism, his ability to avoid didacticism, and his understanding of the motives and feelings of youth.

(See also *Something about the Author*, Vol. 41.)

AUTHOR'S COMMENTARY

[Media & Methods]: How do you conduct your research for your books?

[Todd Strasser]: I have no children of my own, so I eavesdrop on teenagers whenever I have the opportunity. Also, I have a few nephews and nieces in the 11 to 13 year-old range who supply me with information, whether they know it or not. I speak at schools a lot and sometimes I hang around for a few periods, go to some classes and listen to the kids.

M & M: So, where do the ideas come from?

TS: My first book, *Angel Dust Blues*, is about a group of fairly well-to-do, suburban teenagers who get into trouble with drugs. (I grew up in a fairly well-to-do, suburban community and a group of kids I knew got into trouble with drugs.) My first story was based on that experience . . . and watching it occur.

My second book, *Friends Till The End*, is about a healthy teenager who has a friend who becomes extremely ill with leukemia. When I moved to New York, I got a roommate . . . an old friend of mine. Within a few weeks, he became very ill. I spent a year visiting him in the hospital, not knowing whether he was going to live or die. I thought it was an experience that teenagers could relate to and one they *should* relate to.

M & M: So you rely heavily on your own experience?

TS: To a point. My most recent book to come out is *Rock and Roll Nights*. It's about a teenage rock and roll band—something with which I have absolutely no *direct* experience. However, I grew up in the 1960s when rock and roll was really our

Photograph by Bill Soiffer. Courtesy of Todd Strasser.

''national anthem.'' I relate much better to rock stars than to movie stars. I always wanted to be in a rock band, as did just about everybody I knew.

M & M: But that is still drawing on an old dream of your own. Do you think that what interests teenagers today is basically the same as 20 years ago?

TS: Absolutely. I think the kind of music changes or what they wear may change, but dealing with being popular, friends or the opposite sex, or questions of morality and decency . . . [I don't think] those things really ever change. I hate to say this, but I think we tell the same stories—just in today's language and in today's settings.

M & M: For what age range do you think you write?

TS: I've been writing almost exclusively for an age range that probably goes from about 11 to 15 or 16. I'd say it's for bright, sophisticated 11 year-olds and not as bright, nor as sophisticated 15 year-olds. There's a real difference in this country, depending on where you live.

M & M: Is it by overhearing and eavesdropping that you get your story ideas and characters?

TS: Characters grow out of the story. Each story requires a certain group of characters to make it progress from beginning to end, and I supply them based on the story. I very rarely will pick a character and create a story around that character.

M & M: I know that you are concerned about the *kinds* of books that are written for girls and the *kinds* of books that are written for boys. How and why do you think they differ?

TS: Teenage boys will not read books about teenage girls. There's a wealth of literature for teenage girls—romance, mysteries, realistic fiction. But if you remove all those books *about* girls (which boys tend not to read), and if you take away science fiction and sports, the amount of contemporary, realistic fiction that recognizes that boys are thinking, feeling, caring people, is practically nil.

My favorite example of this concerns that wonderful affliction called the "crush." There are millions of books about teenage girls with crushes. Teenage girls have crushes on everybody—the boy next door, the brother of the boy next door, the cousin of the boy next door. How many books are there about boys with crushes? There are so few. Does this mean that very few boys have teenage crushes? *I* was a teenage boy and I had lots of crushes—the girl next door, the cousin of the girl next door. . . .

A teenage boy from the age of about 11 to 14 is discovering his masculinity and trying to understand the difference between himself as a male and others as females. In most families, the women are still *the readers*. The boy grows up saying to himself, "Mom is reading and Dad is watching TV. I want to be like Dad." A girl sees her mother reading and says, "I can read just like Mom does." Boys at that age aren't really *against* reading, but they want to do the things they envision as being masculine.

What I try to do in my books is present *boyish* boys, but I try to make them *real* boys, with emotions and sensitivities. If a boy sees a book that says on the cover, "Tommy is a sensitive, caring young boy in a tumultuous relationship with his best friend and his girlfriend," he's not going to pick it up. But if Tommy is the star of the soccer team and is a tough, good-looking guy, but is *still* in "a tumultuous relationship with his best friend and his girlfriend," *then* he's something kids will pick up on.

I do not write books solely for teenage boys, but I write books that teenage boys will read. A greater percentage of my fan mail still comes from teenage girls, but at least I know that boys are reading my books, and that's important to me.

M & M: Do you consider your books educational or entertainment?

TS: Both. Because we're competing against television and video arcade games, we must be entertaining. Up to the time they're teenagers, students have been told what to read by their teachers or their parents. This is the first opportunity they have to voluntarily pick up a book and decide whether they want to read it or not. This is the most important time in terms of getting a reader for life. If we give them books that they are not going to enjoy on a primary level, that they're not going to be entertained by, we may be losing readers for life. I don't think we can afford to do that.

M & M: You wrote the novelization of *The Wave* under the name of Morton Rhue. How do you feel about television as an incentive to reading?

TS: I didn't feel comfortable attaching my name to something that wasn't my original idea so I created 'Morton Rhue.' Any-

thing on TV available in book form, kids will read. It has entertainment appeal, and for kids who are not natural readers, it gets them to enjoy reading as an entertainment.

M & M: What is your main message?

TS: Honesty. Standing up for one's friends, self and beliefs. Even though I grew up in the 1960s with the "new morality," I'm so old-fashioned. I want kids to have the same old-fashioned morals and values that I have. That doesn't mean I can't write about contemporary issues. If you have to deal with drugs or with teenage sexuality, you can have contemporary kids dealing with it, and those kids can still have what we call "old-fashioned" values.

M & M: What do you think is wrong with young adult literature today and where would you like to see it go?

TS: There are too many writers following trends. What we need is more contemporary, realistic, well-written fiction—especially for boys and especially for minorities. (pp. 10-12)

> *Todd Strasser, "I Was a Teenage Boy," in an interview with Nina Piwoz in* Media & Methods, *Vol. 19, No. 6, February, 1983, pp. 10-12.*

It is a sad fact that sooner or later almost every writer of young adult fiction must leave the safe and cozy confines of his or her writing room and face the perilous task of researching the subject—namely, teenagers. Most of us try to avoid such research for as long as possible. Some writers succeed in never confronting it at all. Instead they cling to the age-old writer's adage, "When in doubt, make it up."

But for those of us who try to be factually accurate and who have never taught or had a teenager of our own, there is no avoiding it. I, for one, never even thought of research back in the old days when I was embarking on a career as a fiction writer. I just drew heavily on personal experience. My first couple of young adult books are based almost completely on factual experience and observation.

But then I became intrigued by ideas and situations of which I had no firsthand knowledge. I also grew older, and my memories of my teen years grew dimmer and more difficult to understand. Soon I began to wonder if I really did know anything about teenagers. I worried that I was out of touch; I fretted too long over small details. What clothes should my characters wear? What music should they listen to? How should they speak?

The day finally came when I woke up to the realization that the only way I could continue writing about teens was to leave my IBM PC behind and venture into the turbulent and misty world they inhabited. I put on the only pair of blue jeans left in my closet, grabbed a notebook and some pencils, kissed my wife good-by, and went out the door.

In the last half-dozen years my desire to have realistic and contemporary settings for my books has forced me to infiltrate many bastions of youth. These places have included rock concerts, video arcades, the local Burger King at 3:30 P.M. on a school day, certain parts of public beaches—usually where the music is the loudest—dance clubs catering to the young, high school athletic events, and, of course, high schools. For one month several years ago I even took a job as a beer vendor at Giants Stadium to observe the teens who worked there.

During these forays I am usually uncomfortably aware of my intruder status. Teens almost always become quiet when an older stranger walks among them. For the most part I find myself either ignored or treated in a cordial yet skeptical manner. (pp. 236-37)

I do feel more comfortable when I'm invited to schools to speak on the craft and business of writing. Then I can stroll down crowded hallways and peek over the shoulders of students at their lockers. The boys hang mirrors and tape pictures of motorcycles and athletes inside their locker doors. The girls hang mirrors and paste up photos of bare-chested male movie stars. Schools are also good places to catch the latest developments in word usage. At one school recently I was referred to as "that author dude." At another I listened as a young lady explained why she had rejected an invitation to eat at a nearby diner—"It was too fluorescent."

In my search for clues to the teenage way of life, I have also scoured their hangouts when they were absent. Like an archaeologist I have sorted through the rubble around railroad underpasses searching for clues to what brands of cigarettes and beer were currently in favor. I have wondered at the mysteries of teenagers' spray-painted cave drawings—as in "Led Zep," "Hendrix Lives," and "Black Sabbath." Sometimes the most significant result of my research is simply the reassurance that under the bangles, Walkmans, and spike haircuts today's teenagers are really not so different from their distant ancestors of a few years ago.

With the start of each new book, I find it necessary to interview teens who might have special insights into the subjects or characters I have chosen. Thus, in recent years I have interviewed teenage soccer players, rock musicians, a boy who was in a two-week coma after a car accident, valet parkers, stadium vendors, and Westinghouse Science Prize winners.

It is not easy, however, to get teenagers to speak candidly in any kind of interview situation. Adults are often willing to reveal their inner thoughts when there is a likelihood that what they say will turn up in print. Teens, on the other hand, will speak at length about their favorite rock star, TV show, comic book, and sports team. They will give party-line opinions on controversial issues like drinking, drugs, premarital sex, and abortion. But ask them *why* they feel a certain way and either you will find yourself in the midst of an uncomfortable silence or you will get the standard reply: "I don't know why. I just do."

Unfortunately, more subversive information-gleaning ploys that occasionally work with adults usually fail when applied to teens. With adults it is sometimes possible to relax the subject with ample amounts of small talk, and even a few drinks, and then subtly steer the conversation to subjects they might at first have been reluctant to talk about. With teenagers this is practically impossible, not only because it is reprehensible to ply them with liquor but because teenagers are immediately suspicious of any adult who wants to engage in small talk. This has never been more true than in recent times, when children are taught from an early age to be wary of adult strangers who start up off-the-wall conversations.

Because I've learned that small talk won't get me anywhere with teenagers, I tend to skip the preliminaries and surprise them with direct questions instead. For instance, in an ice cream shop I might purchase a cone and then pause to ask a young employee how many hours a week she works, what she likes and dislikes about the job, whether working leaves her enough time for studying or a social life, and how her parents feel about her working. Not surprisingly, this has become a source of embarrassment to my family and friends. (pp. 237-38)

In my desire to get more inside information on teenagers, I have in recent years tended to go undercover. To this end I have become an almost compulsive eavesdropper. My wife knows that on any bus or subway train or in any diner or pizza place, my choice of seats will not depend on where the ambiance is best but on where the teenagers are. She also knows that should we be walking on the sidewalk talking and I suddenly tune out, I am not being purposefully impolite. My ears have merely picked up the strains of youthful vocal cords.

This form of research has provided me with some fairly interesting material, some of it usable, some of it not. Once in a Greek diner on Broadway I listened to a young man complain to two of his friends that his parents like to smoke marijuana but wouldn't let him have any. Another time I heard one teenage girl chastise another for relying on "mind control birth control." I have listened to boys discussing girls and girls discussing boys. I have listened to many conversations about baseball, SATs, clothes, fights (usually in the future tense), being grounded, and the best places to get your parents to take you on vacation. Much of what I have heard has not been a revelation but more of a confirmation that the teenagers I place in my books are still reasonable reflections of the real thing.

But eavesdropping, like the other forms of research, has its own problems. One is being discovered. It's bad enough being caught eavesdropping in general, but to be an adult discovered by a teenager (usually two teenagers or more) carries an even greater onus: it's not only impolite, it's somehow terribly demeaning.

Over the years I have often complained to my wife that I wished that there were some easier way to do research on teenagers, especially in New York where, except for a few weeks each spring and fall, they seem particularly hard to find. Then last year we had our first child, a daughter. Shortly after we brought her home from the hospital, my wife turned to me and said, "Just think, in thirteen years you won't have to leave the house at all."

Perhaps that's the best solution: grow your own. (pp. 238-39)

Todd Strasser, "Stalking the Teen," in The Horn Book Magazine, *Vol. LXII, No. 2, March-April, 1986, pp. 236-39.*

ANGEL DUST BLUES: A NOVEL (1979)

Not since *Dinkey Hocker Shoots Smack* has so unlikely a title been attached to so genuine an experience. But there's a difference—several years' difference. Alex Lazar does buy and sell some angel dust, though mainly he's into dealing pot. (There's a funny, dead-center description of his one experience with dusted joints.) The novel's outline seems as unpromising as the title: Alex, 17, is the overprivileged offspring of busy absentee parents who, as he puts it, want a "low maintenance" child and react to problems by shipping him off to a shrink to be fixed up like a broken toaster. A hopelessly self-destructive, no-good companion lures him into the dope scene, later rats on Alex and gets him busted, and himself winds up, multi-habituated (as the lawyer puts it), in a possibly fatal coma. And Alex, shaken by the bust and in love (and, at last, in bed) with a reasonably straight rich girl, pulls out of his senior-year funk and applies to college. Alex's sardonic views of his parents, his principal, and adult society at large are also pretty similar to those of other rebellious teens, real and fictitious; but they are expressed with a lot more bite and verve and intelligence. Alex is a mixed-up teenager who is also a wry, refreshing, full-blooded character; and Strasser writes like he knows the scene—from the Brooklyn Rastis to the suburban high school john to family life (or its absence) in upper-income Upper Deepbrook. No trumped-up YA object lesson, this is a real novel with the strength and the sense of real life of a *Hard Feelings* or an *Ordinary People*.

> *A review of "Angel Dust Blues," in* Kirkus Reviews, *Vol. XLVIII, No. 20, October 15, 1979, p. 1213.*

When he is arrested, Alex has a change of heart and, thanks to family connections, is cleared. Michael, the loser, O.D.'s and dies. Does Mr. Strasser mean to imply that wealth and influence, coupled with regret, eradicate the guilt of a drug dealer? I hope not. "Angel dust" in the title is used to exploit the current interest of teens in this powerful drug. Mr. Strasser says nothing to discourage its use.

> *Penny S. Markey, in a review of "Angel Dust Blues,"
> in* Children's Book Review Service, *Vol. 8, No. 4,
> December, 1979, p. 40.*

The secondary characters (Alex's singularly unattractive parents; an unorthodox principal; and Alex's shy intellectual best friend James) don't have the interest and sympathy of Alex and Ellen, whose relationship (including its graphic sexual aspects and Ellen's decision to lose her virginity to Alex) is particularly well handled. The story, which has power, wit, punch and remarkably little sensationalism, could attract kids tired by now of *Go Ask Alice* (Prentice-Hall, 1971).

> *Cyrisse Jaffee, in a review of "Angel Dust Blues,"
> in* School Library Journal, *Vol. 26, No. 5, January,
> 1980, p. 81.*

Phencyclidine, angel dust, is the drug that causes the violent climax of this trenchant and honest story. . . . This is rough and tough, both in subject and language, but it is not didactic although Alex learns something from his bitter experience, and it's not overdone; Strasser's writing has a depth and candor that puts the book's focus on the intricate and at times compassionate development of the characters and their relationships.

> *Zena Sutherland, in a review of "Angel Dust Blues,"
> in* Bulletin of the Center for Children's Books, *Vol.
> 33, No. 6, February, 1980, p. 120.*

The tender, graphically described love affair with Ellen is beautifully handled. The author successfully presents Alex as basically good but heedless; his development into responsible maturity is believable as an outgrowth of his reactions to circumstances. The characterizations are exceptional, and the writing style is clear and fluid.

> *Ann A. Flowers, in a review of "Angel Dust Blues,"
> in* The Horn Book Magazine, *Vol. LVI, No. 2, April,
> 1980, p. 178.*

This is a taut, believable portrayal of teenage alienation and drug abuse. Character development and the portrayal of relationships, especially the one between Alex and Ellen, are well done, and readers will readily understand and sympathize with various characters as the story unfolds. The bitterness Alex feels toward his parents is vividly portrayed. . . . This is strong, candid, informative, but not didactic, material. (p. 361)

> *Sharon Spredemann Dreyer, "Annotations: 'Angel
> Dust Blues'," in her* The Bookfinder, When Kids
> Need Books: Annotations of Books Published 1979
> through 1982, *American Guidance Service, 1985,
> pp. 361-62.*

FRIENDS TILL THE END: A NOVEL   (1981)

David is a high-school senior whose primary interests are soccer and his girlfriend. Howie is a newcomer to New York who has a hard time making friends. David likes Howie but just doesn't have time to get to know him very well. But when Howie is hospitalized with leukemia David is pressured by his parents to go visit him. The visits make David less self-centered and inspire him to re-evaluate his goals for the future. David's other friends cannot understand his interest in Howie, but several of them get to know Howie through David and are also changed. The friendship between David and Howie and the effect of the leukemia on everyone associated with the sick boy are realistically portrayed. Although the reader senses that Howie will die, the story is open-ended. The book is well-written, fast-moving, and thought-provoking.

> *Beth Doyle, in a review of "Friends till the End,"
> in* Children's Book Review Service, *Vol. 9, No. 9,
> April, 1981, p. 80.*

Without probing deeply or pushing too hard, Strasser convincingly links David's new interest in medicine with his rather unusual commitment to Howie. The story is far closer to the YA norm than Strasser's *Angel Dust Blues* . . .—it's as if, after that fresh first novel, Strasser surveyed the field and decided to conform—but it has a spark of particularity that sets it apart from many more maudlin casebook scenarios. (p. 438)

> *A review of "Friends till the End," in* Kirkus Reviews, *Vol. XLIX, No. 7, April 1, 1981, pp. 437-38.*

Strasser focuses mainly on David, who gains, through his relationship with Howie, a better understanding of what is important in his own life. Other strengths of the novel lie in its vivid portrayal of the guilt, fear, and anger Howie feels as a disease victim and its clear picture of the devastating physical and mental toll of the illness.

> *Stephanie Zvirin, in a review of "Friends till the
> End," in* Booklist, *Vol. 77, No. 16, April 15, 1981,
> p. 1148.*

A fair proportion of the first-person narrative is told through dialogue, and the author is clearly attuned to the speech of contemporary teenagers. But he reveals his characters to be not stereotyped suburbanites but caring individuals facing up to the prospect of a classmate's untimely death. The book becomes, then, less a story of a tragedy than an account of the changes one person's life can make on another's.

> *Kate M. Flanagan, in a review of "Friends till the
> End," in* The Horn Book Magazine, *Vol. LVII, No.
> 3, June, 1981, p. 314.*

It is nice to see one of the most promising authors of adolescent fiction . . . live up to his potential in this second novel. . . . As David and his friends renegotiate their relationships, the pain of separating from peers as well as from parents is described beautifully. Told in the first person, this novel shows how well such narrative can be handled. Strasser's style is graceful and understated, and the adults, while not intrusive, are also not the usual cardboard stock characters of the genre. . . . Especially good is David's relationship with Rena who saw him as a boyfriend of convenience until she left for college and the real world, only to realize she loved him when he stood up for his friend. There is one scene where he spends the night with her which is really lovely and definitely in context, a perfect example of a depiction of kids mature enough to handle a sexual relationship well. The ending, in which Howie's parents return him to Florida while David is at a soccer game, without really letting him say goodbye is perfect and heart-rending. The book is well worth YASD Best Books consideration and should be useful in death and values clarification curricula as well as just a good read. I suspect that some creative adolescent medical specialists could also use the scenes at the hospital in medical education for dealing with friends and relatives of dying adolescents. A lovely and highly recommended book.

Mary K. Chelton, in a review of "Friends till the End," in Voice of Youth Advocates, *Vol. 4, No. 2, June, 1981, p. 32.*

Friends till the End attempts to deal with the problems of disease, and the difficulties of accepting death, on a teenage level. It succeeds to the small degree that it presents various situations that a teenager, who has leukemia, might encounter with his friends, parents, doctors, and himself. The book fails in that it icebergs—it only shows us the tip of these relationships and situations; it doesn't go deep enough to tell us what these people really think, how they really feel, and that's very important.

Howie Jamison, the leukemia victim, mentions that he sometimes thinks about what he must have done wrong to deserve the sickness, but that's it, he only mentions it. He doesn't dwell on that point which, in most cases, continually haunts the victim. The same is true of the thought about what happens to one after death. Howie mentions it, and he speaks briefly with David Gilbert, his best friend, about it, but it doesn't get a realistic treatment.

Novelist Todd Strasser hindered this work further by creating too many distractions. Instead of concentrating on the friendship of Howie and David, and exploring all the facets of the problem at hand, he offers a too full world—too many boyfriend-girlfriend arguments. Sure, these things are real, but they all detract from the main subject.

In writing this book, Strasser had a worthy idea, and a noble intention. Unfortunately, the work doesn't come close to its potential.

Mike Klodnicki, in a review of "Friends till the End," in Best Sellers, *Vol. 41, No. 4, July, 1981, p. 159.*

THE WAVE (1981)

Rhue's precipitately resolved and wooden narrative lacks the impact of real, threatening results from an experiment in a California high school. The book is based on ABC-TV's dramatization wherein fictional teacher Ben Ross attempts to discipline careless students. Having stunned a class with films of Nazi atrocities and tried to explain how a minority achieved such power in Germany, Ross reads extensively on third Reich indoctrination methods. They give him the idea for creating "The Wave," a select group who chivvy each other into excelling and bully others into joining them. The Wave's influ-

ence spreads incredibly and frighteningly until Ross takes steps to undo the mischief. What the author fails to clarify is *why* Ross would act on such an "inspiration," why the students who were horrified by the Nazis eagerly aped them.

A review of "The Wave," in Publishers Weekly, *Vol. 220, No. 22, November 27, 1981, p. 88.*

[This] spare, rather slick novel fictionalizes an incident that took place in a California high school in 1969. . . . Characters and plot are merely sketched and the author never really takes advantage of the dramatic potential of the incident, but his fictional reconstruction may encourage investigation into the real incident while it makes the lesson learned from it more accessible for general classroom discussion.

Stephanie Zvirin, in a review of "The Wave," in Booklist, *Vol. 78, No. 10, January 15, 1982, p. 644.*

The dilemma of the teacher and of those students who oppose the increasingly popular movement are made vividly clear. Although this is based on a true incident, here the speed of the conversion and the way in which almost every student is captivated are not quite convincing. Adequately written, this has good if not profound characterization, and an interesting if not always credibly developed plot.

Zena Sutherland, in a review of "The Wave," in Bulletin of the Center for Children's Books, *Vol. 35, No. 7, March, 1982, p. 137.*

One can excuse the light sketching of characters and the action gaps (often found in novelizations) because the story moves fast, holds attention and has political and social implications of great importance.

Jack Forman, in a review of "The Wave," in School Library Journal, *Vol. 28, No. 7, March, 1982, p. 160.*

[**The Wave**] is described by its publishers as "a novelization of a teleplay based on a short story" written about this happening, but as each step is taken away from the original experience, so does any feeling for authenticity give way to the glibly superficial.

As the story now stands, the teacher who set this whole process into play is as unconvincing as is the behaviour of his pupils. Bewitching orator he may have been, but it is not enough to explain the extraordinary effect he has simply in terms of introducing a few slogans and a distinctive salute, while any analogy with popular support for Nazism—which this whole experiment was supposed to illustrate—is absurd. One of the problems is the author's concern to picture the teacher as a comparatively decent figure despite his lapses in judgment, but the benign ineffectual individual that emerges has more in common with Will Hay than Adolf Hitler. Another difficulty is the writing, which limps along after the television version, so far not seen over here, describing personality and motivation rather than revealing it, and adding anxious commentary between dialogue in case readers have still missed the point. In this way, characters become puppets rather than people, except perhaps for Robert, the "class nerd", and the most enthusiastic recruit to the new regime.

Even so, I must also admit to finding **The Wave** compulsively readable while it lasted. But there is a nasty taste in the mouth after finishing it, not simply because of its pretentious plot but also owning to the tacky way this has now been realized in prose. Themes of this importance deserve a more serious treatment, as in P. H. Newby's sadly out of print *The Spirit of Jem*, a wholly imaginary story, but one that still carries far greater conviction.

> *Nicholas Tucker, "Over the Top," in* The Times Educational Supplement, *No. 3469, December 24, 1982, p. 25.*

The book jacket describes this as a 'thought provoking novel', but it is more like a political fable. The people in it are distanced from us by the features of the American high school scene: the importance of dating, beating rivals in a football game, being well liked in class. *The wave* has been made into a one-hour television show for ABC and I can well imagine it: the good young wife pleading with her husband, the history teacher, to desist; the student realising with horror that he has just knocked his girlfriend to the ground; the brainy individualist who will not join in. The message is a worthy one, but comes over more effectively, perhaps, in the story of a boy who refuses to sell chocolates though compelled by both teacher and bully boys (*The chocolate war*, by Robert Cormier).

> *Dorothy Atkinson, in a review of "The Wave," in* The School Librarian, *Vol. 31, No. 2, June, 1983, p. 167.*

ROCK 'N' ROLL NIGHTS: A NOVEL (1982)

This novel about four New York City high-school kids trying to succeed as a rock-and-roll band has two uncommon strengths: realistic views of aspiring musicians' prospects in popular music and of the tough New York club scene and the excellent characterization of its likable protagonist. Gary, 17, is the group's thoughtful leader and manager, initiating the group's play dates, organizing the recording of a single, prodding work from and keeping the peace among the members: Gary's cousin Susan, who tries to grow up too fast by dating a record executive; pot-smoking Karl, whose aging flower-child mother aids Gary in managing the group; and Oscar, a balding, unpleasant keyboard genius-songwriter. All the members, in their own ways, are backward socially. Strasser uses unobtrusive narrative devices to show Gary's loneliness; his fantasies about marrying Susan end in his realization that he perhaps cultivates this notion to avoid dating, with its risks as well as its demands on his time. Though Gary loves the music and the performing and is exuberant about the group's rare, small successes, he always realizes that the odds are against him, and persists despite them; he's so determined and responsible, readers know he might have a chance.

> *Sally Holmes Holtze, in a review of "Rock 'n' Roll Nights," in* School Library Journal, *Vol. 28, No. 7, March, 1982, p. 161.*

This novel about a high school rock band in New York could be seen as an answer to Meyer's fictionalized documentary *Rock Band* (1980). Where Meyer ended realistically with the band breaking up, Strasser follows convention and ends with an evening of raging success for the showcased unknowns; but Strasser, while also avoiding the wilder and seamier side of rock life, conveys a better sense of being there and sharing the group's perceptions. . . . Strasser fills in the background with some family dinner-table conversations and one lovely scene in which Gary's abstracted dentist father shoots some baskets with his sons; but mostly this chronicles the group's often discouraging, often sleazy, but gratifyingly promising road to their breakthrough. Well-tempered wish fulfillment with a true sound. (pp. 278-79)

> *A review of "Rock 'n' Roll Nights," in* Kirkus Reviews, *Vol. L, No. 5, March 1, 1982, pp. 278-79.*

The rock and roll generation (or generations) has stereotypically been surrounded by an air of drug abuse, alcohol consumption and less than discreet sexual practices. In Todd Strasser's children's novel, the author does little to correct this partially inaccurate stereotype and even less to dull the effects of rock's darker side. Possibly I am conservative or just naïve, but after completing the novel I felt reluctant about passing it on to my thirteen year old brother. . . .

Strasser's characters are run-of-the-mill American teenagers drinking beer, smoking pot and laboring over the issue of adolescent sexuality. The question is, how much run-of-the-mill should a twelve year old be exposed to?

The book also seeks support from the current pop/rock stars. Names like Bruce Springsteen, Bob Seger and Tom Petty form a bridge between today's top-forty and the encounters of "The Electric Outlet."

Rock 'n' Roll Nights may or may not be very accurate in its representation of the lives of up and coming rockers, but may overestimate the age group at which it is aimed.

> *John Hambrose, in a review of "Rock 'n' Roll Nights," in* Best Sellers, *Vol. 42, No. 2, May, 1982, p. 79.*

It's a good book in many ways. Gary is stuck with an interesting bunch of teenagers in his band—his cousin Susan, who won't practice and would rather be dating; Karl, the marijuana smoker with acne; and Oscar, the boy genius who helps Gary write the songs. Gary's parents are stereotyped to the point of looking ridiculous. I think some readers would enjoy the book, but it does drag and is limited in appeal. (pp. 99-100)

> *Jennifer Brown, in a review of "Rock 'n' Roll Nights," in* Children's Book Review Service, *Vol. 10, No. 10, May, 1982, pp. 99-100.*

Along with a realistic portrayal of the multifaceted world of hard rock, Strasser has created a complex character with a single-minded purpose who is fully rewarded with an uncertain chance rather than formula superstardom. Gary is ultimately recognized for his talent and his craft rather than his image or other externals of the trade. Consequently, this is an upbeat story for readers as different as the next Mick Jagger or Carl Sagan. (p. 88)

> *Dick Abrahamson, Betty Carter, and Barbara Samuels, "The Music of Young Adult Literature," in* English Journal, *Vol. 71, No. 5, September, 1982, pp. 87-8.**

Obstacles are realistic, and characters are quite well drawn. It is apparent that Gary has talent; success is probable if he can get a break. Whether the break the band gets will suffice is left open, but that is a major strength of the novel.

Younger students should find this an appealing story. It is a realistic career portrayal; being a first rate musician is extremely difficult, but it is not impossible. The story should appeal to both sexes.

> *William G. McBride, in a review of "Rock 'n' Roll Nights," in* Voice of Youth Advocates, *Vol. 5, No. 5, December, 1982, p. 36.*

WORKIN' FOR PEANUTS (1983)

High school graduate Jeff Mead coasts along selling ice cream and "drips" at the stadium for Stotts and Sons concessions, generally resigned to the disparaging attitudes of both company management and fans toward himself and the other working vendors. Therefore, he's particularly surprised when a girl named Melissa, sitting in the Stotts' private box, shows an interest in him. Despite warnings from his friend Rick (who has problems of his own with a local gang), his working-class parents' disapproval, and his own niggling misgivings about dating the daughter of a company vice-president, Jeff pursues Melissa, who, like him, believes that things will work out despite the disparity of their economic backgrounds. Predictably, such is not the case; but if Strasser ties up matters too neatly, his first-person narrative is smoothly written, his stadium background quite vivid, and his message about social class dynamics well balanced by traditional romantic trappings. Melissa is sketched a shade too lightly, but Jeff comes through as a genuinely likable character who grows realistically in the reader's estimation as he learns some of life's harder lessons.

> *Stephanie Zvirin, in a review of "Workin' for Peanuts," in* Booklist, *Vol. 79, No. 13, March 1, 1983, p. 871.*

Realistically—if not happily—resolved, the book draws its strength from skillful characterization rather than from the plot, which is weaker than that of either *Angel Dust Blues* . . . or *Friends Till the End*. . . . The colloquial first-person account is laced with street language. But at the same time the author writes with sensitivity—handling well both the interaction of the boy with his unemployed, rather belligerent father and the relationship between Jeff and Melissa, including the one sex scene.

> *Karen Jameyson, in a review of "Workin' for Peanuts," in* The Horn Book Magazine, *Vol. LIX, No. 2, April, 1983, p. 175.*

At first glance, **Workin' for Peanuts,** with its snappy title and first-person chatter, seems like a typical, trite "confessional effect" novel: poor teen stadium vender Jeff Mead's attraction to rich-girl/boss' daughter Melissa poses problems for his job, family, and future career.

Though the book holds the potential for trashy writings, its ability to portray economic realities and teen relationships in a realistic, moving manner places it a cut above the usual Young Adult problem-solving title. Protagonist Jeff's concerns about his unemployed father, breadwinning bus driver mother, and his own financial future are juxtaposed with Melissa's freer, unconcerned lifestyle, her uncertainties over a future unaffected by money concerns, and her genuine and growing affection for Jeff.

Through such slow and deliberate comparisons of life styles, the reader is led to discern exactly how the presence or absence of money can affect interpersonal relationships and even love. . . .

The result is a readable, engrossing tale which will capture and hold reader attention and provide unusual insight into the differences between poverty and wealth.

> *Diane C. Donovan, in a review of "Workin' for Peanuts," in* Best Sellers, *Vol. 43, No. 2, May, 1983, p. 75.*

This is an honest, vigorous, and perceptive story, convincingly told from Jeff's viewpoint; it has sharp characterization and vivid depictions of Jeff's work situation and his relationship with his father.

> *Zena Sutherland, in a review of "Workin' for Peanuts," in* Bulletin of the Center for Children's Books, *Vol. 36, No. 9, May, 1983, p. 180.*

This is a pleasant enough YA novel that will probably appeal to Strasser's fans, but it does not compare to his earlier books. . . . The social/economic distance between Jeff and Melissa seems exaggerated and a lot of Jeff's and his father's philosophizing about the "big guys" versus the "little guys" is strained and petulant. All in all, a fast, easy read without much depth, peopled with characters who are strictly two-dimensional.

> *Audrey B. Eaglen, in a review of "Workin' for Peanuts," in* School Library Journal, *Vol. 29, No. 10, August, 1983, p. 80.*

With Strasser's usual compassionate humor a story of relationships; the ins vs. the outs, the rich vs. the poor; the ethical vs. the unethical, is quickly unfolded. Strasser is careful not to allow his characters to become caricatures—the bigoted Archie Bunker beer swilling, belching father, the ticket scalping best friend, Rick (Speedy) with larcenous mind and peeping Tom habit bragging about his weekly consumption of prophylactics—each is glimpsed with motivations behind behavior. The use of drugs is prevalent with a skillfully depicted rock concert bringing forth aromas of pot and vomit, and visuals of sex and excesses. Language is vivid, ("pissed off" a favorite expression), as the reader explores the bonds of friendship, motivations, and the distinction of differences. Will be controversial and widely read.

> *Allan A. Cuseo, in a review of "Workin' for Peanuts," in* Voice of Youth Advocates, *Vol. 6, No. 4, October, 1983, p. 209.*

TURN IT UP! A NOVEL (1984)

[In a sequel to **Rock 'n' Roll Nights**] the four high school students (three male, one female) who have a rock group are struggling to become better known. The mother of one of the boys has been acting as manager (and not doing too well in promoting the group), so the young people secretly hire another manager. Mother is hurt, the new man [Barney] proves an expensive disaster, but the book ends with an unexpected gig and a smash performance. The musical ambience should appeal to most readers, as will the humor and vigor of the writing style; the book is given substance, however, by the nicely defined and sympathetic relationships among the younger performers, their friends, and their families. (pp. 156-57)

> *Zena Sutherland, in a review of "Turn It Up!" in* Bulletin of the Center for Children's Books, *Vol. 37, No. 8, April, 1984, pp. 156-57.*

[As in **Rock 'n' Roll Nights**], Strasser introduces the rough edges of rock-music biz yet goes out of his way to brighten and soften them. The kids are decent, relatively innocent and clean-living, mostly drug-free. (Karl smokes a bit of pot—along with cigarette, cigars, *anything*.) So the result is something halfway between *The Partridge Family* and the other, seamy extreme: a likable, predictable slice of show-biz, with just enough convincing details (including the eloquent opposition of Gary's mom) to keep the music more or less on a true pitch.

A review of "Turn It Up!" in Kirkus Reviews, *Juvenile Issue, Vol. LII, Nos. 6-9, May 1, 1984, p. J-52.*

[Gary Specter and his band] dream of rockin' Madison Square Garden and turning thousands on to their wavelength—it's the rock land of fantasy. It is a shallow fantasy.

This superficial world fits the characters—high school seniors and recent grads living for the rock & roll dream. . . . Gary's kid brother begs for attention by becoming a delinquent, but even the narrator fails to notice or care. Gary's parents are either the worst cliches or weak attempts at humor. (Actually, *all* the characters are all the worst cliches.) Allison's penthouse-snobby father, of course, is the *deus ex machina*, teaching the young reader that it's *not* how good you are or how you persevere—it's who you know. Even dumb kids won't buy this story line. By comparison, "The Partridge Family" is extraordinarily deep drama.

Lest the reader be misled, I do have some complaints. The "music world" is a natural setting for drug use, vulgarity, and superficial relationships, but Strasser treats it as innocent and acceptable. His attempts to suggest that a few characters are struggling to define life's goals are his own fantasies. What he shows this reviewer contradicts what he thinks he tells the reader. He misses opportunities to give depth to characters and plot. Consequently, the book is insulting to readers of all ages.

Strasser's *Friends Till the End* and *Rock 'N' Roll Nights* were selected as American Library Association Best Books for Young Adults. As a sequel to the latter book, *Turn It Up!* deserves to be turned off. (pp. 118-19)

Michael Healy, in a review of "Turn It Up!" in Best Sellers, *Vol. 44, No. 3, June, 1984, pp. 118-19.*

This fast-paced, breezy novel features likeable characters, an upbeat theme and a real feel for the details of the rock world. Though less effective as a novel than *Rock 'n' Roll Nights*, fans of the first will enjoy this one, and it will likely serve as an effective bridge to the promised third Gary Specter story.

Christy Tyson, in a review of "Turn It Up!" in Voice of Youth Advocates, *Vol. 7, No. 2, June, 1984, p. 98.*

Strasser's tale about life on the rock and roll scene stresses how easy it is to become a rock loser. Although the subplots are pat, the characterizations are good. The most obvious problem with the book is the totally transparent plot. Early on, Gary learns that his girlfriend's father is the friend of the president of a recording company; when this connection leads to success for the group, Gary is surprised but readers are not. Also, the moral that rock and roll is a hard life gets a bit shopworn. The mood of the rock clubs, the dialogue and the original song lyrics are well-crafted, though, and most readers won't mind the obvious ending.

Fran Wolfe, in a review of "Turn It Up!" in School Library Journal, *Vol. 30, No. 10, August, 1984, p. 87.*

The story is narrowly focused and fast-paced. The adolescent characters are wholesome and engaging. Except for the invisible Mr. Specter, the adults are given chances to redeem themselves. Even Barney's treachery is understandable if not ex-

cusable. The resolution of Gary's problem is satisfying, even though it does strain credulity just a bit.

The only real disappointment is the lack of authentic detail in the depiction of the rock scene. Strasser's lyrics are pretty good imitations of bubble-gum rock, but the descriptions of the concerts repeat clichés. The noise is thunderous; the drums explode and send shock waves; the guitar sizzles. The bass thumps out "an earthquake of bass lines"; later, it blasts out "a hurricane of bass notes." (p. 94)

Beth Nelms, Ben Nelms, and Linda Horton, "A Brief but Troubled Season: Problems in YA Fiction," in English Journal, *Vol. 74, No. 1, January, 1985, pp. 92-5.**

THE COMPLETE COMPUTER POPULARITY PROGRAM (1984)

Tony is a newcomer to the seventh grade in Peekham, where his father has just taken a job as a security engineer at an unpopular nuclear power plant. Strasser mixes the implications of the community's negative attitude toward plant workers with the boy's efforts to secure popularity for himself and his only friend, a "computer nerd" who is more interested in developing his talking synthesizer than being a hit on the social circuit. Bolstered by handily drawn characterizations, these subplots are woven into an amusing tale that is filled with junior high concerns matrixed in the computer age.

Ilene Cooper, in a review of "The Complete Computer Popularity Program," in Booklist, *Vol. 81, No. 4, October 15, 1984, p. 313.*

This slight formula story features stock characters and situations with few surprises other than the protagonists being male rather than the standard female. However, junior high students wanting a quick, easy read will probably enjoy it. *The Complete Computer Popularity Program* does not have the depth one would expect from the author of two ALA "Best Books for Young Adults," but it compares favorably with others of this genre, and Strasser fans will probably be waiting for it. (p. 139)

Maureen S. Dugan, in a review of "The Complete Computer Popularity Program," in School Library Journal, *Vol. 31, No. 3, November, 1984, pp. 138-39.*

[Strasser] has taken two current concerns of teens, popularity and computers and combined them into a winning novel told from the male perspective. He has also explored both sides of the nuclear power controversy that also concerns YAs. Tony and Paul are believable seventh grade boys. . . . This book should appeal to both the popular teens and those computer nerds who are striving for popularity. A definite candidate for YASD Best Books.

Gayle Keresey, in a review of "The Complete Computer Popularity Program," in Voice of Youth Advocates, *Vol. 7, No. 6, February, 1985, p. 333.*

A VERY TOUCHY SUBJECT (1985)

"A lot of this book is about a very touchy subject—sex. Get it? Touchy? Oh, well. I just want to say that if all you're looking for are graphic scenes of people undressing, and a lot of dirty words, you might as well stop reading now." Scott Tauscher, Todd Strasser's 17-year-old narrator-protagonist, is right. His story isn't sexy at all, though there are a lot of comments from him and his buddies about hormones and the torture of going without. Scott has a beautiful, rich girl friend, but lately they are always fighting the same fight. (''If you really loved me, you would.'' ''If you really loved me, it wouldn't be important.'') So they finally break up, as Scott's attention wanders to sexy 15-year-old Paula next door, whose greaser boyfriend he sees climbing out of her bedroom window every morning. At first Scott's attention is drawn to Paula's ''bod,'' but soon he is viewing her as a poor kid who needs help escaping her sluttish rep and her drunken, abusive mother. And so when he is presented with the ''golden opportunity''—an invitation to join Paula in her sleeping bag—Scott says no. By then Paula is on her way to live with her father and change her ways . . . , and Scott doesn't want to set her back.

Strasser fleshes out this conventional exemplar with peer and family interactions, but the viewpoint never transcends the snobby virgin/troubled slut stereotypes.

> *A review of "A Very Touchy Subject," in* Kirkus Reviews, *Juvenile Issue, Vol. LIII, Nos. 5-10, May 15, 1985, p. J-45.*

The author is an acute observer of the teenage scene and presents a humorous, no doubt accurate, rendering of the absorptions and conversations of teenage boys. Scott, though preoccupied with the very touchy subject, is a thoughtful and decent young man, and the value of the book is the author's optimistic view of the basic kindness and good sense of young people.

> *Ann A. Flowers, in a review of "A Very Touchy Subject," in* The Horn Book Magazine, *Vol. LXI, No. 3, May-June, 1985, p. 321.*

[Scott is] really a very nice lad, compassionate, altruistic, willing to become involved. Strasser does a good job of letting Scott, as speaker, define his own personality and comment on others, and the book responds to several concerns and problems of the adolescent: the adjustment to physical changes, the conflict between a need for security and a desire for independence, and the need for loving and being loved.

> *Zena Sutherland, in a review of "A Very Touchy Subject," in* Bulletin of the Center for Children's Books, *Vol. 38, No. 10, June, 1985, p. 196.*

[Scott's] story is realistic, humorous and warm. Sex is a recurrent theme but the situations are reasonable, handled without vulgarity, and when Scott's golden opportunity comes along, he does the honorable thing and refuses. A junior boy read it, enjoyed it, and wanted his girlfriend to read it. I read a galley proof, but if it has an attractive cover, it should be very popular with young adults.

> *Joan Estes, in a review of "A Very Touchy Subject," in* Voice of Youth Advocates, *Vol. 8, No. 2, June, 1985, p. 136.*

Delacorte Press's young adult line has included some real winners. [*A Very Touchy Subject* and Cin Forshay-Lunsford's *Walk Through Cold Fire*] rank high and should gain favor with teens and their parents, for they deal with difficult topics in a clean, wholesome, non-intimate way. And perhaps it is this very cleanness that keeps them from soaring like L'Engle's *Arm of the Starfish* or George's *Julie of the Wolves*. . . .

A Very Touchy Subject has a more ordinary topic [than *Walk Through Cold Fire*] and is less successful . . . [Todd Strasser's] greatest strength is his command of tone; *A Very Touchy Subject* sounds just like a seventeen-year-old Westchester boy talking. . . .

Scott struggles with his ''need'' for sexual release and his compunctions about taking advantage of Paula. The obvious ending would be for him to resist temptation and live happily ever after with Alix; the first-choice surprise ending would be for him to get involved with Paula and eventually marry her. What really happens is more satisfying: Alix drops him, he helps Paula escape to North Carolina, he meets another nice girl to date, and his hormones keep right on paining him.

Through all of this, there isn't a single four-letter word, no mention of the tawdry physical unpleasantnesses of wet dreams and erections. Like *Walk Through Cold Fire*, this book avoids things sordid and physical. But in this book that's a weakness, because it prevents the reader from understanding what Scott is *feeling*. I've always been convinced that the best novels create an identification between reader and hero. So, good as it is, this book isn't a Best.

> *Loralee MacPike, in a review of "A Very Touchy Subject," in* Best Sellers, *Vol. 45, No. 5, August, 1985, p. 197.*

APPENDIX

The following is a listing of all sources used in Volume 11 of *Children's Literature Review*. Included in this list are all copyright and reprint rights and acknowledgments for those essays for which permission was obtained. Every effort has been made to trace copyright, but if omissions have been made, please let us know.

THE EXCERPTS IN CLR, VOLUME 11, WERE REPRINTED FROM THE FOLLOWING PERIODICALS:

Appraisal: Children's Science Books, v. 1, Winter, 1967; v. 1, Spring, 1968; v. 1, Fall, 1968; v. 2, Spring, 1969; v. 4, Spring, 1971; v. 5, Spring, 1972; v. 7, Winter, 1974; v. 8, Fall, 1975; v. 9, Fall, 1976; v. 12, Winter, 1979; v. 13, Spring, 1980; v. 13, Fall, 1980. Copyright © 1967, 1968, 1969, 1971, 1972, 1974, 1975, 1976, 1979, 1980 by the Children's Science Book Review Committee. All reprinted by permission.

Appraisal: Science Books for Young People, v. 14, Fall, 1981; v. 15, Winter, 1982; v. 16, Spring-Summer, 1983; v. 16, Fall, 1983; v. 17, Winter, 1984; v. 18, Summer, 1985. Copyright © 1981, 1982, 1983, 1984, 1985 by the Children's Science Book Review Committee. All reprinted by permission.

Atlantic Provinces Book Review, v. 10, November & December, 1983. © APBR Service. Reprinted by permission.

The Babbling Bookworm, v. 6, February, 1978. Copyright 1978 The Babbling Bookworm Newsletter. Reprinted by permission.

Best Sellers, v. 29, June 1, 1969. Copyright 1969, by the University of Scranton. Reprinted by permission./ v. 38, December, 1978; v. 38, March, 1979; v. 40, November, 1980; v. 41, July, 1981; v. 41, January, 1982; v. 42, May, 1982; v. 42, June, 1982; v. 43, May, 1983; v. 44, June, 1984; v. 44, September, 1984; v. 44, February, 1985; v. 45, August, 1985. Copyright © 1978, 1979, 1980, 1981, 1982, 1983, 1984, 1985 Helen Dwight Reid Educational Foundation. All reprinted by permission.

The Book Buyer, n.s. v. II, May, 1885.

The Book Report, v. 4, November-December, 1985. © copyright 1985 by Linworth Publishing Co. Reprinted by permission.

Book Week—New York Herald Tribune, November 1, 1964. © 1964, *The Washington Post.* Reprinted by permission.

Book Week—The Sunday Herald Tribune, May 30, 1965; August 14, 1966. © 1965, 1966, *The Washington Post.* Both reprinted by permission.

Book Window, v. 8, Spring, 1981. © 1981 S.C.B.A. and contributors. Reprinted by permission.

Book World—The Washington Post, May 2, 1976; September 19, 1976; August 13, 1978; November 12, 1978; November 11, 1979; September 14, 1980; February 14, 1982; November 7, 1982; November 10, 1985. © 1976, 1978, 1979, 1980, 1982, 1985, *The Washington Post.* All reprinted by permission.

Bookbird, n. 4 (December 15, 1980). Reprinted by permission.

Booklist, v. 73, September 1, 1976; v. 73, October 15, 1976; v. 74, October 15, 1977; v. 74, March 15, 1978; v. 75, December 1, 1978; v. 75, June 1, 1979; v. 75, July 1, 1979; v. 76, April 1, 1980; v. 77, November 1, 1980; v. 77, February 15, 1981; v. 77, April 15, 1981; v. 77, May 1, 1981; v. 77, June 15, 1981; v. 77, July 15 & August, 1981; v. 78, September 15, 1981; v. 78, November 15, 1981; v. 78, January 15, 1982; v. 78, February 1, 1982; v. 78, April 1, 1982; v. 79, November 15, 1982; v. 79, December 1, 1982; v. 79, March 1, 1983; v. 79, April 1, 1983; v. 79, April 15, 1983; v. 79, July, 1983; v. 80, November 1, 1983; v. 80, March 15, 1984; v. 80, April 1, 1984; v. 80, May 1, 1984; v. 80, June 1, 1984; v. 81, October 15, 1984; v. 81, November 1, 1984; v. 81, January 15, 1985; v. 81, April 15, 1985; v. 81, May 15, 1985; v. 81, July, 1985; v. 82, January 15, 1986. Copyright © 1976, 1977, 1978, 1979, 1980, 1981, 1982, 1983, 1984, 1985, 1986 by the American Library Association. All reprinted by permission.

The Booklist, v. 40, January 15, 1944; v. 45, September 15, 1948; v. 49, January 15, 1953; v. 52, April 1, 1956./ v. 66, September 1, 1969; v. 69, November 15, 1972; v. 71, September 15, 1974; v. 71, October 1, 1974; v. 70, November 15, 1974; v. 72, December 15, 1975. Copyright © 1969, 1972, 1974, 1975 by the American Library Association. All reprinted by permission.

The Booklist and Subscription Books Bulletin, v. 62, September 15, 1965; v. 64, January 15, 1968. Copyright © 1965, 1968 by the American Library Association. Both reprinted by permission.

The Bookman, London, v. VII, January, 1895.

Books for Keeps, n. 23, November, 1983; n. 25, March, 1984; n. 30, January, 1985; n. 32, May, 1985. © School Bookshop Association 1983, 1984, 1985. All reprinted by permission.

Books for Your Children, v. 13, Summer, 1978; v. 19, Summer, 1984. © *Books for Your Children* 1978, 1984. Both reprinted by permission.

Books in Canada, v. 9, December, 1980 for "Huck Finn in Newfoundland" by Janet Lunn; v. 13, December, 1984 for an interview with Kevin Major by Sherie Posesorski. Both reprinted by permission of the respective authors.

Bulletin of the Center for Children's Books, v. XVI, July-August, 1963; v. 21, October, 1967. Copyright 1963, 1967 by The University of Chicago. Both reprinted by permission of The University of Chicago Press./ v. 23, January, 1970; v. 24, September, 1970; v. 25, January, 1972; v. 25, June, 1972; v. 27, September, 1973; v. 27, January, 1974; v. 27, June, 1974; v. 28, November, 1974; v. 28, December, 1974; v. 28, January, 1975; v. 28, February, 1975; v. 28, June, 1975; v. 28, July-August, 1975; v. 29, July-August, 1976; v. 30, April, 1977; v. 31, January, 1978; v. 32, September, 1978; v. 32, May, 1979; v. 32, July, 1979; v. 32, July-August, 1979; v. 33, October, 1979; v. 33, December, 1979; v. 33, February, 1980; v. 33, May, 1980; v. 33, June, 1980; v. 33, July-August, 1980; v. 34, November, 1980; v. 34, January, 1981; v. 34, March, 1981; v. 34, April, 1981; v. 34, May, 1981; v. 35, November, 1981; v. 35, February, 1982; v. 35, March, 1982; v. 35, July-August, 1982; v. 36, October, 1982; v. 36, April, 1983; v. 36, May, 1983; v. 36, June, 1983; v. 36, July-August, 1983; v. 37, November, 1983; v. 37, January, 1984; v. 37, March, 1984; v. 37, April, 1984; v. 37, May, 1984; v. 37, July, 1984; v. 38, October, 1984; v. 38, December, 1984; v. 38, April, 1985; v. 38, June, 1985; v. 38, July-August, 1985; v. 39, December, 1985; v. 39, February, 1986. © 1970, 1972, 1973, 1974, 1975, 1976, 1977, 1978, 1979, 1980, 1981, 1982, 1983, 1984, 1985, 1986 by The University of Chicago. All reprinted by permission of The University of Chicago Press.

Bulletin of the Children's Book Center, v. VI, September, 1952./ v. XIII, March, 1960. Reprinted by permission of The University of Chicago Press.

Canadian Children's Literature: A Journal of Criticism and Review, n. 14, 1979; n. 22, 1981. Box 335, Guelph, Ontario, Canada N1H 6K5. Both reprinted by permission.

Catholic Library World, v. 40, October, 1968; v. 42, March, 1971; v. 56, November, 1984; v. 56, March, 1985. All reprinted by permission.

Chambers's Journal, v. II, June 17, 1899.

Childhood Education, v. 42 (November, 1965); v. 54 (February, 1978); v. 58 (September-October, 1981). © 1965, 1978, 1981 by the Association for Childhood Education International, 11141 Georgia Ave., Suite 200, Wheaton, MD. All reprinted by permission of the Association.

Children's Book Review, v. VI, October, 1976. © 1976 Five Owls Press Ltd. All rights reserved. Reprinted by permission.

Children's Book Review Service, v. 1, July, 1973; v. 2, December, 1973; v. 2, August, 1974; v. 3, October, 1974; v. 3, December, 1974; v. 4, September, 1975; v. 5, November, 1976; v. 5, January, 1977; v. 6, October, 1977; v. 7, September, 1978; v. 7, August, 1979; v. 8, December, 1979; v. 9, March, 1981; v. 9, April, 1981; v. 10, February, 1982; v. 10, May, 1982; v. 11, May, 1983; v. 12, June, 1984; v. 13, September, 1984; v. 13, November, 1984; v. 13, Winter Supplement, 1985. Copyright © 1973, 1974, 1975, 1976, 1977, 1978, 1979, 1981, 1982, 1983, 1984, 1985 Children's Book Review Service Inc. All reprinted by permission.

Children's Literature: Annual of the Modern Language Association Seminar on Children's Literature and The Children's Literature Association, v. 2, 1973; v. 4, 1975. © 1973, 1975 by Francelia Butler. All rights reserved. Both reprinted by permission of Francelia Butler.

Arbuthnot, May Hill. From *Children and Books*. Scott, Foresman, 1947. Copyright, 1947, renewed 1974, by Scott, Foresman and Company. Reprinted by permission.

Arbuthnot, May Hill and Sutherland, Zena. From *Children and Books*. Fifth edition. Scott, Foresman, 1977. Copyright © 1977, 1972, 1964, 1957, 1947 by Scott, Foresman and Company. All rights reserved. Reprinted by permission.

Arbuthnot, May Hill, Sutherland, Zena, and Monson, Dianne L. From *Children and Books*. Sixth edition. Scott, Foresman, 1981. Copyright © 1981, 1977, 1972, 1964, 1957, 1947 by Scott, Foresman and Company. All rights reserved. Reprinted by permission.

Bader, Barbara. From *American Picture Books from Noah's Ark to the Beast Within*. Macmillan, 1976. Copyright © 1976 by Barbara Bader. All rights reserved. Reprinted with permission of Macmillan Publishing Company.

Baildon, H. Bellyse. From *Robert Louis Stevenson: A Life Study in Criticism*. A. Wessels Company, 1901.

Barrie, J. M. From *An Edinburgh Eleven: Pencil Portraits from College Life*. Lovell, Coryell & Company, 1888.

Baskin, Barbara H. and Karen H. Harris. From *More Notes from a Different Drummer: A Guide to Juvenile Fiction Portraying the Disabled*. Bowker, 1984. Copyright © 1984 by Barbara H. Baskin and Karen H. Harris. All rights reserved. Reprinted with permission of the R.R. Bowker Company, Division of Reed Publishing, USA.

Books for Children: 1967-1968. American Library Association, 1968. Copyright © 1967, 1968 by the American Library Association. Reprinted by permission.

Burton, Virginia Lee. From "Virginia Lee Burton," a promotional piece by Houghton Mifflin, 1968? Reprinted by permission of Houghton Mifflin Company.

Butts, Dennis. From *R. L. Stevenson*. Henry Z. Walck, Incorporated, 1966. © Dennis Butts 1966. Reprinted by permission of the author.

Crouch, Marcus. From *The Nesbit Tradition: The Children's Novel in England 1945-1970*. Ernest Benn Limited, 1972. © Marcus Crouch 1972. Reprinted by permission of the author.

Cullinan, Bernice E, with Mary K. Karrer and Arlene M. Pillar. From *Literature and the Child*. Harcourt Brace Jovanovich, 1981. Copyright © 1981 by Harcourt Brace Jovanovich, Inc. Reprinted by permission of the publisher.

Daiches, David. From *Robert Louis Stevenson*. New Directions Books, 1947. Copyright 1947 by New Directions. Renewed 1975 by David Daiches. Reprinted by permission of the author.

Davis, Enid. From *The Liberty Cap: A Catalogue of Non-Sexist Materials for Children*. Academy Chicago Publishers, 1977. Copyright © 1977 by Academy Chicago Publishers. All rights reserved. Reprinted by permission.

Dreyer, Sharon Spredemann. From *The Bookfinder, a Guide to Children's Literature about the Needs and Problems of Youth Aged 2-15: Annotations of Books Published 1975 through 1978, Vol. 2*. American Guidance Service, Inc., 1981. © 1981 American Guidance Service, Inc. All rights reserved. Reprinted by permission.

Dreyer, Sharon Spredemann. From *The Bookfinder, When Kids Need Books: Annotations of Books Published 1979 through 1982*. American Guidance Service, 1985. © 1985 American Guidance Service, Inc. All rights reserved. Reprinted by permission.

Duff, Annis. From *"Bequest of Wings": A Family's Pleasures with Books*. The Viking Press, 1944. Copyright 1944 by Annis Duff. Copyright renewed © 1972 by Annis Duff. Reprinted by permission of Viking Penguin Inc.

Eaton, Anne Thaxter. From "Poetry for Children in the Nineteenth Century," in *A Critical History of Children's Literature*. By Cornelia Meigs, Anne Thaxter Eaton, Elizabeth Nesbitt, and Ruth Hill Viguers, edited by Cornelia Meigs. Revised edition. Macmillan, 1969. Copyright © 1953, 1969 by Macmillan Publishing Company. All rights reserved. Reprinted with permission of Macmillan Publishing Company.

Egoff, Sheila A. From *Thursday's Child: Trends and Patterns in Contemporary Children's Literature*. American Library Association, 1981. Copyright © 1981 by the American Library Association. All rights reserved. Reprinted by permission.

Fisher, Margery. From *Who's Who in Children's Books: A Treasury of the Familiar Characters of Childhood*. Weidenfeld & Nicolson, 1975. Copyright © 1975 by Margery Fisher. All rights reserved. Reprinted by permission.

Garrod, H. W. From *The Profession of Poetry and Other Lectures*. Oxford at the Clarendon Press, Oxford, 1929.

Gillespie, John and Diana Lembo. From *Introducing Books: A Guide for the Middle Grades*. R. R. Bowker Co., 1970. Copyright © 1970 by R. R. Bowker, Division of Reed Publishing, USA. All rights reserved. Reprinted with permission of the R. R. Bowker Company.

Haugaard, Erik Christian. From *Hakon of Rogen's Saga*. Houghton Mifflin, 1963. Copyright © 1963 Erik Christian Haugaard. All rights reserved. Reprinted by permission of Houghton Mifflin Company.

Hearn, Lafcadio. From *A History of English Literature in a Series of Lectures, Vol. II*. Edited by R. Tanabe and T. Ochiai. The Hokuseido Press, 1927.

Human—And Anti-Human—Values in Children's Books: A Content Rating Instrument for Educators and Concerned Parents. Edited by the Council on Interracial Books for Children, Inc. Racism and Sexism Resource Center for Educators, 1976. Copyright © 1976 by the Council on Interracial Books for Children, Inc. All rights reserved. Reprinted by permission.

Lasky, Kathryn. From *Dollmaker: The Eyelight and the Shadow*. Charles Scribner's Sons, 1981. Copyright © 1981 Kathryn Lasky. Reprinted with the permission of Charles Scribner's Sons.

Lukens, Rebecca J. From *A Critical Handbook of Children's Literature*. Scott, Foresman, 1976. Copyright © 1976 by Scott, Foresman and Company. All rights reserved. Reprinted by permission.

Lystad, Mary. From *From Dr. Mather to Dr. Seuss: 200 Years of American Books for Children*. Schenkman Books, 1980. Copyright © 1980 by Schenkman Books, Inc. Reprinted by permission.

Moss, John. From *A Reader's Guide to the Canadian Novel*. McClelland and Stewart, 1981. Copyright © 1981 by McClelland and Stewart Limited. All rights reserved. Used by permission of The Canadian Publishers, McClelland and Stewart Limited, Toronto.

Norton, Donna E. From *Through the Eyes of a Child: An Introduction to Children's Literature*. Charles E. Merrill Publishing Company, 1983. Copyright © 1983 by Merrill Publishing Company, Columbus, Ohio. All rights reserved. Reprinted by permission.

Noyes, Alfred. From *Some Aspects of Modern Poetry*. Stokes, 1924. Copyright, 1924, by Frederick A. Stokes Company. Copyright renewed © 1952 by Alfred Noyes. Reprinted by permission of the Literary Estate of Alfred Noyes.

Osbourne, Lloyd. From an introduction to *A Child's Garden of Verses*. By Robert Louis Stevenson. Charles Scribner's Sons, 1901.

Peterson, Linda Kauffman. From "The Caldecott Medal and Honor Books, 1938-1981: 'The Little House'," in *Newbery and Caldecott Medal and Honor Books: An Annotated Bibliography*. By Linda Kauffman Peterson and Marilyn Leathers Solt. Hall, 1982. Copyright 1982 by G. K. Hall & Co. Reprinted with the permission of Twayne Publishers, a division of G. K. Hall & Co., Boston.

Provensen, Alice and Martin Provensen. From "Alice and Martin Provensen," a promotional piece by The Viking Press, 1983. Reprinted by permission of Viking Penguin Inc.

Rees, David. From *Painted Desert, Green Shade: Essays on Contemporary Writers of Fiction for Children and Young Adults*. The Horn Book Inc., 1984. Copyright © 1980, 1981, 1983, 1984 by David Rees. All rights reserved. Reprinted by permission.

Sadker, Myra Pollack and David Miller Sadker. From *Now Upon a Time: A Contemporary View of Children's Literature*. Harper & Row, 1977. Copyright © 1977 by Myra Pollack Sadker and David Miller Sadker. All rights reserved. Reprinted by permission of Harper & Row, Publishers, Inc.

Salway, Lance. From "Fiction: 'Handles'," in *The Signal Review 2: A Selective Guide to Children's Books 1983*. Edited by Nancy Chambers. Thimble Press, 1984. Copyright © 1984 The Thimble Press. Reprinted by permission.

Saposnik, Irving S. From *Robert Louis Stevenson*. Twayne, 1974. Copyright 1974 by Twayne Publishers. All rights reserved. Reprinted with the permission of Twayne Publishers, a division of G. K. Hall & Co., Boston.

Schwarcz, Joseph H. From *Ways of the Illustrator: Visual Communication in Children's Literature*. American Library Association, 1982. Copyright © 1982 by the American Library Association. All rights reserved. Reprinted by permission.

Sebesta, Sam Leaton and William J. Iverson. From *Literature for Thursday's Child*. Science Research Associates, 1975. © 1975, Science Research Associates, Inc. All rights reserved. Reprinted by permission of the authors.

Sims, Rudine. From *Shadow and Substance: Afro-American Experience in Contemporary Children's Fiction*. National Council of Teachers of English, 1982. © 1982 by the National Council of Teachers of English. All rights reserved. Reprinted by permission of the publisher and the author.

CUMULATIVE INDEX TO AUTHORS

This index lists all author entries in *Children's Literature Review* and includes cross-references to them in other Gale sources. References in the index are identified as follows:

AITN: *Authors in the News*, Volumes 1-2
CA: *Contemporary Authors* (original series), Volumes 1-116
CANR: *Contemporary Authors New Revision Series*, Volumes 1-17
CAP: *Contemporary Authors Permanent Series*, Volumes 1-2
CA-R: *Contemporary Authors* (revised editions), Volumes 1-44
CLC: *Contemporary Literary Criticism*, Volumes 1-37
CLR: *Children's Literature Review*, Volumes 1-11
DLB: *Dictionary of Literary Biography*, Volumes 1-48
DLB-DS: *Dictionary of Literary Biography Documentary Series*, Volumes 1-4
DLB-Y: *Dictionary of Literary Biography Yearbook*, Volumes 1980-1985
NCLC: *Nineteenth-Century Literature Criticism*, Volumes 1-12
SAAS: *Something about the Author Autobiography Series*, Volume 1-2
SATA: *Something about the Author*, Volumes 1-44
TCLC: *Twentieth-Century Literary Criticism*, Volumes 1-20
YABC: *Yesterday's Authors of Books for Children*, Volumes 1-2

Author Index

Author Index

CUMULATIVE INDEX TO NATIONALITIES

CUMULATIVE INDEX TO TITLES

Title Index